02556

KT-144-291

The Stuart Constitution
1603–1688

LORETTO SCHOOL
VI FORM LIBRARY

SPARTAM·NACTUS·ES
HANC·EXORNA

LORETTO SCHOOL LIBRARY

The Stuart Constitution
1603–1688

Documents and commentary

SECOND EDITION

EDITED AND INTRODUCED BY

J. P. KENYON

LORETTO SCHOOL LIBRARY

SPARTAM·NACTUS·ES
HANC·EXORNA

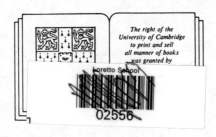

The right of the
University of Cambridge
to print and sell
all manner of books
was granted by

Loretto School

02556

CAMBRIDGE UNIVERSITY PRESS

CAMBRIDGE

NEW YORK   NEW ROCHELLE   MELBOURNE   SYDNEY

Published by the Press Syndicate of the University of Cambridge
The Pitt Building, Trumpington Street, Cambridge CB2 IRP
32 East 57th Street, New York, NY 10022, USA
10 Stamford Road, Oakleigh, Melbourne 3166, Australia

© Cambridge University Press 1986

First published 1986
Reprinted 1987

Printed in Great Britain at
the University Press, Cambridge

British Library cataloguing in publication data

The Stuart constitution 1603–1866: documents
and commentary. – 2nd ed.
1. Great Britain – History – Stuarts, 1603–1714
I. Kenyon, J. P.
941.06   DA375

Library of Congress cataloguing in publication data

Main entry under title:
The Stuart Constitution, 1603–1688.
Bibliography: p.
Includes index.
1. Great Britain – Politics and government – 1603—1714.
2. Great Britain – Constitutional history.
I. Kenyon, J. P. (John Philipps), 1927–
JN191.S78 1985   941.06   85–12773
ISBN 0 521 30810 0 hard covers
ISBN 0 521 31327 9 paperback

FOR
JACK PLUMB

CONTENTS

TABLE OF DOCUMENTS

In chronological order

Throughout the book figures in bold type refer to documents

PREFACE TO THE SECOND EDITION

I am very grateful to the Press for allowing me to revise this book thoroughly, instead of just tinkering with it. Thus I have not only been able to incorporate the results of the latest research – which in any case only called for adjustments of detail – but also to review the selection of documents and adjust the balance of the book.

When I came to re-read *The Stuart Constitution* after a lapse of some years, it was at once apparent that the opening sections were too much influenced by the late J. R. Tanner, not only by the detailed collection of documents for the reign of James I he published in 1930, but also by his approach to the period 1603–25 in general. Such matters as impositions and prohibitions loom less large in our eyes than his, and his treatment of King James, though conventional enough at that time, did him less than justice.

Secondly, it has been pointed out to me many times that my coverage of the period 1647–60 was inadequate. This I accept, and I have done my best to rectify it. But critics must bear in mind that a longer and therefore more expensive book was out of the question, so that for every new document inserted an old one has had to be removed. (As it is, I have ended up with one document more.)

It is also clear to me now, and no doubt to others, that chapters 12 and 13 in the first edition, on 'The Judiciary 1660–1688' and 'The Catholic Problem and the Revolution' respectively, were an indulgence on my part, albeit an unconscious one; they too much reflected my personal research interests at that time. I have pruned them both drastically, and distributed the second across the book.

At an early stage I consulted a cross-section of my colleagues working in the field, either verbally or by correspondence. Some of them gave hugely of their time, all of them went out of their way to be helpful and constructive, and I am very grateful. I gladly list their names here, on the understanding that they bear no responsibility for the final result, especially since I was simply unable to follow all their recommendations. They are: Professor Gerald Aylmer, Professor Geoffrey Elton, Professor Kenneth Haley, Dr John Miller, Dr John Morrill, Professor Ivan Roots, Dr Kevin Sharpe, Dr Nicholas Tyacke and Professor Austin Woolrych. In addition Dr Ian Green, Professor Mark Kishlansky, Dr Sheila Lambert and Dr David Stevenson gave me advice and information on specific points, and Dr Lambert lent me a paper of hers in advance of publication (as did Professor Woolrych).

All of them had kind words to say of the first edition; I can only hope that the second will meet with their approval.

J. P. K.

St Andrews
January 1985

PREFACE TO THE FIRST EDITION

This volume is intended to provide a representative and easily accessible selection of documents concerned with, and often in themselves comprising, the political and constitutional history of the seventeenth century in England. It overlaps two older collections, J. R. Tanner's *Constitutional Documents of the Reign of James I* and S. R. Gardiner's *Constitutional Documents of the Puritan Revolution*. Since they were published in a less affluent society each is comparable in size with the present volume, and they retain their value as source books, as a glance at my footnotes will show. But Tanner's commentary is in many respects out of date, while Gardiner offered none at all, apart from a short introduction, and his choice of documents was geared to the requirements of the Oxford Schools in the closing years of the nineteenth century.

The Civil Wars and the Interregnum make it impossible to submit the seventeenth century to a static analysis, which is why this volume falls into three books, divided at 1640 and 1660, with a fourth book dealing with certain themes that persisted throughout the period. Moreover, the immense volume of printed material produced in an age of almost continuous crisis in Church and state has obliged me to omit a great deal which I regard as desirable and some will think essential.

I have been fortunate in coming after Dr G. R. Elton, whose *Tudor Constitution* not only provided me with a model but also treated of some organs common to the Tudor and Stuart state so fully and admirably that I have been able to omit them altogether or mention them only briefly. My book, therefore, should be read in conjunction with his, even though it must be to my disadvantage. I might add that without Dr Elton's firm encouragement at every stage I doubt whether I would ever have completed this book. He also gave me the benefit of his advice on several specific points, read the whole of the first draft in typescript and helped me to reduce it by one-third to its present size. That is not to say that he, or anyone else mentioned in this preface, is responsible for errors of fact or judgement remaining.

I am also grateful to Professor William Haller, for answering questions on specific points, and to Professor G. E. Aylmer, who discussed the project with me at an early stage, to my great advantage. Mr J. Anthony Williams placed at my disposal his specialised knowledge of seventeenth-century recusancy, and thereby contributed a great deal to chapter 13. I also owe much to the staff of the University Library, Hull, and particularly Mr Peter Sheldon. My wife and my secretary, Mrs Kay Austin, between them typed the final draft of the book; a thankless task performed with great patience and accuracy.

Finally, I must acknowledge the patience and consideration of two successive secretaries to the Syndics, who have waited five years for this book and never doubted that it would be completed.

J. P. K.

Hull
April 1965

ACKNOWLEDGMENTS

Thanks are due to the following for permission to reprint the documents indicated: Yale University Press (**33**), (**57**); Oxford University Press (**41**); Manchester University Press (**81**); Columbia University Press (**85**); Harvard University Press (**94**); Messrs Jackson Son & Co. Ltd (**134**); City of Manchester Leisure Services Committee (**140**); The Chetham Society (**144**); and also to the Public Record Office and Dr Williams' Library for their assistance. Particulars of sources are given at the end of each extract.

ABBREVIATIONS

APC	*Acts of the Privy Council*
BIHR	*Bulletin of the Institute for Historical Research*
CJ	*Commons Journals*
CSPD	*Calendars of State Papers Domestic*
EHR	*English Historical Review*
GCD	S. R. Gardiner (ed.) *Constitutional Documents of the Puritan Revolution*, 3rd edn, Oxford 1906
HLQ	*Huntington Library Quarterly*
HJ	*Historical Journal*
HMC	*Historical Manuscripts Commission*
JBS	*Journal of British Studies*
JMH	*Journal of Modern History*
LJ	*Lords Journals*
OPH	'The Old Parliamentary History'; vere, *The Parliamentary or Constitutional History of England*, 24 vols. London 1751–61
PCD	G. W. Prothero (ed.) *Select Statutes and Other Constitutional Documents Illustrative of the Reigns of Elizabeth and James I*, 4th edn, Oxford 1913
PH	William Cobbett (ed.) *The Parliamentary History of England*, 36 vols. London 1806–20
PRO	Public Record Office, London
SR	*Statutes of the Realm*
SRP	*Stuart Royal Proclamations*, vol. I: *James I*, ed. James F. Larkin and Paul L. Hughes. Oxford 1973, vol. II: *Charles I*, ed. James F. Larkin. Oxford 1983
ST	W. Cobbett and T. B. Howell (eds.) *State Trials*, 33 vols. London 1809–26
TCD	J. R. Tanner (ed.) *Constitutional documents of the Reign of James I*. Cambridge 1930
TRHS	*Transactions of the Royal Historical Society*

The spelling and punctuation in the documents have been modernised wherever it is possible to do so without losing the sense or the emphasis.

All dates are in the old style, but the year is taken as beginning on 1 January.

INTRODUCTION

The study of the seventeenth-century constitution is dominated by the work of the great Victorians, Gardiner and Macaulay, interpreted and to a limited extent amplified by Sir Charles Firth and J. R. Tanner. Both Gardiner and Macaulay were often extremely acute, realistic and, of course, well informed, and they still have a great deal to offer the student; but their Whig interpretation of the seventeenth century in general – of an aggressive but incompetent dynasty, whose attempts to suppress the rights of the subject to free speech, property and due process of law were resisted in manly fashion by a representative assembly which mirrored all that was best or most important in the nation – is long out of date.

Today we believe that there was no right or wrong solution to the problems of the seventeenth century. The Revolution of 1688 stamped England as a wildly eccentric country outside the mainstream of European political development; indeed, it is doubtful if more than half the governing classes accepted it, and if they could have foreseen its consequences, or even if they had realised clearly what they were doing at the time, that proportion would have sunk to 5 per cent or less. The natural bent of European government was towards enlightened despotism and centralisation, which involved the sacrifice of the medieval estates or representative assemblies; England in the 1630s and to some extent in the 1680s was moving down that road. The Diet of Brandenburg was soon to follow the Cortes of Castile and Aragon and the States General of France into obscurity, and the Parliament at Westminster might well be next. Its counterparts at Dublin and Edinburgh were already the obedient tools of king and Council.

But to emulate their European colleagues the Stuarts needed two things they did not possess: a paid bureaucracy in the provinces, and a standing army. (It would be advantageous also to be able to secure a steady supply of money, but this was not essential; most European monarchs were chronically short of money, and periodically went bankrupt altogether, without endangering their regimes.) So, despite a background of contestation over forms of worship, taxation and the administration of justice, which was merely a continuation of similar squabbles under Elizabeth, in the foreground of the disputes between the Stuart kings and their parliaments lay foreign policy and the army. All these kings hoped to fight a successful war, which had always

I

eluded their predecessors, and at the end of that war establish a permanent army. Thus Charles I, Charles II, even James I, spent the greater part of their time and energy – more than is commonly supposed – in fashioning their foreign policy. It was their misfortune that these policies were not only unsuccessful but bitterly unpopular. Up to 1618 James I's attempts at a *rapprochement* with Spain were regarded with indulgence, but the outbreak of the Thirty Years War brought an immediate revulsion of feeling. From then on parliament was obsessed with the danger of the Counter Reformation, and despite the war with Spain from 1625 to 1630 the policy of Charles I was so ambiguous that in 1640 it was easy for his opponents in parliament to associate him in the public mind with the great European conspiracy for the suppression of Protestantism. It was this suspicion that led to the outbreak of the Civil Wars. Of course, Charles I's fiscal and ecclesiastical policies were a source of irritation, and made accommodation much more difficult, but in the summer of 1641 he and the Long Parliament reached agreement on a series of reforms which satisfied all the demands they had put forward, except one. And Charles went to war in 1642, not in defence of his right to levy taxation at will (he had abandoned that), nor in defence of his right to control the Church (he might have done, but parliament had not yet seriously challenged that control), but in defence of his right to command the army and to choose his own advisers. Contemporaries, at any rate, were quite clear on this point.[1]

The Civil Wars broke down temporarily the exceedingly strong and well-organised assumptions that maintained the pre-war social structure, and subsequent inability of parliament to reach agreement with the defeated king or deal effectively with its own captains left the way open for some of the most daring experiments that have ever been made with the English constitution. For a few wild months in 1647 and 1648 it seemed that England might even topple into democracy. But the massive inertia of the class structure was far too strong. The king was executed, but only to make way for a narrow, oligarchic republic on the Dutch or Venetian model. Cromwell overthrew the republic, but by then the messianic radicalism of his fighting years was fast sloughing away, and his consolidation or consummation of the 'Revolution' was only superficially experimental. By 1657 the retreat on monarchy had begun, and on Cromwell's death it became a rout, which ended in the confusion of the Restoration.

The *status quo ante bellum* restored, the situation of 1642 soon recurred. Charles I had tried to rule without parliament, his son kept his parliaments too long; and in 1678 the Popish Plot of 1640 returned in a more virulent and

---

[1] Edmund Ludlow said bluntly in 1659: 'The great quarrel between the king and us was the militia. Either he or we were guilty' (Burton, *Diary*, III, 145). Charles I said on the scaffold, 'All the world knows that I never did begin a war with the two Houses of Parliament . . . They began upon me, it is the militia they began upon' (p. 294 below). It is strange that this is still a matter for debate.

hysterical form. Probably only the cult of the martyred Charles I and visceral fear of another civil war saved the monarchy. James II's remedy, naturally, was to raise an army, which he found it remarkably easy to do, and if he had not at the same time played on his subjects' nerves by attempting to secure complete toleration for his co-religionists, and if he had not quarrelled with the ruling classes in the process, he might well have succeeded.

But even in 1689 the measures taken to deal with the central problem of the seventeenth-century constitution, military power, were feeble and hesitant. It was solved indirectly, even furtively, by parliament's refusal to vote William III a regular income. Because 1689 saw the inauguration of 'parliamentary monarchy' it is too easily assumed that the opposition programme triumphed. In fact, it is difficult to see that the opposition to the Stuarts had any programme, except the preservation of what they conceived to be the 'ancient constitution' and the maintenance of their own class power. The years 1640 to 1645 were the great years of the parliamentary gentry, but then they were swept aside; and they were swept aside not only because there were no leaders to replace Pym and Hampden, but because neither Pym nor Hampden nor their successors had any viable programme for the future. They were 'conservationists' just as much as Charles I or Strafford. And subsequently the quality of the Commons gentry shows a remarkable decline; from Pym's Middle Party to the Exclusionists, and from the Exclusionists to the October Club of 1710. What these groups had in common was a dislike of efficient, centralised government, extreme gullibility and a poor tactical sense. They produced plenty of demagogues and incendiaries, like Eliot, Russell and St John, but only one statesman, John Pym – and even he would have lost his opportunity but for the intervention of the Scots. (It is often forgotten that Charles I's defeat was precipitated by his failure to control Scotland and Ireland, not England.) Pym and his immediate associates were selfish, narrow minded and class orientated, but they had a sense of public and national responsibility lacking in their sons and grandsons. An opposition that became increasingly reactionary and irresponsible won the plaudits of posterity but lost the day, and the broad stream of statesmanship that stemmed from Pym, Hampden, Brooke and Holles petered out in the eighteenth-century inanities of Sir John Hinde Cotton and Sir Watkyn Williams-Wynn. Who gained by the revolution of 1688 has yet to be decided, but it was not the House of Commons.

BOOK I

THE ANCIENT CONSTITUTION 1603–40

He that goeth about to persuade a multitude that they are not so well governed as they ought to be shall never want attentive and favourable hearers; because they know the manifold defects whereunto every kind of regiment is subject, but the secret lets and difficulties, which in public proceedings are innumerable and inevitable, they have not ordinarily the judgement to consider. And because such as openly reprove supposed disorders of state are taken for principal friends to the common benefit of all and for men that carry singular freedom of mind, under this fair and plausible colour whatsoever they utter passeth for good and current. That which wanteth in the weight of their speech is supplied by the aptness of men's minds to accept and believe it.

RICHARD HOOKER

CHAPTER I

THE MONARCHY

Samuel Rawson Gardiner's services to scholarship were many and great; his greatest disservice was his persistence in describing the Great Rebellion as 'The Puritan Revolution', implying that Charles I's opponents were united in a desire to change the nature of the Church and of the state. Nothing could be further from the truth. In fact, the opponents of the monarchy were for the most part sturdy reactionaries who wanted nothing more than to restore the 'ancient constitution' of a century, perhaps even two or three centuries, before. Sir Arthur Haslerigg was one of the most radical men in the Long Parliament, yet in 1659, when he looked back on the crisis of 1642, he was quite sure that 'there was at this time no thought to alter government', and all he and his kind had wanted was 'our ancient liberties with our ancient government'.[1] Perhaps this does not need restating, but Gardiner is certainly not dead when a modern professional historian can entitle his book *The Rise of the Revolutionary Party in the English House of Commons, 1603–1629*.[2]

Political theory in the early seventeenth century was simple, patriarchal and authoritative – but not authoritarian; it was virtually untouched in terms of practical politics by the work of Bodin, for instance. From Adam descended the heads of families, from heads of families chiefs of tribes, and from chiefs of tribes, kings. To this extent the patriarchal theories of Sir Robert Filmer were a commonplace (1). The opposing theory, of elective kingship and government by the people, was familiar enough, too, but sturdily rejected (2).

England had the additional complication of a native system of law which appeared to have grown up with the monarchy. The king enjoyed many privileges at Common Law, but whether he was outside it or above it or not was a question that had never been settled, largely because it had so very rarely been raised. It was raised often in the reigns of James I and Charles I, for three reasons. First, the steady fall in the value of money made it impossible for the king to live on his hereditary revenues, even in peace time, though Elizabeth's financial prudence and the long war against Spain (1587–1604) had disguised the fact. Secondly, James I was uncertain in his handling of the House of Commons, Charles I still more so, yet the Commons was a proud and sensitive body whose members were subject to much the same economic pressures as the Crown. They were reluctant to authorise additional taxation which might become permanent, so in the intervals of parliament the king tried various ways of supplementing his income, including devices like impositions and ship-money, which had never specifically been declared illegal, but which depended on the assumption that the king – in certain matters at least – had absolute power. The next parliament often felt

---

[1] Burton, *Diary*, III, 87 (7 February 1659).   [2] By Williams B. Mitchell (New York 1957).

obliged to debate these illicit methods of supply before it even thought of voting any itself, and a vicious circle was established. At the same time the king's position as supreme governor of the Church was never wholly accepted by the Commons, who argued that since their predecessors had passed the legislation establishing the English Church in 1559 they were free to amend the terms of that establishment. And finally the king, with the support of certain lawyers and clerics, publicly laid claim to powers as full and complete as those of any monarch in Europe.

Some of James I's pronouncements are notorious. In *The Trew Law of Free Monarchies* he asserted that kings were God's vice-gerents on earth, that there were no legal limits to their power, and that the sole function of elected assemblies was to give advice (*TCD*, pp. 9–10). But in the event his absolutism was confined to the realm of theory, and though he continued to believe that he stood in a special relationship with God, in an important and carefully argued speech to parliament in 1610 (**4**) he made a distinction between kings in their first creation, whose powers knew no limit, and kings of settled states, who ought to abide by the law their predecessors had helped create; they were not forced to respect the rights and customs of their subjects, but if they did not they would answer for it to God. He himself regarded his coronation oath with great seriousness, and by that oath he had promised to respect the laws and customs of England (*PCD*, pp. 391–2). Thus he was careful always to operate within the framework of the Common Law, he never promulgated new law of his own accord, though he may have believed he could, and in some ways he was more moderate in his behaviour, more 'constitutional' than Queen Elizabeth.[3] Particularly significant was his reaction in 1610, when the Commons complained that he was abusing his right to issue proclamations, creating new crimes not hitherto recognised in law, and transferring known crimes from one jurisdiction to another. He consulted the two chief justices, Coke and Altham, and meekly accepted their decision against him, though in *The Trew Law of Free Monarchies* he had declared, 'The king makes daily statutes and ordinances, enjoining such pains thereto as he thinks meet, without any advice of parliament or estates.' In the same year Dr John Cowell's law dictionary, *The Interpreter*, said much the same thing, but when parliament objected James himself drew up a proclamation suppressing the book (p. 126 below) and authorised Salisbury to tell parliament that he regarded himself as 'king by the Common Law of the land' (**3**).

In fact, James was sensible enough to realise that England, like Scotland, lacked the practical attributes of despotic monarchy, such as a standing army, and without these it was best to accept with grace what could not be amended, and in his later parliaments he relaxed his theoretical position still further. His opening speech to parliament in 1624 (p. 43 below) is particularly significant in this respect.

Charles I was much less of a theorist, and much more pragmatic than his father. For instance the long *apologia* he published after the dissolution of parliament in 1629 (pp. 71–3 below) reviews recent events in detail, and asserts his immediate right to levy tunnage and poundage, but it does not enunciate any general theory of kingship. Clearly he tended to regard his duties as supreme governor of the Church more

---

[3] F. D. Wormuth, *The Royal Prerogative 1603–1649* (Ithaca, New York 1939), p. 93.

emotionally, more personally than his predecessors, perhaps because he was the first monarch to be raised virtually from birth in that Church, but he did not necessarily agree with the advanced theologians of his reign, like Sibthorpe, Manwaring and Montague, who would have him enforce the royal supremacy in matters temporal as well as spiritual – no doubt he would have liked to do so, but it is not clear that he regarded it as practical politics. The theme of the age was patriarchalism, as we have seen, not absolutism. No doubt Charles listened complacently enough to Manwaring's sermons on *Religion and Allegiance*, delivered before him in 1627, but when the Commons protested the following year he agreed to suppress them without entering upon a discussion of their contents (**5**).

Like his father, he was careful not to stray beyond the pale of the Common Law as he understood it, and though it is dangerous perhaps to lay too much stress on disconnected utterances, his political thought appears to have been entirely conventional, and essentially the same as that voiced by his opponents and critics. With remarkable unanimity early seventeenth-century Englishmen believed that they were bound to abide by the ancient constitution, which had existed without change time out of mind. Under that constitution the ruler had certain prerogatives, his subjects certain rights, and neither could be infringed without a dangerous imbalance resulting.[4] Both sides were aware by the 1620s that an imbalance existed, or was imminent, and this was a decade of tension, a tension evident, for instance, in the clashing phrases of Thomas Wentworth's famous speech to the Council of the North in December 1628 (**7**). Similar tension lay behind Charles's denunciation in 1626 of those 'unquiet and restless spirits' whose sole aim was to 'break that circle of order which without apparent danger to Church and state may not be broken' (p. 139 below).

But if Charles I and Strafford were obsessed with the maintenance of the 'circle of order', 'the arch of government', so was John Pym. In June 1628, in the magnificent speech with which he launched Manwaring's impeachment, he gave one of the best expositions in this era of the classic contemporary view of the constitution (**6**). One of the main burdens of his discourse was that it was perilous to exalt the power either of the king or his people, but in 1641 Charles I, too, sternly warned the Commons of the danger of innovation or change: 'I make a great difference between reformation and alteration of government' (**8**).

Everyone spoke the same language. When Pym opened the case against Strafford on 25 November 1640 his words echoed the earl's in his speech to the Council of the North 12 years before – 'A king and his people make one body; the inferior parts confer nourishment and strength, the superior, sense and motion.' Strafford in his turn echoed Pym when he made his last speech in his own defence, in April 1641 (p. 193 below).

King Charles produced the most elaborate and reasoned exposition of the classic

---

[4] The whole theory is discussed in Pocock, *Ancient Constitution*. At a lower stage of theorising G. L. Harriss argues that the period 1460–1580 was one of stable mixed monarchy, whose incipient breakdown thereafter was a source of bewilderment and fear, 'Medieval Doctrines in the Debates on Supply 1610–29', in Sharpe, *Faction*, pp. 72–103. Also several historians have recently pointed to the contemporary emphasis placed on the *loving* nature of the king–parliament relationship; e.g. Derek Hirst, *ibid.*, p. 109. This is evident even in supposedly confrontational documents like the 'Form of Apology and Satisfaction' (p. 29 below).

theory of the constitution in his Answer to the Nineteen Propositions, in June 1642 (**9**).[5] He insisted that as king he was given certain powers, to defend the people against their social superiors, and the law against the encroachment of parliament, and the 'class' bias thus introduced into the theory of the constitution was again stressed at his trial in 1649, when he once more insisted that he was the only upholder of law and order, 'order' meaning the right order of society.[6] Yet in the main he was only redefining principles already laid down by Pym and Strafford from opposite sides of the gulf which had opened beneath men's feet in 1628.

Wild claims were made by wild men on both sides, by Sir John Eliot as well as Roger Manwaring, but these were ignored, just as the theories of philosophers like Hobbes were rejected. In the sphere of practical politics the disagreement essentially lay in how to operate a constitution of whose nature few had any doubts.

1. Introduction to the Commons Journals, 19 March 1604

Liceat Praefari

The first frame of this earthly body of a Chaos became a distinct essence of Creatures. Man, the most noble by Nature, born to a Law, out of that gave law to others, and to himself. Hence Order, the lustre of Nature, guided by a First Essence, put all government into form: First, in two, who, by procreation, according to the rule of power (increase and multiply) made a Family, with one Head; by propagation, a Tribe, or Kindred, with one Elder, or Chief; by multiplication, a Society, a Province, a Country, a Kingdom, with one or more Guides or Leaders, of spirit aptest, or of choice fittest, to govern.

This division, sorting itself into proprieties, fell in parts of right, greater or smaller, to some Tribe, Kindred, or elective change of Person. *Vicissitudo rerum*, the herald of time, doth warrant this to be the true original pedigree of government; and by a present change, in our own eyes, hath made the demonstration more subject to our sense, by our loss of an excellent princess, by our gain of a successor, for eminent virtue and experience in government famous and peerless, leading us, by a momentary fear, to a better sight of a permanent happiness . . .   *CJ*, I, 139

---

[5] It was written by Culpeper and Falkland in Hyde's absence; Hyde strongly objected to their admission that the king was merely one of the Three Estates (Clarendon, *Life* (1759), I, 130-2), and his suspicions were later confirmed when Sir Henry Vane used it in his defence to a charge of treason, in 1662 (*ST*, VI, 158). It was also pressed into service by the Exclusionists in 1680 (*State Tracts*, I, 477ff.). See Corinne Comstock Weston, *House of Lords*, chs. 1-2.

[6] Muddiman, *Trial of Charles I*, pp. 231-3; 'His Majesty's Reasons against the pretended jurisdiction of the High Court of Justice' (see p. 292 below).

2. The canons of 1606[7]

★　★　★

II. If any man shall affirm that men at the first, without all good education and civility, ran up and down in woods and fields, as wild creatures, resting themselves in caves and dens, and acknowledging no superiority one over another, until they were taught by experience the necessity of government; and that thereupon they chose some among themselves to order and rule the rest, giving them power and authority so to do; and that consequently all civil power, jurisdiction and authority was first derived from the people, and disordered multitude; or either is originally still in them, or else is deduced by their consents naturally from them, and is not God's ordinance originally descending from him and depending upon him; he doth greatly err.

Cardwell, *Synodalia*, 1, 331–2

3. The Earl of Salisbury's speech, 8 March 1610

His Majesty said further that for his kingdom he was beholden to no elective power, neither doth he depend upon any popular applause; and yet he doth acknowledge that, though he did derive his title from the loins of his ancestors, yet the law did set the crown upon his head, and he is a king by the common law of the land. Which as it is most proper and natural for this nation, so it is the most equal and just law in any kingdom in the world. He said further that it was dangerous to submit the power of a king to definition. But withal he did acknowledge that he had no power to make laws of himself, or to exact any subsidies *de jure* without the consent of his three Estates; and therefore he was so far from approving the opinion as he did hate those that believed it; and lastly he said that there was such a marriage and union between the prerogative and the law as they cannot possibly be severed . . .

Gardiner, *Parliamentary Debates in 1610*, p. 24

4. James I on monarchy: speech to Parliament, 21 March 1610

The state of monarchy is the supremest thing upon earth; for kings are not only God's lieutenants upon earth, and sit upon God's throne, but even by God himself they are called gods . . .

[7] James I declined to license these canons, chiefly because of no. XXVIII, which stated, 'If any man shall affirm . . . that when any such new forms of government, begun by rebellion, are after thoroughly settled, the authority in them is not of God, or that any who live within the territories of such new governments are not bound to be subject to God's authority which is there executed, but may rebel against the same . . ., he doth greatly err'. The king was posthumously justified when the canons were at last published in 1690, under the title of 'Bishop Overall's Convocation Book', and promptly used by divines like William Sherlock to justify their support for William III. See Charles F. Mullett, 'William Sherlock and the Revolution of 1688', *HLQ*, x (1946), 83.

Kings are justly called gods for that they exercise a manner or resemblance of divine power upon earth, for if you will consider the attributes to God you shall see how they agree in the person of a king. God hath power to create or destroy, make or unmake, at his pleasure; to give life or send death, to judge all and to be judged not accountable to none; to raise low things and to make high things low at his pleasure; and to God are both soul and body due. And the like power have kings: they make and unmake their subjects; they have power of raising, and casting down; of life, and of death, judges over all their subjects, and in all causes, and yet accountable to none but God only. They have power to exalt low things, and abase high things, and make of their subjects like men at the chess – a pawn to take a bishop or a knight – and cry up or down any of their subjects, as they do their money. And to the king is due both the affection of the soul and the service of the body of his subjects . . .

But now in these our times we are to distinguish between the state of kings in their first original, and between the state of settled kings and monarchies that do at this time govern in civil kingdoms; for even as God, during the time of the Old Testament, spake by oracles and wrought by miracles, yet how soon it pleased him to settle a Church which was bought and redeemed by the blood of his only son Christ, then was there a cessation of both, he ever after governing his people and Church within the limits of his revealed will; so in the first original of kings, whereof some had their beginning by conquest, and some by election of the people, their wills at that time served for law, yet how soon kingdoms began to be settled in civility and policy, then did kings set down their minds by laws, which are properly made by the king only, but at the rogation of the people, the king's grant being obtained thereunto. And so the king became to be *lex loquens*, after a sort, binding himself by a double oath to the observation of the fundamental laws of the kingdom: tacitly, as by being a king, and so bound to protect as well the people as the laws of his kingdom; and expressly, by his oath at his coronation. So, as every just king in a settled kingdom is bound to observe that paction made to his people by his laws, in framing his government agreeable thereto, according to that paction which God made with Noah after the deluge, 'Hereafter seed time and harvest, cold and heat, summer and winter, and day and night shall not cease, so long as the earth remains'; and therefore a king governing in a settled kingdom leaves to be a king, and degenerates into a tyrant, as soon as he leaves off to rule according to his laws . . . As for my part, I thank God I have ever given good proof that I never had intention to the contrary, and I am sure to go to my grave with that reputation and comfort, that never king was in all his time more careful to have his laws duly observed, and himself to govern thereafter, than I.

I conclude then this point touching the power of kings with this axiom of

Divinity, that as to dispute what God may do is blasphemy, but *quid vult Deus*, that divines may lawfully and do ordinarily dispute and discuss, for to dispute *a posse ad esse* is both against logic and divinity; so is it sedition in subjects to dispute what a king may do in the height of his power, but just kings will ever be willing to declare what they will do, if they will not incur the curse of God. I will not be content that my power be disputed upon, but I shall ever be willing to make the reason appear of all my doings, and rule my actions according to my laws.   *Works*, pp. 529-31[8]

5. Roger Manwaring: a sermon preached before the king at Oatlands, 4 July 1627

Among all the powers that be ordained of God the regal is most high, strong and large: kings [are] above all, inferior to none, to no multitudes of men, to no Angels, to no order of Angels. For though in nature, order and place the Angels be superior to men, yet to powers and persons royal they are not, in regard of any dependence that princes have of them. Their power [is] then the highest. No power in the world or in the hierarchy of the Church can lay restraint upon these supremes; therefore theirs [is] the strongest . . .

. . . All the significations of a royal pleasure are, and ought to be to all loyal subjects in the nature and force of a command; as well for that some may nor can search into the high discourse and deep counsels of kings, seeing their hearts are so deep, by reason of their distance from common men, even as the heavens are in respect of the earth. Therefore said he who was wise in heart and deep in counsel, 'The heavens for height, and the earth for depth, and the heart of a king is unsearchable' (Prov. xxv. 3) . . . Who then may question that which God doth proclaim from heaven to be in his hands, and at his guidance?

Nay, though any king in the world should command flatly against the law of God, yet were his power no otherwise at all to be resisted but for the not doing of his will, in that which is clearly unlawful, [and] to endure with patience, whatsoever penalty his pleasure should inflict upon them, who in this case would desire rather to obey God than Man. By which patient and meek suffering of their sovereign's pleasure they should become glorious martyrs, whereas by resisting of his will they should for ever endure the pain and stain of odious traitors and impious malefactors.

But on the other side, if any king shall command that which stands not in

---

[8] Notes taken of this speech at the time (Foster, *Proceedings*, i, 46, ii, 60) suggest that it scarcely mentioned the conditional nature of kingship, if at all. It is suggestive that in the version published soon afterwards, and republished in his *Works* in 1616, James should have adopted a much more whiggish line. In fact, it was reprinted as a pamphlet in 1681 with the title, *Vox Regis: or the Difference betwixt a King ruling by Law and a Tyrant by his own Will . . .* [etc.].

any opposition to the original laws of God, Nature, Nations and the Gospel (though it be not correspondent in every circumstance to laws national and municipal), no subject may, without hazard of his own damnation, in rebelling against God, question or disobey the will and pleasure of his sovereign. For, as a father of the country he commands what his pleasure is, out of counsel and judgement; as a king of subjects, he enjoins it; as a lord over God's inheritance he exacts it; as a supreme head of the body he adviseth it; as a Defender of the Faith he requires it as their homage; as a protector of their persons, lives and estates he deserves it; and as the sovereign, procurer of all the happiness, peace and welfare which they enjoy who are under him he doth most justly claim it at their hands. To kings therefore in all those respects nothing can be denied (without manifest and sinful violation of law and conscience) that may answer their royal estate and excellency, that may further the supply of their urgent necessities, that may be for the security of their royal persons (whose lives are worth millions of others), that may serve for the protection of their kingdoms, territories and dominions, that may enable them to yield relief, aid and succour to their dear and royal confederates and allies, or that may be for the defence and propagation of that sacred and precious truth, the public protection whereof they do maintain by their laws, and prerogatives royal . . .

[As for parliament], though such assemblies as are the highest and greatest representatives of a kingdom be most sacred and honourable, and necessary also for those ends to which they were first instituted, yet know we must that ordained they were not to this end, to contribute any right to kings, whereby to challenge tributary aids and subsidiary helps, but for the more equal imposing, and more easy exacting of that which unto kings doth appertain by natural and original law and justice, as their proper inheritance annexed to their imperial crowns from their very births. And therefore if, by a magistrate that is supreme, if upon necessity, extreme and urgent, such subsidiary helps be required, a proportion being held respectively to the abilities of the persons charged, and the sum, or quantity so required surmount not (too remarkably) the use and charge for which it was levied, very hard would it be for any man in the world that should not accordingly satisfy such demands to defend his conscience from that heavy prejudice of resisting the ordinance of God and receiving to himself damnation, though every of those circumstances be not observed which by the municipal laws is required.

Religion and Allegiance (1627)

6. Pym's speech at Manwaring's impeachment, 4 June 1628

. . . He said there did result three positions, which he was to maintain as the groundwork and foundation of the whole cause.

The first, that the form of government in any state could not be altered without apparent danger of ruin to that state. The second, [that] the law of England, whereby the subject was exempted from taxes and loans not granted by common consent of parliament, was not introduced by any statute, or by any charter or sanction of princes, but was the ancient and fundamental law, issuing from the first frame and constitution of the kingdom. The third, that this liberty of the subject is not only most convenient and profitable for the people, but most honourable, most necessary for the king – yea, in that point of supply for which it was endeavoured to be broken.

The form of government is that which doth actuate and dispose every part and member of a state to the common good; and as those parts give strength and ornament to the whole, so they receive from it again strength and protection in their several stations and degrees. If this mutual relation and intercourse be broken, the whole frame will quickly be dissolved, and fall in pieces, and instead of this concord and interchange of support, whilst one part seeks to uphold the old form of government, and the other part to introduce a new, they will miserably consume and devour one another. Histories are full of the calamities of whole states and nations in such cases. It is true that time must needs bring some alterations, and every alteration is a step and degree towards a dissolution; those things only are eternal which are constant and uniform. Therefore it is observed by the best writers upon this subject that those commonwealths have been most durable and perpetual which have often reformed and recomposed themselves according to their first institution and ordinance; for by this means they repair the breaches and counterwork the ordinary and natural effects of time.

The second question is as manifest. There are plain footsteps of those laws in the government of the Saxons; they were of that vigour and force as to overlive the Conquest, nay, to give bounds and limits to the Conqueror, whose victory gave him first hope. But the assurance and possession of the Crown be obtained by composition, in which he bound himself to observe these and the other ancient laws and liberties of the kingdom, which afterwards he likewise confirmed by oath at his coronation. From him the said obligation descended to his successors. It is true they have been often broken, they have been often confirmed by charters of kings, by acts of parliaments, but the petitions of the subjects upon which those charters and acts were founded were ever petitions of right, demanding their ancient and due liberties, not suing for any new.

To clear the third position (he said) may seem to some men more a paradox: that those liberties of the subject should be so honourable, so profitable for the king, and most necessary for the supply of his Majesty.

It hath been upon another occasion declared that if those liberties were taken away there should remain no more industry, no more justice, no more courage; for who will contend, who will endanger himself for that which is not his own? But (he said) he would not insist upon any of those points, nor yet upon others very important. He said that if those liberties were taken away there would remain no means for the subjects, by any act of bounty or benevolence, to ingratiate themselves to their sovereign . . . The hearts of the people, and their bounty in parliament, is the only constant treasure and revenue of the Crown, which cannot be exhausted, alienated, anticipated, or otherwise charged and encumbered . . .   *ST*, III, 341–3

7. Thomas Lord Viscount Wentworth's speech when he first sate Lord President of the North, December 1628

. . . To the joint individual well being of sovereignty and subjection do I here vow all my cares and diligences through the whole course of this my ministry. I confess I am not ignorant how some distempered minds have of late very far endeavoured to divide the considerations of the two, as if their ends were distinct, not the same, nay in opposition; a monstrous, a prodigious birth of a licentious conception, for so we should become all head or all members. But, God be praised, human wisdom, common experience, Christian religion teach us far otherwise.

Princes are to be indulgent, nursing fathers to their people; their modest liberties, their sober rights, ought to be precious in their eyes; the branches of their government be for shadow, for habitation, the comfort of life, repose, safe and still under the protection of their sceptres. Subjects on the other side ought with solicitous eyes of jealousy to watch over the prerogatives of a crown; the authority of a king is the keystone which closeth up the arch of order and government, which contains each part in due relation to the whole, and which once shaken, infirmed, all the frame falls together into a confused heap of foundation and battlement, of strength and beauty . . .

Verily, these are those mutual intelligences of love and protection descending, and loyalty ascending, which should pass, be the entertainments, between a king and his people. Their faithful servants must look equally on both, weave, twist these two together in all their counsels, study, labour to preserve each without diminishing or enlarging either, and by running in the worn, wonted channels, treading the ancient bounds, cut off early all disputes from between them. For whatever he be which ravels forth into questions the right of a king and of a people, [he] shall never be able to wrap them up again into the comeliness and order he found them . . .

The Academy, VII (1875), 582–3

8. King's speech, 25 January 1641

My Lords and Gentlemen,

I must lay before you the present distractions of government, occasioned partly because of the parliament, not by it; for some men, taking occasion now by the sitting thereof (more maliciously than ignorantly) will put no alteration betwixt reformation and alteration of government. Hence it seems that divine service is irreverently interupted, petitions tumultuously given, and much of my revenue detained or disputed.

More particulars I will not mention, because I will hasten to put you in a way of remedy, which I will do, first, by showing you my clear intentions; then by warning you to eschew those rocks that may hinder this good work.

First then know, that I shall willingly concur with you to find out and inform all innovations in Church and Commonwealth, and consequently, that all courts of justice shall be regulated according to law, my intention being to reduce all matters of religion and government to what they were in the purest times of Queen Elizabeth's days.

Moreover, what parts of my revenue that shall be found illegal or grievous to the public, I shall willingly lay down, relying entirely upon the affections of my people.

Having thus clearly shown you my intentions, I will now tell you what you are to eschew; to which purpose I cannot but take notice of those petitions (I cannot tell how to call them) given in the name of several counties, against the present established government of the Church, and of the greater threats that are given out, that bishops shall be no better than ciphers, if not clean done away.

Now I must clearly tell you, that I make a great difference between reformation and alteration of government; though I am for the first, I cannot give way to the latter. I will not say but that bishops may have overstretched their power, or encroached upon the temporal; which if you find, correct and reform the above, according to the wisdom of former times, so far I am with you.

Nay further, if, upon serious debate, you shall show me that bishops have some temporal authority inconvenient to the state, and not so necessary to the Church for the support of the episcopacy, I shall not be unwilling to persuade them to lay it down; yet, by this, you must not understand that I can consent for the taking away of their voice in parliament, which they have so anciently enjoyed, under so many of my predecessors, even before the Conquest, and ever since; and which I conceive I am bound to maintain, as one of the fundamental institutions of this kingdom.

There is but one other rock, and that not in substance, but in form; yet that form is so essential that, except it be reformed, it will mar the substance. There is a bill given in for frequent parliaments. The thing I like; that is to say, to have often parliaments; but to give power to sheriffs and constables, and I know not whom, to do my office, that I cannot yield unto. But, to show you that I am desirous to please you in forms (which destroy not the substance), I am content you shall have an act for this purpose, but so reformed, it neither trench on mine honour, nor on that inseparable right of my crown concerning parliaments. To which purpose I have commanded my learned counsel to wait on you, my Lords, with such propositions as I hope will give contentment, for I ingenuously confess that frequent parliaments is the best means to preserve that right understanding betwixt me and my subjects which I so heartily desire.

LJ, IV, 142

9. The king's Answer to the Nineteen Propositions,[9] 18 June 1642

★   ★   ★

There being three kinds of government among men, absolute monarchy, aristocracy and democracy, and all these having their particular conveniences and inconveniences, the experience and wisdom of your ancestors hath so moulded this out of a mixture of these as to give to this kingdom (as far as human prudence can provide) the conveniences of all three, without the inconveniences of any one, as long as the balance hangs even between the three estates, and they run jointly on in their proper channel (begetting verdure and fertility in the meadows on both sides) and the overflowing of either on either side raise no deluge or inundation. The ill of absolute monarchy is tyranny, the ill of aristocracy is faction and division, the ills of democracy are tumults, violence and licentiousness. The good of monarchy is the uniting a nation under one head to resist invasion from abroad and insurrection at home; the good of aristocracy is the conjunction of counsel in the ablest persons of a state for the public benefit; the good of democracy is liberty, and the courage and industry which liberty begets.

In this kingdom the laws are jointly made by a king, by a house of peers, and by a House of Commons chosen by the people, all having free votes and particular privileges. The government, according to these laws, is [en]trusted to the king; power of treaties of war and peace, of making peers, of choosing officers and councillors for state, judges for law, commanders for forts and castles, giving commissions for raising men, to make war abroad, or to prevent or provide against invasions or insurrections at home, benefit of confiscations,

---

[9] No. **68** p. 222 below.

power of pardoning, and some more of the like kind are placed in the king. And this kind of regulated monarchy, having this power to preserve that authority without which it would be disabled to preserve the laws in their force and the subjects in their liberties and properties, is intended to draw to him such a respect and relation from the great ones, as may hinder the ills of division and faction, and such a fear and reverence from the people as may hinder tumults, violence and licentiousness.

Again, that the prince may not make use of his high and perpetual power to the hurt of those for whose good he hath it, and make use of the name of public necessity for the gain of his private favourites and followers, to the detriment of his people, the House of Commons (an excellent convener of liberty, but never intended for any share in government, or the choosing of them that govern) is solely entrusted with the first propositions concerning the levy of money (which is the sinews as well of peace as of war), and the impeaching of those who for their own ends, though countenanced by any surreptitiously gotten command of the king, have violated the law, which he is bound (when he knows it) to protect; and to the prosecution of which they are bound to advise him, at least not to serve him to the contrary. And the Lords, being trusted with a judicatory power, are an excellent screen and bank between the prince and people, to assist each against any encroachment of the other, and by just judgments to preserve that law which ought to be the rule of every one of the three . . .

Since therefore the power, legally placed in both houses, is more than sufficient to prevent and restrain the power of tyranny, and without the power which is now asked from us we shall not be able to discharge that trust which is the end of monarchy, since this would be a total subversion of the fundamental laws, and that excellent constitution of this kingdom which hath made this nation so many years both famous and happy to a great degree of envy, since to the power of punishing (which is already in your hands according to law) if the power of preferring be added, we shall have nothing left for us but to look on, since the encroaching of one of these estates upon the power of the other is unhappy in the effects, both to them and all the rest, since this power of at most a joint government in us with our councillors (or rather, our guardians) will return us to the worst kind of minority, and make us despicable both at home and abroad, and beget eternal factions and dissensions (as destructive to public happiness as war) both in the chosen, and in the houses that chose them, and the people who chose the choosers, since so new a power will undoubtedly intoxicate persons who were not born to it, and beget not only divisions among them as equals, but in them contempt of us, as become an equal to them, and insolence and injustice toward our people, as now so much their inferiors, which will be the more grievous unto them, as suffering from those who were so lately of a nearer degree to themselves, and being to have redress only from those that placed them, and fearing they may be inclined to preserve what they have made, both out of kindness and policy, since all great changes are extremely inconvenient, and almost infallibly beget yet greater changes, which beget yet greater inconveniences.

Since as great a one in the Church must follow this of the kingdom, since the second estate would in all probability follow the fate of the first, and by some of the turbulent spirits jealousies would soon be raised against them, and the like propositions for reconciliation of differences would then be sent to them as they now have joined to send to us till (all power being vested in the House of Commons, and their number making them incapable of transacting affairs of state with the necessary service and expedition, these being retrusted to some close committee) at last the common people (who in the meantime must be flattered, and to whom licence must be given in all their wild humours, how contrary soever to established law, or their own real good) discover this *arcanum imperii*, that all this was done by them, but not for them, and grow weary of journey-work, and set up for themselves, call parity and independence liberty, devour that estate which had devoured the rest, destroy all rights and proprieties, all distinctions of families and merit, and by this means this splendid and excellently distinguished form of government end in a dark, equal chaos of confusion, and the long line of our many noble ancestors in a Jack Cade or a Wat Tyler.

★   ★   ★

Rushworth, v, 728, 730-2

CHAPTER 2

PARLIAMENT

I. STATUS AND PRIVILEGE

The status of the seventeenth-century parliament rested on the peers' immemorial right to give counsel to the Crown, and the Commons' role as the representative element in the constitution. In the first statute of James I's reign it was described as:

> This High Court of Parliament, where all the whole body of the realm, and every particular member thereof, either in person or by representation (upon their own free elections), are by the laws of the realm deemed to be personally present.[1]

James acknowledged this in his first speech to the Commons, in March 1604, addressing them as 'you who are presently assembled to represent the body of this whole kingdom and all sorts of people within the same'.[2] By the end of this contumacious session he was by no means so sure of this (**11**), but he returned to the same theme in 1624 (**15**).

In view of the distribution of seats, markedly skewed in favour of the South, and particularly the South-West – not to mention the restricted franchise in most boroughs – James did right to remind the Commons that 'this House doth not so represent the whole commons of the realm as the shadow doth the body, but only representatively' (that is, figuratively). The payment of wages to borough MPs was fast dying out, as was the idea that a knight of the shire must be a native of that county, but in some ways they were both still regarded as delegates. It was not unusual for a session to begin with each Member stepping forward to present the grievances of his own area; in fact this was done as late as 1640. In July 1610 Salisbury deliberately prorogued parliament for three months so that MPs could consult their constituents on new methods of taxation, though the result did not encourage a repetition of the practice.

Yet it was never explicitly stated whom the Commons were representing. In fact apart from the landowning classes the only sizable elements in the House were the professional lawyers, who in 1614 numbered 48 out of 475, and in 1640 75 out of 504, and the merchants, who numbered 42 and 45 respectively.[3] It is significant that in a period when taxes on trade were increasing by leaps and bounds the number of merchants in the Commons remained static. The divine right of landowners to govern the nation was duly accepted by contemporaries; it is surprising that it should have been accepted so complacently by historians. The fact is, seventeenth-century parliaments were not always representative of the upper classes as a whole.

---

[1] The Succession Act, 1 Jac. I, c. 1, printed in *TCD*, pp. 10–12.   [2] *Ibid.*, p. 24.
[3] Figures taken from Keeler, *Long Parliament*, and Moir, *Addled Parliament*.

Yet the House had grown steadily in size in the late sixteenth century, mainly because of the pressure by the landed classes on the Crown to confer parliamentary representation *de novo* by letters patent. Moreover, by a strained construction on the Buckinghamshire Election Case in 1604 (p. 22 below), the Commons began to restore the right to many boroughs which had allowed it to lapse, often for a couple of centuries. James I and Charles I also continued to exercise their own rights with some freedom – with typical donnishness James gave Oxford and Cambridge two Members each – with the result that the Commons swelled from 467 Members in 1604 to 504 in 1640.[4]

Even so, interest in seats for a majority does not imply the electoral engagement of the majority. It has been argued that public interest in elections increased between 1604 and 1640, and so did the number of those contested.[5] The first is notoriously subjective, the second is more precise, but can be deceptively presented; a 100 per cent increase in contested elections does not signify very much when the increase was from about 3.5 per cent to about 7 per cent. In the elections for the Long Parliament in 1640, the most hotly contested of the era, only 62 boroughs out of 214 went to the polls, and 14 counties out of 51. It would be absurd to pretend that the political awareness of the upper classes was not sharpened over this period, but it is difficult to argue that this was expressed at the hustings.

In contrast the House of Lords had remained static during the sixteenth century, and on Elizabeth's death there were only 55 temporal peers. By 1610 James I had raised their numbers to 80, and was proud of it, though the House is still best regarded as an annexe to the Council.[6] However, Buckingham's policy of selling peerages on a large scale brought the number up to 126 by 1628, and shifted the balance in more ways than one; the older peers were alienated, the new peers were not to be relied on, and in 1621, 1626 and 1628 the Lords joined the Commons to inflict a series of heavy political defeats on the Crown. In the crisis of 1628-9 many peers returned to their traditional allegiance, encouraged by Charles's conciliatory attitude and his abandonment of Buckingham's war policy, but in 1640 and 1641 their position is best described as 'delicate'. By putting them forward in his Answer to the Nineteen Propositions (pp. 18-20 above) as an essential buffer or intermediary between king and people Charles's advisers were making a self-conscious bid for their support.

Meanwhile, from the first day of the first session of his first parliament, 19 March 1604, King James's relations with the Commons were distinguished by a fluctuating but persistent degree of low-key contestation which captured the attention of an older school of historians and even led them to discern in this session the origins of the Great Rebellion. A closer examination of the circumstances, however, shows that the king made a constructive effort at reform, and that the Commons, while behaving with customary foolishness and narrow-mindedness at times, were neither so obstructive

---

[4] In 1661 the number was 507. The county and city of Durham were enfranchised in 1672, and Newark in 1677, bringing the total to 513. But the row over Newark discouraged Charles from trying again, and in return for the tacit suspension of his right the Commons suspended theirs. They therefore stuck at 513, apart from the addition of 45 Scots Members in 1707.

[5] Derek Hirst, *The Representative of the People?* (Cambridge 1975). Mark Kishlansky's forthcoming book, *Parliamentary Selection: Social and Political Change in Early Modern England*, will shed new light on this issue.

[6] He told a deputation from the House of Commons as early as April 1604 that since his accession 'the Church was decided, the nobility increased, the burden of the people eased' (*CJ*, I, 192).

nor radical as was once thought.[7] Over the next six years, moreover, the king could usually get his way with parliament if he set his mind to it (and if he stayed in London). But he was persistently let down by his ministers and advisers, and one symptom of this was an obvious deficiency in parliamentary management, which had in fact been very evident in Elizabeth's last parliament, in 1601, and was not rectified in the new reign. It is usual to attribute this to the failure to secure the election of sufficient privy councillors to the Commons, but it must be said that in 1621 and 1628, when the government took care to see that a large number of privy councillors and other placemen were present, the results in terms of guidance and control were disappointing.[8]

However, once we cease to look at the reign of James I from the vantage point of 1640, and once we break ourselves of the habit of picking over the evidence looking for points of disagreement, signs of co-operation and concord are not lacking, and trends which once appeared adverse to the Crown lose much of their sinister aura. The development of parliamentary procedure is a case in point. It used to be argued that the Commons steadily developed and refined their procedure over the period 1604–29 in a self-conscious attempt to wrest control of business from the Crown and its servants.[9] We are coming to realise now that in so far as this was not a random and unplanned natural development it was prompted by the Crown in an attempt to expedite government business; if anything the Commons, though aggressive in short-term episodes, were apprehensive of the long-term results.[10] Yet this is one of the factors which has encouraged so many historians, having at one end of their mental spectrum a (largely imaginary) period of harmony under Elizabeth, and at the other end the outbreak of Civil War in 1642, to posit a steady deterioration in Crown–parliament relations under James I, accelerating under Charles I, and by 1629 fated inevitably to end in a major confrontation.[11] But the school of 'revisionist' historians, emerging in the 1960s, argued that there was no such continuity of deterioration, that contemporaries took each parliament, or even each session, separately, and so must we; that there was no serious breakdown in Crown–parliament relations until the session of 1629, and even in 1641 all but a tiny minority assumed that the breakdown was superficial and temporary.[12]

[7] R. C. Munden, 'James I and "The Growth of Mutual Distrust": King, Commons and Reform 1603–4', in Sharpe, Faction, pp. 43–72.

[8] D. H. Willson, Privy Councillors, pp. 123–5, 225–6, 234–5, argues that Salisbury deliberately attempted to control the Commons from the Lords by the use of conferences between the two houses. This is not entirely convincing. It is a pity that we still lack a thorough study of Salisbury, and that Professor Willson, here and in his biography of James, is heavily biased in his favour.

[9] A thesis most cogently argued by Wallace Notestein, 'The Winning of the Initiative by the House of Commons', Proc. Brit. Academy, XI (1924–5), 125–75, which must rank as one of the most influential historical papers of the century.

[10] See, for instance, Sheila Lambert, 'Procedure in the House of Commons in the early Stuart period', EHR, XCV (1980), 753–81; Elizabeth Read Foster, 'Speaking in the House of Commons', BIHR, XLIII (1970), 35–56, and Sharpe, Faction, p. 27. Sharpe (ibid., p 13), speaks of 'a world of flux and doubt, not one of resolution and certainty, a clash of personality, not principle, a quarrel about forms and methods not about fundamentals'.

[11] The latest manifestation of this outlook is Lawrence Stone's Causes of the English Revolution, in 1972. For important critical assessments, see G. R. Elton, in HJ, XVI (1973), 205–8, and Conrad Russell, in EHR, LXXXVIII (1973), 856–61.

[12] See the works attributed to Russell in the bibliography, also the essays in Sharpe, Faction, and Russell's important paper, 'Parliamentary History in Perspective', History, LXI (1976), 1–27.

Certainly there was no disposition on James I's part to undervalue parliament or to regard it as unworkable. Sometimes he gave way to exasperation, as in 1614, when he told the Spanish ambassador after the fiasco of the Addled Parliament, 'I am surprised that my ancestors should ever have allowed such an institution to come into existence.'[13] But he was equally hysterical the other way in 1605, in the aftermath of the Gunpowder Plot, when he told parliament that if he had been blown up with them, 'Mine end should have been with the most honourable and best company, and in that most honourable and fittest place for a king to be in, for doing the turns most proper to his office', and in 1621, despite the recent impeachment of his lord chancellor, he could say with apparent sincerity, 'the House of Commons at this time have [sic] showed greater love, and used me with more respect in all their proceedings than ever any House of Commons have heretofore done to me'.[14] In fact, in this respect and when every qualification has been made, his reign closed on a happier note than that on which it began.

In the interval questions of privilege were a focus for discontent. Here Elton has taught us to make a crucial distinction between 'privilege' and 'liberties', though the first word often covered both.[15] All Members of Parliament, Lords and Commons, enjoyed important personal privileges, of which the most important was immunity from arrest, except for treason, felony or breach of the peace. As luck would have it, this was infringed in 1604, by the arrest of Sir Thomas Shirley, but the principle was resoundingly confirmed, with the king's ready co-operation, and embodied in a statute (*TCD*, pp. 302–17). However, though it was a bold king who arrested Members during a session, as Charles I did with Eliot and Digges in 1626, he need have no qualms about falling on them when parliament rose; as James grimly remarked in 1604, 'The parliament not sitting, the liberties are not sitting', and it was common enough after a dissolution, or even during a recess, for Members to be hauled before the Council and put under house arrest for a while. In the wake of the Addled Parliament nine Members appeared before the Council, and four of them went to the Tower, where one of them stayed a year. Sir Edwin Sandys spent a month in the Tower during the summer recess in 1621, and after the dissolution in January 1622 Sir Edward Coke and two other MPs were sent there until August, while John Pym spent three months under house arrest.[16] Significantly, the Commons made little attempt to contest this issue; in 1621 they were warned off by Coke himself, and in the same year James remarked, 'We think ourself very free and able to punish any man's misdemeanours in parliament, as well during their sitting and after.'[17] So Charles I's punishment of Sir John Eliot and his fellow 'martyrs' in 1629 was not so outrageous as all that.

Freedom of speech within the House was a privilege, which could be exercised on any matter brought before them; freedom to introduce issues of their own and debate them freely, even to the extent of addressing the Crown on the matter or bringing in bills, was a 'liberty', and though it was always held to be an 'ancient and undoubted

[13] Gardiner, *History*, II, 251.   [14] *LJ*, II, 359 (9 November 1605), III, 69 (26 March 1621).
[15] Elton, *Tudor Constitution*, pp. 260ff.
[16] Gardiner, *History*, II, 249–50, IV, 133, 267; Mitchell, *Revolutionary Party*, pp. 77–8, 147.
[17] *Commons Debates 1621*, II, 57–8.

right', or some such form of words, it was a claim novel to Elizabeth's reign, as Francis Bacon reminded the Commons in 1610 (**12**), and one which she had firmly and on the whole successfully resisted. However, it should be noticed that unlike her James never contested the Commons' right to debate religion and the Church, or introduce bills for church reform, though they were invariably suppressed in the Lords (p. 113 below), and he submitted to, and tried to answer a great variety of addresses and petitions on unwelcome topics. On the other hand, foreign policy, which had been a prime source of friction between Elizabeth and her parliaments, did not become a serious issue until 1621.

On another aspect of privilege altogether, the celebrated Buckinghamshire Election Case of 1604 has loomed large in the minds of an older generation of constitutional historians (*TCD*, pp. 201–71), and is supposed to display James's total ineptitude in his handling of the Commons, resulting in a humiliating defeat for the Crown. However, James's conduct was more judicious and sensible than it has been made to appear, and such mistakes as he made are to be blamed on the bad advice given him by his law officers. Nor is it clear that he sustained a defeat; certainly the Commons did not think so. Chancery's attempt to bar the return of Sir Francis Godwin because of his outlawry on a technicality, and seat Sir John Fortescue, a privy councillor, instead, ended in a compromise, the whole election being quashed. But it now seems extremely doubtful whether James or his ministers wanted Fortescue seated, and as for the Commons' right to arbitrate on returns, this remained in dispute, as it had been under Elizabeth.[18]

Towards the end of the session, in June, the Commons appointed a committee to draw up a 'Form of Apology and Satisfaction' for the king, which laid particular emphasis on the Buckinghamshire Election Case (**10**). The posthumous reputation of this document has been considerably lowered in recent years. It used to be regarded as the first in a series of great constitutional protests which stand as milestones along the road to rebellion, culminating in the Grand Remonstrance of 1641. This will not do at all. It was pegged to the events of this session, and its prime concern was with the problem of the Crown's prerogative rights of wardship and marriage, which had been the subject of an abortive discussion between Commons, Lords and ministers (p. 47 below). The Commons' assertion of their privileges was once thought aggressive; it could equally well be regarded as neurotically defensive. The only sinister note, given the blessing of hindsight, is their identification of their own narrow, pedantic privileges with the rights and liberties of the people in general; an unwarranted construction which was to be one of the theme songs of the Long Parliament. When the committee reported, the House recommitted the whole document, almost certainly because it was regarded as too bold, and it was largely forgotten until it was taken up by the Whig Henry Hallam in 1827.[19] It is not certain that the king ever saw it, though he may well have learned the gist of it; there is a copy in Robert Cecil's

[18] R. C. Munden, 'The Defeat of Sir John Fortescue: Court *versus* Country at the Hustings', *EHR*, XCIII (1978), 811–16; *idem*, in Sharpe, *Faction*, pp. 53–7; Derek Hirst, 'Elections and the Privileges of the House of Commons in the Early Seventeenth Century: Confrontation or Compromise?', *HJ*, XVIII (1975), 851–62. For the Elizabethan precedents see Elton, *Tudor Constitution*, p. 264.

[19] G. R. Elton, 'A High Road to Civil War?', in *Studies*, II, 164–82. First published in 1965, this is not only a destructive analysis of this document, but an early and important statement of the 'revisionist' case in general. See Notestein, *Commons*, pp. 125–40, for a moderate restatement of the conventional view, though acceptive of many of Elton's points (n. 28, p. 520).

papers. Certainly the speech he delivered at the end of the session was belligerent in tone, and less mannered and diplomatic than most of his parliamentary orations; it may well have been delivered extempore (11).

After all this relations between king and parliament could only improve, and did. The sessions of 1605–6, in the shadow of the Gunpowder Plot, and 1606–7, were relatively trouble free, though in 1607 James was finally obliged to abandon his cherished plans for a complete union between England and Scotland.[20] The Commons' grant of three subsidies in 1607, in time of peace, was more generous than anything they had done for Elizabeth (p. 47 below). But the issue of privilege and freedom of speech was on the anvil again in 1610.

In late April 1610, nearly three months into the session, and with the king away at Newmarket, the Commons set about investigating the legality of the new impositions, or import duties, lately imposed by the government. James sent word to the Council that he could not allow parliament to debate any aspect of his prerogative, especially after it had been confirmed by the high court, in Bate's Case (p. 54 below), and on 21 May he returned to London and repeated this prohibition in a speech to both Houses.[21] In a subsequent debate in the Committee for Grievances, Francis Bacon brought forward a whole series of awkward precedents from the previous reign, which showed that Elizabeth had often stopped a debate when she considered that it touched her prerogative (12), but what the House could not deny it was prepared to ignore, and on 23 May it submitted a petition claiming the right to scrutinise any aspect of the royal prerogative which encroached on the subject's liberties (*TCD*, pp. 245–7). James's answer was remarkably conciliatory, but he did not deal with the principle involved. However, the House did get to debate impositions (p. 48 below), and it debated them again in the short-lived parliament of 1614.

By the time the next parliament met, in 1621, the Commons' attention had been drawn away from taxation, towards abuses in government and the king's handling of foreign affairs. The renewal of war between Spain and the Dutch, the outbreak of the Thirty Years War in central Germany and the initial victories of the Counter Reformation – particularly the expulsion of James's son-in-law from Bohemia and the Palatinate – filled them with alarm. Their petition of 3 December 1621 (13) expressed their fears and displayed their simple cunning. After a lengthy exposé of the dangers of popery at home and abroad they exhorted James, grandly but vaguely, 'speedily and effectually to take the sword into your hand', and to direct it 'against that prince . . . whose armies and treasures have first diverted and since maintained the war in the Palatinate'; they also urgently requested that 'our most noble prince may be timely and happily married to one of our own religion', which implied the abandonment of James's cherished plans to marry Charles to the Spanish Infanta. In return all they offered was one subsidy, and that on condition that he passed 'such bills . . . [as] shall be prepared for your Majesty's honour and the good of the people' – in effect, various measures for the relief of landowners, some of which passed by agreement with Buckingham in 1624 (p. 50 below).

---

[20] Notestein, *Commons*, ch. 3, pp. 211–49.
[21] *House of Lords Manuscripts*, XI, no. 3314; Gardiner, *Parliamentary Debates in 1610*, p. 34n.

James, at Newmarket again, wrote the same day forbidding them to 'meddle with anything concerning our government and deep matters of state', and tactlessly referring to the king of Spain as his 'friend and confederate' (*TCD*, pp. 279–88). The Commons at once withdrew their petition and redrafted it in a more tactful form, and appointed a deputation to take it to the king at Newmarket on 11 December. He jocularly ordered 'stools for the ambassadors', but he drafted a long and learned reply. He told them he was 'an old and experienced king, needing no such lessons', and in any case the House of Commons was not equipped to discuss foreign relations. As for their privilege of freedom of speech,

> We cannot allow of the style, calling it 'your ancient and undoubted right and inheritance', but could rather have wished that you had said that your privileges were derived from the grace and permission of our ancestors and us.

This roused a veritable storm in the Commons, and it was useless for James to send another letter on 16 December, expanding his remarks and to some extent modifying them. All other business was shelved for a week, and on the 18th they produced a Protestation in which they claimed the right to debate any matter of state whatsoever (**14**). The king at once ordered them to adjourn, and on 30 December he presided over a meeting of the Privy Council at which the Protestation was formally torn out of the Journals of the House.[22] He then took the unprecedented step, followed by his son in 1629 and his grandson in 1681, of issuing a public declaration reviewing the events of the last session and justifying his decision to dissolve parliament forthwith (*TCD*, pp. 289–95).

It was unfortunate that in the next parliament his son and his favourite should force him to eat his words. Charles and Buckingham sustained a humiliating personal defeat at Madrid in 1623, and they came back determined on war with Spain. Buckingham persuaded James to call another parliament, and even induced him in his speech from the throne, on 19 February 1624, to seek its advice on foreign policy (**15**). James carried it off as best he could, but it set an awkward precedent; in effect parliament was not being asked to approve an arrangement agreed between the king and his advisers, but to arbitrate on a matter on which even the royal family was deeply divided. Parliament humbly requested him to break off all negotiations with Spain; he tried to hedge, but a Joint Address from Both Houses on 22 March kept him in line. When it was all over he had to endure their congratulations on abandoning a policy to which he had devoted much of his energies for many years, and in which (there can be little doubt) he still believed.[23]

This was Prince Charles's doing. But when he came to the throne the following year he showed little disposition to quibble over parliament's conduct provided they granted him money and did not argue about his efforts to obtain more from other sources. He was much brisker than his father, and much less disposed to indulge in theoretical arguments.

---

22 *APC 1621–1625*, pp. 108–10. For a more detailed examination of these events, see Robert Zaller, *The Parliament of 1621*, and Russell, *Parliaments and Politics*, ch. 2.

23 *TCD*, pp. 296–302. See Robert E. Ruigh, *The Parliament of 1624*, *passim*, and Russell, *loc. cit.*

Nevertheless, though he mentioned his own rights much less, he was ready to go farther and strike harder in their defence, as he showed in May 1626, when he committed Sir John Eliot and Sir Dudley Digges to the Tower in the middle of the session for what he regarded as seditious, if not treasonable words used in the management of Buckingham's impeachment. Moreover, he authorised his secretary of state to warn the Commons that he might, like other European monarchs, decide to dispense with elected assemblies altogether (**16**). Digges was released after five days, but the king held on to Eliot another three, arguing that his actions outside the House revealed a conspiracy to wreck the session – an argument he was to use again in 1629. He was forced to give way when the Commons suspended their sitting *sine die*.

But in 1629 Eliot and his associates overreached themselves, when they delayed the adjournment of the House on 2 March by physical coercion of the Speaker. Next day he and eight other Members were arrested by order of the Council. On the 10th parliament was dissolved, and on the 27th Charles issued a proclamation denouncing Eliot as 'an outlawed man, desperate in mind and fortune'. He was determined to make an example of him, despite a division of opinion on the Council, which was reflected in Star Chamber. Informations were laid before Star Chamber in May, but the court was obviously unwilling to rule that it had jurisdiction, and over the Long Vacation the case lapsed. When the prisoners sued out a writ of habeas corpus Charles complied with the Petition of Right by specifying the cause of their imprisonment as 'sedition', and King's Bench ruled that this was not bailable. Further pressure was brought to bear on the judges, and at last, on 25 January 1630, proceedings were opened in King's Bench against Eliot, Denzil Holles and Benjamin Valentine.

The indictment was for seditious words spoken during the actual session, as well as violence to the Speaker. It was open to Charles to argue that from the moment Black Rod knocked on the door of the Commons' House the session stood adjourned, and that anything said or done after that was said or done outside parliament. But he spurned the evasion, and the attorney-general was briefed to argue that parliamentary privilege did not cover seditious words, and that Strode's Case of 1512, pleaded by the defence, did not apply.[24] On the question of jurisdiction, Heath argued that though King's Bench certainly could not reverse judgments of the High Court of Parliament it could take notice of day-to-day events therein. The judges agreed, and gave judgment for the Crown accordingly (**17**). The three men refused to pay their fines, and were imprisoned indefinitely. Holles escaped and went into hiding, and Eliot died in 1632. Valentine was not released until February 1640, when the writs were going out for the Short Parliament. Parliament took up his case, but this did not deter Charles. Immediately after the dissolution, in May 1640, John Crew, chairman of the Committee on Religion, was sent to the Tower for refusing to surrender his papers, and Sir John Hotham and Henry Bellasis followed him there. The houses of John Pym, John Hampden and Sir Walter Erle were searched for incriminating documents.[25]

So, on the very eve of the final crisis the Commons were still unable to defend their privilege of free speech, though the more general privilege of discussing any matter they chose, in any order, had been virtually conceded in practice, Charles's only

[24] Elton, *Tudor Constitution*, p. 266.   [25] Gardiner, *History*, IX, 129–30.

counter being prorogation or dissolution. The Long Parliament was obsessed with its privileges to an unhealthy degree, but it did remarkably little to put the matter on a firm legal footing. In July 1641 it was resolved that the proceedings against Eliot, Holles and Valentine had been a gross breach of privilege, but not until 1668, on a motion by Holles himself – now Lord Holles of Ifield – was the judgment of 1630 reversed on a writ of error.[26]

10. The Form of Apology and Satisfaction, 20 June 1604

The Apology directed to the King's most excellent Majesty from the House of Commons assembled in Parliament[27]

We know, and with great thankfulness to God acknowledge, that he hath given us a king of such understanding and wisdom as is rare to find in any prince in the world. Howbeit, seeing no human wisdom, how great soever, can pierce into the particularities of the rights and customs of people, or of the sayings and doings of particular persons, but by tract of experience and faithful report of such as know them (which it hath pleased your Majesty's princely mouth to deliver), what grief, what anguish of mind hath it been to us at some time in presence to hear, and so in other things to find and feel by effect, your gracious Majesty (to the extreme prejudice of all your subjects of England, and in particular of this House of Commons thereof), so greatly wronged by misinformation as well touching the estate of the one as the privileges of the other, and their several proceedings during this parliament; which misinformations, though apparent in themselves and to your subjects most injurious, yet have we in some humble and dutiful respect rather hitherto complained of amongst ourselves than presumed to discover and oppose against your Majesty.

But now, no other help or redress appearing, and finding these misinformations to have been the first, yea, the chief and almost the sole cause of all the discontentful and troublesome proceedings much blamed in this parliament, and that they might be again the cause of like or greater discontents and troubles hereafter (which the Almighty Lord forbid), we have been constrained, as well in duty to your royal Majesty whom with faithful hearts we serve as to our dear native country for which we serve in this parliament, to break our silence, and freely to disclose unto your Majesty the truth of such matters concerning your subjects the Commons as hitherto by misinformation hath been suppressed or perverted; wherein, that we more plainly proceed

[26] *ST*, III, 310–15, 332–3.

[27] Prefaced by: 'The Form of an Apology and Satisfaction to be presented to his Majesty penned and agreed on by a former select committee, was now reported and delivered into the House by Sir Thomas Ridgeway, one of the committees [*sc.* committee men], twice read, debated and agreed [argued?] *pro et con*. Whether the matter and the manner fit, or what was fit to be done in it.'

(which next to truth we affect in this discourse), we shall reduce these misinformations to three principal heads:

First, touching the cause of the joyful receiving of your Majesty into this kingdom;

Secondly, concerning the rights and liberties of your subjects of England and the privileges of this House;

Thirdly, touching the several actions and speeches passed in the House.

(1) It has been told us to our faces by some of no small place (and the same also spoken in the presence of your Majesty), that on the 24th of March was twelve month[28] we stood in so great fear that we would have given half we were worth for the security wherein we now stand, whereby some misunderstanders of things might perhaps conjecture that fear of our own misery had more prevailed with us in the duty which on that day was performed, than love of your Majesty's virtues and hope of your goodness towards us. We contrariwise most truly protest the contrary, that we stood not at that time, nor of many a day before, in any doubt at all. We all professing true religion by law established (being by manifold degrees the greater, the stronger and more respective part of your Majesty's realm), standing clear in our consciences touching your Majesty's right, were both resolute with our lives and all other our abilities to have maintained the same against all the world; and vigilant also in all parts to have suppressed such tumult as, but in regard of our poor united minds and readiness, by the malcontent and turbulent might have been attempted.

But the true cause of our extraordinary great cheerfulness and joy in performing that day's duty, was the great and extraordinary love which we bore towards your Majesty's most royal and renowned person, and a longing thirst to enjoy the happy fruits of your Majesty's most wise, religious, just, virtuous and gracious heart, whereof not rumour but your Majesty's own writings had given us a strong and undoubted assurance. For from hence, dread Sovereign, a general hope was raised in the minds of all your people that under your Majesty's reign religion, peace, justice and all virtue should renew again and flourish, that the better sort should be cherished, the bad reformed or repressed, and some moderate ease should be given us of those burdens and sore oppressions under which the whole land did groan.

This hope being so generally and so firmly settled in the minds of all your most loyal and most loving people, recounting [sc. remembering] what great alienation of men's hearts and defeating of great hopes doth usually breed, we could not, in duty as well unto your Majesty as to our country, cities and boroughs who had sent us hither not ignorant nor uninstructed of their griefs, of their desires and hopes, but according to the ancient use and liberty of

[28] The day of Queen Elizabeth's death.

parliaments present our several humble petitions to your Majesty of different nature, some for right and some for grace, to the easing and relieving of us of some just burdens and of other some unjust oppressions, wherein what due care and what respect we have had that your Majesty's honour and profit should be enjoyed with the content and satisfaction of your people, shall afterwards in their several places appear.

(2) Now concerning the ancient rights of the subjects of this realm, chiefly consisting in the privileges of this House of Parliament, the misinformation openly delivered to your Majesty hath been in three things:

First, that we held not our privileges of right, but of grace only, renewed every parliament by way of donature upon petition, and so to be limited.

Secondly, that we are no court of record, nor yet a court that can command view of records, but that our proceedings here are only to acts and memorials, and that the attendance with the records is courtesy, not duty.[29]

Thirdly and lastly, that the examination of the return of writs for knights and burgesses is without our compass, and due to the Chancery.

Against which assertions, most gracious Sovereign, tending directly and apparently to the utter overthrow of the very fundamental privileges of our House, and therein of the rights and liberties of the whole commons of your realm of England which they and their ancestors from time immemorable have undoubtedly enjoyed under your Majesty's most noble progenitors, we, the knights, citizens and burgesses of the House of Commons assembled in parliament, and in the name of the whole commons of the realm of England, with uniform consent for ourselves and our posterity, do expressly protest, as being derogatory in the highest degree to the true dignity, liberty and authority of your Majesty's High Court of Parliament, and consequently to the rights of your Majesty's said subjects and the whole body of this your kingdom; and desire that this protestation may be recorded to all posterity.

And contrariwise, with all humble and due respect to your Majesty, our sovereign Lord and Head, against those misinformations we most truly avouch, that our privileges and liberties are our right and due inheritance, no less than our very lands and goods; that they cannot be withheld from us, denied or impaired, but with apparent wrong to the whole state of the realm; and that our making of request in the entrance of parliament to enjoy our privilege is an act only of manners, and doth weaken our right no more than our suing to the king for our lands by petition . . .

We avouch also, that our House is a court of record, and so ever esteemed, and that there is not the highest standing court in this land that ought to enter into competency [sc. competition], either for dignity or authority, with this High Court of Parliament, which with your Majesty's royal assent gives laws to other courts but from other courts receives neither laws nor orders.

[29] In fact James had acknowledged on 11 April that the Commons were a court of record, CJ, I, 168.

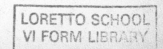
LORETTO SCHOOL
VI FORM LIBRARY

And lastly, we avouch that the House of Commons is the sole proper judge of the return of all such writs and of the election of all such Members as belong unto it (without which the freedom of election were not entire), and that the Chancery, though a standing court under your Majesty, be to send out those writs and receive the returns and to preserve them, yet the same is done only for the use of the Parliament, over which neither the Chancery nor any other court ever had or ought to have any manner of jurisdiction.

From these misinformed positions, most gracious Sovereign, the greatest part of our troubles, distrusts and jealousies have arisen, having apparently [sc. obviously] found that in the first parliament of the happy reign of your Majesty the privileges of our House, and therein the liberties and stability of the whole kingdom, have been more universally and dangerously impugned than ever (as we suppose) since the beginning of parliaments . . .

What cause we your poor Commons have to watch over our privileges is manifest in itself to all men. The prerogatives of princes may easily and do daily grow; the privileges of the subject are for the most part at an everlasting stand. They may be by good providence and care preserved, but being once lost are not recovered but with much disquiet. If good kings were immortal as well as kingdoms, to strive so for privilege were but vanity perhaps and folly; but seeing the same God who in his great mercy hath given us a wise king and religious doth also sometimes permit hypocrites and tyrants in his displeasure and for [the] sins of [the] people, from hence hath the desire of rights, liberties and privileges, both for nobles and commons, had its just original, by which an harmonical and stable state is framed, each member under the Head enjoying that right and performing that duty which for the honour of the head and happiness of the whole is requisite . . .

[The Commons then rehearsed their rights again, and showed how they had been threatened; notably in the Buckinghamshire Election Case, and in the case of Sir Thomas Shirley, MP, arrested earlier in the session for debt. They also complained of being libelled by the Bishop of Bristol in a book advocating Union with Scotland. After excusing at some length their attitude towards Union, they turned to religion.]

. . . For matter of religion, it will appear by examination of truth and right that your Majesty should be misinformed if any man should deliver that the kings of England have any absolute power in themselves either to alter religion (which God defend should be in the power of any mortal man whatsoever), or to make any laws concerning the same otherwise than as in temporal causes, by consent of parliament. We have and shall at all times by our oaths acknowledge that your Majesty is Sovereign Lord and Supreme Governor in both. Touching our own desires and proceedings therein, they have been not a little misconceived and misreported. We have not come in any Puritan or Brownist spirit, to introduce their parity or to work the subversion of the state ecclesiastical as now it standeth; things so far and so clearly from our meaning as that with uniform consent in the beginning of this parliament we committed to the Tower a man who out of that humour in a petition exhibited to our House had slandered the bishops.[30] But according to the tenor of your Majesty's writ of summons directed to the counties from whence we came,[31] and according to the ancient and long continued use of parliaments as by many records from time to time appeareth, we come with another spirit, even with the spirit of peace. We disputed not of matters of faith and doctrine; our desire was peace only and our device of unity, how this lamentable and long-lasting dissension amongst the ministers, from which both atheism, sects and all ill life have received such encouragement and so dangerous increase, might at length, before help came too late, be extinguished. And for the ways of this peace, we are not addicted at all to our own inventions but ready to embrace any fit way that may be offered; neither desire we so much that any man in regard of weakness of conscience may be exempted after Parliament from obedience unto laws established, as that in this Parliament such laws may be enacted as by the relinquishment of some few ceremonies of small importance, or by any way better, a perpetual uniformity may be enjoined and observed. Our desire hath also been to reform certain abuses crept into the ecclesiastical state even as into the temporal; and lastly, that the land might be furnished with a learned, religious and godly ministry; for the maintenance of whom we would have granted no small contributions, if in these (as we trust) just and religious desires we had found that correspondency from others which was expected. These minds and hearts we in secret present to that Sovereign Lord who gave them, and in public profess to your gracious Majesty who we trust will so esteem them.

[The Commons then turned to financial matters; first to a bill they had put up to legalise 'assart' – agricultural encroachment on the royal forests – then to the abuse of purveyance, in lieu of which, they explained, they were reluctant to vote a permanent revenue; at least, they dare not 'impose it by law upon the people without first acquainting them and having their consents unto it'. The feudal incidents of wardship and marriage, however, were another matter.]

[30] In fact, the Rev. Bryan Bridger had been committed to prison in Southwark by the High Commission a year before for stating that the bishops 'defiled the land', and were agents of Anti-Christ. When he petitioned the Commons on 29 March they promptly transferred him to the Tower (*CJ*, I, 157–8).

[31] The reference is rather to his Proclamation of Summons, in which he ordered 'that there be great care taken to avoid the choice of any persons either noted for their superstitious blindness one way, or for their turbulent humours other ways, because their disorderly and unquiet spirits will disturb all the discreet and modest proceedings in that greatest and gravest council'; *SRP*, I, 68. This reinforced his proclamation of 24 October 1603 'concerning such as seditiously seek reformation in Church matters' (*ibid.*, I, 60), and he took up the theme again in his first Speech from the Throne, 22 March 1604, when he denounced 'Puritans and Novelists, who do not so far differ from us in points of Religion, as in their confused form of policy and parity, being ever discontented with the present government [of the Church], and impatient to suffer any superiority, which maketh their sect unable to be suffered in any well-governed commonwealth'; *CJ*, I, 144.

. . . We prepared a petition to your most excellent Majesty for leave to treat with your Highness touching a perpetual composition to be raised by yearly revenue out of the lands of your subjects for wardships and other burdens depending upon them or springing with them; wherein we first entered into this dutiful consideration, that this prerogative of the Crown which we desire to compound for was a matter of mere profit, and not of any honour at all or princely dignity – for it could not then, neither yet can, by any means sink into our understandings that these economical matters of education and marrying of children, which are common also to subjects, should bring any renown or reputation to a potent monarch whose honour is settled on a higher and stronger foundation: faithful and loving subjects, valiant soldiers, an honourable nobility, wise counsellors, a learned and religious clergy, and a contented and a happy people, are the true honour of a king – and contrariwise, that it would be an exceeding great honour and of memorable renown to your Majesty with all posterity, and in [the] present an assured bond of the hearts of all your people, to remit unto them this burden under which our children are born.

This prerogative, then, appearing to be mere matter of profit, we entered into a second degree of consideration; with how great grievance and damage of the subject, to the decay of many houses and disabling of them to serve prince and country, with how great mischief also by occasion of many forced and ill-suited marriages, and lastly, with how great contempt and reproach of our nation in foreign countries; how small a commodity was now raised to the Crown in respect of that which with great love and joy and thankfulness, for the restitution of this original right in disposing of our children, we would be content and glad to assure unto your Majesty.

We fell also from hence into a third degree of consideration: that it might be that, in regard that the original of these wardships was serving of the king in his wars against Scotland,[32] which cause we hope now to be at an everlasting end, and in regard, moreover, of that general hope which at your Majesty's first entry by the whole land was embraced (a thing known unto all men), that they should be now for ever eased of this burden, your Majesty, out of your most noble and gracious disposition and desire to overcome our expectation with your goodness, may be pleased to accept the offer of our perpetual and certain revenue, not only proportionable to the uttermost benefit that any of your progenitors ever reaped thereby but also with such an overplus and large addition as in great part to supply your Majesty's other occasions, that our ease might breed your plenty . . .

And thus, most gracious sovereign, with dutiful minds and sincere hearts towards your Majesty, have we truly disclosed our secret intents and delivered

[32] Untrue, needless to say.

our outward actions in all these so much traduced and blamed matters; and from henceforward shall remain in great affiance that your Majesty resteth satisfied both in your grace and in your judgment, which above all worldly things we most desire to effect before the dissolving of this parliament, where in so long time, with so much pains and endurance of so great sorrow, scarce anything hath been done for their good and content who sent us hither and whom we left full of hope and joyful expectation.

There remaineth (dread Sovereign) yet one part more of our duty at this present which faithfulness of heart, no[t] presumption, doth press upon us. We stand not in place to speak or do things pleasing, our care is and must be to confirm the love and to tie the hearts of your subjects the commons most firmly to your Majesty. Herein lieth the means of our well deserving of both. There was never prince entered with greater love, with greater joy and applause of all his people. This love, this joy, let it now flourish in their hearts for ever. Let no suspicion have access to their fearful thoughts, that their privileges, which they think by your Majesty should be protected, should now by sinister information or counsel be violate or impaired, or that those which with dutiful respect to your Majesty speak freely for the right and good of their country, shall be oppressed or disgraced. Let your Majesty be pleased to refuse [receive?] public information from your Commons in parliament of all the abuses in the Church as in the civil estate and government, for private informations pass often by practice. The voice of the people in things of their knowledge is said to be as the voice of God. And if your Majesty shall vouchsafe at your best pleasure and leisure to enter into gracious consideration of our petitions for ease of these burdens under which your whole people have of long time mourned, hoping for relief by your Majesty, then you may be assured to be possessor of their hearts for ever, and if of their hearts, then of all they can do or have. And so we your Majesty's most humble and loyal subjects, whose ancestors have with loyalty, readiness and joyfulness served your famous progenitors, kings and queens of this realm, shall with like loyalty and joy, both we and our posterity, serve your Majesty and your most royal issue for ever with our lives, lands, goods and all other our abilities, and by all means endeavour to procure your Majesty's honour with all plenty, tranquillity, content, joy and felicity.

[Sir William Strode then moved that it be recommitted, that extra members be appointed to the committee, and that those who took exception to this document should attend the committee to voice their views. The committee was to re-assemble on Monday next, 25 June.]

HMC Salisbury, XXIII, 140–52[33]

---

[33] A few variant readings have been adopted from the Record Office copy, SP14/8:134–9.

11. James I: speech at the prorogation of parliament, 7 July 1604

My Lords, and you the knights and burgesses of the lower House: Though in the true nature of a parliament you are but one body, yet because you are not conjoined as in Scotland, but divided into two houses, I must speak unto you distinctly.

With you (my Lords) I will not be long. I will not flatter, nor by God's grace speak an untruth publicly or privately; less than this I cannot afford you, and give you your due, that you have carried yourselves with discretion, modesty, judgment, care and fidelity. Never king had better subject to praise good subjects than I you. In fine, you have done that both in circumstance and effect that became you.

I have more to say to you, my Masters of the lower House, both in regard of former occasions, and now of your Speaker's speech. It hath been the form of most kings to give thanks to their people however their deserts were; of some, to use sharp admonishment and reproof. Now if you expect either great praises, or reproofs out of custom, I will deceive you in both. I will not thank where I think no thanks due; you would think me base if I should; it were not Christian, it were not kingly. I do not think you, as the body of the realm, undutiful. There is an old rule, *qui bene distinguit, bene docet*. This house doth not so represent the whole commons of the realm as the shadow doth the body, but only representatively. Impossible it was for them to know all that would be propounded here; much more all those answers that you would make to all propositions. So, as I account not all that to be done by the commons of the land which hath been done by you, I will not thank them for what you have well done, nor blame them for what you have done ill. I must say this for you, that I never heard nor read that there were so many wise, and so many judicious men of that house generally. But where many are some must needs be idle heads, some rash, some curious, some busy informers. The greatest part of you were well affected, but where there is a like liberty the worst likely carries away the best. The reason is the corruption of our nature. The pertness and boldness of some cries all modest men down. You see I am not such a stock as to praise fools. I cannot say you all did well, or all ill; and whether well or ill you must not expect I will give you the same answer. There were wise men amongst you; so was there a roll of knavery. I do not think that any of you had seditious minds to overthrow and confound this monarchy, but out of divers humours and respects you were moved to curiosities.

1. Some out of boldness to press upon my lenity, and likewise on the thanks I gave you at the beginning of the parliament. They thought they would put me to it; and now it was time to be done or never.

2. Some wanted fame, and rather than they would not win fame, would do as he that burnt the temple of Ephesus.

3. Some had an itching humour ever to be talking, and this common saying is proper to common babblers, *in multiloquis non deest peccatum.*

4. Some were great populars, that did not cut even way betwixt their duty to their king and love to the country.

5. And some of a new religion, framed to their own appetite, who in all haste would build new Jerusalem, and had not patience to stay for their fellows till Doomsday.

No marvel if such concurrence bred perturbation. Too curious you were, and (God forgive you) too jealous of me. In my government bypast of Scotland (where I ruled amongst men not of the best temper) I was heard not only as a king, but, suppose I say it, as a counsellor. Contrary, here nothing but curiosity from morning to evening to find faults with my propositions. There, all things warranted that come from me; here all things suspected . . .

You had great business amongst yourselves about religion. I can not enough wonder that in three days after the beginning of the Parliament men should go contrary to their oaths of Supremacy. In my first speech I did lightly note those of that novelty; I did not think they had been so great, so proud, or so dominant in your House. This I say of it. It is the most dangerous sect that claims to novelty. Advise unto it. In things that are against the word of God I will with as great humility as any slave fall upon my knees or face; but in things indifferent they are seditious which obey not the magistrate. There is no man half so dangerous as he that repugns against order, yet some which make scruple I would use with clemency; but let them meet me with obedience. To discreet men I say, they shall obtain their desires by grace, but to all I profess, they shall extort nothing by violence.

Touching the Purveyors (who have much busied you this parliament), you have good laws already; see them executed in God's name. Punish them, but wrong not their Master. I were a tyrant if I should uphold those scribes and publicans. I will punish the great officers if they punish not the less. And now you are going into your several countries I would have you advise of the fittest means to ease yourselves of that burden, but so that you lay not a greater burden upon me.

You see how in many things you did not well. The best apology-maker of you all, for all his eloquence, cannot make all good. Forsooth, a goodly matter to make apologies when no man is by to answer. You have done many things rashly. I say not you meant disloyally. I receive better comfort in you, and account better to be king of such subjects than of so many kingdoms. Only I wish you had kept a better form. I like form as much as matter. It shows respect, and I expect it, being a king well born (suppose I say it) as any of my progenitors. I wish you would use your liberty with more modesty in time to come.

PRO SP 14/8, 93

12. Debate in committee, 22 May 1610, on the Commons' Petition of Right

Mr Fuller[34] repeated part of a speech that was formerly spoken by Mr Whitelock,[35] which was that the English nation was accompted in times past by all others in three special respects:

1. That that which is the subjects' cannot be taken from them without their consent, but by due course of law.

2. That laws cannot be made without the consent of the three estates.

3. That the parliament, consisting of these three estates, was the armamentary or storehouse wherein these things were safely reposed and preserved, as well the laws of the land as the rights and proprieties of the subjects to their lands and goods. And that the special privilege of parliament is to debate freely of all things that shall concern any of the subjects in particular, or the commonwealth in general, without any restraint or inhibition.

Secondly, it was said[36] that in all ages the king's prerogative . . . hath been examined and debated in parliament . . . Also it was said that in all the Courts of Justice at Westminster the king's prerogative is there ordinarily disputed, and therefore may much more be debated in parliament, being the highest court of justice in the realm.

But Sir Francis Bacon took upon him to answer these reasons, and said . . . that he had been a parliament man ever since he was seventeen years old, within which time he did observe that the parliament had received divers inhibitions from the queen to restrain them from debating the matter then in question; wherein he took this difference, that if the matter debated concerned the right or interest of any subject or the Commonwealth, if in that case an inhibition came, he for his part would not advise the House to desist, but to inform the king of the liberty of the House, and so to proceed. But if the matter in question were an essential thing which concerned the prerogative and power of the Crown, then the House did always desist from proceeding any further upon such inhibitions received. He gave instance[s] of divers in his time . . .

In answer to this speech divers stood up, by whom it was answered that, as we *ambulare in via recta* so it is an express text also not to remove the ancient landmarks, and therefore we must be careful to follow the steps of our ancestors, but [also] to preserve and maintain the liberties and privileges of our House . . .

[After further speeches] it was moved therefore, that as the king had granted

---

[34] Nicholas Fuller, MP for the City of London.
[35] James Whitelock, MP for Woodstock. The speech that Fuller summarises had actually been delivered that morning in the House.
[36] By Thomas Wentworth, MP for Oxford City.

us freedom of speech at the beginning of the parliament concerning all matters of the Commonwealth (which could not well be taken from us without shaking the foundations of the liberties of parliament), so we should by a Petition of Right make known our liberties to his Majesty, and desire him to remove the impediment, for though it is Solomon's counsel not to move the king, yet it is counsel also, that if his spirit be moved yet leave not thy place.

Gardiner, Parliamentary Debates in 1610, pp. 37–9[37]

13. Commons Petition, 3 December 1621

Most gracious and dread sovereign: We, your Majesty's most humble and loyal subjects, the knights, citizens and burgesses now assembled in parliament, who represent the commons of your realm, full of hearty sorrow to be deprived of the comfort of your royal presence, the rather for that it proceeds from the want of your health, wherein we all unfeignedly do suffer; in all humble manner calling to mind your gracious answer to our former petition concerning religion, which, notwithstanding your Majesty's pious and princely intentions, hath not produced that good effect which the danger of these times doth seem to us to require; and finding how ill your Majesty's goodness hath been requited by princes of different religion, who even in time of treaty have taken [the] opportunity to advance their own ends, tending to the subversion of religion and disadvantage of your affairs and estate of your children; by reason whereof your ill-affected subjects at home, the popish recusants, have taken too much encouragement and are dangerously increased in their number and in their insolencies; we cannot but be sensible thereof, and therefore humbly represent what we conceive to be the causes of so great and growing mischiefs, and what be the remedies.

I. The vigilancy and ambition of the Pope of Rome and his dearest son; the one aiming at as large a temporal monarchy as the other at a spiritual supremacy.

II. The devilish positions and doctrines whereon popery is built, and taught with authority to their followers for advancement of their temporal ends.

III. The distressed and miserable estate of the professors of true religion in foreign parts.

IV. The disastrous accidents to your Majesty's children abroad, expressed with rejoicing, and even with contempt of their persons.

V. The strange confederacy of the princes of the popish religion, aiming mainly at the advancement of theirs and subverting of ours, and taking the advantages conducing to that end upon all occasions.

---

[37] An alternative version is now available in Foster, *Proceedings*, II, 110–12.

VI. The great and many armies raised and maintained at the charge of the king of Spain, the chief of that league.

VII. The expectation of the popish recusants of the match with Spain, and feeding themselves with great hopes of the consequences thereof.

VIII. The interposing of foreign princes and their agents in the behalf of popish recusants for connivance and favour unto them.

IX. Their open and usual resort to the houses and, which is worse, the chapels of foreign ambassadors.

X. Their more than usual concourse to the City, and their frequent conventicles and conferences there.

XI. The education of their children in many several seminaries and houses of their religion in foreign parts appropriated to the English fugitives.

XII. The grants of their just forfeitures intended by your Majesty as a reward of service to the grantees but, beyond your Majesty's intention, transferred or compounded for at such mean rates as will amount to little less than a toleration.

XIII. The licentious printing and dispersing of popish and seditious books, even in the time of parliament.

XIV. The swarms of priests and Jesuits, the common incendiaries of all Christendom, dispersed in all parts of your kingdom.

And from these causes, as bitter roots, we humbly offer to your Majesty that we foresee and fear there will necessarily follow very dangerous effects both to Church and state. For,

I. The popish religion is incompatible with ours in respect of their positions.

II. It draweth with it an unavoidable dependency on foreign princes.

III. It openeth too wide a gap for popularity to any who shall draw too great a party.

IV. It hath a restless spirit, and will strive by these gradations: if it once but get a connivancy, it will press for a toleration; if that should be obtained, they must have an equality; from thence they will aspire to superiority, and will never rest till they get a subversion of the true religion.

The remedies against these growing evils, which in all humility we offer unto your most excellent Majesty, are these:

I. That seeing this inevitable necessity is fallen upon your Majesty which no wisdom or providence of a peaceable and pious king can avoid, your Majesty would not omit this just occasion speedily and effectually to take the sword into your hand.

II. That once undertaken upon so honourable and just grounds, your Majesty would resolve to pursue and more publicly avow the aiding of those of our religion in foreign parts; which doubtless would reunite the princes and states of the Union, by these disasters disheartened and disbanded.[38]

III. That your Majesty would propose to yourself to manage this war with the best advantage, by a diversion or otherwise, as in your deep judgment shall be found fittest, and not to rest upon a war in these parts only, which will consume your treasure and discourage your people.

IV. That the bent of this war and point of your sword may be against that prince (whatsoever opinion of potency he hath) whose armies and treasures have first diverted and since maintained the war in the Palatinate.

V. That for securing of our peace at home, your Majesty would be pleased . . . to put in execution, by the care of choice commissioners to be thereunto specially appointed, the laws already and hereafter to be made for preventing of dangers by popish recusants and their wonted evasions.

VI. That to frustrate their hopes for a future age, our most noble prince may be timely and happily married to one of our own religion.

VII. That the children of the nobility and gentry of this kingdom, and of others ill affected and suspected in their religion, now beyond the seas, may be forthwith called home by your means and at the charge of their parents or governors.

VIII. That the children of popish recusants, or such whose wives are popish recusants, be brought up during their minority with Protestant schoolmasters and teachers, who may sow in their tender years the seeds of true religion.

IX. That your Majesty will be pleased speedily to revoke all former licences for such children and youth to travel beyond the seas, and not grant any such licence hereafter.

X. That your Majesty's learned counsel may receive commandment from your Highness carefully to look into former grants of recusants' lands, and to avoid [sc. cancel] them if by law they can; and that your Majesty will stay your hand from passing any such grants hereafter.

This is the sum and effect of our humble declaration, which we (no ways intending to press upon your Majesty's undoubted and regal prerogative) do with the fullness of our duty and obedience humbly submit to your most princely consideration: the glory of God, whose cause it is; the zeal of our true religion, in which we have been born and wherein (by God's grace) we are resolved to die; the safety of your Majesty's person, who is the very life of your people; the happiness of your children and posterity; the honour and good of the Church and state, dearer unto us than our own lives, having kindled these affections truly devoted to your Majesty.

And seeing out of our duty to your Majesty we have already resolved to give at the end of this session one entire subsidy, for the present relief of the Palatinate only, to be paid in the end of February next, which cannot well be effected but by passing a bill in parliamentary course before Christmas, we most humbly beseech your Majesty (as our assured hope is) that you will then

[38] The Union of Protestant Princes was dissolved in April 1621.

also vouchsafe to give life by your royal assent to such bills as before that time shall be prepared for your Majesty's honour and the general good of your people; and that such bills may also be accompanied (as hath been accustomed) with your Majesty's gracious pardon (which proceeding from your own mere grace, may by your Highness's direction be drawn to that latitude and extent as may best sort with your Majesty's bounty and goodness). And that not only felons and criminal offenders may take benefit thereof, but that your good subjects may receive ease thereby. And if it shall so stand [with] your good pleasure, that it may extend to the relief of old debts and duties to the Crown before the first year of your Majesty's reign, to the discharge of alienations without licence, and misusing of liveries, and *ouster le mains* before the first summons of this parliament, and of concealed wardships, and not suing of liveries, and *ouster le mains* before the twelfth year of your Majesty's reign.[39] Which gracious favour would much comfort your good subjects, and ease them from vexation, with little loss or prejudice to your own profit.

And we by our daily and devout prayers to the Almighty, the great King of Kings, shall contend for a blessing upon our endeavours, and for your Majesty's long and happy reign over us, and for your children's children after you for many and many generations.   Rushworth, I, 40—3

14. The Commons' Protestation, 18 December 1621

The Commons now assembled in parliament, being justly occasioned thereunto concerning sundry liberties, franchises and privileges of parliament, amongst others here mentioned, do make this Protestation following.

That the liberties, franchises, privileges and jurisdictions of parliament are the ancient and undoubted birthright and inheritance of the subjects of England; and that the arduous and urgent affairs concerning the king, state and defence of the realm, and of the Church of England, and the maintenance and making of laws, and redress of mischiefs and grievances which daily happen within this realm, are proper subjects and matters of counsel and debate in parliament; and that in the handling and proceeding of those businesses every Member of the House of Commons hath, and of right ought to have, freedom of speech to propound, treat, reason and bring to conclusion the same; and that the Commons in parliament have like liberty and freedom to treat of these matters in such order as in their judgments shall seem fittest; and that every Member of the said House hath like freedom from all impeachment, imprisonment and molestation (other than by censure of the House itself) for

---

[39] Livery and *ouster le main* were the specialised writs by which a ward regained control of his estate on coming of age, the latter being used by tenants-in-chief. 'Alienations', of course, referred to alienations of Crown lands.

or concerning any speaking, reasoning or declaring of any matter or matters
touching the parliament or parliament business; and that if any of the said
members be complained of and questioned for anything done or said in
Parliament, the same is to be showed to the king by the advice and assent of all
the Commons assembled in parliament before the king give credence to any
private information.   Rushworth, I, 53

15. The king's speech at the opening of parliament, 19 February 1624

It is a true saying and uttered by the spirit of God, that the glory of a king stands
in the multitude of his people. And I am sure it is as true, that the strength of a
kingdom stands next, and immediately after God's protection, in the hearts of
the people. That you may see, and have a proof, that I have not this only in my
tongue but have it likewise settled in my heart (as God can bear me record), and
that every way, I have therefore called you at this time to speak freely my mind
unto you; for remembering many misunderstandings between me and you
before, I am now brought hither with an earnest desire to do my duty that God
hath called me unto, by declaring unto you the verity of this, that God hath put
in my heart, and to manifest my actions to be true by my words. I remember
very well, it is a very fit similitude for a king and his people to be like to a
husband and wife, for even as Christ, in whose throne I sit in this part of the
earth, is husband to the Church, and the Church is his spouse, so I likewise
desire to be your husband and ye should be my spouse; and therefore, as it is the
husband's part to cherish his wife, to entreat her kindly, and reconcile himself
towards her, and procure her love by all means, so it is my part to do the like to
my people . . .

The properties and causes of calling a parliament (and so go the writs) are to
confer with the king and give him their advice in matters of greatest weight
and importance. For this cause have I now called you together, that ye may
have proof of my love, and of my trust; I have now called you to give me your
advice in the greatest matters that ever could concern any king; a greater
declaration of my confidence in you I cannot give.

I have been these many years upon treaties;[40] but so far as I thought (and,
God is my witness, I never had any other intention) for settling a peace in
Christendom, and settling of peace at home. And in these treaties I went long
on, but finding in them a slower success than I expected, or had reason to do, I
was willing, and especially in one thing concerning the estate of my
grandchildren, to see a good and speedy end. And in this finding as great

---

[40] Meaning 'negotiations' throughout.

promises as I could wish, and yet finding their actions clean contrary, it stirred up my son to offer himself to make that journey, and I thank God, having him here now, I have no cause to repent it; for, being of fit age and ripeness for marriage, he urged me to know the certainty in a matter of so great weight, that he might not be put off with long delays, for delay in such a case is more dangerous than denial. In it I was content, as a rare example, to grant his desire, and with him I only sent the man whom I most trusted, Buckingham, commanding him never to leave him, nor to return home without him; and I thank God for it, for it hath learned me a wisdom, for *in generalibus versatur dolus*. I had general hopes before, but particulars will resolve matters, generals will not, and before this journey things came to me as raw, as if I had never treated of them before; and I was as far disappointed of my ends as if I had been wakened out of a dream. Now I have put it into a certainty, and whereas I walked in a mist before I have now brought it to particulars . . . And, when you have heard all *super totam materiam*, I shall then entreat your good and sound advice, for the glory of God, the peace of the kingdom, and the weal of my children. Never king gave more trust to his subjects than to desire their advice in matters of this weight, for I assure you ye may freely advise me, seeing, of my princely fidelity, ye are entreated thereunto. And never subjects had better hearts and experience to give me good advice than you, of which I make no doubt, for if you love yourselves you will give me good advice, your own felicity depending upon it.

One particular I must remember of you, because it hath been much talked of in the country, that I should be slack in my care of religion for other occasions.

My Lords, and you Gentlemen all, I pray you judge me charitably, as you would have me to judge you; for I never made public nor private treaties but I always made a direct reservation for the weal public and [the] cause of religion, for the glory of God [and] the good of my subjects. I only thought good sometimes to wink and connive at the execution of some penal statutes, and not to go on so rigorously as at other times, but to dispense with any, to forbid or alter any that concern religion, I never promised or yielded; I never did think it with my heart, nor speak it with my mouth . . .

★   ★   ★

God judge me, I speak as a Christian prince, never man in a dry and sandy wilderness, where no water is, did thirst more in hot weather for drink, than I do now for a happy conclusion of this parliament. And now I hope, after the miscarriage of three, this may prove happy. I am neither curious nor captious. Eschew all occasions of curious questions, that may hinder you in this great cause for which I have called you; and remember that spending of time is spoiling of business. And this I hope in God, and that by a faith in God, that by your actions this parliament I shall clearly see your hearts, and that you are the true representative body of my subjects. For you know in your consciences that of all the kings that ever were, I dare say, never king was better beloved of his people than I am. Therefore be ye true glasses and mirrors of their faces, and be sure you yield true reflections and representations, as you ought to do. And this doing I hope you shall not only find the blessing of God, but also by these actions procure the thanks and love of the whole people for being so true and faithful glasses. And you shall never find me desire any thing of you, but what shall tend to the common good and weal of the kingdom. *LJ*, III, 209–10

16. Speech by Sir Dudley Carleton, House of Commons, 12 May 1626

. . . I beseech you, gentlemen, move not his Majesty with trenching upon his prerogatives, lest you bring him out of love with parliaments. You have heard his Majesty's often messages to you, to put you forward in a course that will be most convenient. In those messages he told you, that if there were not correspondency between him and you, he should be enforced to use new counsels. Now, I pray you consider what these new counsels are, and may be; I fear to declare those that I conceive. In all Christian kingdoms you know that parliaments were in use anciently, by which their kingdoms were governed in a most flourishing manner, until the monarchs began to know their own strength, and, seeing the turbulent spirit of their parliaments, at length they little by little began to stand upon their prerogatives, and at last overthrew the parliaments throughout Christendom, except here only with us.

And indeed, you would count it a great misery if you knew the subjects in foreign countries as well as myself, to see them look not like our nation, with store of flesh on their backs, but like so many ghosts, and not men, being nothing but skin and bones, with some thin cover to their nakedness, and wearing only wooden shoes on their feet, so that they cannot eat meat or wear good clothes, but they must pay and be taxed unto the king for it. There is a misery beyond expression, and that which yet we are free from. Let us be careful then to preserve the king's good opinion of parliaments, which bringeth this happiness to this nation, and makes us envied of all others, while there is this sweetness between his Majesty and his Commons, lest we lose the repute of a free-born nation by turbulency in parliament. For in my opinion the greatest and wisest part of a parliament are those that use the greatest silence, so as it be not opiniative, or sullen, as now we are by the loss of these our members that are committed.

This good correspondency being kept between the king and his people will so join their love and favour to his Majesty with liking of parliaments, that his prerogative shall be preserved entire to himself, without our touching upon it, and also the privilege of the subject (which is our happiness) inviolated, and both be maintained to the support of each other. *PH*, II, 120–1

17. Proceedings in King's Bench, 12 February 1630

[Against Sir John Eliot, Denzil Holles and Benjamin Valentine]

. . . Inasmuch as the Defendants would not put in any other plea, the last day of the Term judgment was given against them upon a *nihil dicit*, which judgment was pronounced by [Mr Justice William] Jones to this effect:

The matter of the information now, by the confession of the defendants, is admitted to be true, and we think their plea to the jurisdiction insufficient for the matter and manner of it. And we hereby will not draw the true liberties of parliament-men into question; to wit, for such matters which they do or speak in a parliamentary manner. But in this case there was a conspiracy between the defendants to slander the state, and to raise sedition and discord between the king, his peers and people, and this was not a parliamentary course. All the judges of England, except one, have resolved the statute of 4 H. 8 to be a private act, and to extend to Strode only. But every Member of Parliament shall have such privileges as are there mentioned; but they have no privilege to speak at their pleasure. The parliament is a high court, therefore it ought not to be disorderly, but ought to give good example to other courts. If a judge of our court should rail upon the state, or clergy, he is punishable for it. A Member of Parliament may charge any great officer of state with any particular offence, but this was a malevolous accusation in the generality of all the officers of state, therefore the matter contained within the information is a great offence, and punishable in this court.

For the punishment, although the offence be great, yet that shall be with a light hand, and shall be in this manner.

That every of the defendants shall be imprisoned during the king's pleasure: Sir John Eliot to be imprisoned in the Tower of London, and the other defendants in other prisons.   *ST*, III, 309–10

II. FINANCE

The parliaments of the first two Stuarts, like the later parliaments of Elizabeth, spent much of their time and energy on questions of finance, which boiled down to questions of taxation. The general rise in prices had depressed the real income of the Crown, yet it was difficult to convince the taxpayers – which meant in effect the landowning classes – that they should supplement that income on a regular basis, come peace, come war. As a result in her closing years Elizabeth had begun to exploit with greater vigour such fiscal rights as she had; a notable example was her feudal right to the incidents of wardship and marriage. This became especially evident after Robert Cecil succeeded his father, Lord Burleigh, as Master of the Court of Wards in 1598.[41]

[41] Joel Hurstfield, *The Queen's Wards* (1958), and 'The profits of fiscal feudalism', *Econ. Hist. Review*, VIII (1955), 53–61.

Purveyance – the Crown's right to buy victuals and commandeer transport at rock-bottom prices – was still exercised directly in the home counties, though it had supposedly been commuted for a nationwide levy.[42] Her reckless distribution of monopolies, by sale or gift, finally produced a full-scale parliamentary revolt in 1601.

Naturally these grievances were speedily revived in 1604, and by 26 March the situation in the Commons was so alarming that Robert Cecil decided to take the initiative in arranging a conference between the two Houses, and James assured them, with unconscious cynicism, that all his most eminent predecessors had legislated against abuses of purveyance, and he was ready to follow suit. But the end was stalemate. The Commons declined to recognise the Crown's right to purveyance at all, and rejected the Lords' proposals for an annual tax in lieu. They did acknowledge the Crown's right to compensation for its rights of wardship, but the Lords rejected their proposals on the grounds that it would be 'inconvenient and unseasonable' to press such demands in the new king's first parliament.[43]

Thus the chance of initiating serious negotiations on taxation was lost, though there are signs that Cecil realised the need for a comprehensive settlement of the kind he eventually proposed in 1610.[44] The Commons generously voted the king three subsidies in 1606, and naturally looked for corresponding concessions. But a further attempt to deal with purveyance failed,[45] and in March 1606 the Commons submitted a portmanteau list of grievances. The petition itself has not survived, but the king's reply has (19). The Commons were alert to the recent issue of a new Book of Rates, increasing the customs duties, and to the levy of the new impositions, but they were mainly preoccupied with monopolies and special privileges in trade and manufacture. Altogether it is worth the attention of those who still think that parliaments in this period were concerned exclusively, or even preponderantly, with questions of religion, sovereignty and right.[46] James dealt fairly with it, by his own lights, and he was irritated when the same grievances came round again in 1610; he accused them of taking up complaints 'in the streets', just to 'have a show made'.[47]

In fact in 1610 the Commons' attention was focussed on impositions almost entirely, and the fact that a body composed almost entirely of landowners should be so moved on this matter suggests the presence of a powerful merchants' lobby, inside and outside parliament. The Crown had always enjoyed a theoretical right to levy import duties for the regulation of trade and the protection of native manufactures, and Elizabeth's action in imposing a small duty on imported currants in 1601, later extended to tobacco, went unchallenged, in fact was scarcely noticed until the Turkey merchant John Bate refused to pay and was committed in 1606. Horrendous prophecies of doom from the merchants' lobby induced the Commons to include it in their petition in

---

[42] Allegra Woodworth, 'Purveyance for the Royal Household in the Reign of Queen Elizabeth', *Trans. Amer. Phil. Society*, XXXV (1945); G. E. Aylmer, 'The Last Years of Purveyance, 1616–1660', *Econ. Hist. Review*, X (1957) 81–93.

[43] *CJ*, I, 153–4, 204, 207–8; *LJ*, II, 294, 309.

[44] Nicholas Tyacke, 'Wroth, Cecil and the Parliamentary Session of 1604', *BIHR*, L (1977), 120–5.

[45] Notestein, *Commons*, pp. 186–210.

[46] Such petitions were recurrent. In 1621 the Commons descended to such trivia as the lighthouse at Winterton, Norfolk, and the scandalous conduct of the president of Corpus Christi College, Oxford (*PH*, I, 1489–92).

[47] *Works*, p. 356 (21 March 1610).

March.[48] James simply went ahead, and sued Bate in the Exchequer to test his rights. Predictably he won; indeed, Chief Baron Fleming's judgment appeared to give him the power to levy a duty on any commodity at any time (**18**). It is difficult to know what weight to attach to this; as Tanner says, 'It was very usual in this period for judges whose real conclusions were based on the narrowest and most technical grounds to embellish their judgments with vague philosophy.'[49] Sir Edward Coke later claimed that he and his fellow chief justice, Popham, had privately dissented from Fleming's judgment,[50] but William Hakewill and other radical barristers found it perfectly convincing. Moreover, the House of Commons would find it difficult to defend men whose sole preoccupation was quite clearly money, and Fleming's gibe – 'It is well known that the end of every private merchant is not the common good but his particular profit' – must have struck home. The topic did not come up in the following session, 1606–7.

But when Salisbury took over as Lord Treasurer in 1608 he soon extended impositions to cover almost every imported commodity except basic foodstuffs, munitions and ships' stores, and as soon as parliament re-assembled for its fourth session in February 1610 the Commons called for an inquiry.[51] The whole topic was ventilated in a three-day debate on 23, 28 and 29 June, despite James's efforts to stop them (p. 26 above). Here they displayed a new propensity to shift the basis of discussion from the immediate grievance and its effect on individuals – which in the case of impositions was difficult to demonstrate anyway – onto broad and general issues of law and immemorial rights. They were perhaps taking their cue from the judges, perhaps from James himself, whose pronouncements on the Divine Right of Kings in his published works were at last beginning to excite adverse comment. They were further flustered by Cowell's *Interpreter*, which gave the king an absolute right of taxation without consent, and they were not entirely mollified by James's explication of his views in his speech of 21 March (p. 11 above) or his suppression of the book.[52]

Thus we find the Commons seeking to give their arguments a firm historical as well as a legal base. On 28 June Thomas Hedley and William Hakewill delivered long orations tracing the history of English taxation back to Magna Carta, and concluding from this, of course, that impositions were contrary to law and ancient custom.[53] Next day, James Whitelocke made a celebrated speech (**20**) in which he propounded the classic argument that taxation was vested in the Sovereign Authority, and this was neither king nor parliament alone, but king-in-parliament. Some of these speeches were published at the time, and republished in 1641, but their short-term impact is difficult to assess. But it is significant that in the negotiations now proceeding for a 'Great Contract' the king reluctantly agreed to levy no new impositions for the future.[54]

---

[48] 'The merchants offer to leave all rather than this shall stand, go beyond seas', *CJ*, i, 309.

[49] *TCD*, p. 338.   [50] *Reports*, pt XII, §§ 33–5 (VI, 237–40).

[51] Gardiner, *Parliamentary Debates in 1610*, pp. 58ff.; *ST*, II, 407–520. Cf. Dietz, *English Public Finance*, pp. 369–71.

[52] P. 126 below. Cf. S. B. Chrimes, 'The Constitutional Ideas of Dr John Cowell', *EHR*, LXIV (1949), 461–83.

[53] For Hedley's speech see Foster, *Proceedings*, II, 170–98. Notice the strained but ingenious argument by which he associates the introduction of impositions with a decline in military power (pp. 195–6).

[54] Gardiner, *Debates*, pp. 162–5. See also *TCD*, pp. 345–7.

Salisbury's 'Great Contract' envisaged a rationalisation of taxation, and particularly the surrender of the king's contentious feudal rights of wardship, marriage and purveyance in return for a regular income in perpetuity. Negotiations to this end took up most of the first session of 1610, but the Commons' views could not be aligned with Salisbury's, nor his with the king's. In 1604 the Commons had been willing to consider the commutation of wardship, but in the interval their attitude had hardened; they were nervous of making the king financially independent of parliament, and in any case when it came to the point they were extremely reluctant to agree to a permanent land tax or an excise, though these were the only conceivable means by which the money could be raised. James on his side was reluctant to abandon sources of income which were responsive to inflation in return for a fixed annual sum whose real value might well depreciate. After a recess in August and September to consult their constituents the Commons returned in an even less co-operative mood. They were adjourned in some disorder on 24 November and dissolved the following January (1611). Salisbury died discredited a year later.

Some regard the failure of the Great Contract as one of those vital turning-points which are supposed to punctuate the history of the years 1603–40. But the imposition of the kind of graduated taxation, direct and indirect, which the Long Parliament carried through in 1642 and 1643 (p. 243 below) was unthinkable at a time of peace and good order, and James was right in thinking that the kind of fixed annual sum Salisbury had in mind would soon have been overtaken by inflation, leading to further confrontation. As it was, James blundered on in a state of chronic indebtedness common to most European monarchs at this time; actuarially horrifying but in practical terms unimportant. It was a life of swings and roundabouts. For instance, in 1618 the Queen lay in state for ten weeks while the necessary cash was scraped together to pay for her funeral, but when the Whitehall Banqueting House burned down in 1619 its reconstruction began within six months, to the designs of Inigo Jones.

But impositions, it seemed, had come to stay. James fulfilled his promise, made in 1610, to rationalise their distribution, and by weighting them against foreign merchants he did much to pacify the City. There was a hysterical debate on the matter in the Addled Parliament of 1614, but after that they dropped from view. Some merchants renewed their opposition in 1625, simply because James had so often declared that he claimed the right only for his own lifetime; a small minority carried their opposition to extreme lengths in 1627 and 1628, but their demonstrations were swallowed up in the more general resistance to tunnage and poundage.[55] They were retrospectively legalised by the Tunnage and Poundage Act of 1641.

In the interval between the parliaments of 1614 and 1621 James found a new and expensive favourite in George Villiers, ultimately Duke of Buckingham, but also an able financial adviser in Lionel Cranfield, who for the first time succeeded in curbing his reckless overspending, especially in the Household.[56] But in the meanwhile James had also resorted to the issue of patents of monopoly on an unprecedented scale; up to

[55] Dietz, *op. cit.*, pp. 371–5.
[56] Menna Prestwich, *Cranfield*, ch. 5; P. R. Seddon, 'Household Reform in the Reign of James I', *BIHR*, LIII (1980), 44–55.

1612 Salisbury, with the reaction of 1601 against Elizabeth in mind, had firmly restricted their use. The reaction of 1601 was repeated 20 years later, and given added weight by the severe economic crisis of the years 1619–23.[57] James was willing to sacrifice the arch-monopolists, Sir Francis Mitchell and Sir Giles Mompesson, in order to shield Buckingham and the other ministers who had sealed the patents. He also had to stand by while his lord chancellor, Francis Bacon, succumbed to other charges (p. 88 below). But the government's retreat was skilfully conducted, three scapegoats did penance for a host, and Coke's attempt to pass a statute outlawing monopolies failed. James was even voted two subsidies in the first session, which was more than he got in 1610 or 1614. In the second session, of course, parliament was bogged down in questions of foreign policy and free speech (p. 27 above).

In 1624 all was changed. Buckingham and the Prince of Wales, anxious to reverse James's foreign policy, did a covert deal with the Commons' spokesmen. Parliament was allowed to debate foreign relations, Lionel Cranfield, now Lord Treasurer, was removed by impeachment, and Coke at last secured a Monopolies Act (**21**), which confined their use to new inventions – though Charles I's lawyers found a way round it in the 1630s.

But the Monopolies Act was not alone, and the remaining legislation of this parliament reminds us of a substratum of legal and financial grievance which deserves a great deal more attention than it has received. It centred on the king's legal rights as lord of land, which gave him an overwhelming advantage in litigation over property. The work of informers who searched out encroachments on the royal forests or the Crown estates, often committed generations back, or old debts to the Crown long forgotten, was also bitterly resented. A tentative programme of legislation from the back benches in 1604 embodied some of these ideas,[58] and it is noticeable that in the Form of Apology and Satisfaction the Commons committee thought it worth while to request the regulation of 'assarts', or the conversion of forest land, here the royal forest, into arable. The problem was exacerbated by Lord Treasurer Dorset, who in 1604 launched a campaign to maximise the income from Crown lands, a campaign intensified by Salisbury after 1608.[59] In 1610 such issues were pushed aside by impositions and the Great Contract, but in the abortive negotiations which preceded the Addled Parliament the self-nominated Commons spokesman Sir Henry Neville put forward 11 bills of grace along these lines.[60] In 1621 the Commons' mind was still on other things, it seems, but we notice that they incongruously tacked onto their petitition of 3 December 1621, on free speech, a request for a general pardon which would embrace alienation of Crown lands, old debts to the Crown, and technical infraction of the law relating to wardship (p. 42 above). In 1624, with a government anxious to please, the floodgates were open. 21 Jac. I, c. 2, protected the subject against accusations of encroachment on Crown lands and confirmed titles held for 60 years unchallenged; c. 4 relieved him to some extent from the threat of informers under penal statutes; c. 5 protected former sheriffs against a belated scrutiny of their accounts;

[57] B. E. Supple, *Commercial Crisis and Change* (Cambridge 1959), chs. 2–4 *passim*.
[58] Notestein, *Commons*, pp. 47–54.   [59] Dietz, *op. cit.*, pp. 116–18.
[60] Moir, *Addled Parliament*, pp. 16, 69, 200–4; Clayton Roberts and Owen Duncan, 'The Parliamentary Undertaking of 1614', *EHR*, XCIII (1978), 481–98.

five other acts protected landowners from 'troublesome and contentious suits' of a kind likely to be initiated by the Treasury or its agents, and another (c. 23) was designed to prevent the removal of property suits from the jurisdiction of local courts. Another act, against usury (c. 16) fixed the maximum rate of interest at 8 per cent, which was of obvious concern to those seeking a mortgage. Conrad Russell comments that in 1624 many MPs could no longer afford to neglect their provincial power base in the pursuit of high politics, but his treatment of the matter, though far from complete, is a shining exception; most historians are too much concerned with what parliament said, which was usually less important than what it did.[61] In fact this brief parliament passed 35 public statutes, as against seven in 1625, none in 1621, and only 73 between 1604 and 1610, when the highest count in any one session (1604) was 29. The statutes of 1624 included the general pardon requested in 1621, and three acts dear to Puritan hearts, against profane swearing, drunkenness and bigamy.

This was where the heart of the ordinary MP was to be found, not in Cadiz, Prague or Munich. Yet the Commons had endorsed Buckingham's policy of war with Spain, and they now felt obliged to support it, however inadequately, with a grant of three subsidies and three fifteenths and tenths, but the preamble to the Subsidy Act (22) declared that the money collected should be paid to treasurers accountable to parliament, and was to be expended only on the navy, aid to the Dutch, and the defence of the British Isles. This device of 'appropriation' was premature, and lacked bureaucratic reinforcement; the government seems to have ignored it. However, the Lords objected at the time, and James threatened to add the words 'and the recovery of the Palatinate', the ostensible cause of the war.[62] But by the time James died, on 27 March 1625, his son's diplomatic and military policy was going badly astray. Having evaded, to the general rejoicing, one Catholic princess, he was now affianced to another, Henrietta Maria of France, and the money voted in 1624 was being used to finance an expedition to the Palatinate under Count Mansfeldt which got no farther than the Flanders coast.

Thus there was a lot of explaining to do, but Charles I was the last man to do it. There is no greater contrast between James I and his son than in their handling of parliament. At the beginning of almost every session James treated both Houses to an extensive speech in which he outlined his views on kingship and his immediate policy, and also went into great detail on any topic which happened to have taken his fancy. In the course of the session he often intervened with further speeches, almost as long; he sent long letters to the Speaker, he sent impromptu messages by his privy councillors almost every week, and he positively welcomed deputations from the Commons. Charles's conduct was in stark contrast. His speeches were simple, direct and brief; Wentworth told the Irish parliament in 1634, 'I shall, as near as I can, speak in the style of my royal master, which is to be with brevity and clarity.'[63] He regarded the Commons with apparent scorn, and though he would occasionally send down a brief

[61] Russell, *Parliaments and Politics*, pp. 159, 181, 183, 190–4. Ruigh's monograph on this parliament has one slight reference (pp. 223–4). Stephen White (*Sir Edward Coke*, ch. 3 *passim*) is rather better, but he is primarily concerned with Coke's proposed legal reforms.

[62] Gardiner, *History*, V, 234–5.

[63] W. Knowler, *The Earl of Strafforde's Letters and Despatches* (2 vols., 1739), I, p. 287.

message by one of his servants in the House he made little effort to prompt debate or even explain his wishes.

These defects were patently obvious in his first parliament, which assembled in June 1625 in a mood of grudging good will, despite the difficult economic situation, and was abruptly dissolved in mid August in a mood of resentful bewilderment. Starved of information, even the secretaries of state could not explain the king's policy, which now included the suppression of a Huguenot revolt at La Rochelle and *de facto* toleration for Roman Catholics under the terms of the French marriage treaty. Anger which had no other outlet was directed at Buckingham, and the failure of his expedition against Cadiz in the late autumn left him exposed to the new parliament which had to be summoned in 1626. The King compounded his favourite's difficulties by taking steps to exclude from the Commons the leaders of opposition, notably Coke and Wentworth, forgetting that these men were also the spokesmen of the 'war party'. This left the field open for personal enemies of Buckingham like Sir John Eliot. The impeachment of his chief minister and closest friend enraged Charles, and he warned the Commons, 'Parliaments are altogether in my power for their calling, sitting and dissolution; therefore as I find the fruits of them good or evil they are to continue or not to be.'[64]

He already believed that he could rule without parliament, and he authorised his servants to publish his views without reserve.[65] When he was forced to another dissolution in June 1626, without a penny voted for the war, he at once put his vague threats into execution. The successful levy of forced loans on a large scale, and the decision of King's Bench in 1627 that men imprisoned for refusing such loans were not bailable, filled the parliamentary classes with alarm.[66] Like King John, King Charles was probing the wall of law and custom which protected his subjects' purses, hoping to find a gap through which he could press. The gap he had found was not very wide – the prisons were not large enough for him to coerce taxpayers on a large scale – but his success had serious implications. When further disasters in war and diplomacy forced him to summon a third parliament for 17 March 1628 the opposition abandoned its attack on Buckingham and proceeded to examine the Five Knights' Case, as well as the king's recent practice of billeting troops on civilians and subjecting whole areas to martial law.[67]

The tortured manoeuvres which followed cannot be explored in detail here. Charles's opening speech was typically brief and curt, to the point of rudeness; he was always to confuse bravery with courage (23). He only succeeded in incensing the Commons, and though he fought every inch of the way, for ten weeks, the impossibility of continuing the war at all without a parliamentary grant, and the importunities of Buckingham, who never looked beyond the next campaigning season, forced him to give way, and on 7 June he finally gave his assent to the Petition of Right (24). There was some doubt at the time, and there still is, precisely what the petition

---

[64] *PH*, II, 56 (29 March 1626).   [65] As in Carleton's speech, p. 45 above.
[66] For the Five Knights' Case, see p. 89 below.
[67] See Lindsay Boynton, 'Martial Law and the Petition of Right', *EHR*, LXXIX (1964), 255–84.

was, and whether it was a statute, equivalent to a statute, or superior to one.[68] However this may be, it obliged the king not to levy taxation without consent of parliament, not to imprison his subjects without cause shown, not to billet troops on civilians without their consent, and not to subject civilians to martial law. Less than a week later disputes as to its interpretation broke out, but there was no doubt as to its binding force.

The trouble was tunnage and poundage. These customs duties on wine and wool had been granted to each of the Tudors and to James I for life. But in 1625 the Commons had decided to review the whole field of indirect taxation, and, apparently without malicious intent, they had only granted tunnage and poundage for one year, pending further discussions. Those discussions never came, a year elapsed, but Charles continued to collect the duties. The parliament of 1626 declared that he was acting illegally, and brought in a bill to indemnify him, but this was lost on the dissolution. On 8 July 1626 the Privy Council declared that tunnage and poundage was an inseparable part of the king's revenue, which he had enjoyed since Henry VI's reign, and which was independent of any parliamentary grant. In 1628 the Commons was at first prepared to be reasonable; they agreed that Charles ought to have these duties, and they discussed ways and means, but unfortunately nothing was done until after the passing of the Petition of Right, and then the situation suddenly swung out of control.

As soon as the petition was passed Wentworth and Coke relaxed their grip on the House. Pym launched an attack on the royalist divine Roger Manwaring, and Eliot resumed his campaign against Buckingham; this led to a Remonstrance on 17 June severely critical of the conduct of the war.[69] In this unpromising atmosphere discussion of tunnage and poundage was resumed, and the Commons proposed once again to review the whole field of indirect taxation. They suggested, however, that this be left for the next session; in the meanwhile they would pass a simple enabling bill. But Charles chose to insist that parliament had no standing in the case, and with equal folly the Commons replied with a Remonstrance on 25 June which declared that the levy of tunnage and poundage was not only contrary to the Petition of Right but an infraction of 'the fundamental liberties of this kingdom', and asked Charles 'not to take it in ill part from those of your Majesty's loving subjects who shall refuse to make payment' (GCD, p. 73). Next day, when he prorogued parliament, Charles made a surprisingly moderate rejoinder; he affirmed his adhesion to the Petition of Right, but said that no one had thought that it covered tunnage and poundage (GCD, pp. 73–4).

He was probably right. In any case, the action of the Commons in virtually appealing to the people not to pay a tax was unprecedented and indefensible, and the decision of a group of London merchants, led by John Rolles, to take them at their

[68] The bibliography of the Petition of Right is vast, and growing. Frances H. Relf, *The Petition of Right*, is still basic, but for a simpler treatment see Judson, *Crisis of the Constitution*, pp. 240–69, Russell, *Parliaments and Politics*, ch. 6, and Stephen D. White, *Coke*, ch. 7. Also Elizabeth Read Foster, 'Petitions and the Petition of Right', *JBS*, xiv (1974), 21–45; J. A. Guy, 'The origins of the Petition of Right reconsidered', *HJ*, xxv (1982), 289–312; Michael B. Young, 'The Origins of the Petition of Right Reconsidered Further', *ibid.*, xxvii (1984), 449–52; and G. L. Harriss, in Sharpe, *Faction*, pp. 96–8.
[69] Rushworth, I, 631–8.

word only brought them into further disrepute. The Council ordered the merchants' goods to be confiscated, the Court of Exchequer ratified their action, and the responsible public agreed that the Commons were encouraging self-interested men to break the law. Since 1621 the Lords had been in broad sympathy with the Commons, but the Remonstrance of 25 June alienated them completely. The assassination of Buckingham in August removed the main obstacle to domestic concord, and leaders of opposition like the Earls of Bristol and Arundel at once rejoined the king, on a platform that included the strengthening of the Church and the purification of government. When parliament re-assembled in January 1629 the House of Commons found itself isolated; it intensified its isolation by at once espousing the cause of the delinquent merchants and declining to offer the compromise on tunnage and poundage which common sense dictated. It secured no support from the Lords in this, nor in its exaggerated and intemperate attack on Charles's ecclesiastical policy (pp. 133–4 below). Eliot, who had framed this policy of disaster, brought the session to a disgraceful close on 2 March, when he and his supporters held the Speaker down in the Chair to prevent an adjournment, and pushed through three resolutions, on the Church and on tunnage and poundage, which were yet another attempt to impose the will of the Commons – not even parliament as a whole – on the nation (**25**).

Charles at once dissolved parliament in a perfect fury, and in a lengthy *apologia* issued on 10 March he accused a minority of Members of deliberately conspiring to reduce monarchical authority and even usurp executive control (**26**). In a further proclamation, on the 27th, he announced that he had no intention of summoning another parliament until the present ringleaders had received 'condign punishment', and until 'our people shall see more clearly into our intentions and actions'.[70]

18. Bate's Case, 1606

[*Chief Baron Fleming*]

. . . To the king is committed the government of the realm and his people; and Bracton saith that for his discharge of his office God has given to him power, the act of government and the power to govern. The king's power is double, ordinary and absolute, and they have several laws and ends. That of the ordinary is for the profit of particular subjects, for the execution of civil justice, the determining of *meum*; and this is exercised by equity and justice in ordinary courts, and by the Civilians is nominated *jus privatum*, and with us Common Law: and these laws cannot be changed without parliament, and although that their form and course may be changed and interrupted, yet they can never be changed in substance. The absolute power of the king is not that which is converted or executed to private use, to the benefit of any particular person, but is only that which is applied to the general benefit of the people and is *salus populi*; as the people is the body and the king the head; and this power is [not] guided by the rules which direct only at the Common Law, and is most

[70] *Foedera*, XIX, 62–3.

properly named policy and government; and as the constitution of this body varieth with the time, so varieth this absolute law according to the wisdom of the king for the common good; and these being general rules and true as they are, all things done within these rules are lawful. The matter in question is material matter of state, and ought to be ruled by the rules of policy; and if it be so, the king hath done well to execute his extraordinary power. All customs, be they old or new, are no other but the effects and issues of trade and commerce with foreign nations; but all commerce and affairs with foreigners, all wars and peace, all acceptance and admitting for current, foreign coin, all parties and treaties whatsoever, are made by the absolute power of the king; and he who hath power of causes hath power also of effects. No exportation or importation can be but at the king's ports, they are the gates of the king, and he hath absolute power by them to include or exclude whom he shall please; and ports to merchants are their harbours and repose, and for their better security he is compelled to provide bulwarks and fortresses, and to maintain for the collection of his customs and duties collectors and customers; and for that charge it is reason that he should have this benefit. He is also to defend the merchants from pirates at sea in their passage. Also by the power of the King they are to be relieved if they are oppressed by foreign princes . . . [etc.].

It is said that an imposition may not be upon a subject without parliament. That the king may impose upon a subject I omit; for it is not here the question if the king may impose upon the subject or his goods, but the impost here is not upon a subject, but here it is upon Bates, as upon a merchant who imports goods within this land charged before by the king; and at the time the impost was imposed upon them they were the goods of the Venetians and not the goods of a subject, nor within the land, but only upon those which shall after be imported; and so all the arguments which were made for the subject fail. And where it is said that he is a merchant, and that he ought to have the sea open and free for him, and that trades of merchants and merchandise are necessary to export the surplus of our commodities and then to import other necessities, and so is favourably to be respected; as to that, it is well known that the end of every private merchant is not the common good but his particular profit, which is only the means which induceth him to trade and traffic. And the impost to him is nothing, for he rateth his merchandise according to that . . .

And whereas it is said that if the king may impose, he may impose any quantity what he pleases, true it is that this is to be referred to the wisdom of the king, who guideth all under God by his wisdom, and this is not to be disputed by a subject; and many things are left to his wisdom for the ordering of his power, rather than his power shall be restrained. The king may pardon any felon; but it may be objected that if he pardon one felon he may pardon all, to the damage of the commonwealth, and yet none will doubt but that is left in his wisdom . . . And the wisdom and providence of the king is not to be disputed by the subject; for by intendment they cannot be severed from his person, and to argue *a posse ad actum* to restrain the king and his power because that by his power he may do ill is no argument for a subject. To prove the power of the king by precedents of antiquity in a case of this nature may easily be done, and if it were lawful in ancient times it is lawful now, for the authority of the king is not diminished and the Crown hath the same attributes that then it had . . .

[After reviewing the precedents he concluded:]

. . . All these statutes prove expressly, that the king had power to increase the impost, and that upon commodities of the land, and that he continually used this power notwithstanding all acts of parliament against it . . . Wherefore I think, that the king ought to have judgment . . .

ST, ii, 387–94

19. Grievances, 1606

[19 November 1606]

Mr Speaker publisheth, that the Clerk of the higher House, by his Majesty's commandment, had delivered unto him a roll of parchment, written and entitled:

A Memorial of such Resolutions as his Majesty hath taken, with the advice of his Privy Council, assisted with the two chief justices, the Lord Chief Baron, and his Majesty's Counsel at Law, upon examination of those Grievances which were presented to his Majesty by the lower House of Parliament at the last Session[71]. . .

1. *Lord Danvers' Suit*. First, whereas his Majesty hath granted to the Lord Danvers and Sir John Gilbert three parts in four of all such benefit as should arise to his Majesty by fines, issues, amercements, forfeitures, &c., over and above the sum of 2,800*l*., which sum is supposed to be the medium of those profits accruing in former years; although their profit was only to arise by such augmentation as should appear to be made in the Court of Exchequer, upon order given by his Majesty to the barons, and all other officers, for reformation of the great frauds and abuses committed in the levying of the fines and amercements; nevertheless, because the said grant appeareth to be subject to inconvenience in the execution, his Majesty hath been contented to revoke the said Patent . . .

2. *Green Wax*. To the second, which is concerning a patent granted to Sir

[71] *CJ*, i, 309.

Roger Aston for all fines, amercements and other penalties and forfeitures known under the name of Green Wax, growing from the tenants of the Duchy of Lancaster, it is resolved by the judges that they be things grantable by the king, and are enjoyed by a patent of the late queen's. Nevertheless, because this grant . . . dependeth upon some recitals which the judges have not examined, and therefore cannot now determine of it, in point of law, and because there may be some inconvenience to the subject in the execution, except some things may be reformed, his Majesty hath taken order with the patentee for surrender of his patent, and to grant him a new patent upon these conditions: First, that the patentee dispense not aforehand with offences or default of jurors . . .; the second, that upon every General Pardon the subject may enjoy the benefit thereof, as though the things pardoned were not granted, but still in the king's hands . . .

3. *Issues of Jurors*. To the third, which is touching a patent made to Sir Henry Brouncker of the issues of jurors not appearing, throughout England, forasmuch as there are in this patent some such inconveniences as in the former of Sir Roger Aston's, it is also resolved to resume the old patent, which the judges already have determined to be void in law, and to grant a new, with the like provisions as are appointed for . . . Sir Roger Aston.

4. *Licence to sell Wines*. To the fourth, concerning the Lord Admiral, for the licences to sell wines by retail, at a greater price than the laws now in force do allow, the judges resolve the grant to be good in law; and touching the supposed abuses complained of, such are the answers which have been given by the patentees after due examination, as it seemeth that the informers have abused the lower House with many untruths.

5. *Logwood*. To the fifth, concerning a patent which doth permit the use of a stuff for dyeing made of a mixture of logwood, or blockwood, with other things. . .; although both sides have been heard before his Majesty's council, and there received the opinion of the judges that his Majesty's grant is justifiable by the law; and some suggestions made by the dyers, as well concerning the price supposed to be demanded for every ton as touching some other abuses in the execution, proved false upon the hearing; nevertheless, such is and ever shall be his Majesty's precious care to prevent all colour of vexation to his subjects in general, and in this particular, more than in any other, [it] tending to discredit the making of cloth (which is one of the greatest and richest commodities of the kingdom), as he hath been pleased to resume into his hands this grant . . .

6. *Raising of Customs*. To the sixth, concerning the raising of the customs, it is apparent that his Majesty may by the laws of this realm require 12d. in the pound, according to the very value of most merchandises, nevertheless the king hath not done this, neither (according to some use of former times) were

these new rates set by oath; but his Majesty, by his commissioners calling to them principal merchants of all sorts, and using their opinion and advice, caused the old rates to be changed according to the change of times, abating the former customs of divers commodities that are fallen, or too hardly rated, and so likewise advancing some others; and yet with great moderation, far under the due in those commodities that are much risen. Which course, as it hath been used by former kings of this realm from age to age, applying themselves to the times, so is it necessary now in point of state, seeing all the neighbour princes and states have divers times of late mounted their customs; otherwise, if they shall increase theirs, and by consequence raise the price of their commodities, and his Majesty by the contrary course undervalue his, the stranger merchants shall sell dear to his Majesty's subjects and buy cheap of them, whereby the importation shall exceed the exportation, to the exhausting of treasure, and undoing of the state. And therefore the complaint appears to be without cause, and might well have been forborne.

7. *Imposition upon Currants.* To the seventh, which is touching the imposition upon currants, forasmuch as that complaint carried with it among other things a suggestion that this imposition would not be found warrantable by the law, in case the complainants might be permitted to try the right in course of justice, his Majesty, for satisfaction of all parties interested therein, hath remitted the determination thereof to such proceedings in law as is usual in like cases and standeth with the common justice of the realm. Which hath already proceeded so far as it hath been pleaded largely and often against the king, as well as for him, upon his Majesty's special directions to afford the plaintiff free and favourable hearing; and thereupon being publicly argued by all the Barons of the Exchequer, without contradiction it hath received there a final judgment for the king. In the carriage whereof, as his Majesty assureth himself, that those who preferred those complaints unto him have cause to remain satisfied, considering his Majesty's extraordinary and gracious dealing herein, in suffering a case which so nearly toucheth his ancient prerogative in this nature to be disputed in the common form of law. So if any other persons, either out of unquietness or partiality to their own gain, shall further importune them to deal with his Majesty in cases so greatly concerning him, he expecteth they shall be rejected, as persons worthy rather of reproof than to find any favour in that place.

8. *Imposition upon Tobacco.* To the eighth, concerning the imposition set upon tobacco, his Majesty is pleased to leave it to the same course, as a thing depending upon the same reasons.

9. *Sealing of New Draperies.* To the ninth, touching a patent granted to the duke of Lennox for the searching and sealing of divers stuffs by the name of 'new draperies', it is thought fit that the validity thereof be left to be judged by

the law, and whensoever any abuse arising in the execution thereof shall appear it is intended that the same shall be severely punished.[72]

10. *Sheriffs' Accounts.* To the tenth, which is the great charge that sheriffs of counties are put to by the clerks and officers in the Exchequer, upon their accounts, which are made merely for the king's service; forasmuch as those things are to be redressed, upon complaint and proof in the Court of Exchequer, his Majesty hath commanded the Lord Treasurer and that Court to examine the particularities thereof, and to give order for reformation.

11. *Muster Masters.* To the eleventh, concerning muster masters;[73] as his Majesty persuadeth himself that there is no meaning in this complaint, to take exception to those courses which his predecessors have used for the orderly and necessary training up of his subjects, wherein consisteth a great part of the strength of this realm, so whensoever it appears that any [lord] lieutenant, by virtue of his commission, hath taken or shall take any indirect course for the execution of that service, his Majesty is determined, upon proof, to see the same redressed.

12. *Pre-emption of Tin.* To the twelfth, concerning the pre-emption of tin, it is a right of inheritance so anciently and justly appertaining to his Majesty as none can or ought to impugn the same; to which being added, that in the execution thereof it is apparent that a number of his Majesty's good subjects in those parts of Cornwall that live by the labour of their hands receive great relief by receiving reasonable payments, where the merchants used in former times to make what payment they list for that which they bought of them. The exception to this appeareth not to be worthy the name of a grievance, unless some abuses be committed, which shall be reformed upon complaint whensoever any cause shall appear.

13. *Blue Starch.* To the thirteenth, which is concerning the making of smalt, or blue starch; it was granted upon suggestion that it would be a means to set many poor people a-work, which if it shall be found unwarranted by the law it is left free to be called in question, and there determined.

14. *Purveyance.* To the fourteenth, concerning purveyance; his Majesty hath already declared his pleasure, by proclamation, for reformation of any abuses to be offered to his subjects by continuing the ancient use of his prerogative of the same, whereof there is, and hath been always, so great necessity for him and his predecessors as there needs no further answer to that complaint than that his Majesty is graciously pleased to continue the course he hath done, in punishing all that shall abuse the meanest of his subjects in execution thereof.

[72] See Stone, *Crisis of the Aristocracy*, p. 437.

[73] Muster masters were veteran NCOs appointed by the government to drill and train the local militia in each county. It is not clear whether the Commons were complaining, as they often did, of having to pay these men, or whether some lord lieutenants were employing their own servants in this duty.

15. *Iron Ordnance.* To the fifteenth, concerning licence for transportation of iron ordnance and bullets; although his Majesty assureth himself that no man will presume to call in question his power to grant them at his pleasure, yet he is well content to make it known, that as there hath not been of late any grants passed of such nature, so his Majesty will then be sparing; except it be when he shall find it fit in his great judgment and consideration.

16. *Saltpetre.* To the sixteenth, concerning those grievances which his Majesty's subjects have suffered in the execution of a commission granted to certain persons for getting saltpetre; his Majesty granted no other commission than such as was drawn by his learned counsel, and more restrained than the former in the late queen's time. Wherein, as his Majesty had never an intention to make any application of his prerogative further than may stand with the lawful and necessary use thereof, so his Majesty was never minded to show himself so improvident as to suffer his crown and people to depend upon the uncertainty of foreign supply for [gun]powder, which is made of the saltpetre within this realm, the provision and proportion whereof doth so highly concern the defence and safety of the same. Nevertheless, because there never was anything in like cases so well devised and perfected by the wisdom and providence of man which hath not been in time by inferior ministers deputies and servants corrupted, and diverted from the true and original institution (as hath appeared in this particular, wherein divers injuries and grievances have been offered by some of the meanest persons used therein, not only repugnant to the authority of the commission, rightly examined, but merely contrary to his Majesty's meaning . . .), his Majesty, upon consideration of the matter contained in this complaint concerning that particular, and in regard of the reverent form which hath been used in presenting all your petitions, hath been pleased out of his gracious care and goodness to revoke and anull all commissions or grants made to any person or persons for and concerning digging and working for saltpetre, intending to consider of some such course hereafter, as the same may be made without any just cause of complaint . . .

CJ, 1, 316–18

20. James Whitelocke's speech on Impositions[74] (House of Commons, 29 June 1610)

. . . It will be admitted for a rule and ground of state that in every commonwealth and government there be some rights of sovereignty, *jura majestatis*, which regularly and of common right do belong to the sovereign power of that state, unless custom or the provisional ordinance of that state do otherwise dispose of them; which sovereign power is *potestas suprema*, a power

[74] Incorrectly ascribed to Henry Yelverton in *ST*.

that can control all other powers and cannot be controlled but by itself. It will not be denied that the power of imposing hath so great a trust in it, by reason of the mischiefs [that] may grow to the commonwealth by the abuses of it, that it hath ever been ranked among those rights of sovereign power. Then is there no further question to be made but to examine where the sovereign power is in this kingdom, for there is the right of imposition. The sovereign power is agreed to be in the king: but in the king is a twofold power – the one in parliament, as he is assisted with the consent of the whole state; the other out of parliament, as he is sole and singular, guided merely by his own will. And if of these two powers in the king, one is greater than the other and can direct and control the other, that is *suprema potestas*, the sovereign power, and the other is *subordinata*. It will then be easily proved that the power of the king in parliament is greater than his power out of parliament, and doth rule and control it; for if the king make a grant by his letters patent out of parliament, it bindeth him and his successors; but by his power in parliament he may defeat and avoid it; and therefore that is the greater power. If a judgment be given in the King's Bench by the king himself, as may be and by the law is intended, a writ of error to reverse this judgment may be sued before the king in parliament . . . So you see the appeal is from the king out of the parliament to the king in parliament; the writ is in his name; the rectifying and correcting the errors is by him, but with the assent of the Lords and Commons, than which there can be no stronger evidence to prove that his power out of parliament is subordinate to his power in parliament; for in acts of parliament, be they laws, grounds, or whatsoever else, the act and power is the king's but with the assent of the Lords and Commons, which maketh it the most sovereign and supreme power above all and controllable by none. Besides this right of imposing, there be others in the kingdom of the same nature: as the power to make laws, the power of naturalisation, the power of erection of arbitrary government, the power to judge without appeal, the power to legitimate; all which do belong to the king only in parliament. Others there be of the same nature that the king may exercise out of parliament, which right is grown unto him in them more in those others by the use and practice of the common-wealth, as denization, coinage, making war; which power the king hath time out of mind practised without the gainsaying and murmuring of his subjects. But these other powers before mentioned have ever been executed by him in parliament, and not otherwise but with the reluctation [*sc.* opposition] of the whole kingdom . . .

It hath been alleged that those which in this cause have enforced their reasons from this maxim of ours, that the king cannot alter the law, have diverted from the question. I say under favour, they have not, for that in effect is the very question now in hand; for if he alone out of Parliament may impose, he altereth the law of England in one of these two main fundamental points. He must either take his subjects' goods from them without assent of the party, which is against the law; or else he must give his own letters patent the force of a law to alter the property of his subjects' goods, which is also against the law . . .

ST, II, 481–3

21. The Monopolies Act, 1624

21 & 22 Jac. I, c. 3: *An Act concerning Monopolies and Dispensations with Penal Laws and the forfeiture thereof*

I. Forasmuch as your most excellent Majesty in your royal judgment and of your blessed disposition to the weal and quiet of your subjects did, in the year of our Lord God one thousand six hundred and ten, publish in print to the whole realm and to all posterity that all grants of monopolies . . . are contrary to your Majesty's laws,[75] which your Majesty's declaration is truly consonant and agreeable to the ancient and fundamental laws of this your realm. And whereas your Majesty was further graciously pleased expressly to command that no suitor should presume to move your Majesty for matters of that nature; yet nevertheless upon misinformations and untrue pretences of public good many such grants have been unduly obtained and unlawfully put in execution, to the great grievance and inconvenience of your Majesty's subjects, contrary to the laws of this your realm and contrary to your Majesty's royal and blessed intention so published as aforesaid. For avoiding whereof, and preventing of the like in time to come, may it please your most excellent Majesty, at the humble suit of the Lords Spiritual and Temporal and the Commons in this present Parliament assembled, that it may be declared and enacted . . . that all monopolies and all commissions, grants, licences, charters and letters patent heretofore made or granted, or hereafter to be made or granted, to any person or persons, bodies politic or corporate whatsoever, of or for the sole buying, selling, making, working or using of anything within this realm . . . or of any other monopolies, or of power, liberty or faculty to dispense with any others, or to give licence or toleration to do, use and exercise anything against the tenor or purport of any law or statute, or to give or make any warrant for any such dispensation, licence or toleration to be had or made, or to agree or compound with any others for any penalty or forfeitures limited by any statute, or of any grant or promise of the benefit, profit or commodity of any forfeiture, penalty or sum of money that is or shall be due by any statute before judgment thereupon had, and all proclamations, inhibitions, restraints, warrants of assistance, and all other matters and things whatsoever any way tending to the instituting, erecting, furthering or countenancing of the same or

---

[75] I can find no trace of any such statement, though it is unlikely that the Commons invented it and the Lords and the Privy Council failed to notice the fact.

any of them, are altogether contrary to the laws of this realm, and so are and shall be utterly void and of none effect, and in no wise to be but in ure [*sc.* practice] or execution.

[§ II decreed that the validity of monopolies be tried only by common law. § III put an immediate stop to all existing monopolies. § IV enabled complainants to proceed in the high court, and receive treble damages and double costs, offenders being liable to the penalties of praemunire.]

V. Provided nevertheless, and be it declared and enacted, that any declaration before mentioned shall not extend to any letters patent and grants of privilege for the term of one and twenty years or under heretofore made, of the sole working or making of any manner of new manufacture within this realm, to the first and true inventor or inventors of such manufactures which others at the time of the making of such letters patent and grants did not use, so they be not contrary to the law or mischievous to the state by raising of the prices of commodities at home, or hurt of trade, or generally inconvenient . . .

[§ VI extended the same privilege to new inventions in the future, though it reduced the period of grace to a maximum of 14 years. § VII exempted monopolies established by statute. § VIII preserved the rights of the Common Law courts to compound for forfeitures under penal statutes.]

IX. Provided also, and it is hereby further intended, declared and enacted, that this act or anything therein contained shall not in any wise extend or be prejudicial unto the City of London, or to any city, borough or town corporate within this realm for or concerning any grants, charters or letters patent to them or any of them made or granted, or for or concerning any custom or customs used by or within them or any of them, or unto any corporations, companies or fellowships of any art, trade, occupation or mystery, or to any companies or societies of merchants within this realm erected for the maintenance, enlargement or ordering of any trade of merchandise, but that the same charters, customs, corporations, companies, fellowships and societies, and their liberties, privileges, power and immunities shall be and continue of such force and effect as they were before the making of this act, and of none other, anything before in this act contained to the contrary notwithstanding.[76]

[The remaining clauses (X–XIV) excepted certain trades or industries: printing, the manufacture of saltpetre and gunpowder, the casting of ordnance; alum mining; the association of 'hoastmen' which controlled the Newcastle coal trade; glass-making and the export of calfskin; the smelting of iron ore and the manufacture of a blue starch known as 'smalt'.]

SR, IV, 1212

[76] This was used in the 1630s to evade the act, by setting up chartered companies to administer new monopolies.

22. Subsidy Act, 1624

21 Jac. I, c. 33: *An Act for payment of Three Subsidies and Three Fifteenths by the Temporalty*

Most Gracious sovereign, we your Majesty's most faithful and loving subjects, by your royal authority now assembled in your High Court of Parliament, having entered into serious and due consideration of the weighty and most important causes which at this time more than at any other time heretofore do press your Majesty to a much greater expense and charge than your own treasure alone can at this present support and maintain, and likewise of the injuries and indignities which have been lately offered to your Majesty and your children, under colour and during the time of the treaties for the marriage with Spain and the restitution of the Palatinate, which in this parliament have been clearly discovered and laid open unto us; and withal what humble advice with one consent and voice we have given unto your Majesty to dissolve those treaties, which your Majesty hath been graciously pleased to our exceeding joy and comfort fully to yield unto, and accordingly have made your public declaration for the real and utter dissolution of them, by means whereof your Majesty may haply be engaged in a sudden war: we in all humbleness, most ready and willing to give unto your Majesty and the whole world an ample testimony of our dutiful affections and sincere intentions to assist you therein, for the maintenance of that war that may hereupon ensue, and more particularly for the defence of this your realm of England, the securing of your kingdom of Ireland, the assistance of your neighbours the States of the United Provinces and other your Majesty's friends and allies, and for the setting forth of your Royal Navy, we have resolved to give for the present the greatest aid which ever was granted in parliament, to be levied in so short a time. And therefore we do humbly beseech your Majesty that it may be declared and enacted, and be it declared by the authority of this present parliament, that the said two treaties are by your Majesty utterly dissolved, and for the maintenance of the war which may ensue thereupon, and for the causes aforesaid, be it enacted that three whole fifteenths and tenths shall be paid, taken and levied of the moveable goods, chattels and other things usual to such fifteenths and tenths, to be contributory and chargeable within the shires, cities, boroughs, towns and other places of this your Majesty's realm, in manner and form aforetime used . . . to be paid in manner and form following: that is to say, the whole entire payment of the first of the said whole fifteenths and tenths . . . to be paid into the hands of Sir Thomas Middleton knight and alderman of London, Sir Edward Barkham knight and alderman of London, Sir Paul Baning knight and baronet, Sir Richard Grubham knight, James Campbell, George Whitmore and Ralph Freeman, aldermen of

London, and Martin Bond, citizen and haberdasher of London, Treasurers especially appointed in and by this act to receive and issue the same . . ., on or before the 10th of July next coming . . . [The second by 10 December, and the third by 10 May, 1625.]

II. [Collectors are to be appointed in each shire by the Members of Parliament for that shire; their qualifications, duties, etc.]

III. [Such collectors must enter into recognisances for the due payment.]

IV. And furthermore, for the great and weighty considerations aforesaid, we the Lords Spiritual and Temporal and the Commons in this present parliament assembled, do by our like assent and authority of this parliament give and grant to your Highness our said sovereign lord the king's Majesty, your heirs and successors, three entire subsidies, to be rated, taxed, levied and paid at three several payments, of every person spiritual and temporal, of what estate or degree soever he or they be of, according to the tenor of this act, in manner and form following, that is to say: as well that every person born within this realm of England, Wales or other the king's dominions, as all and every fraternity, guild, corporation, mystery, brotherhood and commonalty, corporated or not corporated, within this realm of England, Wales or other the king's dominions, being worth three pounds, for every pound as well in coin and the value of every pound that every such person, fraternity . . . [etc.] hath of his or their own or any other to his or their use, as also plate, stock of merchandise, all manner of corn and grain, household stuff, and of all other goods moveable, as well within this realm as without and of all such sums of money as to him or them is or shall be owing, whereof he or they trust in his or their conscience surely to be paid, except and out of the said premises deducted such sums of money as he or they owe, and in his or their consciences intendeth truly to pay, and except also the apparel of every such person, their wives and children, belonging to their own bodies, saving jewels, gold, silver, stone and pearl, shall pay to and for the first subsidy, at one entire payment, two shillings and eight pence of every pound . . . [And the same for each of the other two subsidies. Aliens are to pay 5s. 4d. in the £.]

V. And be it further enacted by the authority aforesaid, that every person born under the king's obeisance, and every corporation, fraternity, guild, mystery, brotherhood and commonalty, corporate or not corporate, for every pound that every of the same persons, and every corporation . . . [etc.], or any other to his or their use, hath in fee simple or fee tail, for term of life, term of years, by execution, wardship or by copy of court roll, of land in any honours, castles, manors, lands, tenements, rents, services, hereditaments, annuities, fees, corrodies or other yearly profits of the yearly value of twenty shillings, as well within ancient demesne and other places privileged as elsewhere, and so upward, shall pay to and for the said first subsidy, in one entire payment, four shillings of and for every pound . . . [and the same for each of the other two subsidies.]

[§ VI decreed that the three subsidies be finally payed at the same time as the fifteenths and tenths, that is, by 10 July, 10 December and 10 May respectively, and into the hands of the same Treasurers before named.]

* * *

[§ VIII stipulated that the commissioners for the subsidy be appointed by the Lord Chancellor or Lord Keeper, acting with at least one other senior member of the Council.]

XVI. And that all persons of the estate of baron or baroness, and every estate above, shall be charged with their freehold and value as is aforesaid by the Chancellor or Lord Keeper of the Great Seal of England, the High Treasurer for the time being, or one of them, together with other such persons as by the king's Majesty's authority or commandment shall be named or appointed . . .

* * *

XXXVII. And to the end that all and every the sums of money by this present act granted as aforesaid, and also to be collected and expended as aforesaid, may be truly expended for and towards the uses aforesaid and not otherwise, according to your Majesty's own gracious desire, be it further enacted, that the monies to be received by the said Treasurers by virtue of this act shall be issued out and expended for or towards the uses aforesaid to such person and persons, and in such manner and form as by the warrant of George Lord Carew, Fulke Lord Brooke, Oliver Lord Viscount Grandison of Limerick within the realm of Ireland, Arthur Lord Chichester, Sir Edward Cecil, knight, Sir Edward Conway, knight, one of the principal Secretaries to his Majesty, Sir Horace Vere, knight, Sir Robert Mansell, knight, Sir John Ogle, knight, and Sir Thomas Button, knight, which ten persons before mentioned his Majesty hath already nominated and hath made choice of to be his Council for the War, or any five or more of them, whereof two to be of his Majesty's most honourable Privy Council, under their hands and seals shall be directed and not otherwise. And such warrant or warrants of the said Councillors of War or of any five of them, whereof two to be of the Privy Council as aforesaid, together with the acquittances of those persons who shall receive those monies according to those warrants or the enrollment thereof to be for that purpose likewise kept by his Majesty's remembrancer of the said Court of Exchequer, shall be unto the said Treasurers and every one of them, their heirs, executors and administrators, a full and sufficient discharge . . .

XXXIX. And be it further enacted, that as well the said Treasurers as the said persons appointed for the Council of War as aforesaid, and all other persons who shall be trusted with the receiving, issuing, bestowing and employing of these monies or any part thereof, their heirs, executors and administrators, shall be answerable and accountable for their doings or proceedings herein to the Commons in parliament when they shall be hereunto required by warrant under the hand of the Speaker of the House of Commons for the time being, and there they and every one of them, according to their several places and employments, shall give a true and real declaration and account of their several and respective doings and proceedings therein, and that the said Commons in parliament shall have power by this Act to hear and determine the said account and all things thereunto appertaining.

* * *

SR, IV, 1247–62

23. King's speech, 17 March 1628

My Lords and Gentlemen,

These times are for action; wherefore, for example's sake, I mean not to spend much time in words, expecting accordingly, that your (as I hope) good resolutions will be speedy, not spending time unnecessarily, or (that I may better say) dangerously, for tedious consultations at this conjuncture of time is [*sic*] as hurtful as ill resolutions.

I am sure you now expect from me both to know the cause of your meeting, and what to resolve on; yet I think there is none here but knows what common danger is the cause of this parliament, and that supply at this time is the chief end of it; so that I need but to point to you what to do. I will use but few persuasions, for if to maintain your own advices and (as now the case stands by the following thereof) the true religion, the laws, liberties of this state, and the just defence of our true friends and allies, be not sufficient, no eloquence of men or angels will prevail.

Only let me remember you, that my duty most of all, and every one of yours according to his degree, is to seek the maintenance of this Church and Commonwealth; and certainly there was never a time in which this duty was more necessarily required than now.

I, therefore, judging a parliament to be the ancient, speediest and best way, in this time of common danger, to give such supply as to secure ourselves and to save our friends from imminent ruin, have called you together. Every man now must do according to his conscience, wherefore if you (which God forbid) should not do your duties in contributing what this state at this time needs I must in discharge of my conscience use those other means which God hath put into my hands to save that that the follies of particular men may otherwise hazard to lose.

Take not this as a threatening (for I scorn to threaten any but my equals), but an admonition from him that, both out of nature and duty, hath most care of your preservations and prosperities, and hopes (though I thus speak) that your demeanours at this time will be such as shall not only approve your former counsels but lay on me such obligations as shall tie me by way of thankfulness to meet often with you, for be assured that nothing can be more pleasing unto me than to keep a good correspondency with you.

I will only add one thing more, and then leave the Keeper to make a short paraphrase upon the text I have delivered you; which is, to remember a thing to the end we may forget it. You may imagine I came here with a doubt of good success of what I desire, remembering the distractions at the last meeting; but I shall assure you, that I shall very easily and gladly forget and forgive what's past, so that you will at this time leave the former ways of distractions and follow the counsel lately given you, 'To maintain the Unity of the Spirit in the Bond of Peace'.[77]

24. The Petition of Right, 1628

The petition exhibited to his Majesty by the Lords Spiritual and Temporal and Commons in this present parliament assembled concerning divers rights and liberties of the subject.

To the King's Most Excellent Majesty

Humbly show unto our Sovereign Lord the King the Lords Spiritual and Temporal and Commons in parliament assembled, that whereas it is declared and enacted by a statute made in the time of the reign of King Edward the First commonly called Statutum de Tallagio non Concedendo, that no tallage or aid should be laid or levied by the king or his heirs in this realm without the good will and assent of the arch-bishops, bishops, earls, barons, knights, burgesses and other the freemen of the commonalty of this realm; and by authority of parliament holden in the five and twentieth year of the reign of King Edward the Third it is declared and enacted, that from henceforth no person should be compelled to make any loans to the king against his will because such loans were against reason and the franchise of the land, and by other laws of this realm it is provided that none should be charged by any charge or imposition called a benevolence nor by such like charge, by which the statutes before mentioned and other the good laws and statutes of this realm your subjects have inherited this freedom, that they should not be compelled to contribute to any tax, tallage, aid or other like charge not set by common consent in parliament.

[77] Presumably the text of the pre-session sermon.

II. Yet, nevertheless of late divers commissions directed to sundry commissioners in several counties with instructions have issued, by means whereof your people have been in divers places assembled and required to lend certain sums of money unto your Majesty, and many of them upon their refusal so to do have had an oath administered unto them not warrantable by the laws or statutes of this realm, and have been constrained to become bound to make appearance and give attendance before your Privy Council and in other places; and others of them have been therefore imprisoned, confined, and sundry other ways molested and disquieted, and divers other charges have been laid and levied upon your people in several counties by lord lieutenants, deputy lieutenants, commissioners for musters, justices of peace and others by command or direction from your Majesty or your Privy Council against the laws and free customs of the realm.

III. And where also by the statute called the Great Charter of the Liberties of England it is declared and enacted, that no freeman may be taken or imprisoned or be disseised of his freehold or liberties or his free customs or be outlawed or exiled or in any manner destroyed, but by the lawful judgment of his peers or by the law of the land.

IV. And in the eight and twentieth year of the reign of King Edward the Third it was declared and enacted by authority of parliament, that no man, of what estate or condition that he be, should be put out of his land or tenement, nor taken, nor imprisoned, nor disherited, nor put to death without being brought to answer by due process of law.

V. Nevertheless against the tenor of the said statutes and other the good laws and statutes of your realm to that end provided, divers of your subjects have of late been imprisoned without any cause shown; and when for their deliverance they were brought before your justices by your Majesty's writ of habeas corpus there to undergo and receive as the Court should order, and their Keepers commanded to certify the causes of their detainer, no cause was certified, but that they were detained by your Majesty's special command signified by the Lords of your Privy Council, and yet were returned back to several prisons without being charged with any thing to which they might make answer according to the law.

VI. And whereas of late great companies of soldiers and mariners have been dispersed into divers counties of the realm, and the inhabitants against their will have been compelled to receive them into their houses, and there to suffer them to sojourn against the laws and customs of this realm and to the great grievance and vexation of the people.

VII. And whereas also by authority of parliament in the five and twentieth year of the reign of King Edward the Third it is declared and enacted that no man should be forejudged of life and limb against the form of the Great

Charter and the law of the land; and by the said Great Charter, and other the laws and statutes of this your realm, no man ought to be adjudged to death but by the laws established in this your realm, either by the customs of the same realm or by act of parliament, and whereas no offender of what kind soever is exempted from the proceedings to be used and punishments to be inflicted by the laws and statutes of this your realm; nevertheless of late time divers commissions under your Majesty's great seal have issued forth, by which certain persons have been assigned and appointed commissioners with power and authority to proceed within the land according to the justice of martial law against such soldiers or mariners or other dissolute persons joining with them as should commit any murder, robbery, felony, mutiny or other outrage or misdemeanour whatsoever, and by such summary course and order as is agreeable to martial law and as is used in armies in time of war to proceed to the trial and condemnation of such offenders, and them to cause to be executed and put to death according to the law martial.

By pretext whereof some of your Majesty's subjects have been by some of the said commissioners put to death, when and where, if by the laws and statutes of the land they had deserved death, by the same laws and statutes also they might and by no other ought to have been judged and executed.

And also sundry grievous offenders by colour thereof claiming an exemption have escaped the punishments due to them by the laws and statutes of this your realm, by reason that divers of your officers and ministers of justice have unjustly refused or forborne to proceed against such offenders according to the same laws and statutes upon pretence that the said offenders were punishable only by martial law and by authority of such commissions as aforesaid. Which commissions and all others of like nature are wholly and directly contrary to the said laws and statutes of this your realm.

VIII. They do therefore humbly pray your most excellent Majesty that no man hereafter be compelled to make or yield any gift, loan, benevolence, tax or such like charge without common consent by act of parliament, and that none be called to make answer or take such oath or to give attendance or be confined or otherwise molested or disquieted concerning the same or for refusal thereof. And that no freeman in any such manner as is before mentioned be imprisoned or detained. And that your Majesty would be pleased to remove the said soldiers and mariners, and that your people may not be so burdened in time to come. And that the aforesaid commissions for proceeding by martial law may be revoked and annulled. And that hereafter no commissions of like nature may issue forth to any person or persons whatsoever to be executed as aforesaid, lest by colour of them any of your Majesty's subjects be destroyed or put to death contrary to the laws and franchises of the land.

All which they most humbly pray of your most excellent Majesty as their rights and liberties according to the laws and statutes of this realm, and that your Majesty would also vouchsafe to declare that the awards, doings, and proceedings to the prejudice of your people in any of the premises shall not be drawn hereafter into consquence or example. And that your Majesty would be also graciously pleased for the further comfort and safety of your people to declare your royal will and pleasure that in the thing aforesaid all your officers and ministers shall serve you according to the laws and statutes of this realm as they tender the honour of your Majesty and the prosperity of this kingdom.

SR, v, 23–4

25. Protestation of the Commons, 2 March 1629

1. Whosoever shall bring in innovation of religion, or by favour or countenance seek to extend or introduce popery or Arminianism, or other opinion disagreeing from the true and orthodox Church, shall be reputed a capital enemy to this kingdom and Commonwealth.

2. Whosoever shall counsel or advise the taking and levying of the subsidies of tonnage and poundage, not being granted by parliament, or shall be an actor or instrument therein, shall be likewise reputed an innovator in the government, and a capital enemy to the kingom and Commonwealth.

3. If any merchant or person whatsoever shall voluntarily yield, or pay the said subsidies of tonnage and poundage, not being granted by parliament, he shall likewise be reputed a betrayer of the liberties of England, and an enemy to the same.

Rushworth, I, 670

26. His Majesty's Declaration to all his Loving Subjects, of the Causes which moved him to Dissolve the last Parliament, 10 March 1629

Howsoever princes are not bound to give account of their actions, but to God alone; yet for the satisfaction of the minds and affections of our loving subjects, we have thought good to set down thus much by way of declaration, that we may appear to the world in the truth and sincerity of our actions, and not in those colours in which we know some turbulent and ill-affected spirits (to mask and disguise their wicked intentions, dangerous to the state) would represent them to the public view . . .

[He then embarked on a detailed examination of the events of this late parliament, stressing his confidence in the integrity and good will of a majority of the Commons, and lamenting the fact that they have been led astray by a minority of ill-intentioned troublemakers. He particularly deplored the encroachments by the House on the process of law and the operation of government.]

We are not ignorant how much that House hath of late years endeavoured to extend their privileges, by setting up general committees for Religion, for Courts of Justice, for Trade, and the like; a course never heard of until of late: so as, where in former times the knights and burgesses were wont to communicate to the House such business as they brought from their countries, now there are so many chairs erected to make inquiry upon all sorts of men, where complaints of all sorts are entertained, to the insufferable disturbance and scandal of justice and government, which, having been tolerated a while by our father and ourself, hath daily grown to more and more height; insomuch that young lawyers sitting there take upon them to decry the opinions of the judges, and some have not doubted to maintain that the resolutions of the House must bind the judges, a thing never heard of in ages past. But in this last assembly of parliament they have taken on them much more than ever before.

[They have sent messengers to examine the attorney-general, they have questioned and controverted the proceedings and decisions of the Court of Exchequer, the Court of King's Bench and Star Chamber. They have even cross-examined members of the Privy Council as to decisions taken there. They have examined the Sheriff of London in a case in which they had no jurisdiction, and committed him to the Tower. And Charles had no doubt of their ulterior motive:]

In these innovations (which we will never permit again) they pretended indeed our service, but their drift was to break by this means through all respects and ligaments of government, and to erect an universal over-swaying power to themselves, which belongs only to us and not to them.

[After descanting on the Commons' treatment of the customs officials, and reviewing at length the conduct of the House on 2 March, he concluded thus:]

Whilst the Duke of Buckingham lived he was entitled to all the distempers and ill events of former parliaments, and therefore much endeavour was used to demolish him, as the only wall of separation between us and our people. But now he is dead, no alteration was found amongst those envenomed spirits which troubled then the blessed harmony between us and our subjects, and continue still to trouble it. For now under pretence of public care of the Commonwealth they suggest new and causeless fears, which in their own hearts they know to be false; and devise new engines of mischief, so to cast a blindness upon the good affections of our people, that they may not see the truth and largeness of my heart towards them. So that now it is manifest, the Duke was not alone the mark these men shot at, but was only as a near minister of ours taken up, on the by, and in their passage to their more secret designs; which were only to cast our affairs into a desperate condition, to abate the powers of our Crown, and to bring our government into obloquy, that in the end all things may be overwhelmed with anarchy and confusion.

We do not impute these disasters to the whole House of Commons, knowing that there were amongst them many religious, grave and well-minded men; but the sincerer and better part of the House was overborne by the practices and clamours of the other, who, careless of their duties, and taking advantage of the times and our necessities, have enforced us to break off this meeting; which, had it been answered with like duty on their parts as it was invited and begun with love on ours, might have proved happy and glorious both to us and this whole nation.

We have thus declared the manifold causes we had to dissolve this parliament, whereby all the world may see how much they have forgotten their former engagements at the entry into the war, themselves being persuaders to it; promising to make us feared by our enemies and esteemed by our friends, and how they turned the necessities grown by that war to enforce us to yield to conditions incompatible with monarchy.

And now that our people may discern that these provocations of evil men (whose punishments we reserve to a due time) have not changed our good intentions to our subjects, we do here profess to maintain the true religion and doctrine established in the Church of England, without admitting or conniving at any backsliding either to popery or Schism. We do also declare that we will maintain the ancient and just rights and liberties of our subjects, with so much constancy and justice that they shall have cause to acknowledge that under our government and gracious protection they live in a more happy and free estate than any subjects in the Christian world. Yet let no man hereby take the boldness to abuse that liberty, turning it into licenciousness; nor misinterpret the Petition [of Right] by perverting it to a lawless liberty, wantonly or forwardly, under that or any other colour, to resist lawful and necessary authority. For as we will maintain our subjects in their just liberties, so we do and will expect that they yield as much submission and duty to our royal prerogatives, and as ready obedience to our authority and commandments, as hath been promised to the greatest of our predecessors.

★   ★   ★

And now having laid down the truth and clearness of our proceedings, all wise and discreet men may easily judge of those rumours and jealous fears that are maliciously and wickedly bruited abroad, and may discern, by examination of their own hearts, whether (in respect of the free passage of the Gospel, indifferent and equal administration of Justice, freedom from oppression, and the great peace and quietness which every man enjoyeth under his own vine and fig-tree) the happiness of this nation can be paralleled by any of our neighbour countries; and if not, then to acknowledge their own blessedness, and for the same be thankful to God, the author of all goodness.

Rushworth, I, App., pp. I–I2

CHAPTER 3

THE JUDICIARY

I. THE CROWN AND COMMON LAW

The Common Law, civil and criminal, was administered in the high courts of justice, sitting in Westminster Hall; King's Bench, Common Pleas and Exchequer; whose judges departed on circuit each summer and autumn to hold the assizes in the provinces, under special commissions of oyer and terminer and gaol delivery.[1]

To an external observer, distant in time, the system seems to have worked well enough, and because it survived the seventeenth century, and indeed the eighteenth, virtually unscathed, it is natural to assume that its worth was generally acknowledged, and that it was one of the few uncontentious aspects of the Stuart constitution. Natural, but not so. Its decisions dependent on case law, its structure a rank medieval survival, the Common Law was of such treacherous complexity, so restricted by arcane and arbitrary rules of procedure, so expensive to operate, that it often seemed designed to entrap those who resorted to it.[2] It was confined to England and Wales, and it could only entertain cases involving British subjects overseas by the most blatant 'fictions', such as the pretence that the island of Sumatra was in the London borough of Islington. Some of the greatest lawyers of this generation – Coke and Fleming as well as Bacon and Ellesmere – recognised the need for reform, but such remedies as they proposed were often contradictory, and our assessment of their value is often impeded by our ignorance of contemporary legal procedures.[3]

The judges were only notionally salaried, and depended for their (often princely) income on fees. In civil cases this led them grimly to defend their own sphere of jurisdiction and if possible extend it at the expense of other courts. In criminal cases it encouraged an indecent haste. As now, they were appointed from the ranks of the leading barristers, and they had behind them a very narrow and restricted training, largely by rote, in the Inns of Court. Most of them were self-made men, many of them self-conscious *arrivistes*. Like the clergy, they tended to be drawn from the lower gentry, or cadet branches thereof, from within their own class, being sons of lawyers, or even from the lower orders.[4] It was a background and a training which made for

---

[1] The system is outlined in some detail by Elton, *Tudor Constitution*, ch. 5, and by Holdsworth, I, ch. 3. For the assizes see Cockburn.

[2] Especially in the land law, for which see A. W. B. Simpson, *An Introduction to the History of Land Law* (Oxford 1961).

[3] As White remarks, 'Because [Coke's] complaints about legal abuses often concerned complex, obscure and as yet unstudied aspects of legal administration, it is often hard to know precisely what they were about, let alone assess their accuracy', *Coke*, p. 48.

[4] Brian P. Levack, *The Civil Lawyers in England 1603–1641* (Oxford 1973), p. 10, offers some interesting figures. Out of 372 men who passed through the Middle Temple 1599–1642 only 16 had fathers who were commoners or 'unknown', but 115 were sons of 'esquires', and 168 the sons of 'gentlemen', two very elastic and in this context dubious social classifications. Only 30 were the sons of knights or baronets, none the sons of peers.

acute formalism and narrow-mindedness, and it was perhaps fortunate that judges were appointed by the king direct and could be dismissed at will. Whether their patents read *quamdiu se bene gesserit* or *durante bene placito*, a distinction to which much importance was later attached, seems to have been immaterial, at least up to 1640.[5]

Juries were as awkward to deal with as judges, being subject in the provinces to bribery and intimidation, and obstinately attached to their medieval role as witnesses to fact, and even interested parties. Now the supposed glory of the judicial system, they were then one of its main weaknesses. Forthright and authoritative judges could sometimes cow a jury, a technique later refined by Scroggs and Jeffreys, but in the last resort a recalcitrant jury, or the sheriff who had impanelled it, could only be dealt with in Star Chamber.[6]

Star Chamber was also popular with private litigants seeking to undermine their adversaries in civil suits by bringing ancillary criminal charges against them (p. 104 below). Or they could resort to the Lord Chancellor's Court of Chancery, which was supposed to decide civil cases according to principles of common sense and natural justice. In fact by the late sixteenth century the law of Equity was almost as arcane and ossified as Common Law, but under the long reign of the reforming Thomas Egerton, Lord Ellesmere (Lord Keeper and Master of the Rolls 1596–1603, Lord Chancellor 1603–17) a determined effort was made to simplify its rules and speed up its procedure. The judges saw another threat in the ecclesiastical courts, whose jurisdiction over marriage contracts and wills gave them an entrée to the lucrative world of real property litigation. Under Elizabeth and James I the venerable metropolitan Courts of Arches were invigorated by a succession of aggressive archbishops, who also controlled High Commission. The conciliar courts of the Council of the North and the Council of the Marches and Wales also offered growing competition.

As a result, from 1596 onwards, and intensifying with the appointment of Coke as Chief Justice of Common Pleas in 1606, the high court judges began an intermittent guerilla campaign against their rivals, using the writ of prohibition, which stayed process in the other court pending a 'consultation', which could take months or even years to set up. Chancery was not at this stage seriously threatened, but the ecclesiastical and conciliar courts were. A few examples serve to demonstrate the technique (27).

Sir Edward Coke's prominent share in these proceedings has served to dramatise the issue. He was one of the foremost jurists of his generation, and his *Reports*, published in 11 parts 1600–15, were highly controversial but enormously influential. His temper and character were such as to intimidate most of his contemporaries – 'We shall never see his like again', said his harassed widow, 'praises be to god.'[7] To King James he was 'Captain Coke'.

The king's personal intervention dramatised the issue still further. James's restless intellectuality extended to a keen interest in the quality and the administration of the

---

[5] The holder of the former patent could sue out a writ of *scire facias* requiring the king to show cause. Only one man is known to have exercised this right, Chief Baron Fleming in 1629. Charles I riposted by suspending him for life (Gardiner, *History*, VII, 110–15; Aylmer, *King's Servants*. pp. 111–12).

[6] Cockburn, *Assizes*, pp. 123–4. See pp. 392–3 below.

[7] S. E. Thorne, *Sir Edward Coke 1552–1952* (Selden Society 1952), p. 4.

law, which made him almost unique amongst English sovereigns, certainly in the modern era; and he was naturally suspected of favouring the civil law, under which he had been raised in Scotland. He certainly championed the cause of the English civil courts, he resented the attempt of the judges to challenge what he regarded as his own authority expressed through the conciliar courts, and he was particularly responsive to the protests of Archbishop Bancroft, who argued that Coke's campaign was not only undermining ecclesiastical jurisdiction but the Church itself. He was also irritated by the Common Law judges' attempt to oust Chancery by formulating a bastard equity of their own.[8] He also took very literally his role as head of the legal system (an admitted fact which had been largely ignored by his immediate predecessors), and once he had found his feet in England he did not hesitate to interfere even with the details of legal administration. In 1613, for instance, he personally forbad assize judges to ride the circuit of their residence or birth,[9] and in 1616 he even supervised a revision of the Commission of the Peace in the provinces (p. 443 below).

The result was a series of acrimonious confrontations between the king, often flanked by his Council, and his combative chief justice (**28**). James showed remarkable tolerance and common sense under the most intense provocation, but in a characteristically bluff and homely speech to parliament in 1610 he gave his unvarnished opinion of the Common Law and its practitioners, and put forward a number of radical demands for reform, notably for the codification of the law and the substitution of English for Law French in all proceedings (**29**).

In 1611 Ellesmere secured a compromise on the most pressing question, the conflicting jurisdictions of High Commission and Common Pleas (p. 159 below), and in 1613 Coke was transferred against his will to what was hoped would be the less contentious arena of King's Bench. Unfortunately this had the opposite effect to that intended; Coke simply intensified his attack on Chancery, antagonising Ellesmere, and siezed every opportunity to block James's interference with the legal process. In 1615, in Peacham's Case, he insisted in the face of established custom and precedent that the king had no right to consult the judges individually before they tried a case, and in 1616 he refused to postpone the hearing of a case of *commendam* – the Crown's right to collate a bishop to an additional benefice – until the king had taken advice on the matter (*TCD*, pp. 188–98). He was at once suspended, and in June 1616 James harangued the judges in Star Chamber, repeating his views on the relationship of the king to the law and ordering them to keep within their own jurisdictions, which he helpfully outlined for them (**30**). Ellesmere added his own professional gloss in a scathing review of Coke's *Reports* (**31**). It was Ellesmere, Archbishop Abbott and Francis Bacon (now attorney-general) who finally secured his dismissal in November.[10]

Coke's reputation as a great jurist was confirmed by the publication in 1624 of the first part of his *Institutes of the Laws of England*, generally known as 'Coke on Littleton',

[8] G. W. Thomas, 'James I, Equity and Lord Keeper Williams', *EHR*, XCI (1976), 506–28. For a more sympathetic view of Coke see W. J. Jones, 'The Crown and the Courts', in Smith, *James VI and I*, pp. 183–91.

[9] Cockburn, *Assizes*, p. 227.

[10] Knafla, *Law and Politics* ch. 7, esp. pp. 176–7. G. W. Thomas, *art. cit.*, pp. 508–9, 520, makes it clear that his dismissal was provoked by his attitude to Chancery, not his conduct in Peacham's Case.

and his posthumous reputation has been inflated by the assumption that his role as an opposition spokesman in the parliaments of the 1620s was merely an extension or a continuation of the role he had played as Lord Chief Justice. He has an assured place in the mythology of early American history as a spokesman for judicial review, and his insistence on the immemorial antiquity of parliaments in his posthumous *Second* and *Third Institutes*, published in 1642 and 1644, even gave succour to the Levellers. As a result S. R. Gardiner regarded him as a champion of 'liberty' against the rampant 'absolutism' of the Stuart kings, a theme developed by later constitutional historians like J. R. Tanner. Thus the insistence of the judges in 1605 that only parliament could arbitrate between them and the High Commission delighted Gardiner, who remarked: 'It is this appeal to parliament which raises the dispute from a mere quarrel about jurisdiction to the dignity of a constitutional event.'[11] But they were not 'appealing to parliament', they were merely remarking, quite casually, that the body which framed new statutes was the ultimate authority in Common Law. Certainly there is no trace of an alliance between the judges and the parliamentary opposition, and it was generally recognised that their motivation was financial rather than constitutional; James I remarked that 'every court [was] striving to bring most moulture to their own mill'.[12]

In fact the dismissal of an obstructive and impertinent judge who had flouted the king's commands did not alarm contemporaries, and it is posterity that has made it an event of constitutional importance. Coke joined the Privy Council in 1617 and for four years pursued a career at Court, using all the flattery and unction at his command to win over the king's favourite, Buckingham. Had these schemes come to fruition no doubt he would have been less scrupulous in his attitude to government in the 1620s.

As for James I, his suspicion of common lawyers was as deep as ever. Despite Bacon's protests, he insisted on inserting in his proclamation for the summons of a new Parliament in 1621 a warning to the electors not to choose 'curious and wrangling lawyers, who may seek reputation by stirring needless questions',[13] and on Bacon's fall he insisted on appointing as Lord Chancellor a non-lawyer, Bishop Williams of Lincoln, who knew his mind and would do his bidding.[14] But in his old age he lacked the drive to initiate reform, and none of his successors shared his interest in the law for its own sake. However, they continued to consult the judges beforehand, and even secure preliminary rulings from them which governed their subsequent judgments in court. Charles I in 1634, James II in 1685 and 1686, are obvious examples. For their part the judges continued to issue prohibitions, but on a much reduced scale, and usually only where the circumstances of the case genuinely required it. The traditional view of the judicial function, as 'lions under the throne', was reinforced by Lord Chief Justice Hobart in the ironically titled *Sir Edward Coke's Case* in 1623 (**32**).

27. Prohibitions

(a) *Candict and Plomer's Case*. Pasch. 8 Jacobi [1610], Common Pleas

The parishioners had used time out of memory of man to choose the parish

---

[11] *History*, II, 36.   [12] P. 83 below.   [13] *SRP*, I, 494.   [14] G. W. Thomas, *art. cit.*

clerk of the church of St Augustine in Canterbury, and the old clerk being dead they chose a new clerk and the parson by force of a new canon[15] chose another man for the clerk. Upon which the clerk chosen by the parishioners was sued in the Spiritual Court, and he had a prohibition; and afterwards he was sued again in the Spiritual Court, for setting of the bread upon the Communion Table, and for singing in another tune than the parishioners and the other clerk[16] did, and was deprived by sentence there.

Haughton, Serjeant, moved for a prohibition, and said that although the last suit in the Spiritual Court was not directly for the using of the office of clerk, yet by the matters contained in the libel it is drawn in question whether he were lawful clerk or not, and therefore prayed a prohibition.

Coke. You shall have a prohibition, for the canon is against the Common Law, for particular customs are part of the Common Law; and said, that the Canon Law would not endure gun-shot. And he said that by the suit in the Spiritual Court they would examine whether he were a lawful clerk or not, for if he be a lawful clerk, then he hath good authority to set the bread upon the Communion Table.

Haughton. But what shall we do, for we are deprived by sentence given there?

Coke. There is no question but that the prohibition lieth, notwithstanding the sentence there, and for the deprivation it is merely void. For the clerkship is a lay office, and may be executed by a layman, and therefore the Ordinary hath no power to deprive him . . . And I wish that an Information be drawn against them for holding plea of a thing which is a mere lay thing . . .

Warmersley, Justice. The office is lay, and the deprivation by the Ordinary is void; for he cannot deprive him because he hath nothing to do in the election.

And a prohibition was granted.

At another day the case was moved again, and the court was of the same opinion, that the clerk could not be deprived because the clerkship was a lay office . . . But *Coke* said, the same day in another case which was moved in court, and gave it for a rule, that after sentence given in the spiritual court he would not grant a prohibition if there were not matter apparent within the proceedings. For I will not allow [he said] that the party shall, to have a prohibition, show anything not grounded on the sentence, because he hath admitted of the jurisdiction; and there is no reason for him to try if the spiritual court will help him, and afterwards at the Common Law to sue forth a prohibition. All which was agreed by the whole court.[17]

Godbolt, pp. 163-4

[15] By canon XCI of 1604 (Cardwell, *Synodalia*, I, 298), the parson was to appoint the clerk.

[16] One of the clerk's duties, of course, was to set the key and lead the singing.

[17] The inconsistency is only apparent. Coke was not prepared to challenge the verdict of an ecclesiastical court on the petition of the loser unless it could be shown that that court had never possessed jurisdiction.

(b) *The Archbishop of York and Sedgwick's Case.* Trin. 10 Jacobi [1612]

The Archbishop of York and Doctor Ingram brought and exhibited a bill in the Exchequer at York upon an obligation of seven hundred pounds, and declared in their bill [it was] in the nature of an action for debt brought at the Common Law. Which matter being showed unto the Court of Common Pleas by Sedgwick, the defendant there, a prohibition was awarded to the archbishop and to the said court at York.

And *Coke*, Chief Justice, gave the reasons wherefore the court granted the prohibition. He said: (1) because the matter was merely determinable at the Common Law, and therefore ought to be proceeded in according to the course of the Common Law. (2) Although the king had granted to the Lord President and the Council of York to hold pleas of all personal actions, yet (he said) they cannot alter the form of the proceedings. For as 6 Hen. VII, c.5 is, the king by his grant cannot make that inquirable in a Leet which was not inquirable there by the law, nor a Leet to be of other nature than it was at the Common Law. And in 11 Hen. IV it is holden that the Pope nor any other person can change the Common Law, without a parliament. And Coke vouched a record in 8 Hen. IV, that the king granted to both the universities that they should hold pleas of all causes arising within the universities according to the course of the Civil Law; and all the judges of England were then of opinion that the grant was not good, because the king could not by his grant alter the law of the land. With which case agrees 37 Hen. VI, 26, 2 Ed. IV, 16 and 7 Hen. VII. But at this day, by a special act of parliament, made 13 Eliz., not printed, the universities have now power to proceed and judge according to the Civil Law. (3) He said that the oath of judges is, viz. 'You shall do and procure the profit of the king and his Crown, in all things wherein you may reasonably effect and do the same.' And he said that upon every judgment upon debt of forty pounds the king was to have ten shillings paid to the Hanaper, and if the debt were more, then more. But he said by his manner of proceeding by English Bill[18] the king should lose his fine. (4) He said that it was against the statute of Magna Carta, viz., *Nec super eum ibimus, nec super eum mittemus, nisi per legale judicium parium suorum, vel per legem terrae.* And the law of the land is, that matters of fact shall be tried by verdict of twelve men; but by their proceedings by English bill, the party should be examined upon his oath, and it is a rule in law that *nemo tenetur seipsum prodere.* And also he said, that upon their judgment there no writ of error lieth, so as the subject should by such means be deprived of his birthright. (5) It was said by all the justices, with which the justices of the King's Bench did agree, that such proceedings were illegal, and the Lord Chancellor of England would have cast such a bill out of the Court of Chancery. And they

---

[18] The writ or indictment in the Common Law courts was in Latin.

advised the Court of York so to do, and a Prohibition was awarded
accordingly.   *Ibid.*, pp. 201–2

28. Prohibitions del Roy, Michaelmas 5 Jac. I. (1607)

Note, upon Sunday the 10th of November in this same term the king, upon
complaint made to him by Bancroft, Archbishop of Canterbury, concerning
prohibitions, the king was informed that when the question was made of what
matters the ecclesiastical judges have cognisance, either upon the exposition of
the statute concerning tithes, or any other thing ecclesiastical, or upon the
statute 1 Eliz. concerning the High Commission, or in any other case in which
there is not express authority in law, the king himself may decide it in his royal
person, and that the judges are but the delegates of the king, and that the king
may take what causes he shall please to determine from the determination of
the judges, and may determine them himself. And the archbishop said that this
was clear in divinity, that such authority belongs to the king by the word of
God in the Scripture.

   To which it was answered by me, in the presence and with the clear consent
of all the judges of England and barons of the exchequer, that the king in his
own person cannot adjudge any case, either criminal (as treason, felony, &c.)
or betwixt party and party, concerning his inheritance, chattels or goods, &c.,
but this ought to be determined and adjudged in some court of justice
according to the law and custom of England. And always judgments are given,
ideo consideratum est per curiam, so that the court gives the judgment; and the
king hath his court viz., in the Upper House of Parliament, in which he with
his Lords is the supreme judge over all other judges; for if error be in the
Common Pleas, that may be reversed in the King's Bench; and if the Court of
King's Bench err, that may be reversed in the Upper House of Parliament, by
the king with the assent of the Lords spiritual and temporal, without the
Commons, and in this respect the king is called the Chief Justice . . . And it
appears in our books that the king may sit in the Star Chamber, but this was to
consult with the justices upon certain questions proposed to them, and not *in
judicio*; so in the King's Bench he may sit, but the court gives the judgment,
and it is commonly said in our books that the king is always present in court in
the judgment of law, and upon this he cannot be nonsuit[ed]; but the
judgments are always given *per curiam* and the judges are sworn to execute
justice according to law and the custom of England . . . And the judges
informed the king that no king after the Conquest assumed to himself to give
any judgment in any cause whatsoever which concerned the administration of
justice within this realm, but these were solely determined in the courts of
justice . . ., and it was greatly marvelled that the archbishop durst inform the

king that such absolute power and authority, as is aforesaid, belonged to the king by the word of God . . .

Then the king said, that he thought the law was founded upon reason, and that he and others had reason, as well as the judges. To which it was answered by me, that true it was that God had endowed his Majesty with excellent science and great endowments of nature, but his Majesty was not learned in the laws of his realm of England, and causes which concern the life, or inheritance, or goods, or fortunes of his subjects are not to be decided by natural reason but by the artificial reason and judgment of law, which law is an act which requires long study and experience before that a man can attain to the cognisance of it, and that the law was the golden mete-wand and measure to try the causes of the subjects, and which protected his Majesty in safety and peace. With which the king was greatly offended, and said, that then he should be under the law, which [it] was treason to affirm, as he said. To which I said, that Bracton saith, *quod rex non debet esse sub homine, sed sub Deo et lege.*

Coke, Reports, VI, 280–2 (pt XII, 63–5)

29. James I: speech to Parliament, 21 March 1610

. . . Kings' actions (even in the secretest places) are as the action of those that are set upon the stage, or on the tops of houses, and I hope never to speak that in private which I shall not avow in public . . . For it is true that within these few days I spake freely my mind touching the Common Law in my Privy Chamber, at the time of my dinner, which is come to all your ears; and the same was likewise related unto you by my Treasurer;[19] and now I will again repeat and confirm the same myself unto you.

First, as a king I have least cause of any man to dislike the Common Law, for no law can be more favourable and advantageous for a king, and extendeth further his prerogative, than it doth, and for a king of England to despise the Common Law, is to neglect his own crown. It is true, that I do greatly esteem the Civil Law, the profession thereof serving more for general learning, and being most necessary for matters of treaty with foreign nations; and I think that if it should be taken away, it would make an entry to barbarism in this kingdom, and would blemish the honour of England, for it is in a manner *Lex Gentium*, and maintaineth intercourse with foreign nations; but I only allow it to have course here according to those limits of jurisdiction which the Common Law itself doth allow it . . . My meaning therefore, is not to prefer the Civil Law before the Common Law, but only that it should not be extinguished, and yet so bounded (I mean to such courts and causes) as have been in ancient use . . . Nay, I am so far from disallowing the Common Law,

---

[19] Perhaps a reference to Salisbury's message from him on 8 March; Foster, *Proceedings*, I, 30–1, II, 47–52.

as I protest, that if it were in my hand to choose a new law for this kingdom, I would not only prefer it before any national law, but even before the very judicial Law of Moses . . .

[Having made this rash comparison, James had some difficulty extricating himself, but he elaborately explained that the Mosaic Law was only appropriate to a certain time and place, just as the Common Law was, and though the Mosaic Law, in its proper context, was immune from criticism, as part of the law of God, Common Law was not.]

No book nor law is perfect nor free from corruption, except only the book and law of God. And therefore I could wish some three things specially to be purged and cleared in the Common Law; but always by the advice of parliament, for the king with his parliament here are absolute (as I understand) in making or forming of any sort of laws.[20]

First, I could wish that it were written in our vulgar language, for now it is in an old, mixed and corrupt language, only understood by lawyers, whereas every subject ought to understand the law under which he lives. For since it is our plea against the Papists, that the language in God's service ought not to be in an unknown tongue, according to the rule in the Law of Moses, that the law should be written in the fringes of the priest's garment, and should be publicly read in the ears of all the people, so methinks ought our law to be made as plain as can be to the people, that the excuse of ignorance may be taken from them, for conforming themselves thereto.

Next, our Common Law hath not a settled text in all cases, being chiefly grounded upon old customs, or else upon the Reports and Cases of judges, which you call *responsa prudentum*, the like whereof is in all other laws, for they are much ruled by precedents . . . But though it be true, that no text of law can be so certain, wherein the circumstances will not make a variation in the case, . . . otherwise there needed no judges, but the bare letter of the law, yet I could wish that some more certainty were set down in this case by parliament. For since the very Reports themselves are not always so binding but that divers times judges do disclaim them, and recede from the judgment of their predecessors, it were good that upon a mature deliberation the exposition of the law were set down by act of parliament, and such Reports therein confirmed, as were thought fit to serve for law in all times hereafter, and so the people should not depend upon the bare opinions of judges, and uncertain Reports.

And lastly, there be in the Common Law divers contrary Reports and precedents, and this corruption doth likewise concern the statutes and acts of

---

[20] Anticipating Whitelocke's argument in his speech of 29 June (p. 60 above)

parliament, in respect there are divers cross and cutting statutes, and some so penned as they may be taken in divers, yea contrary, senses. And therefore I would wish both those Statutes and Reports, as well in the parliament as Common Law, be once maturely reviewed and reconciled, and that not only all contrarieties should be scraped out of our books, but even that such penal statutes as were made but for the use of the time (from breach of which no man can be free), which do not now agree with the condition of this our time, might likewise be left out of our books, which under a tyrannous or avaricious king could not be endured.[21]

I know now that being upon this point of Common Law, you look to hear my opinion concerning Prohibitions, and I am not ignorant that I have been thought to be an enemy to all Prohibitions, and an utter stayer of them. But I will now shortly inform you what hath been my course in proceeding therein. It is true that in respect of divers honourable courts and jurisdictions planted in this kingdom, I have often wished that every court had its own true limit and jurisdiction clearly set down, and certainly known, which if it be exceeded by any of them, or that any of them encroach one upon another, then I grant that a Prohibition in that case is to go out of the King's Bench, but chiefliest out of the Chancery; [as] for other benches, I am not yet so well resolved of their jurisdiction in that point. And for my part, I was never against Prohibitions of this nature, nor the true use of them, which is indeed to keep every river within its own banks and channels. But when I saw the swelling and overflowing of Prohibitions in a far greater abundance than ever before, every court striving to bring in most moulture to their own mill, by multitudes of causes, which is a disease very natural to all courts and jurisdictions in the world, then I dealt with this cause . . . I told them, as Christ said concerning marriage, *ab initio non fuit sic*. For as God contains the sea within his own bounds and marches (as it is in the Psalms), so it is my office to make every court contain himself within his own limits. And therefore I gave admonitions to both sides: to the other courts, that they should be careful hereafter every of them, to contain themselves within the bounds of their own jurisdictions; and to the courts of Common Law, that they should not be so forward and prodigal in multiplying their Prohibitions. Two cautions I willed them to observe in granting their Prohibitions: first, that they should be granted in a right and lawful form; and next, that they should not grant them but upon a just and reasonable cause . . . I put a difference between the true use of Prohibitions and the superabounding abuse thereof; for as a thing which is good ought not therefore [to] be abused, so ought not the lawful use of a good thing be forborne because of the abuse thereof. *Works* (1616), pp. 532–5

[21] Another contemporary account has him say, 'Now no subject, as the law standeth, can either avoid or escape a tyrannous or an avaricious king' (Foster, *Proceedings*, i, 47).

30. James I: speech to the judges in Star Chamber, June 1616

As kings borrow their power from God, so judges from kings; and as kings are to account to God, so judges unto God and kings; and . . . as no king can discharge his account to God unless he make conscience not to alter, but to declare and establish the will of God, so judges cannot discharge their accounts to kings unless they take the like care, not to take upon them to make law, but joined together after a deliberate consultation, to declare what the law is. For as kings are subject unto God's law, so they to man's law. It is the king's office to protect and settle the true interpretation of the law of God within his dominions, and it is the judges' office to interpret the law of the king, whereto themselves are also subject.

★   ★   ★

I understand the inheritance of the king and subjects in this land must be determined by the Common Law . . . [But] there is another law, of all laws free and supreme, which is God's law, and by this all common and municipal laws must be governed, and except they have dependence on this law, they are unjust and unlawful . . . That law in this kingdom hath been too much neglected, and churchmen too much had in contempt. I must speak truth; great men, lords, judges and people of all degrees from the highest to the lowest have too much contemned them; and God will not bless us in our own laws, if we do not reverence and obey God's law, which cannot be except the interpreters of it be respected and reverenced. And it is a sign of the latter days drawing on, even the contempt of the Church, and of the governors and teachers thereof now in the Church of England, which I say in my conscience, of any church that I ever read or knew of, present or past, is most pure, and nearest the primitive and apostolic church in doctrine and discipline, and is sureliest founded upon the word of God, of any church in Christendom . . . So, speaking of the Common Law, I mean the Common Law kept within her own limits, and not derogating from these other laws, which by longer custom hath been rooted here; first, the law of God and his Church, and next, the Law Civil and Canon, which in many cases cannot be wanting . . .

[He then addressed the judges directly.]

When I bid you do justice boldly, yet I bid you do it fearfully; fearfully in this, to utter your own conceits, and not the true meaning of the law. And remember you are no makers of law, but interpreters of law, according to the true sense thereof; for your office is *ius dicere*, and not *ius dare*. And that you are so far from making law, that even in the Higher House of Parliament you have no voice in making of a law, but only to give your advice when you are required.

And though the laws be in many places obscure, and not so well known to the multitude as to you, and that there are many parts that come not into ordinary practice, which are known to you because you can find out the reason thereof by books and precedents, yet know this, that your interpretations must be always subject to common sense and reason. For I will never trust any interpretation that agrees not with my common sense and reason, and true logic; for *ratio est anima legis* in all human laws, without exception. It must not be sophistry or strains of wit that must interpret, but either clear law or solid reason . . . Curious wits, various conceits, different actions and variety of examples breed questions in law, and therefore when you hear the questions, if they be plain, there is a plain way in itself; if they be such as are not plain (for men's inventions daily abound) then you are to interpret according to common sense, and draw a good and certain minor of natural reason out of the major of direct law, and thereupon to make a right and true conclusion. For though the Common Law be a mystery and skill best known unto yourselves, yet if your interpretation be such as other men which have logic and common sense understand not the reason, I will never trust such an interpretation.

Remember also that you are judges, and not a judge, and divided into benches, which showeth that what you do you should do with advice and deliberation, not hastily and rashly, before you well study the case and confer together, debating it duly, not giving single opinions . . .[22]

Now having spoken of your office in general, I am next to come to the limits wherein you are to bound yourselves . . . First, encroach not upon the prerogative of the Crown. If there fall out a question that concerns my prerogative or mystery of state, deal not with it till you consult with the king or his Council, or both; for they are transcendent matters . . . That which concerns the mystery of the king's power is not lawful to be disputed; for that is to wade into the weakness of princes, and to take away the mystical reverence that belongs unto them that sit in the throne of God.

Secondly, that you keep yourselves within your own benches, not to invade other jurisdictions, which is unfit, and an unlawful thing. In this I must enlarge myself. Besides the courts of Common Law there is the Court of Requests, the Admiralty Court, the Court of the President and Council of Wales, the President of the Council of the North, High Commission Courts, every bishop in his own court.

These courts ought to keep their own limits and bounds of their commission and instructions, according to the ancient precedents. And like as I declare that my pleasure is that every of these shall keep their own limit and bounds, so the courts of Common Law are not to encroach upon them, no more than it is my

---

[22] A palpable hit at Coke, of course, who was wont to give instant decisions on his colleagues' behalf without consulting them.

pleasure that they should encroach upon the Common Law. And this is a thing regal, and proper to a king, to keep every court within its own bounds.

Works (1616), pp. 551, 554–7

31. The Lord Chancellor Egerton [Ellesmere]'s Observations upon the Lord Cooke's Reports[23]

It is to be observed throughout all his books, that he has as it were purposely laboured to derogate much from the rights of the Church and dignity of churchmen, and to disesteem and weaken the power of the king in the ancient use of his prerogative; to traduce or else to cut short the jurisdiction of all other courts but of that court wherein himself doth sit, and in the cases of subject, sometimes to report them otherwise than they were adjudged, sometimes to report them to be adjudged which were not, sometimes by running before the judgment, as in publishing the case depending [on] the writ of error whereby the first judgment should be better examined, and oftentimes in setting down that for resolve which himself draws in upon the by and tendeth nothing to the point in judgment.

In all which points, it is not easily to be discerned whether he hath erred more in setting down the sudden opinions of judges for resolutions, which is more than the judges themselves intended, or in scattering or sowing his own conceits almost in every case, by taking occasion, though not offered, to range and expatiate upon by-matters . . .

*   *   *

So as men had need to be wary what faith they build upon these reports, they being in many places like hollow grounded greenswards, on the top seeming fair to the eye, yet such as they can take little sure footing, they walk so uncertainly among so many novelties, which can never settle their judgments, but rather draw them from the old way in which is best abiding.

Knafla, *Law and Politics*, pp. 297, 318

32. 'Sir Edward Coke's Case' (Pasch: 21 Jacobi [1623] in the Court of Wards)

[The Crown was attempting to recover debts to Queen Elizabeth incurred by Sir Christopher Hatton as Remembrancer and Collector of the First Fruits and Tenths. The issue was complicated by the fact that Hatton had made a deed settling his lands on his son and his son's heirs in tail, with a power of revocation in his own lifetime. Sir Edward Coke represented the interests of his wife Frances, Hatton's daughter. The Court of Wards was assisted by Ley, Chief Justice of

---

[23] Published in the 1650s, undated. Probably written c. 1615.

King's Bench, Hobart, Chief Justice of Common Pleas, Tanfield, Chief Baron of Exchequer, and Dodderidge, Justice of King's Bench.]

Hobart, Lord Chief Justice of the Common Pleas, argued to the same purpose . . . He said in this case it was not material whether the Inquisition find the Deed to be with power of revocation, for he said that the land is extended, and that the extent remains good until it be avoided;[24] and he said that a revocable conveyance is sufficient to bind the parties themselves, but not to bind the king, but that the lands are liable into whose hands soever they come. When a man is said to forfeit his body, it is not to be intended his life, but the freedom of his body; imprisonment. At the Common Law a common person could neither take the body nor the lands in execution, but yet at the Common Law a *capias* lay upon a force,[25] although it did not lie in case of debt, agreement, etc. The king is *parens legum*, because the laws flowed from him; he is *maritus legum*, for the Law is as it were under *covert baron*;[26] he is *tutor legum*, for he is to direct the laws, and they desire aid of him. And he said that all the land of the king's debtor are liable to his debt. The word (*debitor*) is *nomen equivocum*, and he is a debtor who is any way chargeable for debt, damages, duty, rent behind, etc. The Law amplifies everything which is for the king's benefit, or made for the king. If the king releaseth all his debts, he releaseth only debts by recognisance, judgment, obligation, specialty,[27] or contract. Every thing for the benefit of the king shall be taken largely, as every thing against the king shall be taken strictly; and the reason why they shall be taken for his benefit is because the king cannot so nearly look to his particular, because he is intended to consider *ardua regni pro bono publico*. The Prerogative Laws are not the Exchequer Law, but is the Law of the Realm for the king, as the Common Law is the Law of the Realm for the subject. The King's Bench is a Court for the Pleas of the Crown; the Common Pleas is for Pleas betwixt subject and subject; and the Exchequer is the proper court for the king's revenues.

Godbolt, p. 295

II. LAW AND POLITICS

Sir Edward Coke's entry to parliament in 1621 added a new dimension to English politics. It would be reinforcing a distortion often perpetrated by historians in the past to describe him as a 'leader of opposition', and such was certainly not his intention, but his fluency in the invention of legal precedents, his immense knowledge of legal

---

[24] The writ of extent was the peculiar means open to the Crown to sue for debt; it differed from the remedies available to the subject in that the debtor's lands, goods and person could all be seized at the same time.

[25] A writ of *capias* required the sheriff to seize the person of the defendant, and could be used in cases of forcible entry or disseisin.

[26] A *covert baron* was a married woman. Hobart meant that the law stood in relation to the king as a wife to her husband.

[27] A contract under seal.

procedure, his bottomless faith in the Common Law, strongly influenced the tone of parliamentary proceedings, and ultimately the Commons' approach to Charles I.

His assumption of the role of legal guide and mentor to the House was at once evident in the so-called 'revival of impeachment' in 1621.[28] When the Commons asked the Lords to try the delinquent holders of patents of monopoly, notably Sir Francis Mitchell and Sir Giles Mompesson, the medieval precedent of impeachment was in their minds, and here they owed as much to the researches of John Selden as they did to the promptings of Coke, but they were also developing a form of parliamentary judicature which had been employed already, though with ambiguous results, in James's first parliament. They were seeking to punish a crime not covered by Common Law by any method available, and the Lords' powers to act as a court of law, which the Commons did not possess except over their own Members, offered a way out. Coke merely put a legal gloss on a pragmatic solution (33). It was in the king's interest to sacrifice Mitchell and Mompesson, lest the Commons turn on the 'referees', the officers of state who had issued the patents of monopoly in the first place, but his occasional interventions also demonstrate his essential fair-mindedness, his keen professional interest in legal problems and his ability – not always employed in his own best interests – to see more than one side of a question. Later in the session, when the Commons turned on one of his most valued servants, the Lord Chancellor, Francis Bacon, he let justice take its course.

The very word 'impeachment' was not used in 1621, nor in 1624, and the Commons spokesmen were not invited to act as prosecuting counsel until 1626, against Buckingham. Procedure was still comparatively informal. The Commons Committee on Grievances met the equivalent Lords Committee, made a brief statement of their case, then handed over what written evidence they had, together with a list of witnesses, then withdrew, returning later to request a verdict and sentence (33). In the three cases which came before the Lords in 1621 a formal trial was scarcely necessary, since one defendant (Mompesson) had fled abroad, another (Bacon) pleaded guilty, and the guilt of the other (Mitchell) was obvious enough.

In 1624, when the Commons proceeded against Lionel Cranfield, Earl of Middlesex and Lord Treasurer, the case was different. The case against him was far from watertight; he pleaded not guilty and had to have a six-day trial.[29] James's fair-mindedness was strained to the limit, but even if his son Prince Charles and his favourite, Buckingham, had not been ranged with the Commons against Cranfield it is difficult to see what he could have done. Cranfield was sentenced in the name of 'this High Court of Parliament', which may have been intended to associate the Commons with the verdict;[30] certainly Coke claimed in a speech before a Lords committee that the Commons, as the representative element in the constitution, could act as 'inquisitors-general of the grievances of the kingdom' (34).

James warned his son of the dangerous precedent thus created, and his prophecy was

---

[28] Our understanding of this process has been very much deepened by the researches of Colin C. G. Tite, and in what follows I have drawn extensively on his *Impeachment and Parliamentary Judicature*; also on White, *Coke*, ch. 5.

[29] Prestwich, *Cranfield*, ch. 10.

[30] In 1621 the wording was, 'The Lords Spiritual and Temporal of this High Court of Parliament', or just, 'This High Court'.

speedily fulfilled. The impeachment of Buckingham in 1626, in a parliament from which Coke was absent, was the first attempt to remove a minister the king was determined to retain. It was successful to the extent that though Buckingham remained he was denied the money to finance his controversial war policy. The next attempt to remove an unpopular minister by this means was in 1641; but Strafford's impeachment broke down, and the Commons had to resort to an attainder (p.178 below). In the subsequent crisis so many men were impeached – the ship-money judges, virtually the whole bench of bishops, the Five Members, the peers who joined the king at York in 1642 – and so few brought to trial that the process fell into some disrepute. In any case, when it was used against Laud in 1644 it failed again.

Meanwhile Coke was active in 1624 in the passing of legislation for the reform of legal procedure and in forcing through a Monopolies Act, which he had first introduced in 1621.[31] But in 1625, with the advent of a new, vigorous and less tolerant king, embarked on an ambitious European war, the tempo changed.[32] Coke emerged as a serious critic of the government, though of course by no means the only one, but he was excluded from the parliament of 1626, which launched its abortive impeachment of the Duke of Buckingham, and when he returned to Westminster in 1628 it was to face a serious crisis.

Denied parliamentary taxation in 1626, Charles resorted to the use of forced loans, and tried to enforce them by imprisoning those who refused *sine die*. The issue came to trial in the famous Five Knights' Case in 1627, when five gentlemen so imprisoned sued out a writ of habeas corpus in King's Bench. The judges decided for the Crown in the most narrow way available to them. They were given every opportunity to discuss whether the king could levy forced loans or imprison men without cause shown, or whether by Magna Carta the subject had a general right to 'due process of law', but they studiously ignored them. There is something pathetic in Lord Chief Justice Hyde's remark, 'The precedents are all against you, every one of them, and what shall guide our judgments, since there is nothing alleged in this case but precedents?' (35).

Coke's answer was the Petition of Right (p. 68 above), an attempt to produce a set of simple general principles which would be a guide to the judges henceforward, and in some sense binding on them. But he was wasting his time; the judges hearkened only to the king's appeal for their support when he prorogued Parliament in June 1628: 'My lords the judges . . ., to you only, under me, belongs the interpretation of laws.'[33] In the months and years that followed they showed again and again that they were not prepared to abandon the professional mystique of case law, crabbed but certain, for the misty profundities and vague generalisations of the fundamental law. Nor were they prepared to forsake their traditional role as servants of the Crown, comfortable and honourable, for the hazardous demagogic role of arbiters between Crown and parliament. In 1628 the Court of Exchequer ruled that the Petition of Right did not

[31] See above, p. 50. White, *op. cit.*, pp. 62–76, 128–35.

[32] Conrad Russell (*Parliaments and English Politics, passim*) stresses with some truth that the strategic and financial problems posed by an insanely over-ambitious war were more important than the character or the policy of either Charles I or Buckingham, but lacking wider perspectives the Commons pressed its attack *ad hominem*. Russell himself admits that in contrast with his father Charles I 'suffered from energy' (*op. cit.*, p. 422).

[33] *PH*, II, 434 (26 June 1628).

cover tunnage and poundage, enabling Charles to break down the resistance of the merchants. King's Bench also decided that the imprisonment of Eliot and his fellow MPs was not an infraction of the petition, nor of parliamentary privilege (p. 46 above).

Judges who felt a disposition to stray were perhaps deterred by the suspension of the Chief Baron of the Exchequer in 1629, and the dismissal of Sir Robert Heath, Chief Justice of Common Pleas, in 1634.[34] But this does not explain the defection of many younger lawyers who had supported Coke in 1628. Edward Lyttelton, for instance, accepted the Recordership of London in 1631 and the solicitor-generalship in 1634; he prosecuted Hampden in 1637, and was made Lord Keeper in 1641. William Noy, Dudley Digges, John Selden, were others who took the same course. It was not just that these men did not expect another parliament to sit in the near future, they were disillusioned by the manifest failure of the Petition of Right, and probably alienated by the conduct of the Commons opposition in 1629. When Coke died in 1634 his influence was dwindling fast. In the same year Charles consulted the judges before he issued the first writs of ship-money, and again in 1635 before he extended them to the inland counties. This use of prior consultation, which effectively committed the judges before they had heard the point argued in open court, lowered their prestige still further. In 1637, when Hampden and Lord Saye and Sele showed a disposition to contest the issue, he again consulted the judges, and *Rex* v. *Hampden* was finally heard that November before all the judges of the high courts, sitting in the Exchequer Chamber. Hampden's counsel agreed that the king could call on his subjects for aid, in the form of ships, arms, men or money, in a sudden emergency, but they denied that such an emergency existed in the years 1634-6, and they argued that there had been ample time to summon a parliament. The answer was that the king was sole judge of an emergency, and if he was obliged to call parliament on every such occasion this would lead, sooner or later, to disaster (**36**). In many ways the judges were less sweeping in their judgment than their predecessors in Bate's Case; they stuck close to the issue in hand – whether the king, in a war emergency, could demand extra-parliamentary aid – and Mr Justice Berkeley's careful proviso that this did not confer on the Crown a general right of arbitrary taxation was not contradicted by any of his colleagues. Moreover, five out of the 12 judges found for Hampden, though two of them acted on technical grounds.[35] Unfortunately, Sir John Finch, Chief Justice of King's Bench, caused grave offence by reflecting on the past conduct of parliaments in general, and particularly the last parliament, of which he had been Speaker. More generally, Clarendon later pointed out that whereas in 1627 the judges had resolutely declined to consider any issues or factors outside the narrow limits of case law or precedent, ten years later they had no hesitation in discussing the state of Europe or the war in the Narrow Seas, and allowing such considerations to shape their decisions (**37**). He was sharply critical of this, but in some ways the judges were only following Coke's advice, and it was ironic that their new-found boldness should be thus employed.

The case of ship-money finally wrecked the reputation of the bench, at least in this

[34] Gardiner, *History*, VII, 112-13, 361. It may be assumed that Heath was dismissed for his attitude to ship-money, but there is no direct proof of this.

[35] The best discussion of the Hampden Case, and its implications for the judiciary, is by W. J. Jones, *Politics and the Bench*, pp. 123-30.

generation, and brought on their impeachment in the summer of 1641. But the law had suffered, too. In the 1620s the law and lawyers had been regarded with superstitious reverence, as priests who could exorcise the devils that possessed the king and Commonwealth; through the law and the judges the ancient constitution would regain its true balance. Thus the dominance of the lawyers in the parliamentary session of 1628 was notable and almost complete. But Russell reminds us that 'for all the trust Stuart gentlemen had felt in the law, distrust for its practitioners was never very far away from their minds'.[36] The failure of the Petition of Right, and the attitude of the judges towards subjects' rights, were deeply disillusioning, and led to a wholesale assault on the judiciary in the Long Parliament.[37] Ultimately this left the profession barely protected against the criticisms of the lower classes, which were directed against the incomprehensibility of the law, its defectiveness and its expense. In the 1640s men not only demanded the codification of law, the abandonment of Law French and the streamlining of court procedure, they even demanded the exclusion of lawyers from parliament.

33. The revival of impeachment: Sir Giles Mompesson

[Commons, 28 February 1621: in a committee appointed to examine precedents]

Sir Edward Coke. The court of parliament a Court of Counsel and a Court of Pleas. When the Houses were divided the indivisible things remained with the Lords; pleas continued in the upper House long after the statute. Complaints and examinations of grievances have been ancient in the House of Commons, the matter of fact tried there; they have often resorted to the Lords for judicature. The proceedings have been with some variety. In some cases the House of Commons made plaintiffs and delinquents to answer there, sometimes the Steward of the House made a complaint and the Commons were made a party, and sometimes the Commons would have the cognizance alone. Never any that was found guilty hath been able to bear out the storm of the Commons forces. *Commons Debates 1621, IV, 115–16*

[Later, in the House]

Sir Edward Coke made report from the committee for the search of precedents, that the searchers have discharged their duties. I thank God for three unities of this parliament: 1, betwixt our sovereign and us; 2, betwixt the Lords and us; 3, betwixt ourselves. This is as weighty a cause as any in my time, because it concerns not us only but the Lords also. Therefore we are resolved according to former precedents to address ourselves to the Lords, for so it was in Henry the Sixth's time, in whose reign we have two precedents: 2 Hen. 6 [Sir John Mortimer], and the 31 Hen. 6 [Thomas Thorpe].

[36] *Parliaments and Politics,* p. 349.
[37] W. J. Jones reminds us of the seriousness of this assault, *op. cit.,* pp. 137–48.

So it was agreed to go to the Lords, and that the committee examine all his offences.   *Ibid.*, II, 148–9

[3 March] A message from the lower House, delivered by Sir Edward Coke, with divers knights, citizens and burgesses:

That the House of Commons had entered into a due consideration of divers heavy grievances, and about that matter they desired a conference with their Lordships . . .

Answer was returned by the same messengers that the Lords are willing and do yield to such conference as is desired; the number to be the whole house . . . [33]

[12 March] The Lord Chancellor, removing from his place to his seat as a peer, reported what passed at the conference of both houses on Saturday last [10 March], the inducement of which conference was to clear the king's honour touching grants to Sir Giles Mompesson, and the passages procuring the same. The effect of which conference was, . . . that the authority granted by the king was much abused in the execution thereof, to the intolerable grievance of the subject, and much imposture was used in the trade. [42]

[22 March] The Lord Chief Justice related the message delivered yesterday from the lower House by Sir Robert Phelips and others . . . They acknowledged the good correspondence between both the Houses, especially in the examination of the grievances complained of, and presented to the Lords, with humble thanks for the supply the Lords added to their labours in giving the oath unto the examinants, which they cannot do. [61]

[26 March. King's Speech] . . . I am ashamed (these things proving so, as they are generally reported to be) that it was not my good fortune to be the only author of the reformation and punishment of them by some ordinary course of justice. Nevertheless, since these things are now discovered by parliament, which before I knew not of, nor could so well be discovered otherwise, in regard of that representative body of the kingdom which comes from all parts of the country, I will be never a wit the slower to do my part for the execution . . .

I intend not to derogate or infringe any of the liberties or privileges of this House, but rather to fortify and strengthen them, for never any king hath done so much for the nobility of England as I have done, and will ever be ready to do. And whatsoever I shall now say and deliver unto you as my thought, yet, when I have said what I think, I will afterwards freely leave the judgment wholly to your House. I know ye will do nothing but what the like hath been done before, and I pray you be not jealous that I will abridge you in anything that hath been used, for whatsoever the precedents in times of good government can warrant I will allow. For I acknowledge this to be the Supreme Court of Justice, wherein I am ever present by representation, and in this ye may be better satisfied by my own presence, coming divers times amongst you; neither can I give you any greater assurance or better pledge of this my purpose, than that I have done you the honour to set my only son amongst you, and hope that ye with him shall have the means to make this the happiest parliament that ever was in England . . . [69]

[26 March, afternoon] Message sent to the lower House . . ., that if the Commons, with their Speaker, will according to the ancient custom of parliament come to demand of the Lords that judgment be given against Sir Giles Mompesson for the heinous offences by him committed, they shall be heard . . .

The knights, citizens and burgesses of the House of Commons, accompanied with their Speaker, came to the Bar, where the Speaker repeated the message which the Lords had sent unto them, and said:

The Commons, by me their Speaker, demand judgment to be given against Sir Giles Mompesson, according as the heinousness of his offence doth require.

The Lord Chief Justice, being in place of the Lord Chancellor[38] answered:

Mr Speaker, the Lords Spiritual and Temporal have taken knowledge of the great pains the Commons have taken to inform their Lordships of many complaints brought unto them against Sir Giles Mompesson and others, whereof their Lordships received divers instructions from them, and thereupon, proceeding by examinations of divers witnesses upon oath, they find Sir Giles Mompesson, and divers others, guilty of many heinous crimes, against the king's Majesty and against the Commonwealth . . .

And so his Lordship pronounced the judgment of the Lords against Sir Giles Mompesson . . . [72]   *LJ*, III, 33–72

34. The impeachment of Cranfield, 1624

[15 April] Message from the House of Commons, by Lord Cavendish and others: That whereas they have received divers and sundry complaints against a member of this House, which are of a high and grievous nature, they desire a conference, thereby to impart the same unto their Lordships. The time and place, and number of committees, they humbly leave unto their Lordships.

Answered: The Lords will be ready to give them meeting and conference, with a committee of their whole house, about this business, this afternoon at three, in the Hall at Whitehall. [306]

[16 April] The Lord Keeper reported on the conference yesterday at Whitehall between the two Houses in this manner, *videlicet*: At this conference *Sir Edward Coke* (on the behalf of the Commons) showed that the knights, citizens and burgesses assembled in parliament are always elected; the knights

---

[38] Bacon had been accused of corruption the previous week, and had retired to his bed.

by the counties, the citizens by the cities, and the burgesses by the boroughs of the kingdom. That your Highness and my Lords do enjoy your places by blood and descent; some of your Lordships by creation, and the Lords Ecclesiastical by succession; but the members of the House of Commons by free election. They appear for multitudes, and bind multitudes, and therefore they have no proxies. They are the representative body of the realm, for all the people are present in parliament by person representative; and therefore, by the wisdom of the state, and by parliament orders, the Commons are appointed the Inquisitors-General of the grievances of the kingdom, and that for three causes:

1. Because they have best notice from all parts thereof.

2. They are most sensible it is not your Lordships, but the weakest Commons, that go to the wall.

3. As in a natural body, not the disease but the neglect of cure killeth, *non morbus sed morbi neglecta curatio interfecit*; so the long delay of cure of grievances *corpus politicum interfecit*; and this would happen if they were not found out by the Commons.

In their inquisition they found (what they scarce ever did before in this kind) many great, exorbitant and heinous offences against a member of this House, the Lord Treasurer; and they found him guilty after a strange manner, for in all the House no man said 'no' but [it was] concluded against him *nemine dissentiente*.

That the House appointed him (Sir Edward Coke) to present these enormities unto your Lordships, much against his mind; others were far more sufficient, as well in regard of his great years, as of other accidents. Yet, he said, he would do it truly, plainly and shortly.

There were two great offences in general, which they had distributed into two parts, one of them which should be represented by him, and the other by his colleague.

That which he should represent was to consist of two charges: (1) Gross and sordid bribery. (2) For procuring good orders of the Court of Wards to be altered – for it was done by his principal procurement – to the deceit of the King, oppression of the subject, [and] enriching of his own servants.

He would begin with presenting unto your Lordships the bribery . . . [307]

*   *   *

[5 May. King's speech to the Lords]

. . . It is my judgment, next under God, which you are to exercise at this time; and therefore, as a judge instructs the jury before the prisoner departs from the bar, so it becomes me to tell you how to carry yourselves in this great business. And the cause hereof is this, because I am bound in conscience to be careful of your carriage herein, for if your judgment should fall contrary to my approbation I protest to God it would be a great misery to me, and a greater grief unto your hearts. Before the last parliament I never saw any precedents of this nature. In the last, against another great officer of mine, there needed no admonition, because ye had *reum confitentem*. In this the party stands upon his justification, and therefore you have more need to take heed and examine it well. There is no doubt at all of your doing justice, . . . you are the most honourable jury of England; nor do I intend further to instruct you than to open your eyes (many eyes see more than one) . . .

Now I shall recommend unto you some generals, not for his respect or particular but mine own, my son's, and posterity's; and your own (my Lords), whose part, God knows when, it may fall unto. Let no man's particular ends bring forth a precedent that may be prejudicial to you all, and your heirs after you. Precedents there were none, of many years, before this and the last sessions. The informers are the lower House, and the upper House are the judges. If the accusations come in by the parties wronged, then you have a fair entrance for justice; if by men that search and hunt after other men's lives and actions, beware of it; it is dangerous, it may be your own case another time . . . [343–4]

[7 May] The Lord Keeper signified to the Lords that his Majesty said, he did not deliver this speech out of any suspicion of their Lordships, but only in discharge of his own duty and conscience. Which the House ordered to be entered. [344]

> [On 13 May Cranfield was found guilty, and sentenced to be dismissed all his offices, barred from Court and parliament, fined £50,000 and imprisoned during the king's pleasure. James at once cancelled the fine and the imprisonment.]

LJ, III, 306–83

35. The Five Knights' Case, King's Bench, 15–28 November 1627

[Letter from the Council to the Warden of the Fleet, on a writ of habeas corpus from King's Bench]

Whereas Sir Walter Earl, Knight, was heretofore committed to your custody, these are to will and require you still to detain him, letting you know that both his first commitment and this direction for the continuance of him in prison were and are by his Majesty's special commandment.

From Whitehall, 7 November 1627.

To the Guardian of the Fleet or his deputy.   *ST*, III, 12

[Sergeant Bramston, 22 November 1627]

If this return shall be good, then his imprisonment shall not continue on for a

LORETTO SCHOOL
VI FORM LIBRARY

time, but for ever; and the subjects of his kingdom may be restrained of their liberties perpetually, and by law there can be no remedy for the subject: and therefore this return cannot stand with the laws of the realm or that of Magna Carta, nor with the statute of 28 Edw. 3, c. 3; for if a man be not bailable upon this return, they cannot have the benefit of these two laws, which are the inheritance of the subject . . . We are not to reflect upon the present time and government, where justice and mercy floweth, but we are to look what may betide us in the time to come, hereafter.   *Ibid.*, III, 6–8

[John Selden, 22 November]

. . . Now, my Lord, I will speak a word or two to the matter of the return; and that is touching the imprisonment *per speciale mandatum domini regis*, by the Lords of the Council, without any cause expressed . . .

The statute of Magna Carta, cap. 29, that statute [which] if it were fully executed as it ought to be, every man would enjoy his liberty better than he doth . . . out of the very body of this act of parliament, besides the explanation of other statutes, it appears, *nullus liber homo capiatur vel imprisonetur nisi per legem terrae*. My Lords, I know these words, *legem terrae*, do leave the question where it was, if the interpretation of the statute were not. But I think, under your Lordships' favour, there it must be intended, by 'due course of law', to be either by presentment or by indictment.

My Lords, if the meaning of these words *per legem terrae* were but, as we use to say, 'according to the law', which leaves the matter very uncertain; and [if] *per speciale mandatum, &c.* be within the meaning of these words 'according to law', then this act had done nothing.   *Ibid.*, III, 16–18

[Heath, Attorney-General, 26 November]

And now, my Lord, we are where we were, to find out the true meaning of Magna Carta, for there is the foundation of our case; all this that hath been said concerneth other things, and is nothing to the thing in question. There is not a word either of the commitment of the king, or commandment of the Council, in all the statutes and records . . . [and] they on the other side cannot cite one book, statute or other thing to prove that they have been committed *per speciale mandatum* are bailable . . .

My Lords, there be *arcana Dei, et arcana imperii* . . . There shall be as much prejudice come to the kingdom, if God direct not the heart of the king, which is in the hand of God, as the rivers of waters; I say there may as much hazard come to the commonwealth in many other things with which the king is trusted, as in this particular there can accrue to the subject . . . It may be divers men do suffer wrongfully in prison, but therefore shall all prisoners be delivered? That were a great mischief. No doubt but the king's power is absolutely over his coins; if then he shall command his coin shall be turned to brass or leather . . . can your Lordship hinder it, as being an inconvenience?

. . . The king may pardon all traitors and felons; and if he should do it, may not the subjects say, If the king do this, the bad will overcome the good? But shall any say, The king cannot do this? No, we may only say, he will not do this.

Ibid., III, 35–50

[Lord Chief Justice Hyde, 28 November]

. . . I am sure you expect justice from hence, and God forbid we should sit here but to do justice to all men according to our best skill and knowledge, for it is our oaths and duties so to do, and I am sure there is nothing else expected of us. We are sworn to maintain all prerogatives of the king, that is one branch of our oath; and we are likewise sworn to administer justice equally to all people.

. . . That which is now to be judged by us is this: whether one that is committed by the king's authority, and no cause declared of his commitment, according as here it is upon this return, whether we ought to deliver him by bail, or to remand him back again? Wherein you must know this, which your counsel will tell you, we can take notice only of this return; and when the case appears to come to us no otherwise than by the return we are not bound to examine the truth of the return, but the sufficiency of it, for there is a great difference between the sufficiency and the truth.

We cannot judge upon rumours nor reports, but upon that which is before us on record, and therefore the return is examinable by us, where it be sufficient or not . . .

The cause of the detention is sufficiently answered, . . . and therefore we resolve that the form of this return is good. The next thing is the main point in law, whether the substance or matter of the return be good or no, wherein the substance is this, he [the warder] doth certify that they are detained in prison by the special command of the king; and whether this be good in law or no, that is the question . . .

[He then examined in detail all the cases and statutes cited by counsel, and dismissed them.]

. . . Then the precedents are all against you, every one of them, and what shall guide our judgments, since there is nothing alleged in this case but precedents? [We find] that if no cause of the commitment be expressed it is to be presumed to be for matters of state, which we cannot take notice of. You see we find none, no not one, that hath been delivered by bail in the like cases, but by the hand of the king or his direction . . .

[He then examined in detail a number of cases in favour of the Crown, ending with a declaration by the judges in 1592, with which the Attorney-General had made great play.]

. . . You see what hath been the practice in all the kings' times heretofore, and your own records, and this resolution of the judges teacheth us; and what can we do but walk in the steps of our forefathers? . . . If in justice we ought to deliver you, we would do it. But upon these grounds, and these records, and the precedents and resolutions, we cannot deliver you, but you must be remanded . . .   *Ibid.*, III, 51-9

36. *Rex* v *Hampden*, 1637-8 (ship-money)

[Oliver St John, November 1637]

My Lords, . . . it must needs be granted that in this business of defence the *suprema potestas* is inherent in his Majesty, as part of his crown and kingly dignity.

So that as the care and provision of the law of England extends in the first place to foreign defence, and secondly lays the burden upon all, and for ought I have to say against it, it maketh the quantity of each man's estate the rule whereby this burden is to be equally apportioned upon each person; so likewise hath it in the third place made his Majesty the sole judge of dangers from foreigners, and when and how the same are to be prevented, and to come nearer, hath given him power by writ under the Great Seal of England, to command the inhabitants of each county to provide shipping for the defence of the kingdom, and may by law compel the doing thereof.

So that, my Lords, as I still conceive [it] the question will not be *de persona*, in whom the *suprema potestas* of giving the authorities or powers to the sheriff, which are mentioned in this writ, doth lie, for that is in the king; but the question is only *de modo*, by what medium or method this supreme power, which is in his Majesty, doth infuse and let out itself into this particular . . .

His Majesty is the fountain of justice; and though all justice which is done within the realm flows from this fountain, yet it must run in certain and known channels: an assize in the King's Bench, or an appeal of death in the Common Pleas, are *coram non judice*, though the writ be his Majesty's command; and so of the several jurisdictions of each Court . . . If the process be legal, and in a right court, yet I conceive that his Majesty alone, without assistance of the judges of the court, cannot give judgment. I know that King John, H.3 and other kings have sat on the King's Bench, and in the Exchequer; but for ought appears they were assisted by their judges . . .

And as without the assistance of his judges, who are his settled counsel at law, his Majesty applies not the law and justice in many cases unto his subjects; so likewise in other cases neither is this sufficient to do it without the assistance of his great Council in parliament. If an erroneous judgment was given before the Statute of 27 Eliz. in the King's Bench, the king could not relieve his grieved subjects any way but by Writ of Error in parliament; neither can he out of parliament alter the old laws, nor make new, or make any naturalisations or legitimations, nor do some other things; and yet is the parliament his Majesty's court too, as well as other his Courts of Justice. It is his Majesty that gives life and being to that, for he only summons, continues and dissolves it, and by his *le volt* enlivens all the actions of it; and after the dissolution of it, by supporting his Courts of Justice, he keeps them still alive, by putting them in execution. And although in the Writ of Waste, and some other writs, it is called *commune concilium regni*, in respect that the whole kingdom is representatively there, and secondly, that the whole kingdom have access thither in all things that concern them, other courts affording relief but in special causes, and thirdly, in respect that the whole kingdom is interested in, and receive benefit by the laws and things there passed; yet it is *concilium regni* no otherwise than the Common Law is *lex terrae* . . . [484–6]

My Lords, the parliament, as it is best qualified and fitted to make this supply for some of each rank, and that through all the parts of the kingdom being there met, his Majesty having declared the danger, they best knowing the estates of all men within the realm, are fittest, by comparing the danger and men's estates together, to proportion the aid accordingly.

And secondly, as they are fittest for the preservation of that fundamental propriety which the subject hath in his lands and goods, because each subject's vote is included in whatever is there done . . . [505]

My Lords, it appears not by anything in the writ, that any war at all was proclaimed against any state, or that if any his Majesty's subjects had taken away the goods of any prince's subjects in Christendom, but that the party might have recovered them before your Lordships in any his Majesty's courts; so that the case in the first place is, whether in times of peace his Majesty may, without consent in parliament, alter the property of the subject's goods for the defence of the realm.

Secondly, the time that will serve the turn for the bringing in of supplies and means of the defence, appears to your Lordships judicially by the writ, that is seven months within four days, for the writ went out 4 August, and commands the ship to be at Portsmouth, the place of rendezvous, the first of March following; and thereby it appears that the necessity in respect of the time was not such, but that a parliamentary consent might in that time have been endeavoured for the effecting of the supply . . . [526–7]

Rushworth, II, 484–527

The Judgment, 1638

[Sir Robert Berkeley, 10 February 1638]

. . . I hope that none doth imagine that it either is, or can be drawn by consequence, to be any part of the question in this case, whether the king may at all times and upon all occasions impose charges upon his subjects in general, without common consent in parliament. If that were made the question, it is questionless that he may not. The people of the kingdom are subjects, not slaves, freemen, not villeins to be taxed *de alto et basso*.

Though the king of England hath a monarchical power, and hath *jura summae majestatis*, and hath an absolute trust settled in his crown and person for government of his subjects, yet his government is to be *secundum leges regni* . . . By those laws the subjects are not tenants at the kings will, of what they have . . . They have in their goods a propriety, a peculiar interest, a *meum et tuum*. They have a birthright in the laws of the kingdom. No new laws can be put upon them, none of their laws can be altered or abrogated, without common consent in parliament . . . [1090]

> [He then examined the precedents for ship-money, and dismissed the idea that it was an aid or subsidy. He pointed out that ships, not money, were to be provided, and in theory they remained the property of the contributors. He admitted that the kingdom was not on the very verge of war, but he argued that there was sufficient danger on the high seas to warrant the king's action (1090–6).]

Now, whether to set the Commonwealth free and in safety from this peril of ruin and destruction the king may not of his own royal authority, and without common assent in parliament, impose a charge upon his subjects in general to provide such shipping as is necessary in his royal judgment, to join with his Majesty's own ships to attend them for such time as his Majesty in his royal wisdom shall think fit, and also to enjoin them to be themselves at the expenses . . .? [That is the question.]

I would be loth to irritate any differing from me with provoking or odious terms, but I cannot more fully express myself (and so I desire it may be taken as an expression, and not as a comparison) than in saying, that it is a dangerous tenet, a kind of judaizing opinion, to hold that the weal public must be exposed to peril of utter ruin and subversion, rather than such a charge as this, which may secure the Commonwealth, may be imposed by the king upon the subject, without common consent in parliament. So that the security of the Commonwealth, for the very subsistence of it, must stay and expect until a parliament provide for it, in which interim of time it is possible, nay, apparently probable, yea, in a manner to be presumed, that all may be, yea, will be brought to a final period of destruction and desolation . . .

I now come to my second general head, wherein I proposed to consider of the fundamental policy and maxims and rules of law for the government of this realm, and of the reasons of law pertinent to our case, which are very many. I will briefly and severally point at those which make impression on me.

1. It is plain that as originally, even before the Romans' time, the frame of this kingdom was a monarchical state, so for divers hundreds of years past, upon the Romans' desertion of it, and after the heptarchy ended, it was, and

continued and still continueth monarchical. And our gracious sovereign is a monarch, and the rights of free monarchy appertain unto him . . .

2. Where Mr Holborne[39] supposed a fundamental policy in the creation of the frame of this kingdom, that in case the monarch of England should be inclined to exact from his subjects at his pleasure he should be restrained, for that he could have nothing from them, but upon a common consent of parliament, he is utterly mistaken herein. I agree the parliament to be a most ancient and supreme court, where the king and peers, as judges, are in person, and the whole body of the commons representatively. There peers and Commons may, in a fitting way, *parler leur ment*, and shew the estate of every part of the kingdom; and amongst other things, make known their grievances (if there be any) to their sovereign, and humbly petition him for redress.

But the former fancied policy I utterly deny. The law knows no such king-yoking policy. The law is of itself an old and trusty servant of the king's; it is his instrument or means which he useth to govern his people by. I never read nor heard that *lex* was *rex*; but it is common and most true that *rex* is *lex*, for he is *lex loquens*, a living, a speaking, an acting law . . .

There are two maxims of the law of England, which plainly disprove Mr Holborne's supposed policy. The first is, 'that the king is a person trusted with the state of the Commonwealth'. The second of these maxims is, 'that the king cannot do wrong'. Upon these two maxims the *jura summae majestatis* are grounded, with which none but the king himself (not his high court of parliament without leave) hath to meddle, as, namely, war and peace, value of coin, parliament at pleasure, power to dispense with penal laws, and divers others; amongst which I range these also, of regal power to command provision (in case of necessity) of means from the subjects, to be adjoined to the king's own means for the defence of the Commonwealth, for the preservation of the *salus reipublicae*. Otherwise I do not understand how the king's Majesty may be said to have the majestical right and power of a free monarch.

It is agreed that the king is by his regal office bound to defend his people . . . against all disturbers of the general peace amongst them, most chiefly in my judgment against dangerous foreigners . . .

3. Though I have gone already very high, I shall go yet to a higher contemplation of the fundamental policy of our laws, which is this: that the king of mere right ought to have, and the people of mere duty are bound to yield unto the king, supply for the defence of the kingdom. And when the parliament itself doth grant supply in that case it is not merely a benevolence of the people, but therein they do an act of justice and duty to the king . . . [1097–9]

---

[39] One of Hampden's counsel.

4. I confess that by the fundamental law of England the parliament is *commune concilium regis et regni*, that it is the greatest, the most honourable and supreme court in the kingdom, that no man ought to think any dishonourable thing of it. Yet give me leave to say that it is but a *concilium*, to say so is no dishonour to it; the king may call it, prorogue it, dissolve it, at his pleasure, and whatsoever the king doth therein is always to be taken for just and necessary. We must consider that it is a great body, [and] moves slowly; sudden despatches cannot be expected in it. Besides, though the parliament cannot err, parliament men may *de facto*. Every particular member of the House hath his free voice; some of them may chance to make scruples where there is no cause; it is possible some of them may have sinister ends. These things breed delays, so they may disturbances; I would to God the late woeful experience of this kingdom had not verified these speculations . . . [1101]   *ST*, III, 1090–101

[Sir John Finch, Lord Chief Justice of Common Pleas]

. . . A parliament is an honourable court, and I confess it is an excellent means of charging the subject, and defending the kingdom, but yet it is not the only means. An honour the last parliament was pleased to bestow on me, which never any shall with more respect remember than myself, when they were pleased to choose me for their Speaker. And as my brother Hutton said, I conceive it a fit way to charge the subject, and I wish that some, for their private humour, had not sowed the tares of discontent in that field of the Commonwealth, then might we have expected and found good fruit. But now the best way to redeem this lost privilege (for which we may give those thanks only) is to give all opportune appearance of obedience and dutifulness to his Majesty's command. The two Houses of Parliament without the king cannot make a law, nor without his royal assent declare it; he is not bound to call it but when he pleaseth, nor to continue it but at his pleasure. Certainly there was a king before a parliament, for how else could there be an assembly of king, Lords and Commons? And then what sovereignty was there in the kingdom but this? His power then was limited by the positive law; then it cannot be denied but originally the king had the sovereignty of the whole kingdom both by sea and land, who hath a power of charging the whole kingdom.

The law that hath given that power hath given means to the king by this authority to put it in execution. It is a very true rule, the law commands nothing to be done, but it permits the ways and means how it may be done, else the law should be imperfect, lame and unjust. Therefore the law that hath given the interest and sovereignty of defending and governing the kingdom to the king doth also give the king power to charge his subjects for the necessary defence and good thereof. And as the king is bound to defend, so the subjects are bound to obey, and to come out of their own country, if occasion be and so provide horse and arms in foreign war . . . Then if sea and land be but one entire kingdom, and the king lord of both, the subject is bound as well to the defence of the sea as of the land, and then all are bound to provide ships, men, ammunition, victuals and necessaries for that defence . . . But here the maritime towns shall not help the inland, nor the inland the maritime, but each of them bear their own charge . . . [1226-7]

*   *   *

. . . There hath been, and may be, as great danger when the enemy is not discerned as when in arms and on the land. In the time of war when the course of law is stopped, when judges have no power or place, when the courts of justice can send out no process, in this case the king may charge his subjects, you grant. Mark what you grant: when there is such a confusion as no law, then the king may do it . . . Expectancy of danger, I hold, is sufficient ground for the king to charge his subjects, for if we stay till the danger comes it will be then too late, it may be. And his averment of the danger is not traversable, it must be binding when he perceives and says there is a danger; as in 1588, the enemy had been upon us, if it had not been foreseen and provided for before it came.

But I will not determine the danger now. Do not we see our potent neighbours, and our great enemies heretofore, were they not prepared for war; and was there not another navy floated upon the sea? and was not the dominion of the sea threatened to be taken away? As long as this danger remains I shall bless God for such a king as will provide for the defence of the kingdom timely, and rejoice to see such a navy as other nations must veil to; and we are not in case of safety without it, and should lose our glory besides . . . [1234]

Acts of parliament may take away flowers and ornaments of the crown, but not the crown itself; they cannot bar a succession, nor can they be attainted by them, and acts that bar them of possession are void. No act of parliament can bar a king of his regality, as that no lands should hold of him; or bar him of the allegiance of his subjects; or the relative on his part, as trust and power to defend his people. Therefore acts of parliament to take away his royal power in the defence of his kingdom are void . . . They are void acts of parliament to bind the king not to command the subjects' persons and goods, and I say their money too, for no acts of parliament make any difference . . . [1235]

Ibid., 1226-35

37. Clarendon on ship-money

And here the damage and mischief cannot be expressed, that the Crown and state sustained by the deserved reproach and infamy that attended the judges, by being made use of in this and like acts of power; there being no possibility to preserve the dignity, reverence and estimation of the laws themselves but by the integrity and innocency of the judges. And no question, as the exorbitancy of the House of Commons this Parliament[40] hath proceeded principally from their contempt of the laws, and that contempt from the scandal of that judgment, so the concurrence of the House of Peers in that fury can be imputed to no one thing more than to the irreverence and scorn the judges were justly in; who had been always before looked upon there as the oracles of the law, and the best guides and directors of their opinions and actions: and they now thought themselves excused for swerving from the rules and customs of their predecessors (who in altering and making of laws, in judging of things and persons, had always observed the advice and judgment of those sages) in not asking questions of those whom they knew nobody would believe; and thinking it a just reproach upon them (who out of their gentilesses had submitted the difficulties and mysteries of the law to be measured by the standard of general reason and explained by the wisdom of state), to see those men make use of the licence they had taught, and determine that to be law which they thought reasonable or found to be convenient. If these men had preserved the simplicity of their ancestors in severely and strictly defending the laws, other men had observed the modesty of theirs in humbly and dutifully obeying them.

Clarendon, History, bk 1, § 151

III. STAR CHAMBER

The history, functions and procedure of the Court of Star Chamber under the Tudors have now been definitively established, and under the Stuarts there were no new developments.[41] Ostensibly its main purpose remained to punish infractions of the king's peace, whether by riot, assault or intimidation, and in 1633 it was employed to beat down local opposition to Vermuyden's draining of the Fens (**38a**). Since it was composed of the Privy Council (or some of its members), presided over by the Lord Keeper or Lord Chancellor, assisted by the two chief justices, it was also the obvious court to deal with delinquent sheriffs and juries. Some of its most spectacular cases originated with the government, but the great majority of plaintiffs who threw themselves on its jurisdiction were private individuals already engaged in parallel litigation in Chancery or Common Pleas, who sought to strengthen their case or simply harass their opponents by accusing them – often on the flimsiest evidence – of riot, defamation, conspiracy or assault; charges which the Tudor and Stuart monarchy's 'almost compulsive preoccupation with good order' would not allow it to

---

[40] The Long Parliament.

[41] Elton's basic account (*Tudor Constitution*, pp. 163–87) is essential. For the Stuart period see also Thomas G. Barnes, 'Due Process and Slow Process in the late Tudor early Stuart Star Chamber', *Amer. Jnl Legal History* VI (1962), 221, 315; H. E. I. Phillips, 'The Last Years of the Court of Star Chamber 1630–1641', 4 *TRHS*, XXI (1938), 103–31, and W. J. Jones, *op cit.*, pp. 103–6.

ignore.[42] By the end of Elizabeth's reign the court had become so popular that in 1596 Keeper Egerton issued a series of orders clarifying and expediting its procedure, but even then the pressure upon it was so great that in 1632 its doors were closed to common informers under penal statutes, whose suits, initiated merely to substantiate their accusations, rarely proceeded to judgment.[43]

It is clear that right up to 1640 the court retained its popularity with litigants, nor did it arouse any jealousy in the Common Law courts. The Chief Justices commonly sat on it, and its president, the Lord Keeper, was usually a common lawyer, too. Moreover, it was administering the Common Law, though by a different procedure, which admitted written depositions as evidence and permitted the cross-examination of the accused under oath, and it had the unqualified endorsement of Coke, who did not take kindly to conciliar courts.[44] As Professor Barnes remarks:

> Star Chamber was latterly and throughout the period under discussion a court of law, fixed solidly in the firmament of English judicature, administering the historically founded yet changing Common Law by a procedure different from that of Common Law though acceptable to the common lawyers and sanctioned by the judges of the Common Law courts.[45]

With this in mind, it is difficult to explain the precipitate abolition of the court in 1641. Of course, on this occasion the Long Parliament acted with more emotion than logic,[46] but it showed no such reckless animus against the Court of Requests or the Court of Wards, which were most unpopular with lawyers and landowners respectively; in fact, both of them survived into the Civil War.

The explanation may lie in the severe corporal punishments meted out by the court in the 1630s, and its use in the same period to support a controversial religious and economic policy. In the absence of a prison system all seventeenth-century courts had to impose fines, corporal punishment or public penance; this was especially so of Star Chamber, which could not impose the death penalty. But in an age when the Poor Law prescribed that women who would not work should be whipped 'till their backs be bloody', the ear-cropping ordered by Star Chamber was not out of line, and in fact, out of 236 known sentences of the court between 1630 and 1641 only 19 included corporal punishment, and of these only nine or ten roused any great public interest.[47] But William Prynne's second trial in 1637, with Bastwick and Burton, and the trial of that arch-publicist John Lilburne, caught the attention of the people, no doubt in part because they were campaigning against the unpopular bishops. Another factor which inflamed public opinion was the savage sentences imposed on gentlemen, who were rarely sentenced to the pillory or the branding iron by the ordinary courts. Most remarkable in this respect was the case of Sir Thomas Wiseman, who was convicted in 1638 of slandering Lord Keeper Finch and the court of Star Chamber itself. He was

---

[42] Barnes, *art. cit.*, p. 226.   [43] *Ibid.*, pp. 331–3.
[44] See the extract from his *Institutes*, in Elton, *Tudor Constitution*, pp. 168–70.
[45] *Art. cit.*, p. 224.
[46] For the circumstances see Phillips, *art. cit.*, pp. 103–6.
[47] *Ibid.*, p. 118. Cf. Thomas G. Barnes, 'Star Chamber Mythology', *Amer. Jnl Legal History*, v (1961), 1.

fined £10,000, with £7,000 damages; he was degraded from the order of knights bachelor and his patent as a knight baronet was cancelled, his ears were cut off, and he was ordered to be detained during his Majesty's pleasure.[48]

The court was also besmirched by its connexion with the Laudian hierarchy. One of its main uses was to strengthen and sustain other courts, and the ecclesiastical courts often needed its aid to deal with upper-class malefactors. So in 1632 we find Lady Grenville using her husband's casual and almost irrelevant slander on the Earl of Suffolk to enforce her demands for alimony, granted her by High Commission but never paid (38b). This was perhaps not unreasonable; it was a different matter when a minister, having found the High Commission ineffectual, took his parishioners up to Star Chamber for refusing to take the sacrament kneeling (38c), or when another clergyman was arraigned for 'irreligious and profane speeches to the disgrace of the state and his Majesty's government'.[49] When yet another clergyman prosecuted a pedlar for accusing him of adultery with his wife the Lord Keeper protested that the case properly belonged to the ecclesiastical courts, but he did not press the point.[50] Such cases emphasised the presence of bishops on the board. Laud sat regularly, as Bishop of London and later Archbishop, and so did Richard Neile, Bishop of Winchester and subsequently Archbishop of York. Juxon of London also sat occasionally after his appointment to the Treasury in 1635. It was said that the men of the cloth always pressed for the heaviest and cruellest punishments, whether their order was involved or not.

However, the most important single cause of Star Chamber's unpopularity was the role it was called upon to play in the enforcement of the king's social and economic policies in the thirties. In the absence of parliament the government had to resort increasingly to proclamations, and the enforcement of proclamations had always been a function peculiar to Star Chamber. Between 1631 and 1641 the attorney-general brought 175 actions in Star Chamber, most of them on the simplified procedure of *ore tenus* – in itself something of an abuse.[51] Of these 175 about 40 were brought to a conclusion, and the great majority of these concerned breaches of proclamations; proclamations against enclosures, against unlawful residence in London (p. 455 below), against builders of tenements in the suburbs, fraudulent manufacturers, exporters of prohibited commodities and victuallers who sold meat in Lent.[52] Other prosecutions involving questions of public policy were those of sheriffs who failed to collect ship-money, hoarders of corn, and those who infringed the new patents of monopoly. In other words, in the 1630s Star Chamber had become 'a tribunal for the trial of cases of public import, involving profit for and the safety of the State'.[53] Or, as Pym said in 1640 (p. 187 below), 'The Star Chamber now is become a court of revenue . . . it was not used that *meum et tuum* should be disputed there.'

[48] *CSPD 1637–8*, p. 491. This is an obscure case; the savagery of the sentence may have reflected the sensitivity of the judges to accusations of corruption, especially after Bacon's fall.

[49] Gardiner, *Cases in Star Chamber*, p. 89.

[50] *Ibid.*, pp. 70–1.

[51] This was when the accused stood mute, and was then assumed to have confessed. See Phillips, *art. cit.*, pp. 113–14.

[52] Barnes, 'Due Process', p. 336. Cf. Phillips, *art. cit.*, p. 116, where the number of cases arising directly from proclamations is put at seventeen, out of approximately 40 settled.

[53] Barnes, *loc. cit.*

38. Cases before Star Chamber

(a) Attorney-general versus Charles Moody, Richard Strode and others. Michaelmas Term 1633

Present: Lord Keeper   Bishop of London
     Lord Privy Seal   Bishop of Winchester
     Earl of Arundel   Sir Thomas Jermyn
     Earl of Bridgewater Sir John Coke
     Lord Wentworth Sir Thomas Richardson, CJ
     Lord Falkland   Sir Robert Heath, CJ.

The bill set forth that his Majesty, being seized of divers lands and waste grounds called the Fens, in the counties of Lincoln and Nottingham, etc., these lands were surrounded with water and barren, his Majesty by advice of his Council took order with Sir Cornelius Vermuyden for the draining of the Fens if it might be, and articles of agreement were made between his Majesty and the said Sir Cornelius Vermuyden, and authority given by virtue of the King's letters patent under the Great Seal of England for the doing thereof, and a special provision that those that had any title of common should repair to the commissioners appointed for that purpose by commission, and upon their showing their title or interest they should have full recompense. The king's letters were sent to warn them to come to the Commission and demand their recompense 23 February, 3 *Caroli* [1628]. They were all agreed the commoners should have one part of [blank]. The king provided workmen, the work was brought to good forwardness, and divers ditches and banks made, and Sir Cornelius Vermuyden was at great charge thereabouts.

That the defendants, with others, came together in companies to throw down and demolish what was done, although divers proclamations were made, and no right they could pretend, and 4 *Caroli* they made their assemblies by hundreds and five hundreds, they demolish[ed] the work, they beat the workmen, and burne[d] the spades, shovels, wheelbarrows, planks, set up a pair of gallows for to terrify the workmen, threw some of them into the water and held them under a while. They had a signal to assemble themselves by sometimes a bell, sometimes by a horn, they threatened to kill the workmen if they came thither to work again. That they had fourteen several times in riotous and rebellious manner assembled themselves and done these riots, etc., to the slander of his Majesty's government, to the hindrance of the works, and to the damage of Sir Cornelius Vermuyden £5,000, and that some of them put those that served the king's process out of this court upon them into the stocks. [59–60]

★   ★   ★

It was unanimously declared by the whole court that his Majesty proceeded herein legally and rightfully for the benefit of his crown and people, for the draining of these Fens; and many of the defendants were found guilty of the several riots charged in the bill; viz., Toxie, James Moody, Henry Scott, and Hezekias Browne, who were fined £1,000 apiece. The widow Smith, who married the minister after the riots,[54] £500, and the several women who were proved to be at the said riots, 500 marks apiece, and they were adjudged to pay for damages unto Sir Cornelius Vermuyden, the relator, £2,000.

After this sentence Mr Attorney moved the court to take it into their consideration, whether it were not fit to fine the adjoining towns where these riots and rebellious assemblies were made; he showed that here were fourteen several riots, wherein the poorer sorts of people were set on work, but the rich, they escape, and these were committed three years ago, and never any are brought to be presented or indicted at any assizes or sessions. He taketh it that by the law these towns ought to be fined. [The Statute of] Westm[inster] 2, ch. 4, [said] that the towns adjoining shall be distrained in such a case, etc., which was but a declaration of the Common Law. My Lord Keeper directed that the precedents should be considered, and if it agreed therewith they should be fined, but [it was] objected that these towns and villages were not called here to answer. Mr Attorney answered that upon a *rescusse* returned into a court of record if it appeared to be done the village or town where it was done is amerced, though not called, etc. Whereupon my Lord Keeper said it was a good motion and was not fit to die; yet nothing more was done for this time.

Gardiner, *Cases in Star Chamber*, pp. 59–60, 64–5

(b) Theophilus, Earl of Suffolk, versus Sir Richard Grenville, Bt. 3 February 1632
The Earl of Suffolk complained by his bill of Sir Richard Grenville, but [?that] whereas he had been a means to procure his lady, in a just cause, alimony against the said Sir Richard till the cause were heard in the ecclesiastical court, and the said Earl of Suffolk sent a messenger with the order to give Sir Richard notice to pay the said alimony. Whereupon the said Sir Richard broke out in words before the said messenger, and the Lady Grenville, and others, saying: The Earl of Suffolk is a base lord and hath dealt basely with me; and sent a message to him with these reproachful words: Tell him he is a base lord and hath used me basely, and he shall know as much, etc.

The defendant pleaded not guilty, and endeavoured to excuse himself for not defending himself in examining his witnesses to the contrary, and upon the reputation of the witnesses.

This cause came to be heard and sentenced this day.

My Lord Richardson showed that the Earl of Suffolk was a noble lord, and a man of great office and trust, and honourable in his birth and actions, and not

---

[54] 'Katherine Smith had since married with a minister, a grave divine, who was not called to answer . . .' [p. 64].

base. These words were very foul and dishonourable, it is a tainting of all honour. The old law was to cut off the tongues of such men; all honour is founded in the king. This is against the statutes of Westminster 2, ch. 34, and 12 Rich. II, c. 30, and [the] Book of Assizes. [A] Lord Chief Baron brought his writ against a lady that called him traitor, and his declaration was that it was *in despite le Roy*.

The bishop of Winchester said that Sir Richard Grenville had touched the highest blood in the kingdom, that his actions are according to his degree and parentage, and related what he heard the Lord Treasurer Burleigh say long ago, upon the coming forth of Dollmann's book, that he would boldly justify the House of Suffolk from the Earls of Norfolk to be descended of Edward IV. The offices of my Lord Suffolk were great, Captain of the Pensioners and Lord Warden of the Cinque Ports. Sir Richard Grenville is a soldier, and a colonel, a man of good deserts otherwise.

But the tongue should not be the soldier's weapon, said the *Bishop of London*.

So by the vote of the court Sir Richard Grenville was fined £4,000 to the King, and adjudged to pay £4,000 damages to the said earl of Suffolk, and to be imprisoned during the King's pleasure. *Ibid.*, pp. 108–10

(c) Allen versus Jemmat and others[55]

A motion was made by one Allen, a minister of Sudbury in Suffolk, that whereas he had put in a bill in this court against one Samuel Jemmat, clerk, and others for divers riots and misdemeanours committ[ed] by the defendants in the Church, of which they endeavoured to dispossess the pl[ain]tiff because he would not suffer them to receive the sacrament sitting, and for refusing to kneel at the sacrament, and for throwing the holy sacrament most contemptu-ously and irreligiously under their feet. The pl[ain]tiff desired, being admitted to prosecute this cause *in forma pauperis*, that in regard he is poor and hath but £11 a year, that the suit might be undertaken to be presented by the king's attorney.

The Bishop of London commended this cause to the court as concerning the ecclesiastical jurisdiction as much as any ever did.[56]

Mr Prynne for the defend[an]ts showed that this was complained of in the High Commission court, and there dismissed, and that for the same things that are here charged; that Mr Jemmat was lawfully presented, etc., and that therefore the court would dismiss the cause or dispauper the pl[ain]t[iff] for that by his confession he hath £11 *per annum*.

The Bishop of Winchester showed the court that the Archb[isho]p of York

---

[55] This case is undated, but it was heard before 1 February 1633, when Prynne was imprisoned.

[56] Clearly by 'ecclesiastical jurisdiction' Laud meant the dignity and authority of the priesthood rather than the jurisdiction of ecclesiastical courts.

brought this into the High Commission court, that upon the defend[an]ts' submissions and promises of amendment and quietness they were there dismissed; but that since they were more refractory, etc.

My Lord Keeper pronounced this order, that the plaintiff should continue *pauper*, and to be considered if it can be proved by certificate that any of these things being so foul as they seem to be by the charge of the bill; his Lordship thought it a fit thing for Mr Attorney to take care of and to present it.

Mr Prynne desired my Lord Keeper to give him leave to open the truth of the cause to his Lordship shortly. He showed that Allen, being a vicar in Sudbury and beneficed and unqualified, accepted of another living, and his lordship for that cause did grant the first living to another, one Samuel Jemmat; that he was admitted and inducted at five of the clock in the morning, when nobody was there in the church, and this he chargeth as a riot; and that in the afternoon of the same day there was a burial to be solemnised, and there coming the said Jemmat and thirty persons more to bury the dead corpse, when he had locked up the doors, this was the second riot. And for the other things charged, they were exhibited by articles into the High Commission court and there dismissed.

The Bishop of London reproved Mr Prynne for saying that the articles in the Commission court were at the suit of the party; he averred that to his knowledge they were at the preferring of the late [Arch]bishop of York. So the order aforesaid stood.   *Ibid.*, pp. 72–3

CHAPTER 4

THE ESTABLISHED CHURCH

I. THE JACOBEAN CHURCH

In the first edition of this book I found it necessary to issue a stern warning against the orthodox view that the period 1558–1640 was one of steadily mounting tension in church affairs, of steadily increasing pressure by militant Puritanism on the Crown and the established Church. Fortunately my commonsense suggestions have now been overtaken and amplified by the deeper scholarship of others,[1] who have confirmed that between two periods of confrontational church politics, in the 1580s and the 1630s, there was a long lull, and the reign of James I was even a period of eirenic compromise.

The falling-away of Puritanism in Elizabeth's closing years is now well established;[2] long before 1603 serious thoughts of reforming the structure and liturgy of the Church in any radical way had been abandoned, or shelved *sine die*, though some stiff-necked clergymen still balked at the three articles to which they had been obliged to subscribe since 1583, pledging their acceptance of the Book of Common Prayer and the Thirty-Nine Articles *in toto*, including those which upheld the present government of the Church by archbishops and bishops.[3] The same kind of clergyman also objected strongly to the use of the surplice. Otherwise there was a more general desire, difficult to quantify, to launder out of the Prayer Book the last vestiges of popish idolatry or pagan superstition – perhaps the only significant point here being whether or not communion should be received kneeling. Serious-minded laymen, of a type known to the eighteenth and nineteenth centuries as 'evangelical', were much exercised by these problems, and urgently supported the provision in greater numbers of a learned and preaching clergy. They particularly deplored the poor income attached to many benefices, and the resultant evil of pluralism. These points they were prepared to voice frequently and loudly in James I's first parliament, and with an elastic order of business and relaxed Court control there was little to stop them, though any bills they passed relating to the Church were killed in the Lords.

In any case, as in so many aspects of seventeenth-century government, those who were ready to demand reforms were unwilling to provide the money to effect them. The rehabilitation of the clergy depended on two things: better education and higher incomes. The first the Church itself could take care of, and did: by the provision of more places, even more colleges, at Oxford and Cambridge, by stricter screening of ordinands and insistance on their possession of a university degree or its equivalent. So

---

[1] Notably Patrick Collinson, in *The Elizabethan Puritan Movement* (1967), and *The Religion of Protestants* (Oxford 1982).

[2] See Elton, *Tudor Constitution*, pp. 442–8.   [3] *Ibid.*, pp. 455–6

successful were the efforts of Archbishops Whitgift (1583–1604) and Bancroft (1604–11) in this respect that by the end of James's reign there appears to have been if anything a surplus of well-qualified clergymen.[4] However, any better financial provision for the clergy depended to a great part on the generosity of the landowning classes, and it is lamentable but only human that their religious zeal stopped short of financial self-sacrifice. Out of a total of 9,224 livings 3,849 were in the hands of lay patrons, who collected the tithes and usually only passed a proportion of this income on to the incumbent; some were not above holding the living vacant and employing a curate on a starvation wage. And even where there was no lay patron, or a conscientious one, the rate of tithe had often been fixed in the late Middle Ages, and never adjusted to keep pace with inflation. Yet any attempt to remedy the situation, either by raising the rate of tithes or modifying the rights of patrons, was firmly resisted by the Commons.[5]

The new king took a keen professional interest in matters theological and ecclesiastical, which, as in the case of the law, was a mixed blessing. Unlike Elizabeth, he had a great respect for the existing hierarchy; in fact, as is well known, his experience with Scots Presbyterianism had given him a positive fondness for episcopacy. On the other hand, he did not share Elizabeth's neurotic apprehension that the least manifestation of a desire for church reform threatened the very foundations of the English polity. He was relaxed in his attitudes, very willing to discuss any proposals put before him, provided they did not impugn his royal authority, and his general tolerance, good humour and informality, and his initial desire to please, roused expectations of a change.

In these circumstances the first manifestation of Puritan dissent was significantly mild. The Millenary Petition (**39**), submitted to the king on his way south in 1603 – supposedly endorsed by over a thousand ministers, though this is highly unlikely – merely called for cosmetic amendments to the Prayer Book, minor alterations in the administration of episcopal discipline, and (of course) the fostering of a godly, preaching ministry. James easily agreed to a conference, held at Hampton Court 14–16 January 1604, between the bishops and a delegation of reformers mainly drawn from the universities.

Initially the biased reporting of this conference by the conservative William Barlow gave a poor impression of the king's performance.[6] In fact, James was always at his best in face-to-face negotiation, and on this occasion he sent both parties away happy, if not entirely satisfied. He took the opportunity to affirm his belief in episcopacy, though this was not a point at issue – this was the occasion of his famous remark, 'No bishop, no king' – but he was not uncritical of the bishops. He echoed the general concern at the low standard of the parish clergy and the abuses of pluralism, and though he would not contemplate any fundamental alterations in the Church he expressed himself ready to amend anything that was shown to be dissonant with Scripture or with the practice

---

[4] Mark H. Curtis, *Oxford and Cambridge in Transition 1558–1642* (Oxford 1959), and 'The Alienated Intellectuals of Early Stuart England', *Past and Present*, no. 23 (1962), 25–43. But see Ian Green, 'Career prospects and clerical conformity in the early Stuart Church', *ibid.*, no. 90 (1981), 71–115.

[5] Usher, *Reconstruction*, i, 205–43, 352–3. Cf. Hill, *Economic Problems of the Church*, passim.

[6] See Mark H. Curtis, 'The Hampton Court Conference and its Aftermath', *History*, XLVI (1961), 1–16, and Frederick Shriver, 'Hampton Court Revisited', *Jnl Ecclesiastical History*, XXXIII (1983), 48–71.

of primitive Christianity. He agreed to minor changes in the Prayer Book, mainly in the rubrics, ordered the bishops to tidy up procedure in their lower courts, accepted proposals which it was hoped would maximise the income from tithes, and agreed to a new translation of the Bible, which eventually emerged as the Authorised Version of 1611. Typically, he even drew up instructions to the translators.[7]

In pursuance of this policy he commissioned Convocation, which met as usual at the same time as parliament, to draw up new canons for the discipline and governance of the Church, but at the same time he set up a conference between representatives of Convocation and the House of Commons.[8] This broke down on the opposition of the bishops, but James was nettled when the Commons went ahead on their own. After an abortive conference with the Lords, they drew up a whole series of bills which, by seeking to provide for 'a learned and godly ministry', prevent plurality of benefices, remove 'scandalous and unworthy ministers' and prevent clergymen being appointed magistrates, sufficiently expressed the seventeenth-century layman's view of the clergy, that they should be poor, pure, learned and unworldly. They reached the Lords so late in the session that they were not put to the trouble of rejecting them.[9] Irritated by their presumption, James gave them a tongue-lashing at the end of the session (p. 37 above), and a week later, on 16 July, he issued a proclamation which gave the clergy until 30 November to conform or suffer deprivation (40). Moreover, the canons drawn up by Convocation and issued by James in September demanded (canon xxxv) that candidates for holy orders 'willingly and *ex animo* subscribe [in writing], to three articles virtually identical to Whitgift's, accepting that the Prayer Book contained 'nothing contrary to the Word of God' and that all the Thirty-Nine Articles were 'agreeable to the Word of God' (41). In 1605 this was imposed on all university graduates, though Cambridge did not comply until 1613.[10]

However, the Millenary Petition had barely mentioned subscription, nor had it excited much attention at the Hampton Court Conference or in parliament, and while the canons of 1604 were an unqualified endorsement of orthodoxy they did embody some remarkable concessions. For instance, canon LVI, by seeking to control lecturers or preachers without cure of souls, endorsed their existence, and canon LXXII, by requiring 'prophesyings', or meetings of ministers for mutual edification or instruction, to be licensed by a bishop, allowed a practice for which Elizabeth had incontinently suspended her Archbishop of Canterbury 30 years before. Canon LXXXII, though drafted no doubt with deliberate obscurity, substantially adopted the Puritan position on the nature and location of the 'communion table', markedly at variance with the practice of Laud in the 1630s (41).

The enforcement of conformity provoked a minor reaction in the laity, in the form of petitions from some of the leading gentlemen in several counties. This in turn

---

[7] Fuller, *Church History*, III, 255–6.   [8] R. C. Munden, in Sharpe, *Faction*, pp. 66–8.

[9] They are, in the order cited, nos. 3278, 3279, 3287(a) and 3285 in *House of Lords Manuscripts*, XI. Other bills would have prohibited the residence of married men in universities or cathedral precincts, restricted the lease of episcopal lands, and made new provisions against simony (*ibid.*, nos. 3283, 3284, 3288).

[10] Even then, it was only required of graduates in divinity; James had to intervene again, in 1616, before it was extended to MAs. See C. H. Cooper, *Annals of Cambridge* (5 vols., London 1842–1908), III, 59–60, and J. B. Mullinger, *The University of Cambridge 1535–1625* (1884), p. 456–8.

provoked a disproportionate reaction from James; the presenters of the Northampton-shire petition were examined by the Privy Council and banished for a time to the country.[11] But he did not visit his anger on the clergy themselves. At Hampton Court he had commanded the bishops to treat recalcitrant ministers gently – a point he also made in the very proclamation enforcing conformity (40) – and the evidence suggests he was obeyed.[12] Contemporaries put the numbers involved at about 300, a figure whittled down by modern research to 150, of whom only 80 or 90 were deprived.[13] All the same, the conviction of many laymen that these men were the cream of the ministry kept the Commons active on their behalf. In 1606 they struck at the root of the matter by bringing in a bill 'for the more sure establishing and assurance of true religion', which required that 'no alteration should be of any substantial point of religion but by parliament with the advice and consent of the clergy in Convoca-tion'.[14] They then proceeded to bring in measures 'for the providing of a learned and godly ministry' and 'against scandalous and unworthy ministers', very similar to those of 1604, and subject to a similar fate in the Lords.[15] In 1607 and 1610 they brought in bills to make the terms of the Subscription Act of 1571, which merely obliged ministers to accept 'all the Articles of Religion which only concern the true Christian Faith and the doctrine of the sacraments', the sole test of orthodoxy,[16] and they returned to the charge in their Petition on Religion in 1610 (43), though they did admit the king's 'supreme power, as well in the Church as in the Commonwealth'.

James's reply was, that 'there hath never been hitherto any particular church in the world (for aught that we have read or heard) that hath allowed such ministers to preach in it, as have refused to subscribe to the doctrine and discipline settled in it, and maintained by it'; but he shrewdly added that he did not lump all the recalcitrants together, and if he were given a list of the persons concerned he would try to distinguish between them, 'in regard of better hope of conformity in some than in others, although they be in the same degree offenders by our laws'.[17] He was probably as good as his word, because agitation on this point died away.

Increasingly after 1610 the problem was not to ensure more and better preaching, but to restrain and control it. In his dealings with the Church, as with the law, James displayed a strong sense of professionalism. He and his chosen bishops were the only true experts in theology and doctrine, and his impatience with the less well equipped who yet presumed to meddle with the mysteries of the faith is evident in the prologue to one of his most idiosyncratic proclamations, that suppressing Dr Cowell's *Interpreter* in 1610 (42).

---

[11] He regarded this petition as treasonable, perhaps because it contained an implied threat of further action; Gardiner, *History*, I, 198–9. (The original is PRO SP14/12, 69.) See also *HMC Salisbury*, XVII, 7–8, 34–5, 56–7, and Babbage, *Bancroft*, pp. 125ff.

[12] Curtis, 'Hampton Court', p. 9; *HMC Salisbury*, XVII, 34–5, 46–7, 58–9, 133.

[13] R. G. Usher, 'The Deprivation of Puritan Ministers', *EHR*, XXIV (1909), 232–46; *idem, Reconstruction*, bk II, ch. 7; Babbage, *Bancroft*, ch. 6.

[14] Some Members even objected to the last phrase, but Sir Edwin Sandys told them 'that the papists would say, not without show, that we professed only a statute religion'; *The Parliamentary Diary of Robert Bowyer 1606–7*, ed. D. H. Willson (Minneapolis 1931), p. 52 (24 February 1606).

[15] *House of Lords Manuscripts*, XI, nos. 3293, 3287(b).

[16] *Ibid.*, nos. 3307, 3316. The Subscription Act (13 Eliz. c. 12) is printed *PCD*, pp. 64–5.

[17] 23 July 1610, *LJ*, II, 658.

However, much of the foregoing can be classified as superficial irritation on both sides. James's finest achievement was the establishment of a religious *détente* which had entirely eluded Elizabeth. He knew when to yield, and when to stand firm; when to enforce the rules, and when to bend them. He controlled the neurotic propensity to confrontation displayed by that typically Elizabethan prelate Richard Bancroft, Archbishop of Canterbury 1604–11, and on his death replaced him by the eirenic and dispassionate George Abbott. Their authority carefully controlled from above, and their activities watched, the bishops were now generally accepted, if with varying degrees of enthusiasm, and their example respected. Conformity was not pressed to the limit, the quality and numbers of the clergy were visibly improving, and 'the general confidence in freedom to preach the Gospel in a Protestant Church seems to have been at a higher point [in the early 1620s] than it was under Elizabeth or Charles'. John Pym in 1629 even tried to include King James in a roll-call of the 'Fathers of the Church'.[18]

Even then, the situation had begun to deteriorate before James's death. There was still a correlation between the intensity of Puritanism at home and the agressiveness of Catholicism abroad. The death of Philip II in 1598 had led to a relaxation of tension; so had the Edict of Nantes, safeguarding the rights of the French Huguenots, in the same year. The peace between England and Spain in 1604 and the truce between Spain and the Dutch in 1609 confirmed a trend which was only slightly disturbed by isolated acts of regression like the Gunpowder Plot of 1605 and the assassination of Henry IV in 1610 – both of which seemed to frighten James more than they did his subjects. So, the outbreak of the German War in 1618, leading rapidly to the annexation of the Palatinate and the renewal of the Spanish–Dutch War, was a sudden and profound shock to public opinion. There was widespread sympathy for the Elector Palatine and his Electress, James's popular daughter Elizabeth, and a growing fear that the success of the Emperor Ferdinand and Maximilian of Bavaria heralded the ultimate victory of Catholicism. A similar crisis in the 1570s and 1580s had persuaded many Englishmen that the Church of England must be strengthened by an injection of radical reform, and there are signs of this again in the early 1620s. The King's Directions to Preachers in August 1622 (**44**) were provoked by violent attacks from the pulpit on Catholics in general and on Spain in particular, but they were equally concerned to suppress radical Puritan speculation and exhortation. Preachers were confined to the exposition of the Thirty-Nine Articles, and the bishops were sharply ordered to exercise greater care in the licensing of lecturers – 'a new body, severed from the ancient clergy'. The printed word was covered by a proclamation of September 1623, reviving the 'Star Chamber' decree of 1586 against unlicensed printing, though a year later a further proclamation admitted that the number of 'seditious, puritanical books and pamphlets, scandalous to our person and state', had if anything increased, and declared that henceforth no works on religion or government were to be published without the imprimatur of an archbishop, the vice-chancellor of Oxford or Cambridge, or the bishop of London.[19]

---

[18] Russell, *Parliaments and Politics*, pp. 419–20. Sharpe makes the point (*Faction*, p. 21) that the reformers never despaired of James, as they had of Elizabeth.

[19] *SRP*, I, nos. 247 (25 September 1623), 256 (15 August 1624).

Another straw in the wind was the Commons' increasing concern with sabbatarianism, though this was an issue on which they had always been at odds with James. In 1606 a bill for the stricter observance of the Lord's Day was sent up to the Lords as early as 17 February but went no further; in 1614 a similar bill was read on the first day of the session, but it was abortive, of course.[20] But in May 1618, returning via Lancashire from a visit to Scotland, James came to the conclusion that the obstinate survival of Catholicism in that county was due to the Protestants' over-precise enforcement of Lord's Day observance.[21] With typical impulsiveness he at once issued his controversial 'Declaration of Sports', which laid it down that once they had attended Divine Service on a Sunday 'our good people be not disturbed, letted or discouraged from any lawful recreation, such as dancing, either men or women, archery for men, leaping, vaulting or any other such harmless recreation, nor from having May games, Whitsun ales and Morris dances, and the setting of maypoles and other sports therewith used', though it specifically forbad 'bear and bull baitings, interludes [sc. plays], and, at all times in the meaner sort of people by law prohibited, bowling' (TCD, pp. 54–6). The order that this be read in churches caused many a clergyman considerable heart-searching, though some eased their consciences by pretending to believe that it applied only to Lancashire, and others were consoled by the fact that they did not have to signify their agreement with it.[22]

The parliament of 1621 lost no time in debating a bill 'for punishing of abuses on the Sabbath day', but James forbad them to legislate against any pursuits allowed by his Declaration of Sports, and they heeded his recommendation that they turn to more important matters.[23] In 1624 James was happy to pass an act 'for repressing of drunkenness', and another 'to prevent and reform profane swearing and cursing' (21 Jac. I, cc. 7, 20), but he vetoed another bill to punish abuses committed on the Lord's Day. He was ever ready to join with the governing classes in regulating the private morals of the poor – in 1604 he had consented to no less than four statutes in this vein, for repressing drunkenness, regulating alehouses, and restraining 'inordinate haunting and tippling in inns, alehouses and other victualling houses' – but he was not willing to make Sunday a social desert. His son took the same view, and though the first act of Charles I's reign (1 Car. I, c. 1) was for the better observance of the Lord's Day, it merely enforced the exclusions and inclusions of the Declaration of Sports.[24] We are coming to realise that in the seventeenth century strict Lord's Day observance was a minority fad. But it was a fad disproportionately represented amongst the upper classes, and in their care for the comfort and enjoyment of the people at large the first two Stuart kings were making concessions which would bring them no political return.

---

[20] House of Lords Manuscripts, XI, no. 3291; Commons Debates 1621, VII, 634. Cf. Foster, Proceedings, II, 408.

[21] James Tait, 'The Declaration of Sports for Lancashire', EHR, XXXII (1917), 561–8.

[22] Fuller, Church History, III, 303–6.

[23] The Commons took the occasion humourlessly to expel an over-clever young lawyer from Lincoln's Inn who pointed out that the Sabbath was properly Saturday, and that King David had danced before the Ark of the Lord; Commons Debates 1621, II 82, IV, 52–3.

[24] Whereas the abortive bill of 1606 would have prohibited 'morris dances, hunting, coursing, hawking, church ales, dancing, rush-bearing, may games, whitsun ales, outhurlings, inhurlings and wakes'. The problem was that the Declaration of Sports by implication licensed any activity it did not specifically prohibit.

But the most significant straw in the wind was the attack launched in 1624 on Richard Montague, rector of Stanford Rivers, for his pamphlet *A New Gag for an Old Goose*. His rejection of predestination, his acceptance of a modified form of transubstantiation in the elements, his allowance of the use of pictures, images or statues in churches, were to some extent dictated by circumstances – he was engaged in a violent polemic against the Catholic controversialist Matthew Kellison – but they were an extreme example of the kind of position now being adopted by the more advanced right-wing thinkers in the Church, whose most prominent spokesman was William Laud, bishop of St David's. James's comment, typically enough, was, 'If that is to be a papist, so am I a papist', and in the closing weeks of the parliament of 1624 the Commons were content to refer the matter to Archbishop Abott.[25] In the next parliament, in the next reign, they were not to be so easily satisfied.

39. The Millenary Petition, 1603

The humble petition of ministers of the Church of England, desiring reformation of
certain ceremonies and abuses of the Church

To the most Christian and excellent prince, our gracious and dread sovereign, James, by the grace of God, [etc.], We, the ministers of the Church of England that desire reformation, wish a long, prosperous and happy reign over us in this life, and in the next everlasting salvation.

Most gracious and dread sovereign, seeing it hath pleased the Divine Majesty, to the great comfort of all good Christians, to advance your Highness according to your just title, to the peaceable government of this Church and Commonwealth of England; we the ministers of the gospel in this land, neither as factious men affecting a popular parity in the Church, nor as schismatics aiming at the dissolution of the state ecclesiastical; but as the faithful servants of Christ, and loyal subjects to your Majesty, desiring and longing for the redress of divers abuses of the Church, could do no less, in our obedience to God, service to your Majesty, love to his Church, than acquaint your princely Majesty with our particular griefs. For, as your princely pen writeth: 'The king, as a good physician, must first know what peccant humours his patient naturally is most subject unto, before he can begin his cure.' And, although divers of us that sue for reformation have formerly, in respect of the times, subscribed to the [Prayer] Book, some upon protestation, some upon exposition given them, some with condition[s], rather than the Church should have been deprived of their labour and ministry; yet now we, to the number of more than a thousand, of your Majesty's subjects and ministers, all groaning as under a common burden of human rites and ceremonies, do with one joint consent, humble ourselves at your Majesty's feet to be eased and relieved in this

[25] Gardiner, *History*, v, 351–4.

behalf. Our humble suit, then, unto your Majesty is, that [of] these offences following, some may be removed, some amended, some qualified:

I. *In the church-service.* That the cross in baptism, interrogatories ministered to infants, confirmation, as superfluous, may be taken away: baptism not to be ministered by women, and so explained: the cap and surplice not urged: that examination may go before the communion: that it be ministered with a sermon; that divers terms of *priests* and *absolution*, and some others used, with the ring in marriage, and other such like in the Book, may be corrected: the longsomeness of service abridged: church-songs and music moderated to better edification: that the Lord's day be not profaned, the rest upon holy-days not so strictly urged: that there may be a uniformity of doctrine prescribed: no popish opinion to be any more taught or defended: no ministers charged to teach their people to bow at the name of Jesus: that the canonical scripture only be read in the church.

II. *Concerning church ministers.* That none hereafter be admitted into the ministry but able and sufficient men; and those to preach diligently, and especially upon the Lord's day: that such as be already entered, and cannot preach, may either be removed, and some charitable course taken with them for their relief; or else be forced, according to the value of their livings, to maintain preachers: that non-residency be not permitted: that King Edward's statute for the lawfulness of ministers' marriage be revived: that ministers be not urged to subscribe but according to the law to the Articles of Religion, and the King's Supremacy only.

III. *For church-livings and maintenance.* That bishops leave their commendams; some holding prebends, some parsonages, some vicarages with their bishoprics: that double-beneficed men be not suffered to hold some two, some three, benefices with cure, and some two, three, or four dignities besides: that impropriations annexed to bishoprics and colleges be demised only to the preachers-incumbents, for the old rent: that the impropriations of laymen's fees may be charged with a sixth or seventh part of the worth, to the maintenance of the preaching minister.

IV. *For church-discipline.* That the discipline and excommunication may be administered according to Christ's own institution; or, at the least, that enormities may be redressed: as, namely, that excommunication come not forth under the name of lay persons, chancellors, officials, &c.: that men be not excommunicated for trifles, and twelve-penny matters: that none be excommunicated without consent of his pastor: that the officers be not suffered to extort unreasonable fees: that none having jurisdiction, or registers' places, put out the same to farm: that diverse popish canons (as for restraint of marriage at certain times) be reversed: that the longsomeness of suits in ecclesiastical courts, which hang sometimes two, three, four, five, six, or seven years, may be restrained: that the oath *ex officio*, whereby men are forced to accuse themselves, be more sparingly used: that licences for marriage, without banns asked, be more cautiously granted.

These, with such other abuses yet remaining, and practised in the Church of England, we are able to show not to be agreeable to the scriptures, if it shall please your Highness farther to hear us, or more at large by writing to be informed, or by conference among the learned to be resolved. And yet we doubt not but that, without any farther process, your Majesty, of whose Christian judgment we have received so good a taste already, is able of yourself to judge the equity of this cause. God, we trust, hath appointed your Highness our physician to heal these diseases. And we say with Mordecai to Esther, 'Who knoweth, whether you are come to the kingdom for such a time?' Thus your Majesty shall do that which, we are persuaded, shall be acceptable to God; honourable to your Majesty in all succeeding ages; profitable to his Church, which shall be thereby increased; comfortable to your ministers, who shall be no more suspended, silenced, disgraced, imprisoned, for men's traditions; and prejudicial to none, but to those that seek their own quiet, credit and profit in the world. Thus, with all dutiful submission, referring ourselves to your Majesty's pleasure for your gracious answer, as God shall direct you; we most humbly recommend your Highness to the Divine Majesty; whom we beseech for Christ's sake to dispose your royal heart to do herein what shall be to his glory, the good of his Church, and your endless comfort.

Your Majesty's most humble subjects, the ministers of the gospel, that desire not a disorderly innovation, but a due and godly reformation.

Fuller, Church History, III, 215–17

40. A proclamation enjoining conformity to the form of the service of God established, 16 July 1604

The care which we have had, and pains which we have taken, to settle the affairs of this Church of England in a uniformity, as well of doctrine as of government, both of them agreeable to the Word of God, the doctrine of the primitive Church, and the laws heretofore established for these matters in this realm, may sufficiently appear by our former actions. For no sooner did the infection of the plague, reigning immediately after our entry into this kingdom, give us leave to have any assembly, but we held at our honour of Hampton Court for that purpose a conference between some principal bishops and deans of this Church and such other learned men as understood or favoured the opinions of those that seek alteration, before ourself and our Council.

Of which conference the issue was, that no well-grounded matter appeared to us or our said Council why the state of the Church here by law established should in any material point be altered. Nor did those that before had seemed to affect such alteration, when they heard the contrary arguments, greatly insist upon it, but seemed to be satisfied themselves, and to undertake within reasonable time to satisfy all others that were misled with opinion that there was any just cause of alteration. Whereupon we published by our proclamation[26] what had been the issue of that conference, hoping that when the same should be made known, all reasonable men would have rested satisfied with that which had been done, and not have moved further trouble or speech of matters whereof so solemn and advised determination had been made.

Notwithstanding, at the late assembly of our parliament there wanted not many that renewed with no little earnestness the questions before determined, and many more as well, about the Book of Common Prayer, as other matters of church government, and importuned us for our assent to many alterations therein; but . . . the end of all their motions and overtures falling out to be none other in substance than was before at the conference at Hampton Court, that is, that no apparent or grounded reason was shown why either the Book of Common Prayer or the church discipline here by law established should be changed, which were unreasonable considering that particular and personal abuses are remediable otherwise than by making general alterations, we have thought good once again to give notice thereof to all our subjects by public declaration, who we doubt not but will receive great satisfaction when they shall understand that after so much impugning there appeareth no cause why the form of the Service of God wherein they have been nourished so many years should be changed; and consequently to admonish them all in general to conform themselves thereunto, without listening to the troublesome spirits of some persons who never receive contentment, either in civil or ecclesiastical matters, but in their own fantasies, especially of certain ministers who, under pretended zeal of reformation, are the chief authors of divisions and sects among our people. Of many of which we hope that now, when they shall see that such things as they have proposed for alteration prove upon trial so weakly grounded as [to] deserve not admittance, they will out of their own judgment conform themselves to better advice, and not omit the principal and substantial parts of their duties for shadows and semblances of zeal, but rather bend their strength with our intent to join in one end, that is, the establishing of the Gospel and recovering of our people seduced out of the hands of the common adversaries of our religion, which shall never be well performed but by a uniformity of our endeavours therein.

But if our hope herein fail us, we must advertise them that our duty towards

[26] Of 5 March 1604, SRP, I, no. 35.

God requireth at our hands that what intractable men do not perform upon admonition they must be compelled unto by authority, whereof the supreme power resting in our hands by God's ordinance we are bound to use the same in nothing more than in preservation of the Church's tranquillity, which by God's grace we are fully purposed to do. And yet by advice of our Council, and opinion of the bishops, although our former proclamations, both before the conference and since, ought to be a sufficient warning and admonition to all men who are within the danger of them, we have thought good to give time to all ministers disobedient to the orders of the Church and to ecclesiastical authority here by law established, and who for such disobedience, either in the days of the queen our sister of famous memory deceased or since our reign, have incurred any censures of the Church or penalties of laws, until the last of November now next ensuing to bethink themselves of the course they will hold therein.

In which mean time both they may resolve either to conform themselves to the Church of England and obey the same, or else to dispose of themselves and their families some other ways as to them shall seem meet, and the bishops and others whom it concerneth provide meet persons to be substitutes in the place of those who shall wilfully abandon their charges upon so slight causes, assuring them that after that day we shall not fail to do that which princely providence requireth at our hands, that is, to put in execution all ways and means that may take from among our people all grounds and occasions of sects, divisions and unquietness; whereof, as we wish there may never be occasion given us to make proof, but that this our admonition may have equal force in all men's hearts to work a universal conformity, so we do require all archbishops, bishops and other ecclesiastical persons to do their utmost endeavours, by conferences, arguments, persuasions, and by all other ways of love and gentleness, to reclaim all that be in the ministry to the obedience of our church laws, for which purpose only we have enlarged the time formerly prefixed for their remove or reformation, to the end that if it be possible that uniformity which we desire may be wrought by clemency and by weight of reason, and not by rigour of law. And the like advertisement do we give to all civil magistrates, gentlemen, and others of understanding, as well abroad in the counties as in cities and towns, requiring them also not in any sort to support, favour or countenance any such factious ministers in their obstinacy, of whose endeavours we doubt not but so good success may follow, as this our admonition, with their endeavours, may prevent the use of any other means to retain our people in their due obedience to us, and in unity of mind to the service of Almighty God.

SRP, I, no. 41

41. The canons of 1604

OF THE CHURCH OF ENGLAND

* * *

V. *Impugners of the Articles of Religion established in the Church of England censured*

Whosoever shall hereafter affirm, That any of the nine and thirty Articles agreed upon by the archbishops and bishops of both provinces and the whole clergy in the Convocation holden at London in the year of our Lord God 1562, for avoiding diversities of opinions and for the establishing of consent touching true religion, are in any part superstitious or erroneous, or such as he may not with a good conscience subscribe unto; let him be excommunicated . . . [etc.]

VI. *Impugners of the rites and ceremonies established in the Church of England censured*

Whosoever shall hereafter affirm, That the rites and ceremonies of the Church of England by law established are wicked, anti-Christian, or superstitious, or such as, being commanded by lawful authority, men who are zealously and godly affected may not with any good conscience approve them, use them, or, as occasion requireth, subscribe unto them; let him be excommunicated . . . [etc.]

VII. *Impugners of the government of the Church of England by archbishops, bishops, &c., censured*

Whosoever shall hereafer affirm, That the government of the Church of England under his Majesty by archbishops, bishops, deans, archdeacons and the rest that bear office in the same, is anti-Christian or repugnant to the Word of God; let him be excommunicated . . . [etc.]

* * *

MINISTERS, THEIR ORDINATION, FUNCTION AND CHARGE

* * *

XXXIV. *The quality of such as are to be made ministers*

No bishop shall henceforth admit any person into sacred orders, which is not of his own diocese, except he be either of one of the universities of this realm, or except he shall bring letters dimissory (so termed) from the bishop of whose diocese he is; and desiring to be a deacon is three and twenty years old, and to be a priest four and twenty years complete; and hath taken some degree of school in either of the said universities; or at the least, except he be able to yield an account of his faith in Latin, according to the Articles . . . [of 1562], and to confirm the same by sufficient testimonies out of the Holy Scriptures . . .

* * *

XXXVI. *Subscription required of such as are to be made Ministers*

No person shall hereafter be received into the ministry, nor either by institution or collation admitted to any ecclesiastical living, nor suffered to preach, catechise, or to be a lecturer or reader of divinity in either university, or in any cathedral or collegiate church, city or market-town, parish church, chapel or in any other place within this realm, except he be licensed either by the archbishop, or by the bishop of the diocese where he is to be placed, under the hands and seals, or by one of the two universities under their seal likewise; and except he shall first subscribe to these three articles following, in such manner and sort as we have here appointed.

(I) That the king's Majesty, under God, is the only supreme governor of this realm, and of all other his Highness's dominions and countries, as well in all spiritual or ecclesiastical things or causes as temporal; and that no foreign prince, person, prelate, state or potentate hath, or ought to have, any jurisdiction, power, superiority, pre-eminence or authority, ecclesiastical or spiritual, within his Majesty's said realms, dominions and countries.

(II) That the Book of Common Prayer, and of ordering of bishops, priests and deacons, containeth in it nothing contrary to the Word of God, and that it may lawfully so be used; and that he himself will use the form in the said Book prescribed in public prayer and administration of the sacraments, and none other.

(III) That he alloweth the Book of Articles of Religion agreed upon by the archbishops and bishops of both provinces, and the whole clergy, in the Convocation holden at London in the year of our Lord God 1562; and that he acknowledgeth all and every the articles therein contained, being in number nine and thirty, besides the ratification, to be agreeable to the Word of God.

To these three articles whosoever will subscribe, he shall, for the avoiding of all ambiguities, subscribe in this order and form of words, setting down both his Christian and surname, viz.:

'I, N. N., do willingly and *ex animo* subscribe to these three articles above mentioned, and to all things that are contained in them.'

And if any bishop shall ordain, admit or license any as is aforesaid, except he first have subscribed in manner and form as here we have appointed, he shall be suspended from giving of orders and licenses to preach for the space of twelve months. But if either of the universities shall offend therein, we leave them to the danger of the law, and his Majesty's censure.

* * *

XLI. *Licences for plurality of benefices limited, and residence enjoined*

No licence or dispensation for the keeping of more benefices with cure than one shall be granted to any but such only as shall be thought very well worthy for his learning, and very well able and sufficient to discharge his duty; that is, who shall have taken the degree of Master of Arts at the least in one of the universities of this realm, and be a public and sufficient preacher licensed. Provided always that he be by a good and sufficient caution bound to make his personal residence in each of his said benefices for some reasonable time in every year, and that the said benefices be not more than thirty miles distant asunder; and lastly, that he have under him in the benefice where he doth not reside a preacher lawfully allowed, that is able sufficiently to teach and instruct the people.

★   ★   ★

L. *Strangers not admitted to preach without showing their licence*

Neither the minister, churchwardens, nor any other officers of the Church shall suffer any man to preach within their churches or chapels but such as by showing their licence to preach shall appear unto them to be sufficiently authorised thereunto, as is aforesaid.

★   ★   ★

LVI. *Preachers and lecturers to read Divine Service and administer the Sacraments twice a year at the least*

Every minister being possessed of a benefice that hath cure and charge of souls, although he chiefly attend to preaching, and hath a curate under him to execute the other duties which are to be performed for him in the church, and likewise every other stipendiary preacher that readeth any lecture, or catechiseth, or preacheth in any church or chapel, shall twice at the least every year read himself the Divine Service upon two several Sundays publicly, and at the usual times, both in the forenoon and afternoon, in the church which he so possesseth, or where he readeth, catechiseth, or preacheth, as is aforesaid; and shall likewise as often in every year administer the sacraments of baptism (if there be any to be baptised), and of the Lord's Supper, in such manner and form, and with the observation of all such rites and ceremonies, as are prescribed by the Book of Common Prayer in that behalf; which if he do not accordingly perform, then shall he that is possessed of a benefice (as before) be suspended; and he that is but a reader, preacher, or catechiser, be removed from his place by the bishop of the diocese, until he or they shall submit themselves to perform all the said duties in such manner and sort as before is prescribed.

★   ★   ★

LVIII. *Ministers reading Divine Service and administering the Sacraments to wear surplices, and graduates therewithal hoods*

Every Minister saying the public prayers, or ministering the Sacraments, or other rites of the Church, shall wear a decent and comely surplice with sleeves, to be provided at the charge of the parish. And if any question arise touching the matter, decency, or comeliness thereof, the same shall be decided by the discretion of the ordinary. Furthermore, such ministers as are graduates shall wear upon their surplices at such times, such hoods as by the orders of the universities are agreeable to their degrees, which no minister shall wear (being no graduate) under pain of suspension . . .

★   ★   ★

LXXII. *Ministers not to appoint public or private Fasts or Prophecies, or to exorcise, but by authority*

No minister or ministers shall, without the license and direction of the bishop of the diocese first obtained and had under his hand and seal, appoint or keep any solemn fasts, either publicly or in any private houses, other than such as by law are, or by public authority shall be appointed, nor shall be wittingly present at any of them, under pain of suspension for the first fault, of excommunication for the second, and of deposition from the ministry for the third. Neither shall any minister not licensed, as is aforesaid, presume to appoint or hold any meetings for sermons, commonly termed by some prophecies or exercises, in market-towns, or other places, under the said pains: nor, without such licence, to attempt upon any pretence whatsoever, either of possession or obsession, by fasting and prayer, to cast out any devil or devils, under pain of the imputation of imposture or cosenage, and deposition from the ministry.

★   ★   ★

THINGS APPERTAINING TO CHURCHES

★   ★   ★

LXXXII. *A decent communion table in every church*

Whereas we have no doubt but that in all churches within the realm of England convenient and decent tables are provided and placed for the celebration of the Holy Communion, we appoint that the same tables shall from time to time be kept and repaired in sufficient and seemly manner, and covered in time of Divine Service with a carpet of silk or other decent stuff thought meet by the ordinary of the place, if any question be made of it, and with a fair linen cloth at the time of the ministration, as becometh that table, and so stand, saving when the said Holy Communion is to be administered, at which time the same shall be placed in so good sort within the church or chancel as thereby the minister may be more conveniently heard of the communicants in his prayer and ministration, and the communicants also more conveniently and in more number may communicate with the said minister . . .   Cardwell, *Synodalia*, I, 250-93 *passim*

42. A Proclamation touching Dr Cowell's book called the Interpreter, 25 March 1610

This later age and times of the world wherein we are fallen, is so much given to verbal profession, as well of religion, as of all commendable moral virtues, but wanting the actions and deeds agreeable to so specious a profession, as it hath bred such an insatiable curiosity in many men's spirits, and such an itching in the tongues and pens of most men, as nothing is left unsearched to the bottom, both in talking and writing. For from the very highest mysteries in the Godhead, and the most inscrutable counsels in the Trinity, to the very lowest pit of Hell, and the confused actions of the devils there, there is nothing now unsearched into by the curiosity of men's brains, men not being contented with the knowledge of so much of the will of God as it hath pleased him to reveal, but they will needs sit with him in his most privy closet, and become privy of his most inscrutable counsels. And therefore it is no wonder, that men in these our days do not spare to wade in all the deepest mysteries that belong to the persons or state of kings or princes, that are gods upon earth, since we see (as we have already said) that they spare not God himself . . . *SRP*, I, no. 110

43. Commons' Petition on Religion, July 1610

Most Gracious and Dread Sovereign,

Since it hath pleased Almighty God of his unspeakable goodness and mercy towards us to call your Majesty to the government of this kingdom, and hath crowned you with supreme power, as well in the Church as in the Commonwealth, for the advancement of his glory and the general benefit of all the subjects of this land, we do in all humility present at the feet of your excellent Majesty ourselves and our desires, full of confidence in the assurances of your religious mind and princely disposition that you will be graciously pleased to give life and effect to these our petitions, greatly tending (as undoubtedly we conceive) to the Glory of God, the good of his Church, and safety of your most royal person, wherein we acknowledge our greatest happiness to consist.

I. Whereas good and provident laws have been made for the maintenance of God's true religion, and safety of your Majesty's royal person, issue and estate, against Jesuits, seminary priests and popish recusants; and although your Majesty by your godly, learned and judicious writings have declared your Christian and princely zeal in the defence of the religion established, and have very lately (to the comfort of your best affected subjects) published to both Houses of Parliament your princely will and pleasure that recusants should not be concealed, but detected and convicted; yet for that the laws are not executed against the priests, who are the corrupters of the people in religion and loyalty, and many recusants have already compounded, and (as it is to be feared) more and more (except your Majesty in your great wisdom prevent the same) will compound with those that beg their penalties, which maketh the laws altogether fruitless, or of little or none effect, and the offenders to become bold, obdurate and unconformable.[27]

Your Majesty therefore would be pleased, at the humble suit of your Commons in this present parliament assembled, in the causes so highly concerning the Glory of God, the preservation of true religion, of your Majesty and state, to suffer your Highness's natural clemency to retire itself, and give place to justice, and to lay your royal command upon all your ministers of justice, both ecclesiastical and civil, to see the laws made against Jesuits, seminary priests and recusants (of what kind and sort soever) to be duly and exactly executed without dread or delay; and that your Majesty would be pleased likewise to take into your own hands the penalties due for recusancy, and that the same be not converted to the private gain of some, to your infinite loss, the emboldening of the papists, and decay of true religion.

II. Whereas also divers painful and learned pastors, that have long travailed in the work of the ministry with good fruit and blessing of their labours, who were ever ready to perform the legal subscription appointed by the statute of the 13th of Elizabeth, which only concerneth the confession of the true Christian Faith, and doctrine of the Sacraments; yet for not conforming in points of ceremonies, and refusing the subscription directed by the late Canons, have been removed from their ecclesiastical livings, being their freehold, and debarred from all means of maintenance, to the great grief of sundry your Majesty's well-affected subjects, seeing the whole people that want instructions are by this means punished, and through ignorance lie open to the seducements of popish and ill-affected persons.

We therefore most humbly beseech your Majesty would be graciously pleased that such deprived and silenced Ministers may, by licence or

[27] Petyt has *uncomfortable*.

permission of the Reverend Fathers, in their several dioceses, instruct and preach unto the people, in such parishes and places where they may be employed, so as they apply themselves in their Ministry to wholesome doctrine and exhortation, and live quietly and peaceably in their callings, and shall not by writing or preaching impugn things established by public authority.

III. Whereas likewise through plurality of benefices, and toleration of non-residency in many who possess not the meanest of livings with cure of souls, the people in divers places want instruction, and are ignorant and easy to be seduced, whereby the adversaries of our religion gain great advantage; and although the pluralities and non-residents do frame excuse of the smallness[28] of some livings, and pretend the maintenance of learning, yet we find by experience that they, coupling many of the greatest livings, do leave the least helpless, and the best as ill served and supplied with preachers as the meanest. And where[as] pluralists, heaping up many livings into one hand, do by that means keep divers learned men from maintenance, to the discouragement of students and the hindrance of learning, and the non-residents (forsaking or absenting themselves from their pastoral charges) do leave the people as a prey to the popish seducers; it might therefore please your most excellent Majesty, for remedy of those evils in the Church, to provide that dispensations for plurality of benefices with cure of souls may be prohibited, and that the toleration of non-residency may be restrained. So shall all true religion be better upheld, and the people more instructed in divine and civil duties.

★ ★ ★

Petyt, Jus Parliamentarium, pp. 318-21

44. Directions to preachers, 1622

[The king to the Archbishop of Canterbury, 4 August 1622]

Most Reverend Father in God, right trusty and entirely beloved counsellor, we greet you well.

Forasmuch as the abuses and extravagances of preachers in the pulpit have been in all times suppressed in this realm by some act of council or state with the advice and resolution of grave and learned prelates, . . . and whereas at this present divers young students, by reading of late writers and ungrounded divines, do broach many times unprofitable, unsound, seditious and dangerous doctrines, to the scandal of the Church and disquiet of the state and present government, we upon humble representation unto us of these inconveniences by yourself and sundry other grave and learned prelates of this Church, as also

---

[28] Petyt has *smallest*.

of our princely care and zeal for the extirpation of schism and dissension growing from these seeds, and for the settling of a religious and peaceable government both in Church and Commonwealth, do by these our special letters straitly charge and command you to use all possible care and diligence that these limitations and cautions herewith sent unto you concerning preachers be duly and strictly from henceforth put in practice and observed by the several bishops within your jurisdiction. And to this end our pleasure is, that you send them forthwith copies of these directions, to be speedily sent and communicated unto every parson, vicar, curate, lecturer and minister, in every cathedral or parish church within their several dioceses; and that you do earnestly require them to employ their utmost endeavours in the performance of this so important a business, letting them know that we have a special eye unto their proceedings and expect a strict account thereof, both from you and every of them. And these our letters shall be your sufficient warrant and discharge in that behalf.

[Directions enclosed]

I. That no preacher under the degree and calling of a bishop or dean of a cathedral or collegiate church (and they upon the king's days and set festivals) do take occasion, by the expounding of any text of scripture whatsoever, to fall into any set discourse or common place [*sc.* theme], otherwise than by opening the coherence and division of the text, which shall not be comprehended and warranted, in essence, substance, effect or natural inference, within some one of the Articles of Religion . . ., or in some of the homilies set forth by authority of the Church of England not only for a help for the non-preaching but withal for a pattern and boundary (as it were) for the preaching ministers . . .

II. That no parson, vicar, curate or lecturer shall preach any sermon or collation hereafter upon Sundays and holy days in the afternoon in any cathedral or parish church throughout the kingdom but upon some part of the Catechism or some text taken out of the Creed, Ten Commandments, or the Lord's Prayer (funeral sermons only excepted) . . .

III. That no preacher of what title soever under the degree of bishop, or dean at the least, do from henceforth presume to preach in any popular auditory the deep points of predestination, election, reprobation, or of the universality, efficacy, resistibility or irresistibility, of God's grace; but leave those themes rather to be handled by the learned men, and that moderately and modestly by way of use and application rather than by way of positive doctrines, being fitter for the schools and universities than for simple auditories.

IV. That no preacher, of what title or denomination soever, from henceforth shall presume in any auditory within this kingdom, to declare, limit, or bound out, by way of positive doctrine, in any lecture or sermon the power, prerogative, and jurisdiction, authority, or duty of sovereign princes, or otherwise meddle with these matters of state and the differences betwixt princes and the people . . .

V. That no preacher, of what title or denomination soever, shall presume causelessly (and without invitation from the text) to fall into bitter invectives and indecent railing speeches against the persons of either papists or Puritans, but modestly and gravely (when they are occasioned thereunto by the text of Scripture), free both the doctrine and discipline of the Church of England from the aspersions of either adversary, especially where the auditory is suspected to be tainted with the one or the other infection.

VI. Lastly, that the archbishops and bishops of the kingdom (whom his Majesty hath good cause to blame for their former remissness) be more wary and choice in licensing of preachers, . . . and that all the lecturers throughout the kingdom of England (a new body severed from the ancient clergy, as being neither parsons, vicars, nor curates) be licensed henceforward in the Court of Faculties only by recommendation of the party from the bishop of the diocese under his hand and seal, with a *fiat* from the Lord Archbishop of Canterbury, and a confirmation under the Great Seal of England . . .

Cardwell, Documentary Annals, II, 198–203

II. THE LAUDIAN REVOLUTION

The rise of 'Laudianism' – for want of a better term – had its beginning in James I's reign; when Charles came to the throne the leaders of the movement; Buckeridge, Howson, Neile, Cosin, Laud himself; were already quite high on the ladder of preferment.

The new king had many advantages. As we have seen, he was the first monarch to be raised from childhood in the Church of England, and we need not doubt that he sincerely loved it and found his inner satisfaction there. But for all his sincerity he lacked the deep theological expertise which had enabled his father to impose his will on warring churchmen, and unlike his father he made the mistake of committing himself wholeheartedly to one faction.

The strength of that faction – if 'faction' it was – has been underestimated until quite recently. The Church of England incorporated within it many different strands or elements, and the scholarship of the past hundred years has been too much focussed on the Puritan element. There were many who rejected the kind of hair-splitting pulpit exegesis, the laborious Bible-reading, associated with Puritanism, in favour of a less didactic, more sacramental approach, which placed the emphasis of worship on the communion service (whether communion was actually received or not), on corporate singing and on the recital of set prayers from Cranmer's book. Such men found the Puritan approach to eschatology essentially a matter of accountancy; the minute assessment of one's personal conduct, on a strict profit and loss basis, had to be measured against biblical texts of transcendant obscurity whose correct interpretation was nevertheless vital. They preferred, with Laud and the king, to rest their hopes on blind faith, supported by ritual observance.

The verdict handed down in 1662 was essentially in favour of the Laudian style, though not of Laud himself, of course. Puritanism, however vocal and at times influential, was essentially a minority movement; the 'Laudian' form of worship, glamorous, emotionally satisfying, morally undemanding, met the needs of a majority. Moreover, it was more nationalistic than Puritanism; it taught that the *ecclesia anglicana* was the only true heir to the primitive church of the Apostles and the Fathers, preserved by its isolation and independence from the fatal corruptions of the medieval papacy. Other churches should learn from her, not vice versa. In contrast, though some Elizabethan Puritans had seen England as the Elect Nation, especially called for God's higher purpose, Puritanism was essentially a branch of an international movement in which England occupied a subordinate place. In fact, she was a backward pupil, who could and must learn from 'the example of the best reformed churches' on the Continent. In the long run this was not calculated to appeal to a majority of patriotic, chauvinistic Englishmen.

So it is possible to envisage the preservation of a religious balance down the seventeenth century, with Puritanism steadily withering away. But Laud was not a man for Fabian tactics; the Puritans, in a famous phrase, were 'tarrying for the magistrate', he already had the magistrate's support, and he was determined to use it to reform the Church in his own image. It was a policy of aggression which suited his suspicious, embattled temper; instead of viewing his opponents as what they were, a collection of fearful, puzzled, by his own standards deluded men, he saw them as a gang of radical, conspiratorial zealots intent on the overthrow of Church and state. For his part Charles made the same mistake as Edward VI, with less excuse; he lent his full support to one particular party in the Church instead of playing one off against another, as James and Elizabeth had done, and for that matter Henry VIII. Ultimately he created the very situation Laud's policy was supposed to prevent; he gave some men at least a doctrinal or spiritual motive for opposing his secular rule.

This latent problem was exacerbated by the outbreak of the Thirty Years War, and England's involvement from 1625 in a war against one Catholic power (Spain) and from 1626 against two (Spain and France) which she showed no signs of winning. In particular, Charles and Buckingham's abject failure to relieve the Huguenot citadel of La Rochelle was heavy with symbolism, but it was also of considerable material import. England's patent inability to defend herself and her Protestant allies intensified her fear of Catholicism; not only must popery as such be eradicated – a recurrent theme in parliament's pronouncements on religion – it must be winnowed out of the Church of England, and in this atmosphere any emphasis on ceremony and ritual, any compromise with the claims of the papacy, such as could be detected in the writings of Richard Montague, was immediately suspect.

In this scheme of things the role of Arminianism, of which Laud and his associates were often accused, is widely misunderstood. Since 1558 at least the theology of the Church of England had always been firmly Calvinist, but on some questions, and particularly the key question of predestination, Calvin's precise stance was in some doubt – and still is.[29] But he was held to have taught that a minority of sinful men, the Elect, were predestined to salvation by the intervention of saving Grace, while the rest were reprobated to damnation, this selection being made antecedently – before the Fall, said the prelapsarians; after the Fall, said the supralapsarians, though not long after. Strictly speaking this was a random process, but to suppose it was entirely random might lead men into the revolting heresy of Antinomianism (which taught that any carnal sin was permitted to the Elect), and it was allowed that though absolute certainty was never attainable presumption of Grace was related to one's earthly conduct; thus it was highly likely that a sober and honest Christian was one of the Elect, and a fornicator and a drunkard was manifestly not. Arminius of Leyden (1560–1609) took this a step further. Christ, he argued, had died for all men, therefore all men could embrace salvation by the exercise of free will; though it was true that whether they did so, or whether they pressed on down the road to the Everlasting Fire, was predestined in the mind of God, whose ways were inscrutable. These humane propositions split the Calvinist Movement, particularly in the Netherlands, where they were formally condemned at the Synod of Dort in 1619, and many of the more obstinate Remonstrants (Arminians) executed, even the Pensionary of the Republic, John Oldenbarneveldt.

James I's representatives at Dort, as might have been expected, presented a straight bat, retreating on the Church of England's only valid pronouncement on the question of Predestination and Election, number XVII of the Thirty-Nine Articles.[30] This dealt with Predestination, but not Reprobation. It allowed that Predestination was a doctrine 'full of sweet, pleasant and unspeakable comfort to godly persons, and such as feel in themselves the working of the spirit of Christ', but it added that for 'curious and carnal persons ... to have continually before their eyes the sentence of God's predestination' might easily drive them 'either into desperation, or into wretchlessness [sic] of most unclean living, no less perilous'. Under Puritan pressure Archbishop Whitgift had moved towards a more austere standpoint, and the Lambeth Articles of 1595, opening up the question of Reprobation, comfortably concluded that the great majority of mankind was irreversibly damned. But these articles had no public standing, they were not authorised by Convocation, still less the queen, and they were not even published at the time; they merely represented the agreed views of a committee of leading theologians.[31] The Articles of the Irish Church, in 1615, went even further than the Lambeth Articles, but they had no standing in England either.

The issue was ventilated in the case of Richard Montague (p. 117 above), which was prolonged into the new reign, when he appealed to Charles I for justice in a new pamphlet, *Appello Caesarem*. Laud, Buckeridge and Howson exhorted the king, through the Duke of Buckingham, to stand firm on the doctrine of the Church of England, in a letter which is supposed to prove Laud's commitment to Arminianism

---

[29] See the useful summary by François Wendel, *Calvin* (Fontana 1965), pp. 263–84. Predestination was much less important to Calvin than it was to his disciples, and the Thirty-Nine Articles follow his thought fairly accurately.

[30] Peter White, 'The Rise of Arminianism Reconsidered', *Past and Present*, no. 101 (1983), 41–5.

[31] Whitgift described them as, 'Our private judgments, thinking them to be true and correspondent to the doctrine professed in the Church of England, and established by the laws of the land, and not as laws and decrees', qu. H. C. Porter, *Reformation and Reaction in Tudor Cambridge* (Cambridge 1958), p. 372.

(45). In fact it shows that he was determined to maintain the ambiguous compromise established in article XVII above, which was still the only legal basis of Anglican belief. The dispute dragged on into the parliament of 1626, and after the dissolution Charles issued a proclamation setting his face against any innovations in religion, from whatever quarter, and threatening with condign punishment those who set out 'wilfully [to] break that circle of order, which without apparent danger to Church and state may not be broken' (46).

After that Montague dropped out of sight, but the pot was kept on the boil by the indiscreet sermons of ultra-royalist divines like Roger Manwaring, reputed to be Arminian (p. 13 above). Manwaring was impeached in 1628, and the Commons sent up a Remonstrance in which they complained bitterly of the growth of popery and Arminianism, mentioning Laud by name. 'It being now generally held the way to preferment and promotion in the Church', they said, 'many scholars do bend the course of their studies to maintain those errors.'[32]

Like his father, Charles I was impatient with religious debate unless it was conducted by professional experts, preferably of his own choosing. Soon after the prorogation in the summer of 1628 he suppressed Manwaring's sermons,[33] and in November, 'with the advice of so many of our bishops as might conveniently be called together', he republished the Thirty-Nine Articles and announced that any differences as to their interpretation must be settled by Convocation (GCD, p. 75). Finally, in January 1629 he made what he regarded as a final gesture of conciliation; he appointed Montague Bishop of Chichester, but he called in all the copies of Appello Caesarem, 'hoping thereby, that men will no more trouble themselves with these unnecessary questions'; but, he added:

> If we shall be deceived in this our expectation, and that by reading, preaching, or making books, either pro or contra, concerning these differences, men begin to dispute, we shall take such order with them, and those books, that they shall wish they had never thought upon these needless controversies.[34]

But in the eyes of his opponents men, not measures, were now the danger. The House of Commons when it re-assembled was alarmed at the great episcopal reshuffle that had taken place during the recess. In June 1628 Richard Neile was already installed at Winchester, Joseph Hall at Exeter and John Buckeridge at Ely, while Laud had moved from St David's to Bath and Wells. Now Laud moved on to London, Samuel Harsnet to the archbishopric of York, Walter Curle (after a brief interregnum) to Bath and Wells, John Howson to Durham, Richard Corbet to Oxford, Francis White to Norwich and the controversial Richard Montague, as we have seen, to Chichester. Apart from Lincoln, Salisbury and Worcester, and Canterbury itself, where Archbishop Abbott lived on until 1633, all the English sees were now occupied by allies of Laud or men prepared to accede to the king's will. In January 1629 the Commons began an investigation of the state of the Church during which Neile and Montague came in for particular criticism; but it was difficult to contest the king's use of his prerogative as Supreme Governor, and the Resolutions on Religion prepared in

[32] Rushworth, I, 633.   [33] SRP, II, no. 92 (24 June 1628).   [34] Ibid., II, no. 105 (17 January 1629).

committee on 24 February merely moved that the king 'be graciously pleased to confer bishoprics, and other ecclesiastical preferments, with the advice of his Privy Council, upon learned, pious and orthodox men'. However, they then asserted that the doctrine and practice of the Church was properly defined by the Lambeth Articles, the Irish Articles of 1615 and the decrees of the Synod of Dort (47). This was the most extreme pronouncement on religion made by the Commons in this period.

In the heroic age of Stuart historiography, represented by Gardiner and his followers, it was assumed that Arminianism was the root cause of Laud's unpopularity, and of the divisions in the Church in the 1630s and 1640s. An attempt has recently been made to revive this thesis, though with limited success.[35] But the fact is that after 1629 little more is heard of Arminianism; it did not feature at Laud's trial, when the 'innovations' he was accused of were mainly in ceremonial, and the most serious charge against him was that he had tried to re-unite the Church of England with Rome, not merely undermine its Calvinist orthodoxy.[36] Nor did he mention it in his various apologias (50). This is best regarded as an academic dispute between professional theologians which did not concern practising clergymen – certainly not Laud himself – and which never really expanded, as it did in the Netherlands, to embrace the laity.

From a study of the impeachment proceedings against Laud in 1640 and 1644 it appears that there were more substantial grievances against him, especially after he was promoted to Canterbury in 1633. For a start, he rejected the aimable compromises sanctioned by James I and continued by Abbott. One of his first acts as archbishop was to secure new instructions from the king which placed further restrictions on lecturers without cure of souls and ordered the bishops to monitor the sermons of their parish clergy. He was particularly concerned, also, with the activities of the private chaplains to the nobility and gentry, who like their Catholic counterparts in some areas constituted a kind of 'anti-clergy' (48). The bishops' reports were subsumed in an annual report from the archbishop to the king, who took a keen personal interest (49). Such evidence as we have suggests that this campaign was more of a harassment than a persecution, and the much publicised exodus to New England in these years, when it was not prompted by chronic under-employment in the cloth-working districts and in the Fens, was undertaken more in fear of what was to come than of what was actually happening. Some of these emigrants should also be classified as sectaries, members of independent, breakaway congregations which were regarded with aversion by churchmen of all persuasions. Laud haled more than one such group of

[35] Nicholas Tyacke, 'Puritanism, Arminianism and Counter-Revolution', in Russell, *Origins*, pp. 119–43, and 'Arminianism and English Culture', in *Britain and the Netherlands VII*, ed. A. C. Duke and C. A. Tamse (1981), pp. 94–117. But see Peter White, *art. cit.* (The unnecessary confusion which surrounds this question is betrayed by the approach of textbook authors. Robert Ashton, in *Reformation and Revolution 1558–1660* (1984), pp. 280–1, adopts an alarmist interpretation which might have been penned by J. R. Tanner, but Barry Coward, *The Stuart Age* (1980), pp. 148–52, is much more cautious.

[36] It was not listed in the charges against him, but it arose in cross-examination. Laud said, 'I have nothing to do to defend Arminianism, no man having yet charged me with the abetting any point of it.' He added, 'I do heartily wish these differences were not pursued with such heat and animosity, in regard that all the Lutheran Protestants are of the very same opinions, or with very litle differences from those which are now called Arminians', Laud, *Works*, IV, 267–8 (17 June 1644).

sectaries before the High Commission (p. 163 below), and the events of the 1640s show that his concern for this problem was justified.

His attitude to ceremony and ritual, though of less importance in our eyes, was in the circumstances of the time decidedly controversial. The siting of the communion table was a particularly sensitive point. The Injunctions of 1559 thought the matter 'of no great moment, so that the sacrament be duly and referently administered', but decreed that the table be kept along the east wall of the chancel, and brought down to the junction with the nave for the actual communion.[37] This had been confirmed by canon LXXXII of 1604, (p. 125 above). But in fact practice varied – as we must assume it did in all matters liturgical – and in some churches the table had become fixed along the east wall, covered with a carpet, and often railed in, so that it resembled the stone altars of yore, still surviving in cathedral churches. Laud openly favoured this arrangement, but this, and his requirement that communion be taken kneeling, laid him open to the accusation that like the papists he was acknowledging a Real Presence in the elements. In return he could point to horrific instances of the communion table being lodged in the nave, and there used as a repository for hats, sticks and cloaks, or worse (50b). In 1637, when he defended his policy before Star Chamber, he maintained that this was 'a thing indifferent' (50a), and in answer to the charges laid against him in 1640 he stressed the need for uniformity (50b). His response when the Recorder of Salisbury smashed a stained-glass window in the cathedral which represented God as 'an old gaffer in red and blue' is significant. He insisted that the Recorder be punished, but he ordered that the window be not replaced. The Elizabethan Injunctions were firmly against images of this kind.[38]

But the most unpopular aspect of the Laudian Revolution was probably his exaltation of the bishops, and his insistence on the primitive antiquity of their order, which meant that it was of the *esse*, not the *bene esse*, of the Church; an integral and necessary element, not a useful and acceptable addition (50a). His belief that they acted by direct Divine Right even seemed to place them on a level with the king, though this apparently left Charles I unmoved. Such claims were distinctly inflammatory, especially bearing in mind that this was an age peculiarly sensitive to distinctions of rank and status, and that a majority of the bishops were of rather mean parentage.[39]

This was but one aspect of his general policy of discouraging lay interference in church affairs at all levels. As we have seen, he tried to restrict the right of the gentry to appoint their own chaplains, and he lost no time in suppressing the Lay Feoffees, an association of gentry formed to purchase impropriations as they came onto the market and use the income to finance lectureships.[40] When Richardson, Chief Justice of Common Pleas, tried to suppress the Somersetshire wakes, or church ales, and caused an order to this effect to be read in churches, he was savagely criticised by Laud at the

[37] Cardwell, *Documentary Annals*, II, 233–4.   [38] Cardwell, *op. cit.*, II, 221 (no. XXIII).

[39] In fact, of the 34 clergymen promoted to sees between 1625 and 1641 only one stemmed from the nobility or gentry, and this was John Williams of Lincoln, who said he was 'of an ancient Welsh family'. Harsnet, Archbishop of York, was a baker's son, and Corbet of Oxford a gardener's. The rest were of yeoman or merchant stock, or sons of clergy; Laud's father was a clothier (as was Wolsey's).

[40] E. W. Kirby, 'The Lay Feoffees', *JMH*, XIV (1942), 1–25; Isabel M. Calder, *The Activities of the Puritan Faction of the Church of England 1625–1633* (1957); Hill, *Economic Problems*, ch. 11.

Council table, and barred from the Western Circuit.[41] The following year Charles re-issued his father's Declaration of Sports, which roused a much greater furore than it had in 1618, though it had received statutory confirmation in 1625 (p. 116 above).

But most serious of all was the association of Laudianism with Catholicism in the public mind, encouraged by his views on ritual, by his supposed Arminianism, and by the trafficking of Charles's court with Rome through emissaries such as Con and Panzani – not to mention the influence of the queen. The canard that Charles and Laud planned to return the nation to the Roman obedience is incredible to any one who has studied their mind and will to any depth, but we have to acknowledge that there was some excuse.[42]

In the end it was Laud's passion for uniformity which proved his undoing. Emboldened by his success in forcing the Irish Church to abandon the Articles of 1615, in 1637 he tried to impose a modified version of the Book of Common Prayer on the Scots, and this brought the whole edifice crashing down.

He was well aware of his own unpopularity (50a), but he was defiant to the last. The Convocation of Canterbury which assembled with the Short Parliament in 1640 took the unprecedented step of remaining in session after the dissolution, mainly to pass a controversial series of new canons, which included an elaborate defence of the Laudian standpoint on 'innovations', and an 'explanation' of the Divine Right of Kings and the unlawfulness of resistance to constituted authority, which every clergyman was to read out from the pulpit four times a year (51). But the most controversial of these canons was number VI, which imposed on all clergymen the notorious 'etcetera oath', which bound them not to consent to the alteration of the government of the Church by 'archbishops, bishops, deans and archdeacons, etc.' It was primarily directed at lurking romanists, and indeed, it soon revealed Goodman, Bishop of Gloucester, as a secret convert, and thus confirmed the general suspicion of the Laudian hierarchy. On 11 December 1640 a petition supposedly signed by 15,000 Londoners was presented to the House of Commons calling for the extirpation of episcopacy 'root and branch' (52). On the 15th the Commons declared the late canons of non effect, and next day they voted them illegal, since Convocation had no power to legislate without consent of parliament.[43] On the 18th Laud was impeached of high treason and taken into custody. The authoritarian rule he had established over the Church now proved its greatest weakness, for with his disappearance into the Tower the machinery of ecclesiastical discipline promptly collapsed.

45. Letter to the Duke of Buckingham, 2 August 1625

The cause [of Richard Montague], we conceive . . . concerns the Church of England nearly; for that church, when it was reformed from the superstititious opinions broached or maintained by the Church of Rome, refused the

---

[41] Thomas G. Barnes, 'County Politics and a Puritan *cause célèbre*: Somerset Church Ales 1633', 5 *TRHS*, IX (1959), 103–32.

[42] See Caroline Hibbard's excellent study of *Charles I and the Popish Plot*, and p. 168 below.

[43] *CJ*, II, 51, 52.

apparent and dangerous errors, and would not be too busy with every particular school-point. The cause why she held this moderation was, because she could not be able to preserve any unity amongst Christians, if men were forced to subscribe to curious particulars disputed in the schools.

Now, may it please your Grace, the opinions which at this time trouble many men in the late work of Mr Montague, are, some of them, such as are expressly the resolved doctrine of the Church of England, and those he is bound to maintain. Some of them, such as are fit only for schools, are to be left at more liberty for learned men to abound in their own sense, so they keep themselves peaceable, and distract not the Church; and therefore, to make any man subscribe to school-opinions may justly seem hard in the Church of Christ, and was one great fault of the Council of Trent. And to affright them from those opinions in which they have (as they are bound) subscribed to the Church, as it is worse in itself, so it may be the mother of greater danger.

May it please your Grace further to consider, that when the clergy submitted themselves in the time of Henry the Eighth, the submission was so made, that if any difference, doctrinal or other, fell in the Church, the king and the bishops were to be judges of it in a National Synod or Convocation; the king first giving leave, under his broad seal, to handle the points in difference.

But the Church never submitted to any other judge, neither indeed can she, though she would. And we humbly desire your Grace to consider, and then to move his most gracious Majesty . . . what dangerous consequences may follow upon it. For, first, if any other judge be allowed in matter of doctrine, we shall depart from the ordinance of Christ, and the continual course and practice of the Church.

2. Secondly, if the Church be once brought down beneath herself, we cannot but fear what may next be struck at.

3. Thirdly, it will some way touch the honour of his Majesty's dear father, . . . who saw and approved all the opinions of this book; and he in his rare wisdom and judgment would never have allowed them, if they had crossed with truth and the Church of England.

4. Fourthly, we must be bold to say, that we cannot conceive what use there can be of civil government in the Commonwealth, or of preaching and external ministry of the Church, if such fatal opinions, as some which are opposite and contrary to these delivered by Mr Montague are and shall be publicly taught and maintained.

5. Fifthly, we are certain that all or most of the contrary opinions were treated of at Lambeth [in 1595], and ready to be published, but then Queen Elizabeth of famous memory, upon notice of how little they agreed with the practice of piety and obedience to all government, caused them to be suppressed; and so they have continued ever since, till of late some of them

have received countenance at the Synod of Doort. Now this was a synod of that nation, and can be of no authority in any other national church till it be received there by public authority; and our hope is that the Church of England will be well advised, and more than once over, before she admit a foreign synod, especially of such a church as condemneth her discipline and manner of government, to say no more . . .

[Buckeridge, bishop of Rochester, Howson, bishop of Oxford, Laud bishop of St David's]
Laud, *Works*, VI, 244–6

46. A proclamation for the establishing of the peace and quiet of the Church of England, 16 June 1626

The king's most excellent Majesty, in his most religious care and princely consideration of the peace of this Church and Commonwealth of England and other his dominions, whereof God in his goodness hath, under his son Christ Jesus, made him his Supreme Governor, observing that in all ages great disturbances both in Church and state have ensued out of small beginnings when the seeds of contention were not timely prevented, and finding that of late some questions and opinions seem to have been broached or raised in matters of doctrine and the tenets of our religion, which at first only being meant against the papists, but afterwards by the sharp and indiscreet handling and maintaining some of either parts have given much offence to the sober and well-grounded readers and hearers of these late written books on both sides, which [it] may justly be feared will raise some hopes in the professed enemies of our religion, the Romish Catholics, that by degrees the professors of our religion may be drawn first to schism and after to plain popery.

His Majesty therefore, in the integrity of his own heart and singular providence of the peaceable government of that people which God hath committed to his charge, hath thought fit, by the advice of his reverend bishops, to declare and publish not only to his own people but also to the whole world his utter dislike to all those who, to show the subtlety of their wit, or to please their own humours, or vent their own passions, do or shall adventure to stir or move any new opinions not only contrary [to] but differing from the sound and orthodoxal grounds of the true religion sincerely professed and happily established in the Church of England; and also to declare his full and constant resolution that neither in matter of doctrine or discipline of the Church, nor in the government of the state, he will admit of the least innovation, but by God's assistance will so guide the sceptre of these his kingdoms and dominions, by the Divine Providence put into his hand, as shall be for the comfort and assurance of his sober, religious and well-affected subjects, and for the repressing and severe punishing of the insolencies of such as out of any sinister respects or disaffection to his person and government shall dare either in Church or state to disturb or disquiet the peace thereof.

And therefore his most excellent Majesty doth hereby admonish, and also straightly charge and command all his subjects of this realm and of his realm of Ireland, of whatsoever degree, quality or condition they be of, especially those who are churchmen, and by their profession and places ought to be lights and guides to others, that from henceforth they carry themselves so wisely, warily and conscionably that neither by writing, preaching, printing, conferences or otherwise they raise any doubts, or publish or maintain any new inventions, or opinions concerning religion than such as [are] clearly grounded and warranted by the doctrine and discipline of the Church of England heretofore published and happily established by authority. And if any person of what degree soever shall at any time hereafter adventure to break this rule of sobriety and due obedience to his Majesty and his laws, and to this religious duty to the Church of God, his Majesty doth hereby straitly charge and command all his reverend archbishops and bishops, in their several dioceses, speedily to reclaim and repress all such spirits as shall in the least degree attempt to violate this bond of peace.

And his Majesty doth also charge and command all his councillors of estate, judges, justices and ministers of justice whatsoever, that they in their several places take especial care to observe and execute his Majesty's pious and royal pleasure herein expressed.

And lastly, his Majesty doth hereby give assurance to all to whom it may concern, that such as shall take the boldness wilfully to neglect this his Majesty's gracious admonition, and for the satisfying of their unquiet and restless spirits, and to express their rash and undutiful insolencies, shall wilfully break the circle of order, which without apparent danger to Church and state may not be broken, that his Majesty shall and will proceed against all such offenders and wilfull contemners of his gracious and religious government with that severity as upon due consideration had of the quality of their offences and contempts they shall deserve, that so by the exemplary punishment of some few, who by lenity and mercy cannot be won, all others may be warned to take heed how they fall into the just indignation of their Sovereign, and that all his Majesty's good and loving subjects who are studious of the peace and prosperity of this Church and Commonwealth may bless God for his Majesty's pious, religious, wise, just and gracious government.

SRP, II, no. 44

47. Heads of articles to be insisted on, and agreed upon, at a sub-committee for religion (House of Commons, 24 February 1629)

I. That we call to mind, how that, in the last session of this parliament, we presented to his Majesty a humble declaration of the great danger threatened to this Church and state, by divers courses and practices tending to the change and innovation of religion.[44]

II. That what we then feared, we do now sensibly feel; and therefore have just cause to renew our former complaints herein.

III. That yet, nevertheless, we do with all thankfulness acknowledge the great blessing we have received from Almighty God, in setting a king over us, of whose constancy in the profession and practice of the true religion here established, we rest full assured; as likewise of his most pious zeal and careful endeavour for the maintenance and propagation thereof; being so far from having the least doubt of his Majesty's remissness therein that we, next under God, ascribe unto his own princely wisdom and goodness, that our holy religion hath yet any countenance at all amongst us.

IV. And for that the pious intention and endeavours, even of the best and wisest princes, are often frustrated through the unfaithfulness and carelessness of their ministers; and that we find a great unhappiness to have befallen his Majesty this way; we think that, being now assembled in parliament to advise of the weighty and important affairs concerning Church and state, we cannot do a work more acceptable than, in the first place, according to the dignity of the matter, and necessity of the present occasions, faithfully and freely to make known, what we conceive may conduce to the preservation of God's religion, in great peril now to be lost; and, therewithal, the safety and tranquillity of his Majesty and his kingdoms now threatened with certain dangers. For the clearer proceedings therein, we shall declare: (1) What those dangers and inconveniences are. (2) Whence they arise. (3) In some sort, how they may be redressed.

The dangers may appear partly from the consideration of the state of religion abroad; and partly from the condition thereof within his Majesty's own dominions, and especially within this kingdom of England.

From abroad we make these observations: (1) By the mighty and prevalent party, by which true religion is actually opposed, and the contrary maintained. (2) Their combined counsels, forces, attempts, and practices, together with a most diligent pursuit of their designs, aiming at the subversion of all the Protestant Churches in Christendom. (3) The weak resistance that is made against them. (4) Their victorious and successful enterprises, whereby the

---

[44] The Remonstrance of 11 June 1628; Rushworth, I, 631.

Churches of Germany, France, and other places, are in a great part already ruined, and the rest in the most weak and miserable condition.

* * *

Here in England we observe an extraordinary growth of popery, insomuch that in some counties, where in Queen Elizabeth's time there were few or none known recusants, now there are above 2,000, and all the rest generally apt to revolt. A bold and open allowance of their religion, by frequent and public resort to mass, in multitudes, without control, and that even to the Queen's Court, to the great scandal of his Majesty's government. Their extraordinary insolence; for instance, the late erecting of a College of Jesuits in Clerkenwell, and the strange proceedings thereupon used in favour of them. The subtle and pernicious spreading of the Arminian faction; whereby they have kindled such a fire of division in the very bowels of the state, as if not speedily extinguished, it is of itself sufficient to ruin our religion; by dividing us from the Reformed Churches abroad, and separating amongst ourselves at home, by casting doubts upon the religion professed and established, which, if faulty or questionable in three or four articles, will be rendered suspicious to unstable minds in all the rest, and incline them to popery, to which those tenets, in their own nature, do prepare the way: so that if our religion be suppressed and destroyed abroad, disturbed in Scotland, lost in Ireland, undermined and almost outdared in England, it is manifest that our danger is very great and imminent.

* * *

The points wherein the Arminians differ from us and other the Reformed Churches, in the sense of the articles confirmed in parliament, 13 Eliz., may be known and proved in these controverted points, viz.: (1) By the Common Prayer, established by Parliament. (2) By the book of Homilies, confirmed by the Articles of Religion. (3) By the Catechism concerning the points printed in the Bible, and read in churches, and divers other impressions published by authority. (4) Bishop Jewel's works, commanded to be kept in all churches, that every parish may have one of them. (5) The public determination of divinity professors, published by authority. (6) The public determination of divines in both the universities. (7) The Resolution of the Archbishop of Canterbury and other reverend bishops and divines assembled at Lambeth, for this very purpose, to declare their opinions concerning those points, anno 1595, unto which the Archbishop of York and all his province did likewise agree. (8) The Articles of Ireland, though framed by the Convocation there, yet allowed by the clergy and State here. (9) The suffrage of the British divines, sent by King James to the Synod of Dort. (10) The uniform consent of our writers published by authority. (11) The censures, recantations, punishments, and submissions made, enjoined and inflicted upon those that taught contrary thereunto, as Barrow and Barrett in Cambridge, and Bridges in Oxford.

The remedy of which abuses we conceive may be these:

1. Due execution of laws against papists.

2. Exemplary punishments to be inflicted upon teachers, publishers, and maintainers of popish opinions, and practising of superstitious ceremonies, and some stricter laws in that case to be provided.

3. The orthodox doctrine of our Church, in these now controverted points by the Arminian sect, may be established and freely taught, according as it hath been hitherto generally received, without any alteration or innovation; and severe punishment, by the same laws, to be provided against such as shall, either by word or writing, publish anything contrary thereunto.

*   *   *

5. That such as have been authors, or abettors, of those Popish and Arminian innovations in doctrine, may be condignly punished.

*   *   *

7. That his Majesty would be graciously pleased to confer bishoprics, and other ecclesiastical preferments, with the advice of his Privy Council, upon learned, pious and orthodox men.

8. That bishops and clergymen being well chosen, may reside upon their charge, and with diligence and fidelity perform their several duties, and that accordingly they may be countenanced and preferred.

9. That some course may in this parliament be considered of, for providing competent means to maintain a godly, able minister in every parish church of this kingdom.

10. That his Majesty would be graciously pleased to make a special choice of such persons, for the execution of his ecclesiastical commissions, as are approved for integrity of life and soundness of doctrine.   *PH*, II, 483–7

48. The instructions of 1633

Instructions for the most Reverend Father in God our right trusty and right entirely
beloved counsellor William lord archbishop of Canterbury, concerning certain
orders to be observed and put in execution by the several bishops of his province,
Anno Dom. 1633

I. That the Lords the Bishops respectively be commanded to their several sees, there to keep residence, excepting those which are in necessary attendance at our court.

*   *   *

III. That they give charge in their triennial Visitations, and at other convenient times, both by themselves and the archdeacons, that our declaration for settling all questions in difference[45] be strictly observed by all parties.

IV. That there be a special care taken by them all, that their ordinations be solemn, and not of unworthy persons.

V. That they likewise take great care concerning the lecturers within their several dioceses, for whom we give them special directions following.

(1) That in all parishes the afternoon sermons be turned into catechising by questions and answers, where and whence ever there is not some great cause apparent to break this ancient and profitable order.

(2) That every bishop take care in his diocese that all the lecturers do read Divine Service according to the liturgy printed by authority, in their surplices and hoods, before the lecture.

(3) That where a lecture is set up in a market town it may be read by a company of grave and orthodox divines near adjoining and of the same diocese, and that they ever preach in such seemly habits as belong to their degrees, and not in cloaks.

(4) That if a corporation maintains a single lecturer he be not suffered to preach till he professes his willingness to take upon him a living with cure of souls within that corporation, and that he do actually take such benefice or cure so soon as it shall be fairly procured for him.

* * *

VII. That the bishops suffer none under noblemen or men qualified by law, to keep any private chaplain in his house.

* * *

XIV. Lastly, we command every bishop respectively to give his account in writing to his Metropolitan of all these our instructions, or as many of them as may concern him, at or before the tenth day of December yearly, and likewise that you out of them make a brief of your whole province, and present it to us yearly by the second day of January following, that so we may see how the Church is governed and our commands obeyed. And hereof in any wise fail you not.   *Foedera*, XIX, 470–2

49. My Lord of Canterbury's return to his Majesty's instructions, for the year 1636

May it please your sacred Majesty,

According to your royal commands expressed in your late instructions for the good of the Church, I do here most humbly present my yearly account for

---

[45] In 1628; see p. 133 above.

my diocese and province of Canterbury for this last year, ending at Christmas 1636.

And first for my own diocese.

I have every year acquainted your Majesty, and so must do now, that there are still about Ashford and Edgerton divers Brownists and other Separatists; but they are so very mean and poor people that we know not what to do with them. They are said to be the disciples of one Turner and Fenner, who were long since apprehended and imprisoned by order of your Majesty's High Commission Court; but how this part came to be so infected with such a humour of Separation I know not, unless it were by too much connivance at their first beginning, neither do I see any remedy like to be, unless some of their chief seducers be driven to abjure the kingdom, which must be done by the Judges at the Common Law, but it is not in our power. [*Inform me of the particulars and I shall command the judges to make them abjure.*] . . .[46]

There have been heretofore many in Canterbury that were not conformable to church discipline, and would not kneel at the Communion, but they are all now very conformable, as I hear expressly by my officers, and that there is no falling away of any to recusancy . . .

In the diocese of *London* I find that my lord the bishop there (now by your Majesty's grace and favour Lord High Treasurer of England) hath very carefully observed those instructions which belong to his own person, and for the diocese his lordship informs me of three great misdemeanours: the one committed by Dr Cornelius Burgess, who in a Latin sermon before the clergy of London uttered divers insolent passages against the bishops and government of the Church, and refused to give his lordship a copy of the sermon, so there was a necessity of calling him into the High Commission Court, which is done.

The second misdemeanour is of one Mr Wharton, a minister in Essex, who in a sermon at Chelmsford uttered many unfit and some scurrilous things, but for this he hath been convented, and received a canonical admonition, and upon his sorrow and submission any further censure is forborne.

The third misdemeanour which my Lord complains of is the late spreading and dispersing of some factious and malicious pamphlets against the bishops and government of the Church of England, and my lord further certifies that he hath reasonable ground to persuade him that those libellous pamphlets have been contrived, or abetted and dispersed, by some of the clergy of his diocese; and therefore desires me to use the authority of the High Commission for the discovery of this notorious practice, to prevent the mischiefs that will otherwise ensue upon the government of the Church. This, God willing, I shall see performed; but if the High Commission shall not have power enough,

---

[46] These are marginal comments by the king.

because one of these libels contains seditious matter in it, and that which is very little short of treason (if any thing at all), then I humbly beg leave to add this to my Lord Treasurer's motion, and humbly to desire, that your Majesty will call it into a higher court, if you find cause, since I see no likelihood but that these troubles in the Church, if they be permitted, will break out into some sedition in the Commonwealth . . . [*What the High Commission cannot do in this I shall supply as I shall find cause, in a more powerful way.*]

*   *   *

[*Norwich.*] His Lordship found a general defect in catechising quite through the diocese, but hath settled it. And in Norwich, where there are thirty four churches, there was no sermon in the morning on Sundays save only in four, but all put off till the afternoon, and so no catechising; but now he hath ordered that there shall be a sermon every morning and catechising in the afternoon in every church.

For lectures, they abound in Suffolk, and many set up by private gentlemen, even without so much as the knowledge of the Ordinary, and without any due observation to the canons of the discipline of the Church. Divers of these his Lordship hath carefully regulated according to order, especially at St Edmundsbury [Bury St Edmunds], and with their very good content, and suspended no Lecturer of whom he might obtain conformity . . . At Yarmouth, where there was great division heretofore for many years, their lecturer being censured in the High Commission about two years since went into New England, since which time there hath been no lecture, and very much peace in the town, and all ecclesiastical orders well observed. [*Let him go, we are well rid of him.*] But in Norwich one Mr Bridge, rather than he would conform, hath left his lecture and is gone into Holland, the lecturers in the Country generally observing no Church Orders at all; and yet the bishop hath carried it with that temper, and upon their promise and his hope of conformity, that he hath inhibited but three in Norfolk and as many in Suffolk, of which one is no graduate and hath been a common stage-player.

His Lordship humbly craves direction what he shall do with such scholars (some in Holy Orders and some not) as knights and private gentlemen keep in their houses, under pretence to teach their children, as also with some divines that are beneficed in towns, or near, but live in gentlemen's houses. For my part, I think it very fit the beneficed men were presently commanded to reside upon their cures, and for the rest, your Majesty's Instructions allow none to keep chaplains but such as are qualified by law; all which notwithstanding, I most humbly submit (as the bishop does) to your Majesty's judgment. [*I approve your judgment in this. I only add that care must be taken that even those qualified by law keep none but conformable men.*] . . .

Worcester. My lord the bishop of this see certifies that your Majesty's instructions are carefully observed, and that there are only two lectures in the city of Worcester, but very conformable, and that they shall no longer continue than they are so, and that one of them preaches on Sundays in the afternoons after catechising and service in the parish churches, and ending before evening prayers in the Cathedral . . .

*　*　*

[*St Davids*] Baronet Ridd is in this diocese, the son of a late bishop there, who is a sober gentleman. He hath built him a chapel, and desires the bishop to consecrate it, but his lordship finding one of your Majesty's Instructions to be, that none shall keep a chaplain in this house but such as are qualified by law, which he conceives a baronet is not, hath hitherto forborne to consecrate this chapel, as being to be of small use without a chaplain, and humbly craves direction herein, what he shall do.

I humbly propose to your Majesty, whether, considering the charge this gentleman hath been at, and the ill ways which many of them there have to church, it may not be fit to consecrate this chapel, and then that he may have a licence to use the minister of the parish, or any other lawfully in orders; always provided that he use this chapel but at times of some necessity, and not making himself and his family strangers to the Mother Church, and that there be a clause expressed in the licence for recalling thereof, upon any abuse there committed, and that this licence be taken, either from the bishop under his seal, or from the archbishop of the province. [*Since he hath been at the charge and hath so good testimony, let him have his desire, with those restrictions mentioned.*]

*　*　*

St Asaph. In the diocese of St Asaph there is no complaint but the usual, that there is great resort of recusants to Holy Well, and that this summer the Lady Falkland and her company came as pilgrims thither, who were the more observed because they travelled on foot, and disembled neither their quality nor their errand; and this boldness of theirs is of very bad construction among your Majesty's people. My humble suit to your Majesty is, that whereas I complained of this in open council in your Majesty's presence you would now be graciously pleased that the order then resolved on for her confinement may be put in execution. [*It is done.*]

Bangor. For Bangor, I find that the catechising was quite out of use in those remote parts (the more the pity), but the bishop is now in hope to do much good, and seeth some reformation in that particular already. And I would say for this and the other dioceses in Wales, that much more good might be done there in a Church way if they were not overborne by the Court of the Marches there. And this present year in this diocese of Bangor my commissioner for my Metropolitical Visitation there complains unto me that the power which

this church might be kept in uniformity and decency, and in some beauty of holiness. And this the rather because, first, I found that with the contempt of the worship of God the inward fell away apace, and profaneness began boldly to show itself. And secondly, because I could talk with no conscientious persons almost, that were wavering in religion, but the great motive which wrought upon them to disaffect, or think meanly of the Church of England, was that the external worship of God was so lost in the Church (as they conceived it) and the churches themselves, and all things in them, suffered to lie in such a base and slovenly fashion in most places of the kingdom. These, and no other considerations, moved me to take such care as I did of it, which was with a single eye, and most free from any romish superstition in anything.

As for ceremonies, all that I enjoined were according to law. And if any were superstitious, I enjoined them not. As for those which are so called by some men, they are no innovations, but restorations of the ancient approved ceremonies in and from the beginning of the Reformation, and settled either by law or custom; till the faction of such as now openly and avowedly separate from the Church of England did oppose them, and cry them down.

Works, III, 407–8

51. The canons of 1640

Constitutions and canons ecclesiastical, treated upon by the . . . convocations . . . of Canterbury and York, . . . and now published for the due observation of them by his Majesty's authority under the great seal of England [16 June 1640]

Charles, by the Grace of God king of England, Scotland, France and Ireland, Defender of the Faith, etc., to all to whom these presents shall come, greeting . . . Forasmuch as we are given to understand that many of our subjects, being misled against the rites and ceremonies now used in the Church of England, have lately taken offence at the same, upon an unjust supposal that they are not only contrary to our laws but also introductive unto popish superstitions; whereas it well appeareth unto us . . . that the authors and fomenters of these jealousies, though they colour the same with a pretence of zeal, and would seem to strike only at some supposed iniquity in the said ceremonies, yet, as we have cause to fear, aim at our own royal person, and would fain have our good subjects imagine that we ourselves are perverted, and do worship God in a superstitious way, and that we intend to bring in some alteration of the religion here established. Now, how far we are from that, and how utterly we detest every thought thereof, we have by many public declarations and otherwise upon sundry occasions given such assurance to the world, as that from thence we also assure ourself, that no man of wisdom and discretion could ever be so beguiled as to give any serious entertainment to such brainsick jealousies; and for the weaker sort, who are prone to be misled by crafty seducers, we rest no less confident that even of them as many as are of loyal, or indeed but of charitable, hearts, will from henceforth utterly banish all such causeless fears and surmises, upon these our sacred professions so often made by us, a Christian Defender of the Faith, their King and Sovereign . . .

We therefore, out of our princely inclination to uniformity and peace, in matters especially that concern the holy worship of God, . . . and . . ., having fully advised herein with our metropolitan, and with the commissioners authorised under our Great Seal for causes ecclesiastical, have thought good to give them free leave to treat in Convocation, and agree upon certain other canons necessary for the advancement of God's glory, the edifying of his Holy Church, and the due reverence of his blessed Mysteries and Sacraments; that, as we have ever been and by God's assistance (by whom alone we reign) shall ever so continue, careful and ready to cut off superstition with one hand, so we may no less expel irreverence and profaneness with the other . . .

★   ★   ★

I. Concerning the regal power

Whereas sundry laws, ordinances and constitutions have been formerly made for the acknowledgment and profession of the most lawful and independent authority of our dread sovereign lord the king's most excellent Majesty, over the state ecclesiastical and civil, . . . for the fuller and clear instruction and information of all Christian people within this realm in their duties in this particular we do further ordain and decree that every parson, vicar, curate or preacher upon some one Sunday in every quarter of the year, at morning prayer, shall, in the place where he serves, treatably and audibly read these explanations of the regal power here inserted:

The most high and sacred Order of Kings is of Divine Right, being the ordinance of God himself, founded in the prime laws of nature, and clearly established by express texts both of the Old and New Testaments. A supreme power is given to this most excellent Order by God himself in the Scriptures, which is, that kings should rule and command in their several dominions all persons of what rank or estate soever, whether ecclesiastical or civil, and that they should restrain and punish with the temporal sword all stubborn and wicked doers.

The care of God's Church is so committed to kings in the Scripture that they are commended when the Church keeps the right way, and taxed when it runs amiss, and therefore her government belongs in chief unto kings; for otherwise one man would be commended for another's care, and taxed but for another's negligence, which is not God's way.

The power to call and dissolve Councils, both national and provincial, is the true right of all Christian kings within their own realms and territories; and when in the first times of Christ's Church prelates used this power, it was therefore only because in those days they had no Christian kings; and it was then so only used as in times of persecution, that is, with supposition (in case it were required) of submitting their very lives unto the very laws and commands even of those pagan princes that they might not so much as seem to disturb their civil government, which Christ came to confirm, but by no means to undermine.

For any person or persons to set up, maintain or avow in any their said realms or territories respectively, under any pretence whatsoever, any independent coactive power, either papal or popular (whether directly or indirectly), is to undermine their great royal office, and cunningly to overthrow that most sacred ordinance which God himself hath established, and so is treasonable against God as well as against the king.

For subjects to bear arms against their kings, offensive or defensive, upon any pretence whatsoever, is at least to resist the powers which are ordained of God; and though they do not invade but only resist, St Paul tells them plainly they shall receive to themselves damnation.

And although tribute, and custom, and aid, and subsidy, and all manner of necessary support and supply be respectively due to kings from their subjects by the Law of God, Nature and Nations, for the public defence, care and protection of them; yet nevertheless subjects have not only possession of but a true and just right, title, and property to and in all their goods and estates, and ought to have. And these two are so far from crossing one another that they mutually go together for the honourable and comfortable support of both. For as it is the duty of the subjects to supply their king so it is part of the kingly office to support his subjects in the property and freedom of their estates . . .

[Canons II, III, IV and V were, respectively, 'For the better keeping of the day of his Majesty's most happy Inauguration', 'For the suppressing of the growth of Popery', 'Against Socinianism' and 'Against Sectaries'.]

VI. An oath enjoined for the preventing of all innovations in doctrine and government

This present synod (being desirous to declare their sincerity and constancy in the profession of the doctrine and discipline already established in the Church of England, and to secure all men against any suspicion of revolt to Popery, or any other superstition) decrees, that all archbishops and bishops, and all other priests and deacons, in places exempt or not exempt, shall before the second day of November next ensuing take this oath following, against all innovation of doctrine or discipline, and this oath shall be tendered [to] them and every of them, and all others named after in this canon, by the bishop in person, or his chancellor, or some grave divines named and appointed by the bishop under the seal; and the said oath shall be taken in the presence of a public notary, who is hereby required to make an act of it, leaving the universities to the provision which follows.

The oath is:

I, A. B., do swear that I do approve the doctrine and discipline, or government established in the Church of England, as containing all things necessary to salvation, and that I will not endeavour by myself or any other, directly or indirectly, to bring in any popish doctrine, contrary to that which is so established; nor will I ever give my consent to alter the government of this Church by archbishops, bishops, deans and arch-deacons, etc.[48] as it stands now established, and as by right it ought to stand, nor yet ever subject it to the usurpations and superstitions of the See of Rome. And all these things I do plainly and sincerely acknowledge and swear, according to the plain and common sense and understanding of the same words, without any equivocation, or mental evasion, or secret reservation whatsoever. And this I do heartily, willingly and truly, upon the faith of a Christian. So help me God in Jesus Christ.

★　★　★

We likewise constitute and ordain that all masters of arts (the sons of noblemen only excepted), all bachelors and doctors in divinity, law or physic, all that are licensed to practise physic, all registrars, actuaries and proctors, all schoolmasters, all such as being natives or naturalised do come to be incorporated into the universities here, having taken a degree in any foreign university, shall be bound to take the said oath. And we command all governors of colleges and halls in either of the universities that they administer the said oath to all persons resident in their several houses that have taken the degrees before-mentioned in this canon within six months after the publication hereof.

And we likewise constitute, that all bishops shall be bound to give the said oath unto all those to whom they give Holy Orders at the time of their ordination, or to whomsoever they give collation, institution, or licence to preach or serve any cure.

VII. A declaration concerning some rites and ceremonies

Because it is generally to be wished that unity of faith were accompanied with

---

[48] This is what made it notorious as the 'Etcetera Oath'.

uniformity of practice in the outward worship and service of God, chiefly for the avoiding of groundless suspicions of those who are weak, and the malicious aspersions of the professed enemies of our religion; the one fearing the innovations, the other flattering themselves with the vain hope of our backslidings unto their popish superstition, by reason of the situation of the Communion Table, and the approaches thereunto, the synod declareth as followeth:

That the standing of the Communion Table sideway[s] under the east window of every chancel or chapel is in its own nature indifferent, neither commanded nor condemned by the word of God, either expressly or by immediate deduction, and therefore that no religion is to be placed therein, or scruple to be made thereon. And albeit at the time of reforming this Church from that gross superstition of popery it was carefully provided that all means should be used to root out of the minds of the people both the inclination thereunto and memory thereof, especially of the idolatry committed in the Mass, for which cause all popish altars were demolished; yet notwithstanding it was then ordered by the Injunctions and Advertisements of Queen Elizabeth of blessed memory, that the Holy Tables should stand in the place where the altars stood, and accordingly have been continued in the royal chapels of three famous and pious princes, and in most cathedral and some parochial churches, which doth sufficiently acquit the manner of placing the said tables from any illegality, or just suspicion of popish superstition or innovation. And therefore we judge it fit and convenient that all churches and chapels do conform themselves in this particular to the example of the cathedral or mother-churches, saving always the general liberty left to the bishop by law, during the time of administration of the Holy Communion. And we declare that this situation of the Holy Table doth not imply that it is or ought to be esteemed a true and proper altar, whereon Christ is again really sacrificed, but it is and may be called an altar by us in that sense in which the Primitive Church called it an altar, and in no other.

And because experience hath shewed us how irreverent the behaviour of many people is in many places, some leaning, others casting their hats, and some sitting upon, some standing [on], and others sitting under the Communion Table in time of Divine Service, for the avoiding of these and the like abuses it is thought meet and convenient by this present synod that the said Communion Tables in all chancels or chapels be decently severed with rails, to preserve them from such or worse profanations . . .

* * *

Cardwell, *Synodalia*, I, 380–92, 402–6

52. The Root and Branch Petition, 11 December 1640

To the Right Honourable the Commons House of Parliament.

The humble petition of many of his Majesty's subjects in and about the City of London, and several counties of the kingdom, showeth,

That whereas the government of archbishops and lord bishops, deans and archdeacons, etc., with their courts and ministrations in them, have proved prejudicial and very dangerous both to the Church and Commonwealth, they themselves having formerly held, that they have their jurisdiction or authority of human authority, till of these later times, being further pressed about the unlawfulness, that they have claimed their calling immediately from the Lord Jesus Christ, which is against the Laws of this kingdom, and derogatory to his Majesty and his state royal. And whereas the said government is found by woeful experience to be a main cause and occasion of many foul evils, pressures and grievances of a very high nature unto his Majesty's subjects in their own consciences, liberties and estates, as in a schedule of particulars hereunto annexed may in part appear.

We therefore most humbly pray and beseech this honourable assembly, the premisses considered, that the said government, with all its dependencies, roots and branches, may be abolished, and all laws in their behalf made void, and the government according to God's Word may be rightly placed amongst us. And we your humble suppliants, as in duty we are bound, will daily pray for his Majesty's long and happy reign over us, and for the prosperous success of this high and honourable Court of Parliament.

A particular of the manifold evils, pressures and grievances caused, practised and occasioned by the prelates and their dependants

1. The subjecting and enthralling all ministers under them and their authority, and so by degrees exempting them from the temporal power; whence follows:

2. The faint-heartedness of ministers to preach the Truth of God, lest they should displease the prelates; as namely, the doctrine of Pre-destination, of Free-Grace, of Perseverance, of Original Sin remaining after baptism, of the Sabbath, the doctrine against Universal Grace, Election for Faith foreseen, Free Will, against Anti-Christ, Non-Residents, human Inventions in God's Worship; all which are generally withheld from the people's knowledge, because not relishing to the bishops.

3. The encouragement of ministers to despise the temporal magistracy, the nobles and gentry of the land, to abuse the subjects and live contentiously with their neighbours, knowing that they, being the bishops' creatures, shall be supported.

4. The restraint of many godly and able men from the ministry, and

thrusting out of many congregations their faithful, diligent and powerful ministers, who lived peaceably with them, and did them good, only because they cannot in conscience submit to and maintain the bishops' needless devices; nay, sometimes for no other cause but for their zeal in preaching or great auditories.

* * *

6. The great increase of idle, lewd and dissolute, ignorant and erroneous men in the ministry, which swarm like the locusts of Egypt over the whole kingdom, and will they but wear a canonical cap, a surplice, a hood, bow at the name of Jesus, and be zealous of superstitious ceremonies, they may live as they list, confront whom they please, preach and vent what errors they will, and neglect preaching at their pleasures without control.

* * *

9. The hindering of godly books to be printed, the blotting out or perverting those which they suffer, all or most of that which strikes either at popery or Arminianism, the adding of what or where pleaseth them, and the restraint of reprinting books formerly licensed, without relicensing.

* * *

11. The growth of popery and increase of papists, priests and Jesuits in sundry places, but especially about London since the Reformation; the frequent venting of crucifixes and popish pictures both engraved and printed, and the placing of such in Bibles.

* * *

13. Moreover, the offices and jurisdictions of archbishops, lord-bishops, deans, archdeacons, being the same way of Church government which is in the Romish Church, and which was in England in the time of popery, little change thereof being made (except only the head from whence it was derived), the same arguments supporting the Pope which do uphold the prelates, and overthrowing the prelates which do pull down the Pope; and other Reformed Churches having, upon their rejection of the Pope, cast the prelates out also, as members of the Beast; hence it is that the prelates here in England, by themselves or their disciples, plead and maintain that the Pope is not Anti-Christ, and that the Church of Rome is a true Church, hath not erred in fundamental points, and that salvation is attainable in that religion, and therefore have restrained to pray for the conversion of our Sovereign Lady the Queen. Hence also hath come:

14. The great conformity and likeness both continued and increased of our Church to the Church of Rome, in vestures, postures, ceremonies and administrations, namely as bishops' rotchets and the lawn-sleeves, the four-

cornered cap, the cope and surplice, the tippet, the hood and the canonical coat, the pulpits clothed, especially now of late, with the Jesuits' badge upon them every way.

15. The standing up at *Gloria Patri*, and at the reading of the Gospel, praying towards the east, bowing at the name of Jesus, the bowing to the altar towards the east, cross in baptism, the kneeling at the Communion.

16. The turning of the Communion Table altar-wise, setting images, crucifixes and conceits over them, and tapers and books upon them, and bowing or adoring to, or before them, . . . which is a plain device to usher in the Mass.

* * *

19. The multitude of canons formerly made, wherein among other things excommunication, *ipso facto*, is denounced for speaking of a word against the devices above said, or subscription thereunto, though no law enjoined a restraint from the ministry without subscription, and appeal is denied to any that should refuse subscription or unlawful conformity, though he be never so much wronged by the inferior judges. Also the canons made in the late sacred synod, as they call it, wherein are many strange and dangerous devices to undermine the Gospel, and the subjects' liberties, to propagate popery, to spoil God's People, ensnare ministers and other students, and so to draw all into an absolute subjection and thraldom to them and their government, spoiling both the king and the parliament of their power.

20. The countenancing plurality of benefices, prohibiting of marriages without their licence, at certain times almost half the year, and licensing of marriages without banns asking.

21. Profanation of the Lord's Day, pleading for it, and enjoining ministers to read a declaration set forth (as 'tis thought) by their procurement for tolerating of sports upon that day, suspending and depriving many godly ministers for not reading the same, only out of conscience, because it was against the Law of God so to do, and no law of the land to enjoin it.

* * *

25. . . .The pride and ambition of the prelates being boundless, unwilling to be subject either to man or laws, they claim their office and jurisdiction to be *jure divino*, exercise ecclesiastical authority in their own names and rights, and under their own seals, and take upon them temporal dignities, places and offices in the Commonwealth, that they may sway both Swords.

26. Whence follows the taking commissions in their own courts and consistories, and where else they sit, in matters determinable of right at Common Law, the putting of ministers upon parishes without the patron's and people's consent.

* * *

28. The exercising of the oath *ex officio*, and other proceedings by way of Inquisition, reaching even to men's thoughts, the apprehending and detaining of men by pursuivants, the frequent suspending and depriving of ministers, fining and imprisoning of all sorts of people, breaking up of men's houses and studies, . . . and the doing of many other outrages, to the utter infringing of the laws of the realm and the subjects' liberties, and ruining of them and their families; and of later time the judges of the land are so awed with the power and greatness of the prelates, and other ways promoted, that neither prohibition, *habeas corpus*, nor any other lawful remedy can be had, or take place, for the distressed subjects in most cases; only papists, Jesuits, priests and such others as propagate popery or Arminianism, are countenanced, spared, and have much liberty; and from hence followed amongst others these dangerous consequences:

First, The general hope and expectation of the Romish party, that their superstitious religion will ere long be fully planted in this kingdom again, and so they are encouraged to persist therein, and to practice the same openly in divers places, to the high dishonour of God, and contrary to the laws of the realm.

2. The discouragement and destruction of all good subjects, of whom are multitudes, both clothiers, merchants and others, who being deprived of their ministers and overburdened with these pressures have departed the kingdom, to Holland and other parts, and have drawn with them a great manufacture of cloth, and trading, out of the land into other places where they reside, whereby wool, the great staple of the kingdom, is become of small value, and vends not, trading is decayed, many poor people want to work, seamen lose employment and the whole land is much impoverished, to the great dishonour of this kingdom, and blemishment to the government thereof.

3. The present wars and commotions happened between his Majesty and his subjects of Scotland, wherein his Majesty and all his kingdoms are endangered, and suffer greatly, and are like to become a prey to the common enemy, in case the wars go on, which we exceedingly fear will not only go on, but also increase, to an utter ruin of all, unless the prelates with their dependencies be removed out of England, and also they and their practises, who, as we under your Honours' favours do verily believe and conceive, have occasioned the quarrel.

All which we humbly refer to the consideration of this Honourable Assembly, desiring the Lord of Heaven to direct you in the right way to redress all these evils.   Rushworth, v, 93–6

III. HIGH COMMISSION[49]

High Commission is linked in the popular mind with Star Chamber, but the basis of their authority was quite different. Star Chamber was an expression of the almost limitless juridical authority of the king in Council; High Commission was a manifestation of the king's powers as Supreme Governor of the Church of England, which could be held not to extend to the laity, and in fact were arguably defined and restricted by § VIII of the Act of Supremacy of 1559.[50] However, one of its main targets, the popish priesthood, were not clergy of the Church of England, even if they were not exactly laymen, and under Elizabeth its scope had been extended to sectaries and other external enemies of the Church. Moreover, it had come to be regarded as a court of appeal from the lower ecclesiastical courts which routinely sat in judgment in cases of matrimonial and family law usually involving laymen exclusively. In fact, it had mutated from a visitatorial commission dealing only with the clergy into a full-blown court with jurisdiction over almost any crime which could be brought within the purview of Christian morality and able to award almost any punishment short of mutilation or death – not just the ecclesiastical sanctions of deprivation, excommunication and penance. Successive commissions under the great seal reflected this trend.[51]

The issue had been tested in 1592, in Caudry's Case, when the judges had declared the High Commission a valid court of law,[52] but in the early years of James I's reign the Common Law judges began to issue writs of prohibition on a large scale against the High Commission, ordering cases pending before it to be halted while they determined whether they belonged to the lay or the clerical jurisdiction – an arbitration which very rarely went in favour of the Commission (p. 75 above). To their general desire at this time to curb competing jurisdictions there was probably added an element of anti-clerical, especially anti-episcopal, prejudice, and there was also a disruptive personality clash between those two aggressive and opinionated men Chief Justice Coke and Archbishop Richard Bancroft – an echo, in fact, of similar clashes between Burleigh and Whitgift in the 1580s. In 1605 Bancroft presented to the king the *Articuli Cleri*, 25 leading questions on the relationship of the lay to the clerical jurisdiction, implying that writs of prohibition did not lie against a spiritual court, and that it was the duty of the judges to support the royal supremacy (*TCD*, pp. 177–86).

Coke rebutted this with his usual vigour, and for once James's powers as a peacemaker were unavailing. In 1606 the House of Commons took up the attack, their main target being the oath *ex officio mero*, which obliged the defendant to answer questions of which he had no prior knowledge, even if his answers incriminated him. During the recess the Privy Council asked the two chief justices for a ruling, and they replied that the oath could only be administered after the accused had been given a list

---

[49] R. G. Usher, *The Rise and Fall of the High Commission* (Oxford 1913) is still the basic authority, though it should be consulted in the 1968 reprint, which has an important revisionary introduction by Philip Tyler. See also Elton, *Tudor Constitution*, pp. 221–32, and Babbage, *Bancroft*, ch. 9.

[50] Elton, *op. cit.*, pp. 374–5.

[51] The very restricted Commission of 1559 is printed in Elton, *op. cit.*, pp. 226–30; for the subsequent Commissions of 1562, 1572, 1576 and 1601 see *PCD*, pp. 232–41.

[52] Elton, *op. cit.*, pp. 225–6.

of heads under which he was to be examined, nor could a layman be questioned in this way on his political or religious beliefs.[53] In December the Commons passed a bill which sought to make the oath illegal altogether, and six months later (June 1607) another which would have confined the Commission to the powers granted it in 1559.[54]

In the next two years the flood of prohibitions continued, despite James's efforts to stop it. Worse still, the judges declared that it was for them to interpret the Act of Supremacy, and that act gave the Commission no power to imprison.[55] Yet this power was crucial, for if the accused refused to take the oath *ex officio*, then he could only be imprisoned for contumacy. A compromise of sorts was finally reached in 1611, when James issued a new Commission (53), which specifically empowered it to imprison and to use the *ex officio* oath. Whom it could punish and for what was still not entirely clear; the clergy were still ostensibly its main target, though it could now deal with schismatics and conventiclers, with 'infamous and notorious' adulterers, with those who assaulted bishops or archbishops or interrupted church services, and with those who dug up bodies from churchyards. Not a very wide mandate, but no doubt after a decent interval the Commission simply ignored it. Coke refused to sit on the new Commission, but the other judges complied, and with the death of Bancroft in 1611 some of the sting seems to have gone out of the controversy. All the same, High Commission remained one of the most ambiguous of the king's courts, and it is safe to say that it was the most unpopular, especially after Laud breathed fresh life into it in the 1630s.

But the general impression, then and later, that it was a key weapon in Laud's campaign against the Puritans is on the whole false. It proceeded against non-conforming clergymen, and against sectaries, who were universally odious (54a), but the most notorious cases in Laud's drive for conformity – the prosecution of Leighton, Prynne and Bastwick, the proceedings against the lay feoffees, and so on – were heard in Star Chamber. The minute books of the Commission for 1634 to 1636 reveal a wide variety of business, much of it trivial or uncontentious (54), and Usher points out that 80 per cent of the cases heard between 1611 and 1640 were initiated by private litigants, mostly parishioners trying to winkle out drunken, immoral, eccentric or violent clergymen. Of the remaining 20 per cent only a quarter were brought in by the commissioners, and these often of a trifling nature.[56] (We find Laud, for instance, when Bishop of London, hauling an unfortunate peasant before the Commission for relieving himself in St Paul's Cathedral.)[57] However, it was noticeable that it was dealing with an increasing number of cases which could loosely be called 'matrimonial'.

[53] Coke, *Reports*, pt XII, 26 (vi, 227–8). Usher, *op. cit.*, p. 169, questions the authenticity of this report, but it was consistent with Coke's known views, and with standard Star Chamber procedure. Cf. Mary H. Maguire, 'The Attack of the Common Lawyers on the Oath *ex officio*', in *Essays in History and Political Thought presented to C. H. McIlwain* (Cambridge, Mass. 1936), pp. 221–2.

[54] Bowyer, *Diary*, pp. 344–9; *House of Lords Manuscripts*, XI, 3305.

[55] Usher, *Reconstruction*, bk 3, ch. 10.

[56] Usher, *High Commission*, ch. 12, and particularly the table on p. 279.

[57] Gardiner, *Cases in Star Chamber*, pp. 380, 298. See also the case of the men arraigned for christening a cat; *ibid.*, p. 275.

The trial of matrimonial offences and the imposition of alimony was the business of the lower Church courts, but they found it difficult to enforce their judgments, especially against members of the upper classes. In 1613, to ease the strain on the Privy Council, which was besieged by injured husbands and starving wives, the High Commission was empowered to hear such appeals. With the power to fine and imprison it reduced many recalcitrant spouses to order, and the successful prosecution of Sir Giles Allington for incest and Viscountess Purbeck for adultery showed that the wealthy and the well born could no longer order their private lives as they wished, irrespective of the laws of God and the Church.[58] It was not a welcome discovery.

In any case, many men, and not just radicals or sectarians, objected to divines exercising any jurisdiction at all. So general was the belief that the bishops had no power to hold courts in their own name that in 1637 Laud asked Charles to consult the judges, whose reply, of course, was favourable. The king publicised the result by proclamation.[59] In 1638, in response to their complaints that the court was being frustrated by those who stood mute, defying the threat of imprisonment, he sent the commissioners a letter authorising them 'of our own mere motion and knowledge, and by our supreme power ecclesiastical' to proceed against those who refused to take the oath as though they had confessed to the crimes of which they stood accused – the procedure *ore tenus*.[60] The Common Law judges responded by attacking ecclesiastical jurisdiction at the root, in the lower courts, but it is not surprising that the High Commission found no defenders in 1641, and that even the Cavalier Parliament in 1661 thought only of confirming its abolition (p. 338 below).[61]

53. High Commission, 29 August 1611

James, by the Grace of God . . . [etc.], to the most reverend father our right and trusty and right well-beloved councillor, George, lord Archbishop of Canterbury, . . . [and 89 others], greeting.

[1.] Whereas at the parliament holden at Westminster in the first year of the reign of our dear sister Elizabeth late queen of England one act was made amongst others entitled, An act restoring to the Crown the ancient jurisdiction over the state ecclesiastical . . .,[62] by the express words of which said act, authorising our said dear sister, her heirs and successors, to grant such commissions when and as often and for such and so long time as should be thought meet and convenient, it appeareth that the said parliament purposed plainly . . . that such commissions . . . might be accommodated to the accidents and varieties of times and occasions; we have now thought good, for

---

[58] Gardiner, *History*, VII, 251, VIII, 145. See also Grenville *v.* Grenville, in Gardiner, *Cases*, pp. 265–8. The Commission of 1613 is printed in *PCD*, pp. 431–2.

[59] *SRP*, II, no. 244 (18 August 1637).   [60] *Foedera*, XX, 190–1 (4 February 1638).

[61] I have discussed the High Commission for the province of Canterbury, but there were also similar commissions established at York and Durham. See R. A. Marchant, *The Puritans and the Church Courts in the Diocese of York 1560–1642* (1960), and Philip Tyler's introduction to the 1968 reprint of Usher's *High Commission*.

[62] Act of Supremacy, 1559; Elton, *Tudor Constitution*, pp. 372–7.

divers weighty causes, and out of our princely care and desire to ease and content our loving subjects as far as may stand with good government and justice, by the advice of our Privy Council to grant forth our commissions in manner and form following.

[2.] Know ye therefore that we for sundry good, weighty, and necessary causes and considerations us thereunto especially moving, of our own mere motion and certain knowledge, by force and virtue of our supreme authority and prerogative royal and of the said act, do by these our letters patent under our Great Seal of England give and grant full, free and lawful power and authority unto you the said . . . [commissioners] . . . to inquire as well by examination of witnesses or presentments as also by examination of the parties accused themselves upon their oath . . . of all and singular apostacies, heresies, great errors in matters of faith and religion, schisms, unlawful conventicles tending to schisms against the religion or government of the Church now established, and also of all other persons which have or shall refuse to have their children baptised, or which have or shall administer or procure or willingly suffer the sacrament of baptism to be administered by any Jesuit, seminary or other popish priest, or which have or shall celebrate the mass or procure the same to be celebrated, or willingly hear or be present at the same, and of their said offences, and also of all blasphemous and impious acts and speeches, scandalous books, libels and writings against the doctrine of religion, the Book of Common Prayer, or ecclesiastical state or government now established in the Church of England, or against any archbishop or bishop touching any offence or crime of ecclesiastical cognisance, profanation of the sacraments of baptism and the Lord's Supper and of all other things and places consecrated or dedicated to divine service, wilful and unlawful digging up of buried bodies in any church or chapel or churchyard, violent and wilful disturbances and interruptions of divine service or sermons in any church, chapel or public preaching place, violent and wilful laying of hands upon the person of any archbishop or bishop, simonies, incests, infamous and notorious adulteries, and also of all corruptions, contempts and abuses in any ecclesiastical judges, officers or their deputies or clerks or other ministers whatsoever belonging to any ecclesiastical courts or attending or . . . employed in or by the same, committed . . . within these our realms . . .

*　*　*

[6.] And we do further give . . . authority unto you . . . to send your letters missive to or for any person which shall be charged, accused or upon notorious fame suspected to have offended in any of the premises, thereby willing, requiring and commanding them to appear before you . . . at a day and place certain to answer thereunto; and where you . . . shall find it necessary in any of the cases aforesaid only we give you . . . authority, by our messengers or pursuivants or by attachment to be directed to the sheriff to whom the execution in that behalf shall appertain, to cause such person so charged . . . to be arrested . . . and kept in safe custody till he shall be brought before you . . .

*   *   *

[10.] And we do also give full power and authority unto you . . . to call before you . . . all and every offender and offenders in any of the premises and also all such as shall be charged, accused or upon notorious fame suspected to have offended in any of the premises and every of them, to examine [them] upon their corporal oaths touching every or any of the premises which you shall object against them, in case it do first appear that the parties unto which the said oath shall be so ministered are thereof detected either by examination of witnesses or by presentments or by public or notorious fame or by information of the Ordinary where the offence was committed. And if any person or persons shall refuse to take the said oath in the cases aforesaid or having taken the oath shall refuse to answer upon their oath directly and fully unto the articles and matters objected against them . . ., then it shall and will be lawful to and for you . . . to apprehend . . . such persons . . . and to commit them to prison, there to remain . . . until they have taken the said oath and made full and direct answer respectively unto the said articles . . .

*   *   *

[13.] And if you . . . shall find by confession of the party or other sufficient proof any person to have offended in the premises, . . . or refusing to obey or perform your orders, decrees and commandments in anything touching the premises, that then you . . . shall have full power and authority . . . to punish the same person so offending by censures ecclesiastical or by reasonable fine or imprisonment according to the quality and quantity of their offence, or by all or any the said means according to your discretions.

*   *   *

[24.] Provided always . . . that no sentence definitive of any cause or matter determinable by virtue of this commission shall hereafter be given without the personal presence, hearing and full assent of five or more of you, whereof . . . [the Archbishop of Canterbury, the Lord Chancellor, Lord Treasurer, Lord Privy Seal, the Bishops of London, Winchester, Exeter, Lichfield, Chichester, Rochester or Gloucester, and five other named persons] to be one, anything before in these presents contained to the contrary in anywise notwithstanding.

*   *   *

[26.] And our will and pleasure is, and we do hereby signify and declare unto you our said commissioners and to all other our loving subjects, that it shall be lawful for any persons that shall hereafter be sentenced by you by virtue of this our commission which shall find themselves grieved by reason of any such sentence, to become suitors unto us by way of supplication as of our grace to have a commission of review to be granted by us for the re-examination of their cause.

⋆　⋆　⋆

PRO Patent Roll, 9 Jac. I

54. Cases before High Commission

(a) 'The Newington Sectaries', 14 June 1632

Rawlins, Harvy, Arthur Goslin, Howland, Robert Bye, John Smith and others were taken at a conventicle in a wood near Newington, in Surrey, upon the Sabbath day last, and being now brought to the court they were required to take their oaths to answer the articles put in against them. Two of them answer[ed] they will not swear at this time, and as they were going out Harvy put on his hat, which was presently taken off and he was complained on, and being called back to answer it, he said he was shifting away, and put on his hat. Another saith that a lawful magistrate had examined them already, and therefore he will not swear to be here examined.

[*The Bishop of*] *London* [Laud]: 'Your examinations taken before Sir [blank] he sent to me; there is nothing in it but that you met together to confer upon the word of God as far as you understand the same, and to pray, which you might answer here. But you tell this court that it is not a lawful power and authority, and of the same mind are those that were taken at Blackfriars, for they petitioned the king to be tried by his judges, by his lords, declining the ecclesiastical jurisdiction. This they tendered the last Sunday. This your obstinacy will cause you to be proceeded against at the Common Law, and be made [to] abjure the kingdom, and if you return, be hanged.'

[*The*] *King's Advocate* speaketh to another of them: 'You are required to take your oath to answer the articles put in against you.'

Prisoner: 'I cannot swear, because I know them not in certainty . . .'

Andrew Sherle will not lay his hand upon the book.

Robert Bye coming into the court, the *Bishop of London* spoke kindly to him, saying: 'Come, thou lookest like a good fellow, that will take thy oath.' *Bye*: 'I am Christ's freeman; I owe obedience to God and the king, and those that are lawfully sent by him, but to no others.' At which there being some laughter, he said: 'I am indeed in good earnest, I dare not take this oath. An oath is for the ending of a controversy, but this is made to be but the beginning of the controversy.'

[*The*] *Archbishop of Canterbury*: 'You do show yourselves the most ungrateful to God and to his Majesty the king and to us the fathers of the Church. If you have any knowledge of God, it hath come through and by us, or some of our predecessors. We have taken care, under God, to give milk to the babes and younglings and strong meat for the men of understanding; you have the word of God to feed you, the Sacraments to strengthen you, and we support you by prayer. For all this what despite do you return us? You call us abominable men, to be hated of all, that we carry the mark of the Beast, that we are his members. We do bear this patiently, not because we have no law to right us, but because of your obstinacy. But for your dishonouring of God and disobeying the king, it is not to be endured. When you have reading, preaching, singing, teaching, you are your own ministers; the blind lead the blind. Whereas his Majesty is God's vice-gerent in the Church, the Church is nothing with you, and his ministers not to be regarded, and you run into woods as if you lived in persecution. Such a one you make the king, to whom we are so much bound for his great care for the truth to be preserved among us; and you would have men believe he is a tyrant – this besides your wickedness, unthankfulness and ungraciousness towards us, the fathers of the Church. Therefore let these men be put two and two in several prisons.'

Gardiner, *Cases in Star Chamber*, pp. 308–10

(b) *Peter Kirby, 2 July 1634*

Being apprehended by John Wragg the messenger, it appeared that he had travelled beyond seas with leave, and now on his return was found with a Roman breviary about him, which is the book generally used by Romish priests, and being tendered the oath of allegiance he refused to take the same. He was committed to the Gatehouse as vehemently suspected to be a Romish priest.

CSPD 1634–35, p. 177

(c) *Anthony Lapthorne, rector of Tretire with Michael Church, co. Hereford, 9 October 1634*

Defendant was charged that since . . . his promotion to Tretire about three years ago he has not usually read divine service, nor administered the sacraments, according to the prescript form appointed in the Book of Common Prayer . . . He had seldom read the Litany, unless in Lent, and usually omitted sundry parts of the service, as for example, when he came to the Psalms, or to one of the Lessons, he would leave off reading and fall to expounding the Psalms or Lessons, and that done go up to the pulpit and begin his sermon. In expounding he inveighed at some of his parishioners with whom he was offended. He never observed any holy days or fasting days except at Christmas, Easter and Whitsuntide. At baptism he refused to take the child into his arms, or to sign it with the cross. In Holy Communion, after having said the words of benediction to one or two, to the rest he said 'Take and eat', or 'Take and drink.' He reviled some of his parishioners who bowed at the name of Jesus . . . Examples were adduced of his terming the clergy of the realm the Great Rabbis, the Great Clergy-monsters, and the neighbouring ministers, Idol Shepherds, Dumb-dogs and Soul-murderers, and that their sermons were strawberry sermons and dawbing sermons. He had also taught that Christ did not descend into Hell . . . The Court pronounced him a man incorrigible, and ordered him to be deprived and suspended from his ministry, and to appear the next court day to hear his sentence.   *Ibid.*, p. 263

(d) John Elkins, of Isham, co. Northampton, 16 October 1634

Charged with irreverent behaviour in wearing his hat during divine service, in causing 100*l.* to be told over the communion table, and tendered to the use of John Pickering in performance of a bargain for houses and lands, and in saying in the streets of Isham in scorn that a ploughman is as good as a priest. Fined 100*l.*, ordered to make a public submission in the church of Isham, and condemned in costs.   *Ibid.*, p. 268

(e) Sir Alexander Cave, of Rotherby, co. Leicester, Richard Roe, and Amy, his wife, 13 November 1634

Before July 1619 Sir Alexander had been several times convented in this court for adultery with the said Amy Roe, and for avoiding future scandal was tied by bond not to remain in her company, but notwithstanding the same had for eight years past lived and cohabited with the said Amy. The court finding that he had shown himself incorrigible ordered him to do penance in his parish church in a form to be prescribed, fined him 500*l.* to the king, condemned him in costs, and lastly committed him until he should give bond with sureties for the performance of this order. Richard Roe was admonished to appear personally on the next court day and produce Amy his wife to hear the further judgment of the court.   *Ibid.*, p. 325

(f) Rowland Chedle, DD, 13 November 1634

Ordered that the cause depending in the Court of Arches for a separation for cruelty proceed with all expedition, and that the suit in this court do stand in statu quo till that cause be sentenced. Dr Chedle is not to molest his wife in her proceedings in the Court of Arches.   *loc. cit.*

IV. THE CATHOLIC PROBLEM

The Roman Catholics were not, of course, of the Established Church, but they constituted one of its abiding problems. Apart from a negligible minority of Brownists, or Independents, they were the only element in English society in 1603 which totally rejected the Protestant Settlement. And they were a much greater threat than any Protestant deviants because of the support they could expect from foreign powers, and from powerful international organisations like the papacy and the Society of Jesus; indeed the papal bull *Regnans in Excelsis* of 1570[63] made them all potential traitors.

The battery of legislation brought to bear on them by Elizabeth's parliaments ought to have been sufficient to eliminate them.[64] They incurred cumulative fines of £20 a month for non-attendance at church, which for landowners could lead to the permanent sequestration of two-thirds of their estates. Severe penalties were imposed for attending mass, or even possessing any of the apparatus of Catholic devotion; it was felony to be converted to Rome, treason to convert others; Catholic priests could be convicted of high treason simply for being in orders. But it seems that even at the height of anti-Catholic agitation, in the 1580s, this legislation was never efficiently, consistently and ruthlessly enforced, except against the clergy. It virtually eliminated working-class Catholicism, but this only meant that it was now concentrated on the wealthier and more influential landed classes. Even so, their numbers were probably not large. Our best guess now puts the Catholic adult male population at about 40,000, but any figure is very difficult to establish, and hostile contemporaries are to be forgiven if they believed the papists to be a much larger minority than they actually were.[65]

The very persistence of the English Catholics, the failure to eliminate them as the Protestants had been eliminated in Italy and Spain, for instance, and were shortly to be eliminated from South Germany, was exasperating and alarming; but much of the blame for this lay with the amateur officials of local government. Parliament had provided them with sufficient legislation, but JPs were strangely reluctant to enforce it against their neighbours, often their relations by marriage, despite their near-paranoid fear of popery as a national or international phenomenon. A few known or suspected Catholics even survived in local government itself.[66]

On the accession of James I, like all the Stuarts ecumenical in spirit and easy-going in his attitude to Catholicism, there was even the prospect of a formal *détente*. With Philip II dead and Europe turning towards peace, even Elizabeth I and Robert Cecil had been trying to detach the native Catholic community and its clergy from the ultramontane influence of the Jesuits and the papacy – a solution which also appealed to Charles II and Clarendon in 1660. Unfortunately, James's talk of toleration was premature, and when parliament in 1604 forced him to pass an act enforcing the existing law[67] the result was the Gunpowder Plot of 1605, which provoked a new burst of penal legislation. A new act of 1606 (**55**) attempted *inter alia* to smoke out church-papists by obliging suspected recusants not only to attend church but to take communion regularly. A second act penalised Protestants incautious enough to take Catholic

[63] Elton, *Tudor Constitution*, pp. 423–8.

[64] *Ibid.*, pp. 419–42. There is also a useful analytical summary in Havran, *Catholics in Caroline England*, ch. 1.

[65] The latest and most thorough assessment of numbers is by John Bossy, *The English Catholic Community 1570–1850* (1975), ch. 8. But the situation is fluid enough for Usher to suggest that there were as many as a million of them in 1603, roughly one-quarter of the population (*Reconstruction*, I, 156–9). This we can discount, but it shows how easy it was for contemporaries to deceive themselves. See also Caroline Hibbard, 'Early Stuart Catholicism: Revisions and Re-revisions', *JMH*, LII (1980), 1–34.

[66] Kenyon, *Popish Plot*, pp. 6–8.

[67] 'An Act for the due execution of the Statutes against Jesuits, Seminary Priests, Recusants, etc.', 1 & 2 Jac. I, c. 4, printed *TCD*, pp. 83–5.

wives; the husbands were barred from public office, and the wives forfeited two-thirds of their dowers and jointures. Further attempts were made to reinforce the Elizabethan legislation forbidding recusants to travel overseas, to keep arms or to baptise their children as Catholics; provisions which were so rarely enforced that they are scarcely worth reciting.[68]

But, terrified as he was by the Plot, James still strove for conciliation, and he personally framed a new oath of allegiance, embodied in the first statute of 1606 (55), which he hoped Catholics might be persuaded to take with a clear conscience, perhaps even with the permission of their Church.[69] To his disappointment it was steadily rejected by successive popes, and the attempt made by a further act of 1610[70] to impose it not only on all office-holders but on the population in general was predictably not pressed to a conclusion. But it remained in force until 1689, as the standard oath of allegiance, and in the second half of the century there is evidence that an increasing number of lay Catholics felt themselves able to take it, with or without the permission of their priests.[71]

Meanwhile James's tolerance of crypto-Catholics like the Howards, Earls of Northampton, Suffolk and Arundel, in prominent positions at his court – it was virtually impossible to enforce any penal law for religion against the nobility – aggravated the general suspicion of his soundness on this question, as did his intimacy with the Spanish ambassador Sarmiento, later Gondomar. His queen, Anne of Denmark, was secretly converted to Rome, as was the Countess of Buckingham, mother of his prime favourite. Indeed, the famous conference between William Laud and the Jesuit Fisher in 1622 was designed to rescue Buckingham himself from temptation.[72] There was much that was attractive, even glamorous, in Catholicism; its bland assurances, its majestic antiquity, its cosmopolitanism, its status as the only religion fit for princes. Moreover the exigencies of foreign policy in a Europe still dominated by the Catholic powers made it impossible for James I or his son to persecute their Catholic subjects too blatantly. Thus the Spanish Marriage negotiations in 1623 and the French Marriage treaty in 1625 both led to the clandestine suspension of the penal laws, at least for a time. This is reflected in the figures for the execution of Catholic priests: 124 under Elizabeth, 19 under James I, only two between 1625 and 1640.[73] In fact, the reign of James saw a notable increase in the strength of the Jesuit mission in England, and, for all the legislation against it, the establishment of a string of English religious houses and new contemplative orders on the Continent.[74]

Given the contemporaneous revival of Catholic power in France and Germany in the 1620s, it is not surprising that parliament after parliament demanded the sterner

---

[68] 'An Act to prevent and avoid dangers which may grow by Popish recusants', 3 & 4 Jac. I, c. 5, printed TCD, pp. 94–104.

[69] David Harris Willson, James VI and I (1956), pp. 227–8.

[70] 7 & 8 Jac. I, c. 6, printed TCD, pp. 105–9.

[71] Kenyon, Popish Plot, pp. 229–31; Miller, Popery and Politics, pp. 30–3.

[72] Gardiner, History, IV, 279–81; Roger Lockyer, Buckingham (1981), p. 115; Trevor-Roper, Archbishop Laud, pp. 59–60.

[73] Havran, op. cit., pp. 111–12; David Mathew, Catholicism in England (1955), p. 82.

[74] Hugh Aveling, The Handle and the Axe, ch. 3; John Bossy, 'The English Catholic Community 1603–25', in Smith, James VI and I, pp. 91–105.

enforcement of the penal laws, the removal of Catholics from Court, and the suppression of clergymen like Richard Montague, who discerned points of contact, even a certain identity of interest, between Rome and Canterbury (p. 117 above). Charles I's intensification of persecution in the 1630s, like Danby's in the 1670s, was obviously undertaken for financial reasons, or as a sop to public opinion,[75] and did nothing to offset the impression created by the presence at Court of a prominent and self-confident Catholic element, which was adding to its numbers by conversion, of clandestine emissaries from the Holy See, and of a number of bishops who seemed prepared to compromise with Rome, if not worse.[76] By 1639 and 1640 this had become a first-class political issue, though Charles's government was slow to realise it.

55. 3 Jac. I, c. 4: An Act for the better discovering and repressing of Popish recusants, 1606

Forasmuch as it is found by daily experience that many his Majesty's subjects that adhere in their hearts to the popish religion, by the infection drawn from thence, and by the wicked and devilish counsel of Jesuits, seminaries and other like persons dangerous to the Church and state, are so far perverted in the point of their loyalties and due allegiance unto the king's Majesty and the Crown of England, as they are ready to entertain and execute any treasonable conspiracies and practices, as evidently appears by that more than barbarous and horrible attempt to have blown up with gunpowder the king, queen, prince, Lords and Commons in the House of Parliament assembled, tending to the utter subversion of the whole state, lately undertaken by the instigation of Jesuits and seminaries, and in advancement of their religion by their scholars taught and instructed by them to that purpose, which attempt by the only goodness of Almighty God was discovered and defeated; and where[as] divers persons popishly affected do nevertheless, the better to cover and hide their false hearts, and with the more safety to attend the opportunity to execute their mischievous designs, repair sometimes to church to escape the penalties of the laws in that behalf provided; for the better discovery therefore of such persons and their evil affections to the king's Majesty and the state of this his realm, to the end that being known their evil purposes may be the better prevented; be it enacted . . . that every popish recusant convicted or hereafter to be convicted which heretofore hath conformed him or herself, or which shall hereafter conform him or herself, and repair to church . . . shall within the first year next after the end of this session of parliament . . . or within the first year next after that he or she shall . . . conform his or herself, and after the first said year shall

---

[75] The picture presented by Havran, op. cit., ch. 6, is not entirely clear. We can only conclude that in certain areas there was an increased drive for enforcement, but this was limited in scope, and as always the machinery available was never very efficient. See Hugh Aveling, in Catholic Record Society, LIII (1961), 291ff., and Thomas G. Barnes, Somerset, pp. 14-15.

[76] Aveling, Handle and Axe, ch. 5; Hibbard, Charles I and the Popish Plot, passim.

once in every year following at the least, receive the blessed sacrament of the Lord's Supper . . . And if any recusant so conformed shall not receive the sacrament . . . accordingly, he or she shall . . . forfeit for the first year twenty pounds, and for the second year . . . forty pounds, and for every year after . . . threescore pounds, until he or she shall have received the said sacrament as is aforesaid . . .

★   ★   ★

[§ v re-enacted, with slight alterations, the provisions of 23 Eliz., c. 1 and 29 Eliz., c. 6,[77] which imposed a fine of £20 a month on recusants, and permitted the government to take the income from two-thirds of their estates in default.]

VI. . . . Now forasmuch as the said penalty of twenty pounds monthly is a greater burden unto men of small living than unto such as are of better ability . . ., who, rather than they will have two parts of their lands to be seized, will be ready always to pay the said twenty pounds . . ., and yet retain the residue of their living and inheritance in their own hands, being of great yearly value, which they do for the most part employ (as experience hath taught) to the maintenance of superstition and the popish religion, and to the relief of Jesuits, seminaries, popish priests and other dangerous persons to the state; therefore to the intent that hereafter the penalty . . . might be inflicted in better proportion upon men of great ability, be it enacted . . . that the king's Majesty, his heirs and successors, shall from and after the Feast of St Michael the Archangel [29 September] next coming after the end of this session of parliament, have full power and liberty to refuse the penalty of twenty pounds a month, though it be tendered . . ., and thereupon to seize and take to his own use . . . two parts in three parts to be divided as well of all the lands, tenements and hereditaments, leases and farms that at the time of such seizure shall be or afterwards shall come to any the said offenders . . ., or any other to his or her use, or in trust for him or her, or at his or her disposition, or whereby or wherewith, or in consideration whereof, such offender or his family or any of them shall be relieved, maintained or kept . . .

★   ★   ★

VIII. And for the better trial how his Majesty's subjects stand affected in point of their loyalty and due obedience, be it also enacted . . . that from and after the end of this present session of parliament it shall be lawful to and for any bishop in his diocese, or any two justices of the peace, whereof one of them to be of the quorum, within the limits of their jurisdiction out of sessions, to require any person of the age of eighteen years or above, being or which shall be convict or indicted of or for any recusancy, other than noblemen or

[77] Elton, *Tudor Constitution*, p. 431, and *PCD*, p. 88, respectively.

noblewomen, . . . or any person passing in or through the county, shire or liberty, and unknown, except as is last before excepted, that being examined by them upon oath, shall confess or not deny himself or herself to be a recusant, or shall confess or not deny that he or she has not received the said sacrament twice within the year when last past, to take the oath hereafter following, upon the Holy Evangelist, which said bishop or two justices of peace shall certify in writing . . . at the next General or Quarter Sessions . . . the Christian name, surname and place of abode of every person which shall so take the oath, which certificate shall be there recorded by the clerk of the peace . . .

IX. . . . The tenor of which said oath hereafter followeth:

I, A. B., do truly and sincerely acknowledge, profess, testify and declare in my conscience before God and the world, that our Sovereign Lord King James is lawful and rightful king of this realm and of all other his Majesty's dominions and countries, and that the pope, neither of himself nor by any authority of the Church or See of Rome, or by any other means with any other, hath any power or authority to depose the king, or to dispose [of] any of his Majesty's kingdoms or dominions, or to authorise any foreign prince to invade or annoy him or his countries, or to discharge any of his subjects of their allegiance and obedience to his Majesty, or to give licence or leave to any of them to bear arms, raise tumult, or to offer any violence or hurt to his Majesty's royal person, state or government, or to any of his Majesty's subjects within his Majesty's dominions. Also I do swear from my heart that notwithstanding any declaration or sentence of excommunication or deprivation made or granted or to be made or granted by the pope or his successors, or by any authority derived or pretended to be derived from him or his see, against the said king, his heirs or successors, or any absolution of the said subjects from their obedience, I will bear faith and true allegiance to his Majesty, his heirs and successors, and him or them will defend to the uttermost of my power against all conspiracies and attempts whatsoever which shall be made against his or their persons, their crown and dignity, by reason or colour or any such sentence or declaration or otherwise, and will do my best endeavour to disclose and make known unto his Majesty, his heirs and successors, all treasons and traitorous conspiracies which I shall know or hear of to be against him or any of them. And I do further swear, that I do from my heart abhor, detest and abjure as impious and heretical this damnable doctrine and position that princes which be excommunicated and deprived by the pope may be deposed or murdered by their subjects or any other whatsoever. And I do believe and in my conscience am resolved, that neither the pope nor any person whatsoever hath power to absolve me of this oath or any part thereof, which I acknowledge by good and full authority to be lawfully ministered unto me, and do renounce all pardons and dispensations to the contrary. And all these things I do plainly and sincerely acknowledge and swear, according to these express words by me spoken, and according to the plain and common sense and understanding of the same words without any equivocation or mental evasion or secret reservation whatsoever. And I do make this recognition and acknowledgment heartily, willingly and truly, upon the true faith of a Christian. So help me God.

Unto which oath so taken, the said person shall subscribe his or her name or mark.

★ ★ ★

SR, IV, 1071–7

BOOK II

THE ERA OF EXPERIMENT
1640–60

Men go away, but constitutions never fall.
GEORGE DOWNING

CHAPTER 5

THE BREAKDOWN 1640-2

We have a much better understanding now of the mechanism by which a total breakdown in political conventions occurred in 1640 and 1641, leading to rebellion in 1642,[1] but the reasons for it are still difficult to determine. In the sphere of constitutional law, the proper concern of this book, there was singularly little disagreement, as I have attempted to show (p. 9 above); if there was a dispute at all it was focussed on the *use* of the constitution, not its nature.

In fact, the assumption which is implicit in the work of Gardiner and the Whig historians, that Charles I's personal rule in the 1630s was doomed from the beginning, that from 1629 he was on a downward path, lurching from expedient to expedient towards a disastrous and all but inevitable confrontation, must now be considerably modified. Though this 'experiment' was not a resounding success from the king's point of view it was certainly not a failure, and if he had been able to avoid a foreign war his regime might have continued indefinitely.[2]

Certainly all the attempts which have been made to locate the causes of the Great Rebellion in class conflict and economic strain have been unavailing. In fact, with the rest of Europe at war in the 1630s England enjoyed a mild trading boom, and agriculture flourished in a series of long, hot summers. Contemporaries as diverse as Clarendon and Harrington were later to look back on this as a golden age, at least in its physical aspects. (Though Clarendon was not the only one who thought it had been *too* prosperous, to such an extent that it had corrupted the ruling classes.) There was some grumbling at the petty fiscal expedients adopted by the government, such as distraint of knighthood or the enforcement of antique forest laws, but no concerted resistance. The revival of monopolies was an irritation, but the continued levy of tunnage and poundage and impositions did not even merit comment, even when the latter were increased; and by the time he died in 1635 Lord Treasurer Portland had succeeded in balancing the royal budget. Nor was there much opposition to the government's most comprehensive, onerous and controversial tax, ship-money – not until 1638, and then it is difficult to say whether this was in reaction to the verdict in *Rex* v. *Hampden* (the commonly received doctrine until a few years ago) or to the outbreak of the Scots

---

[1] Notably through the efforts of Anthony Fletcher, *The Outbreak of the English Civil War*; but see also Donald Pennington, 'The Making of the War 1640–42', in Pennington and Thomas, *Puritans and Revolutionaries*, and Brian Manning, *The English People and the English Revolution*.

[2] Even Lawrence Stone, *The Causes of the English Revolution* (1972), pp. 132–4, makes some concessions in this direction. See also Robert Ashton, *Reformation and Revolution 1558–1660* (1984), p. 296, and Kevin Sharpe, 'The Personal Rule of Charles I', in Tomlinson, *Before the Civil War*, pp. 53–78. It is fair to say that there is another school of thought which is engaged in refining the Whig interpretation in order to accommodate it to twentieth-century theories of rebellion. This is represented to some extent by Stone, above, also by Perez Zagorin, *The Court and the Country* (1969) and *Rebels and Rulers* (Cambridge 1982), vol. 2.

Rebellion only a few months later.[3] Above all, the absence of parliament, which seems to us the most significant aspect of the whole period, occasioned very little comment. Even in 1639 and early 1640 there was no general call for a meeting of parliament to remedy the nation's ills, as there was in 1679 and 1680.[4]

It is too easy to take the legal and fiscal reforms adumbrated in the Short Parliament, and partly implemented in the first session of the Long Parliament, and assume that these had been serious and important issues for the past ten years, or that they constituted a kind of 'reform programme'. The truth is, the banning of ship-money by statute, the abolition of Star Chamber, the Forest Laws and so on, were random, piecemeal measures which did not even begin to cope with a general crisis which was outside parliament's competence to deal with, and did not meet any of the deep anxieties and suspicions now prevalent; the best that could be said of them is that they were better than doing nothing.[5]

We are driven back, in fact, on an interpretation based on politics, war and religion. The root of the crisis is to be found in the Bishops' Wars of 1639 and 1640. These cut both ways: they put an intolerable strain on Charles's administrative machine, which was no more able to wage war than it had been under Buckingham; but on the other hand his possession of an army, however ineffective, and the possibility – however remote – that he might reconquer Scotland, was infinitely alarming to a generation accustomed to operating in a demilitarised political situation. This is why the pace of the crisis visibly accelerated in 1640, and why the elections to the Long Parliament in October were conducted in a much more excited and combative atmosphere than those for the Short Parliament in March.[6] The year 1640 merits more attention than it has so far received, but it is obvious that the recall of Strafford from Dublin, the abrupt dissolution of the Short Parliament and the king's blatant attempts to secure aid from Spain exacerbated his subjects' worst suspicions, and led some of them to dealings with the Scots enemy which at the time were very far from being as natural or forgiveable as they appear in retrospect.[7]

Nor could the original cause of the Bishops' Wars – Charles's attempt to impose an

[3] M. D. Gordon, 'The Collection of Ship Money', 3 *TRHS*, IV (1910), 141–62. N. P. Bard, 'The Ship Money Case and William Fiennes, Viscount Saye and Sele', *BIHR*, L (1977), 177–84, shows the unavailing attempts of one of the leading obstructionists to publicise the issue. Fletcher (*Sussex*, p. 208) reminds us that opposition was particularly slow to arise in the seaboard counties.

[4] Esther Cope, 'Public Images of Parliament During its Absence', *Legislative Studies Quarterly*, VII (1982), 221–34. Conrad Russell points out that a belief in the need for regular parliaments did not arise until 1641. 'The Nature of a Parliament in Early Stuart England', in Tomlinson, *op. cit.*, pp. 146–50.

[5] It is worth noting that this reform legislation was far from comprehensive, though we often assume that it was. There was no attempt to reinforce the Monopolies Act of 1624, though one would regard the revival of monopolies as much more important than, say, distraint of knighthood. Similarly wardship, which was on the tapis in 1641, but was left over until 1646. Enclosures were not dealt with at all, though this was the one issue which had roused general opposition in the previous decade. (See Keith Lindley, *Fenland Riots and the English Revolution* (1982).) In fact, it is a point of some general significance that the Long Parliament had no economic or fiscal programme at all, and the Grand Remonstrance had virtually nothing to say on such matters. Parliament even failed to deal properly with the key question of general taxation; Conrad Russell, 'Parliament and the King's Finances, in *Origins*, pp. 108–16.

[6] John K. Gruenfelder, 'The Election to the Short Parliament', in *Early Stuart Studies*, ed. Howard S. Reinmuth (Minneapolis 1970), pp. 188–230; Keeler, *Long Parliament*, pp. 6–11.

[7] John Elliott's 'The Year of the Three Ambassadors', in *History and Imagination*, ed. Hugh Lloyd-Jones *et al.* (1981), pp. 165–81, throws new light on Charles's negotiations with Spain.

English-style prayer book on the Scots – easily be forgotten. It is arguable that Laud's ecclesiastical policy in general roused a sharper resentment than any of this government's secular measures, though we should still be sceptical of any corporate, dynamic movement labelled 'Puritan'. The bishops in themselves provoked feelings of frustrated rage in many quarters, but this did not reach boiling point and spill over until Convocation passed its insanely provocative series of canons in 1640.[8] Again, this was the critical year.

Yet time was to show that though there was a very strong and very general feeling in 1640 and 1641 that the Church was in need of reform of some kind, a majority could never be found for any one solution. Nor were most MPs willing to look beyond 'reformation' to 'alteration'; that is, a complete change in the nature of the Church of England. The most serious complaint in 1640 was that the word 'Puritan' was being used by the enemies of Protestantism to libel its defenders – the effect being to enhance the prestige of 'Puritanism' and enlist on its side a great deal of bi-partisan support which was not basically 'Puritan' at all. As Francis Rous told the Short Parliament:

> The word Puritan is an essential engine . . . For this word in the mouth of a drunkard doth mean a sober man, in the mouth of an Arminian, an orthodox man, in the mouth of a Papist, a Protestant. And so it is spoke to shame a man out of all religion.[9]

In an age when the issue Catholicism versus Protestantism was still in the balance in Europe, with neither side willing to compromise, the Church of England's ability to lead the defence against Rome was crucial, and it seemed to many, and not the most bigoted, that in this respect Laud had treacherously weakened it; indeed the main charges against him at his trial in 1644, and those most vigorously pressed, were that he had himself planned to renege to Rome and so far as possible take the Church with him. Nineteenth and twentieth-century historians, by nature and training liberal in their outlook, have been reluctant to face the fact that by 1640, and increasingly in the course of that year, Charles and his ministers – for the pretence that his ministers were acting independently of the king was never more than a legal fiction or a polite convention – were suspected of planning a total subversion of Church and state, to bring them into line with the Church of Rome and with the continental autocracies of France and Spain. But this 'conspiracy theory' has now been unravelled and fully documented, and must be accepted as the mainspring of action in the Long Parliament.[10] This is why one of the first acts of the Long Parliament, on 11 November 1640, was to impeach Strafford for high treason and send him to the Tower, closely followed by Archbishop Laud.

The deterioration in the situation over the summer and autumn of 1640 is evident from a comparison of two 'keynote' speeches made by John Pym, one to the Short Parliament on 17 April (**56**), the other to the Long Parliament on 7 November (**57**).

---

[8] The latest examination of this problem is by Michael G. Finlayson, *Historians, Puritanism and the English Revolution* (Toronto 1983).

[9] Cope, *Proceedings*, p. 147.

[10] Hibbard, *Charles I and the Popish Plot*, also Robin Clifton, 'Fear of Popery', in Russell, *Origins*, pp. 144–67. (See p. 168 above.)

The first was concerned, rather laboriously, to tabulate grievances in a way familiar in previous Stuart parliaments, and concerned the interaction of government and people. The second, much shorter and more trenchant, strongly hinted at the existence of a conspiracy to subvert government altogether.[11] It led to the appointment on 10 November of a Committee on the State of the Kingdom which a year later produced the Grand Remonstrance.

But it was the attempt to destroy the Earl of Strafford which dominated politics over the winter of 1640-1 and well into the spring. It revealed the weakness of the impeachment process, confirmed time and again under the later Stuarts; yet if the Commons could not remove one of the most feared and hated men in England it could not hope to influence, let alone reverse the king's policy. Pym opened the proceedings on 25 November 1640 by arguing that it was the blackest treason to sow discord between king and people as Strafford had done; and if he had succeeded England would have succumbed to 'the ecclesiastical tyranny of the pope' and 'the civil tyranny of an arbitrary, unlimited, confused government', (58a).

Strong stuff indeed, but it was not reflected in the Articles of Impeachment, which were delayed until 28 January. These accused Strafford of erecting an 'arbitrary and tyrannical government' in the North and in Ireland, of deliberately provoking a further war with the Scots in 1640, when the dispute between them and the king was about to be composed, and of advising Charles to break the Short Parliament and rule arbitrarily, 'loosed and absolved from all rules of government', a process in which he then played a leading part.[12] However, none of these acts individually, even if they could be proved, amounted to treason, and the Lords were reluctant to allow the Commons' argument that they constituted a kind of 'cumulative treason'; they were also sympathetic to the counter-argument that if it were allowed no future minister could serve the king in safety. Two powerful closing speeches, by Strafford himself and Pym, brought the proceedings to deadlock, (58b, c).[13] The Commons had to resort to the dubious expedient of an act of attainder, simply asserting Strafford's guilt and sentencing him to death, which was forced past the Lords and the king under the pressure of mob violence. He was executed on 12 May 1641. But no further proceedings were taken against Laud or Finch, the former Lord Keeper, who also stood impeached.

Meanwhile the process by which public confidence in the king was undermined, and the political temperature of the capital was raised by apocalyptic preaching and mob rioting, has been sufficiently explained.[14] It is possible to impugn, as Clarendon

---

[11] In the first edition of this book I discovered a much stronger and more marked contrast between these two speeches. I now think I read into them more than I should have done, but to my mind they still suggest a change of stance as well as a deterioration in the political situation, and since together they embody the opposition's case against Charles's government I have decided to retain them. Pym's role in these proceedings has now been considerably clarified by Sheila Lambert, 'The Opening of the Long Parliament', *HJ*, 27 (1984), 265-87.

[12] Rushworth, II, 61-75.

[13] C. V. Wedgwood's *Strafford: a Revaluation* (1961) is still valuable, but the fullest account of the trial is by John H. Timmis, *Thine is the Kingdom* (Alabama 1974). See also Conrad Russell, 'The Theory of Treason in the Trial of Strafford', *EHR*, LXXX (1965), 30-50, who argues that in fact Strafford's 'crime' of coming between the king and his people *was* treasonable as the law was then understood.

[14] Fletcher, *Outbreak*, chs. 1-3; Ashton, *The English Civil War*, ch. 6; Manning, *The English People and the English Revolution*; Valerie Pearl, *London and the Outbreak of the Puritan Revolution* (Oxford 1961), ch. 6.

very vigorously did, the sincerity of the parliamentary leaders who fomented public alarms, but the Queen's confused intrigues with officers of the army, the king's negotiations with the Dutch Stadholder, his repeated refusal to disband the Irish army and his continued clemency towards Catholic priests, gave them plenty of ammunition. Whether he ought, as Clarendon thought, to have taken some of these spokesmen into his government, is doubtful;[15] certainly it would have been to fly in the face of the accepted conventions of the age. To suppose that opposition to the king's government in parliament was the road to preferment is to transfer eighteenth-century practice back to the seventeenth. (And even this was firmly rejected by George III.)

Moreover, by May 1641 Charles had been forced to make significant concessions, which, however grudging, he could not but regard as binding upon him. On 25 January, in a speech to both Houses, he agreed in general terms to cancel all innovations in Church and state, to reform the courts of law, and strip the bishops of their temporal authority; but he warned them that he would never consent to the exclusion of the bishops from parliament, nor would he consent to the Triennial Bill, then before the Lords, which he characterised as a direct encroachment on his prerogative.[16] However, this bill, which obliged him to meet all subsequent parliaments at least once in three years for a session of 50 days, and set up independent machinery to ensure this (59), passed the Lords, and such was the public agitation in the City and at Westminster that on 16 February he gave way. Arguably this was not a crucial measure; it did not come into effect until the next parliament, and the machinery for enforcing it would almost certainly have broken down in practice. He was much more dismayed by a subsequent bill forbidding the prorogation or dissolution of the present parliament without its own consent (GCD, p. 158). Both acts reflect a profound mistrust of the king, but the majority of the Commons fell in with them on the plea that without them it was becoming increasingly difficult to borrow money to pay off the Scots and disband the English army. But it was not until June that taxation was regularised by the Tunnage and Poundage Act, which gave Charles the ancient customs, plus all the impositions which were being levied when parliament met, but for two months only; it was subsequently renewed at two-monthly intervals until July 1642 (GCD, p. 159).

The redress of other grievances continued throughout July and August rather episodically, and apparently without any predetermined plan.[17] The Court of Star Chamber was abolished on a number of flimsy and unhistorical excuses, and with it went the Councils of the North and of the Marches and Wales, (62); another statute disposed of High Commission (63). In addition the levy of ship money was declared illegal, and the verdict in Rex v. Hampden reversed (GCD, p. 189), the limits of the royal forest were defined once and for all (ibid., p. 192), and the levy of fines in distraint of knighthood prohibited (ibid., p. 196). The Court of Requests, moribund for some

---

[15] Clarendon, History, iv, 75–7; B. H. G. Wormald, Clarendon: Politics, History and Religion (Cambridge 1951), pt I, § 1, pt II, §2.

[16] No. 8, p. 17 above.

[17] Dr Lambert points out (art. cit., p. 274) that many of these bills did not originate in the committees appointed to consider the grievances in question. Clarendon's account of how a bill to regulate procedure in Star Chamber was incontinently turned into one to abolish the court altogether is well known; History, III, 262.

years, was apparently overlooked; so, more surprisingly, was the Court of Wards and the feudal rights it administered – such a bone of contention under James I. Purveyance was another such issue; a bill to abolish it was in progress at the end of the first session, but then lapsed; all that survived was an act to restrict the powers of the Clerk of the Market.[18] Wardship was abolished by ordinance in 1646, confirmed by Cromwell ten years later and by the Cavalier Parliament in 1661.[19] These statutes were never repealed. In fact, they were the basis of the Restoration Settlement, and in that sense the constitution just marked time from August 1641 until May 1661. But it seemed a poor return for seven or eight months' effort on the part of a parliament supposedly united in the cause of reform and a king supposedly disposed to grant it.

The truth is, parliament was far from united. It was divided on the attainder of Strafford; it continued to be divided on Church reform (ch. 6 below); two good reasons, incidentally, for postponing Laud's trial. The Commons' Protestation of 3 May 1641, appealing for national support against a supposed popish conspiracy, savoured of desperation more than aggression, and was itself divisive (60). By the summer the Scots army was ready to retire and the English army was on the point of being disbanded, but the king's decision to visit Edinburgh, obviously to seek support there, kept up the tension. The Ten Propositions, drawn up by the Commons and sent to the Lords on 24 June, was a confused and rambling document, but by implication it confirmed the House's belief in a popish conspiracy, and the demand that the king employ only 'such councillors and officers as the parliament may have cause to confide in' was a bid for control of the executive which would have been undreamt-of six months before. The demand that the lord lieutenants 'may be faithful and trusty, and careful of the peace of the kingdom' even foreshadowed the Militia Ordinance of the following year (61).

Charles's ill-judged conduct in Edinburgh, particularly his attempt to arrest the Earl of Argyll and the Duke of Hamilton, further clouded his reputation; but the decisive event, of course, was the Irish Rebellion, news of which reached London on 1 November. It confirmed and at the same time extended the idea of a great Catholic conspiracy, and put Charles's persistent refusal to disband the Irish army in a most sinister light. Moreover, it raised the whole question of executive power and military command in its most acute form: could Charles be trusted with the substantial army which must now be raised to pacify Ireland? Pym argued not, to the extent that on 5 November he brought in an Additional Instruction to the joint parliamentary committee in attendance on the king at Edinburgh, that they were to inform the king that unless he changed his policy and his advisers parliament must decline to assist him in the reconquest of Ireland. The House would not stomach this, but on 8 November it was stampeded into accepting a new draft embodying a much more revolutionary proposition, that if Charles did not comply with their request they would take their own measures to suppress the rebellion.[20]

[18] 17 Car. I, c. 19. Purveyance was suspended by order of Parliament in December 1642 and abolished by ordinance in 1657; G. E. Aylmer, 'The Last Years of Purveyance 1610–1660', *Econ. Hist. Review*, X (1957), 84, 90.
[19] Firth and Rait, I, 833, II, 1043; 12 Car. II, c. 4.
[20] *D'Ewes Journal*, ed. Coates, pp. 94–105; Fletcher, *Outbreak*, pp. 143–5.

The Lords rejected this Instruction, and it is doubtful if the Commons would have pursued it anyway. But if parliament was confused and divided, the king seemed to have no substantial following at all. His one hope was the religious question, which had seriously divided the Commons in February and March, and had divided Lords from Commons in August and September (p. 231 below). At the end of October he announced from Edinburgh, 'I am constant for the doctrine and discipline of the Church of England as it was established by Queen Elizabeth and my father, and resolved (by the Grace of God) to live and die in the maintenance of it.'[21] The Commons' answer was to bring on at last the Grand Remonstrance on the state of the kingdom which had been in gestation since the previous November (64). In it was now incorporated the demand that the king employ only ministers trusted by parliament, subject to removal at parliament's request without a formal case being made out against them (§§ 197–8), and its sponsors tried to smother the Church question by referring it to a synod of divines drawn not only from England but from the other Protestant communities of Europe (§ 185). It led to one of the fiercest and longest debates in this parliament, and it finally passed, on 22 November, by a mere 11 votes.

Three days later Charles returned to London at last and came to terms with the 'constitutional royalists' headed by Edward Hyde and the Earl of Bristol. On his arrival he repeated to the aldermen of London his pledge to the established Church, and on 10 December he ordered that religious services be conducted according to law. His answer to the Grand Remonstrance, on 23 December, also stressed his responsibility for the preservation of the Church (GCD, p. 233). Meanwhile the increasingly violent rioting round the palaces of Westminster and Whitehall convinced Charles that the Commons intended to force his hand as they had in May, by an oblique threat to the queen, and the Common Council elections in December showed that he was losing such influence as he had on the City government. On their side the opposition leaders were alarmed at the assembly in London of large numbers of gentlemen volunteers and soldiers of fortune, ostensibly for service in Ireland or in the Portuguese War of Independence. With some reason they feared a military *coup d'état*, and Charles's attempt on 23 December to replace the governor of the Tower by one of his own creatures roused such fierce opposition that he had to give way. On 28 December Lord Digby took the alternative, constitutionalist line by proposing to the Lords that in view of the persistent rioting round Westminster their deliberations were not free, and they should adjourn to a place of safety. Unfortunately, these same riots had caused most of the bishops to stay away, and the motion was lost by four votes. When the bishops returned the following day and tried to have the vote set aside, the Lords suddenly lost patience with these unpopular and troublesome ecclesiastics. They sent the bishops' petition down to the Commons, who gratefully impeached the lot, and the Lords at once sequestered them.

This sudden volte-face on the part of the Lords, and the serious reduction of his

---

[21] *Memoirs Illustrative of the Life and Writings of John Evelyn*, ed. W. Bray, 2nd edn (London 1819), II, App., p. 37. This was a marginal note to a letter from Edward Nicholas dated 12 October, received back the 23rd.

majority there, panicked the king. On 3 January 1642, the Lord Keeper was instructed to impeach Lord Kimbolton and five members of the Commons – Pym, Hampden, William Strode, Denzil Holles and Sir Arthur Haslerigg – on the grounds that they had 'endeavoured to subvert the fundamental laws and government of the kingdom', almost exactly the same charge as had been levelled against the bishops a few days before (65). Next day, 4 January, the king appeared at Westminster with a posse of his gentlemen volunteers, and burst into the House of Commons to arrest the five Members. Forewarned, they had already fled downriver to the City. This gross violation of parliamentary privilege lost Charles London, and did his reputation permanent harm. Such was the reaction of the Lords as well as the Commons, the Inns of Court and the City government, that he left with the queen on 10 January.

During the succeeding nine months the struggle revolved round the control of the forces which both sides wanted to raise for the relief of Ireland. Other questions which had hitherto seemed incapable of solution were simply pushed aside; the bill to exclude the bishops from the House of Lords, for instance, which had been bouncing to and fro between the two Houses for nearly a year, passed the Lords on 5 February, and received the king's assent a week later (p. 237 below). Meanwhile on 31 January the Commons drew up a Militia Bill giving parliament the power to name the lord lieutenant in each county. The Lords hesitated to pass the bill, but they associated themselves with the demand which lay behind it, and on 12 February a list of lord lieutenants was drawn up for submission to the King.

Charles refused point-blank to surrender control of the only armed forces now available, and withdrew north to York.[22] But on 5 March parliament passed the Militia Bill as an Ordinance, nominating their own lord lieutenants (66), and on 23 April the new parliamentary governor of Hull, Sir John Hotham, denied Charles access to this important royal arsenal. A flurry of protests and counter protests on this and cognate issues culminated in a parliamentary Remonstrance on 26 May which anticipated some of the charges levelled at Charles at his trial in 1649 (67). Emboldened by the king's continued weakness, on 1 June parliament proceeded to issue the Nineteen Propositions, which were effectively terms of unconditional surrender (68). The king must accept the Militia Ordinance, consent to the reform of the Church by synod, place the upbringing and the marriage of his children in parliament's hands, and surrender his rights of appointment in every sphere of government, even his right to issue patents of nobility. But on 27 May Charles had already issued a proclamation forbidding his subjects to obey the Militia Ordinance (GCD, pp. 248–9), and in their reply, on 6 June, parliament finally enunciated the doctrine that was to see them through the first Civil War – that the person of the king was distinguishable from his office, and the functions of that office could be exercised by parliament 'after a more eminent and obligatory manner than it can be by personal act or resolution of his own' (69).

In his Answer to the Nineteen Propositions, on 18 June, Charles's advisers produced

---

[22] For a discussion of the constitutional issues involved see Lois G. Schwoerer, 'The Fittest Subject for a King's Quarrel', JBS, XI (1971), 45–76.

a most remarkable document, upon which they never succeeded in improving.[23] They argued that England's was a mixed constitution, of monarchy, aristocracy and democracy, and that no one of those elements could be too closely restricted without unbalancing the whole structure. They re-affirmed the king's acceptance of the Triennial Act, and the act preventing the dissolution of this parliament, but they insisted that if parliament secured the right to appoint ministers of the state this would be an unwarranted encroachment on the executive and could only lead to anarchy and disorder. (Indeed, they forecast the general course of events for the next few years with remarkable accuracy.)

On any academic judgment, there can be no doubt that the king had won this legal and constitutional debate. Parliament, stripped of more and more of its Members, was soon in danger of losing all credibility, and it made its position no better by declining to assert its own sovereignty and hiding under the king's skirts instead. But this dialectical victory was not so easily translated into military terms. Reverence for the kingly office was universal, but so was distrust of the kingly person (which was why parliament wanted to separate the two), and when Charles raised his standard at Nottingham on 22 August the response was lukewarm.[24] It needed parliament to provide him with a nucleus of supporters, which they did with incomparable clumsiness on 6 September, when they declared that the charges and expense of the war must be borne by those persons who had been, or were to be, voted delinquents by both Houses – which was a suspended sentence on any man of property who did not at once join them (**70**).

56. Pym's speech on Grievances, 17 April 1640[25]

He that takes away weights from the motions doth as good service as he that adds wings unto them. These weights are old grievances. He therefore will do a good work for the king who, to expedite his designs, will set good rules and patterns for effecting thereof.

When God made the world he did it by a pattern which [he] himself had conceived, and Moses did according to the pattern he saw on the Mount. I shall therefore offer you a model of the grievances which afflict the Common-wealth, and which have disabled us to administer any supply until they be redressed, and which still disable us; which grievances may be reduced to three heads.

[23] No. **9**, p. 18 above. Though it was not so epoch-making and original as is often assumed. In many statements issued during the spring and early summer Charles or his speechwriters had been moving towards a more relaxed and liberal position. For instance, 'The King's answer to the Parliament's Votes and Declarations concerning Sir J. Hotham and Hull', 7 May 1642, had a nasty sting in the tail: 'We conclude with Mr Pym's own words: "If the prerogative of the king overwhelm the liberty of the subject, it will be turned to tyranny; if liberty undermine the prerogative, it will grow into anarchy" – and we would say, confusion' (*PH*, II, 216).
[24] Joyce L. Malcolm, *Caesar's Due*, esp. ch. 2; though Ronald Hutton gives a more favourable picture, in *The Royalist War Effort 1642–1646* (1982), chs. 1–2.
[25] As in the first edition, I have continued to use Rushworth's version, supplemented occasionally from the very similar draft now published in Cope, *Proceedings*.

The first are those grievances which during these eleven years' interval of parliaments are against the liberties and privileges of parliament.

The second are innovations in matters of religion.

The third, grievances against the propriety of our goods.

Which grievances I will first propound, and secondly show that the permission of them is as prejudicial to his Majesty as to the Commonwealth; and thirdly, I will show in what way they may be remedied.

In all these I shall take care to maintain the great prerogative of the king, which is, that the king can do no wrong.

And first, I will begin with the grievances against the privileges and liberties of parliament. We all know that the intellectual part, which ought to govern the rest, ought to be kept from distemper, for it is that which purgeth us from all errors, and prevents other mischiefs for time to come. If the understanding part be hurt the mind cannot perform her function. A parliament is that to the Commonwealth which the soul is to the body, which is only able to apprehend and understand the symptoms of all such diseases which threaten the body politic. It behoves us therefore to keep the faculty of that soul from distempers.[26] I shall briefly therefore give you a view of such occurrences as have altered the happy and healthful constitution of it; and in the first place I must remember the breaches of our liberties and privileges of parliament, which are:

First, in that the Speaker the last parliament (the last day of it), being commanded to put the question, the House was commanded they should not speak. These are conceived to be the grounds of whatsoever befell those gentlemen which so lately suffered. 'Tis true, the House was commanded to adjourn presently, yet whilst the House sat God forbid we should be barred from offering the last sighs and groans to his Majesty.

Secondly, in that the parliament was then dissolved, before our grievances had redress, or before we could make our wills known, which is the privilege of dying men; and to be heard before [being condemned] is not denied to private persons.[27]

Thirdly, that the judges presume to question the proceedings of the House. It is against nature and order that inferior courts should undertake to regulate superior. The Court of Parliament is a court of the highest jurisdiction, and cannot be censured by any other law or sentence but by its own.

---

[26] 'And although religion is in truth the greatest grievance to be looked into after, and also should claim the precedence in that respect before either of the other generals, yet inasmuch [as] that verity in religion receives an influence from the free debates in parliament, and consequently from the privileges in parliament without which men will be afraid to speak, I think it fit in order to privileges in parliament to have priority' (Cope, p. 149).

[27] 'Here he applied it some way to the present Speaker in telling him the rights that appertain to the House even at a dissolution of a parliament' (loc. cit.).

Fourthly, the several imprisonments of divers gentlemen, for speaking freely in parliament.

Fifthly, that inferior courts should be informed to punish acts done in this court, whereby divers members of the House were so kept in prison till they had put in security for their good behaviour; and some of them died in prison, others not released until writs came for this parliament.

Lastly (which I conceive to be the greatest), that the parliament was punished without being suffered to make its own defence. I call the dissolution of the parliament a punishment, and justly; the breaking of the parliament is death to a good subject.

But it is to be observed that in this and the other grievances, though the king be no party (for his Highness's prerogative is to do no wrong) yet most of these distempers of state arise and do invade the subjects by means of misinforming him; as the celestial bodies of themselves send forth nothing but wholesomeness to man, but by the ill distemper in inferior bodies much hurt ariseth from them.

The next sort of grievances I deliver are those that concern matters of religion. Wherein I will first observe the great encouragement which is given to them of the popish religion by a universal suspension of all laws that are against them, and some of them admitted into public places of trust and power.[28] I desire not to have any new laws made against them (God be thanked, we have enough), nor a strict execution of the old ones, but only so far forth as tends to the safety of his Majesty, and such a practice of them that the religion that can brook no co-rival may not be the destruction of ours by being too concurrent with it. There is an intention of a Nuncio from the Pope, who is to be here to give secret intelligence to Rome how we incline here, and what will be thought fit to win us thither.

I observe as a great grievance, there are divers innovations in religion amongst ourselves, to make us more capable of a translation,[29] to which purpose popish books have been published in print, and disputations of popish points are and have been used in the universities and elsewhere with privilege, and preached in the pulpit, and maintained for sound doctrine, whereby popish tenets are maintained. The introducing of popish ceremonies, as altars, bowing towards the east, pictures, crosses, crucifixes and the like, which of themselves considered, are so many dry bones, but being put together make

---

[28] 'Divers of them might be of themselves I confess of peaceable dispositions and good natures, but we must not look upon them [as] they are in their natures, for the planets of themselves are of a slow and temperate motion, were they not hurried about by the rapid motion of the spheres, and they carried about by the violence of the *primum mobile*; so are all these papists at the Pope's command at any time, who only waits for blood. I may instance in Hen. 3 and 4 of France, that were both taken away for allowing of Protestants' (*ibid.*, p. 150).

[29] The phrase 'an applying of us towards a conversion to Rome' (*ibid.*, p. 151), makes his meaning more explicit.

the man. We are not now contented with the old ceremonies, I mean such as the constitution of the reformed religion hath continued unto us, but we must introduce again many of those superstitious and infirm ceremonies which accompanied the most decrepit age of popery – bowing to the altar, and the like.

I shall observe the daily discouraging of all godly men who truly profess the Protestant religion, as though men could be too religious. Some things are urged by ecclesiastical men without any ground by any canon or article established, and without any command from the king, either under his Great Seal or by proclamation. The parliament ever since Queen Elizabeth's time desired the bishops to deal moderately, but how they have answered those desires we all know, and these good men for the most part feel. I may not forget that many of the ministers are deprived for refusing to read the Book for Sports and Recreation upon the Sabbath, which was a device of their own heads, which book I may affirm hath many things faulty in it.

Then the encroaching upon the king's authority by ecclesiastical courts, as namely the High Commission, which takes upon it to fine and imprison men, enforcing them to take the oath *ex officio*, with many of the like usurpations, which are punishments belonging only to temporal jurisdiction, and it hath been resolved in the time of King James that the statute of 1 Eliz., c. 1 gives them no such power; moreover, the power which they claim they derive not from the king, nor from any law or statute, but they will immediately have it from heaven *jure divino*. Divers particular ordinaries, chancellors and archdeacons take upon them to make and ordain constitutions within their particular limits. All these things are true to the knowledge of most that hear me.

I now come to the general head of grievances, which is the grievances belonging to our goods, and are in civil matters. The heads thereof are too many.

[1.] The taking of tunnage and poundage, and divers other impositions, without any grant or law for to do so, is a great grievance. There are divers ancient customs due to the king, but they are certain what they are and are due by prescription. These customs being too narrow for his service, and the affections of the people growing stronger and stronger to their prince, tunnage and poundage were granted for years to the king, and afterwards by this House granted for lives, but never were taken by the king's own act without a parliament, for doing which there is no precedent, unless a year or two in the latter end of Queen Elizabeth.

[2.] In the next place of these grievances I rank knighthood, the original whereof was, that persons fit for chivalry might be improved. But this after was stretched for another end, for money, and extended not only to terre tenants [sc. freeholders] but to lessees and merchants, who were first to appear, and then to plead for themselves, at the Council board, but were delayed from day to day, to their great charge and inconvenience, and notwithstanding the just defence they have made for themselves there have been infinite distresses laid upon them until the fines were paid, which were imposed not by courts but by commissioners assigned for that purpose, and this being a continuing offence they are by the same rule as liable now to fines as ever.

[3.] Monopolies, and inundations of them, whereby a burden is laid not only upon foreign but upon native commodities, as soap, salt, drink, etc., the particulars whereof are fit for the Committee of Grievances.[30]

[4.] Fourthly, ship-money, and although there be a judgment for it, yet I dare be bold to say it's against all former precedents and laws, and not one judgment that ever maintained it. This is a grievance that all are grieved at, having no limits either for time or proportion; if therefore any shall endeavour to defend this he must know that both his reputation and conscience lie at stake in the defence.

[5.] The enlarging the bounds of the Forest. Though our ancestors were heretofore questioned for the same thing, yet upon the satisfaction of all the objections that were or could be made they then saved themselves. Yet now the same things are turned upon us.

[6.] The sale of public nuisances, for so they are pretended to be. Many great nuisances have been complained of, but when there hath been money given, and compositions made, then they are no more nuisances, as buildings and depopulations.

[7.] Military charges and impositions upon counties, by letters only from the council table, whereby soldiers' conduct money and coats are to be provided at the county's charge, and horses also provided without ground or law, many things in this kind being done by deputy-lieutenants of their own accord.

[8.] Extrajudicial judgments and impositions of the judges without any cause before them, whereby they have anticipated the judgment which is legal and public and circumvented one of the parties of just remedies, in that no writ of error lies, but only upon the judicial proceedings.

The next sort of grievances is that the great courts do countenance the oppressions, as I may instance in the Court of Star Chamber advancing and countenancing of monopolies, which should be instead of this great council of the kingdom; and the Star Chamber now is become a court of revenue, informations there being put in against sheriffs for not making returns of

---

[30] This and subsequent references in this speech to monopolies, make it more difficult to understand why the Long Parliament did not tackle the problem. See p. 176, n. 5 above.

money upon the writs of ship-money. It was not used that *meum et tuum* should be disputed there.

The Privy Councillors should be Lights of the Realm. Sure in them is the greatest trust, and they by Magna Carta are to do justice (as was urged by one in this House the last parliament), but now if these councillors should so far descend below themselves as to countenance, nay, to plot projects and monopolies, what shall we think of this? Surely it is much beneath their dignity. This is a great grievance, but I must go higher.

I know the king hath a transcendent power in many cases, whereby by proclamation he may prevent and guard against sudden accidents, but that this power should be applied to countenance monopolies (the projectors being not content with their private grants without a proclamation) is without precedent. But yet I must go higher than this; it hath been in the pulpit applied and also published in books and disputations, asserting a power unlimited in the king, that he may do what he pleaseth. This grievance was complained of in the last parliament, in the case of Dr Manwaring, who for maintaining that opinion in a sermon, that a subject had no propriety in his goods, but that all was at the king's pleasure, made his submission upon his knees in this place, and then was brought so low that I thought he would not have leaped so soon into a bishopric.[31]

I have by this time wearied you as well as myself, but I am come to the last grievance, which is the fountain of all these, and that is the intermissions of parliaments, whereas by two statutes not repealed or expired, a parliament ought to be once in a year.

These grievances are as prejudicial to his Majesty as to the Commonwealth. The breach of parliaments is much prejudicial, for by this means the great union and love which should be kept and communicated betwixt the king and his subjects is interrupted. They cannot make known their petitions, nor the king his wants, to have supplies. Where the intercourse of the spirits betwixt the head and the members is hindered the body prospers not. If parliaments had been more frequent the king had had more supplies.

By our grievance in religion the king's party abroad is much weakened, and that great part of this aids [*sc.* allies] abroad do forsake us is for that they think we are forsaking our religion.[32]

Many of the king's subjects, for that they cannot be quiet in things

---

[31] Manwaring was now Bishop of St Davids. For an extract from his famous sermon, and Pym's speech on his impeachment in 1628, see nos. **5, 6** pp. 13–16 above.

[32] The version printed by Cope, in note form, is fuller on this point: '3. Loss of his reputation abroad, and had it not been for this, I believe the Palatinate had now not been in whose hands it is. Queen Elizabeth never did things on her private purse. Moreover the Kings of England had as great advantage over the House of Austria as any prince whatsoever, and I think it may be recovered still. 4. Loss of regard of religion, which hath lost us much alliance. We have not that intelligence and party as before we had, because our change is feared'; *ibid.*, p. 155. On 22 April a royalist MP took him up on this last point, but he brazenly denied it, and got away with it (*ibid.*, pp. 168–9).

indifferent, and know not where they shall have an end of them, have departed this land with their goods, estates and posterities.

The preferment of men ill-deserving, and neglecting others of great integrity and merit, hath much weakened and discouraged us. There are but a few now that apply themselves either to do well or to deserve well, finding flattery and compliance to be the easier way to attain their ends and expectations.

The not observing of laws, but countenancing of monopolies and such like, breeds jealousies in the minds of many, and may prepare a way for distempers, though (thanks be to God) as yet there have been none; our religion hath preserved us. But if anything but well should happen one summer's distempers would breed great change, and more than all unlawful courses would recompense. We know how unfortunate Henry III and other princes have been, by the occasion of such breaking of their laws. I pray God that we never see such times . . .

I come now to the last thing, the remedy of these grievances.

First, I advise to present them to the House of Peers, that they may join with us to go to the king, and pray that these grievances being clear in fact may be voted. If anything in the vote be stuck upon, that it may be debated and drawn according to the course of the House, into a remonstrance, with a humble petition of both Houses for redress. I hope the wisdom of this House will prepare such a remedy as will make the king a great king, and the people happy.   Rushworth, IV, 1131–6

57. Pym's speech, 7 November 1640[33]

Mr Pym moved for a reformation, etc., finding out authors and punishment of them. [The] actual declaration of offences needs no statutes, and that is a step to reformation.[34]

[There is] a design to alter the kingdom both in religion and government. This is the highest of treason, this blows up by piecemeal, and almost goeth through [to] their ends. This concerns the king as well as we, and that I say with reverence and care of his Majesty.

So there are many heads of grievances.[35]

33 This is the fullest version available. I have omitted the more obscure passages, and supplemented others by quotations, usually in the footnotes, from the brief version published in *Speeches and Passages* the following year (pp. 458–60), which I have also compared with the MS in PRO, SP 16/472, 81–2.

34 'The distempers of this kingdom are well known, they need no repetition, for though we have good laws yet they want their execution; if they are executed it is in a wrong sense.'

35 This hackneyed reference to grievances may have been inserted by d'Ewes or his informant. Pym had already swept the usual grievances aside, and in the printed version he firmly couples the papists with the design to alter the government: 'There is a design to alter law and religion. That party that affects this are papists, who are obliged by a maxim in their doctrine, that they are not only to maintain their religion, but also extirpate others.'

1. The papists' party alter religion, and this by setting differences between the King and his subjects; and tenets of papists undermine our religion.

2. The corrupt part of our clergy[36] that make things for their own ends and with a union between us and Rome.

3. Agents for Spain and other kingdoms by pensions to alter religion and government.[37]

4. Those that [are] for their own preferments and further all bad things are worse than papists; those [who] are willing to run with popery.[38] Steps of these things that have proceeded in motion, first softly, now by strides, which are near their end if they be not prevented.

[These] designs [are] carried upon four feet.

The first foot is [religion].
1. Ecclesiastical courts.
2. Discountenancing of forward men in our religion.
3. Countenancing their own party, or else no promotion.
4. By negotiating agents from hence to Rome and from Rome to this place to extirpate our religion, [of which] proof will appear.
5. Frequent preaching for monarchy, Doctor Beale[39] and others.

The second foot: policy for [the] state and Courts of Justice.
1. The Council endeavouring to make [a] difference between king and people by taxes against laws and wrong ways . . .
2. By keeping the king in constant necessity, [that he may seek their counsels for relief; to this purpose to keep the parliaments in distaste,][40] that he might be for them. Still, [there is] no imputation to be laid upon the king for any irregular actions, but upon them that he entrusted.
3. Arbitrary proceedings of courts of justice; law and precedent were nothing, expunging of matters, all defence of the subject taken away for the dissolution of the kingdom.
4. To make a difference between England and Scotland, [that when we had well wearied ourselves against one another we might be both brought to what scorn they pleased].[41] A sermon [was] preached in the North before the king [that] to make an agreement between popery and our religion the partition wall must be pulled down, which was the Puritans. The Scots have been [made] the first authors of all.

---

[36] 'Our hierarchy, which cannot amount to the height they aim at without a breach of our law.'

[37] 'There they intend chiefly the Spanish white gold, works which are of most effect.'

[38] The printed version refers directly to Charles's ministers: 'Favourites, such as for promotion prize not conscience; and such are our judges spiritual and temporal, such are also our councillors of state.'

[39] Dr William Beale of Paulersbury, Northants.

[40] From *Speeches and Passages*.   [41] From *Speeches and Passages*.

5. By misguiding the king's approbation. [Ingratiating of papists and saying they are the best subjects, to bring the king in love with them].[42]

The third foot: discontent and breach of parliaments.

1. He would not mention the breach of old privileges, but late instances in new, as Mr Crewe's case.[43] The Clerk is not bound to deliver any petitions, nor so any member. If no safety here, then nowhere.

2. Great slanders in the declaration[44] for which he desired reparation. The king took it upon credit of others, he never saw it.

[3.] By moulding the Irish government into an illegal course, with intent to do [the same] here, [and] so we [ought] to have an interest with them; we are all the same subjects and no new thing.

The fourth foot: military steps.

1. Putting papists or suspected persons into command of armies.

2. Power to papists to muster by commission.[45]

3. To bring soldiers from beyond sea, and endeavours have been and haply are, but that means are wanted to do it. No account of Spaniards coming here.[46] Great jealousies.

4. The Irish army to bring us to a better order; we are not fully conquered . . .

He moved that there might be a settled committee to find out the danger the king and kingdom is in. *D'Ewes Journal*, ed. Notestein, pp. 7–11

58. Strafford's impeachment, 1640–1

(a) John Pym's speech to the preliminary charges, 25 November 1640

These articles have expressed the character of a great and dangerous treason, such a one as is advanced to the highest degree of malice and mischief. It is enlarged beyond the limits of any description or definition, it is so heinous in itself as that it is capable of no aggravation; a treason against God, betraying his truth and worship; against the king, obscuring the glory and weakening the foundations of his throne; against the Commonwealth, by destroying the

---

[42] This sentence has been transferred from the next paragraph, on Parliament.

[43] After the dissolution of the Short Parliament John Crew, chairman of the Committee on Religion, had been brought before the Council and committed to the Tower for refusing to surrender his papers; *CSPD 1640*, pp. 141–2.

[44] Giving the king's reasons for dissolving parliament, May 1640, *PH*, II, 572–9.

[45] 'To whom their armour is delivered contrary to the statute.'

[46] An obscure reference to Strafford's negotiations with the Spanish government, or to the arrival of a Spanish fleet in English territorial waters in the autumn of 1639.

principles of safety and prosperity. Other treasons are against the rule of the law: this is against the being of the law. It is the law that unites the king and his people, and the author of this treason hath endeavoured to dissolve that union even to break the mutual, irreversible, indissoluble band [?bond] of protection and allegiance whereby they are, and I hope ever will be, bound together.

If this treason had taken effect our souls had been enthralled to the spiritual tyranny of Satan, our consciences to the ecclesiastical tyranny of the Pope, our lives, our persons and estates, to the civil tyranny of an arbitrary, unlimited, confused government.

Treason in the least degree is an odious and horrid crime. [But] other treasons are particular: if a fort be betrayed, or an army, or any other treasonable fact committed, the kingdom may outlive any of these. This treason would have dissolved the frame and being of the Commonwealth; it is a universal, a Catholic treason; the venom and malignity of all other treasons are abstracted, digested, sublimated into this.

The law of this kingdom makes the king to be the fountain of justice, of peace, of protection; therefore we say, the king's courts, the king's judges, the king's laws; the royal power and majesty shines upon us in every public blessing and benefit we enjoy. But the author of this treason would make him the fountain of injustice, of confusion, of public misery and calamity . . . There cannot be a greater lesion or diminution of majesty, than to bereave a king of the glory of his goodness. It is a goodness, my lords, that can produce not only to his people, but likewise to himself honour and happiness. There are principalities, thrones and dominions amongst the devils, greatness enough; but being incapable of goodness they are made incapable both of honour and happiness.

The laws of this kingdom have invested the royal crown with power sufficient for the manifestation of his goodness and of his greatness; if more be required it is like to have no other effects but poverty, weakness and misery, whereof of late we have had very woeful experience. It is far from the Commons to desire any abridgement of those great prerogatives which belong to the king; they know that their own liberty and peace are preserved and secured by his prerogative . . . A king and his people make one body: the inferior parts confer nourishment and strength, the superior, sense and motion. If there be an interruption of this necessary intercourse of blood and spirits, the whole body must needs be subject to decay and distemper. Therefore obstructions are first to be removed before restoratives can be applied. This, my lords, is the end of this accusation, whereby the Commons seek to remove this person, whom they conceive to have been a great cause of the obstructions between his Majesty and his people; for the effecting whereof they have commanded me to desire your lordships that your proceedings against him may be put into as speedy a way of despatch as the courses of parliament will allow . . . *Somers Tracts*, IV, 216–17

(b) Strafford's last speech in his defence, 13 April 1641[47]

. . . My lords, I have all along my charge watched to see that poisoned arrow of treason that some would have to be feathered in my breast, and that deadly cup of wine that hath so intoxicated some petty mis-alleged errors as to put them in the elevation of high treason; but in truth it hath not been my quickness to discern any such monster yet within my breast, though perhaps now by a sinister imputation sticking to my clothes. They tell me of a twofold treason, one against the statute, another by the Common Law; this direct, that constructive; this individual, that accumulative; this in itself, that by way of construction . . . To make up this constructive treason, or treason by accumulation, many articles are brought against me, as if in a heap of felonies or misdemeanours – for in their own conceit they reach no higher – some prolific seed apt to produce what is treasonable could lurk.

Here I am charged to have designed the overthrow both of religion and the state. The first seemeth to me to have been used rather for making me odious than guilty, for there is not the least probation alleged concerning my confederacy with the popish faction, nor could there be any indeed. Never a servant in authority beneath the king my master who was more hated and maligned, and am still, by these men than myself, and that for a strict and impartial execution of the laws against them. Hence your Lordships may observe that the greater number of the witnesses used against me either from Ireland or Yorkshire are men of that religion; and for my own resolution I thank God I am ready every minute of the day to seal my disaffection to the Church of Rome with my dearest blood . . .

As to my designs about the state, I dare plead as much innocency here as in the matter of my religion. I have ever admired the wisdom of our ancestors, who have so fixed the pillars of this monarchy that each of them keeps due measure and proportion with [the] other, and have so handsomely tied up the nerves and sinews of the state that the straining of one may bring damage and sorrow to the whole economy. The prerogative of the Crown and the propriety of the subject have such mutual relations that this took protection from that, that foundation and nourishment from this; and as on the lute, if anything be too high or too low wound up you have lost the harmony, so here the excess of a prerogative is oppression, of a pretended liberty in the subject disorder and anarchy. The prerogative must be used, as God doth his omnipotency, at extraordinary occasions; the laws . . . must have place at all

---

[47] From a MS in the Public Record Office drawn up by or for Sir Edward Nicholas. Rushworth (II, 633–60) prints another version of the speech with very different wording but much the same sense.

other times, and yet there must be a prerogative if there must be extraordinary occasions. The propriety of the subject is ever to be maintained if it go in equal pace with this; they are fellows and companions that have been and ever must be inseparable in a well-governed kingdom; and no way so fitting, so natural to nourish and intertex both as the frequent use of parliaments. By this a commerce and acquaintance is kept between the king and the subject; this thought hath gone along with me these fourteen years of my public employments, and shall, God willing, to my grave. God, his Majesty and my own conscience, yea, all who have been accessory to my most inward thoughts and opinions, can bear me witness I ever did inculcate this: the happiness of a kingdom consists in [the] just poise of the kings prerogative and the subject's liberty, and that things should never be well till these went hand in hand together. I thank God for it, by my master's favour and the prudence of my ancestors I have an estate which so interests me in the Commonwealth that I have no great mind to be a slave, but a subject. Nor could I wish the cards to be shuffled over again upon hope to fall on a better set; neither did I ever keep such base mercenary thoughts as to become a pander to the tyranny, the ambition of the greatest man living. No, I have and shall ever aim at a fair but a bounded liberty, remembering always that I am a freeman, but a subject; that I have a right, but under a monarch. But it hath been my misfortune now under my grey hairs to be charged with the mistakes of the times, which are now so high bent that all appears to them to be in the extremes for monarchy which is not for themselves . . .

My lords, you see what may be alleged for this constructive, rather this destructive treason. For my part, I have not the judgment to conceive that such a treason is either agreeable to the fundamental grounds of reason or law. Not of reason, for how can that be treason in the whole which is not in any of the parts? Or how can that make a thing treasonable which in itself is nothing so? Nor of law, since neither statute, Common Law nor practice hath from the beginning of this government ever mentioned such a thing. And where, I pray you, my lords, hath this fire without the least token of smoke lain his so many hundreds of years, and now breaks forth in a violent flame to destroy me and my posterity from the earth? My lords, do we not live by laws, and must we be punishable by them ere they be made? Far better it were to live by no law at all, but be governed by those characters of discretion and virtue stamped in us, than to put this necessity of divination upon a man and to argue him of the breach of a law ere it be a law at all . . . My lords, if this crime which they call arbitrary treason had been marked by any discernment of the law, the ignorance of the same should not excuse me; but if it be no law at all, how can it in rigour, in strictness itself, condemn me?

Beware you do not awake these sleeping lions by the raking up of some neglected, some moth-eaten records – they may sometime tear you and your posterity in pieces. It was your ancestors' care to chain them up within the barrier of a statute; be not you ambitious to be more skilful, more curious than your fathers were in the art of killing . . . I leave it to your lordships' consideration to foresee what may be the issue of so dangerous, so recent precedencies. These gentlemen tell me they speak in defence of the commonweal against my arbitrary laws; give me leave to say that I speak in defence of the commonweal against their arbitrary treason. For if this latitude be admitted, what prejudice shall follow to the king, to the country, if you and your posterity be disabled by the same from the great affairs of the kingdom? . . . Let me be a Pharos to keep you from shipwreck, and do not put such rocks in your own way, which no prudence nor circumspection can eschew or satisfy but by utter ruin. And whether judgment in my case – I wish it were not the case of you all – be it life or death, it shall be righteous in mine eyes, and received with a *te deum laudamus*. Now, *in te Domine confido, ne confundar in eternum.*   *CSPD, 1640–41*, pp. 540–5

(c) John Pym's reply

. . . We have passed through our evidence, and the result of all this is, that the Earl of Strafford hath endeavoured by his words, actions and counsels to subvert the fundamental law of England and Ireland, and to introduce an arbitrary and tyrannical government. This is the envenomed arrow for which he inquired, in the beginning of this replication this day, which hath infected all his blood; this is that intoxicating cup (to use his own metaphor) which hath tainted his judgment and poisoned his heart; from hence was infused that specifical difference, which turned his speeches, his actions, his counsels into treason – not cumulative, as he expressed it, as if many misdemeanours could make one treason; but formally and essentially. It is the end that doth inform actions, and doth specificate the nature of them, making not only criminal but even indifferent words and actions to be treason, being done and spoken with a treasonable intention.

That which is given to me in charge, is to show the quality of the offence, how heinous it is in the nature, how mischievous in the effect of it, which will best appear if it be examined by that law to which he himself appealed, that universal, that supreme law, *salus populi*. This is the element of all laws, out of which they are derived, the end of all laws, to which they are designed, and in which they are perfected. How far it stands in opposition to this law I shall endeavour to show in some considerations which I shall present to your lordships, all arising out of the evidence which hath been opened.

The first is this, it is an offence comprehending all other offences; here you will find several treasons, murders, rapines, oppressions, perjuries. The earth has a seminary virtue, whereby it doth produce all herbs and plants, and other vegetables. There is in this crime a seminary of all evils hurtful to a state; and if you consider the reasons of it it must needs be so. The law is that which put as difference between good and evil, between just and unjust; if you take away the law all things will fall into a confusion, every man will become a law to himself, which in the depraved condition of human nature must needs produce many grave enormities. Lust will become a law, and envy will become a law, covetousness and ambition will become laws; and what dictates, what decisions such laws will produce may easily be discerned in the late government of Ireland. The law hath a power to prevent, to restrain, to repair evils; without this all kinds of mischief and distempers will break in upon a state.

It is the law that doth entitle a king to the allegiance and service of his people; it entitles the people to the protection and justice of the king . . . The law is the boundary, the measure between the king's prerogative and the people's liberty. Whilst these move in their own orbs they are a support and a security to one another; the prerogative a cover and defence to the liberty of the people, and the people by their liberty are entitled to be a foundation to the prerogative; but if these bounds be so removed that they enter into contestation and conflict one of these mischiefs must ensue: if the prerogative of the king overwhelm the liberty of the people it will be turned into tyranny; if liberty undermine the prerogative, it will grow into anarchy . . .

The second consideration is this: this arbitrary power is dangerous to the king's person, and dangerous to his crown; it is apt to cherish ambition, usurpation and oppression in great men, and to beget sedition and discontent in the people, and both these have been, and in reason must ever be, causes of great trouble and alteration to princes and states. If the histories of those eastern countries be perused, where princes order their affairs according to the mischievous principles of the Earl of Strafford, loose and absolved from all rules of government, they will be found to be frequent in combustions, full of massacres and of the tragical ends of princes. If any man shall look into our own stories, in the times when the laws were most neglected, he shall find them full of commotions, of civil distempers, whereby the kings that then reigned were always kept in want and distress, the people consumed with civil wars; and by such wicked counsels as these some of our princes have been brought to such miserable ends as no honest heart can remember without horror, and earnest prayer that it may never be so again.

The third consideration is this: the subversion of the laws. And this arbitrary power, as it is dangerous to the king's person, and to his crown, so is it in other respects very prejudicial to his Majesty in his honour, profit and greatness. And yet these are the gildings and paintings that are put upon such counsels: 'These are for your honour, for your service' – whereas in truth they are contrary to both. But if I shall take off this varnish I hope they shall then appear in their own native deformity . . .

It cannot be for the honour of the king that his sacred authority should be used in the practice of injustice and oppression, that his name should be applied to patronise such horrid crimes as have been represented in evidence against the Earl of Strafford. And yet how frequently how presumptuously, his commands, his letters, have been vouched throughout the course of this defence? Your lordships have heard, when the judges do justice, it is the king's justice, and this is for his honour, because he is the fountain of justice; but when they do injustice the offence is their own. But those officers and ministers of the king who are most officious in the exercise of this arbitrary power, they do it commonly for their advantages, and when they are questioned for it, then they fly to the king's interest, to his direction. And truly, my lords, this is a very unequal distribution for the king, that the dishonour of evil courses should be cast upon him, and they to have the advantage . . .   Rushworth, II, 661-3

59. The Triennial Act, 1641

16 Car. I, c. 1: *An Act for the preventing of inconveniences happening by the long intermission of parliaments.*

Whereas by the laws and statutes of this realm the parliament ought to be held at least once every year for the redress of grievances, but the appointment of the time and place for the holding thereof has always belonged, as it ought, to his Majesty and his royal progenitors; and whereas it is by experience found that the not holding of parliaments accordingly hath produced sundry and great mischiefs and inconveniences to the king's Majesty, Church and Commonwealth, for the prevention of the like mischiefs and inconveniences in time to come:

II. Be it enacted . . . that in case there be not a parliament summoned by writ under the Great Seal of England and assembled and held before the tenth day of September which shall be in the third year next after the last day of the last meeting and sitting in this present parliament, . . . and so from time to time and in all times hereafter if there shall not be a parliament assembled and held . . . [as aforesaid], then . . . the parliament shall assemble and be held in the usual place at Westminster in such manner and by such means only as is hereafter in this present act declared and enacted and not otherwise, on the second Monday which shall be in the month of November then next ensuing.

And in case this present parliament now assembled and held, and any other parliament which shall at any time hereafter be assembled and held, . . . shall be prorogued or adjourned or continued by prorogation or adjournment until the tenth day of September which shall be in the third year next after the last day of the last meeting and sitting in parliament, . . . that then in every such case every such parliament . . . shall from the said tenth day of September be thenceforth clearly and absolutely dissolved. And the lord chancellor of England, the lord keeper of the Great Seal of England, and every commissioner and commissioners for the keeping of the Great Seal of England for the time being shall within six days after the said tenth day of September . . . in due form of law and without any further warrant or direction from his Majesty, his heirs or successors, seal, issue forth and send abroad several and respective writs to the several and respective peers of this realm, commanding every such peer that he personally be at the parliament to be held at Westminster on the second Monday which shall be in November next following the said tenth day of September, . . . and shall also seal, issue forth and send abroad several and respective writs to the several and respective sheriffs of the several and respective counties, cities and boroughs of England and Wales . . . for the electing of the knights, citizens, barons and burgesses of and for the said counties . . . [etc.] in the accustomed form, to sit and serve in parliament to be held at Westminster on the second Sunday . . . in November . . . Which said peers after the said writs received, and which said knights, citizens, barons and burgesses chosen by virtue of the said writs shall then and there appear and serve in parliament accordingly. And the said lord chancellor . . . [etc.] shall respectively take a solemn oath upon the Holy Evangelist for the due issuing of writs according to the tenor of this act, . . . which oath is forthwith to be taken by the present lord keeper. . . . And if the said lord chancellor . . . [etc.] shall fail or forbear so to issue out the said writs . . ., then he or they respectively shall beside the incurring of the grievous sin of perjury be disabled and become by virtue of this act incapable *ipso facto* to bear his and their said offices respectively, and be further liable to such punishments as shall be inflicted on him or them by the next or any ensuing parliament.

And in case the said lord chancellor, lord keeper, commissioner or commissioners aforesaid shall not issue forth the said writs as aforesaid, or in case that the parliament do not assemble and be held at the time and place before appointed, then the parliament shall assemble and be held in the usual place at Westminster in such manner and by such means only as is hereafter in this present Act declared and enacted and not otherwise, on the third Monday which shall be in the month of January then next ensuing. And the peers of this realm shall by virtue of this act be enabled and are enjoined to meet in the Old Palace of Westminster in the usual place there on the third Monday in the said month of November, and they or any twelve or more of them then and there assembled shall, on or before the last Monday of November next following the tenth day of September aforesaid, by virtue of this act without other warrant issue out writs in the usual form in the name of the king's Majesty, his heirs or successors, attested under the hands and seals of twelve or more of the said peers, to the several and respective sheriffs . . . for the electing of the knights, citizens, barons and burgesses . . . to be and appear at the parliament . . . on the third Monday in January . . . And it is enacted that the said writs so issued shall be of the same force and power to all intents and purposes as the writs or summons to parliament under the Great Seal of England have ever been . . .

[III. If the peers fail to act, and no parliament assembles by 23 January, then a parliament must be elected in the following manner, to assemble on the second Tuesday in March, when the peers must also assemble as if summoned by writ.]

IV. And for the better assembling of the knights, citizens, barons and burgesses to the said parliament as aforesaid, it is further enacted that the several and respective sheriffs of their several and respective counties, cities and boroughs of England and Wales, and the chancellor, masters and scholars of both and every of the universities, and the mayor and bailiffs of the borough of Berwick upon Tweed, shall at the several courts and places to be held and appointed for their respective countries, universities, cities and boroughs next after the said three and twentieth day of January cause such knight and knights, citizen and citizens, burgess and burgesses of their said counties, universities, cities and boroughs respectively, to be chosen by such persons and in such manner as if several and respective writs of summons to parliament under the Great Seal of England had issued and been awarded. And in case any of the several sheriffs, or the chancellor, masters and scholars of either of the universities, or the mayor and bailiffs of Berwick respectively do not before ten of the clock in the forenoon of the same day wherein the several and respective courts and places shall be held or appointed for their several and respective counties, universities, cities and boroughs, begin and proceed on according to the meaning of this law in causing elections to be made . . . as aforesaid, then the freeholders of each county, and the masters and scholars of every of the universities, and the citizens and others having voices in such election respectively in each university, city and borough, that shall be assembled at the said courts or places . . . shall forthwith without further warrant or direction proceed to the election of such knight or knights, citizen or citizens, burgess or burgesses aforesaid in such manner as is usual in case of writs of summons issued and awarded.

VI. And it is further enacted that no parliament henceforth to be assembled shall be dissolved or prorogued within fifty days at the least after the time appointed for the meeting thereof, unless it be by assent of his Majesty, his heirs or successors, and of both Houses of Parliament assembled. And that neither the House of Peers nor the House of Commons shall be adjourned within fifty days at least after the meeting thereof unless it be by the free consent of every the said houses respectively.

★   ★   ★

XI. And it is lastly provided and enacted that his Majesty's royal assent to this bill shall not thereby determine this present session of parliament, and that all statutes and acts of Parliament which are to have continuance unto the end of this present session shall be of full force after his Majesty's assent until this present session be fully ended and determined. And if this present session shall determine by dissolution of this present parliament then all the acts and statutes aforesaid shall be continued until the end of the first session of the next parliament.   *SR*, v, 54-7

60. Protestation of the House of Commons, 3 May 1641

We the knights, citizens and burgesses of the Commons House in Parliament, finding to the grief of our hearts that the designs of the priests and Jesuits, and other adherents to the see of Rome, have of late been more boldly and frequently put in practice than formerly, to the undermining and danger of the ruin of the true Reformed Religion in his Majesty's dominions established, and finding also that there hath been, and having cause to suspect there still are, even during the sitting in parliament, endeavours to subvert the fundamental laws of England and Ireland, and to introduce the exercise of an arbitrary and tyrannical government by most pernicious and wicked counsels, practices, plots and conspiracies; and that the long intermission and unhappier breach of parliaments hath occasioned many illegal taxations, whereby the subjects have been prosecuted and grieved; and that divers innovations and superstitions have been brought into the Church, multitudes driven out of his Majesty's dominions, jealousies raised and fomented between the king and people, a popish army levied in Ireland, and two armies brought into the bowels of this kingdom, to the hazard of his Majesty's royal person, the consumption of the revenue of the Crown and the treasure of this realm; and lastly, finding the great causes of jealousy, [that] endeavours have been, and are used, to bring the English army into [a] misunderstanding of this parliament, thereby to incline that army by force to bring to pass those wicked counsels, have therefore thought good to join ourselves in a declaration of our united affections and resolutions; and to make this ensuing Protestation:

I, A. B., do, in the presence of God, promise, vow and protest to maintain and defend, as far as lawfully I may, with my life, power and estate, the true reformed religion, expressed in the doctrine of the Church of England, against all popery and popish innovation within this realm, contrary to the said doctrine, and according to the duty of my allegiance to his Majesty's royal person, honour and estate; as also the power and privilege of parliament, the lawful rights and liberties of the subjects, and every person that shall make this Protestation in whatsoever he shall do, in the lawful pursuance of the same: And to my power, as far as lawfully I may, I will oppose, and, by all good ways and means, endeavour to bring to condign punishment all such as shall by force, practice, counsels, plots, conspiracies or otherwise do anything to the contrary in this Protestation contained:

And further, I shall in all just and honourable ways endeavour to preserve the union and peace betwixt the three kingdoms of England, Scotland and Ireland, and neither for hope, fear, nor other respect, shall relinquish this promise, vow and protestation.   *CJ*, II, 132

61. The Ten Propositions

A large conference with the Lords, touching several particulars about disbanding the Army, the Capuchins, &c. [24 June 1641]

I. The First Head, concerning the disbanding of the Armies; and under this there are several particulars.

1. That five regiments, according to the former order of both Houses, be first disbanded.

2. That the commissioners for Scotland be entreated to retire some part of their army.

3. That their lordships will join with us in a petition to his Majesty, to declare his pleasure concerning the disbanding of the five regiments for which there is present money provided, and of the rest of the Army as soon as money is ready.

4. And to declare if any be refractory, and contemn his Majesty's authority, that he will use it for the punishment of them.

5. And that the Lord General [the Earl of Holland] go down to his charge of the army, and begin his journey on Saturday next [26 June]; and that the Master of the Ordnance go then down also to take care of his Charge of Artillery.

II. The Second Head is concerning his Majesty's journey to Scotland.

That his Majesty will be pleased to allow a convenient time before his journey into Scotland; that both armies be first disbanded, and some of the business of importance concerning the peace of the kingdom, depending in parliament, may be despatched before his going. This is seconded with divers reasons.

1. The safety of his Majesty's person.

2. Preventing the jealousies [suspicions] of his subjects.

3. Suppressing the hopes of persons ill affected, that may have designs upon the army to disturb the peace of the kingdom.

4. Great advantage to the king's affairs, and contentment to his people.

5. That some of the bills now depending in parliament, whereof divers are sent up already to the Lords, and some proceeding in this House, may receive his royal assent before he go to Scotland; and that we may have time to pass the bill of tunnage [and poundage] to his Majesty for supporting of the royal estate, and to settle his Majesty's revenues for the best advantage to his service; and for these reasons to allow some time before he go into the North.

III. The Third Head, concerning his Majesty's Council and Ministers of State.

1. Both Houses to make suit to his Majesty to remove from him all such councillors as I am commanded to describe, viz., such as have been active for the time past in furthering those courses contrary to religion, liberty, good government of the kingdom, and as have lately interested themselves in those counsels, to stir up division between him and his people.

2. As we desire [the] removal of those that are evil, so [he is] to take into his Council for managing of the great affairs of this kingdom such officers and councillors as his people and parliament may have just cause to confide in. This is all concerning the third head.

IV. The Fourth Head, touching the queen's most excellent Majesty, which containeth divers particulars.

1. That his Majesty be pleased, by advice of his parliament, to persuade the queen to accept some of the nobility, and others of trust, into her Majesty's service, into such places as are now in her disposal.

2. That no Jesuit, or any in orders, what countrymen soever, whether French or Italian, be received into her Majesty's service; nor any priests of his Majesty's dominion, English, Scottish or Irish; and that they be restrained from coming to Court.

3. That the College of Capuchins at Somerset House may be dissolved and sent out of the kingdom.

These two which I last mentioned, concerning the queen, priests, Jesuits and Capuchins, I am commanded to deliver you some particulars for.

1. Public danger and scandal of this kingdom, and peace of the kingdom.

2. The disaffection of some of those wicked conspirators is expressed in two letters, which letters were here read openly.

3. A particular letter of Father [Robert] Phillips here also read.[48]

---

[48] See Gardiner, *History*, x, 42, 54; Hibbard, *Popish Plot*, pp. 201–2.

4. Because of the priests, Jesuits and the College, there are divers great quantities of gold transported frequently.

5. Particular[ly] touching the queen is upon special occasions of his Majesty's absence; that their lordships will be pleased to join with us to advise the king that some of the nobility, and others of quality, with competent guards, may be appointed to attend the queen's person, against all designs of papists, and of ill affected persons, and of [sic] restraining resort thither in his absence.

V. The Fifth Head concerns the king's children, that some persons of public trust, and well affected in religion, may be placed about the Prince [of Wales], who may take care of his education, and of the rest of his children, especially in matters of religion and liberty.

VI. The Sixth Head concerneth such as shall come into the kingdom with titles of being the Pope's Nuncio, that it may be declared that if any man come into this kingdom with instructions from the Pope of Rome, it be a case of high treason; and that he be out of the King's protection and out of the protection of the law; and I am to inform your lordships that there is notice given upon very good grounds, that Count Rossetti doth yet continue in the kingdom and yet resorts unto the Court.[49]

VII. The Seventh Head is concerning the security and peace of the kingdom.

1. That there may be good lord lieutenants, and deputy lieutenants, and such as may be faithful and trusty, and careful of the peace of the kingdom.

2. That the trained bands be furnished with arms and powder and bullets, and exercised and made fit for service; and that a special oath may be prepared, by consent of both Houses, authorised by law; and to be taken by the lord lieutenants and the deputy lieutenants, captains and other officers, such an oath as may be fit to secure us in these times of danger.

3. That the Cinque Ports and all the forts of the kingdom may be put into good hands; and a list of those in whose charge they now are may be presented in parliament, and special care taken for the reparation and provision of those forts.

4. That my Lord Admiral [Earl of Northumberland] may inform the parliament in what case his Majesty's navy is, which is to be provided for out of tunnage and poundage for the security and peace of the kingdom.

[49] As a result of this Carlo Rossetti, who had replaced George Con as unofficial papal representative at the English Court in 1639, incontinently fled the country; Hibbard, *Popish Plot*, pp. 201-3.

VIII. The Eighth Head, that his Majesty be pleased to give directions to his learned counsel to prepare a general pardon in such a large manner as may be, for the relief of his Majesty's subjects.

IX. The Ninth Head doth concern a committee of both Houses, that their lordships would appoint a number of their members to join together with a proportionable number of this House, who from time to time may confer upon some particular causes, as shall be most effectual for the common good.

X. The Tenth and last Head, that his Majesty be moved that he would be pleased to be very sparing in sending for papists to Court; and that if any should come without being sent for, that the laws be severely put in execution against them; and that the English ladies that are recusants, be removed from Court; and that his Majesty be moved to give his assent that the persons of the most active papists, either lords or commons, may be so restrained as may be most necessary for the safety of the kingdom; and that no pensions be allowed to such recusants as are held dangerous to the state.   Rushworth, IV, 298–301

62. 17 Car. I, c. 10: An Act for regulating the Privy Council and for taking away the court commonly called the Star Chamber

. . . Whereas by the statute made in the third year of King Henry the Seventh[50] power is given to the Chancellor, the Lord Treasurer of England for the time being, and the Keeper of the King's Privy Seal, or two of them, calling unto them a bishop and a temporal lord of the king's most honourable council and the two chief justices of the King's Bench and Common Pleas for the time being or other two justices in their absence, to proceed as is in that act expressed for the punishment of some particular offences therein mentioned, . . . but the said judges have not kept themselves to the points limited by the said statute, but have undertaken to punish where no law doth warrant, and to make decrees for things, having no such authority, and to inflict heavier punishments than by any law is warranted: And forasmuch as all matters examinable or determinable before the said judges or in the court commonly called the Star Chamber may have their proper remedy and redress, and their due punishment and correction, by the Common Law of the Land and in the ordinary course of justice elsewhere; and forasmuch as the reasons and motives inducing the erection and continuance of the court do now cease, and the proceedings, censure and decrees of that court have by experience been found to be an intolerable burden to the subjects, and the means to introduce an arbitrary power and government; and forasmuch as the Council Table hath of

---

[50] 3 Hen. VII, c. 1, printed Elton, *Tudor Constitution*, pp. 166–7.

late times assumed unto itself a power to intermeddle in civil causes and matters only of private interest between party and party, and have adventured to determine of the estates and liberties of the subject, contrary to the law of the land and the rights and privileges of the subject, by which great and manifold mischiefs and inconveniences have arisen and happened, and much more uncertainty by means of such proceedings hath been conceived concerning men's rights and estates.

For settling whereof and preventing the like in time to come, be it ordained and enacted by the authority of this present parliament that the said court commonly called the Star Chamber, and all jurisdiction, power and authority belonging unto or exercised in the same court or by any the judges, officers or ministers thereof be from the first day of August in the year of our Lord God 1641 clearly and absolutely dissolved, taken away and determined . . .

II. And be it likewise enacted that the like jurisdiction now used and exercised in the court before the President and Council in the Marches of Wales, and also before the President and Council established in the Northern Parts, and also in the court commonly called the Court of the Duchy of Lancaster held before the chancellor and council of the court, and also in the Court of Exchequer of the County Palatine of Chester held before the chamberlain and council of that court, the like jurisdiction being exercised there, shall from the same first day of August 1641 be also repealed and absolutely revoked and made void, any law, prescription, custom or usage, or the said statute made in the third year of King Henry the Seventh, . . . or any act or acts of parliament heretofore had or made to the contrary thereof in any wise notwithstanding, and that from henceforth no court, council or place of judicature shall be erected, constituted or appointed within this realm of England or dominion of Wales which shall have use or exercise the same or the like jurisdiction as is or hath been used, practised or exercised in the said Court of Star Chamber.

III. Be it likewise declared and enacted by authority of this present parliament, that neither his Majesty nor his Privy Council have or ought to have any jurisdiction, power or authority by English bill, petition, articles, libel or any other arbitrary way whatsoever to examine or draw into question, determine or dispose of the lands, tenements, hereditaments, goods or chattels of any the subjects of this kingdom, but that the same ought to be tried and determined in the ordinary courts of justice and by the ordinary course of the law.

★   ★   ★

SR, v, 110–12

63. 17 Car. I, c. 11: An Act for repeal of a branch of a statute primo Elizabeth concerning commissioners for causes ecclesiastical

[The preamble rehearses § VIII of the Act of Supremacy of 1559[51] then proceeds:]

. . . And whereas by colour of some words in the foresaid branch of the said act whereby commissioners are authorised to execute their commission according to the tenor and effect of the King's Letters Patent . . ., the said commissioners have to the great and insufferable wrong and oppression of the king's subjects used to fine and imprison them, and exercise another authority not belonging to [the] ecclesiastical jurisdiction restored by that act, and divers other great mischiefs and inconveniences have also ensued to the king's subjects by occasion of the said branch and commissions issued thereupon, and the executions thereof; Therefore, for the repressing and preventing of the foresaid abuses, mischiefs and inconveniences in time to come, be it enacted by the king's most excellent Majesty and the Lords and Commons in this present parliament assembled and by the authority of the same, that the foresaid branch, clause, article or sentence contained in the said act, and every word, matter and thing contained in that branch, clause, article or sentence, shall from henceforth be repealed, annulled, revoked, annihilated and utterly made void for ever, any thing in the said Act to the contrary in any wise notwithstanding.

II. And be it also enacted by the authority aforesaid that no archbishop, bishop or vicar-general, nor any ordinary whatsoever, nor any other spiritual or ecclesiastical judge, officer, or minister of justice, nor any other person or persons whatsoever exercising spiritual or ecclesiastical power, authority or jurisdiction by any grant, licence or commission of the king's Majesty, his heirs or successors, or by any power or authority derived from the king, his heirs or successors, or otherwise, shall from and after the first day of August which shall be in the year of our Lord God 1641 award, impose or inflict any pain, penalty, fine, amercement, imprisonment or other corporal punishment upon any of the king's subjects for any contempt, misdemeanour, crime, offence, matter or thing whatsoever belonging to spiritual or ecclesiastical cognisance or jurisdiction, or shall *ex officio* or at the instance or promotion of any other person whatsoever urge, enforce, tender, give or minister unto any church-warden, sideman or other person whatsoever any corporal oath whereby he or she shall or may be charged or obliged to make any presentment of any crime or offence or to confess or to accuse him or herself of any crime, offence, delinquency or misdemeanour, or any neglect, matter or thing whereby or by reason whereof he or she shall or may be liable or exposed to any censure, pain, penalty or punishment whatsoever . . .

★ ★ ★

[51] See Elton, *Tudor Constitution*, pp. 374–5.

IV. And be it further enacted that from and after the said first day of August no new court shall be erected, ordained or appointed within this realm of England or dominion of Wales which shall or may have the like power, jurisdiction or authority as the said High Commission court now hath or pretendeth to have, but that all and every such letters patent, commissions and grants made or to be made by his Majesty, his heirs or successors, and all powers and authorities granted or pretended or mentioned to be granted thereby and all acts, sentences and decrees to be made by virtue or colour thereof shall be utterly void and of none effect. *SR*, v, 112–13

64. The Grand Remonstrance, 1641

The Petition of the House of Commons which accompanied the Remonstrance of the state of the kingdom, when it was presented to His Majesty at Hampton Court, 1 December 1641

Most Gracious Sovereign,

Your Majesty's most humble and faithful subjects the Commons in this present parliament assembled do with much thankfulness and joy acknowledge the great mercy and favour of God, in giving your Majesty a safe and peaceable return out of Scotland into your kingdom of England, where the pressing dangers and distempers of the state have caused us with much earnestness to desire the comfort of your gracious presence, and likewise the unity and justice of your royal authority, to give more life and power to the dutiful and loyal counsels and endeavours of your parliament for the prevention of that eminent ruin and destruction wherein your kingdoms of England and Scotland are threatened. The duty which we owe to your Majesty and our country cannot but make us very sensible and apprehensive that the multiplicity, sharpness and malignity of those evils under which we have now many years suffered are fomented and cherished by a corrupt and ill-affected party, who amongst other their mischievous devices for the alteration of religion and government have sought by many false scandals and imputations, cunningly insinuated and dispersed amongst the people, to blemish and disgrace our proceedings in this parliament, and to get themselves a party and faction amongst your subjects for the better strengthening themselves in their wicked courses, and hindering those provisions and remedies which might, by the wisdom of your Majesty and counsel of your parliament, be opposed against them.

For preventing whereof, and the better information of your Majesty, your Peers and all other your loyal subjects, we have been necessitated to make a Declaration of the State of the Kingdom, both before and since the assembly of this parliament unto this time, which we do humbly present to your Majesty, without the least intention to lay any blemish upon your royal person, but only to represent how your royal authority and trust have been abused, to the great prejudice and danger of your Majesty, and of all your good subjects.

And because we have reason to believe that those malignant parties whose proceedings evidently appear to be mainly for the advantage and increase of popery, is [*sic*] composed, set up and acted by the subtle practice of the Jesuits and other engineers and factors for Rome, and to the great danger of this kingdom and most grievous affliction of your loyal subjects have so far prevailed as to corrupt divers of your bishops and others in prime places of the Church, and also to bring divers of those instruments to be of your Privy Council, and other employments of trust and nearness about your Majesty, the prince, and the rest of the royal children.

And by this means have had such an operation in your counsel and the most important affairs and proceedings of your government, that a most dangerous division and chargeable preparation for war betwixt your kingdoms of England and Scotland, the increase of jealousies betwixt your Majesty and your most obedient subjects, the violent distraction and interruption of this parliament, the insurrection of the papists in your kingdom of Ireland, and bloody massacre of your people, have been not only endeavoured and attempted but in a great measure compassed and effected.

For preventing the final accomplishment whereof, your poor subjects are enforced to engage their persons and estates to the maintaining of a very expensive and dangerous war, notwithstanding they have already since the beginning of this parliament undergone the charge of 150,000 pounds sterling, or thereabouts, for the necessary support and supply of your Majesty in these present and perilous designs. And because all our most faithful endeavours and engagements will be ineffectual for the peace, safety and preservation of your Majesty and your people of some present, real and effectual course be not taken for suppressing this wicked and malignant party, we your most humble and obedient subjects do with all faithfulness and humility beseech your Majesty:

1. That you will be graciously pleased to concur with the humble desires of your people in a parliamentary way, for the preserving the peace and safety of the kingdom from the malicious designs of the Popish party:

For depriving the bishops of their votes in parliament, and abridging their immoderate power usurped over the clergy, and other your good subjects, which they have perniciously abused to the hazard of religion and great prejudice and oppression to the laws of the kingdom and just liberty of your people;

For the taking away such oppressions in religion, church government and discipline as have been brought in and fomented by them;

For uniting all such your loyal subjects together as join in the same fundamental truths against the papists, by removing some oppressive and unnecessary ceremonies by which divers weak consciences have been scrupled, and seem to be divided from the rest, and for the due execution of those good laws which have been made for securing the liberty of your subjects.

2. That your Majesty will likewise be pleased to remove from your council all such as persist to favour and promote any of those pressures and corruptions wherewith your people have been grieved, and that for the future your Majesty will vouchsafe to employ such persons in your great and public affairs, and to take such to be near you in places of trust, as your parliament may have cause to confide in; [and] that in your princely goodness to your people you will reject and refuse all mediation and solicitation to the contrary, how powerful and near soever . . .

Which humble desires of ours being graciously fulfilled by your Majesty, we will, by the blessings and favour of God, most cheerfully undergo the hazard and expenses of this war, and apply ourselves to such other courses and counsels as may support your real estate with honour and plenty at home, with power and reputation abroad, and by our loyal affections, obedience and service, lay a sure and lasting foundation of the greatness and prosperity of your Majesty, and your royal posterity in future times.

The Grand Remonstrance

The Commons in this parliament assembled, having with much earnestness and faithfulness of affection and zeal to the public good of this kingdom and his Majesty's honour and service, for the space of twelve months wrestled with great dangers and fears, the pressing miseries and calamities, the various distempers and disorders which had not only assaulted but even overwhelmed and extinguished the liberty, peace and prosperity of this kingdom, the comfort and hopes of all his Majesty's good subjects, and exceedingly weakened and undermined the foundation and strength of his own royal throne, do yet find an abounding malignity and opposition in those parties and factions who have been the cause of those evils, and do still labour to cast aspersions upon that which hath been done, and to raise many difficulties for the hindrance of that which remains yet undone, and to foment jealousies between the king and parliament, that so they may deprive him and his people of the fruit of his own gracious intentions, and their humble desires of procuring the public peace, safety and happiness of this realm.

For the preventing of those miserable effects which such malicious endeavours may produce, we have thought good to declare the root and growth of these mischievous designs; the maturity and ripeness to which they have attained before the beginning of the parliament; the effectual means which have been used for the extirpation of those dangerous evils, and the progress which hath therein been made by his Majesty's goodness and the wisdom of the parliament; the ways of obstruction and opposition by which that programme hath been interrupted; the courses to be taken for the removing those obstacles, and for the accomplishing of our most dutiful and faithful intentions and endeavours of restoring and establishing the ancient honour, greatness and security of this Crown and nation.

The root of all this mischief we find to be a malignant and pernicious design of subverting the fundamental laws and principles of government, upon which the religion and justice of this kingdom are firmly established. The actors and promoters thereof have been:

1. The Jesuited papists, who hate the laws, as the obstacles of that change and subversion of religion which they so much long for.

2. The bishops, and the corrupt part of the clergy, who cherish formality and superstition as the natural effects and more probable supports of their own ecclesiastical tyranny and usurpation.

3. Such councillors and courtiers as for private ends have engaged themselves to further the interests of some foreign princes or states to the prejudice of his Majesty and the state at home.[52]

The common principles by which they moulded and governed all their particular counsels and actions were these:

First, to maintain continual differences and discontents between the king and the people, upon questions of prerogative and liberty, that so they might have the advantage of siding with him, and under the notions of men addicted to his service gain to themselves and their parties the places of greatest trust and power in the kingdom.

A second, to suppress the purity and power of religion, and such persons as were best affected to it, as being contrary to their own ends, and the greatest impediment to that change which they thought to introduce.

A third, to conjoin those parties of the kingdom which were most propitious to their own ends, and to divide those who were most opposite, which consisted in many particular observations: to cherish the Arminian part in those points wherein they agree with the papists; to multiply and enlarge the difference between the common Protestants and those whom they call Puritans; to introduce and countenance such opinions and ceremonies as are fittest for accommodation with Popery; to increase and maintain ignorance, looseness and profaneness in the people; that of those three parties, papist, Arminians and Libertines, they might compose a body fit to act such counsels and resolutions as were most conducible to their own ends.

[52] Cf. the similar phraseology used by Pym on 7 November 1640, no. **57** p. 189 above.

A fourth, to disaffect the king to parliaments by slander and false imputations, and by putting him upon other ways of supply, which in show and appearance were fuller of advantage than the ordinary course of subsidies, though in truth they brought more loss than gain both to the king and people, and have caused the great distractions under which we both suffer.

⋆ ⋆ ⋆

[§§ 1–87 of the Remonstrance recount in detail the machinations of the popish faction from the accession of Charles I, reaching a climax in the promulgation of the canons of 1640.]

88. The popish party enjoyed such exemptions from penal laws as amounted to a toleration, besides many other encouragements and court favours.

89. They had a secretary of state, Sir Francis Windebank, a powerful agent for speeding all their desires.

90. A Pope's nuncio residing here, to act and govern them according to such influences as he received from Rome, and to intercede for them with the most powerful concurrence of the foreign princes of that religion.

91. By his authority the papists of all sorts, nobility, gentry and clergy, were convocated after the manner of a Parliament.

92. New jurisdictions were erected of Romish archbishops, taxes levied, another state, moulded within this State, independent in government, contrary in interest and affection, secretly corrupting the ignorant or negligent professors of our religion, and closely uniting and combining themselves against such as were found in this posture, waiting for an opportunity by force to destroy those whom they could not hope to seduce.

93. For the effecting whereof they were strengthened with arms and munitions, encouraged by superstitious prayers, enjoined by the nuncio to be weekly made for the prosperity of some great design.

94. And such power had they at court that secretly a commission was issued out, or intended to be issued to some great men of that profession for the levying of soldiers, and to command and employ them according to private instructions, which we doubt were framed for the advantage of those who were the contrivers of them.

⋆ ⋆ ⋆

[§§ 95–104 deal briefly with the campaign of 1640, leading up to the summons of the Long Parliament.]

105. At our first meeting all oppositions seemed to vanish; the mischiefs were so evident which those evil counsellors produced that no man durst stand up to defend them; yet the work itself afforded difficulty enough.

106. The multiplied evils and corruptions of fifteen years, strengthened by custom and authority, and the concurrent interest of many powerful delinquents, were now to be brought to judgment and reformation . . .

107. The difficulties seemed to be insuperable, which by the Divine Providence we have overcome, the contrarieties incompatible, which yet in a great measure we have reconciled.

★ ★ ★

[§§ 111–36 are a summary of the activities and achievements of this parliament during its first session, particularly its legislative record.]

137. Many excellent laws and provisions are in preparation for removing the inordinate power, vexation and usurpation of bishops, for reforming the pride and idleness of many of the clergy, for easing the people of unnecessary ceremonies in religion, for censuring and removing unworthy and improfitable ministers, and for maintaining godly and diligent preachers through the kingdom.

138. Other things of main importance for the good of this kingdom are in proposition, though little could hitherto be done in regard of the many other more pressing businesses, which yet before the end of this session we hope may receive some progress and perfection.

139. The establishing and ordering the king's revenue, that so the abuse of officers and superfluity of expenses may be cut off, and the necessary disbursements for his Majesty's honour, the defence and government of the kingdom, may be more certainly provided for.

140. The regulating of courts of justice, and abridging both the delays and charges of law suits.

141. The settling of some good courses for preventing the exportation of gold and silver, and the inequality of exchanges between us and other nations, for the advancing of native commodities, increase of our manufacturers, and well balancing of trade, whereby the stock of the kingdom may be increased, or at least kept from impairing, as through neglect hereof it hath done for many years last past.

142. Improving the herring fishing upon our coasts, which will be of mighty use in the employment of the poor, and a plentiful nursery of mariners for enabling the kingdom in any great action.

143. The oppositions, obstructions and the difficulties wherewith we have been encountered, and which still lie in our way with some strength and much obstinacy, are these; the malignant party, whom we have formerly described to be the actors and promoters of all our misery, they have taken heart again.

144. They have been able to prefer some of their own factors and agents to degrees of honour, to places of trust and employment, even during the parliament.

145. They have endeavoured to work in his Majesty ill impressions and opinions of our proceedings, as if we had altogether done our own work, and not his; and had obtained from him many things very prejudicial to the Crown, both in respect of prerogative and profit . . .

★   ★   ★

154. As to the second branch of this slander, we acknowledge with much thankfulness that his Majesty hath passed more good bills to the advantage of the subjects that have been in many ages . . .

★   ★   ★

156. And for both Houses of Parliament we may with truth and modesty say thus much: that we have ever been careful not to desire anything that should weaken the Crown either in just profit or useful power.

157. The triennial parliament [act], for the matter of it, doth not extend to so much as by law we ought to have required (there being two statutes still in force for a parliament to be once a year); and for the manner of it, it is in the king's power that it shall never take effect, if he by a timely summons shall prevent any other way of assembling.

158. In the bill for continuance of this present parliament there seems to be some restraint of the royal power in dissolving of parliaments, not to take it out of the Crown, but to suspend the execution of it for this time and occasion only, which was so necessary for the king's own security and the public peace, that without it we could not have undertaken any of these great charges, but must have left both the armies to disorder and confusion, and the whole kingdom to blood and rapine.

★   ★   ★

161. In the rest there will not be found so much as a shadow of prejudice to the Crown.

162. [Yet] they [the 'malignant party'] have sought to diminish our reputation with the people, and to bring them out of love with parliaments.

163. The aspersions which they have attempted this way have been such as these:

164. That we have spent much time and done little, especially in those grievances which concern religion.

★   ★   ★

166. To which there is a ready answer: if the time spent in this parliament be considered in relation backward to the long growth and deep root of those grievances which we have removed, to the powerful supports of those delinquents which we have pursued, to the great necessities and other charges of the Commonwealth for which we have provided; [167] or if it be considered in relation forward to many advantages, which not only the

present but future ages are like to reap by the good laws and other proceedings in this parliament, we doubt not but it will be thought by all indifferent judgments that our time hath been much better employed than in a far greater proportion of time in many former parliaments put together . . .

★　　★　　★

170. [Moreover], they have had such a party of bishops and popish lords in the House of Peers as hath caused much opposition and delay in the prosecution of delinquents, [and] hindered the proceedings on divers good bills passed in the Commons' House concerning the reformation of sundry great abuses and corruptions both in Church and state.

171. They have laboured to seduce and corrupt some of the Commons' House to draw them into conspiracies and combinations against the liberty of the parliament, [172] and by their instruments and agents they have attempted to disaffect and discontent his Majesty's army, and to engage it for the maintenance of their wicked and traitorous designs: the keeping up of bishops in votes and functions, and by force to compel the parliament to order, limit and dispose their proceedings in such manner as might best concur with the intentions of this dangerous and potent faction.

★　　★　　★

[§§ 173–4 are concerned with the First and Second Army Plots.]

175. Thus they have been continually practising to disturb the peace, and plotting the destruction even of all the king's dominions; and have employed their emissaries and agents in them all for the promoting their devilish designs, which the vigilancy of those who were well affected hath still discovered and defeated before they were ripe for execution in England and Scotland.

176. Only in Ireland, which was farther off, they have had time and opportunity to mould and prepare their work, and had brought it to that perfection that they had possessed themselves of that whole kingdom, totally subverted the government of it, rooted out religion, and destroyed all the Protestants whom the conscience of their duty to God, their king and country, would not have permitted to join with them, if by God's wonderful providence their main enterprise, upon the city and castle of Dublin, had not been detected and prevented upon the very eve before it should have been executed.

177. Notwithstanding, they have in other parts of that kingdom broken out into open rebellion, surprising towns and castles, committed murders, rapes and other villainies, and shaken off all bonds of obedience to his Majesty and the laws of this realm; [178] and in general have kindled such a fire as

nothing but God's infinite blessing upon the wisdom and endeavours of this State will be able to quench it.

*   *   *

179. And certainly had not God in his great mercy unto this land discovered and confounded their former designs we had been the prologue to this tragedy in Ireland, and had by this been made the lamentable spectacle of misery and confusion.

180. And now what hope have we but in God, when as the only means of our subsistence and power of reformation is under him in the parliament?

181. But what can we the Commons [do] without the conjunction of the House of Lords, and what conjunction can we expect there, when the bishops and recusant lords are so numerous and prevalent that they are able to cross and interrupt our best endeavours for reformation, and by that means give advantage to this malignant party to traduce our proceedings?

182. They infuse into the people that we mean to abolish all church government, and leave every man to his own fancy for the sacrifice and worship of God, absolving him of that obedience which he owes under God unto his Majesty, whom we know to be entrusted with the ecclesiastical law as well as with the temporal, to regulate all the members of the Church of England by such rules or order and discipline as are established by parliament, which is his great council, in all affairs both in Church and state.

183. We confess our intention is, and our endeavours have been, to reduce within bounds that exorbitant power which the prelates have assumed unto themselves, so contrary to the Word of God and to the laws of the land, to which end we passed the bill for the removing them from their temporal power and employments, that so the better they might with meekness apply themselves to the discharge of their functions, which bill themselves opposed, and were the principal instruments of crossing it.

184. And we do here declare that it is far from our purpose or desire to let loose the golden reins of discipline and government in the Church, to leave private persons or particular congregations to take up what form of Divine Service they please, for we hold it requisite that there should be throughout the whole realm a conformity to that order which the laws enjoin according to the Word of God. And we desire to unburden the consciences of men of needless and superstitious ceremonies, suppress innovations, and take away the monuments of idolatry.

185. And the better to effect the intended reformation, we desire there may be a general synod of the most grave, pious, learned and judicious divines of this island, assisted with some from foreign parts professing the same religion with us, who may consider of all things necessary for the peace and good

government of the Church, and represent the results of their consultations unto the parliament, to be there allowed of and confirmed, and receive the stamp of authority, thereby to find passage and obedience throughout the kingdom.

186. They have maliciously charged us that we intend to destroy and discourage learning, whereas it is our chiefest care and desire to advance it, and to provide a competent maintenance for conscionable and preaching ministers throughout the kingdom, which will be a great encouragement to scholars, and a certain means whereby the want, meanness and ignorance to which a great part of the clergy is now subject will be prevented.

187. And we intend likewise to reform and purge the fountains of learning, the two universities, that the streams flowing from thence may be clear and pure, and an honour and comfort to the whole land.

★ ★ ★

191. For the perfecting of the work begun, and removing all future impediments, we conceive these courses will be very effectual, seeing the religion of the papists hath such principles as do certainly tend to the destruction and extirpation of all Protestants whom they shall have opportunity to effect it.

192. It is necessary in the first place to keep them in such condition as that they may not be able to do us any hurt, and for avoiding of such connivance and favour as hath heretofore been shown unto them.

193. That his Majesty be pleased to grant a standing commission to some choice men named in parliament, who may take notice of their increase, their counsels and proceedings, and use all due means by execution of the laws to prevent all mischievous designs against the peace and safety of this kingdom.

194. That some good course be taken to discover the counterfeit and false conformity of papists to the Church, by colour whereof persons very much disaffected to the true religion have been admitted into places of greatest authority and trust in the kingdom.

195. For the better preservation of the laws and liberties of the kingdom, that all illegal grievances and exactions be presented and punished at the sessions and assizes.

196. And that judges and justices be very careful to give this in charge to the grand jury, and both the sheriff and justices to be sworn to the due execution of the Petition of Right and other laws.

197. That his Majesty be humbly petitioned by both Houses to employ such councillors, ambassadors and other ministers, in managing his business at home and abroad, as the parliament may have cause to confide in, without which we cannot give his Majesty such supplies for support of is own estate, not such assistance to the Protestant party beyond the sea, as is desired.

198. It may often fall out that the Commons may have just cause to take exception at some men for being councillors, and yet not charge those men with crimes, for there be grounds of difference which lie not in proof, [and, 199,] there are others which, though they may be proved, yet are not legally criminal.

200. To be a known favourer of papists, or to have been very forward in defending or countenancing some great offenders questioned in parliament; or to speak contemptuously of either House of Parliament, or parliamentary privilege; [201,] or such as are factors or agents for any foreign prince of another religion; such [as] are justly suspected to get councillors' places, or any other of trust concerning public employment, for money: for all these and divers others we may have great reason to be earnest with his Majesty not to put his great affairs into such hands, though we may be unwilling to proceed against them in any legal ways of charge or impeachment.

202. That all Councillors of State may be sworn to observe those laws which concern the subject in his liberty, that they may likewise take an oath not to receive or give reward or pension from any foreign prince, but such as they shall within some reasonable time discover to the lords of his Majesty's Council.

203. And although they should wickedly forswear themselves, yet it may herein do good to make them known to be false and perjured to those who employ them, and thereby bring them into as little credit with them as with us.

204. That his Majesty may have cause to be in love with good counsel and good men, by showing him in a humble and dutiful manner how full of advantage it would be to himself to see his own estate settled in a plentiful condition to support his honour; to see his people united in ways of duty to him, and endeavours of the public good; to see happiness, wealth, peace and safety derived to his own kingdom, and procured to his allies by the influence of his own power and government.   Rushworth, IV, 437–51

65. The impeachment of the Five Members, 3 January 1642

The lord keeper signified to the House [of Lords], that he was commanded by the king, to let their lordships know, that his Majesty hath given Mr Attorney-General command to acquaint their lordships with some particulars from him. Hereupon Mr Attorney, standing at the Clerk's table, said that the king had commanded him to tell their lordships, that divers great and treasonable designs and practices against him and the state have come to his Majesty's knowledge, for which the king hath given him command, in his name, to accuse, and did accuse, six persons of high treason, and other high misdemeanours, by delivery of the articles in writing which he had in his hand, which he received from his Majesty, and was commanded to desire your lordships to have it read, in which articles the persons' names, and the heads of the treason, were contained. Which articles were commanded to be read, *in haec verba*.

Articles of high treason and other high misdemeanours against the Lord Kimbolton, Mr Denzil Holles, Sir Arthur Haslerigg, Mr John Pym, Mr John Hampden and Mr William Strode.

1. That they have traitorously endeavoured to subvert the fundamental laws and government of the kingdom of England, to deprive the King of his regal power, and to place in subjects an arbitrary and tyrannical power over the lives, liberties and estates of his Majesty's liege people.

2. That they have traitorously endeavoured, by many foul aspersions upon his Majesty and his government, to alienate the affections of his people, and to make his Majesty odious unto them.

3. That they have endeavoured to draw his Majesty's late army to disobedience to His Majesty's commands, and to side with them in their traitorous designs.

4. That they have traitorously invited and encouraged a foreign power to invade his Majesty's kingdom of England.

5. That they have traitorously endeavoured to subvert the rights and the very being of parliaments.

6. That for the completing of their traitorous designs they have endeavoured (as far as in them lay) by force and terror to compel the parliament to join with them in their traitorous designs, and to that end have actually raised and countenanced tumults against the king and parliament.

7. And that they have traitorously conspired to levy, and actually have levied, war against the king.

★　★　★

Ordered, That this business shall be taken into consideration by a committee of the whole House, and to consider whether this accusation of Mr Attorney-General, of the Lord Kimbolton and others, of high treason, be a regular proceeding, according to law, . . . and whether an accusation of treason may be brought into this House by the king's attorney against a Peer in parliament and whether any person ought to be committed to custody upon a general accusation from the king or the House of Commons, before it be reduced into particulars. *LJ*, IV, 500–1

66. The Militia Ordinance, 5 March 1642

An Ordinance of the Lords and Commons in Parliament for the safety and defence of the kingdom of England and dominion of Wales[53]

Whereas there hath been of late a most dangerous and desperate design upon the House of Commons, which we have just cause to believe to be an effect of the bloody counsels of papists and other ill-affected persons, who have already raised a rebellion in the kingdom of Ireland; and by reason of many discoveries we cannot but fear they will proceed not only to stir up the like rebellion and insurrections in this kingdom of England, but also to back them with forces from abroad;

For the safety therefore of his Majesty's person, the parliament and kingdom in this time of imminent danger; it is ordained by *the king's most excellent Majesty and* the Lords and Commons now in parliament assembled, that Henry Earl of Holland shall be Lieutenant of the county of Berks, Oliver Earl of Bolingbroke shall be Lieutenant of the county of Bedford, William lord Paget shall be Lieutenant of the county of Bucks . . . [etc.][54] and *shall* severally and respectively have power to assemble and call together his Majesty's subjects within the said several and respective counties and places, as well within the liberties as without, that are meet and fit for the wars, and them to train and exercise and put in readiness, and them after their abilities and faculties well and sufficiently from time to time to cause to be arrayed and weaponed, and to take the muster of them in places most fit for that purpose, and the aforesaid Henry Earl of Holland . . . [etc.] shall severally and respectively have power within the several and respective counties and places aforesaid to nominate and appoint such persons of quality as to them shall seem meet to be their deputy lieutenants, to be approved of by both Houses of Parliament. And that any one or more of the said deputies so assigned and approved of, in the absence of or by the command of the said Henry Earl of Holland . . . [etc.], shall have power and authority to do and execute within the said several and respective counties and places to them assigned as aforesaid, all such powers and authorities before in this present ordinance contained; And the aforesaid Henry Earl of Holland [etc.], shall have power to make colonels, captains and other officers, and to remove [them] out of their places and make others from time to time, as they shall think fit for that purpose;

And the said Henry Earl of Holland . . . [etc.], their deputy or deputies in their absence or by their command, shall have power to lead, conduct and employ the persons aforesaid arrayed and weaponed, for the suppression of all

[53] This was passed by the Lords on 16 February, and sent on to the king for his assent, though from the beginning it was described as an 'ordinance', not a bill. When he refused it was enacted regardless, with the phrases in italics deleted.

[54] The only commoner was Denzil Holles, for Bristol.

rebellions, insurrections and invasions that may happen within the several and respective counties and places; and shall have power and authority to lead, conduct and employ the persons aforesaid arrayed and weaponed, as well within their several and respective counties and places, as within any other part of this realm of England or dominion of Wales, for the suppression of all rebellions, insurrections and invasions that may happen, according as they from time to time shall receive directions *by his Majesty's authority, signified unto them by*[55] the Lords and Commons assembled in parliament;

And be it further ordained, that Sir John Gayre, Sir Jacob Garret . . .,[56] shall have such power and authority within the City of London as any of the lieutenants before named are authorised to have by this ordinance within the said several and respective counties (the nomination and appointment of deputy lieutenants only excepted);

And it is further ordained, that such persons as shall not obey in any of the premises, shall answer to their neglect and contempt to the Lords and Commons in a parliamentary way, and not otherwise nor elsewhere, and that every the powers granted as aforesaid shall continue until it shall be otherwise ordered or declared by both Houses of Parliament, and no longer.

LJ, IV, 587–9, 625–7

67. Remonstrance of both Houses, in answer to the King's Declaration [of 7 May] concerning Hull, 26 May 1642

Although the great affairs of this kingdom, and the miserable and bleeding condition of the kingdom of Ireland afford us little leisure to spend our time in Declarations, or in Answers and Replies, yet the malignant party about his Majesty taking all occasion to multiply calumnies upon the houses of parliament, and to publish sharp invectives under his Majesty's name against them and their proceedings, . . . we cannot be so wanting to our own innocency, or to the duty of our trust, as not to clear ourselves from these false aspersions.[57]

★   ★   ★

---

[55] The word 'from' was substituted for this whole phrase.

[56] Six aldermen were named, with Philip Skippon, general of the City trained-bands, or any three of them, plus 12 citizens, or any six of them.

[57] Charles grumbled in much the same way. His Declaration of 4 May began: 'We very well understand how much it is below the high and royal dignity wherein God hath placed us, to take notice of, much more to trouble ourselves with answering, those many scandalous pamphlets and printed papers which are scattered with such great license throughout the kingdom, notwithstanding our earnest desire, so often in vain pressed, for a reformation . . .', *PH*, II, 1243.

As for 'the duty and modesty of former times',[58] from which we are said to have varied, and to want the warrant of any precedents therein, but what ourselves have made; if we have made any precedents in this parliament, we have made them for posterity, upon the same or better grounds of reason and law than those were upon which our predecessors first made any for us. And as some precedents ought not to be rules for us to follow, so none can be limits to bound our proceedings, which may and must vary according to the different condition of times . . . If we have done more than ever our ancestors have done we have suffered more than they have ever suffered, and yet, in point of modesty and duty, we shall not yield to the best of former times, and we shall put this in issue: Whether the highest and most unwarrantable proceedings of any of his Majesty's predecessors do not fall short of, and much below, what hath been done to us this parliament; and on the other side, whether, if we should make the highest precedents of other parliaments our pattern, there would be cause to complain of 'want of modesty and duty' in us, when we have not so much as suffered such things to enter our thoughts which all the world knows they have put in action?

Another charge which is laid very high upon us (and which were indeed a very great crime if we were found guilty thereof), is, that by avowing this act of Sir J. Hotham we do in consequence confound and destroy the title and interest of all his Majesty's good subjects to their lands and goods, and that upon this ground, 'that his Majesty hath the same title to his own town of Hull which any of his subjects hath to their houses or lands . . .'[59]

Here that is laid down for a principle which would indeed pull up the very foundation of the liberty, property and interest of every subject in particular, and of all the subjects in general, if we should admit it for a truth that his Majesty hath the same right and title to his towns and magazines (bought with the public monies, as we conceive that at Hull to have been) that every particular man hath to his house, lands and goods, for his Majesty's towns are no more his own than his kingdom is his own, and his kingdom is no more his own that his people are his own . . . This erroneous maxim, being infused into princes, that their kingdoms are their own, and that they may do with them what they will (as if their kingdoms were for them, and not they for their

---

[58] Charles had expressed resentment that parliament had given no direct answer to his protests about Hull, but instead had chosen 'to publish a Declaration concerning that business, as an appeal to the people; as if their intercourse with us, and for our satisfaction, were now to no more purpose, though we knew this course of theirs to be very unagreeable to the modesty and duty of former times, and unwarrantable by any precedents but what themselves have made', 7 May, *ibid.*, 1213.

[59] Charles had said: 'By the same rule of justice which is now offered to us, all the private interest and title of all our good subjects to all their lands and goods are confounded and destroyed . . . And we would fain be answered, what title any subject of our kingdom hath to his home or land, that we have not to our town of Hull?', *ibid.*

kingdoms) is the root of all the subjects' misery, and of all the invading of their just rights and liberties. Whereas, indeed, they are only entrusted with their kingdoms, and with their towns, and with their people, and with the public treasure of the commonwealth and whatsoever is bought therewith. By the known law of this kingdom the very jewels of the crown are not the king's proper goods, but are only entrusted to him for the use and ornament thereof, as the towns, forts, treasure, magazine, offices and people of the kingdom, and the whole kingdom itself, are entrusted unto him for the good and safety and best advantage thereof; and as this trust is for the use of the kingdom, so ought it to be managed by the advice of the Houses of Parliament, whom the kingdom hath trusted for that purpose . . .

But, admitting his Majesty had indeed a property in the town and magazine of Hull, who doubts but that a parliament may dispose of any thing wherein his Majesty or any subject hath a right, in such a way as that the kingdom may not be exposed to hazard or danger thereby? Which is our case in the disposing of the town and magazine of Hull. And whereas his Majesty doth allow this, and a greater, power to a parliament, but in that sense only as he himself is a part thereof, we appeal to every man's conscience that hath observed our proceedings, whether we disjoined his Majesty from his parliament, who have in all humble ways sought his concurrence with us, . . . or whether these evil counsellors about him have not separated him from his parliament, not only in distance of place, but also in the discharge of this joint trust with them for the peace and safety of the kingdom . . .

*   *   *

We are so far from believing 'that his Majesty is the only person against whom treason cannot be committed'[60] that, in some sense, we acknowledge he is the only person against whom it can be committed, that is, as he is king; and that treason which is against the kingdom is more against his person because he is king; for that very treason is not treason as it is against him as a man, but as a man that is a king, and as he hath relation to the kingdom, and stands as a person entrusted with the kingdom, and discharging that trust . . .   *PH*, II, 1298-314

68. The Nineteen Propositions, 1 June 1642

Your Majesty's most humble and faithful subjects, the Lords and Commons in Parliament . . . do in all humility and sincerity present to your Majesty their most dutiful petition and advice, that, out of your princely wisdom, for the

---

[60] 'The case is truly stated: let all the world judge (unless the mere sitting of a parliament doth suspend all laws, and we are the only person in England against whom treason cannot be committed) where the fault is', 7 May, *ibid.*, 1216.

establishing of your own honour and safety, and gracious tenderness of the welfare and security of your subjects and dominions, you will be pleased to grant and accept these our humble desires and propositions, as the most necessary effectual means, through God's blessing, of removing those jealousies and differences, which have unhappily fallen betwixt you and your people, and procuring both your Majesty and them a constant course of honour, peace and happiness.

1. That the Lords and others of your Majesty's Privy Council and such great officers and ministers of state, either at home or beyond the seas, may be put from your Privy Council, and from those offices and employments, excepting such as shall be approved of by both Houses of Parliament; and that the persons put into the places and employments of those that are removed, may be approved of by both Houses of Parliament; and that all Privy Councillors shall take an oath for the due execution of their places, in such form as shall be agreed upon by both Houses of Parliament.

2. That the great affairs of the kingdom may not be concluded or transacted by the advice of private men, or by any unknown or unsworn councillors, but that such matters as concern the public, and are proper for the High Court of Parliament, which is your Majesty's great and supreme council, may be debated, resolved and transacted only in parliament, and not elsewhere: and such as shall presume to do any thing to the contrary shall be reserved to the censure and judgment of parliament: and such other matters of state as are proper for your Majesty's Privy Council shall be debated and concluded by such of the nobility and others as shall, from time to time, be chosen for that place, by approbation of both Houses of Parliament: and that no public act concerning the affairs of the kingdom, which are proper for your Privy Council, may be esteemed of any validity, as proceeding from the royal authority, unless it be done by the advice and consent of the major part of your council, attested under their hands: and that your council may be limited to a certain number, not exceeding twenty-five, nor under fifteen: and if any councillor's place happen to be void in the intervals of parliament, it shall not be supplied without the assent of the major part of the council, which choice shall be confirmed at the next sitting of parliament, or else be void.

3. That the Lord High Steward of England, Lord High Constable, Lord Chancellor, or Lord Keeper of the Great Seal, Lord Treasurer, Lord Privy Seal, Earl Marshall, Lord Admiral, Warden of the Cinque Ports, Chief Governor of Ireland, Chancellor of the Exchequer, Master of the Wards, Secretaries of State, two Chief Justices, and Chief Baron, may always be chosen with the approbation of both Houses of Parliament; and in the intervals of parliament, by assent of the major part of the council, in such manner as is before expressed in the choice of councillors.

LORETTO SCHOOL
VI FORM LIBRARY

4. That he or they, unto whom the government and education of the king's children shall be committed, shall be approved of by both Houses of Parliament; and in the intervals of parliament, by the assent of the major part of the Council, in such manner as is before expressed in the choice of councillors; and that all such servants as are now about them, against whom both Houses shall have any just exception, shall be removed.

5. That no marriage shall be concluded or treated, for any of the king's children, with any foreign prince, or other person whatsoever, abroad or at home, without the consent of parliament, under the penalty of a Praemunire, unto such as shall conclude or treat any marriage as aforesaid; and that the said penalty shall not be pardoned, or dispensed with but by the consent of both Houses of Parliament.

6. That the laws in force against Jesuits, priests, and popish recusants, be strictly put in execution, without any toleration or dispensation to the contrary; and that some more effectual course may be enacted, by authority of parliament, to disable them from making any disturbance in the state, or eluding the law, by trusts, or otherwise.

7. That the votes of the popish Lords in the House of Peers may be taken away, so long as they continue papists; and that His Majesty would consent to such a bill as shall be drawn for the education of the children of papists by Protestants, in the Protestant religion.

8. That your Majesty would be pleased to consent, that such a reformation be made of the Church government and liturgy, as both Houses of Parliament shall advise; wherein they intend to have consultations with divines, as is expressed in their declaration to that purpose; and that your Majesty will contribute your best assistance to them, for the raising of a sufficient maintenance for preaching ministers throughout the kingdom; and that your Majesty will be pleased to give your consent to laws for the taking away of innovations and superstitions, and of pluralities, and against scandalous ministers.

9. That your Majesty will be pleased to rest satisfied with that course that the Lords and Commons have appointed, for ordering the militia, until the same shall be further settled by a bill; and that your Majesty will recall your declarations and proclamations against the ordinance made by the Lords and Commons concerning it.

10. That such Members of either House of Parliament as have, during this present parliament, been put out of any place and office, may either be restored to that place or office, or otherwise have satisfaction for the same, upon the petition of that House whereof he or they are Members.

11. That all privy councillors and judges may take an oath, the form whereof to be agreed on and settled by act of parliament, for the maintaining

of the Petition of Right and of certain statutes made by parliament, which shall be mentioned by both Houses of Parliament: and that an inquiry of all the breaches and violations of those laws may be given in charge by the justices of the King's Bench, every term, and by the judges of assize in their circuits, and justices of the peace at the sessions, to be presented and punished according to law.

12. That all the judges, and all officers placed by approbation of both Houses of Parliament, may hold their places *quam diu bene se gesserint*.

13. That the justice of parliament may pass upon all delinquents, whether they be within the kingdom or fled out of it; and that all persons cited by either House of Parliament may appear and abide the centure of parliament.

14. That the general pardon offered by your Majesty may be granted with such exceptions as shall be advised by both Houses of Parliament.

15. That the forts and castles of this kingdom may be put under the command and custody of such persons as your Majesty shall appoint with the approbation of your parliament: and in the intervals of parliament, with approbation of the major part of the Council, in such manner as is before expressed in the choice of councillors.

16. That the extraordinary guards and military forces now attending your Majesty may be removed, and discharged; and that, for the future, you will raise no such guards or extraordinary forces, but according to the law, in case of actual rebellion or invasion.

17. That your Majesty will be pleased to enter into a more strict alliance with the states of the United Provinces, and other neighbouring princes and states of the Protestant religion, for the defence and maintenance thereof, against all designs and attempts of the Pope and his adherents to subvert and suppress it; whereby your Majesty will obtain a great access of strength and reputation, and your subjects be much encouraged and enabled, in a parliamentary way, for your aid and assistance, in restoring your royal sister and [her] princely issue to those dignities and dominions which belong unto them, and relieving the other Protestant princes who have suffered in the same cause.

18. That your Majesty will be pleased, by act of parliament, to clear the Lord Kimbolton, and the Five Members of the House of Commons, in such manner that future parliaments may be secured from the consequence of that evil precedent.

19. That your Majesty will be graciously pleased to pass a bill for restraining Peers made hereafter from sitting or voting in parliament, unless they be admitted thereunto with the consent of both Houses of Parliament.

And these our humble desires being granted by your Majesty, we shall forthwith apply ourselves to regulate your present revenue in such sort as may be for your best advantage; and likewise to settle such an ordinary and constant increase of it, as shall be sufficient to support your royal dignity in honour and plenty, beyond he proportion of any former grants of the subjects of this kingdom to your Majesty's royal predecessors. We shall likewise put the town of Hull into such hands as your Majesty shall appoint, with the consent and approbation of parliament, and deliver up a just account of all the magazine, and cheerfully employ to the uttermost our power and endeavours, in the real expression and performance of our most dutiful and loyal affections, to the preserving and maintaining the royal honour, greatness and safety of your Majesty and your posterity.   *LJ*, v, 97–9

69. A Declaration of the Lords and Commons in Parliament concerning His Majesty's Proclamation of the 27th May 1642, 6 June 1642

The Lords and Commons, having perused his Majesty's proclamation forbidding all his Majesty's subjects belonging to the trained bands or militia of this kingdom to rise, march, muster or exercise by virtue of any order or ordinance of one or both Houses of Parliament, without consent or warrant from his Majesty, upon pain of punishment according to the laws:

Do thereupon declare, that neither the statute of the seventh of Edward the First, therein vouched, nor any other law of this kingdom, doth restrain or make void the ordinance agreed upon by both Houses of Parliament, for the ordering and disposing the militia of the kingdom in this time of extreme and imminent danger, nor expose his Majesty's subjects to any punishment for obeying the same, notwithstanding that his Majesty hath refused to give his consent to that ordinance, but [it] ought to be obeyed by the fundamental laws of this kingdom . . .

The question is not, whether it belong to the king or no, to restrain such force, but, if the king shall refuse to discharge that duty and trust, whether there is not a power in the two Houses to provide for the safety of the parliament and peace of the kingdom, which is the end for which the ordinance concerning the militia was made, and, being agreeable to the scope and purpose of the law, cannot in reason be adjudged to be contrary to it . . .

It is acknowledged that the king is the fountain of justice and protection, but the acts of justice and protection are not exercised in his own person, nor depend upon his pleasure, but by his courts, and by his ministers, who must do their duty therein, though the king in his own person should forbid them; and therefore if judgments should be given by them against the king's will and personal command, yet are they the king's judgments.

The High Court of Parliament is not only a court of judicature, enabled by the laws to adjudge and determine the rights and liberties of the kingdom, against such patents and grants of his Majesty as are prejudicial thereunto, although strengthened both by his personal command and by his proclamation under the Great Seal; but it is likewise a council, to provide for the necessities, prevent the imminent dangers, and preserve the public peace and safety of the kingdom, and to declare the king's pleasure in those things as are requisite thereunto; and what they do herein hath the stamp of royal authority, although his Majesty, seduced by evil counsel, do in his own person oppose or interrupt the same; for the king's supreme and royal pleasure is exercised and declared in this high court of law and counsel, after a more eminent and obligatory manner than it can be by personal act or resolution of his own.

Seeing therefore, the Lords and Commons, which are his Majesty's great and high Council, have ordained that, for the present and necessary defence of the realm, the trained bands and militia of this kingdom should be ordered according to that ordinance, . . . all his Majesty's loving subjects, as well by that law as by other laws, are bound to be obedient thereunto; and what they do therein is (according to that law) to be interpreted to be done in aid of the king, in discharge of that trust which he is tied to perform; and it is so far from being liable to punishment, that, if they should refuse to do it, or be persuaded by any commission or command of his Majesty to do the contrary, they might justly be punished for the same, according to the laws and usages of the realm; for the king, by his sovereignty, is not enabled to destroy his people, but to protect and defend them; and the High Court of Parliament, and all other his Majesty's officers and ministers, ought to be subservient to that power and authority which the law hath placed in His Majesty to that purpose, though he himself in his own person should neglect the same.

Wheretofore the Lords and Commons do declare the said proclamation to be void in law, and of none effect; for that, by the constitution and policy of this kingdom, the king by his proclamation cannot declare the law contrary to the judgment and resolution of any of the inferior courts of justice, much less against the High Court of Parliament . . .

*   *   *

LJ, v, 112–13

70. Answer to the king, from both Houses of Parliament, 6 September 1642

Whereas his Majesty, in a message received the 5th of September, requires that the parliament would revoke their declaration against such persons as have assisted his Majesty in this unnatural war against his kingdom: It is this day ordered and declared by the Lords and Commons that the arms which they have been forced to take up, and shall be forced to take up, for the preservation of the parliament, religion, the laws and liberties of the kingdom, shall not be laid down, until his Majesty shall withdraw his protection from such persons as have been voted by both Houses to be delinquents, or that shall by both Houses be voted to be delinquents, and shall leave them to the justice of parliament, to be proceeded with according to their demerits; to the end that both this and succeeding generations may take warning with what danger they incur the like heinous crimes and also to the end that those great charges and damages wherewith all the Commonwealth hath been burdened in the premises since his Majesty's departure from the parliament may be borne by the delinquents and other malignant and disaffected persons; and that all his Majesty's good and well-affected subjects who, by loans or monies, or otherwise at their charge, have assisted the Comonwealth, or shall in like manner hereafter assist the Commonwealth in time of extreme danger, may be repaid all sums of money by them lent for these purposes, and be satisfied their charges so sustained, out of the estates of the said delinquents and of the malignant and disaffected party in this kingdom.　　　　　　　　　　　　　*LJ*, v, 341

CHAPTER 6

THE PURITAN FAILURE, 1641-8

The Root and Branch Petition[1] submitted to parliament in December 1640 voiced a detestation of the bishops which was general amongst all classes. However, it soon became evident that much of this hostility was directed not against the institution of episcopacy but against its present representatives. In December 1640 the Commons had no hesitation in declaring the canons made in convocation that summer illegal, nor in impeaching Laud, but when they debated the Root and Branch Petition in February 1641 it was soon apparent that the firm majority behind all secular reforms was going to break up on the Church question. The elder Vane remarked soothingly that, 'We all tended to one end, that was reformation, only we differed in the way', a remark which summed up the failure of the Puritans to profit from the opportunity for which they had waited so long.[2]

One influential group, led by Falkland, Hyde and Culpeper, was willing to reduce the bishops' coercive powers and punish individuals for specific crimes, but was not even willing to exclude them from the Lords. Others regarded their exclusion from the Lords as an absolute minimum; others toyed with the concept of a 'primitive reformed episcopacy'; others envisaged them as chairmen of diocesan synods; but only a small minority of 'Root and Branchers', or Independents, wanted them removed altogether. On 30 March a bill to remove the bishops from the House of Lords and the Council was given its first reading, and on 1 May it was sent up to the Lords. On the 24th the Lords informed the Commons that they could not agree to remove members of their own House by statute, and on the 27th, as a result, the Root-and-Branchers introduced a bill to abolish episcopacy altogether. However, it made little progress before the end of the session, and it was not revived. Nothing is more impressive in this parliament than the leaders' skill in suppressing contentious legislation.

However, with the removal of Laud episcopal discipline had virtually collapsed, and it was essential to create some alternative form of church government speedily; for on one thing only did an overwhelming majority of the parliamentary gentry agree with Laud, the need to suppress 'the cankers of public liberty' in religion.[3] Already in London and other large towns congregations were hiving off from the Church, denying the necessity of any superior authority under God, and re-arranging divine service to suit themselves. These separatists or sectarians had a few supporters already in the Commons, but many more Members were under pressure from clergymen they respected who wanted them to reform the liturgy and doctrine of the Church, but

---

[1] No. 52, p. 154 above.

[2] D'Ewes Journal, ed. Notestein, p. 337. Cromwell was still saying the same thing in 1647: 'I cannot see but that we all speak to the same end, and the mistakes are only in the way' (Woodhouse, *Puritanism and Liberty*, p. 104).

[3] *CSPD 1640-41*, p. 307.

who loathed congregational independence almost as much as they did Laudian innovation. As to how to effect this there were almost as many opinions as votes in the House, and none of the Commons leaders were ready with a programme of Church reform. When Edward Hyde asked the influential Puritan Nathaniel Fiennes what he would put in place of the bishops if they were abolished he replied 'that there would be time enough to think of that'.[4] Cromwell returned a similar answer to the same question – 'I can tell you, sir, what I would not have, though I cannot, what I would.'[5]

In secular matters this negative attitude was reasonable enough; there it was considered necessary to remove certain illegal accretions on the body of the constitution, which after this operation would function perfectly. But in the case of the Church there was an apparent need in 1641 for constructive statesmanship of a radical kind, for it had never been settled to any man's satisfaction since the Reformation. The obvious alternative to episcopacy was Presbyterianism, a solution naturally pressed with vigour by the influential Scots Committee in London; but the truth was, Presbyterianism was very little understood in England, and less liked, for the union of the crowns had done nothing to close the gulf between England and Scotland. But the more they saw of Presbyterianism, the less the parliamentarians liked it, and the more they laboured to keep it out of sight. With some success, for as late as 20 November one Member remarked that neither Presbyterianism nor Independency had yet been discussed in the House.[6]

Meanwhile the question of church ceremonial was more immediately imperative than that of church government. Early in 1641 many ministers, churchwardens or even parishioners began removing altars and altar rails and breaking down other recent embellishments to their parish churches, and the Puritan clergy abandoned in whole or in part the form of divine service prescribed by the Book of Common Prayer (and therefore by parliament), despite an Order of the House of Lords on 16 January 1641 that services should be conducted in accordance with the laws of the land (**72**). This Order could be said to be levelled against Puritans equally with Laudians, and another Order by the Lords on 1 March, that the communion table 'should stand in the ancient place where it ought to do by the law, and as it hath done for the great part of these three score years last past',[7] was even more two-faced, for the whole altarian controversy hinged on conflicting interpretations of canon LXXXIII of 1604 (p. 125 above). The Commons were equally cautious. They introduced a bill 'for abolishing superstition and idolatry, and for the better advancing of the true worship and service of God' on 5 February, but the committee to which it was referred on the 13th was not called upon to report until 8 August, six months later.[8] In the interval the Commons swore in their Protestation of 3 May (no. **60**, p. 200 above) to defend 'the true reformed Protestant religion expressed in the doctrine of the Church of England', but a little more than a week later they had to issue an explanation that this did not extend to 'maintaining of any form of worship, discipline or government', nor any particular 'rites or ceremonies' (**71**).

---

[4] Clarendon, *Life* (1759), I, 80–1.
[5] Qu. Perry Miller, *Orthodoxy in Massachusetts* (Cambridge, Mass. 1933), p. 73.
[6] Shaw, *English Church during the Civil Wars*, I, 101.
[7] *Ibid.*, I, 105.   [8] *Ibid.*, I, 104.

However, in late August, with the King in Scotland, they were forced to take notice of the random iconoclasm which was still proceeding, and the introduction of *ad hoc* services; on 1 September they passed a series of resolutions on ecclesiastical innovations which ordered the removal of altars, altar rails and statues, forbad bowing at the name of Jesus, and enjoined the proper observance of the Lord's Day (**73**). The Lords agreed to the destruction of altars, but without discussing the other resolutions they provocatively re-issued their Order of 16 January (**72**), and had it printed. The session ended on 10 September with the Houses deadlocked. In the ecclesiastical sphere the only achievement of this great reforming parliament to date was the abolition of High Commission.

The atmosphere when parliament re-assembled on 20 October was not conducive to reform of any kind, and though the next day a bill was introduced and speedily passed in the Commons to prohibit any clergyman from exercising any temporal jurisdiction whatsoever (commonly described as the Bishops' Exclusion Bill) it was still lingering in the House of Lords at the end of the year. However, the king's announcement in November that he would be steadfast in the defence of the Church as established by law (p. 181 above) rallied his supporters, as was evident in the preliminary debates on the Grand Remonstrance. Indeed, the authors of the Remonstrance were very much on the defensive; they denied any intention 'to let loose the golden reins of discipline and government in the Church', and set forth as their aim 'a conformity to that order which the laws enjoin, according to the Word of God' (§ 184, p. 215 above). The bishops could not have asked for more. Even then, on 15 November strong exception was taken to a clause referring to 'the errors and superstitions' of the Book of Common Prayer, and the following day it was moved 'that the clause that has been now read concerning the liturgy shall be recommended to the same committee, that a clause may be brought in that may not cast any aspersions or scandal upon the Book of Common Prayer established by law'. It was finally decided 'that the clause or anything therein contained that concerns the Common Prayer Book shall be totally left out of this declaration'.[9]

The Commons leaders had to take refuge in a clause which left reform of Church government to a synod whose appointment could be postponed at will (§ 185, p. 215 above). Even the king's departure from London, and the drift into civil war, scarcely touched the Church question. In January 1642 the Lords passed the Bishops' Exclusion Bill, and the king gave his assent, after some hesitation, the following month (**74**) – an indication that the struggle now impending had long since ceased to hinge on religious matters, if it ever had. Nevertheless, the difficulty of reaching agreement with the Lords, and a vain attempt to secure the king's assent, delayed until August the passing of an Ordinance to demolish all 'monuments of superstition and idolatry', which embodied the Commons' Resolutions of the previous September.[10]

However, the secession of the royalist Members and the intervention of the Scots doomed the bishops. When parliament sought assistance from the Edinburgh government in September 1642 it was asked what it proposed to do for the reform of the Church. Both Houses at once docilely agreed that bishops, deans and chapters were

[9] *CJ*, II, 598.   [10] Firth and Rait, I, 265–6.

'a great impediment to the perfect reformation and growth of religion, and very prejudicial to the state and government of this kingdom',[11] but although the military disasters of 1643 made Scots aid ever more desirable, there was an increasing disposition on the part of parliament to evade the establishment of Presbyterian church government, which the Scots would almost certainly make a condition of their alliance. One delaying tactic was to appoint at last the synod of divines called for in the Grand Remonstrance, and an ordinance of 12 June 1643 (**75**) set up an Assembly of 121 ministers, selected by parliament, and stiffened by the addition of ten peers and 20 MPs, all men of influence and power. It could only discuss questions put before it by parliament and make recommendations in return, it had no legislative power of its own, and it was even forbidden to publish its recommendations. The preamble to this ordinance pledged parliament once more to abolish episcopacy, but nothing was done to effect it, and in the Solemn League and Covenant in September 1643 (**76**) their delegates insisted on the insertion of the words 'according to the Word of God' after 'reformed', which meant that they were obliged to accept Presbyterianism only insofar as it was demonstrably sanctioned by Scripture.

Progress towards Presbyterianism was slow and halting. In fact, a majority of the Westminster divines were in favour of it, but an able and voluble minority were not, and they had the support of a majority of the lay members, who were in turn supported by an influential group of Independents in the Commons. The Independents believed in the viability of each separate congregation, though they were not necessarily in favour of complete autonomy (for even Independent congregations could be 'federated' in a national Church), and they were supported by other MPs who feared that the establishment of Presbyterianism would only erect a clerical despotism akin to Archbishop Laud's and perhaps more efficient.

So, it was not until February 1643, after it had been sitting six months, that the Westminster Assembly was asked to test the scriptural authenticity of Presbyterianism, and after five weeks this had to be laid aside while parliament and the Assembly dealt with the immediate problems of ordination and public worship. A scheme for ministerial ordination had been delayed in the hope that it could be administered by the presbyteries, but since the presbyteries were no nearer parliament could only appoint a committee of London ministers to examine the qualifications of ordinands for the time being. Significantly, it declined to impose any doctrinal test, or commit itself to a statement that ministers were ordained of God as well as man.[12]

This done, the debate was resumed, but the Assembly was diverted again in October 1644 by the need to frame a new Directory of Worship to replace the Prayer Book, which could be put before the king in the negotiations now pending at Uxbridge. It was hurried through with remarkable speed and very little debate, and published as a schedule to an ordinance of 4 January 1645. But this ordinance provided no machinery for enforcing its use, nor did it impose penalties for the continued use of the Prayer Book, though it did repeal the legislation making its use compulsory.[13] Thus the

[11] *CJ*, II, 747.
[12] 'An ordinance . . . for the ordination of ministers *pro tempore*', Firth and Rait, I, 521–6. Cf. Shaw, I, 318ff.
[13] Firth and Rait, I, 582ff.

failure of the Uxbridge negotiations left the country with two prayer books, neither of them prescribed by law, and no working system of church government at all; and the only question on which Assembly and parliament seemed able to agree was the imposition of that grim personal austerity commonly associated with the word 'Puritan'. As far back as September 1642 Parliament had forbidden the performance of stage plays, and in April 1644 a new ordinance 'for the better observation of the Lord's Day' even forbad travel on a Sunday.[14] In December 1644 it surpassed itself by abolishing Christmas (77).

Now that the Presbyterian generals had been removed by the Self-Denying Ordinance, and the military importance of the Scots was negligible, the pressure was eased. But parliament had boxed itself into a corner. It could not retreat on episcopacy, so it could only go forward, with manifest reluctance, towards some form of Presbyterianism. So, when the Assembly reported in January 1645 Parliament accepted its recommendations for the introduction of Presbyterianism, but it took it until August to produce an ordinance prescribing the form this was to take, with careful provision for a majority of laymen at all levels, with the National Assembly firmly yoked to parliament.[15] Even so, no means were provided to enforce it, though another ordinance a week later did prescribe the Directory of Worship and outlaw the Book of Common Prayer.[16] As for the clergy, since 1642 the Committee on Plundered Ministers had been removing 'delinquent' clergy, though the evidence suggests that only a minority were accused of Laudianism; most of them were guilty of the kind of eccentricity and scandalous conduct which High Commission had always been anxious to suppress. On the other hand many clergy promptly abandoned Laudian innovations and successfully conformed. Many of the ecclesiastical 'revolutions' at the centre simply passed the parishes by.[17]

Of course, the efforts of parliament and the Assembly were also being sabotaged by the Independents, led by Sir Henry Vane the Younger, allied with the rising star of the army, Oliver Cromwell. But at the same time both were threatened by the emergence of a new kind of 'independency' from below.

The 'classical' Independents can be described as 'decentralised' Calvinists. They rejected the authority of bishop and presbytery alike, yet they accepted the need for a national Church which would broadly define doctrine and belief and help the secular magistrate curb heresy, blasphemy and immorality. Moreover, they accepted the fact that each 'gathered' congregation must include both the elect and the reprobate and serve the needs of both.

However, the relaxation of discipline and the profound social disturbances caused by the Civil War had brought to the surface a lower-class Independency which was in the tradition of sixteenth-century Brownism, and for the sake of clarity is best

---

[14] Ibid., I, 20, 420.

[15] 'An ordinance regulating the election of elders', 19 August 1645, ibid., I, 749–54.

[16] Ibid., I, 755 (26 August 1645). However, no evidence has come to light of any prosecutions under this ordinance (Morrill, Reactions, p. 93).

[17] I. M. Green, 'The Persecution of "Scandalous" and "Malignant" Parish Clergy during the English Civil War', EHR, XCIV (1979), 507–31.

described as 'sectarianism'.[18] The distinguishing mark of these sects was that they consisted (theoretically) only of the elect; they also denied the special validity of orders and permitted, even encouraged, lay preaching. Many sects were convinced that they were not only *of* the elect, they *were* the elect, therefore co-operation with other sects was forbidden; most of them had strong chiliastic tendencies, though few of them were so precise as the Fifth Monarchists, who looked to the Second Coming in 1656.

The mutual intolerance of the sects, and their sublime indifference to political forms – even Cromwell believed that the most perfect secular constitution was 'dross and dung in comparison of Christ' – blunted their impact at national level, and their overall numbers have certainly been exaggerated.[19] But their presence in London was spectacularly evident, and they constituted an apparent threat to the social system, which was accentuated by the emergence of the Levellers. Thus a majority of MPs found themselves committed to Presbyterianism for political and social rather than religious reasons, though they were still hamstrung by their rampant suspicion of clerical power. This is why some 'Presbyterians' can be identified as Independent in belief, and vice versa. Thus much of the year 1646 was taken up to wrangles over the use of the right to withhold the sacrament from members of the congregation: should it be vested in the minister or in the elders, and should there be a right of appeal against their decision, or not – and if so, to whom?

Meanwhile the disorderly legislative procedure of this parliament had left the bishops unscathed in law, though it was generally assumed that they had in fact been abolished; certainly no move was made to replace Laud, who was attainted and executed in 1645.[20] In fact it was not until October 1646 that the offices of archbishop and bishop were finally abolished by ordinance, thus implementing a decision made in September 1642, and even then the first sentence of the ordinance, 'for the abolishing of archbishops and bishops, and providing for the payment of the just and necessary debts of the kingdom', betray the fact that the financial embarrassments of the government were the determining factor.[21]

The negotiations with Charles I in 1646 and 1647, aimed to secure his endorsement of Presbyterianism, had the paradoxical effect of delaying its introduction still further – although the army had now agreed to hold off; and it was not until 29 January 1648, on the eve of the second Civil War, that parliament passed an ordinance implementing the legislation of 1645.[22] But it was then far too late. Hatred of the Scots, and with them their religion, soon reached new heights, and a violent hostility to all clergymen, whether Anglican or Presbyterian, was evident amongst the lower classes, particularly in the New Model Army.[23] The religious settlement

---

[18] See the valuable synthesis by Michael Watts, *The Dissenters*, ch. 2. Murray Tolmie, *The Triumph of the Saints 1616–1649* (Cambridge 1977), traces the underground sectarian movement in London back as far 1612.

[19] The latest historian to tackle the problem tells us that 'it seems probable that at no point in the critical period 1643–54 did more than five per cent attend religious assemblies other than those associated with their parish churches'; Morrill, *Reactions*, p. 90.

[20] Parliament always acted as though it had in fact abolished episcopacy and in an ordinance of 14 March 1646 even congratulated itself on having done so. But see Shaw, I, 119ff.

[21] Firth and Rait, I, 879–83 (9 October 1646). Deans and chapters were not abolished until 1649 (*ibid.*, II, 81).

[22] *Ibid.*, I, 1062–3. See Shaw, *English Church during the Civil Wars*, II, 19ff.

[23] James F. Maclear, 'Popular Anti-Clericalism in the Puritan Revolution', *Jnl of the History of Ideas* XVII (1956), 443–70.

was now at the mercy of the opponents of organised religion, and the attempt to remould the Church of England in a Puritan form had been a miserable failure.

71. An Explanation of the Protestation, 12 May 1641[24]

An Explanation, brought from the Committee for the Bill for the Protestation, was this day reported; and upon the Question, ordered, *in haec verba*:

Resolved, upon the Question, That whereas some doubts have been raised by several persons, out of this House, concerning the meaning of these words contained in the Protestation lately made by the Members of this House, viz. 'the true reformed Protestant religion, expressed in the doctrine of the Church of England, against all popery and popish innovations within this realm, contrary to the same doctrine'. This House doth declare, that by these words was and is meant only, the public doctrine professed in the said Church, so far as it is opposite to popery, and popish innovations; and that the said words are not to be extended to the maintaining of any form of worship, discipline, or government; nor of any rites or ceremonies of the said Church of England.

CJ, II, 144-5

72. The Lords on ecclesiastical innovations

[16 January 1641]

[The king brought to the notice of the House that the previous Sunday the constables and churchwardens of St Saviour's, Southwark, had surprised a large number of sectarians worshipping in a private house.]

1. They [the ringleaders] being brought before Sir John Lenthall [JP], he demanded why they would not go and resort to their parish church, according to the Law of 35 Eliz. They answered that the Law of 35 Eliz. was not a true law, but that it was made by the bishops, and they would not obey it.

2. That they would not go to their parish churches, that those churches were not true churches, and that there was no true church but where the faithful met.

3. That the king could not make a perfect law, for that he was not a perfect man.

4. That they ought not to obey him but in civil things . . .

[Having dealt with the offenders,] upon this occasion the House thought fit, and ordered: That this order following shall be read publicly in all the parish churches of London and Westminster, the borough of Southwark, and all the liberties and suburbs of them;

[24] The Protestation is no. **60**, p. 200 above.

That the Divine Service be performed as it is appointed by the acts of parliament of this realm; and that all such as shall disturb that wholesome order shall be severely punished according to law; and that the parsons, vicars and curates in [the] several parishes shall forbear to introduce any rites or ceremonies that may give offence, otherwise than those which are established by the laws of the land.

[9 September 1641]

It being in debate concerning the printing and publishing of an order touching Divine Service; it was resolved upon the question, by the major part, that this House will vote the printing and publishing of the order made the 16th of January 1640[–1] concerning Divine Service, before this House desires a conference with the House of Commons concerning that particular . . .[25] Resolved upon the question, by the major part, that the order made the 16th of January 1640[–1] . . . shall be printed and published.

Hereupon it is ordered, to have a conference with the House of Commons, to desire them to join herein with this House.   LJ, IV, 133–4, 395

73. Resolutions of the Commons on ecclesiastical innovations, 1 September 1641

Whereas divers innovations in or about the worship of God have been lately practised in this kingdom, by enjoining some things and prohibiting others, without warrant of law, to the great grievance and discontent of his Majesty's subjects; for the suppression of such innovations, and for preservation of the public peace, it is this day ordered by the Comons in parliament assembled:

That the churchwardens of every parish church and chapel respectively do forthwith remove the communion table from the east end of the church, chapel or chancel into some other convenient place, and that they take away the rails, and level the chancels as heretofore they were before the late innovations.

That all crucifixes, scandalous pictures of any one of more persons of the Trinity, and all images of the Virgin Mary, shall be taken away and abolished, and that all tapers, candlesticks and basins be removed from the communion table.

That all corporal bowing at the name Jesus, or towards the east end of the church, chapel or chancel, or towards the communion table, be henceforth forborne.

★　★　★

[25] Six peers – Warwick, Newport, Clare, Bedford, Kimbolton and Wharton – entered a protest; not against the order, but against reissuing it without consulting the Commons.

That the Lord's Day shall be duly observed and sanctified; all dancing, or other sports, either before or after divine service, be forborne and restrained, and that the preaching of God's word be permitted in the afternoon in the several churches and chapels of this kingdom, and that ministers and preachers be encouraged thereunto.

★   ★   ★

CJ, II, 279

74. The Bishops' Exclusion Act

17 Car. I, c. 27: *An Act for disenabling all persons in Holy Orders to exercise any temporal jurisdiction or authority*

Whereas bishops and other persons in holy orders ought not to be entangled with secular jurisdiction, the office of the ministry being of such great importance that it will take up the whole man, and for that it is found by long experience that their intermeddling with secular jurisdictions hath occasioned great mischiefs and scandal both to Church and state, his Majesty, out of his religious care of the Church, and [the] souls of his people, is graciously pleased that it be enacted, that no archbishop or bishop or other person that now is or hereafter shall be in holy orders shall at any time after the 15th day of February in the year of Our Lord one thousand six hundred [and] forty-one [1642] have any seat or place, suffrage or voice, or use or execute any power or authority in the parliaments of this realm, nor shall be of the Privy Council of his Majesty, his heirs or successors, or justice of the peace of *oyer and terminer* or gaol delivery, or execute any temporal authority by virtue of any commission, but shall be wholly disabled and be incapable to have, receive, use or execute any of the said offices, places, powers, authorities and things aforesaid.

★   ★   ★

SR, V, 138

75. The Westminster Assembly

An ordinance for the calling of an assembly of learned and Godly divines, to be consulted with by the Parliament, for the settling of the government of the Church
[12 June 1643]

Whereas amongst the infinite blessings of Almighty God upon this nation none is or can be more dear unto us than the purity of our religion; and for that as yet many things remain in the liturgy, discipline and government of the Church which do necessarily require a further and more perfect reformation than as yet hath been attained; and whereas it hath been declared and resolved by the

Lords and Commons assembled in parliament that the present Church government by archbishops, bishops, their chancellors, commissaries, deans, deans and chapters, archdeacons, and other ecclesiastical officers depending upon the hierarchy is evil, and justly offensive and burdensome to the kingdom, a great impediment to reformation and growth of religion, and very prejudicial to the state and government of this kingdom, and that therefore they are resolved that the same shall be taken away, and that such a government shall be settled in the Church as may be most agreeable to God's Holy Word, and most apt to procure and preserve the peace of the Church at home, and nearer agreement with the Church of Scotland, and other reformed churches abroad; and for the better effecting hereof, and for the vindicating and clearing of the doctrine of the Church of England from all false calumnies and aspersions, it is thought fit and necessary to call an assembly of learned, godly and judicious divines, to consult and advise of such matters and things, touching the premises, as shall be proposed unto them by both or either of the Houses of Parliament, and to give their advice and counsel therein to both or either of the said Houses when and as often as they shall be thereunto required.

Be it therefore ordained by the Lords and Commons in this present parliament assembled, that all and every the persons hereafter in this present ordinance named, that is to say: Algernon, Earl of Northumberland, William, Earl of Bedford, Philip, Earl of Pembroke and Montgomery, William, Earl of Salisbury, Henry, Earl of Holland, Edward, Earl of Manchester, William, Lord Viscount Saye and Sele, Edward, Lord Viscount Conway, Philip, Lord Wharton, Edward, Lord Howard of Escrick; John Seldon, esquire, Francis Rouse, esquire, Edmund Prideaux, esquire, Sir Henry Vane, knight, senior, John Glyn, esquire, Recorder of London, John White, esquire, Bulstrode Whitelocke, esquire, Hymphrey Salloway, esquire, Mr Serjeant Wilde, Oliver St John, esquire, his Majesty's solicitor, Sir Benjamin Rudyard, knight, John Pym, esquire, Sir John Clotworthy, knight, John Maynard, esquire, Sir Henry Vane, knight, junior, William Pierrepoint, esquire, William Wheller, esquire, Sir Thomas Barrington, knight, Mr Young, esquire, Sir John Evelyn, knight . . . [and 121 named clergymen] and such other person and persons as shall be nominated and appointed by both Houses of Parliament, or so many of them as shall not be letted by sickness or other necessary impediment shall meet and assemble, and are hereby required and enjoined upon summons signed by the Clerks of both Houses of Parliament, left at their several respective dwellings, to meet and assemble themselves at Westminster, in the chapel called King Henry the Seventh's Chapel, on the first day of July in the year of Our Lord one thousand six hundred and forty three. And after the first meeting, being at least of the number of forty, shall from time to time sit, and be removed from place to place, and also that the said assembly shall be dissolved in such manner as by both Houses of Parliament shall be directed.

And the said persons, or so many of them as shall be so assembled or sit, shall have power and authority, and are hereby likewise enjoined from time to time during this present parliament, or until further order be taken by both the said Houses, to confer and treat amongst themselves of such matters and things touching and concerning the liturgy, discipline and government of the Church of England, or the vindicating and clearing of the doctrine of the same from all false aspersions and misconstructions as shall be proposed unto them by both or either of the said Houses of Parliament, and no other, and to deliver their opinions and advices of or touching the matters aforesaid, as shall be most agreeable to the Word of God, to both or either of the said Houses from time to time, in such manner and sort as by both or either of the said Houses of Parliament shall be required; and the same not to divulge by printing, writing or otherwise without the consent of both or either House of Parliament.

And be it further ordained by the authority aforesaid, that William Twist, Doctor in Divinity, shall sit in the Chair as prolocutor of the said assembly; and if he happen to die, or be letted by sickness or other necessary impediment, then such other person to be appointed in his place as shall be agreed on by both the said Houses of Parliament. And in case any difference of opinion shall happen amongst the said persons so assembled, touching any of the matters that shall be proposed to them as aforesaid, that then they shall represent the same, together with the reasons thereof, to both or either the said Houses respectively, to the end such further direction may be given as shall be requisite in that behalf.

★   ★   ★

Provided always, that this ordinance, or anything therein contained, shall not give unto the persons aforesaid, or any of them, nor shall they in this assembly assume to exercise, any jurisdiction, power or authority ecclesiastical whatsoever, or any other power than is herein particularly expressed.

Firth and Rait, i, 180-4

76. 'A solemn league and covenant for reformation and defence of religion, the honour and happiness of the King, and the peace and safety of the three kingdoms of England, Scotland and Ireland'[26]

We noblemen, barons, knights, gentlemen, citizens, burgesses, ministers of the Gospel, and commons of all sorts in the kingdoms of England, Scotland and Ireland, by the providence of God living under one king, and being of one

[26] Taken by the Convention of Estates, 17 August 1643, and by the Westminster Assembly and the House of Commons, 25 September.

reformed religion; having before our eyes the glory of God and the advancement of the kingdom of Our Lord and Saviour Jesus Christ, the honour and happiness of the king's Majesty and his posterity, and the true public liberty, safety and peace of the kingdom, wherein everyone's private condition is included; and calling to mind the treacherous and bloody plots, conspiracies, attempts and practices of the enemies of God against the true religion and professors thereof in all places, especially in these three kingdoms, ever since the reformation of religion; and how much their rage, power and presumption are of late at this time increased and exercised, whereof the deplorable estate of the Church and kingdom of Ireland, the distressed esate of the Church and kingdom of England, and the dangerous estate of the Church and kingdom of Scotland, are present and public testimonies: we have now at last, after other means of supplication, remonstrance, protestation and sufferings, for the preservation of ourselves and our religion from utter ruin and destruction, according to the commendable practice of these kingdoms in former times, and the example of God's people in other nations, after a mature deliberation, resolved and determined to enter into a mutual and solemn league and covenant, wherein we all subscribe, and each one of us for himself, with our hands lifted up to the most high God, do swear:

I. That we shall sincerely, really and constantly, through the grace of God, endeavour in our several places and callings, the preservation of the reformed religion in the Church of Scotland, in doctrine, worship, discipline and government, against our common enemies; the reformation of religion in the kingdoms of England and Ireland in doctrine, worship, discipline and government, according to the Word of God and the example of the best reformed churches; and we shall endeavour to bring the churches of God in the three kingdoms to the nearest conjunction and uniformity in religion, confessing of faith, form of church government, directory for worship, and catechising, that we and our posterity after us may, as brethren, live in faith and love, and the Lord may delight to dwell in the midst of us.

II. That we shall in like manner, without respect of persons, endeavour the extirpation of popery, prelacy (that is, Church government by archbishops, bishops, their chancellors and commissaries, deans, deans and chapters, archdeacons, and all other ecclesiastical officers depending on that hierarchy), superstition, heresy, schism, profaneness, and whatsoever shall be found to be contrary to sound doctrine and the power of godliness, lest we partake in other men's sins, and thereby be in danger to receive of their plagues; and that the Lord may be one and his name one in the three kingdoms.

III. We shall with the same sincerity, reality and constancy in our several vocations endeavour with our estates and lives mutually to preserve the rights and privileges of the parliaments, and the liberties of the kingdoms, and to preserve and defend the king's Majesty's person and authority, in the preservation and defence of the true religion and liberties of the kingdoms, that the world may bear witness with our consciences of our loyalty, and that we have no thoughts or intentions to diminish his Majesty's just power and greatness.

IV. We shall also with all faithfulness endeavour the discovery of all such as have been or shall be incendiaries, malignants, or evil instruments, by hindering the reformation of religion, dividing the king from his people, or one of the kingdoms from another, or making any faction or parties amongst the people, contrary to the league and covenant, that they may be brought to public trial and receive condign punishment, as the degree of their offences shall require or deserve, or the supreme judicatories of both kingdoms respectively, or others having power from them for that effect, shall judge convenient.

V. And whereas the happiness of a blessed peace between these kingdoms, denied in former times to our progenitors, is by the good providence of God granted to us, and hath been lately concluded and settled by both parliaments; we shall each one of us, according to our places and interest, endeavour that they may remain conjoined in a firm peace and union to all posterity, and that justice may be done upon the wilful opposers thereof, in manner expressed in the precedent articles.

VI. We shall also, according to our places and callings, in this common cause of religion, liberty and peace of the kingdoms, assist and defend all those that enter into this league and covenant in the maintaining and pursuing thereof, and shall not suffer ourselves, directly or indirectly, by whatsoever combination, persuasion or terror, to be divided and withdrawn from this blessed union and conjunction, whether to make defection to the contrary part, or give ourselves to a detestable indifferency or neutrality in this cause, which so much concerneth the glory of God, the good of the kingdoms and the honour of the king; but shall all the days of our lives zealously and constantly continue therein, against all opposition, and promote the same according to our power, against all lets and impediments whatsoever; and what we are not able ourselves to suppress or overcome we shall reveal and make known, that it may be timely prevented or removed; all which we shall do as in the sight of God.

And because these kingdoms are guilty of many sins and provocations against God and his son Jesus Christ, as is too manifest by our present distress and dangers, the fruits thereof, we profess and declare before God and the world our unfeigned desire to be humbled for our own sins and for the sins of these kingdoms, especially that we have not as we ought valued the inestimable benefit of the Gospel, that we have not laboured for the purity and power thereof, and that we have not endeavoured to receive Christ in our hearts, nor to walk worthy of Him in our lives, which are the causes of other sins and transgressions so much abounding amongst us; and our true and unfeigned purpose, desire and endeavour, for ourselves and all others under our power and charge, both in public and in private, in all duties we owe to God and man, to amend our lives, and each one to go before another in the example of a real reformation, that the Lord may turn away his wrath and heavy indignation, and establish these Churches and kingdoms in truth and peace. And this covenant we make in the presence of Almighty God, the searcher of all hearts, with a true intention to perform the same, as we shall answer at that great day when the secrets of all hearts shall be disclosed, most humbly beseeching the Lord to strengthen us by his Holy Spirit for this end, and to bless our desires and proceedings with such success as may be a deliverance and safety to his people, and encouragement to the Christian Churches groaning under or in danger of the yoke of anti-Christian tyranny, to join in the same or like association and covenant, to the glory of God, the enlargement of the kingdom of Jesus Christ, and the peace and tranquillity of Christian kingdoms and commonwealths.   Rushworth, VI, 478–9

77. An ordinance for the better observation of the monthly fast; and more especially the next Wednesday, commonly called the Feast of the Nativity of Christ, throughout the kingdom of England and dominion of Wales, 19 December 1644

Whereas some doubts have been raised whether the next fast shall be celebrated, because it falleth on the day which heretofore was usually called the Feast of the Nativity of Our Saviour, the Lords and Commons in Parliament assembled do order and ordain that public notice be given that the fast appointed to be kept on the last Wednesday in every month ought to be observed until it be otherwise ordered by both Houses of Parliament; and that this day in particular is to be kept with the more solemn humiliation, because it may call to remembrance our sins, and the sins of our forefathers, who have turned this feast, pretending the memory of Christ, into an extreme forgetfulness of him, by giving liberty to carnal and sensual delights, being contrary to the life which Christ himself led here upon earth, and to the spiritual life of Christ in our souls, for the sanctifying and saving whereof Christ was pleased both to take a human life, and to lay it down again.

Firth and Rait, I, 580

CHAPTER 7

GOVERNMENT AND ARMY 1642–49

During the first Civil War no theoretical advance was made on the messages and declarations exchanged in the summer of 1642. Charles, of course, regarded the Long Parliament as being in revolt, but he dare not take the obvious step of dissolving it by proclamation, because that would infringe the act of May 1641 and thereby jeopardise the whole programme of reform legislation upon which his moderate support depended. Parliament, on the other hand, continued to insist that it was exercising the office of the king because the person of its holder had been led astray by evil counsels. Thus the courts of law, despite the king's attempts at interference, continued to function at Westminster, and though the assizes were interrupted in 1642, and abandoned 1643–5, they promptly resumed in 1646, except in the West.[1] The Solemn League and Covenant of 1643 (p. 239 above) had as one of its principal aims an accommodation with the king, and it was not until June 1644 that the royalist Members who had deserted were expelled from the Commons and by-elections ordered.[2] Even then, parliament's avowed policy almost to the bitter end was to reach agreement with Charles and re-establish government by king, Lords and Commons.

Such innovations as it attempted were in the field of administration and taxation. In March 1642 an act was passed to raise £400,000, half by June, the other half by December, to pay the troops now being raised.[3] Somewhat ironically it was modelled on ship-money, in that a lump sum was first named, then divided amongst the counties, leaving each to levy the tax as best it could. For this purpose a committee of 12 to 15 gentry was appointed in each county. Subsequent ordinances for the assessment and sequestration of royalists' estates named other committees, with roughly the same personnel, and these County Committees in the areas under parliament's control soon came to administer every aspect of local government: the levy of troops, and sometimes even their deployment, the collection of taxes, and the implementation of the various ordinances on religion. The minutes of the Committee for Staffordshire give an idea of the scope of their work (81).[4] Despite its success in passing the Militia Ordinance, Parliament abandoned the use of the lord lieutenancy at an early stage. Instead in December 1642 it began grouping counties well affected to its

[1] Cockburn, *Assizes*, p. 272; Donald Pennington, 'The War and the People', in Morrill, *Reactions*, pp. 132–3.

[2] R. N. Kershaw, 'The Recruiting of the Long Parliament 1645–47', *History*, VIII (1924), 169–79.

[3] 16 Car. I, c. 32, *SR*, V, 145; one of the last bills to which Charles gave his assent, these troops being ostensibly bound for Ireland.

[4] See also Alan Everitt, *The County Committee of Kent* (Leicester 1957), and *Suffolk and the Great Rebellion* (Suffolk Records Society 1960); Holmes, *Eastern Association*, ch. 6, and *Lincolnshire*, ch. 11; Fletcher, *Sussex*, ch. 15; Morrill, *Cheshire*, ch. 3, and *Provinces*, chs. 2–3; Underdown, *Somerset*, *passim*; and Donald Pennington, 'The Accounts of the Kingdom 1642–49', in *Essays in the Economic and Social History of Tudor and Stuart England*, ed. F. J. Fisher (Cambridge 1961), pp. 182–203.

cause into Associations, though the only one which was of more than transitory importance was the famous Eastern Association, formed on 20 December 1642 from the counties of Norfolk, Suffolk, Essex, Cambridge and Hertford, with Huntingdon added soon after.

Meanwhile in June 1642 parliament decided to raise a special force of 10,000 men in the London area, and soon found itself short of money. In November it passed an ordinance to raise money, plate, horses and arms by voluntary contribution, as the royalists were doing,[5] but such old-fashioned remedies were no longer adequate, and an ordinance of 24 February 1643 established the weekly Assessment (**78**), which later became monthly and persisted with little change right up to the Restoration.[6] Like the Act of March 1642, the new ordinance simply ordered each county to pay a weekly sum, and the county committee then appointed assessors to levy a rate. Attempts were made to include personal property and income from fees and offices, but like all seventeenth-century direct taxes it soon became in effect a land tax.[7]

The novelty of the assessment was its efficiency, which was achieved by the devolution of responsibility onto the local authorities, who soon found themselves saddled with even more onerous duties by the Sequestration Ordinance of 27 March 1643 (**79**), which ordered the estates of all those who had given money to the king or appeared in arms with him to be confiscated and placed in the charge of the county committees, who managed them and remitted the profits to the parliamentary treasurers at the Guildhall. A second ordinance, in August, bore down on the Catholics, who were naturally but on the whole unjustly suspected of aggressive and whole-hearted royalism.[8] It replaced James I's oath of allegiance by a confessional test, which was a precedent for the more famous and lasting test introduced in 1673 (p. 385 below).[9]

But all this was not enough to meet the rising cost of war, and in March 1643 Pym proposed an excise on alcoholic beverages manufactured in England. A similar proposal had been discussed in 1628, and the principle of the excise was familiar enough, but the more familiar the notion the less it was liked, and it was already firmly linked in the public mind with arbitrary government. But parliament accepted it in 1643 for the same reason as its successors reluctantly continued it after 1660; because the only alternative was another direct tax on property. An ordinance of 22 July 1643

---

[5] Firth and Rait, I, 38 (26 November 1642).   [6] It became monthly in 1645; *ibid.*, I, 630.

[7] From 1649 to 1653 the Commonwealth tried to levy a pound rate on every £20 personalty, but it was not a success. All the same, the very idea of a land tax was so abhorrent that the pretence that the Assessment was a general tax had to be maintained. In 1657 Sir William Strickland told parliament, 'I am sorry to hear any land tax mentioned here. The people would never have chosen us if they had thought we would have moved that. Nothing is so like to blast your settlement as a land tax. Pardon me if I speak confusedly; any man will justify my distraction in this' (Burton, *Diary*, II, 24). For the expression of similar views in 1670, see Grey, *Debates*, I, 314ff.

[8] Carol Z. Wiener, 'The Beleaguered Isle: A Study of Elizabethan and early Jacobean Anti-Catholicism', *Past and Present*, no. 52 (1971), 27–62; Robin Clifton, 'Popular Fear of Catholics during the English Revolution', *ibid.*, no. 53 (1971), 23–55; Keith Lindley, 'The Part Played by the Catholics', in Brian Manning, ed., *Politics, Religion and the English Civil War* (1973), pp. 127–78; and Aveling, *The Handle and the Axe*, pp. 164–70. On the other hand, there is no doubt that that the king's willingness to recruit Catholics damaged his cause; Malcolm, *Caesar's Due*, pp. 51–2, 94–6. (As a result of a new drive against priests 21 were executed between 1640 and 1646, as against two in the preceding 15 years.)

[9] Firth and Rait, I, 254–6.

(80) established a 'new impost' (the word 'excise' being carefully avoided in the title) on tobacco, wine, cider and beer, on imported silks, furs, hats, leather, lace and linen, and on imported 'grocery' – raisins, figs, currants, pepper and sugar. To supervise its collection eight commissioners were established in London, with subordinate officers in the provinces, who were given those broad powers of entry to premises and the authority to examine suspects under oath which were always to be the main grievances against the excise. They even had the power to summon troops to their aid. On 8 September the ordinance was re-enacted, with the addition of soap, paper, cloth and imported glassware to the schedule, and from then on new commodities were added almost every year: in January 1644, meat and salt;[10] in July 1644, industrial chemicals like alum, copperas, hops and saffron, as well as hats and English-made silks; in November 1645, lead, gold and silver thread, fish and vegetable oils and imported cloth; and so on. The new tax, and the men who levied it, were always bitterly unpopular, especially when it was continued into the peace. It was denounced by the Levellers, and by February 1647 riots against the excise were so frequent and so menacing that parliament issued a declaratory ordinance justifying its imposition, promising to abandon it as soon as the army was demobilised, and in the meanwhile establishing special machinery for the investigation of complaints.[11] Even then, in June 1647 it felt obliged to cancel the two most unpopular duties, on meat and salt. But the salt duty was re-imposed in 1649, and in March 1654 Cromwell extended the excise to cover virtually all saleable commodities.[12]

Meanwhile, the principle of sequestration was pressed to its logical conclusion. Royalist prisoners were soon given the opportunity to 'compound' for their delinquency by paying a fine proportionate to their participation in the war. In September 1644 the committee at Goldsmith's Hall (it appears to have had no formal name) was authorised by parliament to negotiate with other delinquents who now wished to withdraw.[13] The following March the committee suggested to parliament that it extend its operations to cover voluntary applications from those not actually named as delinquent. In August the minimum composition was fixed at two years' rent, and the proportion could be as much as two-thirds of the estimated value of the estate.[14] After the Civil Wars the estates of those who had gone abroad or refused to compound were confiscated outright, and most of them were eventually sold on the open market, with the lands of Crown and Church.[15]

In short, parliament's administration was amazingly efficient and comprehensive, but the manner in which it operated was all too reminiscent of the king at his very worst, as its critics never ceased pointing out.[16] Its supporters were increasingly disillusioned, too, by its failure to settle the Church and its patent lack of war aims –

[10] Here the word 'excise' appeared for the first time in the title; Firth and Rait, i, 364.

[11] Ibid., i, 916–20.

[12] Kennedy, English Taxation, pp. 52–5; M. P. Ashley, Financial and Commercial Policy under the Cromwellian Protectorate (Oxford 1934), pp. 62–71; Edward Hughes, Studies in Administration and Finance (Manchester 1934), pp. 120ff. Parliament also continued to collect tunnage and poundage; see Firth and Rait, i, 16, 627.

[13] Calendar of the Committee for Compounding, i, 10.　　[14] Ibid., i, 17, 24. Cf. p. vii.

[15] Hardacre, The Royalists during the Puritan Revolution, ch. 2, has a good summary of the situation.

[16] Robert Ashton, 'From Cavalier to Roundhead Tyranny 1642–49', in Morrill, Reactions, pp. 185–207.

apart from defeating the king. The death of Pym, Hampden and Lord Brooke, all in 1643, removed the ablest and most respected of the Commons leaders, and they were not replaced. Sir Henry Vane was the most able speaker and tactician left, but his radical views put him in a minority, and it was only natural that he and the other Independents should look for support from the army, and especially from Oliver Cromwell, who was emerging as the best general on either side. The alliance with the Scots was never popular, and the first great parliamentary victory, at Marston Moor in 1644, was not followed up. The epilogue to Marston Moor in the South exposed the incompetence and indecisiveness of the 'Presbyterian' generals, Essex, Manchester and Waller, and the following winter parliament decided to hand over the conduct of the war to those who were prepared to prosecute it to the bitter end without regard to the ultimate result. On 17 February 1645 an ordinance was passed creating a new army of mercenaries, 6,600 horse, 14,400 foot and 1,000 dragoons, to replace the 'volunteer' armies of the county Associations. Raised 'for the defence of the king and parliament, the true Protestant religion, and the laws and liberties of the kingdom', it was to remain in commission for the duration of hostilities, and new taxation was specifically appropriated to its pay.[17] It was placed under the command of the youthful Yorkshire general Sir Thomas Fairfax, with Oliver Cromwell as his Lieutenant-General of Horse. The Self-Denying Ordinance passed in April obliged all other Members of both Houses to resign all their offices, military and civil (*GCD*, pp. 287–8).

The resounding victories of the New Model at Naseby and Langport that summer, and the collapse of the king's cause in 1646, ending with his surrender to the Scots, enhanced its prestige and that of its generals to a degree which any civilian government must regard as unhealthy, but the maladroitness with which the Long Parliament approached the transition from war to peace only perpetuated its existence and positively invited its interference in national politics.

The old-fashioned view that the New Model was the peculiar breeding-ground of left-wing democracy and extreme religious radicalism has been subject to considerable modification in recent years,[18] but the myth that this was a God-besotted army of Saints, in which each soldier had enlisted to fight for England's freedom and her people's natural rights, and to fulfil God's Intentions for His Nation, was one which was propagated in many of the army's own pronouncements, was encouraged for their own ends by the Levellers, and was undoubtedly shared by at least some of the troops. But in fact many of these troops were pressed men, many more had simply enlisted for pay in a period of high unemployment; they would follow whomever could satisfy their demands for areas of pay and indemnity from civil action.[19] Nevertheless, as John Pocock remarks, 'Enrolment in the Army had intensified their political awareness; the exercise of arms now gave them the means of political

---

[17] Firth and Rait, I, 614.

[18] Leo F. Solt, *Saints in Arms* (Stanford 1959); also 'Puritanism and Democracy in the New Model Army', *Archiv für Reformationsgeschichte*, L (1959), 234; Kishlansky, *Rise of the New Model Army*.

[19] It is worth noting that even S. R. Gardiner did not regard this as an army of fanatics or reformers; he remarks that arrears and indemnity 'were all that the greater number of the soldiers really cared for', and that 'the religious enthusiasts' were in a minority (*Civil War*, III, 228).

action.'[20] Moreover, the army was a privileged enclave in that it enjoyed complete freedom of preaching and theological speculation, immune from interference by magistrates, county committees, presbyterian clerics, even parliament; and the continuance of this *de facto* toleration was always high on its list of priorities, for officers as well as men.

Meanwhile the growing strength of the army was matched by the growing weakness of parliament. As soon as the war ended its lack of war aims, formerly an embarrassment, became a grievance. By assessment and excise, not to mention sequestration and confiscation, it had imposed on the nation taxation of an unprecedented intensity and efficiency; it had killed thousands of men; it had ridden roughshod over legal and constitutional forms – but why it had done all this it had never clearly explained, and the Levellers were not the only ones who were disillusioned with rulers whose sole aim seemed to be the perpetuation of their own authority. Intellectual republicans like John Milton shared this disillusion.[21] The Long Parliament had long ago exceeded the mandate given it in October 1640 (and half the men elected then had fallen by the way), and it would be difficult to find any element in the nation, apart perhaps from the Presbyterian clergy, that supported it out of conviction. The Propositions for a settlement which it presented to the king at Newcastle in July 1646 (*GCD*, p. 290) were conceived in a narrow spirit of revenge and repression, padded out with so many exceptions that they would have removed from public life any and every person who had ever opposed it or even disagreed with it. They also demanded that he accept the Solemn League and Covenant, and a Presbyterian Church.

Yet it was essential that parliament reach agreement with the king. Any permanent government without him was unthinkable, and in any case the paradox of war had left the vanquished more popular than the victor, as his public reception on his return from Newcastle showed. On the other hand, if they did not insist on Presbyterianism, they would lose all credibility, yet both sides knew that it had very little public support and would attract the particular disfavour of the army. The army was also probably more disenchanted with Charles, as the author of the war, than the civilians were, and the publication of his correspondence, captured at Naseby, confirmed his duplicity. Even so, all might have been well had parliament been able or willing to pay the soldiers' arrears of wages – 18 weeks for the infantry, 43 for the cavalry – and pass an ordinance indemnifying them for crimes committed during the war. But it hesitated to pass such an Act of Oblivion, which might encourage the king to demand similar treatment for the royalists, and at this stage the Presbyterian leaders in parliament decided on a showdown with the New Model. They attempted to ship some of the regiments to Ireland to deal with the continuing rebellion there and demobilise the rest without arrears of pay, in contrast with other, less successful and celebrated units whose

---

[20] *The Political Works of James Harrington* (Cambridge 1977), Intro., p. 25. Elsewhere, however, he comments that after 1647 the army was 'perpetually and vainly in search of an executive able to maintain it', (*ibid.*, p. 131).

[21] See Milton's remarkable 'Character of the Long Parliament', too long for inclusion here (*Works*, x, 318), and his poem 'On the New Forcers of Conscience' (*ibid.*, I, 71). The most cogent Leveller attack was by William Walwyn in *The Bloody Project*, August 1648, printed by Haller and Davies, *Leveller Tracts*, pp. 135–40.

commanders could be relied on to toe the party line, especially in matters of religion.[22] This roused the New Model to a course of political action devastating in its effect, accompanied by a series of ringing pronouncements remarkable for their sophistication as well as their improvisational volubility. But the machinery by which this was effected is still in doubt.[23]

In April 1647 the regiments began spontaneously to elect representatives, a process they described themselves thus:

> The soldiers of this army (finding themselves so stopped in their due and regular way of making known their just grievances and desires to and by their officers) were enforced to an unusual but in that case necessary way of correspondence and agreement amongst themselves; to choose out of the several troops and companies several men, and those out of their whole number to choose two or more for each regiment, to act in the name and behalf of the whole soldiery . . . in the prosecution of their rights and desires.[24]

It was an astonishing development, and we can no longer assume that it was due to the sophisticated influence of the Levellers, from London; this was not effective until October. The name 'agitators' which was attached to these representatives is also deceptive; the word is synonymous with 'agents', and is better translated as 'shop stewards'. It was they plus a few radical officers, acting as a kind of soviet, who authorised the notorious Cornet Joyce to seize the king at Holdenby on 4 June and bring him to the army headquarters at Newmarket. In order to preserve discipline, Fairfax then agreed to the formation of a General Council, consisting of himself, Cromwell and Ireton, and two officers and two soldiers from each regiment, thus institutionalising the agitators. Meanwhile he approved the Solemn Engagement of 5 June, a comparatively straightforward and businesslike document announcing their refusal to disband unless their just demands, especially for indemnity, were met.[25] However, they already identified themselves with 'the free-born people of England, to whom the consequence of our case does equally extend', and promised to vindicate themselves against the accusation of favouring 'the overthrowing of magistracy, the suppressing or hindering of Presbyterian government and establishing of Independent, or upholding of a general licentiousness under pretence of liberty of conscience'. The result was the Declaration of 14 June (82), in which it claimed to speak for and to a wider audience, appealing to 'the law of nature and nations', the example of the Netherlands and Portugal, and 'the proceedings of our ancestors of famous

---

[22] This hardening of the Westminster line is clarified by Valerie Pearl, 'London's Counter-Revolution', in Aylmer, *Interregnum*, pp. 29–56, and Patricia Crawford, *Denzil Lord Holles* (1979), ch. 8.

[23] The prime authority is now Kishlansky's *Rise of the New Model Army*. For other recent work see his bibliography, particularly *sub* 'Gentles' and 'Morrill'. To this should be added Kishlansky's further papers on 'The Army and the Levellers: the Roads to Putney', *HJ*, xxii (1979), 795–824, 'Consensus Politics and the Structure of Debate at Putney,' *JBS*, xx (1981), 50–69, 'What happened at Ware?', *HJ*, xxv (1982), 827–39, and 'Ideology and Politics in the Parliamentary Armies', in Morrill, *Reactions*, pp. 163–84. I have also profited greatly from the generosity of Professor Austin Woolrych, in allowing me to use his unpublished paper 'Putney Revisited', which summarises the conclusions reached in his forthcoming book *Soldiers and Statesmen: the General Council of the Army 1647–48*.

[24] *A Solemn Engagement*, 5 June 1647, *OPH*, xv, 425–6.   [25] *Ibid.*, pp. 424–30.

memory', claiming by inference to represent the people more adequately than the present parliament. 'We are not a mere mercenary army', they said, 'hired to serve any arbitrary power of a state, but called forth and conjured by the several Declarations of Parliament to the defence of our own and people's just rights and liberties.' In this role they demanded that parliament publish its accounts, restrict the power of the county committees, pass a comprehensive Act of Oblivion, then dissolve itself, having made provision for future elections. Predictably parliament did nothing to meet these demands, and increasing pressure was brought to bear on the generals to intervene. This became imperative on 30 July, when the House of Commons was invaded by a violent mob in support of the Presbyterian leaders, and the Speaker and most of the Independent Members fled to St Albans, appealing to the army for help. On 6 August army contingents entered London, restored order and reinstated the Speaker; the Presbyterian leaders fled in their turn.

Meanwhile, on 17 July the General Council met and discussed The Heads of the Proposals, drawn up by Ireton and submitted to Charles on the 23rd. They were published on 1 August (83). They differed most noticeably from parliament's proposals in their leniency to the royalists and their demand for religious toleration. Only a handful of major delinquents was to be subject to the full rigour of the law, as a public example; the rest were to compound on easy terms and were only to be excluded from public office for five years. No provision was made for church government, but all legislation compelling attendance at church was to be repealed, and other means found to deal with the Catholics and the 'prelatists'. For the rest, the Army Council put its faith in biennial parliaments, with the king sharing executive authority with a Council of State; control of the militia and the appointment of the great officers of state were to be in parliament's hands for ten years, and after that under its close supervision. Perhaps the most interesting proposals, reflecting the influence of the lesser gentry, were those calling for the reform of the electoral system (1, 5) and for the election of sheriffs and justices of the peace by the county freeholders, albeit indirectly (1, 11). Finally, like the Declaration, The Heads had to take notice of popular grievances voiced by the Levellers in London.

The Levellers were unique in that they were the only 'party' thrown up during these troubles that did not also constitute a religious sect or impose religious qualifications on its members. However, they were committed to religious toleration, and one of the factors which provoked them to action was parliament's attempt to restrict unlicensed preaching in London. They owed much to the demagogic genius of John Lilburne, who constituted himself the spokesman of the London tradesmen and workpeople, badly hit by a slump which had deepened with the coming of peace; thus the important place allotted to social reform in the Leveller programme: the abolition of monopolies, the improvement of the poor laws, the reduction of indirect taxation, and so on (85). But Lilburne and other Leveller spokesmen, like William Walwyn and John Wildman, had already moved beyond this. Profiting from a study of Coke's *Institutes*, Lilburne had evolved a theory of natural right which asserted that from time immemorial every free man in England had enjoyed full political rights; suppressed by the Norman Conquest, these must now be revived, and the period of foreign tyranny introduced by the Conqueror and still continuing must be brought to an end. For a start he and his followers demanded a large extension of the franchise and the abolition of the monarchy and the House of Lords.[26]

Because of certain obvious identity of interest, it has been customary to ante-date and exaggerate Leveller influence on the army agitators. In fact, this did not become apparent until 9 October, when after some obscure manoeuvering which involved the election of new 'agents' from five of the regiments they produced a bellicose document entitled The Case of the Army Truly Stated, which accused the General Council of backsliding on the Solemn Engagement and the Declaration of June, presumably by entertaining The Heads of the Proposals, and calling for the implementation of the full Leveller programme of political, legal, fiscal and social reform before negotiations were opened with Charles for a binding settlement.[27] It was effectively disowned at the next meeting of the General Council on 21 October, and the new agents with it, but it was agreed that The Case and The Heads would be debated at a full meeting of the Council, with civilian Leveller representatives present, in Putney Church on 28 October. However, the day before the Levellers presented a further, much more radical document, which was tabled at the meeting: The Agreement of the People (**84**), which called for a unicameral legislature elected on a broad franchise, which was to be omnipotent except in certain reserved matters, such as religion and military conscription. King and House of Lords were abolished by default.

The resulting debates were confused and inconclusive.[28] The essential points were: was the Agreement consonant with the previous Declarations and Engagements to which the army was pledged, and should negotiations be continued with the king, something which the Agreement by its very nature appeared to prohibit? The long and rancorous debate on the franchise, which has captured the imagination of the twentieth century, took place at an unofficial committee meeting on Saturday, 30 October, and was inconclusive, though it now seems that the Levellers were not committed to universal adult male suffrage, and accepted the exclusion of wage-earners, servants and paupers; copyholders were in a twilight zone.[29] This was largely irrelevant to the main points above, which appear to have been debated in a series of General Council meetings on 2, 5, 6 and 8 November which are virtually unreported. The Council seems to have been persuaded of the need to keep channels of communication open with the king, and it was fortunate that news of his escape to Carisbrooke on 11 November arrived after it had dispersed, on the promise of a rendezvous of the army in three sections on the 15th, 17th and 18th. For this Fairfax

---

[26] G. E. Aylmer, The Levellers in the English Revolution (1975) provides an analytical bibliography as well as an excellent summary and some well-chosen documents.

[27] Printed by Haller and Davies, Leveller Tracts, pp. 65ff., Stuart Prall, The Puritan Revolution (1968), pp. 125ff.; excerpts in Woodhouse, Puritanism and Liberty, pp. 429ff.

[28] I have decided to omit the extracts from these debates printed in the first edition; they are widely available, in Woodhouse, op. cit., Aylmer, op. cit., and A. L. Morton, Freedom in Arms (1975). Moreover, the account we have, from the Clarke Papers, deals with only two out of six days' debate and it focusses on matters which, while of the greatest interest to political scientists and modern socialists, had little practical contemporary relevance.

[29] C. B. Macpherson, The Political Theory of Possessive Individualism (Oxford 1962), ch. 3; Keith Thomas, 'The Levellers and the Franchise', in Aylmer, Interregnum, pp. 57–78.

prepared a new Remonstrance and Engagement which disowned the Levellers and their allies, the new, intruded agents, and accused them of dividing the army, 'which is as bad and destructive as disbanding, even the dissolution of all that order, combination and government which is the essence of an army'. He disowned 'any such low thoughts as to court or woo the army to continue him their general', but he undertook to do his best to secure regular pay, the issue of accounts, indemnity for acts of war, provision for the disabled, subsequent freedom from conscription, and relaxation of apprenticeship regulations for ex-servicemen. 'For the kingdom', he undertook to work for the speedy dissolution of the Long Parliament, with statutory provision for the regular assembly of others, and 'the freedom and equality of elections thereto, to render the House of Commons (as near as may be) an equal representative of the people that are to elect', and to mediate with parliament for 'redress of the common grievances of the people'. In return for these vague assurances on national politics, plus his very specific assurances as their future personal welfare, he demanded that every soldier subscribe to an undertaking that they would acquiesce in the decisions of the General Council and give unquestioning obedience to him and his Council of War. (He was in effect appropriating the Levellers' device, in the Agreement of the People, of individual and corporate subscription.)[30]

This *démarche* was resoundingly successful. At the first rendezvous, at Corkbush Field, near Ware, a brief Leveller demonstration was suppressed with ease by Fairfax himself, and here and at the other two rendezvous the troops pledged their obedience as required. The army remained quiescent over the winter, despite a barrage of Leveller propaganda accusing the high command of truckling to the king, and despite the increasingly suspect conduct of Charles himself. Indeed, on 26 December at Carisbrooke Charles signed a secret Engagement with representatives of the Scots nobility, who offered him military aid. In return for the establishment of the constitution as in 1641 he bound himself to introduce Presbyterianism for a trial period of three years and suppress all sectarian deviation (*GCD*, pp. 347–52). Two days later he rejected parliament's latest proposals outright, and on 17 January 1648 parliament replied with the Vote of No Addresses (*ibid.*, pp. 353–6). When realisation dawned a few months later that he had deliberately provoked another civil war feeling ran high in the army, and communicated itself to its leaders. On 1 May 1648, at a general rendezvous held at Windsor, it was agreed 'that it was our duty, if ever the Lord brought us back again in peace, to call Charles Stuart, that man of blood, to an account for that blood he had shed, and mischief he had done to his utmost against the Lord's cause and people in these poor nations'.[31]

The utter defeat of the invading Scots at Preston in August, and the speedy repression of sporadic outbreaks in Wales and southern England, gave the army

---

[30] *A Remonstrance from his Excellency Sir Thomas Fairfax and his Council of War, concerning the late Discontent and Distraction in the Army, with his Excellency's Declaration of himself, and Expectation from the Army thereupon, for the future uniting of the Army,* 14 November 1647, printed Abbott, *Cromwell,* I, 557–60. There is no reason to attribute this, as Abbott does, to Cromwell; it was very much a personal demand for a vote of confidence by Fairfax, whose enigmatic character has caused his prestige and powers of leadership to be undervalued.

[31] *Somers Tracts,* ed. Walter Scott (1809–15), IV, 501. This account was not set down by William Allen, the then adjutant-general, until 1659, but there is no reason to doubt its essential truth.

another 'mandate', but parliament's reaction was to re-open negotiations with Charles at Newport, Isle of Wight, for a 'personal treaty' on the same lines as in 1647. This, countered by pressure from their own troops, drove the Council of Officers nearer to the Levellers, whose principles and programme were trenchantly restated by Lilburne in September, in a Humble Petition which was the opposite of humble (85). The Levellers argued that the army should appeal beyond parliament to the people, but they were frustrated by Fairfax's insistence on preserving constitutional forms, a stand to some extent supported by the more radical Ireton. (Cromwell was still in Scotland.) Eventually Ireton, with some Leveller assistance, got his way, and on 20 November a delegation of officers presented to the House of Commons his remarkable Remonstrance of the Army, which demanded that Charles and his leading supporters be brought to justice and that for the future supreme power be vested in a new parliament, elected on a broad franchise, which could elect a new king if it wished, apparently as an administrative convenience (86).[32] On general grounds it is not surprising that the Commons flinched at the idea of hearing this verbose and long-winded document read out to them – it runs to over 25,000 words – or debating it at once. It was shelved for a week, then shelved again until 1 December, when no debate apparently took place.[33] By then, of course, it was too late. Next day the Army Council took Charles into custody and sent troops back into London. Ireton pleaded with the Council now that parliament be dispersed by force, but he was overruled, and on 6 December Colonel Thomas Pride was merely ordered to exclude the 'Presbyterian' Members who had voted for the Newport treaty.

Pride's Purge seemed a dreadful blow to the independence of parliament, but the opposite was the case; by proceeding to these lengths the army betrayed its absolute need of the sanction of the House of Commons, *some* House of Commons, any House of Commons. When the Lords declined to follow, on 4 January 1649 the Rump, as it was now known, passed three resolutions; that ultimate power resided in the people, that the people had delegated this power to them, and that legislation by the Commons alone, without king or Lords, was legally valid (87). Two days later it passed an act – the term 'ordinance' was henceforth abandoned – setting up a High Court of Justice to try the king (*GCD*, pp. 357–8).

Ironically enough, parliament had now accepted the Levellers' main tenet – that all power was derived from the people – but because of the maladroitness and misplaced constitutionalism of the army officers it was now being used to prop up a mere oligarchy, a handful of discredited men (it was said) who dare not face the electors. It had been the army's aim to force a dissolution of the Long Parliament, but they had made the elementary mistake of first seeking from it authority to try the king. Once it had authorised the trial of the Lord's anointed it was itself unassailably the chief legal authority in the land. Yet the High Court of Justice was a farce, so the officers did not even have the satisfaction of giving Charles a dignified public trial. They would have done much better to try him by court-martial and shoot him.

The lost ground could never be regained. In December a joint committee drew

---

[32] For the circumstances see Underdown, *Pride's Purge*, pp. 115–23.
[33] *CJ*, VI, 81, 90; *OPH*, XVIII, 238–9.

up an amended and expanded version of the Agreement of the People, which now offered a complete working constitution, without king or lords. It was further amended by the Council of Officers and presented by them to the Commons on 20 January.[34] It was to be of use to the men who drew up the Instrument of Government four years later, but for the moment it was a dead letter. The Rump was not obliged to accept it, and had no intention of setting a term to its own power now the army had exhausted its means of coercion; and if it needed an excuse for delay it could always plead the necessity of dealing with the king first.

Charles was in a handsome position legally, too, though it was obvious that he had only a week or two to live. He had pursued a perfectly consistent policy ever since 1642, ignoring or rejecting all proposals which limited his command of the armed forces or his choice of ministers. The only treaty he had signed, the Engagement with the Scots, was the only one which did not impose such restrictions. (It did commit him to a trial period of Presbyterian church government, but he was never so committed to episcopacy as his subsequent, mainly Anglican, apologists pretended; on the scaffold he proposed the settlement of the Church by a national synod, and he clearly had reservations about the policy of William Laud.)[35] Moreover, he could plausibly argue that the army's every action since June 1647 had been illegal and unconstitutional, and therefore offered no sound basis for a permanent settlement. The Remonstrance of the Army itself warned of the strength of his position, which he reinforced at his trial and on the scaffold itself. His argument that if the army could arbitrarily put him on trial no man was safe, his insistence that for the mass of the people liberty consisted in having government, not in governing, had a potent appeal for the conservative gentry who had rebelled in 1642 and now found themselves under a military yoke. His words established a programme on which his son was to be restored in 1660 (**88**).

78. An Ordinance for the speedy raising and levying of money for the maintenance of the army raised by the Parliament, and other great affairs of the Commonwealth, by a weekly assessment upon the cities of London and Westminster, and every county and city of the kingdom of England, and dominion of Wales, 24 February 1643

The Lords and Commons now assembled in parliament, being fully satisfied and resolved in their consciences that they have lawfully taken up arms, and may and ought to continue the same for the necessary defence of themselves and the parliament from violence and destruction, and of this kingdom from foreign invasion, and for the bringing of notorious offenders to condign

[34] *GCD*, pp. 359–71, Woodhouse, *Puritanism and Liberty*, pp. 355–67. For a listing and some description of the various documents bearing this title, see J. W. Gough, 'The Agreements of the People 1647–1649', *History*, xv (1931), 334–41.

[35] He made little effort to intervene on Laud's behalf in 1644–5 (Morrill, *Reactions*, pp. 98–9), and in his last letter to the Prince of Wales he warned him 'to beware of exasperating any factions by the crossness and asperity of some men's passions, humours or private opinions employed by you, grounded only upon the differences in lesser matters, which are but the skirts and suburbs of religion'; Philip Knachel, ed., *Eikon Basilike* (Ithaca, New York 1966), p. 164.

punishment, which are the only causes for which they have raised and do continue an army and forces which cannot possibly be maintained, nor the kingdom subsist, without the speedy raising of large and considerable sums of money proportionable to the great expenses which now this kingdom is at for the supporting of the said army, and for the saving of the whole kingdom, our religion, laws and liberties from utter ruin and destruction; which, that it may be done with as much ease and indifferency to the good subject as the exigency of the time will permit, the said Lords and Commons do ordain, and be it ordained by the said Lords and Commons in the present parliament assembled, that for the intents and purposes aforesaid the several and weekly sums of money hereafter in this ordinance mentioned shall be charged, rated, taxed and levied upon all and every the several counties, cities, towns, liberties, places and persons hereafter mentioned, according to the proportions, rates and distributions in this present ordinance expressed, the same to be paid in weekly to the several collectors appointed by this ordinance for the receiving hereof; that is to say, upon the city of London the weekly sum of ten thousand pounds . . .

[Westminster, £1,250; Anglesey, £25; Bedford, £250; Berkshire, £550; Brecon, £50; Bristol, £55. 15s.; Buckingham, £420; Caernarvon, £35; Cambridge, £375; Carmarthen, £50; Cardigan, £62. 10s.; Cheshire, £175; Chester, £62; Cornwall, £625; Coventry, £37. 10s.; Cumberland, £37. 10s.; Denbigh, £25; Derby, £175; Devon, £1,800; Dorset, £437. 10s.; Durham, £62. 10s.; Essex, £1,125; Exeter, £50. 10s.; Flint, £16. 10s.; Glamorgan, £67. 10s.; Gloucestershire, £750; Gloucester, £62. 10s.; Hampshire, £750; Haverfordwest, £5; Hereford, £437. 10s.; Hertford, £450; Hull, £25; Huntingdon, £220; Isle of Ely, £147. 10s.; Kent, £1,250; Lancashire, £500; Leicester, £187. 10s.; Lichfield, £5; Lincoln, £812. 10s.; Merioneth, £12. 10s.; Middlesex, £750; Monmouth, £62. 10s.; Montgomery, £62. 10s.; Newcastle, £25; Norfolk, £1,250; Northampton, £425; Northumberland, £50; Nottingham, 187. 10s.; Oxford, £650; Poole, £5; Radnor, £37. 10s.; Rutland, £62. 10s.; Shropshire, £375; Somerset, £1,050; Southwark, £300; Stafford, £212. 10s.; Suffolk, £1,250; Surrey, £400; Sussex, £625; Warwick, £562. 10s.; Westmorland, £27. 5s.; Wiltshire, £725; Worcester (city), £16. 13s.; Worcester, £550; York, £62. 10s.; Yorkshire, £1,062. 10s.]

And be it further ordained, that as well every person of the estate of baron or baroness, and every estate above, and all and every other person and persons born within this realm of England, Wales or other the king's dominions, as well ecclesiastical as temporal, and every fraternity, guild, corporation, mystery, brotherhood and commonalty corporate or not corporate, as well ecclesiastical as temporal, within the realm of England, Wales or other the king's dominions, for the value of every pound which every such person, fraternity, guild . . . [etc.] hath of his or their own, or that any other hath to his or their use or uses, as well in coin, in plate, stock of merchandise, any manner of corn or grain, household stuff, and of all other goods, moveables, as well within this realm as without, and of all such sum and sums of money as to him or them is, are or shall be owing, whereof he or they trust in his or their conscience to be paid, . . . shall pay towards the said weekly sum and sums of money so assessed as aforesaid. And every alien and stranger born out of the king's obedience, as well denizens as others, inhabiting within the realm, and also every popish recusant convict or not convict, shall pay towards the sums aforesaid a proportion double to those of the like estates being no aliens or recusants.

And that every person born within the king's obedience, as well ecclesiastical as temporal, and every corporation, fraternity . . . [etc.], for every estate that every such person or persons, and every corporation, fraternity . . . [etc.] or any other to his or their use in trust or otherwise, hath in fee-simple, fee-tail, for term of life, term of years, by execution, wardship, or by copy of court-roll, of and in any honours, castles, manors, lands, tenements, rents, services, tithes, oblations, obventions, annuities, offices of profit, fees, corrodies, or other yearly profits or hereditaments, as well within ancient demesne and other places privileged as elsewhere, shall pay to and towards the said weekly sums his and their proportionable part and proportion of such sum or sums of money as are imposed, charged and set upon each several county, according as the same shall be divided, distributed, taxed or set upon each several town, hamlet, parish or place where such person or persons, is or shall be chargeable by this ordinance . . .

And the said several sums so charged, set upon the said several counties, cities, towns, liberties, places and persons aforesaid, shall by authority of this ordinance be taxed, cessed and rated according to this ordinance, in every shire, riding, lathe, wapentake, rape, city, borough, town, and every other place within this realm of England and dominion of Wales, before the twenty-sixth day of February in the year of Our Lord 1642[–3]. And the first payment of the said weekly sums so assessed by this ordinance shall be made at or before the first day of March 1642[–3], and the said weekly payments to continue weekly for three months next ensuing from the said first day of March, unless the king's army shall be disbanded in the meantime. And for the better expediting of the said service, be it further ordained by the said Lords and Commons, that the persons hereafter named shall be committees for the several and respective counties and places hereafter mentioned: That is to say . . . [The names of the members of the committee in each county and county borough follow.]

Which said several committees[36] of the said several and respective counties and places, or the greatest part of them, shall with all convenient speed after

---

[36] That is, 'committee men'.

notice of this ordinance given to them, or any two of them, meet together within the several counties and places respectively, where they are committees, in some convenient place within the same counties or places, and may there agree to sever and divide themselves for the execution of the said service, unto such hundreds, places and divisions within their respective counties and places as to them shall seem meet and expedient; and afterwards the said committees, or any two of them, respectively, shall direct their warrants to such number of persons as they shall think fit within their several and respective divisions, to appear before them, or any two of them, and upon their appearance the said respective committees, or any two of them, shall nominate and appoint such persons as they shall think fit within their respective divisions; which said persons so nominated, or any two of them, shall have power to assess all and every person or persons, fraternity, guild . . . [etc.] chargeable by this ordinance, according to the weekly rates and proportions in this ordinance mentioned.

★ ★ ★

Firth and Rait, I, 85–100

79. An Ordinance for sequestring notorious delinquents' estates, 27 March 1643

The Lords and Commons assembled in parliament, taking into their serious consideration the heavy pressures and calamities which now lie upon this kingdom by this unnatural war raised against the parliament; and that notwithstanding all their faithful and incessant endeavours for the preserving of his Majesty and the whole kingdom from the mischievous and restless designs of papists and ill affected persons whose aim is the extirpation of our religion, laws and liberties, yet their counsels and practices are still so prevalent with his Majesty, and the hearts of so many people so misled and beguiled by their false pretences and insinuations, that nothing can be expected but ruin and desolation unless God in mercy prevent it, and incline his Majesty's heart to the faithful advice of his great council of parliament, which hath ever been and is under God the chief support of his royal dignity and the security of all that we have or can enjoy. And for that it is most agreeable to common justice that the estates of such notorious delinquents as have been the causers or instruments of the pubic calamities, which have been hitherto employed to the fomenting and nourishing of these miserable distractions, should be converted and applied towards the support of the great charges of the Commonwealth, and for the easing of the good subjects therein, who have hitherto borne the greatest share in these burdens.

Be it therefore ordained by the said Lords and Commons, that the estates as well real as personal of the several bishops hereafter mentioned, that is to say, of William, Archbishop of Canterbury, John, Archbishop of York, . . . and of all such bishops, deans, deans and chapters, prebends, archdeacons, and of all other person and persons, ecclesiastical or temporal, as have raised or shall raise arms against the parliament, or have been, are or shall be in actual war against the same, or have voluntarily contributed, or shall voluntarily contribute (not being under the power of any part of the king's army at the time of such contributing) any money, horse, plate, arms, munition or other aid or assistance, for or towards the maintenance of any forces raised against the parliament, or for the opposing of any force or power raised by authority of both Houses of Parliament, and of all such as have joined or shall join in any oath, or act of association against the parliament, or have imposed, or shall impose any tax or assessment upon his Majesty's subjects for or towards the maintenance of any forces against the parliament, or have, or shall use any force or power to levy the same, shall be forthwith seized and sequestered into the hands of the sequestrators and committees hereafter in this ordinance named, and of such other persons as shall at any other time hereafter be appointed and nominated by both Houses of Parliament, for any county, city or place within the realm of England or dominion of Wales. Which said sequestrators and committees, or any two or more of them, in each several county, city or place respectively are hereby authorised and required by themselves, their agents and deputies, to take and seize into their hands and custodies as well all the money, goods, chattels, debts and personal estate, as also all and every the manors, lands, tenements and hereditaments, rents, arrearages of rents, revenues and profits of all and every the said delinquents, or persons before specified . . .; and also two parts of all the money, goods, chattels, debts, and personal estate, and two parts of all and every the manors, lands, tenements and hereditaments, rents, arrearages of rents, revenues and profits of all and every papist, or which any other person hath in trust for any papists, or to the use or uses of any papists, and to let, set and demise the same, or any part thereof, as the respective landlord or owner thereof may or might have done from year to year; and shall have power to call before them, or any two of them, all stewards, bailiffs, rent gatherers, auditors or other officers or servants, as well of the said archbishops, bishops, deans, deans and chapters, prebends, archdeacons, as of all and every other of the said delinquents or persons before specified, and to send for or take any books of accounts, rentals, copies of court rolls, or other evidences, writings, or memorials touching the premises or any of them, and thereby, and by all other ways and means which to the said sequestrators, or any two or more of them, shall seem meet and necessary to inform themselves, as well of the said several delinquents and every of them as of their several estates and possessions, rents, arrearages of rents, revenues and profits, goods and chattels, estates real and personal, and the true value thereof, and of all things concerning the same or any part thereof, and to appoint any officer or officers, or other person or persons under them, for the better expediting of this service . . .

*   *   *

And the said sequestrators . . . shall be accountable from time to time for the same, and for all such other things as shall be had or taken by them, their agents or deputies; and for all their receipts and payments and other acts, for or in respect of the premises, to both Houses of Parliament, or to such as they shall appoint; and shall pay in all such sums of money as they or any of them shall receive out of the said estates unto the treasurers at Guildhall, London, and shall keep books of accounts, and shall be from time to time subject to the further orders and directions of both Houses of Parliament, . . . as cause shall require . . .

*   *   *

Firth and Rait, 1, 106–10

80. An Ordinance for the speedy raising and leavying of monies, set by way of charge or new impost, . . . as well for . . . the maintenance of the forces raised for the defence of the King and Parliament, both by sea and land, as for and towards the payment of the debts of the Commonwealth, 22 July 1643

. . . Forasmuch as many great levies have been already made for the purpose first above mentioned, which the well-affected party to the Protestant religion have hitherto willingly paid, to their great charge, and the malignants of this kingdom have hitherto practised by all cunning ways and means how to evade and elude the payment of any part thereof, by reason whereof the Lords and Commons do hold it fit that some constant and equal way for the levying of monies for the future maintenance of the parliament forces, and other great affairs of the Commonwealth, may be had and established, whereby the said malignants and neutrals may be brought to and compelled to pay their proportionable parts of the aforesaid charge, and that the levies hereafter to be made for the purposes aforesaid may be borne with as much indifferency to the subject in general as may be.

I. Be it therefore ordered, ordained and declared by the said Lords and Commons, that the several rates and charged in a schedule hereunto annexed and contained, shall be set and laid, and are hereby set and laid, charged and imposed upon all and every the commodities in the said schedule particularly expressed, as the same are particularly therein taxed and rated, as well upon those that are already brought into this realm, or the dominion of Wales, and town of Berwick, and every of them, and are remaining in the hands of any merchant, buyer or seller, or other owner thereof respectively, as upon any of the commodities in the schedule mentioned which hereafter shall be imported into this kingdom of England, dominion of Wales, and town of Berwick, or any of them.

II. And be it further ordained by the said Lords and Commons, that for the better levying of the monies hereby to be raised, that an office from henceforth by force and virtue of these presents shall be and is hereby erected, made and appointed in the city of London, called or known by the name of the Office of Excise or New Impost, whereof there shall be eight commissioners to govern the same, and one of them to be treasurer, with several registers, collectors, clerks and other subordinate officers, as the eight commissioners (or the major part of them) for the time being shall with the approbation of the Committee of Lords and Commons appointed for the Advance of Money, and making of other provisions for the army (sitting at Haberdashers' Hall, London) nominate and appoint . . .

★   ★   ★

IV. And it is further ordered and ordained that the said commissioners and treasurer shall be from time to time nominated by both Houses of Parliament . . . And all parts of the cities of London and Westminster, with their several suburbs, and all other places within seven miles of either of the said cities and suburbs, shall be subject to the rule and government of the said Office.

V. That the like Office, and so many of such Officers, shall be and is hereby erected, and appointed in all and every the counties of the realm of England, dominion of Wales and town of Berwick, and in all other the cities and such other places thereof as the said eight commissioners, or the major part of them, shall for the time being think fit . . .

★   ★   ★

X. That all and every the merchants and importers of any of the several foreign commodities in the schedule mentioned, and all ale and common beer brewers shall weekly cause to be entered into the said office a true and perfect list or account, as well of all and every the said commodities by them respectively and weekly sold, as of the names of the buyers thereof, and of those to whose use the same is bought, and that they shall not deliver any of the said commodities unto any of the buyers thereof, or other person or persons, until the same shall be so entered, and that the buyer hath procured a ticket under the hand of the treasurer for the time being signifying that he hath paid the rates set upon the said commodities, or given security for the same.

XI. That if any of the sellers of the said commodities shall refuse or neglect to make a true entry of the said commodities, according to the next precedent article, or do anything contrary to the said article, that then he or they so refusing, neglecting or doing contrary to the said article, shall forfeit to the use of the Commonwealth four times the true value or worth of the goods and commodities so by him or them neglected to be entered or delivered contrary to the said article, for which he shall be distrained . . . And if it shall happen that no distress can be conveniently taken of the goods of the party so offending, that then it may and shall be lawful to and for the said commissioners, or the major part of them, their deputy or deputies, by some one or more of their officers, to arrest the party so offending, and commit him to some common prison next adjoining to his place of dwelling or abode, there to remain without bail or mainprize until he pay the penalties by him forfeited as aforesaid . . .

XII. That if any common brewer, alehouse keeper, cider or perry maker, in the country or in any city, town or place therein, which doth brew ale or beer, or make cider and perry, in their houses or elsewhere, do not make a true entry in manner aforesaid, . . . then they shall incur the like penalty as aforesaid . . .

XIII. That all and every person and persons whatsoever that keep or shall keep private houses and families, . . . which brew, or shall cause to be brewed their own ale and beer for the sustenance of their families, . . . shall monthly cause the like entries to be made . . . or the like penalties to be levied on the offenders herein . . .

★   ★   ★

XX. That the said commissioners . . . shall have power and authority to call before them any person or persons whom they shall think fit, to inform or testify touching the premises, and to examine them upon oath for the better discovery of any fraud or guile in the not entering, or not payment, of the rates of excise or new impost herein mentioned, and that the testimony of two credible witnesses shall be sufficient, and that the said commissioners . . . shall have full power by virtue of this ordinance to administer an oath to any person or persons for the purposes aforesaid.

XXI. That the said commissioners . . . shall from time to time appoint any officer or officers belonging to the said office to enter into cellars, shops, warehouses, store-houses, or other places of every person or persons that selleth, buyeth or spendeth any of the said commodities, to search and see what quantities of any of the said commodities every such hath on his hands, or any other person or persons to his use.

★   ★   ★

XXIV. That the said commissioners and other officers, and every of them appointed by this ordinance, shall have power to call the trained bands, volunteers or other forces of any county, city or place respectively to be aiding and assisting to them, to compel obedience in this ordinance, where any resistance shall be made, which said trained bands, volunteers and other forces, and their several commanders, and other officers, are hereby required and enjoined to give their aid and assistance accordingly, as need shall require.

XXV. And be it further ordained that as well all and every the said commissioners, deputies, treasurer, registers, receivers or other officers whatsoever belonging to the said several offices, as all and every other person and persons which shall do anything in execution or performance of this present ordinance, shall be therein from time to time protected and saved harmless by the power and authority of both Houses of Parliament.

*　*　*

Firth and Rait, 1, 202–9

81. Minutes of the Committee for Staffordshire

[18 March 1643]

The fornicator gunner

Ordered that the gunner which did commit fornication shall be set upon the great gun with a mark upon his back through the garrison and then disgracefully expulsed . . .

Brett

Whereas Alexander Brett of Pencle holds a farm there of Mr Ralph Keeling of Newcastle and is behind of his rent, as the said Mr Keeling informs, the sum of £18, for which he took a distress of his cattle, which he afterwards by the help of the enemy then in those parts rescued and took again: It is therefore now ordered that the said Mr Keeling shall have liberty to distrain for the said arrears, and to take to his assistance so many of Captain Stone's soldiers as shall be thought necessary, giving them satisfaction for their pains therein . . . [75].

[24 April]

1. That Mr Ferne of Crackmarsh be committed to the marshal to bide in prison until he pay the sum of one hundred pounds demanded of him upon the proposition according to the ordinance of parliament.

2. That Jo. Hichecok [sic] be desired to fetch the cistern of lead, three long ladders, and a pair of gates from the Grange and bring them to Stafford.

3. That Mrs Eliz. Hamersley quietly enjoy those lands formerly by deed made over to her by her husband for the maintenance of her and children, she

paying all levies assessed upon those lands by the committee of parliament. And that the remainder of Mr Hamersley's estate only be sequestered . . .

Beer at 1d. the quart

Forasmuch as there hath been of late much drunkenness in the soldiers, which hath been occasioned by the excessive strong beer brewed contrary to the rate ordained by the statute. It is therefore ordered that no inn or alehouse keepers shall brew any ale or beer other than what they will sell for a penny a quart *intus et foras* [*sc.* on or off the premises]. And if they shall demand more, for every such offence that shall pay 10*s.*, to be levied on their goods, and not suffered to brew any more . . . [103].

[7 May 1645]

Tovey

Ordered that Capt. Tovey (in respect his troop is wholly squandered and lost, and that there is not horse in the county to recruit nor need of more officers, the contribution of the county not being able to bear those we have already) be dismissed his attendance here for command, and if he stay to have no more allowance from the committee.

M. Snowe

Ordered that Major Snowe's Company march to the leaguer at Chester, and that Major Snowe himself march with them and command all the Staffordshire Foot in the absence of Colonel Bowyer, and when Col. Bowyer comes he to stay with those companies until he be dismissed by Sir Will. Brereton.

Winkle and Lees

Whereas it is informed that there are two orchards, the one of Mrs Winkles and the other of Mrs Dorothy Lees, which have been converted to the state's use ever since the taking of this garrison by the parliament's forces, which orchards were formerly valued at 40*s.* per annum as is informed. It is ordered that the solicitors for sequestration shall pay yearly to the said Mrs Winkle and Mrs Lees the sum of £1. 13*s.* 4*d.* out of delinquents' rents to be equally divided betwixt them. And likewise shall pay the arrears for the time past, and the £1. 13*s.* 4*d.* so long as the state holdeth them.

[8 May]

Davenport

Ordered that Mr Bargh shall let widow Davenport have a cow's grass rent free, for the maintaining of two poor orphans whose father was killed in service.

Blakemore

Ordered that Mr Blakemore look to the buildings, grass and corn which belong to the parsonage of Swynerton and preserve them for the next incumbent [303–4].

Pennington and Roots, *The Committee at Stafford*, pp. 75, 103, 303–4

82. A declaration, or representation from His Excellency Sir Thomas Fairfax, and of the army under his command, Humbly tendered to the Parliament, St Albans, 14 June 1647

That we may no longer be the dissatisfaction of our friends, the subject of our enemies' malice (to work jealousies and misrepresentations) and the suspicions (if not the astonishment) of many in the kingdom, in our late or present transactions and conduct of business, we shall in all faithfulness and clearness profess and declare unto you those things which have of late protracted and hindered our disbanding, the present grievances which possess our army and are yet unremedied, with our desires as to the complete settlement of the liberties and peace of the kingdom, which is that blessing of God than which (of all worldly things) nothing is more dear unto us, or more precious in our thoughts, we having hitherto thought all our present enjoyments, whether of life, or livelihood, or nearest relation, a price but sufficient to the purchase of so rich a blessing, that we and all the free-born people of this nation may sit down in quiet under our vines, under the glorious administration of justice and righteousness, and in the full possession of those fundamental rights and liberties without which we can have little hopes (as to human considerations) to enjoy either any comforts of life or so much as life itself, but at the pleasures of some men ruling merely according to will and power.

It cannot be unknown what hath passed betwixt the parliament and the army as to the service of Ireland. By all which, together with the late proceedings against the army in relation to their petition and grievances, all men may judge what hath hindered the army from a ready engagement in that service; and without further account or apology as to that particular, than what passages and proceedings themselves already made public do afford, we do appeal to yourselves whether those courses to which the parliament hath (by the designs and practices of some) been drawn, have rationally tended to induce a cheerful and unanimous undertaking of the army to that service, or rather to break or pull the army in pieces with discontent and dishonour, and to put such disobligations and provocations upon it as might drive it into distemper, and indeed discourage both this army and other soldiers from any further engagement in the parliament's service . . .

★   ★   ★

Nor will it now, we hope, seem strange or unseasonable to rational and honest men, who consider the consequence of our present case to their own and the kingdom's (as well as our) future concernment in point of right, freedom, peace and safety, if from a deep sense of the high consequence of our present case, both to ourselves in [the] future and all other people, we shall before disbanding proceed in our own and the kingdom's behalf to propound and plead for some provision for our and the kingdom's satisfaction and future security in relation to those things, especially considering that we were not a mere mercenary army, hired to serve any arbitrary power of a state, but called forth and conjured by the several Declarations of parliament to the defence of our own and the people's just rights and liberties. And so we took up arms in judgment and conscience to those ends, and have so continued them, and are resolved, according to your first just desires in your Declarations, and such principles as we have received from your frequent informations, and our own common sense concerning those our fundamental rights and liberties, to assert and vindicate the just power and rights of this kingdom in parliament, for those common ends premissed against all arbitrary power, violence and oppression, and against all particular parties or interest whatsoever. The said Declarations still directing us to the equitable sense of all laws and constitutions, as dispensing with the very letter of the same, and being supreme to it when the safety and preservation of all is concerned, and assuring us that all authority is fundamentally seated in the office, and but ministerially in the person; neither do or will these our proceedings (as we are fully and in conscience persuaded) amount to any thing not warrantable before God and Men, being thus far much short of the common proceedings in other nations to things of a higher nature than we have yet appeared to. And we cannot but be sensible of the great complaints that have been made generally to us of the kingdom, from the people where we march, of arbitrariness and injustice to their great and insupportable oppressions.

And truly such kingdoms as have, according both to the Law of Nature and Nations, appeared to the vindication and defence of their just rights and liberties, have proceeded much higher; as our brethren of Scotland, who in the first beginning of these late differences associated in Covenant from the very same gounds and principles, having no visible form either of parliament or king to countenance them; and as they were therein justified and protected by their own and this kingdom also, so we justly shall expect to be.

We need not mention the state of the Netherlands, the Portugals, and others, all proceeding from the same principles of right and freedom; and accordingly the parliament hath declared it no resistance of magistracy to side with the just principles and the Law of Nature and Nations, being that law upon which we have assisted you, and that the soldiery may lawfully hold the hands of the general who will turn his cannon against his army on purpose to destroy them, the seamen the hands of the pilot who wilfully runs the ship upon a rock (as our brethren of Scotland argued). And such were the proceedings of our ancestors of famous memory, to the purchasing of such rights and liberties as they have enjoyed through the price of their blood, and we (both by that and the later blood of our dear friends and fellow soldiers, with the hazard of our own) do now lay claim to.

Nor is that supreme end (the glory of God) wanting in these cases, to set a price upon all such proceedings of righteousness and justice, it being one witness of God in the world to carry on a testimony against the injustice and unrighteousness of men, and against the miscarriages of governments, when corrupted or declining from their primitive or original glory.

These things we mention but to compare proceedings, and to show that we are so much the more justifiable and warranted in what we do by how much we come short of that height and measure of proceedings which the people in free kingdoms and nations have formerly practised.

Now, having thus far cleared our way in this business, we shall proceed to propound such things as we do humbly desire for the settling and securing of our own and the kingdom's common right, freedom, peace and safety, as followeth.

First, That the Houses may be speedily purged of such members as for their delinquency, or for corruptions, or abuse to the State, or undue exactions, ought not to sit there; whereof the late elections in Cornwall, Wales and other parts of the kingdom afford too many examples to the great prejudice of the people's freedoms in the said elections.

Secondly, That those persons who have in the unjust and high proceedings against the army appeared to have the will and confidence, credit and power to abuse the parliament and the army, to endanger the kingdom, in carrying on such things against us (while an army), may be some way speedily disabled from doing the like or worse to us when disbanded and dispersed . . .

But because neither the granting of this alone would be sufficient to secure our own and the kingdom's rights, liberties and safety, either for the present age or posterity, nor would our proposing of this singly be free from the scandal and appearance of faction and design, only to weaken one party (under the notion of unjust or oppressive) that we may advance another (which may be imagined more our own), we therefore declare:

That indeed we cannot but wish that such men and such only might be preferred to the great power and trust of the Commonwealth as are approved at least for moral righteousness; and of such we cannot but in our wishes prefer those that appear acted [*sc.* activated] thereunto by a principle of conscience and religion in them. And accordingly we do and ever shall bless God for those many such worthies who through his providence have been chosen into this parliament . . . But yet we are so far from designing or complying to have an absolute or arbitrary power settled, for continuance, in any persons whatsoever, as that (if we might be sure to obtain it) we cannot wish to have it so in the persons of any whom we could most confide in, or who should appear most of our own opinions or principles, or whom we might have most personal assurance of, or interest in. But we do and shall much rather wish that the authority of this kingdom, in parliaments rightly constituted – that is, freely, equally and successively chosen, according to its original intention – may ever stand and have its course; and therefore we shall apply our desires chiefly to such things as, by having parliaments settled in such a right constitution, may give most hopes of justice and righteousness to flow down equally to all in that its ancient channel, without any overtures tending either to overthrow that foundation of order and government in this kingdom, or to engross that power for perpetuity into the hands of any particular persons or party whatsoever . . .

We therefore humbly conceive that . . . the main thing to be intended in this case . . . seems to be this, viz., to provide that however unjust or corrupt the persons of parliament men in present or future may prove, or whatever ill they may do to particular parties (or to the whole in particular things) during their respective terms or period, yet they shall not have the temptation or advantage of an unlimited power fixed in them during their own pleasure, whereby to perpetuate injustice or oppression upon any, without end or remedy, or to advance or uphold any one particular party, faction or interest whatsoever, to the oppression or prejudice of the community and the enslaving of the kingdom to all posterity . . . Yet in this we would not be misunderstood in the least, to blame those worthies of both Houses whose zeal to vindicate the liberties of this nation did procure that act for the continuance of this parliament, whereby it was secured from being dissolved at the king's pleasure, as former parliaments had been, and reduced to such a certainty as might enable them the better to assert and vindicate the liberties of this nation, immediately before so highly invaded, and then also so much endangered. And this we take to be the principal ends and grounds for which in that exigency of time and affairs it was procured, and to which we acknowledge it hath happily been made use of; but we cannot think it was by those worthies intended or ought to be made use of to the perpetuating of that supreme trust and power in the persons of any during their own pleasures, or to the debarring of the people from their right of elections totally now, when these dangers or exigencies were past, and the affairs and safety of the Commonwealth would admit of such a change.

Having thus cleared our grounds and intentions, as we hope, from all scruples and misunderstandings, . . . we further humbly desire as followeth:

Thirdly, That some determinate period of time may be set for the continuance of this and future parliaments, beyond which none shall continue, and upon which new writs may of course issue out, and new elections successively take place, according to the intent of the bill for triennial parliaments.

And herein we would not be misunderstood to desire a present or sudden dissolution of this parliament, but only, as is expressed before, that some certain period may be set for the determining of it, so as it may not remain, as now, continuable for ever, or during the pleasure of the present Members . . . And for further securing the rights and liberties, and settling the peace of the kingdom . . . we further humbly offer:

Fourthly, That secure provision may be made for the continuance of future parliaments so that they may not be adjournable or dissolvable at the king's pleasure, or any other ways than by their own consent during their respective periods, but at those periods each parliament to determine of course as before. This we desire may be now provided for, if it may be, so as to put it out of dispute for [the] future, though we think of right it ought not to have been otherwise before . . .

These things we desire may be provided for by bill or ordinance of parliament, to which the royal assent may be desired; and when his Majesty in these things, and what else shall be proposed by the parliament necessary for securing the rights and liberties of the people, and for settling the militia, and peace of the kingdom, shall have given his concurrence to put them past dispute, we shall then desire that the rights of his Majesty and his posterity may be considered of and settled in all things so far as may consist with the right and freedom of the subject, and with the security of the same for the future.

Fifthly, We desire that the right and freedom of the people to represent to the parliament, by way of humble petition, their grievances, in such things as cannot otherwise be remedied than by parliament, may be cleared and vindicated. That all such grievances of the people may be freely received and admitted into consideration, and put into an equitable and speedy way to be heard, examined and redressed, if they appear real; and that in such things for which men have remedy by law, they may be freely left to the benefit of the law, and the regulated course of justice, without interruption or check from the parliament . . .

Sixthly, That the large powers given to the committees, or deputy-lieutenants, during the late time of war and distraction may be speedily taken into consideration; that such of those powers as appear not necessary to be continued may be taken away, and such of them as are necessary may be put into a regulated way, and left to as little arbitrariness as the nature and necessity of the things wherein they are conversant will bear.

Seventhly, We could wish that the kingdom might both be righted and publicly satisfied in point of accounts for the vast sums that have been levied and payed; as also in divers other things wherein the Commonwealth may be conceived to have been wronged and abused . . .

Eighthly, That public justice being first satisfied by some few examples to posterity, out of the worst of excepted persons, and other delinquents having passed their composition, some course may be taken by a general Act of Oblivion, or otherwise, whereby the seeds of future war or fears, either to the present age or posterity, may the better be taken away, by easing that sense of present and satisfying those fears of future ruin or undoing to persons or families which may drive men into any desperate ways for self-preservation or remedy; and by taking away the private remembrances and distinctions of parties, as far as may stand with safety to the rights and liberties we have hitherto fought for.

. . . These proposals aforegoing being the principal things we bottom and insist upon, we shall, as we have said before, for our parts acquiesce for other particulars in the wisdom and justice of parliament. And whereas it has been suggested or suspected, that in our late or present proceedings our design is to overthrow Presbytery or hinder the settlement thereof, and to have the Independent Government set up, we do clearly disclaim and disavow any such design. We only desire that, according to the declarations promising a provision of tender consciences there may be some effectual course taken according to the intent thereof, and that such who upon conscientious grounds may differ from the established forms may not for that be debarred from the common rights, liberties or benefits belonging equally to all, as men and members to the Commonwealth, while they live soberly and inoffensively towards others, and peaceably and faithfully towards the state.

★   ★   ★

Rushworth, VII, 564–70

83. The Heads of the Proposals, 1 August 1647

The Heads of the Proposals agreed upon by his Excellency Sir Thomas Fairfax and the Council of the Army, to be tendered to the Commissioners of Parliament residing with the army, and with them to be treated on by the Commissioners of the Army: containing the particulars of their desires in pursuance of their former declarations and papers, in order to the clearing and securing of the rights and liberties of the kingdom; and the settling a just and lasting peace . . .

I. That (things hereafter proposed being provided for by this parliament) a certain period may by act of parliament be set for the ending of this parliament (such period to be put within a year at most), and in the same Act provision to be made for the succession and constitution of parliaments in future, as followeth:

1. That parliaments may biennially be called and meet at a certain day, with such provision for the certainty thereof as in the late act was made for triennial parliaments; and what further or other provision shall be found needful by the parliament to reduce it to more certainty; and upon the passing of this, the said act for triennial parliaments to be repealed.

2. Each biennial parliament to sit 120 days, unless adjourned or dissolved sooner by their own consent; afterwards to be adjournable or dissolvable by the king; and no parliament to sit past 240 days from the first meeting, or some other limited number of days now to be agreed on; upon the expiration whereof each parliament to dissolve of course, if not otherwise dissolved sooner.

3. The king, upon the advice of the Council of State, in the intervals betwixt biennial parliaments, to call a parliament extraordinary, provided it meet above 70 days before the next biennial day, and be dissolved at least 60 days before the same, so as the course of biennial elections may never be interrupted.

4. That this parliament and each succeeding biennial parliament, at or before adjournment or dissolution thereof, may appoint committees to continue during the interval for such purposes as are in any of these proposals referred to such committees.

5. That the elections of the Commons for succeeding parliaments may be distributed to all counties, or other parts or divisions of the kingdom, according to some rule of equality or proportion, so as all counties may have a number of parliament members allowed to their choice proportionable to the respective rates they bear in the common charges and burdens of the kingdom, according to some other rule of equality or proportion, to render the House of Commons as near as may be an equal representative of the whole; and in order thereunto, that a present consideration be had to take off the elections of burgesses for poor, decayed or inconsiderable towns, and to give some present addition to the number of parliament members for great counties that have now less than their due proportion, to bring all at present, as near as may be, to such a rule of proportion as aforesaid.

6. That effectual provision be made for future freedom of elections, and certainty of due returns.

7. That the House of Commons alone have the power from time to time to set down further orders and rules for the ends expressed in the two last

preceding articles, so as to reduce the elections of members for that House to more and more perfection of equality in the distribution, freedom in the election, order in the proceeding thereto, and certainty in the returns, with orders and rules in that case to be in laws.

8. That there be a liberty for entering dissents in the House of Commons, with provision that no member be censurable for ought said or voted in the House further than to exclusion from that trust; and that only by the judgment of the House itself.

9. That the judicial power, or power of final judgment, in the Lords and Commons (and their power of exposition and application of law, without further appeal) may be cleared; and that no officer of justice, minister of state or other person adjudged by them, may be capable of protection or pardon from the king without their advice or consent.

10. That the right and liberty of the commons of England may be cleared and vindicated as to a due exemption from any judgment, trial or other proceedings against them by the House of Peers, without the concurring judgment of the House of Commons; as also from any other judgment, sentence or proceeding against them, other than by their equals, or according to the law of the land.

11. The same act to provide that grand jurymen may be chosen by and for [the] several parts or divisions of each county respectively in some equal way, and not to remain as now, at the discretion of an under-sheriff to be put on or off, and that such grand jurymen for their respective counties may at each assize present the names of persons to be made justices of the peace from time to time, as the county hath need for any to be added to the commission, and at the summer assize to present the names of three persons, out of whom the king may prick one to be sheriff for the next year.

II. For the future security of parliament and the militia in general, in order thereunto, that it be provided by act of parliament:

1. That the power of the militia by sea and land during the space of ten years next ensuing shall be ordered and disposed by the Lords and Commons assembled, and to be assembled, in the parliament or parliaments of England, by such persons as they shall nominate and appoint for that purpose from time to time during the said space.

2. That the said power shall not be ordered, disposed or exercised by the king's Majesty that now is, or by any person or persons by any authority derived from him, during the said space, or at any time hereafter by his said Majesty, without the advice and consent of the said Lords and Commons, or of such committees or council in the intervals of parliament as they shall appoint.

3. That during the same space of ten years the said Lords and Commons may by bill or ordinance raise and dispose of what moneys and for what forces

they shall from time to time find necessary; as also for payment of the public debts and damages, and for all other the public uses of the kingdom.

4. And to the end that the temporary security intended by the three particulars last precedent may be the better assured, it may therefore be provided, that no subjects that have been in hostility against the parliament in the late war shall be capable of bearing any office of power or public trust in the Commonwealth during the space of five years without the consent of parliament or of the Council of State; or to sit as members or assistants of either House of Parliament until the second biennial parliament be passed.

III. For the present form of disposing the militia in order to the peace and safety of this kingdom and the service of Ireland:

> [The navy was to be put under commissioners, the army under a general, the militia under county commissioners. A Council of State, for seven years in the first instance, was to control the militia and conduct foreign policy, subject to parliament's ultimate control over war and peace.]

IV. That an act be passed for disposing the great offices for ten years by the Lords and Commons in Parliament; or by such committees as they shall appoint for that purpose in the intervals (with submission to the approbation of the next parliament), and after ten years they to nominate three, and the king out of that number to appoint one for the succession upon any vacancy.

★ ★ ★

XI. An act to be passed to take away all coercive power, authority and jurisdiction of bishops and all other ecclesiastical officers whatsoever, extending to any civil penalties upon any; and to repeal all laws whereby the civil magistracy hath been, or is bound upon any ecclesiastical censure to proceed *ex officio* unto any civil penalties against any persons so censured.

XII. That there be a repeal of all acts or clauses in any act enjoining the use of the Book of Common Prayer, and imposing any penalties for neglect thereof; as also of all acts or clauses of any act imposing any penalty for not coming to church, or for meetings elsewhere for prayer or other religious duties, exercises or ordinances; and some other provision to be made for discovering of papists and popish recusants, and for disabling of them, and of all Jesuits or priests, from disturbing the state.

XIII. That the taking of the Covenant be not enforced upon any, nor any penalties imposed on the refusers, whereby men might be restrained to take it against their judgments or consciences, but all orders and ordinances tending to that purpose to be repealed.

XIV. That (the things herebefore proposed being provided, for settling and securing the rights, liberties, peace and safety of the kingdom) his Majesty's person, his queen and royal issue, may be restored to a condition of safety, honour and freedom in this nation, without diminution to their personal rights, or further limitation to the exercise of the regal power than according to the particular foregoing.

XV. For the matter of composition.

[The proposals here were complicated, but much more merciful than those put forward by parliament in 1646. Apart from the Irish rebels – whom everyone regarded as lepers – only five persons were to be totally excepted from pardon, as against 38 named by parliament. The rates at which other royalists could compound were slashed, and those having less than £200 in land or goods were to be discharged without further penalty.

Lastly, this section ended with a proposal to which the army officers attached the highest importance:]

6. That the faith of the army, or other forces of the parliament, given in articles upon surrenders to any of the king's party, may be fully made good; and where any breach thereof shall appear to have been made, full reparation and satisfaction may be given to the parties injured and the persons offending, being found out, may be compelled thereto.

XVI. That there may be a general Act of Oblivion to extend unto all (except the persons to be continued in exception as before), to absolve from all trespasses, misdemeanours &c., done in prosecution of the war; and from all trouble or prejudice for or concerning the same (after their compositions passed), and to restore them to all privileges, &c., belonging to other subjects, provided as in the fourth particular under the second general head aforegoing concerning security.

And whereas there have been of late strong endeavours and practices of a factious and desperate party to embroil this kingdom in a new war, and for that purpose to induce the king, the queen and the prince to declare for the said party, and also to excite and stir up all those of the king's late party to appear and engage for the same, which attempts and designs many of the king's party, out of their desires to avoid further misery to the kingdom, have contributed their endeavours to prevent (as for divers of them we have had particular assurance): we do therefore desire that such of the king's party who shall appear to have expressed, and shall hereafter express, that way their good affections to the peace and welfare of the kingdom, and to hinder the embroiling of the same in a new war, may be freed and exempted from compositions, or to pay but one year's revenue, or a twentieth part.

Next to the proposals aforesaid for the present settling of a peace, we shall desire that no time may be lost by the parliament for despatch of other things tending to the welfare, ease and just satisfaction of the kingdom, and in special manner:

I. That the just and necessary liberty of the people to represent their grievances and desires by way of petition may be cleared and vindicated, according to the fifth head in the late Representation or Declaration of the Army sent from St Albans[37]

II. That in pursuance of the same head in the said Declaration the common grievances of this people may be speedily considered of, and effectually redressed, and in particular:

1. That the excise may be taken off from such commodities whereon the poor people of the land do ordinarily live, and a certain time to be limited for taking off the whole.

2. That the oppressions and encroachments of forest laws may be prevented for the future.

3. All monopolies (old or new) and restraints on the freedom of trade be taken off.

4. That a course may be taken and commissioners appointed to remedy and rectify the inequality of rates lying upon several counties, and several parts of each county in respect of others, and to settle the proportion of land rates to more equality throughout the kingdom; in order to which we shall offer some further particulars, which we hope may be useful.

5. The present unequal, troublesome and contentious way of ministers' maintenance by tithes to be considered of, and some remedy applied.

6. That the rules and course of law, and the officers of it, may be so reduced and reformed as that all suits and questions of right may be more clear and certain in the issues, and not so tedious nor chargeable in the proceedings as now; in order to which we shall offer some further particulars hereafter.

7. That prisoners for debt or other creditors, who have estates to discharge them, may not by embracing imprisonment, or any other ways, have advantage to defraud their creditors, but that the estates of all men may be some way made liable to their debts (as well as tradesmen are by commissions of bankrupt), whether they be imprisoned for it or not; and that such prisoners for debt who have not wherewith to pay, or at least do yield up what they have to their creditors, may be freed from imprisonment or some way provided for, so as neither they nor their families may perish by their imprisonment.

8. Some provision to be made that none may be compelled by penalty or

---

[37] Printed above, no. **82**.

otherwise to answer unto questions tending to the accusing of themselves or their nearest relations in criminal causes; and no man's life to be taken away [by] under two witnesses.

9. That consideration may be had of all statutes, and the laws and customs of corporations, imposing any oaths; either to repeal or else to qualify and provide against the same, so far as they may extend or be construed to the molestation or ensnaring of religious and peaceable people merely for nonconformity in religion.

[§§ III and IV repeated, respectively, sections six and seven of the Declaration of 15 June (pp. 267–8 above).]

*   *   *

V. That provision may be made for payment of arrears to the army, and the rest of the soldiers of the kingdom who have concurred with the army in the late desires and proceedings thereof; and in the next place for payment of the public debts and damages of the kingdom; and that to be performed first to such persons whose debt or damages upon the public account are great, and their estates small, so as they are thereby reduced to a difficulty of subsistence: in order to all which, and to the fourth particular last preceding, we shall speedily offer some further particulars (in the nature of rules) which we hope will be of good use towards public satisfaction.

August 1, 1647   Signed by the appointment of his Excellency
                                  Sir Thomas Fairfax and the Council of War
                                                      Rushworth, VII, 731–4

84. The First Agreement of the People, 28 October 1647

An Agreement of the People for a firm and present peace upon grounds of common right
    Having by our late labours and hazards made it appear to the world at how high a rate we value our just freedom, and God having so far owned our case as to deliver the enemies thereof into our hands, we do now hold ourselves bound in mutual duty to each other to take the best care we can for the future to avoid both the danger of returning into a slavish condition and the chargeable remedy of another war; for, as it cannot be imagined that so many of our countrymen would have opposed us in this quarrel if they had understood their own good, so may we safely promise to ourselves that, when our common rights and liberties shall be cleared, their endeavours will be disappointed that seek to make themselves our masters. Since therefore our former oppressions and scarce-yet-ended troubles have been occasioned either by want of frequent national meetings in council, or by rendering those meetings ineffectual, we are fully agreed and resolved to provide that hereafter

our representatives be neither left to an uncertainty for the time nor made useless to the ends for which they are intended. In order whereunto we declare:

That the people of England, being at this day very unequally distributed by counties, cities and boroughs for the election of their deputies in parliament, ought to be more indifferently proportioned according to the number of the inhabitants; the circumstances whereof for number, place and manner are to be set down before the end of this present parliament.

II. That, to prevent the many inconveniences apparently arising from the long continuance of the same persons in authority, this present parliament be dissolved upon the last day of September which shall be in the year of Our Lord 1648.

III. That the people do of course choose themselves a parliament once in two years, viz., upon the first Thursday in every second March, after the manner as shall be prescribed before the end of this parliament, to begin to sit upon the first Thursday in April following at Westminster, or such other place as shall be appointed from time to time by the preceding representatives, and to continue till the last day of September then next ensuing, and no longer.

IV. That the power of this and all future representatives of this nation is inferior only to theirs who choose them, and doth extend, without the consent or concurrence of any other person or persons, to the enacting, altering and repealing of laws, to the erecting and abolishing of offices and courts, to the appointing, removing and calling to account magistrates and officers of all degrees, to the making war and peace, to the treating with foreign states, and generally to whatsoever is not expressly or implicitly reserved by the represented to themselves.

Which are as followeth:

1. That matters of religion and the ways of God's worship are not at all entrusted by us to any human power, because therein we cannot remit or exceed a tittle of what our consciences dictate to be the mind of God without wilful sin. Nevertheless, the public way of instructing the nation (so it be not compulsive) is referred to their discretion.

2. That the matter of impressing and constraining any of us to serve in the wars is against our freedom; and therefore we do not allow it in our representatives; the rather because money (the sinews of war) being always at their disposal, they can never want numbers of men apt enough to engage in any just cause.

3. That after the dissolution of the present parliament no person be at any

time questioned for anything said or done in reference to the late public differences, otherwise than in execution of the judgments of the present representatives, or House of Commons.

4. That in laws made or to be made every person may be bound alike, and that no tenure, estate, charter, degree, birth or place do confer any exemption from the ordinary course of legal proceedings whereunto others are subjected.

5. That as the laws ought to be equal, so they must be good, and not evidently destructive to the safety and well-being of the people.

These things we declare to be our native rights, and therefore are agreed and resolved to maintain them with our utmost possibilities against all opposition whatsoever; being compelled thereunto not only by the examples of our ancestors, whose blood was often spent in vain for the recovery of their freedoms, suffering themselves through fraudulent accommodations to be still deluded of the fruit of their victories, but also by our own woeful experience, who, having long expected and dearly earned the establishment of these certain rules of government, are yet made to depend for the settlement of our peace and freedom upon him that intended our bondage and brought a cruel war upon us.   Gardiner, *Civil War*, III, 392–4

85. The Leveller programme: the Humble Petition

To the Right Honourable the Commons of England in Parliament assembled, the humble petition of divers well-affected persons inhabiting the City of London, Westminster, the Borough of Southwark, hamlets and places adjacent. [Presented 11 September 1648]
Showeth,

That although we are as earnestly desirous of a safe and well-grounded peace, and that a final end were put to all the troubles and miseries of the Commonwealth, as any sort of men whatsoever, yet considering upon what grounds we engaged on your part in the late and present wars, and how far (by our so doing) we apprehend ourselves concerned, give us leave (before you conclude us by the treaty in hand)[38] to acquaint you first with the ground and reason which induced us to aid you against the king and his adherents; secondly, what our apprehensions are of this treaty; thirdly, what we expected from you, and do still most earnestly desire.

Be pleased therefore to understand that we had not engaged on your part, but that we judged this honourable House to be the supreme authority of England, as chosen by and representing the people, and entrusted with

---

[38] The negotiations between parliament and the king which opened at Newport, IOW, on 18 September (Gardiner, *Civil War*, IV, 214).

absolute power for redress of grievances and provision for safety; and that the king was but at most the chief public officer of this kingdom, and accountable to this House (the representative of the people, from whom all just authority is or ought to be derived) for discharge of his office. And if we had not been confident hereof we had been desperately mad to have taken up arms or to have been aiding and assisting in maintaining a war against him, the laws of the land making it expressly a crime no less than treason for any to raise war against the king.

But when we considered the manifold oppressions brought upon the nation by the king, his lords and bishops, and that this honourable House declared their deep sense thereof; and that (for continuance of that power which had so oppressed us) it was evident the king intended to raise forces and to make war, and that if he did set up his standard it tended to the dissolution of the government – upon this, knowing the safety of the people to be above law, and that to judge thereof appertained to the Supreme Authority, and not to the Supreme Magistrate, and being satisfied in our consciences that the public safety and freedom was in imminent danger, we concluded we had not only a just cause to maintain but the Supreme Authority of the nation to justify, defend and indemnify us in time to come, in what we should perform by direction thereof, though against the known law of the land or any inferior authority, though the highest.

And as this our understanding was begotten in us by principles of right reason, so were we confirmed therein by your own proceedings: as by your condemning those judges who in the case of ship-money had declared the king to be judge of safety; and by your denying him to have a negative voice in the making of laws, where you wholly exclude the king from having any share in the Supreme Authority; and by your declaring to the Lords that if they would not join with you in settling the militia (which they long refused) and would settle it without them,[39] which you could not justly have done had they had any share in the Supreme Authority.

★   ★   ★

But to our exceeding grief we have observed that no sooner God vouchsafeth you victory, and blesseth you with success, and thereby enableth you to put us and the whole nation into an absolute condition of freedom and safety, but, according as you have been accustomed, passing by the ruin of a nation, and all the blood that hath been spilled by the king and his party, you

---

[39] The farthest the Commons went in this direction was on 1 February 1642, when they sent an oral message to the Lords asking them to join in a petition to the king requesting him to put the militia into the hands of men acceptable to parliament. The messenger was instructed to say that, 'if they will not join with this House now that things are brought to the last gasp . . . they must not expect this House to come to them again in this business' (*CJ*, II, 408). The Lords complied.

betake yourselves to a treaty with him, thereby putting him, that is but one single person, and a public officer of the Commonwealth, in competition with the whole body of the people, whom you represent, not considering that it is impossible for you to erect any authority equal to yourselves; and declared to all the world that you will not alter the ancient government from that of king, Lords and Commons, not once mentioning (in case of difference) which of them is supreme, but leaving that point (which was the chiefest cause of all our public differences, disturbances, wars and miseries) as uncertain as ever.

*   *   *

And whereas a personal treaty, or any treaty with the king, hath been long time held forth as the only means of a safe and well-grounded peace, it is well known to have been cried up principally by such as have been disaffected unto you, and though you have contradicted it yet it is believed that you much fear the issue; as you have cause sufficient, except you see greater alteration in the king and his party than is generally observed, there having never yet been any treaty with him but was accompanied with some underhand dealing; and whilst the present force upon him (though seeming liberty) will in time to come be certainly pleaded against all that shall or can be agreed upon. Nay, what can you confide in if you consider how he hath been provoked, and what former kings upon less provocations have done, after oaths, laws, charters, bonds, excommunications and all ties of reconciliations, to the destruction of all those that had provoked and opposed them; yea, when yourselves so soon as he had signed those bills in the beginning of this parliament saw cause to tell him that even about the time of passing those bills some design or other was on foot, which if it had taken effect would not only have rendered those bills fruitless but have reduced you [to] a worse condition of confusion than that wherein the parliament found you.

*   *   *

The truth is (and we see we must either now speak it [or] for ever be silent), we have long expected things of another nature from you, and such as we are confident would have given satisfaction to all serious people of all parties:

1. That you would have made good the Supreme [Authority] of the people in this honourable House from all pretence of negative voices, either in king or Lords.

2. That you would have made laws for election of representatives yearly and of course, without writ or summons.

3. That you would have set express times for their meeting, continuance and dissolution, [so] as not to exceed 40 or 50 days at the most, and to have fixed an expressed time for the ending of this present parliament.

4. That you would have exempted matters of religion and gospel from the

compulsive or restrictive power of any authority upon earth, and reserved to the Supreme Authority an uncompulsive power only of appointing a way for the public [worship], whereby abundance of misery, persecution and heart-burning would for ever be avoided.

5. That you would have disclaimed in yourselves and all future representatives a power of pressing and forcing any sort of men to serve in wars . . .

6. That you would have made both kings, queens, princes, dukes, earls, lords and all persons alike liable to every law of the land, made or to be made . . .

7. That you would have freed all commoners from the jurisdiction of the Lords in all cases, and to have taken care that all trials should be only of twelve sworn men, and no conviction but upon two or more sufficient known witnesses.

8. That you would have freed all men from being examined against themselves, and from being questioned or punished for doing of that against which no law hath been provided.

9. That you would have abbreviated the proceedings in law, mitigated and made certain the charge thereof in all particulars.

10. That you would have freed all trade and merchandising from all monopolising and engrossing, by companies or otherwise.

11. That you would have abolished excise, and all kinds of taxes except subsidies, the old and only just way of England.

12. That you would have laid open all late enclosures of fens and other commons, or have enclosed them only or chiefly to the benefit of the poor.

13. That you would have considered the many thousands that are ruined by perpetual imprisonment for debt, and provided to their enlargement.

14. That you would have ordered some effectual course to keep people from begging and beggary in so fruitful a nation as through God's blessing this is.

15. That you would have proportioned punishments more equal[ly] to offences, that so men's lives and estates might not be forfeited upon trivial and slight occasions.

16. That you would have removed the tedious burden of tithes, satisfying all impropriators and providing a more equal way of maintenance for the public ministers.

17. That you would have raised a stock of money out of those many confiscated estates you have had, for payment of those who contributed voluntarily above their abilities, before you have provided for those that disbursed out of their superfluities.

18. That you would have bound yourselves and all future parliaments from abolishing propriety, levelling men's estates, or making all things common.

19. That you would have declared what the duty or business of the kingly office is, and what not, and ascertained the revenue, past increase or diminution, that so there might never be more quarrels about the same.

20. That you would have rectified the election of public officers for the City of London, [and] of every particular company therein, restoring the commonalty thereof to their just rights, most unjustly withheld from them, to the producing and maintaining of corrupt interest opposite to common freedom, and exceedingly prejudicial to the trade and manufactures of this nation.

21. That you would have made full and ample reparations to all persons that had been oppressed by sentences in High Commission, Star Chamber and Council Board, or by any kind of monopolisers or projectors, and that out of the estates of those that were authors, actors or promoters of so intolerable mischiefs, and that without much attendance.

22. That you would have abolished all Committees, and have conveyed all businesses into the true method of the usual trials of the Commonwealth.

23. That you would not have followed the example of former tyrannous and superstitious parliaments, in making orders, ordinances or laws, or in appointing punishments concerning opinions or things supernatural, styling some blasphemies, others heresies,[40] when as you know yourselves easily mistaken, and that divine truths need no human helps to support them, such proceedings having been generally invented to divide the people amongst themselves and to affright men from that liberty of discourse by which corruption and tyranny would be soon discovered.

24. That you would have declared what the business of the Lords is, and ascertained their condition, not derogating from the liberties of other men, that so there might be an end of striving about the same.

25. That you would have done justice upon the capital authors and promoters of the former or late wars, many of them being under your power, considering that mercy to the wicked is cruelty to the innocent, and that all your lenity doth but make them the more insolent and presumptuous.

26. That you would have provided constant pay for the army, now under the command of the Lord General Fairfax, and given rules to all judges, and all other public officers throughout the land, for their indemnity, and for the saving harmless all that have any ways assisted you, or that have said or done anything against the king . . .

27. That you would have laid to heart all the abundance of innocent blood that hath been spilled, and the infinite spoil and havoc that hath been made of peaceable, harmless people by express commissions from the king, and seriously to have considered whether the justice of God be likely to be satisfied, or his yet continuing wrath appeased, by an Act of Oblivion.

---

[40] The reference is to an ordinance of 2 May 1648, Firth and Rait, I, 1133-6.

These and the like we have long time hoped you would have minded, and have made such an establishment for the general peace and contentful satisfaction of all sorts of people, as should have been to the happiness of all future generations, and which we most earnestly desire you would set yourselves speedily to effect, whereby the almost dying honour of this most honourable House would be again revived, and the hearts of your petitioners and all other well affected people be afresh renewed unto you . . .

Haller and Davies, *Leveller Tracts*, pp. 148–55

86. The Remonstrance of the Army, November 1648

A Remonstrance of his Excellency Thomas Lord Fairfax, Lord General of the Parliament's Forces, and of the General Council of Officers, held at St Albans the 16th of November 1648

Our tender regard to the privileges and freedom of parliament, on which our hopes of common freedom and right do much depend, and our late experience of what offence many, even honest men seem to have taken, and what advantage evil men have made, of our least interposing in any thing of civil consideration to the parliament, hath made us for a long time hitherto, as it should always make us even to the utmost extremity, to attend in silence the counsels and determinations of parliament concerning all matters of that nature whatsoever; but, finding you to have been of late upon those transactions of highest moment, whereupon the life or death of all our civil interest does depend, and that the public affairs in your hands . . . are brought to the utmost crisis of danger, which calls upon every man to contribute what help he can, and seeing no effectual help from elsewhere to appear, we cannot be . . . altogether silent, or wanting in aught we can honestly say or do to hold off impending ruin from an honest people and a good cause.

[This point was then developed, first in general terms, on the conditions under which it was legitimate for men to interfere in government, secondly in a review of the army's actions over the previous two years, stressing its public-spiritedness at all times, and deploring the campaign of slander against it, particularly in parliament (pp. 161–70). It then considered the personal treaty being negotiated with the king at Newport, and marshalled the arguments against it at great length, beginning (p. 174) with a discussion of ideal government.]

The sum of the public interest of a nation, in relation to common right and freedom, which has been the chief object of our contest, and in opposition to the tyranny and injustice of kings or others, we take to lie in these things following:

1st, That for all matters of supreme trust, or concernment to the safety and welfare of the whole, they have a common and supreme Council or parliament, and that as to the common behalf, who cannot all meet together themselves, to consist of Deputies or Representers, freely chosen by them, with as much equality as may be; and those elections to be successive and renewed, either at times certain and stated, or at the call of some subordinate standing Officer or Council instructed by them for that purpose, in the intervals of the Supreme, or else at both.

2dly, That the power of making laws, constitutions and offices, for the preservation and government of the whole, and of altering or repealing and abolishing the same, for the removal of any public grievance therein, and the power of final judgment concerning war or peace, the safety and welfare of the people, and all civil things whatsoever, without further appeal to any created standing power, and the supreme trust in relation to all such things, may rest in that Supreme Council, so as:

1. That the ordinary ordering and government of the people may be by such offices and administrations, and according to such laws and rules, as by that Council, or the Representative Body of the People therein, have been prescribed or allowed, and not otherwise.

2. That none of those extraordinary or arbitrary powers aforementioned may be exercised towards the People by any as of right, but by that Supreme Council, or the Representative Body of the People therein; nor without their advice and consent may any thing be imposed upon or taken from the People; or if it be otherwise attempted by any, that the People be not bound thereby but free, and the attempters punishable.

3. That those extraordinary powers, or any of them, may be exercised by that Supreme Council, or by the Representative Body of the People therein; and where they shall see cause to assume and exercise the same, in a matter which they find necessary for the safety or well being of the People, their proceedings and determinations therein may be binding and conclusive to the People, and to all officers of justice and ministers of state whatsoever; and that it may not be left in the will of the king, or any particular persons standing in their own interest, to oppose, make void or render ineffectual such their determinations or proceedings, and . . . that therefore the same Council or Representative Body therein, having the supreme trust, in all such cases where the offence or default is in public officers, abusing or failing their trust, or in any person whatsoever, if the offence extend to the prejudice of the public, may call such offenders to account, and distribute punishments to them, either according to the law, where it has provided, or their own judgment where it has not, and they find the offence, though not particularly provided against by particular laws, yet against the general Law of Reason or Nations, and the vindication of the public interest to require justice; and that in such case no

person whatsoever may be exempt from such account or punishment . . .

These things contain the sum or main of public interest; and as they are the ordinary subject of civil contests in all mixed states, where they happen betwixt the People and those that have assumed or claimed a standing privilege or prerogative over them, so they have been in this of ours. And against these matters of public interest this king hath, all along his reign, opposed, and given himself up to uphold and advance the interest of his and his posterity's will and power; first, that there might be no such Common Council, no parliaments at all to restrain or check him, but that all these matters of supreme trust, concerning safety and all things else, might rest in him and his breast alone, without limit from, or account to, any on earth; and that all those extraordinary and arbitrary powers over the People, their laws, liberties, properties, yea, their persons and consciences too, might be exercised at pleasure by himself, and such as he pleased to derive [?devise] the same unto; and as they were assumed, so how vastly and sadly ill they were exercised by him, to the prejudice and oppression of the People in general, and the ruin or persecution of all the Godly of the land, . . . surely . . . we need not yet make any verbal remembrance.

To support himself in that state or height of tyranny, and to make it absolute, he raised his first and second armies against his People in both kingdoms. When he found he could not keep up to that height to have all those extraordinary powers and matters of supreme absolute trust in himself alone, then he fell to play lower, that at least none of them might be exercised by any other without him, no not by all the trustees of the land, nor in any case, though ever so necessary for the relief or saving of the People; that if, according to his former claim, his People and parliament would not admit him positively to oppress or destroy them at his will, yet by this latter, they should have no power to redress a grievance, to provide for the freedom, welfare or so much as [the] immediate safety of themselves or the kingdom, but at and according to his pleasure; and for this . . . he raised his third army, and held them up so long and so much, to the spoil and near desolation of the kingdom, till God wholly broke them, and brought himself captive into your hands.

[Yet even then he had blocked all attempts to establish a permanent settlement, and had given himself no rest (p. 178) until he had secured help from abroad.]

. . . It came to this, he that before would not have allowed the parliament or kingdom a power for safety but at his will, would at least make you know that neither you nor the kingdom should have any peace or quiet without him, and that neither parliament nor any power on earth, whatever ills he had done, might for it attach or meddle with his sacred person, no, not so much as to secure him from opportunities of doing more. And for this last part of his interest his fourth army, the last war, was raised by commissions from himself to the prince, and from him to as many more as would take any, and for the same the Scots invasion was procured.

The pretext or quarrel in this last engagement seemed, as it were, to reach no higher than only to rescue his privileged person, and force the parliament yet, in a personal treaty, to seek peace at his will, and to let them see they could not otherwise have it, nor might do aught against his person, . . . though he make war and refuse peace never so long.

And for this last piece of his interest, as opposite and destructive to that of the public as any of the former, though a Divine Testimony has been borne against it, as full and more glorious, if possible, than before against any of the rest, as if God would thereby declare his designing of that person to justice; yet the parliament, after all this, restoring him, without any pre-satisfaction or security, unto a kind of liberty and state, only that he might appear in a capacity to treat, and then by treaty seeking their peace, and all their matters before contended for, and, through God, gained against him, to come now as concessions from his will, do clearly yield back that last piece of his claimed interest into his hands again . . .

[Aftr a brief excursus on religion (pp. 179–81) and Charles's particular iniquity in this regard, the Remonstrance turned (p. 182) to consider the Newport Treaty more closely.]

First, therefore, as to the goodness (which first implies the justness) of such an accommodation, we cannot but suppose,

1. That where a person, trusted with a limited power to rule according to laws, and by his trust, with express covenant and oath also, obliged to preserve and protect the rights and liberties of the People, for and by whom he is intrusted, shall not only pervert that trust, and abuse that power to the hurt and prejudice of the generality, and to the oppression, if not destruction, of many of them, but also by the advantage of that trust and power he hath shall rise to the assuming of hurtful powers which he never had committed to him, and indeed take away all those foundations of right and liberty, and of redress and remedy too, which the People had reserved from him, and to swallow up all into his own absolute will and power, to impose or take away, yea, to destroy at pleasure; and declining all appeal herein to the established equal judgment agreed upon, as it were betwixt him and his People in all emergent matters of difference between them, or to any judgment of men at all, shall fly to the way of force upon his trusting people, and attempt by it to uphold and establish himself in that absolute tyrannical power so assumed over them, and in the exercise thereof at pleasure – such a person, in so doing, does forfeit all that trust and power he had, and, absolving the People from the bonds of covenant

and peace betwixt him and them, does set them free to take their best advantage, and if he fall within their power to proceed in judgment against him, even for that alone, if there were no more.

2. That if after he is foiled in such an attempt, brought to quit that claim, to confess his offence therein, and give some verbal and legal assurances of remedy and future security, and his Parliament and People thereupon remitting or willing to forbear that advantage against him, the same person, so soon as he finds himself a little freed from the advantage which drew those confessions and concessions from him, shall go about to avoid or overthrow all again, . . . and resume and exercise again above, even sitting a parliament, all the exorbitant and unlimited powers he had so lately disclaimed, . . . and on these terms maintain a war many years against them, to the spilling of much blood, and desolation or spoil of a great part of the kingdom, try all means and interests, by divisions and parties stirred up within, and invasions from abroad, to lengthen it out longer, and after he was subdued, wholly in their power and at their mercy, to revive and renew it, multiplying disturbances, and never ceasing till he had wearied all friends in his own and neighbour nations, or so long as any hopes were left whereby possibly to prolong it; and all this merely to uphold the interest of his will and power against the common interest of his People; such a person in so doing (we may justly say is guilty of the highest treason against the highest law among men, but however) must needs be the author of that unjust war, and therein guilty of all the innocent blood spilt thereby, and of all the evils consequent or concomitant thereunto . . .

If indeed he hath acted such things, and . . . all for the particular interest of his will and power against the public interest of the kingdom, then (without mention or consideration of ought he has done against God and godliness, or godly men, and though we have touched but a few of those many moral or civil evils acted by him, which have been judged capital in several of his predecessors from whom he claims, yet) from that alone which is before spoken of, we may . . . conclude that he has been the author and continuer of a most unjust war, and is consequently guilty of all the treason it contains, and of all the innocent blood, rapine, spoil and mischief to the kingdom acted or occasioned thereby; and if so, how far the public justice of the kingdom can be satisfied, the blood, rapine, &c., avenged or expiated, and the wrath of God for the same appeased, without judgment executed against him, and consequently, how far an accommodation with him implying a restitution of him, when God hath given him so clearly into your power to do justice, can be just before God or good men (without so much as a judicial trial, or evident remorse appearing in him proportionable to the offence) we thus recommend to your saddest and most serious consideration, who must one day be accountable for your judgments here on earth to that which is the highest and most just.

[Charles's utter lack of remorse and contrition was then explored in detail (pp. 185–7), the conclusion being that any accommodation with him was pointless.]

What fruits can be hoped from such a reunion or renewed communion betwixt those contraries God hath once so separated, viz., of principles or affections of liberty, with principles of tyranny; principles of public interest, with principles of prerogative or particular interest; principles of zeal and power of godliness, with principles of formality and superstition in religion; we might say indeed, of Light with Darkness, Good with Evil; as would be implied in his restitution; to be, as it were, your head, your king again, and to have that high trust and influence in relation to our peace, rights and liberties, civil and religious, with the same principles and affections from which he hath so much and so long opposed them? For if his kingly office be not of use or trust in relation to them, what needs his restitution?

[History shows in general terms that unrepentant tyrants with their backs to the wall are never to be trusted (pp. 188–91), and Charles's own unreliability has been evident throughout his reign, and especially over the past two years (pp. 192–3). He is at liberty to argue, and is already arguing, that any treaty now signed is wrung from him by force, and can be renounced as soon as he is a free agent again (pp. 193–8). Moreover, they would play into Charles's hands by confirming his factitious reputation as a man of peace.]

The king comes in with the reputation among the People of having long graciously sought peace, though indeed ever since he found you in condition to oppose his force it was his interest and best play, and especially since you had beaten his force it was his necessary and only play. He comes with the reputation of having long sought it by a personal treaty, which at last has proved, as he prophecied, the only effectual means; and so you having so long denied that, and only plied him with peremptory propositions, and yet at last granting it, are in that self-condemnation rendered by his friends, as having deceitfully or unnecessarily continued burdens, and refused peace so long, in refusing that the king's way, in which you might as well have had it sooner as now . . . He comes also with the reputation of having granted, for peace sake, all that you, as unwilling to peace, have rigidly stood upon, although, when it is summed up, it will appear of very little advantage or security to the public interest . . . However, with the People he carries these and the like points of reputation before him, and wants not trumpets everywhere to blaze them sufficiently to his renown, and your own reproach. Under such banners of love and honour, he comes in the only true Father of his People, you being proved the cruel foster-fathers, he the repairer of the breaches which you had made, he the restorer of their beloved peace, ease and freedoms, which you, as his creatures render it, had ravished or cheated them of thus long, he the restorer of their trade and plenty too, which you had thus long obstructed, he as a conqueror in sufferings and patience, a denyer of himself for the good of his People, and what not that is glorious and endearing.

[In these circumstances it would be impossible for parliament to curb the king if he went back to his old ways; indeed, the signing of such a treaty would be followed by a demobilisation, and any attempt to keep a precautionary army in being would be deeply resented, if only because it would imply the continuance of high taxation (pp. 200–4.) The king's potential support was considerable, in Scotland and Ireland as well as in England, despite his poor showing in the Second Civil War, and peace would give him the opportunity of fomenting divisions amongst his opponents which were already evident (pp. 204–8). Moreover, if the present parliament were continued indefinitely – and the Newport Treaty made no provision for its dissolution, or the proper and recurrent election of its successors – the patronage at the king's disposal, and the weight of his influence, in by-elections as well as at Westminster, would soon give him complete control of it (pp. 208–10). But above all, an accommodation with Charles was prohibited by basic considerations of justice.]

Suppose the best constitutions and strictest laws imaginable in any state, yet their insufficiency and impotency as to the preserving of public interest, without a power to punish those that violate it and them, or where persons in power to prejudice the same, especially if in fixed and lasting power, shall stand privileged from being punishable, whatever they do, is obvious to each considering man . . . Now in our present case, after so many, so great and lasting violations [of the public interest] committed by the king and by his procurement, and after his so long and obstinate maintenance thereof, and persistance therein, and so many refusals of that poor satisfaction and security you now desire, . . . we say, after all this, for you, the Supreme Judicatory of the kingdom, when he is, through the just hand of God, in your power to do justice upon, yet still to decline that way, and instead thereof, to seek again to him your prisoner in the way of treaty, to receive what satisfaction and security you can get as concessions from him, and thereupon . . . to re-admit himself to the throne with safety, freedom and honour; what can this be understood to speak less than that . . . he is indeed above any human justice, and not accountable to or punishable by any power on earth, whatever he does . . . You would also by such exemption of him, and in such a case, proclaim the like perpetual exemption to him and his posterity, . . . since none can be imagined more pregnant or ripe for justice than this already is, and would therein give the most authentic testimony and seal that ever was to all those destructive court maxims concerning the absolute impunity of kings, their accountableness to none on earth, and that they cannot err, do wrong, &c., which principles, . . . as they were begot by the blasphemous arrogance of tyrants upon servile parasites, and fostered only by slavish or ignorant people, and remain in our law books as heirlooms only of the Conquest, so they serve for nothing but to establish that which begot them, tyranny, and to give kings (who, so far as they claim otherwise than by conquest, are but ministers intrusted for righteousness and peace), the highest privilege, encouragement and invitation to do wrong, and make war, even upon their own People, as their corrupt wills or lusts shall prompt them. If therefore our kings claim by right of conquest, God hath given you the same against them, and more righteous, by how much that, on their parts, was extended to a forcible dominion over the People, which originally or naturally they had not, and ours but to a deliverance from that bondage, into that state of right and freedom which was naturally and morally due to us before. If they claim from immediate divine designation, let them show it; if from neither, but as by consent entrusted by and for the People, let them embrace and partake the conditions of such; and not as if the whole People were made only for them, and to serve their lusts, or had, if not their being, yet all their civil endowments by and from them.

[Returning to the current negotiations, the Remonstrance pointed out that no agreement would necessarily bind Charles's followers (pp. 231–15), who were as dangerous as he, and could claim the same immunity. Having finally denounced these negotiations (p. 216) as evil and dangerous, it proceeded to show at great length how they differed from previous negotiations with the king in which the army itself had taken part (pp. 216–18). It also demonstrated (pp. 219–26) that the Solemn League and Covenant, which had pledged them all to seek an accommodation with the king, was no longer applicable. Having thus cleared the way, it called upon parliament to abandon its present policy (p. 226).]

We conceive and hope that, from what hath before been said, you may find abundant cause to forbear any further proceeding in this evil and most dangerous treaty, and to return to your former grounds in the Votes of No Addresses, and thereupon proceed to the settling and securing of the kingdom without and against the king, upon such foundations as hereafter are tendered . . . [and] that it may be expressly declared and provided by you that . . . the person of the king may and shall be proceeded against in a way of justice, for the blood spilt, and the other evils and mischiefs done by him, or by his commission, command or procurement, and in order thereto that he be kept in safe custody as formerly . . . [and that this extend to all his followers, servants and agents].

[It then (pp. 228ff) made the following specific proposals.]

1. That the capital and grand author of our troubles, the person of the King, by whose commissions, commands or procurement, and in whose behalf, and

for whose interest only, of will and power, all our wars and troubles have been, with all the miseries attending them, may be speedily brought to justice for the treason, blood and mischief he is therein guilty of.

2. [That the Prince of Wales and Duke of York be outlawed, though with some prospect of pardon on submission, and the Crown estates be confiscated for public uses.]

3. That, for further satisfaction to public justice, capital punishment may be speedily executed upon a competent number of his chief instruments also, both in the former and latter war; and for that purpose, that some such, of both sorts, may be pitched upon to be made examples of justice in that kind, as are really in your hands or reach, so as their exception from pardon may not be a mockery of justice in the face of God and men.

4. [That a day be set for the submission of the remaining royalists, who, after paying their fines, should be restored to their estates and given legal immunity and full civil rights, except that they should be barred from public office and from voting in parliamentary elections, 'at least for a competent number of years'. The remainder to be attainted in perpetuity, and their estates confiscated.]

5. [That the arrears of army pay, and other public debts, be speedily settled.]

[Next (pp. 232ff.) the Remonstrance made its proposals 'in order to the general satisfaction and settling of the kingdom'.]

1. That you would set some reasonable and certain period to your own power, by which time that great and supreme trust reposed in you shall be returned into the hands of the People, for and from whom you received it, that so you may give them satisfaction and assurance, that what you have contended for against the king, for which they have been put to so much trouble, cost and loss of blood, hath been only for their liberties and common interest, and not for your own personal interest or power.

2. That with a period to this parliament, to be assigned as short as may be with safety to the kingdom and public interest thereof, there may be a sound settlement of the peace and future government of the kingdom, upon grounds of common right, freedom and safety, to the effect here following:

First, That from the end of this, there may be a certain succession of future parliaments, annual or biennial, with secure provision,

1st, For the certainty of their sitting, meeting and ending.

2dly, For the equal distribution of elections thereunto, to render the House of Commons, as near as may be, an equal Representative of the whole People electing.

3dly, For the certainty of the People's meeting, according to such distribution, to elect, and for their full freedom in elections, [it be] provided, that none who have engaged or shall engage in war against the right of the parliament, and interest of the kingdom therein, or have adhered to the enemies thereof, may be capable of electing or being elected, at least during a competent number of years, nor any other who shall oppose, or not join in agreement to this settlement.

4thly, For future clearing and ascertaining the power of the said Representatives, in order to which that it be declared that, as to the interest of the People of England, such Representatives have, and shall have, the supreme power and trust as to the making of laws, constitutions and offices, for the ordering, preservation and government of the whole, and as to the altering, repealing or abolishing of the same, the making of war or peace, and as to the highest and final judgment in all civil things, without further appeal to any created standing power; and that all the People of this nation, and all officers of justice and ministers of state, as such, shall in all such things be accountable and subject thereunto, and bound and concluded thereby. Provided that,

1. They may not censure or question any man after the end of this parliament for any thing said or done in reference to the late wars, or public differences, saving in execution of such determinations of this Parliament, as shall be left in force at the ending thereof, in relation to such as have served the king against parliament.

2. They may not render up, or give, or take away any of the foundations of common right, liberty or safety contained in this settlement and Agreement, but that the power of these two things last mentioned shall be always understood to be reserved from, and not entrusted to, the said Representatives.

5thly, For liberty of entering dissents in the said Representatives, that in case of corruption or abuse in these matters of highest trust, the People may be in capacity to know who are free thereof and who guilty; to the end only they may avoid the further trusting of such; but without further penalty to any for their free judgments there.[41]

Secondly, That no king be hereafter admitted but upon the election of, and as upon trust from the People, by such their Representatives, nor without first disclaiming and disavowing all pretence to a negative voice, against the determinations of the said Representatives or Commons in Parliament; and that to be done in some certain form, more clear than heretofore in the Coronation Oath.

These matters of general settlement, viz., that concerning a period to this parliament, and the other particulars thence following hitherto, we propound

---

[41] The Levellers and their allies seemed to be under the impression that this was allowed in the Scots Estates, as it was in the English House of Lords, but they were mistaken. (I am grateful for the advice of Dr David Stevenson on this point.)

to be declared and provided by this parliament, or by authority of the Commons therein, and to be further established by a Contract or Agreement of the People, with their subscriptions thereunto; and that withal it may be provided that none be capable of any benefit by the Agreement who shall not consent and subscribe thereunto, nor any king be admitted to the crown, or other person to any office or place of public trust, without express accord and subscription to the same.

[All this being done, the kingdom would be returned to peace and quiet, and the army itself could be disbanded; a prospect it viewed with equanimity provided its just demands as to pay and indemnity were met. The Remonstrance closed (pp. 235ff.) with a final exhortation to parliament to address itself to its proper business.]

We shall therefore earnestly desire that these things may be minded and prosecuted effectually, and that nothing may interrupt them, save what shall be for immediate and necessary safety; and that to avoid interruptions from such things as are not necessary, or less proper for parliamentary considerations or debates, you will leave all private matters, and things of ordinary justice and right, to the laws and present proper officers and administrations [*sic*] thereof, until better can be provided, and commit all ordinary matters of state to the management of a fit Council of State, sufficiently empowered for that purpose, and assisted with the addition of some merchants, in relation to the balancing, security and advance of trade, so as you may be more free for the present to attend those aforesaid considerations of public justice, and the settlement of the kingdom upon just and safe foundations of public interest; and that when you have effectuated them, or put them into a way of effect, you may, for the aftertime of this parliament's continuance, more entirely apply your counsels to such other things as are the most proper work of parliaments, and by and for which parliaments have had their esteem in this nation, and the kingdom most benefit by them, viz., the reformation of evils and inconveniences in the present laws and administration thereof, the redress of abuses and supplying of defects therein, and the making of better constitutions for the well government and prosperity of the nation, as also the due proportioning of rates, and providing of monies, in the most equal and least grievous ways, for all the necessary uses of the public, and the like. And in order to such things, that you would, in due time and place, viz., after public justice and the general settlement, consider such special overtures of that kind as have been tendered to you in the Petitions of well-wishers to the public good, and particularly in that large Petition from many about London, dated the 11th of September last,[42] and also what shall be tendered of the like kind from others, that so what is really for the remedy of common grievances, or

---

[42] The Levellers' Humble Petition, of course, no. **85** above.

the advancement of common good, may not be slighted or neglected, but that evils in that kind being removed, and good things ordained and provided by you for the ease, benefit and prosperity of the People in all things possible, you may, when you come to lay down your trust, leave a good savour behind you, both to the name of parliaments, and also of men professing godliness, so much as this House hath done, and therein chiefly to the honour of Almighty God, who hath, in his rich grace and mercy, done such wonders for you and us.

OPH, xviii, 161-238

87. Commons' Resolutions, 4 January 1649

Resolved, &c. That the Commons of England, in parliament assembled, do declare, That the people are, under God, the original of all just power:

And do also declare, That the Commons of England, in parliament assembled, being chosen by, and representing the people, have the supreme power in this nation:

And do also declare, That whatever is enacted, or declared for law, by the Commons, in parliament assembled, hath the force of law; and all the people of this nation are concluded thereby, although the consent and concurrence of king, or House of Peers, be not had thereunto.   *CJ*, vi 111

88. The end of Charles I

(a) *His Majesty's Reasons against the Pretended Jurisdiction of the High Court of Justice, which he intended to have delivered in writing on Monday, January 22, 1648[9] but was not permitted.*[43]

Having already made my protestations not only against the illegality of this pretended court, but also that no earthly power can justly call me, who am your king, in question as a delinquent, I would not any more open my mouth upon this occasion, more than to refer myself to what I have spoken, were I in this case alone concerned. For how can any free-born subject of England call life, or anything he professeth [?possesseth] his own, if power without right daily make new, and abrogate the old and fundamental, law of the land, which I now take to be the present case? . . . I will show you the reason why I am confident you cannot judge me, nor indeed the meanest man in England, for I will not (like you) without showing a reason seek to impose a belief upon my subjects.

There is no proceeding just against any man but what is warranted either by God's laws or the municipal laws of the country where he lives. Now I am

[43] Published, illegally of course, on 5 February. The indictment, the sentence of the court and the death warrant are printed in *GCD*, pp. 371-4, 377-80.

most confident this day's proceedings cannot be warranted by God's law, for on the contrary the authority of obedience unto kings is clearly warranted and strictly commanded both in the Old and New Testaments . . . Then for the law of the land, I am no less confident that no learned lawyer will affirm that an impeachment can lie against the king, they all going in his name . . . Besides, the law upon which you ground your proceedings must be either old or new: if old, show it; if new, tell what authority warranted by the fundamental laws of the land hath made it, and when. But how the House of Commons can erect a court of judicature, which was never one itself, . . . I leave to God and the world to judge . . .

And admitting, but not granting, that the people of England's commission could grant your pretended power, I see nothing you can show for that. For certainly you never asked the question of the tenth man in the kingdom. And in this way you manifestly wrong even the poorest ploughman, if you demand not his free consent. Nor can you pretend any colour for this your pretended commission without the consent at least of the major part of every man in England, of whatsoever quality or condition, which I am sure you never went about to seek, so far are you from having it. Thus you see I speak not for my own right alone, as I am your king, but also for the true liberty of all my subjects, which consists not in the power of government, but in living under such laws, such a government, as may give themselves the best assurance of their lives and the propriety of their goods . . .

I am against my will brought hither, where, since I am come, [I] cannot but to my power defend the ancient laws and liberty of this kingdom, together with my own just right . . . Besides all this, the peace of the kingdom is not the least in my thoughts, and what hope of settlement is there so long as power reigns without rule or law, changing the whole frame of that government under which this kingdom hath flourished for many hundred years? . . . And believe it, the commons of England will not thank you for this change, for they will remember how happy they have been of late years under the reign of Queen Elizabeth, the king my father, and myself, until the beginning of these unhappy troubles, and will have cause to doubt that they shall never be so happy under any new. And by this time it will be too sensibly evident, that the arms I took up were only to defend the fundamental laws of the kingdom against those who have supposed my power hath totally changed the ancient government.   Muddiman, *Trial of Charles I*, pp. 231–2

(b) King Charles his Speech, made upon the Scaffold at Whitehall Gate immediately before his Execution, on Tuesday the 30th of January 1648[9][44]

. . . I could hold my peace very well, if I did not think that holding my peace would make some men think I did submit to the guilt as well as the

[44] Published the same day, and in a second edition on 23 February.

punishment. But I think it is my duty, to God first and to my country, to clear myself both as an honest man and a good king, and a good christian.

I shall begin first with my innocence. In truth I think it not very needful for me to insist long upon this, for all the world knows that I never did begin a war with the two Houses of Parliament. And I call God to witness, to whom I must shortly make an account, that I never did intend for to encroach upon their privileges. They began upon me; it is the militia they began upon. They confessed that the militia was mine, but they thought it fit for to have it from me. And, to be short, if anybody will look at the dates of commissions, of their commissions and mine, and likewise to the declarations, [they] will see clearly that they began these unhappy troubles, not I. So that as [to] the guilt of these enormous crimes that are laid against me, I hope in God that God will clear me of it – I will not, I am in charity. God forbid that I should lay it upon the two Houses of Parliament; there is no necessity of [that] either. I hope they are free of this guilt. For I believe that ill instruments between them and me has [sic] been the chief cause of all this bloodshed . . .

Now, for to show you that I am a good christian. I hope there is a good man [indicating Bishop Juxon, who was with him] that will bear me witness that I have forgiven all the world, and even those in particular that hath been the chief causes of my death. Who they are, God knows, I do not desire to know; God forgive them. But this is not all, my charity must go further. I wish that they may repent, for indeed they have committed a great sin in that particular. I pray God, with St Stephen, that this be not laid to their charge. Nay, not only so, but that they may take the right way to the peace of the kingdom, for my charity commands me not only to forgive particular men, but my charity commands me to endeavour to the last gasp the peace of the kingdom . . .

Now sirs, I must show you both how you are out of the way and [what] will put you in a way. First, you are out of the way, for certainly all the way you have ever had yet, as I could find by anything, is by way of conquest. Certainly this is an ill way, for conquest, sir, in my opinion is never just, except there be a good just cause, either for matter of wrong or just title. And then if you go beyond it, the first quarrel that you have to it, that makes it unjust at the end that was just at the first . . . Believe it, you will never do right, nor God will never prosper you, until you give God his due, the king his due (that is, my successors) and the people their due. I am as much for them as any of you.

You must give God his due by regulating rightly his Church (according to the Scripture), which is now out of order . . . A national synod freely called, freely debating among themselves, must settle this, when that every opinion is freely and clearly heard.

For the king, . . . the laws of the land will clearly instruct you for that. Therefore because it concerns my own particular, I only give you a touch of it.

For the people. And truly I desire their liberty and freedom as much as anybody whomsoever. But I must tell you that their liberty and freedom consists in having of government; those laws by which their life and their goods may be most their own. It is not for having share in government, sir, that is nothing pertaining to them. A subject and a sovereign are clean different things. And therefore until they do that – I mean, that you do put the people in that liberty as I say, certainly they will never enjoy themselves.

Sirs, it was for this that now I am come here. If I would have given way to an arbitrary way, for to have all the laws changed according to the power of the sword, I needed not to have come here. And therefore I tell you, and I pray God it be not laid to your charge, that I am the martyr of the people . . .

I have delivered my conscience. I pray God that you do take those courses that are best for the good of the kingdom and your own salvation.

Ibid., pp. 261–3

CHAPTER 8

THE INTERREGNUM 1649-60

On 6 February 1649 the House of Commons voted to abolish the House of Lords, thus constituting itself the whole of parliament, and next day the monarchy, though the necessary statutes were not passed until mid March, (89). On 11 February, however, an act was passed changing the name of King's Bench to 'Upper Bench', and on the 17th another act removed the word 'king' from all legal documents and substituted the grandiose term 'The Keepers of the Liberties of England'; even the King's Highway was re-named 'The Common Highway'.[1] On 13 February the executive functions of monarchy were vested for one year in a Council of State numbering 40, 31 of them Members of Parliament (*GCD*, pp. 381-3), and on 10 March the Council elected its first president. However, the process of constitutional revision was ragged and haphazard, and it was not until 19 May that an act was passed declaring England to be 'a Commonwealth or Free-State' (*GCD*, p. 388).

The institution of this narrow, oligarchic, self-perpetuating government brought a howl of protest from the Levellers,[2] but a series of mutinies in May led Fairfax to purge them from the army altogether and on 30 July Cromwell sailed for Dublin. During the next two years he and his generals carried the arms of the republic to success after success. Irish resistance was smashed by Cromwell in 1649 and 1650, and mopped up by Ireton in 1651. The Scots were defeated at Dunbar in 1650, and again at Worcester a year later, when they were led by Charles II in person. Both countries were put under military rule and in 1654 Scotland and England were united, in ironic fulfilment of James I's plans. Meanwhile the outlying islands – Jersey, Scilly, Man – were cleared, and the Caribbean plantations and the colonies of the American South came to heel after Worcester, that 'crowning mercy'.

But the regicides found it more difficult to establish their authority in England itself. Six High Court judges refused to accept their new patents, and their places were not filled until June 1649. Even greater difficulty was experienced in finding a City government that would support the new order.[3] In October Lilburne was brought to trial before a special judicial commission on a charge of treason, only to be acquitted; at the other extreme it was well known that Fairfax had not approved Charles's execution and was unwilling to give his unqualified support to the republic. In these circumstances the government decided (with no great reluctance) that it could not fulfil its pledge to dissolve parliament as soon as possible and hold fresh elections. Moreover, the maintenance of large forces by land and sea, in Ireland and Scotland as

---

[1] Firth and Rait, II, 6-9; *CJ*, VI, 138.

[2] See Lilburne's *England's New Chains Discovered*, presented to the Rump on 26 February, printed Haller and Davies, *Leveller Tracts*, pp. 156ff.

[3] Gardiner, *Commonwealth and Protectorate*, I, 42-3, 65.

well as in England, obliged them to continue the bitterly unpopular taxation of the war years, and in this way the officers and civilians at Westminster became ever more dependent one upon the other; and though parliament had to make concessions here and there, the steady pressure of the Council of Officers for the implementation of the programme of social and legal reform which they had expected would follow the inauguration of the new millennium had little effect.[4]

In September 1649 Parliament passed an act to relieve those imprisoned for debt,[5] but it was not until November 1650 that the courts were ordered to abandon the use of Law French.[6] On the key question of religion the Rump was particularly dilatory, and in June 1649 it passed an act 'for the maintenance of preaching ministers' which made express provision for the payment of tithe, though ever since 1647 the army had been on record as demanding its abolition.[7] In August parliament grudgingly decided that in the future government of the Church (not yet decided) tithes would not be compulsory, but until then they were, and it ignored a petition from the Council of Officers on 16 August requesting the active suppression of drunkenness, swearing and 'uncleanness' in general. On 28 September it even issued a public declaration that it would never allow 'a universal toleration'.[8]

Meanwhile the unpopularity of the government, and the threat from Scotland, had the paradoxical effect of setting the Rump more firmly in the saddle. On 11 October 1649, ostensibly in an attempt to frustrate a hostile electorate, it decreed that all its Members, present and future, must take an Engagement to the Commonwealth without king or House of Lords. The following day this was extended to all office-holders, state pensioners, local government officials, army and navy officers, judges, barristers, clergy, schoolmasters, and fellows of the universities.[9] On 2 January 1650 an act was passed confirming this, and imposing the oath on the whole of the male population over the age of 18 (**90**). How far this was enforced it is difficult to say; partly as a result of Fairfax's uncooperative attitude an act had to be passed postponing the deadline for a month;[10] but evidently parliament wanted to divide the whole nation into the sheep and the goats as the Act of Classes had divided Scotland. Meanwhile the House adopted a recommendation from its standing committee on elections that sitting Members should retain their seats even at a general election.[11]

This was not enacted as law, but the Rump's intentions were now clear, and the army was not pacified by an act for the better observation of the Lord's Day, in April 1650,[12] followed the next month by a remarkable statute which made incest and adultery punishable by death and fornication by three months' imprisonment,[13] and

[4] The prime authority for this and all other aspects of the Rump is now Blair Worden's *The Rump Parliament* (Cambridge 1974).

[5] An act 'for discharging poor prisoners unable to satisfy their creditors' (Firth and Rait, II, 240–1). Re-enacted in an expanded form on 21 December (*ibid.*, 321–4).

[6] *Ibid.*, II, 455–6 (22 November 1650).

[7] *Ibid.*, II 142–8. Cf. The Heads of the Proposals, p. 273 above, and Margaret James, 'The Tithes Controversy in the English Revolution', *History*, XXVI (1941), 1–18.

[8] Gardiner, *op. cit.*, I, 192–3.   [9] *CJ*, VI 306–7.   [10] Firth and Rait, II, 348 (23 February).

[11] *CJ*, VI, 345.   [12] Firth and Rait, II, 383–7 (19 April).

[13] *Ibid.*, 387–9 (10 May). See Keith Thomas, 'The Puritans and Adultery: the Act of 1650 Reconsidered', Pennington and Thomas, *Puritans and Revolutionaries*, pp. 257–82.

in June by an act laying down fines, graduated according to rank and social status, for 'profane swearing and cursing'.[14] It was not until the autumn, with Charles II at Edinburgh and an invasion imminent, that parliament turned to the more serious part of the army's religious programme. The Blasphemy Act of 9 August, by outlawing only those who asserted that they or their leader was the reincarnation of Christ and those who taught that any sin was permitted the Elect, legalised by implication any less outrageous religious deviation.[15] On 27 September, in the wake of Dunbar, all standing legislation enforcing attendance at church was at last repealed (GCD, pp. 391–4). Under further pressure from the army, parliament even revitalised its standing committee on the reform of the Common Law.

But it took another 12 months, and the victory at Worcester, to produce another reluctant jerk forward. In November 1651 a rough bargain was struck. The army establishment was to be reduced, and in return the Rump abandoned its plan to give its Members seats in perpetuity; but even then it postponed the date of its dissolution to 3 November 1654. The demand that it account in detail for all the taxes collected in its name since 1642 speeded the passage of a long-delayed Act of Oblivion in February 1652.[16]

Religion, however, remained the most controversial topic, and one which divided the Council of Officers as well as parliament. Cromwell supported the dean of Christ Church, John Owen, who favoured a state church accompanied by a broad degree of toleration, and he strongly influenced the Committee for the Propagation of the Gospel appointed by parliament in February 1652, which made its report a year later. It recommended no doctrinal test, though it added socinianism (unitarianism) to the heresies already proscribed in the Blasphemy Act. It advised the creation of two committees, of laymen and clergy, to examine candidates for the ministry and remove incumbent clergymen deemed unsuitable – the 'Triers' and the 'Ejectors', as they were later called. Most controversial of all, it assumed the continuance of tithes and private patronage.[17] The Rump's deliberations on the matter were interrupted in April 1653, and it was left to Cromwell to set up the Triers and the Ejectors the following year (92).

The outbreak of war with Holland in June 1652 might have been expected to damp down the controversy between the army and parliament, but in fact the nature of the war left the land forces as idle as ever, and a prey to all manner of frustrations and discontents. Thus on 13 August the Council of Officers presented yet another strongly worded petition to the Rump calling for the implementation of the programme of 1647: that parliament dissolve itself, handing over to its successor the task of reforming the law, reducing the excise, publishing its accounts, settling the army's arrears of pay, abolishing tithes, suppressing vagabondage, and so on.[18] It is an astonishing demonstration of the army's impotence, at a time when it was supposed to be in a position to dictate its own terms, that it had been pushing this programme for five years now without result.

---

[14] Firth and Rait, II, 393–6 (28 June).   [15] Ibid., 409–12.

[16] Ibid., 565. Even then, this did not satisfy one of the officers' main grievances, parliament's setting aside of articles of surrender concluded in good faith with royalist commanders.

[17] CJ, VII, 258–9.

[18] Summarised in Gardiner, Commonwealth and Protectorate, II, 167–8.

Cromwell persuaded the Council of Officers to drop their peremptory demand for an immediate dissolution, but parliament tacitly abandoned the terminal date 3 November 1654 and on 14 September appointed a new Committee on Elections. Much now depended on Cromwell. His prestige, high enough in 1649, had been rising steadily ever since, and the retirement of Fairfax in 1650 had left him without a rival. But he was always aware of the fact that what little constitutional or legal authority survived in the England of 1652 was still vested in the Rump, that tiny fragment of a freely elected parliament. He made no move, and he restrained his followers from moving, until his hand was forced. In April 1653 the leaders of the Rump produced another Bill of Elections. It has not survived, and its contents are still a matter for speculation. It almost certainly did not perpetuate the sitting Members, though Cromwell may have thought it did. Alternatively, he may have thought it offered insufficient safeguards against a royalist, or at least a conservative, reaction in the elections; his subsequent explanation (93) suggests that what he most objected to was the Rump's proposal to hand over power directly to its successor, thus evading any attempt to screen its membership or impose terms upon it.[19] However this may be, and despite his famous saying, 'I have sought the Lord night and day, that he would rather slay me than put me upon the doing of this work', his decision to come down to Westminster on 20 April 1653 with a company of soldiers and expel parliament by force has all the marks of haste and lack of judgment.

He was fortunate. There was very little public reaction, and even the judges soothed their consciences by pretending that parliament was only temporarily interrupted. The Long Parliament had long outlived its usefulness, and the remark of Marchamount Nedham that, 'Parliaments always sitting are no more agreeable to the temper of this people, than it is to a natural body to take always physic instead of food', no doubt struck a popular chord, and the events of 1647 to 1653 had consistently shown that it was unwilling to effect the fundamental reforms of the constitution which the radicals, in the army and without, felt to be morally imperative. As Worden has remarked, 'Parliament's objection to both Charles I and the Cromwellian Army was that they had policies: that they wished to change the world rather than leave it as it was'; its preferred aim was 'to create, through political means, a world safe from politics'.[20]

But the forcible dissolution of the Rump had serious constitutional implications, of which Cromwell was well aware. When the Council of Officers had called on 11 March for just this course of action he and Desborough had asked them, 'if they destroyed that parliament what they should call themselves, a State they could not be? They answered that they would call a new parliament. Then, says the general, the parliament is not the supreme power, but that is the supreme power that calls it.'[21]

Cromwell was right. All the constitutional experiments that followed were initiated by him and his officers, and the supreme authority they assumed was always

[19] Worden, *op. cit.*, pp. 372ff. The whole question is re-examined by A. H. Woolrych, *Commonwealth to Protectorate* (Oxford 1982), ch. 3. (There were, of course, other apologias than Cromwell's own; one of them, issued only two days later by the Council of Officers, is printed in *GCD*, pp. 400–4.)

[20] Worden *op. cit.*, p. 379. For Nedham see *A True State of the Case of the Commonwealth* (1653), p. 23.

[21] Qu. C. H. Firth, 'Cromwell and the Expulsion of the Long Parliament', *EHR*, VIII (1893), 528.

resisted by elected parliaments which claimed to represent the nation at large. The removal in 1654 of religious visionaries like Thomas Harrison and dedicated republicans like Edmund Ludlow only exposed the rest of the army high command as ruthless politiques, without principles or convictions, determined to secure by any means that offered the continuation of their own authority. They were every bit as bad, in fact, as the Rump. Cromwell might have retired into private life, as Fairfax had done, but that would have been to abandon the nation to probable chaos and the possible return of the Stuarts. Moreover, he was inspired by the sincere belief that he had been singled out by God for a high purpose, a belief confirmed by his great victories in 1650 and 51.

Indeed, from April to July 1653 England was simply ruled by Cromwell in his capacity as commander-in-chief of the armed forces. His first thought was to summon a nominated assembly, previously in his mind as a bridge between the Long Parliament and the new. In June 1653 140 men (129 from England and Wales, five for Scotland and six for Ireland) were selected by Cromwell and the Council of Officers, and summoned to Whitehall on 4 July, 'that the peace, safety and good government of this Commonwealth should be provided for'.[22] The use of the term 'parliament' was carefully avoided, but the new assembly at once assumed that title and removed itself to the Parliament House at Westminster.

The experiment was a dismal failure. The Nominated Parliament[23] was swayed by a minority of fanatics, which at once began to put into operation the radical reforms demanded by so many of the sects. They alienated the lawyers by abolishing the Court of Chancery outright and bringing forward proposals to codify the Common Law. They offended the army by suggesting that to reduce taxation all officers should serve for a year without pay, and early in December they rejected the report of the Committee for the Propagation of the Gospel and brought in a bill to abolish all ecclesiastical patronage. This was enough for the moderates. Despite the *ad hoc* method of selection from above, this assembly still contained a majority of 'normal' parliamentary gentry, of the kind which had been elected for generations before and would be elected for generations after. They went down to the House early on 12 December and voted to surrender their authority to the Lord General, whence it came.

Cromwell was disappointed, but not surprised, and he was ready with an Instrument of Government, which had been prepared by John Lambert and the Council of Officers (**91**). On 16 December Cromwell took the oath as Lord Protector and the Instrument was published.

It was a sensible, workmanlike document which tried to translate into action, in very different circumstances, the Heads of the Proposals of 1647 (no. **83**, p. 268 above). The executive was vested in a Protector, advised and assisted by triennial parliaments, which must each sit for at least five months. Parliament – consisting only of a lower house, of course – was to be elected from constituencies redistributed and reformed along lines laid down by Ireton and the Levellers. Some 'decayed' boroughs were

---

[22] *GCD*, p. 405. The hardy myth that the Members were chosen from lists sent up by sectarian congregations in the provinces has been dispelled by Woolrych, *op. cit.*, ch. 4.
[23] The nickname 'Barebones' came later. The prime authority now, of course, is Woolrych, *op. cit.*, chs. 6–10.

suppressed, many more were reduced to one Member each, and some of the surplus seats thus created were distributed amongst the counties (§ x), where the franchise was now limited to those having £200 in real or personal property (§ XVIII). Yet the overall number of Members was reduced to 400 from England and Wales, plus 30 each from Scotland and Ireland (§ IX). Those elected must be 'of known integrity', etc. (§ XVII), but otherwise there were few restrictions on candidates, except that royalist 'delinquents' could not elect or be elected to the first four parliaments.[24]

The resultant changes in the composition of the House were more startling than might appear at first glance. The number of borough Members was reduced from 419 to 136, while county Members now took 264 out of 400 seats, as against 90 out of 509 in the Long Parliament. The percentage of borough Members dropped from 83 to 34, while the percentage of county Members rose from 17 to 66.[25] The result was a parliament of more than ordinarily independent country gentry. The officers had planned an independent parliament, of course; they had not foreseen that it would be independent of them. A machinery devised by Ireton to guard the liberties of the people from Charles I was now used to harass Cromwell.

To parliament, when it was elected, the most offensive aspect of the Instrument was its exaltation of the Protector's authority; the more so since this was a constitution built around one man. Had Cromwell not been available, the settlement would clearly have been very different. He had no veto on legislation, unless it infringed the Instrument itself, but he could issue ordinances which had the force of law until or unless they were rejected by his first parliament, which in this case was not due to sit until September 1654 (§ XXX). Moreover, the Instrument granted him £200,000 a year for the expenses of the civil administration, plus maintenance for a standing army of 10,000 horse and 20,000 foot, none of which was subject to amendment by parliament (§ XXVII); he was also granted the remainder of the Crown lands and other perquisites of royalty (§ XXXI). The Council of State was designed as a brake on executive authority, but 15 of its members were named in the Instrument, and subsequent vacancies were to be filled by a cumbersome method obviously open to manipulation (§ XXV). The chief officers of state were to be chosen with 'the approbation of parliament', a sufficiently vague term (§ XXXIV), and in the absence of any statement to the contrary it must be assumed that all other appointments were in the hands of the Protector. Finally, though this was a constitution imposed by men having no relevant legal authority, there was no provision for its revision or amendment; indeed, the Protector had a veto over legislation to that end (§ XXIV). Difficulties were foreseen, and the returning officers were required to certify, on the electors' behalf, 'that the person elected shall not have power to alter the government as it is hereby settled in one single person and parliament' (§ XII).[26] The great questions which had provoked the Civil Wars, and were summed up in the Militia Ordinance of 1642, the control of the army and the

[24] Gardiner offers two different interpretations of the relevant section (XIV), in *Commonwealth and Protectorate*, II, 286, and *GCD*, p. liv, and indeed everything hinges on the placing of a comma.

[25] Vernon F. Snow, 'Parliamentary Reapportionment Proposals in the Puritan Revolution', *EHR*, LXXIV (1959), 420.

[26] However, this was not mentioned in the writs for the first parliament (Abbott, *Cromwell's Writings*, III, 307–8).

negative voice, were not settled in a way satisfactory to any sincere patriot who had fought in those wars.

This was not all. In the first six months of 1654 Cromwell used the powers granted him by the Instrument to promulgate a whole series of ordinances. For many of them there was a good case; it was clearly essential that the customs and excise and the monthly assessment should continue to be collected, and it was only logical, as well as sensible, to repeal the act imposing the Engagement, though it left the nation without a public loyalty oath. But by redefining treason so as to include the public assertion 'that the Lord Protector and the people in parliament assembled are not the supreme authority of this Commonwealth', the Treason Ordinance of 19 January 1654[27] begged a most important question; and the decision to settle religion by ordinance was more controversial still. The Instrument declared (§ xxxv) that tithes should continue to be paid until an alternative could be found, and called for the regulation of the public ministry. Accordingly in March 1654 Cromwell began to implement the recommendations of the Committee for the Propagation of the Gospel, though they had been rejected by the Nominated Parliament with contempt. He set up by ordinance a central committee of 'Triers' to investigate the backgrounds and assess the qualifications of candidates for collation to benefices or appointment to lectureships (92a), and in August a further ordinance appointed commissioners in each county to eject 'scandalous, ignorant and insufficient ministers and schoolmasters' (92b). The government was silent on tithes, but it could take advantage of the fact that the public was deeply divided on this question, many feeling that he only alternative – voluntary contributions – would give the congregation an improper coercive power over the minister. In fact, tithes continued to be collected.[28]

The fact that the first parliament of the Protectorate, to the horror of the righteous, was ordered to assemble on the Lord's Day, 3 September 1654, just because it was the anniversary of Dunbar and Worcester, was an unfortunate beginning, and the extraordinary precautions taken when the Protector ventured down to Westminster to address them indicated the precarious dependence of the regime on one man. The Members were locked out of their own House, which was guarded by troops, and soldiers also patrolled the corridors; Cromwell arrived at the Painted Chamber flanked by his senior officers and surrounded by guards.[29] His opening speech, on the theme that protectoral government had brought order out of chaos, was calculated to appeal to the conservative instincts of his audience:

> 'What was the face that was upon affairs', he said, 'as to the interest of the nation?
> to the authority of the nation? to the magistracy? to the ranks and orders of men
> whereby England hath been known for hundreds of years? A nobleman, a
> gentleman, a yeoman? (That is a good interest of the nation, and a great one.) The
> magistracy of the nation, was it not almost trampled under foot, held in despite
> and contempt by men of Levelling principles?'[30]

---

[27] Firth and Rait, II, 831–5.   [28] James, art. cit.
[29] Burton, Diary, I, p. xxxiii (Guibon Goddard's account).
[30] Abbott, op. cit., III, 435.

But it was of no avail. Parliament insisted on debating the 'fundamentals' of the Instrument – the provision for a standing army, the protectoral veto and his entrenched income – and a week later he treated them to a long, detailed *apologia* and bound them to an undertaking to recognise the Instrument (**93**). All the same, he dissolved them at the earliest opportunity, on 22 January 1655, with 'turbid oratory, protestations of his own virtue and their waywardness, romantic reminiscences, proprietory appeals to the Lord, and great broken gobbets from the Pentateuch and the Psalms'.[31]

Two months later the first considerable royalist rising of the Interregnum, though it fizzled out in a pathetic rural *émeute* in Wiltshire,[32] called attention to the government's pressing security problems. Nevertheless, Cromwell was determined to reduce the numbers of the army, which was not only a serious drain on the national finances but the principal cause of the government's unpopularity, and on 31 July 1655 he cut back the army establishment, reduced its pay, and promulgated measures designed to strengthen the local militia. But at the same time he allowed the Council of Officers to perpetrate their most unpopular move. In August they divided England and Wales into ten districts and placed each under a senior army officer, whose duty it was not only to reinvigorate the militia but to oversee the work of the justices of the peace in suppressing royalism (**94**). This resort to naked military rule was bad enough, but the major generals were financed by a tax of 10 per cent on the estates of royalists, who were thus suffering double jeopardy. Moreover, their instructions also saddled them with the execution of the intemperate anti-vice laws of the Commonwealth, and this, together with the government's decision to close race-meetings and brothels, as being habitual haunts of royalists, set the seal on their unpopularity.[33]

Cromwell survived this; he even survived a serious mutiny in the judiciary. Nothing is more remarkable than the way in which the administration of justice had proceeded under the old forms, or something very close to them, through every constitutional and military upheaval. Individual judges might object and lay down their commissions, but suitable replacements were always available; the terms were kept, the high courts sat in Westminster Hall, the assize judges rode their circuits, the Commissioners of the Great Seal continued to appoint sheriffs and justices of the peace, who maintained the fabric of the legal system in the localities.[34] At the same time the legal profession resisted the demand first voiced by the Levellers, and taken up with increasing insistance by the army, for the reform of legal procedure and above all the reduction of costs.[35] The Nominated Parliament had posed the most serious threat, but Cromwell had apparently abandoned that line of policy; his ordinance reforming

---

[31] H. R. Trevor-Roper, 'Oliver Cromwell and his Parliaments', in *Religion, the Reformation and Social Change* (1967) p. 346. Cf. Abbott, *op. cit.*, III, 579–83. Parliament's proposed amendments to the Instrument were collected into a 'constitutional bill', printed *GCD*, pp. 427–47 (see also pp. lviii–lix).

[32] A. H. Woolrych, *Penruddock's Rising 1655* (1955).

[33] See Ivan Roots, 'Swordsmen and Decimators', in R. H. Parry, ed., *The English Civil War and After* (1970), pp. 78–92.

[34] Though there was a slight downward shift in the social status of JPs. See p. 445 below.

[35] See Stuart Prall, *Agitation for Law Reform*, and Donald Veall, *Popular Movement for Law Reform*.

the Court of Chancery in 1654 was therefore all the greater shock.[36] In 1655 an increasing number of judges in effect served notice that although for the sake of good government they had accepted an illegal constitution they would not allow the executive to override that constitution.[37] Cromwell had scrupulously refrained from issuing further ordinances, but dispute now arose as to whether his earlier ordinances, never confirmed by parliament, were valid – particularly the taxation ordinances. It was also becoming increasingly difficult to find judges and juries who would convict under the Treason Ordinance. The only solution was another parliament, which would confirm the Instrument or extend it, and it was summoned for 17 September 1656, well within the three-year limit.

Cromwell was unusually cunning. The major-generals were encouraged to influence the elections as much as they could, and the Council of State was induced to remove about a hundred of the more obstreperous Members;[38] then Cromwell disowned them both, and viewed with complacency the storm of complaint against them. Apparently he did not foresee a monarchist reaction, but it was inevitable now the republicans had been excluded and Cromwell had now so far dissociated himself from his officers that he could almost be regarded as a spokesman of opposition to them. As early as 28 October one back-bencher proposed to make the Protectorate hereditary, and on 19 January 1657 James Ashe moved that Cromwell 'take upon him the government according to the ancient constitution'. The discovery of a Leveller plot for his assassination caused a stampede; on 29 January parliament snubbed the major-generals by throwing out a bill to legalise the decimation tax, and on 23 February it took into consideration a Remonstrance, later entitled The Humble Petition and Advice, calling upon Cromwell to assume the crown, and revising the Instrument in such a way as to give him every inducement to do so.

The events of the next two or three months are still the subject of controversy.[39] It is still in doubt whether Cromwell declined the crown because of army pressure, and, if he did, whether he was wise to do so. However this may be, a compromise was eventually arrived at. On 25 May Cromwell accepted an amended Humble Petition, clarified by an Additional and Explanatory Petition on 26 June (95). This left him as Protector, but with the right to nominate his successor; it also provided him with an upper House of 40, nominated by him, though it would henceforth fill any gaps in its ranks by co-option. He was also granted an increased income of £1,300,000 a year, of which one million was appropriated to the armed forces, though it was stipulated that this was not to be raised by a land tax.

[36] 21 August 1654, Firth and Rait, II, 949–67. See Stuart E. Prall, 'Chancery Reform and the Puritan Revolution', *Amer. Jnl Legal History*, VI (1962), 28, and Ivan Roots, 'Cromwell's Ordinances', in Aylmer, *Interregnum*, pp. 153–4, 159–60.

[37] Gardiner, *Commonwealth and Protectorate*, III, 149ff.; Roots, *op. cit.*, pp. 160–1; Stephen F. Black, '*Coram protectore*: the Judges of Westminster Hall under the Protectorate of Oliver Cromwell', *Amer. Jnl Legal History*, XX (1976), 32–64.

[38] About 100 were excluded, then 50 or 60 voluntarily stayed away in protest; exact figures cannot be established. See Firth, *Last Years*, I, 12–16.

[39] The most recent discussion is by Trevor-Roper, *op. cit.*, pp. 40–1. See also Firth, *Last Years*, I, chs. 5–6, and 'Cromwell and the Crown', *EHR*, XVII (1902), 429–42, XVIII (1903), 52–80; Robert S. Paul, *The Lord Protector* (1955), pp. 366ff.

But the amended constitution had a short life. During the recess, beginning 26 June, the members of the 'Other House' were chosen, removing from the Commons some of Cromwell's ablest supporters. He also failed to enlist some of the more important hereditary peers (no. **127**, p. 420 below). When the Commons met again on 20 January 1658 the excluded Members were re-admitted on swearing a simple oath of loyalty to the Protector (**96**). But the republicans did not feel bound to accept the Other House, and their provocative criticism of this institution so angered Cromwell that he dissolved them on 4 February.

Cromwell's death on 3 September 1658, and the accession of his son Richard, only exacerbated the problem. The Instrument of Government had never been approved by parliament, and the Humble Petition had not been passed in a full parliament, and so little confidence did the Council of State feel in either document that they abandoned the system of representation introduced in 1654 and summoned a parliament for January 1659 on the old franchise, with the Other House.[40] From the beginning its debates were monopolised by the republicans, who refused to recognise Richard Cromwell as his father's lawful successor. In April the general staff forced him to dissolve parliament, and then acceded to the general demand, from within the army as well as outside, for the return of the Rump. But the Rump, like the Bourbons, had learned nothing and forgotten nothing, and in October it was once more dispersed by the army.[41] By this time, however, the irresponsibility of the republicans, the self-seeking and the sheer incompetence of the general staff, and the threat of a recession in trade had strained the patience of the public beyond endurance. George Monk, commander of the army of Scotland, now came forward as the spokesman of those who demanded a return to constitutional government in whatever form. His demand that the Rump be recalled in December was at once met, and on 1 January 1660 he crossed the Tweed with his hand-picked, firmly disciplined troops.

On his arrival in London Monk assumed responsibility for public order, and rapidly dispersed the English army to the provinces. But he soon realised, if he did not know already, that the Rump had nothing to offer, and on 21 February he recalled the Members excluded by Colonel Pride in 1648. He thus enabled the Long Parliament to dissolve itself at last, and order a general election. On 4 April Charles II, acting on suggestions secretly conveyed by Monk himself, issued a pacific Declaration from Breda. Subject to the approval of a freely elected parliament he offered a free pardon to all, full payment of the army's arrears, the confirmation of land sales concluded since 1642, and the prospect of a general toleration (**97**). On these terms the new parliament, or Convention, which assembled on 25 April, voted to recall him. He landed at Dover on 27 May, and entered London on the 29th.

---

[40] The reasons for this are unknown. See Godfrey Davies, 'The Elections to Richard Cromwell's Parliament', *EHR*, LXIII (1948), 488–501.

[41] The most detailed account of these complicated manoeuvres is by Godfrey Davies, *The Restoration of Charles II* (San Marino 1955). For a more perceptive discussion see Austin Woolrych, 'Last Quests for a Settlement', in Aylmer, *Interregnum*, pp. 181–204, amplified in his introduction to *The Prose Works of John Milton*, ed. Don M. Wolfe, vol. VII (revised edn, New Haven 1980).

89. An Act for the abolishing the kingly office in England and Ireland, and the dominions thereunto belonging, 17 March 1649

Whereas Charles Stuart, late king of England . . . [etc.], hath by authority derived from parliament been, and is hereby declared to be justly condemned, adjudged to die, and put to death, for many treasons, murders and other heinous offences committed by him, by which judgment he stood, and is hereby declared to, be attainted of high treason, whereby his issue and posterity, and all other pretending title under him, are become incapable of the said crowns, or of being king or queen of the said kingdom or dominions, or either or any of them; be it therefore enacted and ordained . . . by this present parliament and by the authority thereof, that all the people of England and Ireland . . ., of what degree or condition soever, are discharged of all fealty, homage and allegiance which is or shall be pretended to be due unto any of the issue and posterity of the said late king, or any claiming under him; and that Charles Stuart, eldest son, and James called Duke of York, second son, and all other the issue and posterity of him the said late King, and all and every person and persons pretending title from, by or under him, are and be disabled to hold or enjoy the said Crown of England and Ireland . . .

And whereas it is and hath been found by experience that the office of a king in this nation and Ireland, and to have the power thereof in any single person, is unnecessary, burdensome and dangerous to the liberty, safety and public interest of the people, and that for the most part use hath been made of the regal power and prerogative to oppress and impoverish and enslave the subject, and that usually and naturally any one person in such power makes it his interest to encroach upon the just freedom and liberty of the people, and to promote the setting up of their own will and power above the laws, that so they might enslave these kingdoms to their own lust, be it therefore enacted and ordained by this present parliament . . . that the office of a king in this nation shall not henceforth reside in or be exercised by any one single person, and that no one person whatsoever shall or may have or hold the office, style, dignity, power or authority of king of the said kingdoms and dominions, or any of them, or of the Prince of Wales, any law . . . notwithstanding.

And whereas by the abolition of the kingly office provided for in this act a most happy way is made for this nation (if God see it good) to return to its just and ancient right of being governed by its own Representatives or National Meetings in Council, from time to time chosen and entrusted for that purpose by the people; it is therefore resolved and declared by the Commons assembled in parliament, that they will put a period to the sitting of this present parliament, and dissolve the same, so soon as may possibly stand with the safety of the people that hath betrusted them, and with what is absolutely necessary for the preserving and upholding the government now settled in the way of a Commonwealth, . . .

And it is hereby further enacted and declared, notwithstanding anything contained in this act, [that] no person or persons of what condition and quality soever, shall be discharged from the obedience and subjection which he and they owe to the government of this nation, as it is now declared, but all and every of them shall in all things render and perform the same, as of right is due unto the Supreme Authority hereby declared to reside in this and the successive Representatives of the people of this nation, and in them only.

Firth and Rait, ɪɪ, 18-20

90. An Act for subscribing the Engagement, 2 January 1650

Whereas divers disaffected persons do by sundry ways and means oppose and endeavour to undermine this present government, so that unless special care be taken a new war is likely to break forth, for the preventing whereof, and also for the better uniting of this nation, as well against all invasions from abroad as the common enemy at home, and to the end that those which receive benefit and protection from this present government may give assurance of their living quietly and peaceably under the same, and that they will neither directly or indirectly contrive or practice anything to the disturbance thereof, the parliament now assembled do enact and ordain, . . . that all men whatsoever within the Commonwealth of England, of the age of eighteen years and upwards, shall as is hereafter in this present act directed take and subscribe this Engagement following, viz., *I do declare and promise, that I will be true and faithful to the Commonwealth of England as it is now established, without a king or House of Lords.*

And for the due taking and subscribing thereof, be it further enacted . . ., that all and every person and persons that now hath, or hereafter shall have, hold or enjoy any place or office of trust or profit, or any place or employment of public trust whatsoever within the said Commonwealth, . . . that hath not formerly taken the said Engagement, by virtue of any order or direction of parliament, shall take and subscribe the said Engagement at or before the twentieth day of February, 1650 . . .

★   ★   ★

And it is further enacted and declared, that all and every person or persons that expects benefit from the courts of justice of this Commonwealth, and that either now are or hereafter shall be plaintiff or plaintiffs, demandant or demandants, in any suit, plaint, bill, action, information, writ, demand, execution, or any other process whatsoever, in any of the courts . . . [of justice] within the Commonwealth of England . . . shall take and subscribe, and are hereby required to take and subscribe the aforesaid Engagement . . . And that it shall be lawful for all and every person or persons that are or shall be defendant or defendants, or that are or shall be sued, impleaded, attached, arrested, molested or complained against in any such courts . . . from and after the twentieth of April, 1650, to plead, aver, or to move in arrest of judgment . . . that the plaintiff or plaintiffs . . . have not taken and subscribed the said Engagement . . .

★ ★ ★

Firth and Rait, I, 325–8

91. The Instrument of Government, 1653

The government of the Commonwealth of England, Scotland and Ireland, and the
dominions thereunto belonging [16 December 1653]

I. That the supreme legislative authority of the Commonwealth of England . . . [etc.] shall be and reside in one person, and the people assembled in parliament; the style of which person shall be, 'The Lord Protector of the Commonwealth of England, Scotland and Ireland'.

II. That the exercise of the chief magistracy, and the administration of the government over the said countries and dominions, and the people thereof, shall be in the Lord Protector, assisted with a Council, the number whereof shall not exceed twenty-one nor be less than thirteen.

III. That all writs, process[es], commissions, patents, grants and other things, which now run in the name and style of the Keepers of the Liberties of England by Authority of Parliament, shall run in the name and style of the Lord Protector, from whom for the future shall be derived all magistracy and honours in these three nations; and [he] shall have the power of pardons (except in case of murders and treason) and benefit of all forfeitures for the public use; and shall govern the said countries and dominions in all things by the advice of the Council, and according to these presents, and the laws.

IV. That the Lord Protector, the parliament sitting, shall dispose and order the militia and forces, both by sea and land, for the peace and good of the three nations, by consent of parliament; and that the Lord Protector, with the advice and consent of the major part of the Council, shall dispose and order the militia for the ends aforesaid in the intervals of parliament.

V. That the Lord Protector, by the advice aforesaid, shall direct in all things concerning the keeping and holding of a good correspondency with foreign kings, princes and states; and also, with the consent of the major part of the Council, have the power of war and peace.

VI. That the laws shall not be altered, suspended, abrogated, or repealed, nor any new law made, nor any tax, charge or imposition laid upon the people, but by common consent in parliament (save only as is expressed in the 30th article).

VII. That there shall be a parliament summoned to meet at Westminster upon the third day of September, 1654, and that successively a parliament shall be summoned once in every third year, to be accounted from the dissolution of the present parliament.[42]

VIII. That neither the parliament to be next summoned, nor any successive parliaments, shall during the time of five months, to be accounted from the day of their first meeting, be adjourned, prorogued or dissolved, without their own consent.

IX. That as well the next as all other successive parliaments shall be summoned and elected in manner hereafter expressed. That is to say, the persons to be chosen within England, Wales, the isles of Jersey, Guernsey and the town of Berwick upon Tweed . . . shall be and not exceed the number of four hundred. The persons to be chosen within Scotland . . . shall be and not exceed . . . thirty; and . . . for Ireland . . . thirty.

X. That the persons to be elected to sit in Parliament from time to time for the several counties of England [and] Wales . . . and all places within the same respectively, shall be according to the proportions and numbers hereafter expressed [43]

[XI. If the Protector fails to issue the writs, they are to be issued by the Commissioners of the Great Seal.]

[XII. That at the day and place of elections the sheriff of each county, and . . . mayors . . . [etc.] within their cities . . . [etc.] shall take view of the said elections, and shall make return into the Chancery within twenty days after the said elections of the persons elected, . . . wherein shall be contained [an acknowledgment] that the persons elected shall not have power to alter the government as it is hereby settled in one single person and a parliament.

[XIII. Sheriffs neglecting their duty to be punished.]

XIV. That all and every person and persons who have aided, advised, assisted or abetted in any war against the parliament since the first day of January 1641 [1642] (unless they have been since in the service of the parliament, and given signal testimony of their good affection thereunto) shall be disabled and incapable to be elected, or to give any vote in the election of

---

[42] That is, the parliament to assemble in 1654.

[43] This redistribution is discussed in detail by Vernon F. Snow, 'Parliamentary Re-apportionment Proposals in the Puritan Revolution', *EHR*, LXXIV (1959), 409–42.

any Members to serve in the next parliament, or in the three succeeding triennial parliaments.

XV. That all such who have advised, assisted or abetted the Rebellion of Ireland shall be disabled and incapable for ever to be elected or to give any vote in the election of any Member to serve in parliament; as also all such who do or shall profess the Roman Catholic religion.

[XVI. Heavy penalties to be imposed on disqualified men who vote.]

XVII. That the persons who shall be elected to serve in parliament shall be such (and no other than such) as are persons of known integrity, fearing God, and of good conversation, and being of the age of twenty-one years.

XVIII. That all and every person and persons seized or possessed to his own use of any estate, real or personal, to the value of £200, and not within the aforesaid exceptions, shall be capable to elect Members to serve in parliament for counties.

[XIX. For failing to do their duty under § XI above, the Commissioners of the Great Seal shall be liable to the penalties of high treason.

XX. If no writs are issued, elections are to be held by the returning officers notwithstanding.]

XXI. That the clerk called the Clerk of the Commonwealth in Chancery for the time being, and all others who shall afterwards execute that office, to whom the returns shall be made, shall for the next parliament, and the two succeeding triennial parliaments, the next day after such return, certify the names of the several persons so returned . . . unto the Council, who shall peruse the said returns, and examine whether the persons so elected and returned be such as is agreeable to the qualifications, and not disabled to be elected; and that every person and persons being so duly elected, and being approved of by the major part of the Council to be persons not disabled, but qualified as aforesaid, shall be esteemed a Member of Parliament and be admitted to sit in parliament, and not otherwise.

XXII. That the persons so chosen and assembled in manner aforesaid, or any sixty of them, shall be and be deemed the parliament of England, Scotland and Ireland; and the supreme legislative power to be and reside in the Lord Protector and such parliament, in manner herein expressed.

XXIII. That the Lord Protector, with the advice of the major part of the Council, shall at any other time than is before expressed, when the necessities of the state shall require it, summon parliaments in manner before expressed, which shall not be adjourned, prorogued, or dissolved without their own consent during the first three months of their sitting; and in case of future war with any foreign state a parliament shall be forthwith summoned for their advice concerning the same.

XXIV. That all bills agreed unto by the parliament shall be presented to the Lord Protector for his consent, and in case he shall not give his consent thereto within twenty days after they shall be presented to him, or give satisfaction to the parliament within the time limited, that then upon declaration of the parliament that the Lord Protector hath not consented nor given satisfaction, such bills shall pass into and become law, although he shall not give his consent thereunto; provided such bills contain nothing in them contrary to the matters contained in these presents.

XXV. That Henry Lawrence, Esq., [John Lambert, Charles Fleetwood, Philip Skippon, John Desborough, Edward Montague, William Sydenham,[44] Philip Sydney (Viscount Lisle), Sir Anthony Ashley Cooper, Sir Charles Wolseley, Sir Gilbert Pickering, Francis Rous, Richard Major and Walter Strickland], or any seven of them, shall be a Council for the purposes expressed in this writing and upon the death or other removal of any of them the parliament shall nominate six persons of ability, integrity, and fearing God, for every one that is dead or removed; out of which the major part of the Council shall elect two and present them to the Lord Protector, of which he shall elect one. And in case the parliament shall not nominate within twenty days after notice given unto them thereof, the major part of the Council shall nominate three as aforesaid to the Lord Protector, who out of them shall supply the vacancy . . .

XXVI. That the Lord Protector and the major part of the Council aforesaid may, at any time before the meeting of the next parliament, add to the Council such persons as they shall think fit, provided the number of the Council be not made thereby to exceed twenty-one; and the quorum to be proportioned accordingly by the Lord Protector and the major part of the Council.

XXVII. That a constant yearly revenue shall be raised, settled and established for maintaining of 10,000 horse and dragoons and 20,000 foot, in England, Scotland and Ireland, for the defence and security thereof, and also for a convenient number of ships for guarding of the seas; besides £200,000 per ann. for defraying the other necessary charges of administration of justice, and other expenses of the government; which revenue shall be raised by the customs, and such other ways and means as shall be agreed upon by the Lord Protector and the Council, and shall not be taken away or diminished, nor the way agreed upon for raising the same altered, but by the consent of the Lord Protector and the parliament.

XXVIII. That the said yearly revenue shall be paid into the public treasury, and shall be issued out for the uses of aforesaid.

XXIX. That in case there shall not be cause hereafter to keep up so great a defence both at land or sea, but that there be an abatement made thereof, the

---

[44] The first seven were army officers.

money which will be saved thereby shall remain in bank for the public service, and not be employed to any other use but by consent of parliament; or, in the intervals of parliament, by the Lord Protector and major part of the Council.

XXX. That the raising of money for defraying the charge of the present extraordinary forces, both at sea and land, in respect of the present wars, shall be by consent of parliament and not otherwise; save only that the Lord Protector, with the consent of the major part of the Council, for preventing the disorders and dangers which might otherwise fall out both by sea and land, shall have power, until the meeting of the first parliament, to raise money for the purposes aforesaid; and also to make laws and ordinances for the peace and welfare of these nations, where it shall be necessary, which shall be binding and in force until order shall be taken in parliament concerning the same.

XXXI. That the lands, tenements, rents, royalties, jurisdictions and hereditaments which remain yet unsold or undisposed of by act or ordinance of parliament, belonging to the Commonwealth . . . shall be vested in the Lord Protector to hold, to him and his successors Lords Protectors of these nations, and shall not be alienated but by consent in parliament . . .

[XXXII. On the Protector's death his successor shall be elected by the Council, with a quorum of thirteen.]

XXXIII. That Oliver Cromwell, Captain General, . . . shall be, and is hereby declared to be, Lord Protector . . .

XXXIV. That the chancellor, keeper or commissioners of the Great Seal, the treasurer, admiral, chief governors of Ireland and Scotland, and the chief justices of both the Benches, shall be chosen by the approbation of parliament, and in the intervals of parliament by the approbation of the major part of the Council, to be afterwards approved by the Parliament.

XXXV. That the Christian religion, as contained in the Scriptures, be held forth and recommended as the public profession of these nations; and that as soon as may be a provision, less subject to scruple and contention, and more certain than the present, be made for the encouragement and maintenance of able and painful teachers, for instructing the people, and for discovery and confutation of error, heresy and whatever is contrary to sound doctrine. And that until such provision be made the present maintenance shall not be taken away nor impeached.

XXXVI. That to the Public Profession held forth none shall be compelled by penalties or otherwise; but that endeavours be used to win them by sound doctrine and the example of a good conversation.

XXXVII. That such as profess faith in God by Jesus Christ (though differing in judgment from the doctrine, worship or discipline publicly held forth) shall not be restrained from, but shall be protected in, the profession of the Faith, and exercise of their religion; so as they abuse not this liberty to the civil injury of others, and to the actual disturbance of the public peace on their parts. Provided this liberty be not extended to popery nor Prelacy, nor to such as, under the profession of Christ, hold forth and practice licentiousness.

XXXVIII. That all laws, statutes and ordinances, and clauses in any law, statute or ordinance to the contrary of the aforesaid liberty, shall be esteemed as null and void.

[XXXIX. Confirmed financial engagements entered into by the Long Parliament.

XL. Confirmed treaties and agreements undertaken by the Long Parliament.]

★   ★   ★

Firth and Rait, II, 813–22

92. The Church Settlement
(a) The Triers

An Ordinance for appointing Commissioners for approbation of Publique Preachers,
[20 March 1654]

Whereas for some time past hitherto there hath not been any certain course established for the supplying vacant places with able and fit persons to preach the Gospel, by reason whereof not only the rights and titles of patrons are prejudiced, but many weak, scandalous, popish and ill-affected persons have intruded themselves, or been brought in, to the great grief and trouble of the good people of this nation; For remedy and prevention whereof, Be it ordained by his Highness the Lord Protector, by and with the consent of his Council, that every person who shall from and after the five and twentieth day of March instant be presented, nominated, chosen or appointed to any benefice (formerly called benefice with cure of souls), or to preach any public settled lecture in England and Wales, shall, before he be admitted into any such benefice or lecture, be judged and approved by the persons hereafter named to be a person for the Grace of God in him, his holy and unblameable conversation, as also for his knowledge and utterance, able and fit to preach the Gospel; and that after the said five and twentieth day of March no person but such as shall upon such approbation be admitted by the said persons, shall take any public lecture having a constant stipend legally annexed and belonging thereunto, or take or receive any such benefice as aforesaid, or the profits thereof.

And be it further ordained that . . . [38 named persons] shall be and are hereby nominated commissioners for such approbation and admission as is above said . . . And the said commissioners, or any five or more of them, met together at some certain place in the City of London or Westminster, as his Highness shall appoint, are hereby authorised to judge and take knowledge of the ability of any person so presented . . ., according to the qualifications above-mentioned, and upon their approbation of such his ability and fitness, to grant unto such person admission to such benefice or lecture by an instrument in writing under a Common Seal to be appointed by his Highness . . .

[If patrons fail to nominate candidates to the vacant benefices within six months, the presentations will revert to the Protector.]

[If persons placed in benefices since 1 April 1653 have not by 20 June next obtained the approbation of the commissioners, then the patron can present another candidate.]

★   ★   ★

And it is hereby lastly declared and ordained, that the approbation or admittance aforesaid . . . is not intended nor shall be construed to be any solemn or sacred setting apart of a person to any particular office in the ministry; but only by such trial and approbation to take care that places destitute may be supplied with able and faithful preachers throughout this nation; and that such fit and approved persons faithfully labouring in the work of the Gospel may be in a capacity to receive such public stipend and maintenance, as is or shall be allotted to such places.

Firth and Rait, II, 855–8

(b) The Ejectors

An Ordinance for ejecting Scandalous, Ignorant and Insufficient Ministers and Schoolmasters, [28 August 1654]

Whereas by the continuance of divers scandalous and insufficient ministers and schoolmasters in many churches, chapels and public schools within this nation, the more effectual propagation of the Gospel, and [the] settlement of a godly and painful ministry is much obstructed, and no authority [is] now in force for removing such ministers and schoolmasters, for remedy thereof, Be it ordained by his Highness . . . [etc.], that the persons hereafter named shall be and are hereby appointed and constituted commissioners for and within the respective counties within England and Wales for the ends and purposes hereafter in and by this ordinance expressed and directed . . .[45]

And the said commissioners for the respective counties aforesaid, or any five of them, are hereby authorised and empowered to call before them . . . any

---

[45] The four northern counties, Cumberland, Durham, Northumberland and Westmoreland, were grouped together, as were Derby and Nottingham, and Cambridge, Huntingdon and the Isle of Ely. Wales was divided into two groups, north and south. The number of commissioners for each county or group fluctuates enormously, and for no very obvious reason.

public preacher, lecturer or other persons formerly called parsons, vicars or curates, settled, or which hereafter shall be settled, in any benefice, commonly called a benefice with cure of souls, or public lecture having any stipend or salary legally annexed or belonging thereunto, and all and every schoolmasters, who are or who shall be ignorant, scandalous, insufficient or negligent in their several and respective places; and shall and may receive all articles or charges which shall be exhibited against them, for ignorance, insufficiency, scandal in their lives and conversations, or negligence in their respective callings and places, and proceed to examination and determination of such offences, according to the rules and directions hereafter specified, viz., such ministers and schoolmasters shall be deemed and accounted scandalous in their lives and conversations as shall be proved guilty of holding or maintaining such blasphemous and atheistical opinions as are punishable by an act entitled, *An Act against several Atheistical, Blasphemous and execrable opinions, derogatory to the Honour of God, and destructive to human society*,[46] or guilty of profane cursing or swearing, perjury, subornation of perjury, such as shall hold, teach or maintain any of those popish opinions required in the oath of abjuration (mentioned in an ordinance of parliament of the 19th of August 1643) to be abjured,[47] or be guilty of adultery, fornication, drunkenness, common haunting of taverns or alehouses, frequent quarrelling or fighting, frequent playing at cards or dice, profaning of the Sabbath day, and such as do or shall allow the same in their families, or countenance the same in their parishioners or scholars; such as have publicly and frequently read or used the Common Prayer Book since the first of January last, or shall at any time hereafter do the same; such as do publicly and profanely scoff at or revile the strict profession or professors of religion or godliness, or do encourage or countenance by word or practice any Whitsun-ales, wakes, morris dances, maypoles, stage plays, or such like licentious practices, by which men are encouraged in a loose and profane conversation; such as have declared or shall declare by writing, preaching or otherwise publishing their disaffection to the present government. Such ministers shall be accounted negligent as omit the public exercises of preaching and praying upon the Lord's day . . . or that are or shall be nonresident; such schoolmasters shall be accounted negligent as absent themselves from their schools, and do wilfully neglect their duties in teaching their scholars.

And such minister or schoolmaster shall be accounted ignorant and insufficient, as shall be so declared and adjudged by the commissioners in every county, or any five of them, together with any five or more of the ministers

---

[46] The Blasphemy Act of 1650, Firth and Rait, II, 409–12.

[47] The Sequestration Ordinance of 18 August 1643, requiring suspected Catholics to abjure the doctrines of transubstantiation, purgatory and justification by works. See p. 244 above.

hereafter nominated in this present ordinance to be assistant to the said commissioners, viz. . . .

[The number of ministers tended to be less than that of the commissioners; for example, seven for Bedfordshire, nine each for Bedfordshire and Bucks, eighteen for the four northern counties together.]

[A detailed procedure was laid down for hearings before the commissioners and their assistants and no action could be taken except on the testimony of two separate witnesses under oath.]

[Where a minister is ejected, the patron must nominate a replacement to the 'Triers' appointed under the previous ordinance within six months, with the implication that otherwise the presentation will revert to the government, though this is not stated.]

[In cases of proven hardship, an ejected minister may receive an allowance of one-fifth of the income of the benefice.]

[Ministers or Schoolmasters appointed by virtue of this ordinance, or any other, shall keep the buildings in their charge in good repair and sound condition. If they fail to do so, the justices of the peace may defray the cost by distress and sale of goods and chattels.]

★   ★   ★

Firth and Rait, ii, 968–90

93. Cromwell's *apologia*

His Highness the Lord Protector's speech to the Parliament in the Painted Chamber, on Tuesday, the 12th of September, 1654

I called not myself to this place. I say again, I called not myself to this place; of that God is witness. And I have many witnesses who, I do believe, could readily lay down their lives to bear witness to the truth of that; that is to say, that I called not myself to this place . . .

If my calling be from God, and my testimony from the people, God and the people shall take it from me, else I will not part with it. I should be false to the trust that God hath placed upon me, and to the interest of the people of these nations, if I should . . .

I was by birth a gentleman, living neither in any considerable height, nor yet in obscurity. I have been called to several employments in the nation – to serve in parliaments – and (because I would not be over tedious) I did endeavour to discharge the duty of an honest man in those services, to God, and His People's interest, and of the Commonwealth; having, when time was, a competent acceptation in the hearts of men, and some evidences thereof. I resolve not to recite the times and occasions and opportunities that have been appointed me by God to serve him in, nor the presence and blessings of God bearing then testimony to me.

I, having had some occasions to see (together with my brethren and countrymen) a happy period put to our sharp wars and contests with the then common enemy, hoped, in a private capacity, to have reaped the fruit and benefit, together with my brethren, of our hard labours and hazards; to wit, the enjoyment of peace and liberty, and the privileges of a Christian and of a man, in some equality with others, according as it should please the Lord to dispense unto me.

And when, I say, God had put an end to our wars, [or] at least brought them to a very hopeful issue, very near an end (after Worcester fight), I came up to London to pay my service and duty to the parliament that then sat. And hoping that all minds would have been disposed to answer that which seemed to be the mind of God, viz., to give peace and rest to His People, and especially to those who had bled more than others in the carrying on of the military affairs, I was much disappointed of my expectation, for the issue did not prove so. Whatever may be boasted or misrepresented, it was not so.

I can say in the simplicity of my soul, I love not, I love not (I declined it in my former speech)[48] I say I love not to rake into sores or discover nakednesses. That which I drive at is this; I say to you, I hoped to have had leave to have retired to a private life. I begged to be dismissed of my charge; I begged it again and again. And God be judge between me and all men if I lie in this matter! That I lie not in matter of fact is known to very many; but whether I tell a lie in my heart, as labouring to represent to you that which was not upon my heart, I say, the Lord be judge. Let uncharitable men, that measure others by themselves, judge as they please; as to the matter of fact, I say it is true. As to the ingenuity and integrity of my heart in that desire, I do appeal as before upon the truth of that also. But I could not obtain what my soul longed for, and the plain truth is, I did afterwards apprehend that some did think (my judgment not suiting with theirs) that it could not well be. But this, I say to you, was between God and my soul, between me and that assembly.

I confess I am in some strait to say what I could say, and what is true of what then followed.

I pressed the parliament, as a member, to period themselves, once, and again, and again, and ten and twenty times over. I told them (for I knew it better than any one man in the parliament could know it, because of my manner of life, which was to run up and down the nation, and so might see and know the temper and spirits of all men, the best of men) that the nation loathed

---

[48] His speech opening this parliament, on 4 September.

their sitting; I knew it. And so far as I could discern, when they were dissolved, there was not so much as the barking of a dog, or any general and visible repining at it. You are not a few here present that can assert this as well as myself.

And that there was high cause for their dissolving is most evident, not only in regard there was just fear of the parliaments perpetuating themselves, but because it was their design. And had not their heels been trod upon by importunities from abroad [*sc.* outside], even to threats, I believe there would never have been thoughts of rising or going out of that room to the world's end.

I myself was sounded, and by no mean persons tempted, and addresses were made to me to that very end, that it might have been thus perpetuated, that the vacant places might be supplied by new elections, and so continue from generation to generation.

* * *

It's true, this will be said, that there was a remedy to put an end to this perpetual parliament endeavoured, by having a future Representative. How it was gotten, and by what importunities that was obtained, and how unwillingly yielded unto, is well known.

What was this remedy? It was a seeming willingness to have successive parliaments. What was that succession? It was, that when one parliament had left their seat, another was to sit down immediately in the room thereof, without any caution to avoid that which was the danger, viz., perpetuating of the same parliaments; which is a sore now that will ever be running, so long as men are ambitious and troublesome, if a due remedy be not found. So then, what was the business? It was a conversion from a parliament that should have been and was perpetual, to a Legislative Power always sitting, and so the liberties and interests and lives of people not judged by any certain known laws and power, but by an arbitrary power – which is incident and necessary to parliaments – by an arbitrary power, I say, to make men's estates liable to confiscation, and their persons to imprisonments, sometimes by laws made after the fact committed, often by taking the judgment both in capital and criminal things to themselves, who in former times were not known to exercise such a judicature.

This I suppose was the case, and in my opinion the remedy[49] was fitted to the disease, especially coming in the rear of a parliament so exercising the power and authority as this had done but immediately before.

Truly I confess, upon these grounds, and with the satisfaction of divers other persons, seeing nothing could be had otherwise, that parliament was dissolved.

---

[49] Cromwell's own remedy, of course: forcible dissolution.

We, desiring to see if a few might have been called together for some short time, who might put the nation into some certain way of settlement, did call those gentlemen out of the several parts of the nation for that purpose.

And as I have appealed to God before you already, . . . though it be a tender thing to make appeals to God, . . . especially to make them before persons that know God, and know what conscience is, and what it is to lie before the Lord, I say that, as a principal end to myself was that I might have opportunity to lay down the power that was in my hands. I say to you again, in the presence of that God who hath blessed and been with me in all my adversities and successes, that was, as to myself, my greatest end. A desire perhaps . . . sinful enough to be quit of the power God had most providentially put into my hand, before he called for it, and before those honest ends of our fighting were attained and settled . . .

What the event and issue of that meeting was, we may sadly remember; it hath much teaching in it, and I hope will make us all wiser for the future.

*   *   *

When this was so [the resignation of Barebones], we were exceedingly to seek how to settle things for the future. My power again by this resignation was as boundless and unlimited as before, all things being subjected to arbitrariness, and [I] a person having power over the three nations boundlessly and unlimited, and upon the matter, all government dissolved, all civil administration at an end . . .

The gentlemen that undertook to frame this government did consult divers days together (they being of known integrity and ability), how to frame somewhat that might give us settlement, and they did so; and that I was not privy to their counsels, they know it.

When they had finished their model in some measure, or made a very good preparation of it, it became communicative. They told me that except I would undertake the government, they thought things would hardly come to a composure and settlement, but blood and confusion would break in upon us. I denied it again and again, as God and those persons know, not compliment-ingly, as they also know and God knows.

I confess, after many arguments, and after the letting of me know that I did not receive anything that put me into any higher capacity than I was in before, but that it limited me and bound my hands to act nothing to the prejudice of the nations without consent of a Council until the parliament, and then limited by the parliament as the act of government expresseth, I did accept it . . .

I did, at the entreaty of divers persons of honour and quality, at the entreaty of very many of the chief officers of the army then present, I did accept of the place and title of Protector, . . . [and] took my oath to this government. This was not done in a corner; it was open and public.

[He then rehearsed at great length the evidence he saw of God's approval of these proceedings, and of the general acceptance of the new government by the people, as well as by the judges, the City of London, the officers of local government in the counties, etc., and resumed as follows.]

Now if this be thus – and I am deriving a title from God and men upon such accounts as these are, though some men be forward – yet that [you in] your judgments, that are persons sent from all parts of the nation under the notion of acceptance of the government, for you to disown or not to own it, for you to act [with] parliamentary authority, especially in the disowning of it, contrary to the very fundamental things, yea, against the very root itself of this Establishment; to sit, and not own the authority by which you sit; that, I believe, astonisheth more men than myself, and doth as dangerously disappoint and discompose the nation, as anything [that] could have been invented by the greatest enemy to our peace and welfare, or could well have happened.

It is true, there are some things in the Establishment that are fundamental, and some things are not so, but are circumstantial. Of such, no question but I shall easily agree to vary or leave out, as I shall be convinced by reason. Some things are fundamentals, about which I shall deal plainly with you; they may not be parted with, but will (I trust) be delivered over to posterity, as being the fruits of our blood and travail.

The government by a single person and parliament is a fundamental; it is the *esse*, it is constitutive. And for the person, though I may seem to plead for myself, yet I do not, ... I plead for this nation, and all honest men therein who have borne their testimony as aforesaid, and not for myself. And if things should do otherwise than well, . . . and the common enemy and discontented persons take advantage at these distractions, the issue will be put up before God. Let him own or let him disown it, as he please.

In every government there must be somewhat fundamental, somewhat like *Magna Charta*, that should be standing and be unalterable. Where there is a stipulation on one part, and that fully accepted, as appears by what hath been said, surely a return ought to be [owing]; else what does that stipulation signify? If I have upon the terms aforesaid undertaken this great trust, and exercised it, and by it called you, surely it ought to be owned?

That parliaments should not make themselves perpetual is a fundamental. Of what assurance is a law to prevent so great an evil, if it lie in one or the same Legislator to unlaw it again? Is this like to be lasting? It will be like a rope of sand; it will give no security, for the same men may unbuild what they have built.

Is not liberty of conscience in religion a fundamental? So long as there is liberty of conscience for the supreme magistrate to exercise his conscience in erecting what form of church government he is satisfied he should set up, why should not he give it to others? Liberty of conscience is a natural right, and he that would have it ought to give it, having liberty to settle what he likes for the public.

Indeed, that hath been one of the vanities of our contests. Every sect saith, Oh! Give me liberty. But give him it, and to his power he will not yield it to anybody else. Where is our ingenuity? Truly, that's a thing ought to be very reciprocal. The magistrate hath his supremacy, and he may settle religion according to his conscience. And I may say it to you, I can say it; all the money of this nation would not have tempted men to fight upon such an account as they have engaged, if they had not had hopes of liberty, better than they had from Episcopacy, or than would have been afforded them from a Scottish Presbytery, or an English either, if it had made such steps or been as sharp and rigid as it threatened when it was first set up.

This I say is a fundamental. It ought to be so: it is for us, and the generations to come. And if there be an absoluteness in the imposer, without fitting allowances and exceptions from the rule, we shall have our people driven into wilderness, as they were when those poor and afflicted people, that forsook their estates and inheritances here, where they lived plentifully and comfortably, for the enjoyment of their liberty, and were necessitated to go into a vast howling wilderness in New England, where they have for liberty['s] sake stripped themselves of all their comfort and the full enjoyment they had, embracing rather loss of friends and want than to be so ensnared and in bondage.

Another, which I had forgotten, is the militia. That's judged a fundamental, if anything be so. That it should be well and equally placed, is very necessary. For put the absolute power of the militia into one without a check, what doth it? I pray you, what doth your check upon your perpetual parliaments, if it be wholly stripped of this? It is equally placed; and desires were to have it so, viz., in one Person and the parliament, sitting the parliament. What signifies a provision against perpetuating of parliaments, if this be solely in them? Whether, without a check, the parliament have not liberty to alter the frame of government to Aristocracy, to Democracy, to Anarchy, to anything, if this be fully in them, yea, into all confusion, and that without remedy? And if this one thing be placed in one, they or he hath power to make what they please of all the rest . . .

The Council are the trustees of the Commonwealth, in all intervals of parliaments, who have as absolute a negative upon the supreme officers in the said intervals, as the parliament hath while it is sitting. It [the militia] cannot be made use of, a man cannot be raised nor a penny charged upon the people, nothing [can be] done without consent of parliament, and in the intervals of parliament without consent of the Council . . .

Give me leave to say that there is very little power, none but what is co-ordinate, in the supreme officer, and yet enough in him that hath the chief government. In that particular he is bound in strictness by the parliament, out of parliament by the Council, that do as absolutely bind him as the parliament, when parliament is sitting.

For that of money, I told you some things are circumstantials. To have two hundred thousand pounds, to defray civil officers, to pay the judges, and other officers, defraying the charges of the Council in sending their embassies, in keeping intelligence, and doing that that's necessary, and for supporting the Governor-in-Chief – all this is by the Instrument supposed and intended, but it is not of the *esse* so much, and so limited. As to so many soldiers, 30,000 – twenty thousand foot and ten thousand horse – if the spirits of men be composed, five thousand horse and ten thousand foot may serve. These are things between the Chief Officer and the parliament, to be moderated as occasion shall offer.

So there are many other circumstantial things, which are not like the laws of the Medes and Persians. But the things which shall be necessary to deliver over to posterity, these should be unalterable, else every succeeding parliament will be disputing to change and alter the government, and we shall be as often brought into confusion as we have parliaments, and so make our remedy our disease. The Lord's providence . . . and [our] better judgment will give occasion for the ordering of things for the best interest of the people; and those things are the matter of consideration between you and me.

★   ★   ★

Abbott, *Cromwell's Writings*, III, 451–62

94. Instructions to the major-generals, October 1655

1. They are to endeavour the suppressing all tumults, insurrections, rebellions or other unlawful assemblies which shall be within the said counties respectively, as also all invasions from abroad, and to that purpose shall have power to draw together the said forces or troops, and march in such places as they shall judge convenient in England and Wales.

2. They are to take care and give order, that all papists and others who have been in arms against the parliament, or assisted the late king or his son in the late wars, as also all others who are dangerous to the peace of the nation, be disarmed, and their arms secured in some adjacent garrisons, or otherwise disposed of, as may be for the public service.

3. And to the end that all the highways and roads may be more safe for travellers, and the many robberies and burglaries daily committed may be prevented, they with the said captains and officers shall use their best endeavours to find out all such thieves, robbers, highwaymen and other dangerous persons as lurk and lie hid in any place within the several counties, and the houses and places which they frequent and usually lodge in, and take such course for the apprehending of them, and also for the prosecuting them and their receivers, as is agreeable to law. And they have hereby power to appoint such reward, not exceeding ten pounds, to such person or persons as shall discover and apprehend any such thief, highwayman or robber, to be paid into them after the conviction of the party so discovered and apprehended, which the sheriff for the time being shall pay . . .

4. They are to have a strict eye upon the conversation and carriage of all disaffected persons within the several counties; and they shall give the like direction to all the said captains and officers at their meetings, to be watchful and diligent in the same kind. As also that no horse-races, cock-fighting, bear-baitings, stage plays, or any unlawful assemblies be suffered or permitted within their counties, forasmuch as treason and rebellion is usually hatched and contrived against the state upon such occasions, and much evil and wickedness committed.

5. They and the aforesaid officers shall labour to inform themselves of all such idle and loose people that are within their counties who have no visible way of livelihood, nor calling or employment, and shall consider by what means they may be compelled to work, or be sent out of the Commonwealth; as also how the poor and impotent of those counties may be employed and better provided for than now they are, and certify the same to us and the Council, for our further direction thereupon; and in the meantime shall endeavour as far as in them lies that the laws in such cases made and provided be put in effectual execution.

6. They shall in their constant carriage and conversation encourage and promote godliness and virtue, and discourage and discountenance all profaneness and ungodliness; and shall endeavour with the other justices of the peace, and other ministers and officers who are entrusted with the care of those things, that the laws against drunkenness, blaspheming and taking of the name of God in vain, by swearing and cursing, plays and interludes, and profaning the Lord's Day, and such-like wickedness and abominations, be put in more effectual execution than they have been hitherto.

7. They shall take an exact account of what proceedings have been put upon the ordinance for ejecting of ignorant, insufficient and scandalous ministers and schoolmasters, and take care that the same be effectually put in execution for the time to come . . .

[8. The servants of delinquents or suspect persons, as defined in § 2, to be bound over.

9–15. A central registry is to be set up for recording the existence and the movements of all papists, delinquents, and suspect persons.]

16. That a more than ordinary regard be had to the securing of the roads, chiefly about London.

17. That no house standing alone and out of a town be permitted to sell ale, beer or wine, or to give entertainment, but that such licenses be called in and suppressed.

[18. Riding post is to be restricted and closely regulated.]

19. And for the effecting more particularly a reformation in the city of London and Westminster, that all gaming houses and houses of evil fame be industriously sought out and suppressed within the cities of London and Westminster and all the liberties thereof.

20. That all house keepers within the same who have no trade or calling, or do not labour in such trade or calling, or have no other visible estate, but are observed generally to lodge and harbour loose and dissolute persons, be bound to their good behaviour and compelled to work, and for want of security be sent to Bridewell.

21. That all alehouses, taverns and victualling houses towards the outskirts of the said cities, or either of them, be suppressed, except such as are necessary and convenient to travellers; and that the number of alehouses in all other parts of the town be abated, and none continued but such as can lodge strangers and are of good repute.   Abbott, *Cromwell's Writings*, III, 844–8

95. The Humble Petition and Advice, 25 May 1657

To his Highness the Lord Protector of the Commonwealth of England, Scotland and Ireland, and the dominions thereto belonging, The Humble Petition and Advice of the knights, citizens and burgesses now assembled in the Parliament of this Commonwealth

We, the knights, citizens and burgesses in this present parliament assembled, taking into our most serious consideration the present state of the three nations joined and united under your Highness's protection, cannot but in the first place with all thankfulness acknowledge the wonderful mercy of Almighty God in delivering us from that tyranny and bondage, both in our spiritual and civil concernments, which the late king and his party designed to bring us under, and pursued the effecting thereof by a long and bloody war; and also that it hath pleased the same gracious God to preserve your person in many battles, to make you an instrument for preserving our peace, though environed with enemies abroad and filled with turbulent, restless and unquiet spirits in our own bowels, that as in the treading down the common enemy and restoring us to peace and tranquility the Lord hath used you so eminently, and the worthy officers and soldiers of the army (whose faithfulness to the common cause we and all good men shall ever acknowledge, and put a just value upon); so also that he will use you and them in the settling and securing our liberties as we are men and Christians to us and our posterity after us, which are those great and glorious ends which the good people of these nations have so freely, with the hazard of their lives and estates, so long and earnestly contended for. We consider likewise the continual danger which your life is in from the bloody practices both of the malignant and discontented party (one whereof through the goodness of God you have been lately delivered from), it being a received a principle amongst them that, no order being settled in your lifetime for the succession in the government, nothing is wanting to bring us into blood and confusion, and them to their desired ends, but the destruction of your person. And in case things should thus remain at your death we are not able to express what calamities would in all human probability ensue thereupon, which we trust your Highness (as well as we) do hold yourself obliged to provide against, and not to leave a people, whose common peace and interest you are entrusted with, in such a condition as may hazard both, especially in this conjecture, when there seems to be an opportunity of coming to a settlement upon just and legal foundations. Upon these considerations we have judged it a duty incumbent upon us to present and declare these our most just and necessary desires to your Highness.

1. That your Highness will be pleased, by and under the name and style of Lord Protector of the Commonwealth of England, Scotland and Ireland, and the dominions and territories thereunto belonging, to hold and exercise the office of chief magistrate of these nations, and to govern according to this Petition and Advice in all things therein contained, and in all other things according to the laws of these nations, and not otherwise. That your Highness will be pleased during your lifetime to appoint and declare the person who shall immediately after your death succeed you in the government of these nations.

2. That your Highness will for the future be pleased to call parliaments consisting of two Houses (in such manner as shall be more particularly afterwards agreed and declared in this Petition and Advice) once in three years at furthest, or oftener, as the affairs of the nations shall require . . .

3. That . . . those persons who are legally chosen by a free election of the people to serve in parliament may not be excluded from sitting in parliament to do their duties, but by judgment and consent of that House whereof they are members.

4. That those who have advised, assisted or abetted the Rebellion of Ireland, and those who do or shall profess the popish religion, be disabled and made incapable for ever to be elected or to give any vote in the election of any Member to sit and serve in parliament; . . . [also] all and every person and persons who have aided, abetted, advised or assisted in any war against the parliament since the first day of January 1641[–2] (unless he or they have since borne arms for the parliament or your Highness, or otherwise given signal testimony of his or their good affection to the Commonwealth, and continued faithful to the same), and all such as have been actually engaged in any plot, conspiracy or design against the person of your Highness, or in any insurrection or rebellion in England or Wales since the 16th day of December 1653 . . .

★   ★   ★

And that the persons who shall be elected to serve in parliament be such, and no other than such as are persons of known integrity, fearing God, and of good conversation, and being of the age of twenty-one years, and not such as are . . . in Holy Orders, . . . ministers, or public preachers of the Gospel. Nor such as are guilty of any of the offences mentioned in an act of parliament bearing date the 9th of August 1650 entitled, an Act against several atheistical, blasphemous and execrable opinions derogatory to the honour of God and destructive to human society, no common scoffer nor reviler or religion, or of any person or persons for possessing thereof, no person that hath married or shall marry a wife of the popish religion, or hath trained or shall train up his child or children, or any other child or children under his tuition or government, in the popish religion, or that shall permit or suffer such child or children to be trained in the said religion, or that hath given or shall give his consent that his son or daughter shall marry any of that religion, no person that shall deny the Scriptures to be the Word of God, or the Sacraments, prayer, magistracy and ministry to be of the Ordinances of God, no common profaner of the Lord's Day, no profane swearer or cursers, no drunkard or common haunter of taverns or alehouses.

[Commissioners were instituted to scrutinise returns and inform parliament if men so disqualified were elected. Elaborate precautions were taken to control these commissioners, but in the *Additional Petition and Advice*[50] the whole clause was repealed and a fine of £1,000 was merely imposed on offenders.]

★   ★   ★

5. That your Highness will consent that none be called to sit and vote in the Other House but such as are not disabled . . . in the former article, being such

[50] Firth and Rait, II, 1183–4.

as shall be nominated by your Highness and approved by this House,[51] and that they exceed not seventy in number, nor be under the number of forty (whereof the quorum to be one and twenty) who shall not give any vote by proxies; and that as any of them do die, or be legally removed, no new ones be admitted to sit and vote in their rooms but by consent of the House itself.[52]

That the Other House do not proceed in any civil causes, except in writs of error, in cases adjourned from inferior courts into the parliament for difficulty, in cases of petition against proceedings in courts of equity, and in cases of the privileges of their own House. That they do not proceed in any criminal causes whatsoever, against any person criminally, but upon an impeachment of the Commons assembled in parliament, and by their consent. That they do not proceed in any cause, either civil or criminal, but according to the known laws of the land, and the due course and custom of parliament. That no final determinations or judgments be by any Members of that House, in any cause there depending either civil, criminal or mixed, as commissioners or delegates, to be nominated by that House; but all such final determinations and judgments to be by the House itself, any law or usage to the contary notwithstanding.

6. That in all other particulars which concern the calling and holding of parliaments, your Highness will be pleased that the laws and statutes of the land be observed and kept, and that no laws be altered, suspended, abrogated or repealed, or new law made, but by act of parliament.

7. And to the end that there may be a constant revenue for support of the government, and for the safety and defence of these nations by sea and land, we declare our willingness to settle forthwith a yearly revenue of £1,300,000, whereof £1,000,000 for the navy and army, and £300,000 for the support of the government, and no part thereof to be raised by a land-tax, and this not be altered without the consent of the three estates in parliament;[53] and to grant such other temporary supplies according to the Commons assembled in parliament shall from time to time adjudge the necessities of these nations to require; and do pray your Highness that it be enacted and declared that no charge be laid, nor person be compelled to contribute to any gift, loan,

[51] However, the Additional Petition and Advice authorised Cromwell to summon the Members of the Other House during the next recess, and declared that at the beginning of the next session 'the persons so summoned and assembled together shall be, and are hereby declared to be the Other House of Parliament, and shall and may without further approbation of this House . . . proceed to do and perform all such matters and things as the other House of Parliament ought to do and perform . . . by the aforesaid Humble Petition and Advice . . .' (Firth and Rait, II, 1186).

[52] The Additional Petition and Advice added: 'That the nomination of the persons to supply the place of such Members of the House as shall die or be removed shall be by your Highness and your successors' (ibid., 1184).

[53] 'That the monies directed to be for the supply of the sea and land forces be issued by advice of the Council, and that the treasurer, or commissioners of the treasury, shall give an account of all the said money to every parliament' (ibid., 1184).

benevolence, tax, tallage, aid or any other like charge, without common consent by act of parliament, which is a freedom the people of these nations ought by the laws to inherit.

8. That none may be admitted to the Privy Council of your Highness or successors, but such as are of known piety and undoubted affection to the rights of these nations, and a just Christian liberty in matters of religion, nor without consent of the Council to be afterwards approved by both Houses of Parliament, and shall not afterwards be removed but by consent of parliament, but may in the intervals of parliament be suspended from the exercise of his place by your Highness, by your successors and the Council, for just cause; and that the number of the Council shall not be above twenty-one, whereof the quorum be seven, and not under; as also that after your Highness's death [the appointment of] the commander-in-chief under your successors of such army or armies as shall be necessary to be kept in England, Scotland or Ireland, as also all such field-officers at land, or generals at sea, which after that time shall be newly made and constituted by your successors be by consent of the Council and not otherwise. And that the standing forces of this Commonwealth shall be disposed of by the chief magistrate by the consent of both Houses of Parliament, the parliament sitting, and in the intervals of parliament by the chief magistrate by the advice of the Council; and also that your Highness and successors will be pleased to exercise your government over these nations by the advice of your Council.

9. And that the chancellor, keeper or commissioners of the Great Seal of England, the treasurer, or commissioners of the treasury, the admiral, the chief governor of Ireland, the chancellor, keeper or commissioners of the Great Seal of Ireland, the chief justices of both the Benches, and the chief baron in England and Ireland, the commander-in-chief of the forces in Scotland, and such officers of state there as by act of parliament in Scotland are to be approved by parliament, and the judges in Scotland hereafter to be made, shall be approved by both Houses of Parliament.[54]

10. And whereas your Highness, out of your zeal to the glory of God and the propagation of the Gospel of the Lord Jesus Christ, hath been pleased to encourage a godly ministry in these nations, we earnestly desire that such as do openly revile them or their assemblies, or disturb them in the worship and service of God, to the dishonour of God, scandal of good men, or breach of the peace, may be punished according to law, and where the laws are defective, that your Highness will give consent to such laws as shall be made in that behalf.

11. That the true Protestant Christian religion, as it is contained in the Holy

---

[54] The Additional Petition and Advice provided that in the intervals of Parliament these officers should be chosen 'by the consent of the Council, to be afterwards approved by Parliament' (*ibid.*, 1184).

Scriptures of the Old and New Testament, and no other, be held forth and asserted for the public profession of these nations; and that a Confession of Faith, to be agreed by your Highness and the Parliament, according to the rule and warrant of the Scriptures, be asserted, held forth and recommended to the people of these nations, that none may be suffered or permitted by opprobrious words or writing maliciously or contemptuously to revile or reproach the Confession of Faith to be agreed upon as aforesaid. And such who profess faith in God the Father, and in Jesus Christ his eternal Son, the true God, and in the Holy Spirit, God co-equal with the Father and the Son, One God blessed for ever, and do acknowledge the Holy Scriptures of the Old and New Testament to be revealed Will and Word of God, and shall in other things differ in doctrine, worship or discipline from the public profession held forth, endeavours shall be used to convince them by sound doctrine and the example of a good conversation, but they may not be compelled thereto by penalties, nor restrained from their profession, but protected from all injury and molestation in the profession of the faith, and exercise of their religion, whilst they abuse not this liberty to the civil injury of others or the disturbance of the public peace; so that this liberty be not extended to popery or Prelacy, or to the countenancing such who publish horrid blasphemies, or practise to hold forth licentiousness or profaneness under the profession of Christ.

And that those ministers or public preachers who shall agree with the public profession aforesaid in matters of faith, although in their judgment and practice they differ in matters of worship and discipline, shall not only have protection in the way of their churches and worship respectively, but be esteemed fit and capable, notwithstanding such difference (being otherwise duly qualified and duly approved) of any trust, promotion or employment whatsoever in these nations that any ministers who agree in doctrine, worship and discipline with the public profession aforesaid are capable of. And all others who agree with the public profession in matters of faith, although they differ in matters of worship and discipline as aforesaid, shall not only have protection as aforesaid, but be esteemed fit and capable (notwithstanding such difference, being otherwise duly qualified) of any civil trust, employment or promotion in these nations. But for such persons who agree not in matters of faith with the public profession aforesaid, they shall not be capable of receiving the public maintenance appointed for the ministry.

Provided, that this clause shall not be construed to extend to such ministers or public preachers, or pastors of congregations; but that they be disenabled to hold any civil employment which those in holy orders were or are disenabled to hold by an act entitled, an act for disenabling all persons in holy orders to exercise any temporal jurisdiction or authority.

And that your Highness will give your consent that all laws, statutes, ordinances, and clauses in any law, statute and ordinance, so far as they are contrary to the aforesaid liberty, be repealed.

[12. Reconfirmed the financial obligations of the Long Parliament, the sale of lands and the abolition of episcopacy, etc.

13. Those excluded from parliament by § 4 above are also excluded from public service.]

14. And that your Highness will be pleased to consent that nothing in this Petition and Advice contained, nor your Highness's assent thereto, shall be construed to extend to the dissolving of this present parliament . . .

15.[55] And that nothing contained in this Petition and Advice, nor your Highness's consent thereunto, shall be construed to extend to the repealing or making void of any act or ordinance which is not contrary hereunto, or to the matters herein contained . . .

[16. Confirmed the validity of all existing writs, indictments, etc., and the efficacy of the actions started by them.]

17. And that your Highness and your successors will be pleased to take an oath in such a form as shall be agreed upon by your Highness and this present parliament.[56]

And in case your Highness shall not be satisfied to give your consent to all the matters and things in this Humble Petition and Advice, that then nothing in the same be deemed of force to oblige the people of these nations in any particulars therein contained.

★　★　★

Firth and Rait, II, 1048–56

96. The Oath to the Lord Protector, 18 January 1658

I, A. B. do, in the presence and by the name of God Almighty, promise and swear that to the utmost of my power, in my place, I will uphold and maintain the true, reformed, Protestant, Christian religion, in the purity thereof, as it is contained in the Holy Scriptures of the Old and New Testaments, and encourage the profession and professors of the same; and that I will be true and faithful to the Lord Protector of the Commonwealth of England, Scotland and Ireland, and the dominions and territories thereunto belonging, as Chief Magistrate thereof; and shall not contrive, design or attempt any thing against the person or lawful authority of the

---

[55] This and the following clauses are misnumbered in the original, 16, 17, etc.
[56] This was set out in the Additional Petition and Advice; see the next document.

Lord Protector; and shall endeavour, as much as in me lies, as a Member of Parliament, the preservation of the rights and liberties of the People.

Firth and Rait, II, 1185

97. The Declaration of Breda, 4 April 1660

Charles, by the Grace of God, king of England, Scotland, France and Ireland, Defender of the Faith, &c., to all our loving subjects, of what degree or quality soever, greeting. If the general distraction and confusion which is spread over the whole kingdom doth not awaken all men to a desire and longing that those wounds which have so many years together been kept bleeding may be bound up, all we can say will be to no purpose. However, after this long silence we have thought it our duty to declare how much we desire to contribute thereunto, and that, as we can never give over the hope in good time to obtain the possession of that right which God and Nature hath made our due, so we do make it our daily suit to the Divine Providence that he will, in compassion to us and our subjects, after so long misery and sufferings, remit and put us into a quiet and peaceable possession of that our right, with as little blood and damage to our people as is possible. Nor do we desire more to enjoy what is ours, than that all our subjects may enjoy what by law is theirs, by a full and entire administration of justice throughout the land, and by extending our mercy where it is wanted and deserved.

And to the end that the fear of punishment may not engage any, conscious to themselves of what is passed, to a perseverance in guilt for the future, by opposing the quiet and happiness of their country in the restoration both of king, peers and people to their just, ancient and fundamental rights, we do by these presents declare, that we do grant a free and general pardon, which we are ready upon demand to pass under our Great Seal of England, to all our subjects, of what degree or quality soever, who within forty days after the publishing hereof shall lay hold upon this our grace and favour, and shall by any public act declare their doing so, and that they return to the loyalty and obedience of good subjects (excepting only such persons as shall hereafter be excepted by parliament). Those only excepted, let all our loving subjects, how faulty soever, rely upon the word of a king, solemnly given by this present Declaration, that no crime whatsoever committed against us or our royal father before the publication of this shall ever rise in judgment or be brought in question against any of them, to the least endamagement of them either in their lives, liberties or estates, or (as far forth as lies in our power) so much as to the prejudice of their reputations by any reproach or term of distinction from the rest of our best subjects, we desiring and ordaining that henceforward all notes of discord, separation and difference of parties be utterly abolished among all our subjects, whom we invite and conjure to a perfect union among themselves, under our protection, for the resettlement of our just rights and theirs in a free parliament, by which, upon the word of a king, we will be advised.

And because the passion and uncharitableness of the times have produced several opinions in religion, by which men are engaged in parties and animosities against each other, which, when they shall hereafter unite in a freedom of conversation, will be composed and better understood, we do declare a liberty to tender consciences, and that no man shall be disquieted or called in question for differences of opinion in matter of religion which do not disturb the peace of the kingdom; and that we shall be ready to consent to such an act of parliament as, upon mature deliberation, shall be offered to us, for the full granting that indulgence.

And because, in the continued distractions of so many years and so many and great revolutions, many grants and purchases of estates have been made, to and by many officers, soldiers and others, who are now possessed of the same, and who may be liable to actions at law upon several titles, we are likewise willing that all such differences, and all things relating to such grants, sales and purchases, shall be determined in parliament, which can best provide for the just satisfaction of all men who are concerned.

And we do further declare, that we will be ready to consent to any act or acts of parliament to the purposes aforesaid, and for the full satisfaction of all arrears due to the officers and soldiers of the army under the command of General Monk, and that they shall be received into our service upon as good pay and conditions as they now enjoy.

Given under our Sign Manual and Privy Signet, at our Court at Breda, this 4/14 day of April, 1660, in the twelfth year of our reign.   *LJ*, XI, 7–8

BOOK III

THE RESTORED CONSTITUTION

A constitution cannot make itself; somebody made it, not at once but at several times. It is alterable, and by that draweth nearer perfection; and without suiting itself to differing times and circumstances, it could not live.

HALIFAX

CHAPTER 9

THE RESTORATION SETTLEMENT

The Restoration Settlement was based on the undertakings given in the Declaration of Breda, and on the legislation of 1641 and 1642 to which Charles I had given his assent. Only two of these statutes were repealed: the Act of 1642 excluding bishops from the House of Lords,[1] and the Triennial Act of 1641, which was hastily repealed in 1664 on the mistaken ground that it might oblige Charles to dissolve his present parliament.[2] It was replaced by a simple declaratory act, which obliged the king to meet parliament every three years, but provided no machinery of compulsion and laid down no minimum period for a session.[3] It is worth noting that Charles II did not begin to infringe this act until March 1684, James II not until November 1688.

Nothing more was heard, or was to be heard, of the insistent demand, voiced in every constitutional schema put forward by the Long Parliament from 1642 to 1648, for parliamentary control of the executive. As for the experiments undertaken by the Instrument of Government in the field of parliamentary representation, they were doomed by association with the Levellers, and Clarendon's view, put forward in his opening speech to the Cavalier Parliament in 1661 (**101**), was never seriously contested. These significant lacunae should always be kept in mind when considering the post-1660 constitution.

On the other hand, very little of the new legislation of 1660–2 was designed to strengthen or protect the executive. The Act for the Preservation of the King's Person and Government[4] confirmed the existing law of treason, and *inter alia* imposed heavy penalties on those who declared the King to be a papist, or who upheld the jurisdiction and authority of the Long Parliament. Another act of 1661, forbidding the submission of petitions to king or parliament by more than ten persons, was obviously framed with the events of 1641 in mind.[5] Also the dispute which had led to the outbreak of civil war was finally settled by the Militia Act of 1661 (**102**), which unequivocally vested the command of the armed forces in the king. Meanwhile the Convention Parliament of 1660 completed the work of reform which the Long Parliament had abandoned in the autumn of 1641 by abolishing purveyance and feudal tenures in return for the grant in perpetuity of a portion of the excise.[6]

Meanwhile the implementation of the Declaration of Breda did not prove easy. By

---

[1] By 13 Car. II, c. 12, *SR*, v, 306.

[2] Caroline Robbins, 'The Repeal of the Triennial Act in 1644', *HLQ*, XII (1948), 121–40. It should be noted that the Acts of 1641 and 1664, unlike the act of 1695, did not lay down any maximum period for a parliament, provided the king met it at least once every three years.

[3] 16 Car. II, c. 1, *SR*, v, 513.

[4] 13 Car. II, st. 1, c. 1, printed Browning, *Documents*, p. 63.

[5] *Ibid.*, p. 66. The preamble to the act reversing Strafford's attainder (*SR*, v, 424) makes the same point.

[6] 12 Car. II, c. 24. The important sections are printed by Costin and Watson, I, 2–5. See p. 180 above.

a prodigious burst of taxation in 1660 and 1661 the greater part of the army and navy was demobilised with full arrears of pay, and a serious and successful effort was made to re-absorb the veterans into civil society.[7] Charles II also fulfilled in a handsome manner his promise of full pardon and indemnity. The Act of Indemnity and Oblivion (98), for which he and Clarendon fought hard in the Convention, is a remarkable document. Only those who had signed Charles I's death warrant or been involved in his execution, and those responsible for the Irish Rebellion of 1641, plus a few particularly obnoxious individuals, like Vane, Lambert and Sir Arthur Haslerigg, were exempted from its very full and ample provisions, and all process of revenge or retribution was halted. More remarkable still, for three years penalties were imposed for reflecting by speech or writing on any man's conduct over the past 20 years.

But the government's approach to the land question was tentative and hesitant, as well it might be. The wholesale confiscation and sale of lands during the Interregnum had left a tangled situation, and Charles's undertaking at Breda to recognise all existing titles to land implied that he would not inquire into their origin. He and his Lord Chancellor, Clarendon, soon decided that they must distinguish between those whose estates had been forcibly confiscated and sold over their heads and those who had sold them voluntarily, even to pay delinquency fines. Any other course would impugn all legal proceedings under the usurping governments, with chaotic results. But the government was not anxious to parade its decision. By reversing all treasons and attainders since 1642, and proceedings on them, § II of the Act of Oblivion (98) freed the estates of prominent royalists who had been formally proscribed by the Long Parliament, but those seeking further enlightenment had to read through to § XLVIII, which declared that those who had purchased estates not previously belonging to the Crown or the Church and not sold by order of one of the Interregnum governments had a sound title. Similarly, § X of the Act confirming Judicial Proceedings (99) again safeguarded the lands of Crown and Church, but § VI specifically excluded all other land sales from its scope. This left the legal situation so uncertain that many leading royalists, particularly those who had gone into exile during the late troubles, secured private acts of parliament for the recovery of their estates. Though there was some grumbling, of course, it never came to a head, or looked like doing so, and the former assumption that large amounts of land changed hands permanently between 1642 and 1660, causing major changes in the composition of the landed classes, can now be dismissed. Very few new landed families appeared in the reign of Charles II whose rise can be attributed to the purchase of royalists' estates, and even fewer royalist families dropped out of the upper classes for this reason.[8]

---

[7] For instance, parliament at last passed an act for which the army had agitated since 1647, obliging gilds and corporations to waive or modify apprenticeship rules for veterans (12 Car. II, c. 16; *SR*, v, 237). For the taxation involved, see Chandaman, *Public Revenue*, pp. 143–4.

[8] Joan Thirsk, 'The Sale of Royalist Land during the Interregnum', *Econ. Hist. Review*, 2nd ser., v (1952), 188–207, and 'The Restoration Land Settlement', *JMH*, xxv (1945), 315–28; and H. J. Habakkuk, 'The Land Settlement and the Restoration of Charles II', 5 *TRHS*, xxviii (1978), 201–22. However, indebtedness incurred during the Civil Wars and Interregnum may have contributed to what some see as a 'Decline of the Gentry' in the next generation; Habakkuk, 'English Landed Families II', *ibid.*, xxx (1980), 200–2, and G. E. Mingay, *The Gentry* (1976), pp. 68–71.

Charles II's final undertaking at Breda, that he would give his assent to any legislation that offered a measure of religious toleration, was never implemented at all, because no such legislation was ever presented. The position of the Puritans, apparently so strong even in 1660, rapidly crumbled. The majority of sectarians or congregationalists were members of the working classes, divided amongst themselves and regarded with aversion by both sides. The Presbyterian ministers were deluded by hopes of 'comprehension' within a reformed Church – bishoprics were offered to the more prominent among them, and Edward Reynolds accepted – and betrayed by the leading 'Presbyterian' laymen, like Monk, Edward Montagu and Anthony Ashley Cooper, on whose support they relied. The Convention contained a powerful Presbyterian element in Lords and Commons, and was without the bishops, but it was skilfully prevented from legislating for the Church by the promise of a national synod.[9] Moreover, the Fifth Monarchy uprising in London in January 1661 compromised all Dissent, however respectable and law-abiding, and the elections of March and April 1661 returned a parliament opposed to any compromise. One of their first Acts sent the bishops back to the House of Lords, and they were only restrained from introducing a new, stringent Uniformity Bill by the need to await the result of the Savoy Conference between the bishops and the leading Dissenting ministers. The failure of this conference gave the extremists their head, and in November 1661 they produced the Corporations Act (**104**), which excluded from the government or management of borough corporations those who would not take the Anglican sacrament, plus the oaths of allegiance and supremacy, plus two solemn declarations, one abjuring the Solemn League and Covenant, the other avowing that it was in no circumstances lawful to take up arms against the king – the notorious 'non-resistance oath'. Moreover, for three years the act was to be administered by Crown commissioners, who had the power to remove members of corporations without cause shown. Secondly, in May 1662 a new Uniformity Act (**105**) laid it down that all those in holy orders, with or without cure of souls, must take all the oaths and declarations imposed on members of corporations, plus a declaration of their 'unfeigned acceptance' of the whole of the Book of Common Prayer – though it was silent on the Thirty-Nine Articles. Those who failed to comply by 24 August 1662, a remarkably short deadline, were removed, and patrons could present to their livings as if they were legally dead. Finally, an act of 1663 compelled vestrymen to take the non-resistance oath and an oath 'to conform to the liturgy of the Church of England as it is now by law established'.[10]

There is still some room for argument between those who believe that this reactionary church settlement was planned with machiavellian cunning from the beginning, and those who think that Charles and Clarendon were forced to accept a

[9] Louise F. Brown, 'Religious Factors in the Convention Parliament', *EHR*, XXII (1907), 51–63; G. F. Trevallyn Jones, 'The Composition and Leadership of the Presbyterian party in the Convention', *ibid.*, LXXIX (1964), 307–54; George R. Abernethy, 'The English Presbyterians and the Stuart Restoration', *Trans. Amer. Philosophical Society*, vol. LV, pt 2 (Philadelphia 1965).

[10] 15 Car. II, c. 5, 'An Act for regulating select vestries', *SR*, V, 446–7.

much narrower solution than that which they had originally contemplated.[11] Indeed, the Worcester House Declaration of 25 October 1660 shows that Charles and his advisers were willing, under pressure, to concede a remarkable degree of Presbyterianism in the government and administration of the Church, and adopt a distinctly relaxed view on subscription to the Thirty-Nine Articles. But his remarks on episcopacy:

> Since by the wonderful blessing of God the hearts of this whole nation are returned to an obedience to monarchic government in the state, it must be very reasonable to support that government in the Church which is established by law, and with which the monarchy hath flourished through so many ages;[12]

betray the bent of his thinking, and no doubt Clarendon's, and probably neither of them was particularly disturbed at being driven steadily to the right. Certainly the speech with which Clarendon dismissed the Convention Parliament in December 1660 does not suggest a disposition to compromise (**100**). It is also important to remember that direct persecution of Nonconformists was not part of the original settlement, and was only introduced in 1664.

However, what is certain is that the Church as re-established would have pleased John Pym more than William Laud. This was evident in the first session of 1661, when the Commons firmly resisted an attempt on the part of the bishops to revive the High Commission. Moreover, though it agreed to repeal those parts of the act of 1641 which might be said to impugn the bishops' powers to hold their ordinary ecclesiastical courts, parliament expressly stated that the clause in Elizabeth's Act of Supremacy which was held to authorise the High Commission was still repealed, and it again forbad – rather neurotically – the use of the *ex officio* oath. Finally, in the same statute it settled an old dispute in its own favour by declining to authorise the canons of 1640, or any other canons promulgated without its approval (**103**).

So, it had been decided that parliament would henceforward control the discipline of the Church, arbitrate on the qualifications demanded of the clergy, and lay down the form of public worship – even if this last had been drawn up by Convocation. But in 1664, by a private agreement with Clarendon, Archbishop Sheldon abandoned the clergy's immemorial right to tax themselves, and as a result Convocation did not meet again until 1689. Nor was the government's control over the Church what it was. Clarendon's attempt to use the Corporation Act as a means of increasing the government's electoral influence in the name of religious orthodoxy was handsomely defeated,[13] and so, too, was the king's attempt to secure a measure of toleration for Catholics and Dissenters (p. 375 below). So little regard did Charles have for his right

---

[11] R. S. Bosher, *The Making of the Restoration Settlement: The Influence of Laudians* (1951), is the chief exponent of the 'planned coup' theory, but his views are contested by every other historian in the field: by George R. Abernethy, 'Clarendon and the Declaration of Indulgence', *Jnl Eccl. Hist.*, XI (1960), 55–73, and 'The English Presbyterians and the Stuart Restoration', *Trans. Amer. Philosophical Soc.*, LV, pt 2 (Philadelphia 1965); by Anne Whiteman, 'The Re-establishment of the Church of England 1660–63', 5 *TRHS*, V (1955), 111–31, and 'The Restoration of the Church of England', in Nuttall and Chadwick, pp. 19ff; and by I. M. Green, *The Re-establishment of the Church of England* (Oxford 1978).

[12] Cardwell, *Documentary Annals*, II, 292.

[13] J. H. Sacret, 'The Restoration Government and the Municipal Corporations', *EHR*, XLV (1933), 232–59.

of appointment to bishoprics and other benefices that in 1681 he turned it over to a committee.[14]

The settlement could not help but diminish the Church. For the first time it was admitted that she did not command a monopoly of all English Protestants, and whereas Laud had always tried to coerce the Puritans into conformity and obedience, Sheldon simply abandoned them. The Uniformity Act of 1662 was far from producing uniformity, and it is doubtful how far it was intended to, and the Conventicles Act of 1664, which forbad meetings held 'under colour or pretence of any exercise of religion' of five or more persons not members of the same household, implied the acceptance of private dissenting worship. This act expired in 1668, and though it was re-enacted in an amended form in 1670 (**106**) the effect of the two-year intermission was disastrous; so, too, was the shorter intermission imposed by the Declaration of Indulgence in 1672 (p. 376). The Elizabethan Acts enforcing church attendance, originally directed at papists, were inadequate, and it proved particularly difficult to deal with ministers ejected by the Uniformity Act. By the Five Mile Act of 1665[15] such ministers, and other unlicensed preachers, were forbidden to come within five miles of the parish where they had been incumbent, or of any city or corporate borough. (It is significant, however, that the government never invoked the draconian act of 1593 against sectaries, though it was still on the statute book, and parliament tried to repeal it in 1680.)[16]

However, as fear of Rome mounted again in the late sixties and early seventies, so did the desire for the reunion of the Protestant nation. § x of the Conventicles Act of 1670 (**106**) was a public admission of the fact that many constables and even some magistrates were failing to enforce persecuting legislation.[17] During the Exclusion Crisis the opposition called for the repeal of this legislation, with the paradoxical result that in the subsequent reaction, beginning in 1681, a serious attempt was made to enforce it. This left it open for James II, with what sincerity it is impossible to say, to appeal for the support of the Dissenters in his Declaration of Indulgence in 1687 (p. 389 below). The apparent ability of a Catholic king to split the Protestant nation led straight to the comprehension proposals of 1689 and the Toleration Act, which were foreshadowed even in the Petition of the Seven Bishops in 1688 (p. 406 below).

98. 12 Car. II, c. 11: An Act of free and general pardon, indemnity and oblivion, 1660

The king's most excellent Majesty, taking into his gracious and serious consideration the long and great troubles, discords and wars that have for many years past been in this kingdom, and that divers of his subjects are by occasion thereof and otherwise fallen into and be obnoxious to great pains and

---

[14] R. A. Beddard, 'The Commission for Ecclesiastical Promotions 1681–84', *HJ*, x (1967), 11–40.

[15] Printed Browning, *Documents*, p. 382.

[16] Henry Horwitz, 'Protestant Reconciliation in the Exclusion Crisis', *Jnl Eccl. History*, xv (1964), 201–17. The act of 1593 is printed in Elton, *Tudor Constitution*, pp. 458–61.

[17] See the remarks of Sir Peter Leicester, p. 459 below.

penalties, out of a hearty and pious desire to put an end to all suits and controversies that by occasion of the late distractions have arisen and may arise between all his subjects, and to the intent that no crime whatsoever committed against his Majesty or his Royal Father shall hereafter rise in judgment or be brought in question against any of them to the least endamagement of them either in their lives, liberties, estates or to the prejudice of their reputations by any reproach or term of distinction, and to bury all seeds of future discords and remembrance of the former, as well in his own breast as in the breasts of his subjects one towards another, and his performance of his royal and gracious word signified by his letters to the several Houses of Parliament now assembled, and his declarations in that behalf published, is pleased that it may be enacted, and be it enacted by the King's most excellent Majesty with the advice and consent of the Lords and Commons in this present parliament assembled, first that all and all manner of treasons, misprisions of treason, murders, felonies, offences, crimes, contempts and misdemeanours coun- selled, commanded, acted or done since the first day of January in the year of Our Lord 1637[–8] by any person or persons before the twenty-fourth day of June in the year of Our Lord 1660 (other than the persons hereafter by name excepted, in such manner as they are hereafter excepted) by virtue or colour of any command, power, authority, commission, warrant or instructions from his late Majesty King Charles or his Majesty that now is, or from any other person or persons deriving or pretending to derive authority mediately or immediately from both or either of their Majesties, or by virtue or colour of any authority derived mediately or immediately of or from both Houses or either House of Parliament, or of or from any convention or assembly called or reputed or taking on them the name of a parliament, or by, from or under any authority styled or known by the name of The Keepers of the Liberty of England by Authority of Parliament, or by virtue or colour of any writ, commission, letters patents, instruction or instructions of or from any person or persons titled, reputed or taken to be Lord Protector of the Commonwealth of England, Scotland and Ireland . . ., or assuming the authority or reputed to be Chief Magistrate of the Commonwealth, or Commander in Chief of the Forces or Armies of this nation by sea or land, or by any pretended warrant or command whatsoever from them or any of them, or their or either of their respective councils or council, or any members of such council or councils, or from any person or persons whatsoever deriving or pretending to derive authority from them or any of them, be pardoned, released, indemnified, discharged and put in utter oblivion.

II. And that all and every the person and persons acting, advising, assisting, abetting and counselling the same, they, their heirs, executors and administra- tors (except as before is excepted) be and are hereby pardoned, released, acquitted, indemnified and discharged from the same, and of and from all pains of death and other pains, judgments, indictments, convictions, attainders, outlawries, penalties, escheats and forfeitures therefore had or given, or that might accrue for the same and that all such judgments . . . [etc.], and all grants thereupon made, and all estates derived under the same, be . . . from henceforth null and void, and that all mesne profits not yet received by such grantees shall be and are here hereby discharged; and that all and every person and persons, bodies politic and corporate, their and every of their heirs, executors, administrators and successors shall be and are hereby restored to all and every their lands, tenements and hereditaments, goods, chattels and other things forfeited, which to his Majesty do or shall appertain by reason of any offence herein before mentioned, and not hereafter in this present act excepted and foreprised.

★   ★   ★

V. And it is further by the authority aforesaid enacted in the second place that all and every the subject of these his Majesty's realms of England and Ireland, the dominion of Wales, the Isles of Jersey and Guernsey and the town of Berwick upon Tweed, and other his Majesty's dominions, the heirs, executors and administrators of them and every of them, and all and singular bodies in any manner or wise corporated, cities, boroughs, shires, ridings, hundreds, lathes, rapes, wapentakes, towns, villages, hamlets and tithings and every of them, and the successors and successor of every of them, shall be and are by the authority of this present parliament acquitted, pardoned, released, indemnified and discharged against the king's Majesty, his heirs and successors and every of them, of and from all manner of treasons, misprisions of treason, felonies, offences, contempts, trespasses, entries, wrongs, deceits, misdemeanours, forfeitures, penalties and sums of money, intrusions, mesne profits, wardships, marriages, reliefs, liveries, ouster le maines, mesne rates, respites of homage, fines and seizures for alienation without licence, arrearages of rents (other than the arrearages of rents due from the late farmers or pretended farmers of the excise or customs . . .), and of and from all arrearages of tenths and first-fruits, fines, post-fines, issues and amercements, and all recognisances, bonds or other securities given for payment of them or any of them, concealments of customs and excise, arrearages of purveyance and of compositions for the same, and of and from all pains of death, pains corporal and pecuniary, and generally of and from all other things, causes, quarrels, suits, judgments and executions in this present act hereafter not excepted nor foreprised which may be or can be by his Majesty in any wise or by any means pardoned before and unto . . . 24 June 1660, to every or any of his said subjects, bodies corporate, cities, boroughs, shires, ridings, . . .[etc.].

★   ★   ★

XXIII. And be it further enacted by the authority aforesaid that all acts of hostility and injuries, whether between the late king and the Lords and Commons then in parliament assembled, or between any of the people of this nation, which did arise upon any action, attempt, assistance, counsel or advice having relation unto or falling out by reason of the late troubles or in the late wars and public differences between the late king and parliament or between his now Majesty or any of his subjects, and which are not in this act excepted, that the same and whatsoever hath ensued thereupon, whether trenching upon the laws and liberties of this nation or upon the honour of his Majesty, or upon the honour or authority of the parliament, or to the prejudice of any particular or private person, shall in no time from and after . . . 24 June 1660 be called in question, whatsoever be the quality of the person, or of whatsoever kind or degree, civil or criminal, the injury is supposed to be, and that no mention be made thereof in time to come in judgment or judicial proceedings.

XXIV. And to the intent and purpose that all names and terms of distinction may likewise be put into utter oblivion, be it furher enacted by the authority aforesaid that if any person or persons within the space of three years next ensuing shall presume maliciously to call or allege of, or object against any other person or persons, any name or names, or other word of reproach anyway tending to revive the memory of the late differences or the occasions thereof, that then every such person so as aforesaid offending shall forfeit and pay unto the party grieved, in case such party offending shall be of the degree of gentleman or above, ten pounds, and if under that degree, forty shillings, to be recovered by the party grieved by action of debts to be therefore brought in any of his Majesty's Courts of Record . . .

X.[18] Except and always foreprised out of this free and general pardon . . . [murder or piracy unconnected with the late wars, buggery, rape, forced marriage, bigamy, and witchcraft]; and also excepted all and singular the accounts of all and every person and persons appointed by any of the authorities or pretended authorities aforesaid to be treasurer, receiver, farmer or collector (other than the subcollectors of the several parishes, towns and hamlets . . . [before 24 June 1659]) who have received or collected any subsidy, custom, subsidy of tunnage and poundage, prize-goods, assessment, sequestration, new impost or excise, or any of the rents and revenues of any land or hereditaments of or belonging to the late king, queen or prince or king that now is, or belonging to the late archbishoprics, bishoprics, deans or deans and chapters, canons, prebends and other officers belonging to any cathedral or collegiate church, or popish recusants convict, or of persons sequestered for their recusancy, or other sequestered estates received or collected by or paid

---

[18] The order of the clauses has been rearranged in the interests of clarity.

unto them since . . . 30 January 1643, and of all monies and other duties grown due or contracted upon the sale or disposition of them or any of them.[19]

* * *

XXIX. And be it further enacted by the authority aforesaid that no person or persons who by virtue of any order or warrant mediately or immediately derived from his late Majesty or his Majesty that now is, or by virtue of any act, ordinance or order of any or both Houses of parliament, or any of the authorities aforesaid, or any committee or committees acting under them or any of them, have seized, sequestered, levied, advanced or paid to any public use or into any public treasury within this kingdom any goods, chattels, debts, rents, sum or sums of money belonging to any person or persons whatsoever shall hereafter be sued, molested or drawn into question for the same, but that they and every of them shall be discharged against all persons for so much and no more of the said goods, chattels, debts, rents, sum or sums of money as their several and respective orders of discharge or acquittances extend unto.

* * *

XLVIII. Provided always . . . that no conveyance, assurance, grant, bargain, sale, charge, lease, assignment of lease, grants and surrenders by copy of court roll, estate, interest, trust or limitation of any use or uses of any manors, lands, tenements or hereditaments, not being the land nor hereditaments of the late king, queen, prince or of any archbishops, bishops, deans, deans and chapters, nor being land or hereditaments sold or given or appointed to be sold or given for the delinquency or pretended delinquency of any person or persons whatsoever by virtue or pretext of any act, order or ordinance, or reputed act, order or ordinance, since . . . 1 January 1642, nor any statute, judgment, or recognisance had, made, acknowledged or suffered to any person or persons, bodies politic or corporate before . . . 29 September 1659 by any of the persons before in this act by name excepted or their heirs . . ., nor any conveyance, assurance, grant or estate made before 25 April 1660 by any person or persons to any such person or persons excepted by name as aforesaid, in trust and for the benefit of any other person or persons, bodies politic or corporate not excepted by name as aforesaid, shall be impeached, defeated, made void, or frustrated hereby, or by the attainder or conviction of any such excepted person or persons, but that the same shall be held and enjoyed by the purchasers, grantees, lessees, assignees, *cestuy que use, cestuy que trust*, and every of them their heirs, executors, administrators and assigns respectively, as if this act had not been made, and as if the said person or persons had not been

---

[19] But no proceedings could be taken under this clause after 24 June 1662 (§ XIV), and military and naval officers could not be called to account for the pay or allowances or subsistence of their men (§ XIII).

excepted, attainted or convicted, any law, statute, usage or custom to the contrary thereof in any wise notwithstanding.

★ ★ ★

[The statute was full of exceptions, though in total the number of men involved was few and their importance slight.

It was natural that those guilty of bribery, forgery, perjury and subornation of witnesses should be excepted (§ xv), and Roman Catholic priests and Jesuits (xviii), and those committing thefts and felonies since 4 March 1660 (xxvii). Charles also took care to make his own servants responsible for money collected on his behalf since his accession in 1649 (xxx) and for traitorous correspondence with foreign powers over the same period (xxxii).

The general moratorium on debts and receipts also had many exceptions. The proceeds of the Decimation Tax of 1655–6 could be recovered (xxxi), and so could the ancient rents collected by sheriffs (xvii), and tithes (xliv). The proceeds of the excise since 1658, and debts against the excise since 1657, were accountable for (xxxiii, xlvi), as were sums owed by the army for billeting since 2 July 1659 (xlvii). Charles also gave himself the power to proceed against those who had stolen or confiscated the goods and chattels of the Royal Family, except munitions and stores, at any time since 1642 (xvi).

But the most important exceptions were penal. The only general category of men excepted were those responsible for the Irish Rebellion of 1641, which still generated more heat than any other single incident in the past 20 years (xxv), and even those responsible for trying, sentencing or executing Charles I were listed by name in so far as they were known (xxxiv). Cromwell, Ireton and John Bradshaw were excepted entirely out of the act (xxxvi), as were the other regicides who had died (xxxvii), and John Lambert and Sir Henry Vane (xli). Six men whose conduct in January 1649 was doubtful (xxxviii) and Sir Arthur Haslerigg (xxxxi) were excepted, but with the proviso that they should not be subject to the death penalty. In addition a number of men who were not regicides but who were regarded as particularly dangerous, such as Lenthall, Speaker of the Long Parliament, Oliver St John, Henry Ireton's brother John, Fleetwood, Desborough, Cobbet and several other army officers, were forbidden to take office under the government or any public employment under pain of exclusion from the benefits of the act (xlii).]   SR, v, 226–34

99. 12 Car. II, c. 12: An Act for confirmation of judicial proceedings, 1660

Be it enacted and it is enacted by his Majesty and the Lords and Commons in parliament assembled and by the authority of the same, that no fines, nor final concords, chirographs nor proclamations of fines, nor any recoveries, verdicts, judgments, statutes, recognisances nor enrolments of any deed or wills or of any such fines, proclamations, recoveries, verdicts, judgments, statutes, or recognisances, nor any exemplifications of them nor any of them, nor any inquisitions, indictments, presentments, informations, decrees, sentences, probates of will, nor letters of administration, nor any writs nor actings on, nor returns of writs, orders or other proceedings in law and equity, had, made, given, taken or done or depending in the Courts of Chancery, King's Bench, Upper Bench, Common Pleas and Court of Exchequer and Courts of Exchequer Chamber or any of them, sitting at Westminster or in the Courts of the Great Sessions in Wales, the Courts of any Counties Palatine or Duchy of Lancaster or town of Berwick-upon-Tweed, or in any other inferior courts of law or equity, or by any the judges, clerks, officers, sheriffs, coroners or ministers or others acting in obedience to them or any of them, or by any the Courts of Admiralty, Delegates, Justices of Assize, Nisi Prius, Oyer and Terminer, Gaol Delivery, Justices of the Peace, Commissioners of Sewers, Bankrupts or Charitable Uses, nor any actings, process, proceedings, nor executions thereupon had, made, given, done or suffered in the kingdom of England since the first of May 1642 shall be avoided for any want or defect of any legal power in the said courts, judges, commissioners, justices or any of them, or for or by reason that the premisses or any of them were commenced, prosecuted, had, made, held or used in the name, style or title of the late king, or in the name, style, title or test of *custodes libertatis angliae authoritate parliamenti*, or . . . of the Keepers of the Liberties of England, or . . . of Oliver, Lord Protector . . ., or . . . of Richard, Lord Protector . . ., or for or by reason of any alteration of the said names, styles or titles, or for that the said fines, recoveries, process, pleadings, proceedings and other things before mentioned, or the entry and enrolment of them or any of them were in the Latin or English tongue; but that all and every such fines, recoveries and other things above mentioned, and the actings, doings and proceedings thereupon, shall be of such and of no other force, effect and virtue than as if such courts, judges . . . [etc.] had acted by virtue of a true, just and legal authority, and as if the same and the entry and enrolment thereof were in Latin, and as if the several acts and ordinances or pretended acts or ordinances made by both or either Houses of Parliament, or any Convention assembled under the name of a parliament, or by Oliver Cromwell . . . and his Council warranting or directing such proceedings had been good, true and effectual acts of parliaments.

* * *

V. And whereas since the first day of May 1641, and before the five and twentieth day of April 1660, there were divers persons that adhered to both Houses of Parliament who for or in respect of such their adherence were indicted, charged or impeached of treason; and whereas . . . [during the same period] divers persons who adhered to his Majesty or to the late king were for such their allegiance charged, impeached or indicted of high treason, be it further provided and enacted that the said charges, impeachments, indictments, and all exigents, outlawries, convictions and attainders thereupon, and all letters patents and grants thereupon made of any manors, lands, tenements or hereditaments escheated or forfeited by reason of such attainder, and all title to any mesne profits by reason of such conviction, outlawry, attainder or grant be from henceforth repealed and discharged, and that all escheats, forfeitures and confiscations by reason of such outlawries, conviction or attainder be and are hereby restored unto such persons so outlawed, convicted or attainted, their heirs, executors and administrators respectively, as if no such attainder had been.

VI. Provided nevertheless . . . that this act or anything herein contained shall not extend to avoid or confirm any sales of estates made by virtue of any act, order or ordinance, or reputed act, order or ordinance of parliament since the first day of May 1642, nor any confirmation thereof made, or to be made thereof in this present parliament, but that such sales stand and be in the same plight and condition as they should or might have done if this act had not been made.

★ ★ ★

X. Provided always . . . that no non-claim upon or after any fine or fines hereby made good or confirmed shall extend or be construed to bar or prejudice any person or persons, their heirs or successors, or their feoffees or trustees . . . as concerning such right, claim and interest as they had in or to any land, tenements or other hereditaments which by colour of any act, order or ordinance of both or either Houses of Parliament or any Convention sitting at Westminster under the name or style or assuming the name or style or assuming the name or style of a parliament since . . . 1 May 1642 and before . . . 25 April 1660, were sold, conveyed or disposed [of, such] as then or late the land, tenements and hereditaments of the king, queen or prince, or of archbishops, bishops, deans, deans and chapters, or other ecclesiastical persons, or [such] as the lands, tenements and hereditaments of any other persons for their adherency to the late king or his Majesty that now is, or for any their actings relating to or in respect of the late Troubles, so always that the said person or persons aforesaid, their heirs or successors, pursue their title, claim or interest by way of action of lawful entry within five years next after . . . 29 May 1660.

XI. And although in this confirmation of Judicial Proceedings it was necessary to mention divers pretended acts and ordinances by the names and styles which those persons then usurped . . . took upon them to pass the same,

. . . yet this present parliament doth declare, and it is enacted by authority of the same, that the names and styles aforesaid and every of them are most rebellious, wicked, traitorous and abominable usurpations, detested by this present parliament as opposite in the highest degree to his sacred Majesty's most just and undoubted right, to whom and to his heirs and lawful successors the imperial crowns of the realms of England, Scotland and Ireland, with their and every of their dominions and territories, do of right appertain, and as violating and infringing the just rights and privileges of parliament and of both Houses thereof now assembled, or that hereafter shall be called and assembled.   SR, v, 234–6

100. Clarendon and the Church of England

Speech to both Houses on the dissolution of the Convention Parliament, 29 December 1660[20]

. . . We may tell those who still contrive the ruin of the Church, the best and the best-reformed church in the Christian World, reformed by that authority, and with those circumstances, as a reformation ought to be made, that God would not so miraculously have snatched this Church as a brand out of the fire, would not have raised it from the grave, after he had suffered it to be buried so many years, by the boisterous hands of profane and sacrilegious persons, under its own rubbish, to expose it again to the same rapine, reproach and impiety. That Church which delights itself in being called Catholic was never so near expiration, never had such a resurrection. That so small a pittance of meal and oil should be sufficient to preserve and nourish the poor widow and her family so long, is very little more miraculous than that such a number of pious, learned and very aged bishops should so many years be preserved, in such wonderful straits and oppressions, until they should plentifully provide for their own succession; that after such a deep deluge of sacrilege, profaneness and impiety had covered, and to common understanding swallowed it up, that that Church should again appear above the waters, God be again served in that Church, and served as he ought to be; and that there should be still some revenue left, to support and encourage those who serve him; nay, that many of those who seemed to thirst after that revenue till they had possessed it, should conscientiously restore what they had taken away, and become good sons and willing tenants to that Church they had so lately spoiled, may make us all piously believe that God Almighty would not have been at the expense and charge of such a deliverance, but in the behalf of a Church very acceptable to him, and which shall continue to the End of the World, and against which the Gates of Hell shall not be able to prevail . . .   LJ, xi, 239

---

[20] A further section of this speech is printed as no. **128**, p. 421 below.

101. Clarendon on Democracy

Speech at the opening of Parliament, 10 May 1661

. . . You have made, Mr Speaker, a very lively description of the extravagancy of that confusion which this poor nation groaned under, when they would throw off a government they had lived and prospered under so many ages, indeed from the time of being a nation, and which is as natural to them as their food or their raiment, to model a new one for themselves, which they knew no more how to do, than the naked Indians know how to dress themselves in the French fashion; when (as you say) all ages, sexes and degrees, all professions and trades, would become reformers, when the common people of England would represent the Commons of England, and abject men, who could neither write nor read, would make laws for the government of the most heroic and the most learned nation in the world – for sure none of our neighbours will deny it to have a full excellency and perfection both in arms and letters. And it was the grossest and most ridiculous pageant that great imposter ever exposed to public view, when he gave up the nation to be disposed of by a handful of poor mechanic persons, who, finding they knew not what to do with it, would (he was sure) give it back to him again, as they shortly did, which made his title complete to the government he meant to exercise.

No man undervalues the common people of England, who are in truth the best and the honestest, aye, and the wisest common people in the world, when he says they are not fit to model the government they are to live under, or to make the laws they are to obey . . . It is the privilege, if you please the prerogative (and it is a great one) of the common people of England to be represented by the greatest, and learnedest, and wealthiest and wisest persons that can be chosen out of the nation; and the confounding the Commons of England, which is a noble Representative, with the common people of England, was the first ingredient into that accursed dose, which intoxicated the brains of men with that imagination of a commonwealth; a commonwealth, Mr Speaker, a government as impossible for the spirit and temper and genius of the English nation to submit to, as it is to persuade them to give their cattle and their corn to other men, and to live upon roots and herbs themselves. I wish heartily that they who have been most delighted with that imagination knew in truth the great benefit under the government. There is not a commonwealth in Europe, where every man that is worth £100 doth not pay more to the government than a man of £1000 a year did ever to the Crown here before these Troubles. And I am persuaded that the monster Commonwealth cost this nation more, in the few years she was begot, born and brought up, and in her funeral (which was the best expense of all) than the monarchy hath done these six hundred years . . .

★　★　★

102. 13 Car. II, c. 6: An Act declaring the sole right of the militia to be in the King, 1661

Forasmuch as within all his Majesty's realms and dominions the sole supreme government, command and disposition of the militia and of all forces by sea and land and of all forts and places of strength is and by the laws of England ever was the undoubted right of his Majesty and his royal predecessors, kings and queens of England, and that both or either of the Houses of Parliament cannot nor ought to pretend to the same, nor can nor lawfully may raise or levy any war, offensive or defensive, against his Majesty, his heirs or lawful successors, and yet the contrary thereof hath of late years been practised, almost to the ruin and destruction of this kingdom, and during the late usurped governments many evil and rebellious principles have been distilled into the minds of the people of this kingdom, which unless prevented may break forth, to the disturbance of the peace and quiet thereof; and whereas an Act is under consideration for exercising the militia with most safety and ease to the king and his people,[21] which act cannot as yet be perfected, be it therefore enacted by the king's most excellent Majesty, by and with the advice and consent of the Lords and Commons assembled in parliament, that the militia and land forces of this kingdom, and of the dominion of Wales and town of Berwick-upon-Tweed, now under the power of Lieutenants or their Deputies, shall be exercised, ordered and managed until the 25th day of March next ensuing in such manner as the same now is actually exercised, ordered and managed, according to such commissions and instructions as they formerly have or from time to time shall receive from his Majesty.[22]

★　★　★

---

[21] This emerged as the Militia Act of 1662 (*SR*, v, 358).

[22] The act was occasioned not so much by the king's desire to settle a question which had brought about civil war in 1642 – though that was undoubtedly a part of it – but by Venner's rising in London in January 1661, and the need to indemnify the trained bands which had helped suppress it.

103. 13 Car. II, c. 12: An Act for explanation of a clause contained in an Act of Parliament made in the seventeenth year of the late King Charles . . . concerning commissioners for causes ecclesiastical, 1661

Whereas in an act of parliament made in the seventeenth year of the late King Charles entitled 'An Act for repeal of a branch of a statute primo Elizabethae concerning commissioners for causes ecclesiastical'[23] it is amongst other things enacted that no . . . person or persons whatsoever exercising spiritual or ecclesiastical power, authority or jurisdiction by any grant, licence or commission of the king's Majesty, his heirs or successors or otherwise shall, from and after . . . [1 August 1641] award, impose or inflict any pain, penalty, fine, amercement, imprisonment or other corporal punishment upon any of the king's subjects for any contempt, misdemeanour, crime, offence, matter or thing whatsoever belonging to spiritual or ecclesiastical cognisance or jurisdiction; whereupon some doubt hath been made that all ordinary power of coercion and proceedings in causes ecclesiastical were taken away, whereby the ordinary course of justice in causes ecclesiastical hath been obstructed; be it therefore enacted . . . that neither the said act nor anything therein contained doth or shall take away any ordinary power or authority from any of the said archbishops, bishops or any other person or persons named as aforesaid, but that they and every of them exercising ecclesiastical jurisdiction may proceed, determine, sentence, execute and exercise all manner of ecclesiastical jurisdiction . . . in as ample manner and form as they did and might lawfully have done before the making of the said act.

II. And be it further enacted . . . that the afore-recited act of decimo septimo Caroli and all the matters and clauses therein contained) excepting what concerns the High Commission Court, or the erecting of some such like court by commission) shall be and is hereby repealed . . .

III. Provided always, and it is hereby enacted, that neither this act nor anything herein contained shall extend or be construed to revive or give force to the said branch of the said statute made in the first year of the reign of the said late Queen Elizabeth mentioned in the said act of parliament [above] . . ., but that the said branch of the said statute made . . . shall stand and be repealed in such sort as if this [present] act had never been made.

IV. Provided also, and it is hereby further enacted, that it shall not be lawful for any archbishop, bishop, vicar-general, chancellor, commissary or other spiritual or ecclesiastical judge, officer, or minister, or any other person having or exercising spiritual or ecclesiastical jurisdiction to tender or administer unto any person whatsoever the oath usually called the oath *ex officio* . . .

---

[23] 17 Car. I, c. 11, no. **63**, p. 206 above.

V. Provided always that this act or anything therein contained shall not extend or be construed to extend . . . to confirm the canons made in the year 1640 nor any of them, nor any other ecclesiastical laws or canons not formerly confirmed, allowed or enacted by parliament or by the established laws of the land as they stood in the year . . . 1639. *SR*, v, 315–16

104. 13 Car. II, st. 2, c. 1: An Act for the well governing and regulating of corporations (The Corporation Act, 1661)

Whereas questions are likely to arise concerning the validity of elections of magistrates and other officers and members in corporations, as well in respect of removing some as placing others during the late Troubles, contrary to the true intent and meaning of their charters and liberties, and to the end that the succession in such corporations may be most probably perpetuated in the hands of persons well affected to his Majesty and the established government, it being too well known that notwithstanding all his Majesty's endeavours and unparalleled indulgence in pardoning all that is past nevertheless many evil spirits are still working, wherefore for prevention of the like mischief for the time to come and for preservation of the public peace both in Church and State, be it enacted . . . that commissions shall before 24 February next be issued forth under the Great Seal of England unto such persons as his Majesty shall appoint for the executing of the powers and authorities hereinafter expressed . . .

II. And be it enacted . . . that no charter of any corporation . . . shall at any time hereafter be avoided for or by reason of any act or thing done or omitted to be done before the first day of this present parliament.

III. And be it further enacted . . . that all persons who upon 24 December, 1661, shall be mayors, aldermen, recorders, bailiffs, town clerks, common councilmen and other persons then bearing any office or offices of magistracy, or places or trusts or other employment relating to or concerning the government of the said respective cities, corporations and boroughs and cinque ports and their members, and other port towns, shall at any time before 25 March 1663, when they shall be thereunto required by the said respective commissioners or any three of them, take the Oaths of Allegiance and Supremacy and this oath following:

I, A. B., do declare and believe that it is not lawful upon any pretence whatsoever to take arms against the king, and that I do abhor the traitorous position of taking arms by his authority against his person or against those that are commissioned by him. So help me God.

And also at the same time shall publicly subscribe before the said commissioners or any three of them the following declaration:

I, A. B., do declare that I hold that there lies no obligation upon me or any other person from the oath commonly called the Solemn League and Covenant, and that the same was in itself an unlawful oath and imposed upon the subjects of this realm against the known laws and liberties of the kingdom.

IV. And that all such of the said mayors and other the persons aforesaid . . . who shall refuse to take and subscribe the same within the time and in manner aforesaid shall from and immediately after such refusal be by authority of this act (*ipso facto*) removed and displaced of and from the said offices and places respectively; and the said offices and places from and immediately after such refusal shall . . . be void to all intents and purposes as if the said respective persons so refusing were naturally dead.

V. And nevertheless be it enacted . . . that the said commissioners or any five or more of them shall have full power by virtue of this act by order and warrant under their hands and seals to displace or remove any of the persons aforesaid from the said respective offices . . . if the said commissioners or the major part of them then present shall deem it expedient for the public safety, although such persons shall have taken and subscribed or be willing to take and subscribe the said oaths and declaration.

VI. And be it also enacted that the said respective commissioners or any five or more of them as aforesaid shall have power to restore such person or persons as have been illegally or unduly removed into the places out of which he or they were removed, and also to put and place into the offices and places which by any of the ways aforesaid shall be void respectively some other person or persons then being or which have been members or inhabitants of the said respective cities . . . [etc.], and that the said persons, from and after the taking of the said oaths and subscribing the said declaration shall hold and enjoy and be vested in the said offices and places as if they had been duly elected and chosen according to the charters and former usages of the said respective cities . . . [etc.]

VII. And be it further enacted . . . that . . . from and after the expiration of the said respective commissions the said three oaths and declaration shall be from time to time administered . . . by such person or persons respectively who by the charters or usages of the said respective cities . . . [etc.] ought to administer the oath for due executing the said places or offices respectively, and in default of such by two justices of the peace of the said cities . . . [etc.] if any such there be, or otherwise by two justices of the peace for the time being of the respective counties where the said cities . . . [etc.] are.

★ ★ ★

IX. Provided also . . . that from and after the expiration of the said commissions no person or persons shall for ever hereafter be placed, elected or chosen in or to any the offices or places aforesaid that shall not have within one year next before such election or choice taken the Sacrament of the Lord's Supper according to the rites of the Church of England, . . . and in default hereof every such placing, election and choice is hereby enacted and declared to be void.

★　★　★

XI. Provided also . . . that the powers granted to the commissioners by virtue of this act shall continue and be in force until 25 March 1663 and no longer.   *SR*, v, 321–3

105. 14 Car. II, c. 4: An Act for the uniformity of public prayers and administration of sacraments and other rites and ceremonies (The Uniformity Act, 1662)

Whereas in the first year of the late Queen Elizabeth there was one uniform Order of Common Service and Prayer and of the administration of Sacraments, Rites and Ceremonies in the Church of England (agreeable to the Word of God and usage of the Primitive Church) compiled by the reverend bishops and clergy, set forth in one book, entitled 'The Book of Common Prayer and Administration of Sacraments and other Rites and Ceremonies in the Church of England', and enjoined to be used by act of parliament holden in the said first year of the said late queen entitled 'An Act for the Uniformity of Common Prayer and Service in the Church, and Administration of the Sacraments',[24] very comfortable to all good people desirous to live in Christian conversation and most profitable to the estate of this realm, . . . and yet, this notwithstanding, a great number of people in divers parts of this realm, following their own sensuality and living without knowledge and due fear of God, do wilfully and schismatically abstain and refuse to come to their parish churches . . ., and whereas by the great and scandalous neglect of ministers in using the said order or liturgy so set forth and enjoined as aforesaid great mischiefs and inconveniences during the times of the late unhappy troubles have arisen and grown, and many people have been led into factions and schisms, to the great decay and scandal of the reformed religion of the Church of England, and to the hazard of many souls; for prevention whereof in time to come, for settling the peace of the Church, and for allaying the present distempers which the indisposition of the time hath contracted, the

---

[24] 1 Eliz., c. 2, printed Elton, *Tudor Constitution*, pp. 410–13.

king's Majesty, according to his Declaration of 25 October, 1660, granted his commission under the Great Seal of England to several bishops and other divines to review the Book of Common Prayer and . . . make such additions and alterations . . . as to them should seem meet and convenient, and should exhibit and present the same to his Majesty in writing for his further allowance or confirmation. Since when time, upon full and mature deliberation, they . . . have accordingly reviewed the said books, and have made some alterations . . . and have exhibited and presented the same unto his Majesty in writing in one book, entitled 'The Book of Common Prayer and Administration of the Sacraments and other Rites and Ceremonies of the Church according to the use of the Church of England, together with the Psalter or Psalms of David appointed as they are to be sung or said in churches, and the form and manner of making, ordaining and consecrating of Bishops, Priests and Deacons'. All which his Majesty having duly considered, hath fully approved and allowed the same, and recommended to this present parliament . . .

Now in regard that nothing conduceth more to the settling of the peace of this nation (which is desired by all good men) nor to the honour of our religion and the propagation thereof than a universal agreement in the public worship of Almighty God, and to the intent that every person within this realm may certainly know the rule to which he is to conform in public worship . . ., be it enacted . . . that all and singular ministers in any cathedral, collegiate or parish church or chapel or other place of public worship within this realm . . . shall be bound to say and use the Morning Prayer, Evening Prayer, celebration and administration of both the Sacraments, and all other the public and common prayer in such order and form as is mentioned in the said Book annexed and joined to this present act and entitled . . . [as above]. And that the Morning and Evening Prayers therein contained shall upon every Lord's day and upon all other days and occasions and at the times therein appointed be openly and solemnly read by all and every minister or curate in every church, chapel or other place of public worship . . . aforesaid.

II. And to the end that uniformity in the public worship of God (which is so much desired) may be speedily effected, be it further enacted . . . that every parson, vicar or other minister whatsoever who now hath and enjoyeth any ecclesiastical benefice or promotion within this realm of England or places aforesaid shall in the church, chapel or place of public worship belonging to his said benefice or promotion upon some Lord's day before the Feast of St Bartholomew [24 August], 1662, openly, publicly and solemnly read the Morning and Evening Prayer appointed to be read by and according to the said Book of Common Prayer at the times thereby appointed, and after such reading thereof shall openly and publicly before the congregation there assembled declare his unfeigned assent and consent to the use of all things in the said Book contained and prescribed, in these words and no other:

I, A. B., do declare my unfeigned assent and consent to all and every thing contained and prescribed in and by the book entitled the Book of Common Prayer and . . . [etc., as above.].

III. And that all and every such person who shall . . . neglect or refuse to do the same within the time aforesaid . . . shall *ipso facto* be deprived of all his spiritual promotions, and that from henceforth it shall be lawful to and for all patrons and donors of all and singular the said spiritual promotions or any of them according to their respective rights and titles to present or collate to the same as though the person or persons so offending or neglecting were dead.

[IV. Henceforward any new incumbent was obliged to make this declaration within two months of entering upon his benefice, under pain of deprivation as above.]

*   *   *

VI. And be it further enacted . . . that every dean, canon and prebendary of every cathedral or collegiate church, and all masters and other heads, fellows, chaplains and tutors of or in any college, hall, house of learning or hospital, and every public professor and reader in either of the universities and in every college elsewhere, and every parson, vicar, curate, lecturer and every other person in holy orders, and every schoolmaster keeping any public or private schools, and every person instructing or teaching any youth in any house or private family as a tutor or schoolmaster, who upon the first day of May, 1662, or at any time thereafter shall be incumbent or have possession of any deanery, canonry, prebend, mastership, headship, fellowship, professor's place or reader's place, parsonage, vicarage, or any other ecclesiastical dignity or promotion, or of any curate's place, lecture or school, or shall instruct or teach any youth as tutor or schoolmaster, shall before the Feast Day of St Bartholomew [24 August], 1662, or at or before his or their respective admission to be incumbent or have possession aforesaid subscribe the Declaration or Acknowledgement following:

I, A. B., do declare that it is not lawful upon any pretence whatsoever to take arms against the king, and that I do abhor that traitorous position of taking arms by his authority against his person or against those that are commissioned by him, and that I will conform to the liturgy of the Church of England as it is now by law established. *And I do declare that I do hold there lies no obligation upon me or on any other person from the oath commonly called the Solemn League and Covenant to endeavour any change or alteration of government either in Church or state. And that the same was in itself an unlawful oath and imposed upon the subjects of this realm against the known laws and liberties of this kingdom.*[25]

[To be subscribed before the vice-chancellor, the archbishop, bishop or other ordinary as appropriate under pain of deprivation as above.]

VII. . . . And after such subscription made every such parson, vicar, curate and lecturer shall procure a certificate under the hand and seal of the respective . . . ordinary . . ., and shall publicly and openly read the same, together with the Declaration and Acknowledgment aforesaid upon some Lord's day within three months then next following in his parish church where he is to officiate in the presence of the congregation there assembled in the time of Divine Service . . . [under pain of deprivation as above].

★   ★   ★

SR, v, 364–8

106. 22 Car. II, c. 1: An Act to prevent and suppress seditious conventicles[26] (The Conventicles Act, 1670)

For providing further and more speedy remedies against the growing and dangerous practices of seditious sectaries and other disloyal persons, who under pretence of tender consciences have or may at their meetings contrive insurrections (as late experience hath shown), be it enacted . . . that if any person of the age of sixteen years or upwards, being a subject of this realm, at any time after May 10th next shall be present at any assembly, conventicle or meeting under colour or pretence of any exercise of religion in other manner than according to the liturgy and practice of the Church of England . . ., at which conventicle . . . there shall be five persons or more assembled together over and besides those of the same household if it be in a house where there is a family inhabiting – or if it be in a house, field or place where there is no family inhabiting, then where any five persons or more are so assembled as aforesaid – it shall and may be lawful for any one or more justices of the peace of the county, limit, division, corporation or liberty wherein the offence aforesaid shall be committed, . . . and he and they are hereby required and enjoined, upon proof to him or them respectively made of such offence, either by confession of the party, or oath of two witnesses, . . . or by notorious evidence and circumstance of the fact, to make a record of every such offence under his or their hands and seals respectively, which . . . shall to all intents and purposes be in law taken and adjudged to be a full and perfect conviction . . . And

---

[25] § VIII of the act decreed that the sentences in italics should be dropped after 25 March 1682.

[26] The marked differences between this and the act of 1664 for the same purpose (16 Car. II, c. 4, *SR*, v, 516–20), which had expired in 1668, are outlined in the footnotes.

thereupon the said justice . . . shall impose on every such offender so convicted as aforesaid a fine of five shillings for such first offence,[27] which record and conviction shall be certified by the said justice . . . at the next Quarter Sessions of the Peace . . .

II. And be it further enacted . . . that if such offender so convicted as aforesaid shall at any time again commit the like offence or offences . . . and be thereof in manner aforesaid convicted, then such offender . . . shall for every such offence incur the penalty of ten shillings,[28] which fine and fines for the first and every other offence shall be levied by distress and sale of the offender's goods and chattels; or in case of the poverty of such offender upon the goods and chattels of any other person or persons who shall be then convicted in manner aforesaid of the like offence at the same conventicle at the discretion of the said justice . . ., so as the sum to be levied on any one person in case of the poverty of other offenders amount not in the whole to above the sum of ten pounds upon occasion of any one meeting . . .[29]

II. And be it further enacted by the authority aforesaid that every person who shall take upon him to preach or teach in any such meeting, assembly or conventicle and shall thereof be convicted as aforesaid shall forfeit for every such first offence the sum of twenty pounds . . .[30] And if the said preacher or teacher so convicted be a stranger, and his name and habitation not known, or is fled and cannot be found, or in the judgment of the justice . . . shall be thought unable to pay the same, the said justice, justices or chief magistrate respectively are hereby empowered and required to levy the same by warrant as aforesaid upon the goods and chattels of any such persons who shall be present at the same conventicle, anything in this or any other act, law or statute to the contrary notwithstanding . . .[31] And if such offender so convicted as aforesaid shall at any time again commit the like offence . . . and be thereof convicted . . . then [he] . . . shall for every such offence incur the penalty of forty pounds . . .

IV. And be it further enacted . . . that every person who shall wittingly and willingly suffer any such conventicle, meeting or unlawful assembly aforesaid to be held in his or her house, outhouse, barn, yard or backside, and be convicted thereof in manner aforesaid, shall forfeit the sum of twenty pounds, to be levied in manner aforesaid . . .

★ ★ ★

[27] In 1664 a maximum of three months' imprisonment or a £5 fine.

[28] In 1664 a maximum of six months' imprisonment or a £10 fine; and for the third offence he was sent to the assizes, and if convicted, sentenced to seven years' transportation or £100 fine. (It is probable that his last proviso was dropped partly because of the difficulty of persuading the colonies to accept such convicts; as it was, Virginia and New England were excluded from the Act.)

[29] Despite the much higher fines imposed, the act of 1664 did not offer this device.

[30] The act of 1664 did not proceed against preachers.

[31] However, § v of this act again restricts the liability of any one person to £10.

VI. Provided also, and be it further enacted, that in all cases of this Act where the penalty or sum charged upon any offender exceeds the sum of ten shillings, and such offender shall find himself aggrieved, it shall and may be lawful for him within one week after . . . to appeal in writing . . . to the judgment of the justices of the peace in their next Quarter Sessions, . . . whereupon such offender may plead and make [his] defence and have his trial by a jury . . . [which shall be final].

★   ★   ★

VIII. And be it further enacted . . . that the justice, justices of the peace and chief magistrates respectively, or the respective constables, head-boroughs and tithingmen by warrant from the said justice, justices or chief magistrate respectively, shall and may, with what aid, force and assistance they shall think fit for the better execution of this Act after refusal or denial to enter, break open and enter into any house or other place where they shall be informed any such conventicle as aforesaid is or shall be held, as well within liberties as without, and take into their custody the persons there unlawfully assembled, to the intent that they may be proceeded against according to this act. And that the lieutenants or deputy-lieutenants or any commissioned officer of the militia or other of his Majesty's forces, with such troops or companies of horse and foot, and also the sheriffs and other magistrates and ministers of justice, or any of them, jointly or severally, within any the counties or places within this kingdom . . ., with such other assistance as they shall think meet or can get in readiness with the soonest, on certificate of that peace or chief magistrate, of his particular information or knowledge, of such unlawful meeting or conventicle held or to be held in their respective counties or places, and that he with such assistance as he can get together is not able to suppress and dissolve the same, shall and may and are hereby required and enjoined to repair unto the place where they are so held or to be held, and by the best means they can to dissolve, dissipate or prevent all such unlawful meetings, and take into their custody such and so many of the said persons so lawfully assembled as they shall think fit . . .

IX. Provided always that no dwelling house of any peer of this realm where he or his wife shall be then resident shall be searched by virtue of this act but by immediate warrant from his Majesty . . . or in the presence of the lieutenant or one deputy-lieutenant or two justices of the peace, whereof one to be of the quorum of the same county or riding.

X. And be it further enacted . . . that if any constable, headborough, tithingman, churchwarden or overseer of the poor who shall know or be credibly informed of any such meetings or conventicles held within his precincts, parish or limits, and shall not give information thereof to some justice of the peace . . . and endeavour the conviction of the parties according to his duty, . . . he shall forfeit for every such offence the sum of five pounds . . . And that if any justice of the peace or chief magistrate shall wilfully and wittingly omit the performance of his duty in the execution of this act he shall forfeit the sum of £100 . . .[32]

*　　*　　*

XVII. Provided also that neither this act nor anything therein contained shall extend to invalidate or avoid his Majesty's supremacy in ecclesiastical affairs, but that his Majesty and his heirs and successors may from time to time and at all times hereafter exercise and enjoy all powers and authorities in ecclesiastical affairs as fully and as simply as himself or any of hs predecessors have or might have done the same, anything in this act notwithstanding.[33]

SR, v, 648–51

---

[32] This clause had no counterpart in the act of 1664, and obviously reflects the sympathy of many magistrates and constables for the Dissenters.

[33] Not found in the act of 1664.

AREAS OF CONFLICT 1661–88

Just as historical studies prior to 1640 tend to focus on the Great Rebellion as if it were the inevitable outcome of events, so the reign of Charles II is often treated as a mere prologue to the Revolution of 1688.

But this takes no account of the great potential strength of the restored monarchy in 1660. An overwhelming majority of the ruling classes, and probably a majority of the people at large in so far as their attitude can be assessed, had fallen back on monarchy as an absolutely essential element in the constitution, and attempts to impose restrictions on its authority, over and above those imposed in 1641, failed ignominiously. It was emphatically and vociferously supported by the restored Church, before which Puritanism, rather surprisingly, shrank to a discredited and politically impotent remnant, and under Charles II the doctrine of Divine Right and Passive Obedience was given its highest and most extreme expression. He retained complete control of foreign policy and war, in 1664 he regained almost complete control of the period and timing of parliaments,[1] and despite the efforts which had been made in the 1640s to restrict the Crown's right of appointment to offices of state, and royal patronage generally, his freedom of operation in this important field was not challenged in 1660 or thereafter. Finally, the Militia Act confirmed his absolute control of the armed forces, and he now had what all his predecessors had lacked, a small but well-trained regular army, with reserves in Portugal as well as in Scotland and Ireland.[2] In fact, the basic apparatus existed for the establishment of authoritarian government on the now fashionable Continental model, of which Charles and his brother James were enviously aware. Charles failed to exploit the potentialities of his position partly through indolence, partly because he was afraid of provoking a reaction he could not handle, but mainly because except for the period 1667–72 and perhaps 1683–5, he lacked ministers and advisers with the necessary ruthlessness and indifference to convention.[3] His longest serving ministers, Clarendon (1660–7) and Danby (1673–9) were firmly wedded to a kind of low church constitutional royalism which inhibited extreme measures.[4]

---

[1] Above, p. 335.

[2] J. C. R. Childs, *The Army of Charles II* (1976); also Stephen Saunders Webb, *The Governors-General: the English Army and the Definition of Empire 1569–1681* (Chapel Hill 1979), which further explores the militarist ethos of the later Stuart state. For the Militia Act, see no. **102**, p. 349 above.

[3] See Maurice Lee, *The Cabal* (Urbana, Illinois 1965); J. R. Western, *Monarchy and Revolution: the English State in the 1680s* (1972); and John Miller, 'The Later Stuart Monarchy', in Jones, *Restored Monarchy*, pp. 30–47, and 'The Potential for "Absolutism" in Later Stuart England', *History*, LXIX (1984), 187–207.

[4] In fact, their brand of royalism would probably not have been uncongenial to some of the Civil War leaders such as Oliver St John. See Valerie Pearl, 'The "Royal Independents" in the English Civil War', 5 *TRHS*, XVIII (1968), 69–96.

As for parliament, any consideration of its activities in the period 1660–85 is hampered by our comparative ignorance, and there is little to match the stream of monographs and articles on the parliaments of James I and Charles I, which is still flowing.[5] There is also none of that plethora of parliamentary diaries and accounts of debates which distinguishes the earlier period; perhaps a significant fact in itself – did MPs consider their work less important than did their fathers and grandfathers in the 1620s and 1640s?[6] All we can hazard at this stage are a few general remarks.

The surprising thing is the sheer ineffectiveness of parliament in the later seventeenth century. It was as if the Long Parliament had never been, never fought and defeated the king, administered the country with assurance and on the whole success, terrorised Scotland and Ireland into submission. In 1661 it subsided rather limply into the kind of role it had played under James I, even under Elizabeth I, which could without unkindness be described as pottering: cavilling at government expenditure, grumbling at court extravagance, sniping desultorily at ministers of state. It could paralyse government policy, but it could not change it, even supposing it had an alternative policy to offer. It was comparatively powerless. The threat to withhold taxation could only be used in time of war, and in fact was only once effective, in forcing the passage of the Test Act in 1673.[7] The battering ram of impeachment was no more effective now than it had been in the 1620s, unless the government co-operated. It served to remove Clarendon in 1667, Danby in 1679, but it could not secure their replacement by more acceptable candidates, and both these ministers had survived previous attempts at impeachment, in 1663 and 1675 respectively. In fact, between 1660 and 1710 only one man was impeached, tried and convicted, and that was the unusual case of the Catholic Lord Stafford in 1680.

Despite the inefficiency, the ineffectuality and the ill-judgment of the government in the 1660s, a formed opposition was slow to develop. There was always a sizeable dissentient group in the so-called Cavalier Parliament; in 1661 103 voted against the burning of the Solemn League and Covenant, a dead document if ever there was one, and the Corporation Act only passed by 185 votes to 136.[8] But the only tangible success registered by this 'Old Parliamentary Party' was the failure to renew the Conventicles Act in 1668, and this was reversed two years later. The Country Party which subsequently emerged succeeded in frustrating Charles's foreign ambitions in

---

[5] See, however, D. T. Witcombe, *Charles II and the Cavalier House of Commons 1663–1674* (Manchester 1966); J. R. Jones, *The First Whigs*, and 'Parties and Parliament', in Jones, *Restored Monarchy*, pp. 48–70, and John Miller, 'Charles II and his Parliaments', 5 *TRHS*, xxxii (1982), 1–24. My debt to these will be obvious in what follows. Wilbur C. Abbott's 'The Long Parliament of Charles II', *EHR*, xxi (1906), 21–56, 254–85, is still very useful.

[6] We are heavily reliant on Anchitel Grey's highly selective account (*Debates of the House of Commons 1667–1694*, 10 vols., 1763), and it is difficult to check its accuracy except for the brief periods covered by *The Diary of John Milward* [1666–8], ed. Caroline Robbins (Cambridge 1938), *The Parliamentary Diary of Sir Edward Dering 1670–73*, ed. B. D. Henning (New Haven 1940), and *The Diaries and Papers of Sir Edward Dering 1664–1684*, ed. Maurice F. Bond (1976). Some information can also be gleaned from newsletters, of which the most important collection is that of Andrew Marvell, printed in his *Poems and Letters*, ed. H. M. Margoliouth (Oxford 1952), vol. ii. However, we now have the official history of parliament for this period, *The House of Commons 1660–1690*, ed. B. D. Henning (3 vols., 1983), which is a mine of information on electioneering, and politics in general at constituency level.

[7] P. 376 below.   [8] Abbott, *art. cit.*, pp. 28, 29.

1673–4, but it could not force him over the next four years to dissolve them.[9] Nor could it force him in the Exclusion Crisis to adopt a policy which undoubtedly enjoyed considerable public support. The fear of another civil war, reinforced by constant and specific warnings against a return to 1641, made it unthinkable for parliament to move out of its proper sphere or to act independently of the king.[10] As a result direct conflict between king and parliament was rare, and never came to an explosive climax.

I. FINANCE

The financial provisions of the Restoration Settlement were generous enough.[11] The Commons budgeted for a Crown income of £1,200,000 a year, principally provided by indirect taxation. The king was voted the customs for life, thus settling a quarrel which had begun on his father's accession, and what was called the 'Hereditary Excise', on beer, cider, mead, unrefined spirits, coffee, chocolate, sherbert and tea, to him and his successors in perpetuity, in consideration of their surrender of the feudal incidents of wardship, marriage and purveyance. (Its perpetual nature was in fact ignored, or overlooked, in 1689.) The slack was then taken up by the Additional Excise, on various other commodities, voted for life, in preference to direct taxation, which was reserved for wartime emergency. It is easy to assume, and it has been generally assumed, that this represented a desire on the part of the landed classes to shift the burden of taxation onto the lower classes, but it was a device which had the strong support of government.[12]

In the short term government's expectations were dashed. Direct collection of customs and excise had to be abandoned in 1662 and the revenue farmed out to private cartels. The Lord Treasurer, the ageing Earl of Southampton, had been chosen for his impeccable royalism, not for any fiscal experience or administrative ability. As a result, the 'settled revenue' fell far short of expectations, and had to be supplemented by a resort to the old pre-war Subsidy and in 1662 to the Hearth Tax, an extremely unpopular innovation, though it was not abandoned until 1689.[13] The constitutional implications of this are difficult to fathom, but they cannot be described as crucial.

The impetus to reform came from the government itself, and originated with Sir George Downing, Envoy to The Hague and Teller of the Exchequer. When the outbreak of the Second Dutch War in 1665 called for the revival of the assessment, or land tax, he persuaded Arlington and Sir William Coventry that the receipts should be subject to a separate system of account, and that those lending money on the security of this tax should be repaid 'in course', that is, in rotation according to the date of their

---

[9] Andrew Browning, 'Parties and Party Organisation in the Reign of Charles II', 4 *TRHS*, xxx (1948), 21–36, and *Thomas Osborne Earl of Danby* (3 vols., Glasgow 1944–51), I, chs. 9–12.

[10] The most significant incident is Charles's veto of the Militia Bill of November 1678, using much the same words as his father's in 1642; Kenyon, *Popish Plot*, pp. 102, 104–5.

[11] The prime authority is C. D. Chandaman, *Public Revenue*, supplemented by H. G. Roseveare, *The Treasury 1660–1870: the Foundations of Control* (1973). Howard Tomlinson provides a very useful review of 'Financial and Administrative Developments' in Jones, *Restored Monarchy*, pp. 94–117, and Christopher Clay's *Public Finance and Private Wealth: the Career of Sir Stephen Fox 1627–1716* (Oxford 1978) gives us an inside view of the workings of government finance through the eyes of one of its most successful exponents.

[12] Chandaman, *op. cit.*, p. 37–9.   [13] *op. cit.*, pp. 203–9.

loan (**107**). A similar act the following year appropriated part of the proceeds to the navy under conditions of strict accountability (**108**).[14]

These reforms were not the product of Commons' initiative at all, and were designed not to curb the Crown, but Lord Treasurer Southampton and the Treasurer of the navy, Sir George Carteret. However, the practice of appropriation was taken up by the Commons in the Third Dutch War (1672–4), and in 1677, when they voted the very precise sum of £584,978. 2s. 2d. 'for the speedy building 30 ships of war', their appropriation clauses were equally precise.[15] In 1678, when they voted money for the disbandment of the army raised for the abortive Flanders campaign that spring they even wrote into the Assessment Act the date of demobilisation; a clear infringement of the royal prerogative of peace and war, though one which passed without comment.[16] Charles having used the money to retain the army, in 1679 parliament passed another Assessment Act, this time writing in the names of the specific regiments, and the order in which they were to be demobilised.[17]

The parliament of 1685, subservient in most things, abandoned these precautions, and granted James II impositions on tobacco, sugar, wines and vinegar for eight years without appropriation. The preambles to these supply bills stated that the money was to be used for the navy and the ordnance, but there was no effort to supervise its expenditure.[18] Since James used a great deal of this money to build up a standing army, after the Revolution strict appropriation became the rule.

The Commission for taking the Public Accounts in 1667 (**109**) was another matter entirely. It was forced upon the government by the Commons' angry suspicion that much of the money voted for the war had been embezzled or diverted to other purposes, and pushed through in the wake of Clarendon's fall. Its powers of summons and investigation were much stronger than those allowed to the parliamentary commissions of the 1690s, for which it offered a precedent, and its brief extended to the customs and excise, and even to naval prize money, which Charles regarded as part of his private income. However, by the time it made its report, in the session of 1669–70, the government had rallied, and it was able to turn it into an issue of confidence in Carteret and secure a narrow majority in his favour.[19] The experiment was not repeated.

But the most important financial reforms undertaken in this reign were in the administration of the Treasury. On Southampton's death in May 1667 Clarendon was so weakened that he had to acquiesce in the appointment of a vigorous, reformist Treasury Commission, with George Monk, Duke of Albemarle, as figurehead, but staffed by the Chancellor of Exchequer, Lord Ashley (later Earl of Shaftesbury), Sir Thomas Clifford, Sir John Duncomb and Sir William Coventry, with Downing as

---

[14] There was an immediate precedent for this in the Assessment Act of 1660, for paying off the arrears of pay to the army and navy: 12 Car. II, c. 20, *SR*, v, 250–1.

[15] 29 Car. II, c. 1, particularly §§ xxv, xliii–iv, *SR*, v, 834, 835.

[16] 30 Car. II, c. 1, *ibid.*, 871.

[17] 31 Car. II, c. 1, § xxiv, *ibid.*, 930–2.

[18] 1 Jac. II, cc. 3–4 (*SR*, vi, 2–7). Another act of the same session, granting the Crown further impositions, on imported silks, linens and brandies, for five years to pay for the suppression of Monmouth's Rebellion, did have a clause (§ 10) requiring debts to be repaid 'in course', but that was all (1 Jac. II, c. 5, *ibid.*, 7–9).

[19] Witcombe, *op. cit.*, pp. 52–3, 76, 93–4; Roseveare, *op. cit.*, p. 52.

Secretary. They instituted a method in the Treasury which lasted into the nineteenth century, established its independence of the Privy Council, and set about increasing the yield of indirect taxation.[20] The Customs was brought back under direct control in 1671, and the same year parliament was persuaded to vote extra duties for six years. (Danby secured their renewal in 1677.) When the Treasury Commission was broken in 1672 and Clifford appointed Lord Treasurer he negotiated a more advantageous farm of the Excise, and his successor, Danby, consolidated his work. As a result, the income of the Crown rose above the projected £1,200,000, averaging £1,393,000 over the years 1672–7.

However, the burden of debt accumulated during the 1660s, and increased by the Stop of the Exchequer, the government's inevitable decision to default on its obligations at the opening of the Third Dutch War,[21] still held down the government's real income, and Danby introduced a comprehensive scheme of retrenchment in 1676. Charles II's attempt to intervene in the European War in 1678 was another financial blow, accentuated by parliament's decision, for political reasons, to ban French imports for three years. However, Lawrence Hyde, Earl of Rochester, First Lord of the Treasury 1679–84, Lord Treasurer 1685–7, was the first to succeed in permanently reducing government expenditure while government income was still rising (to an average of £1,377,000 1681–4). Given the generous financial settlement awarded to James II in 1685, this made him the first monarch since Henry VIII to enjoy financial independence – a fact of crucial constitutional importance.[22]

107. Payment in Course, 1665

17 Car. II, c. 1: *An Act for granting the sum of twelve hundred and fifty thousand pounds to the King's Majesty for his present further Supply*

★   ★   ★

V. And that to the intent that all monies to be lent to your Majesty and monies that shall be due upon such contracts for wares and goods which shall be delivered for this service may be well and sufficiently secured out of the monies arising and payable by this act, be it further enacted . . . that there be provided and kept in his Majesty's Exchequer, to wit, in the office of the auditor of the Receipt, one book or register, in which . . . all monies that shall be paid into the Exchequer by this Act shall be entered and registered, apart and distinct from . . . all other monies or branches of your Majesty's revenue

[20] This is a topic which does not lend itself to documentary illustration in a book of this scope and size, but see Roseveare, *op. cit.*, ch. 1, and the documents printed at pp. 111–36. This was accompanied by a corresponding reform of the Privy Council; see pp. 435–7 below.

[21] Chandaman, *op. cit.*, pp. 224–8. For the aftermath see J. Keith Horsefield, 'The Stop of the Exchequer Revisited', *Econ. Hist. Review*, XXXV (1982), 511–28.

[22] Chandaman, *op. cit.*, p. 256–8, argues that the financial settlement of 1685 was not unduly generous, but this seems a piece of special pleading, and he ignores the fact that when it was abruptly prorogued in November parliament was on the point of voting another £700,000 a year for the improvement of the army.

whatsoever; and that also there be one other book or register provided or kept in the said office, of all Orders or Warrants to be made by the Lord Treasurer and Under Treasurer or by the Commissioners of the Treasury for the time being for payment of all and every sum and sums of money to all persons for monies lent, wares or goods bought, or other payments directed by his Majesty relating to the service of this war; and that no monies levyable by this act be issued out of the Exchequer during this war but by such order or warrant mentioning that the monies payable by such order or warrant are for the service of your Majesty in the said war respectively.

★   ★   ★

VII. That it shall be lawful for any person or persons willing to lend any money or to furnish any wares, victuals, necessities or goods on the credit of this act at the usual times when the Exchequer is open to have access unto and view and peruse all or any of the said books for their information of the state of those monies and all engagements upon them, for their better encouragements to lend any monies or furnish any goods or wares as aforesaid. And . . . that all and every person and persons who shall lend any monies to your Majesty and pay the same into the Receipt of the Exchequer shall immediately have a tally of loan struck for the same, and an order for his repayment bearing the same date with his tally, in which order shall be also a warrant contained for payment of interest for forbearance after the rate of 6 per cent per annum for his consideration, to be paid every six months until the repayment of his principal; and that all person and persons who shall furnish your Majesty, your officers[23] of the navy or ordnance with any wares, good, victuals or other necessaries for the service aforesaid shall upon certificate of the commissioners and officers of the navy, or of the masters or commissioners and officers of the ordnance, or some of them, without delay forthwith have made out to them warrants or orders for the payment of the monies due or payable unto them . . . And that all orders for the repayment of money lent shall be registered in course according to the date of the tallies respectively. And that all orders signed by the Lord Treasurer and Under Treasurer for payment of money for goods, wares, victuals and other necessaries furnished to his majesty . . . shall be registered in course according to the time of bringing to the office of the Auditor of Receipt the certificates above mentioned, and that all orders so signed for payments directed by his Majesty shall be entered in course according to their respective dates, and none of the sorts of orders above mentioned . . . shall have preference one before another, but shall all be entered in their course according to the dates of the tallies, the times of bringing

---

[23] That is, the principal administrative officers who comprised the Boards of the navy and the ordinance.

the certificates, and the dates of the orders for payments directed by his Majesty, as they are in point of time respectively before each other. And that all and every person and persons shall be paid in course according as their orders shall stand entered in the said register book . . .

* * *

SR, v, 573–4

108. Appropriation, 1666

18 & 19 Car. II, c. 13: *An Act for granting the sum of twelve hundred, fifty six thousand three hundred forty seven pounds thirteen shillings to the King's Majesty towards the maintenance of the present war*

* * *

X. Provided always and be it enacted by the authority aforesaid, that the sum of £380,000 shall be charged and registered in the Book of Register appointed by this act to be kept in the office of the Auditor of the Receipt of the Exchequer, to be paid to the Treasurer of the navy for the time being out of the money payable for the last ten months of the eleven months' assessment granted by this act, for the salaries and wages of such officers, seamen, mariners and soldiers as are or shall be employed aboard your Majesty's navy for this present winter, beginning at 1 January 1667 and aboard your Majesty's navy for the summer in the year 1667 . . .

XI. And it is hereby further enacted that if the Treasurer of the navy do divert or employ the said £380,000 or any part thereof to any use or service whatsoever other than for the payment of the salaries and wages of such officers, seamen, mariners and soldiers . . . as aforesaid until the said wages and salaries shall be fully and entirely paid and discharged, that then and in such case he shall forfeit treble the value of the money diverted or employed contrary to the intent and meaning hereof, to be recovered in any of his Majesty's courts at Westminster . . ., one moiety whereof to be to such person as shall sue for the same and the other moiety to your Majesty, your heirs and successors.

* * *

SR, v, 621

109. The Commission for Public Accounts, 1667

19 & 20 Car. II, c. 1: *An Act for taking the accounts of the several sums of money therein mentioned*

Whereas many and great aids and provisions have been given, raised and assigned for the necessary defence of your Majesty and your kingdoms in the late great and important wars, to the end that both your Majesty and this whole kingdom may be satisfied and truly informed whether all the same monies and provisions have been faithfully issued out and expended in and about the preparing and setting forth of your Royal Navy, and other the management and carrying on the said war, and with such care, fidelity and good husbandry as the nature of such services would admit of, according to your Majesty's own gracious and princely desires and the earnest expectations of your most loyal subjects, than which nothing can encourage them more cheerfully to undergo the like burdens in time to come for the necessary defence of your Majesty and your realms, may it therefore please your Majesty that it be enacted . . . that William, Lord Brereton, baron of Laughtyn in the kingdom of Ireland, William Pierrepoint, esquire, Sir George Savile, baronet, Giles Dunster, esquire, Sir James Langham, knight, Henry Osborne, esquire, Sir William Turner, alderman of the city of London, George Thompson, esquire, and John Gregory, esquire, or any five or more of them shall be commissioners for the taking of the accounts of . . . [the direct taxation voted since 1664, in total £5,183,847], and of all such monies as have arisen by the Customs granted to his Majesty by an act of the present parliament and have been applied to the service of the war, and such prizes as have been taken during the said late war for his Majesty's use, and of all other monies, provisions and things whatsoever which have been raised or assigned for or towards the fitting, furnishing or setting out to sea any of the navies or ships employed in the said late war, or for or touching the management or maintenance thereof.

And to that end the said commissioners or any five or more of them are hereby authorised and required to call before them all treasurers, receivers, paymasters, principal officers and commissioners of the navy and ordnance respectively, victuallers, pursers, mustermasters and clerks of the cheque, accountants and all officers and keepers of his Majesty's stores and provisions for war, as well for land as sea, and all other persons whatsoever employed in the management of the said war, or requisite for the discovery of any frauds relating thereunto, to make true and perfect accounts of all such of the monies as have come to any of their hands respectively and to bring in and deliver the same to the said commissioners . . . without delay, and also to bring in their several books of accounts, vouchers and acquittances, contracts, muster rolls, cheque rolls, cheque books, and all other books and writings whatsoever touching or concerning the premises, to be perused, tried and examined by the said commissioners:

Whereby it may appear what monies they have received and how the same have been disbursed, and what ammunition, provisions and stores of any kind which were in his Majesty's storehouses or yards or elsewhere have been

LORETTO SCHOOL
VI FORM LIBRARY

employed in the said war after 1 September, 1664, and what ships or other vessels his Majesty then had for the service of the war, together with their several equipages and furniture, and what monies or other provisions or materials have been paid or delivered to the hands of the said treasurers, receivers, paymasters, victuallers, pursers or other accountants, or any of the said officers or keepers of his Majesty's stores, and when the same was so paid and delivered, and how and at what time or times the same have been disposed of and to whom and for what use or uses, and to examine the rates and prices set upon any provisions, wares, or materials bought or provided for the service of the said war, and what the same were then truly worth, and what was really paid for the same, and by whom and to whom, and when the same was so bought or paid for, and how the same provisions, wares and materials have been employed and disposed of and by what warrant.

And [they are] to examine all such merchants and tradesmen, and their books, receipts and acquittances, and all such seamen and others as shall be thought fit to be heard touching any frauds, oppressions or exactions practised or used by any person or persons entrusted or employed in or about the payment or receipt of any of the said monies or the buying or providing of any of the said provisions, wares or materials, or the custody, ordering or disposing of the same and to what value, and what gain or advantage was made thereby and by whom, and where and about what time the same was so done.

And [they are] to inquire and find out whether any and which of the seamen and others have been defrauded of any of their premiums or rewards, victuals, clothes, pillage or other allowances or benefits assigned, promised or appointed to any of them for or in respect of their service in the said war, and by whom and to what value. And [they are] to inquire and find out what monies have been or ought to have been set apart for the Chest[24] from 24 June 1660, and how the same have been paid or disposed of, and whether any part thereof hath been defalked or detained from the persons to whom it was due and payable, and how much, when and by whom and by what pretence the same was done.

And [they are to inquire] whether any sums of money and how much arising by the customs and subsidy of tunnage and poundage ever since 1 September, 1664, hath been issued and allowed for and towards the maintenance of the said war, and also to inquire and find out the numbers and values of all the prize ships and goods which hath been taken for his Majesty's use during the said war, and their several bills of lading, and how the same ships and goods or any of them have been apprised, valued, sold, embezzled or otherwise disposed of, and how the price and monies thereof arising have been accounted for to his Majesty, and what frauds or abuses have been committed

[24] The Chatham Chest: chiefly for the payment of disablement grants and pensions to seamen.

therein and by whom and for what value. And [they are] to inquire whether any and how much of the said monies given for the maintenance of the said war by act of parliament as aforesaid hath been bestowed or disposed of to or for any other use or purpose, and to what other uses or persons the same are or any part thereof was so bestowed and disposed.

And [they are] also to inquire by whose means, counsel or procurement it came to pass that the ships, seamen, mariners and others were generally discharged by tickets and not paid with money, by the cheque roll of the respective ships or vessels wherein they served as formerly, and how any of the land forces came to be so paid, and what loss or disadvantage his Majesty or any of the seamen or land soldiers have sustained thereby, and what advantage or benefit hath been made by any person or persons by means of such payment or by buying, selling or assigning of any such tickets, and by whom particularly and to what value; and how much of the wages due to any of the said seamen or land soldiers is yet remaining unpaid and to whom particularly the same is due or payable.[25]

And further [they are] to search into, examine and find out all other frauds, exactions, negligences and defaults and abuses which have been practised or committed by any person or persons whatsoever touching the premises, and when and by whom the same were so practised and committed, and what damage hath been sustained thereby, and to what value. And for that end and purpose [they are] also to inspect and examine all such former accounts as they shall think necessary, and to send for seamen and cause to appear before . . . [them] all or any of the said accountants and other officers and keepers of stores, and all such merchants, tradesmen, seamen, soldiers and other persons as they shall think meet, and to examine them severally upon their corporal oaths (which the said commissioners or any five or more of them shall and may administer by virtue of this act), and also to send for and peruse all such records, books, vouchers, acquittances and other writings as they shall think fit to be produced for the better discovery of any the said frauds, exactions, negligences and defaults or abuses, and to do, execute and perform all such other act and acts as they . . . in their judgment shall find requisite whereby all such person and persons as shall appear guilty . . . may be brought to condign punishment in parliament or otherwise . . . [And any official refusing to answer under oath, or refusing to produce his books, could be committed to prison by the commissioners indefinitely.]

[II. The commissioners can call upon sheriffs to summon Grand Juries in the provinces, to examine witnesses under oath, and report.]

---

[25] The greatest single scandal of a scandalous war. Paid off at the ports by tickets redeemable only in London, many seamen had sold them at an outrageous discount to waiting profiteers.

III. . . .And the said commissioners are hereby required from time to time as they shall see cause, and at the determination of their examinations and proceedings by virtue of this act, to give an account thereof in writing . . . to the king's Majesty and to both Houses of Parliament if then sitting . . .

★   ★   ★

SR, v, 624–7

II. FOREIGN POLICY

At the Restoration the king's right to control foreign policy had been tacitly confirmed, but ever since 1621 parliament had been demanding that this control be exercised in full view of the public. James I's surrender on this point in 1624 was decisive, and in 1625 we find Buckingham voluntarily expounding his master's policy to a joint session of both Houses. However, after Buckingham's death Charles I returned to secret, or confidential diplomacy, and his son naturally followed. Foreign policy and war were not only amongst the few remaining prerogatives left to the Crown, they were also the most important; a seventeenth-century king was at his most magnificent, and his most effective, when preparing for or prosecuting war.

In the 1660s there was no serious disagreement on foreign policy as such, though Arlington and Clarendon were criticised for allowing the French to ally with the Dutch in 1662, leaving England without allies in the Second Dutch War; but after 1670 the problem became acute. By the Treaty of Dover of that year Charles agreed to join Louis XIV in the forcible partition of the Netherlands. The fact that he had also undertaken to declare himself a Roman Catholic was a profound secret, but it was generally suspected that the treaty contained more than had ever been made public, especially since the heir-presumptive, James, Duke of York, had been converted to Rome and the declaration of war in 1672 was immediately preceded by the Declaration of Indulgence, which favoured Roman Catholics as much as Protestant Dissenters (p. 382 below). Early in 1674 Charles solemnly denied to parliament that there were any secret clauses in the treaty, but the Commons insisted on cross-examining the 2nd Duke of Buckingham on the circumstances leading up to the war (**110**).

Buckingham eventually resigned, and so did Arlington, the secretary of state chiefly responsible for foreign affairs, and Charles was obliged to make peace in 1674. The Commons had won, and for the next four years the king's foreign policy see-sawed to and fro; Charles tempted parliament with the prospect of a war against France, but they were reluctant to provide him with an army, and he was quite content not to be forced, especially since his resistance earned him a small *douceur* from Louis XIV. In May 1677 the Commons tried to break the deadlock by a memorial threatening to withhold supply unless the king made an alliance with Holland against France (**111a**). The secretaries of state, Coventry and Williamson, protested that this was an invasion of one of the Crown's most cherished prerogatives, and Charles rejected it, on the grounds that while they could advise him in general terms they could not force him to make specific alliances (**111b**). When he next met them, in January 1678, it was with the news that he had now concluded an alliance with the Dutch, as they desired. This produced another brisk exchange. The Commons demanded that by the peace treaty Louis XIV be confined to the frontiers established by the Peace of the Pyrenees in 1659, and that England and her allies bar all trade with France. Charles described the first as 'a determination fitting only for God Almighty, for none can tell what can be fitting conditions for a peace, but he that can certainly foretell the events of the war'; as for the second, he found it difficult to believe 'that ever any assembly of men gave so great and public a provocation to the whole world, without either having provided or so much as considered how to provide one ship, one regiment or one penny towards justifying it'.[26] The House buckled to and voted the money, of course, but his last-ditch intervention was rendered nugatory by the conclusion of the Peace of Nimwegen that autumn.[27] His finances were badly strained, and his foreign policy on the point of collapse, a collapse finally precipitated by the revelation in November 1678 of his secret treaty with France in 1676, for which Danby was promptly impeached. His subsequent attempt in 1679 and 1680 to build up a European coalition against France was viewed with the greatest cynicism by the Exclusion Parliaments.[28] The secret agreement with France in March 1681 is sometimes represented as a victory for the king. It was nothing of the sort; it emphasised that he could no longer pursue an independent foreign policy without the approval of parliament, and for the rest of his reign he was regarded as a mere lackey of Louis XIV's, a fact well recognised in Europe.

110. Buckingham's examination: second day: 14 January 1674

. . . Intimation being given to the House, that the duke now had recollected himself, and could give the House information of some matters relating to public affairs; and thereupon several questions being agreed to by the House to be proposed to his lordship, which are as followeth, viz.,

1. Whether any persons have at any time declared to him any of their advices, or evil purposes, against the liberty of this House, or propounded any ways to him for altering our government; and if they did, what was that advice, and by whom?

2. What was meant by this expression yesterday, that he had gotten nothing, and that others had gotten, three, four and five hundred thousand pounds; who they were that had gotten it, and by what means?

3. By whose advice the army was raised, and papists set to officer them, and M. Schomberg to be their general?

[26] *CJ*, IX, 431–2 (4 February 1678).

[27] The best guide to these labyrinthine negotiations is still that provided by David Ogg, *England in the Reign of Charles II* (1955), II, ch. 15, and by Browning, *Danby*, I, chs. 10–12. See also Clyde L. Grose, 'The Anglo-Dutch Alliance of 1678', *EHR*, XXXIX (1924), 349–72, 526–51, and K. H. D. Haley, 'The Anglo-Dutch Rapprochement of 1677', *ibid.*, LXXIII (1958), 614–48.

[28] Kenyon, *Sunderland*, pp. 40–6.

4. Whether he knows that any have advised to make use of the army to awe the debates and resolutions of this House?

5. By whose counsel and ministry the Triple League was made?

6. And the first treaty with France, whereby it was broken, and the articles thereof?

7. And the Orders of Assignment and Credit of the Exchequer broken and destroyed?

8. And the Declaration about matters of religion made?

9. And the Smyrna Fleet fallen upon before war was declared?

10. And the second treaty with the French king, at Utrecht, and the articles thereof?

11. And by whose counsels the war was made without advice of parliament, thereupon prorogued?   *CJ*, IX, 293

III. Commons Address, 25 May 1677

(a) Commons Address

May it please your most excellent Majesty,

Your Majesty's most loyal and dutiful subjects, the Commons in parliament assembled, having taken into their serious consideration your Majesty's gracious speech, do beseech your Majesty to believe, it is a great affliction to them to find themselves obliged at present to decline the granting your Majesty the supply your Majesty is pleased to demand, conceiving it is not agreeable to the usage of parliament to grant suplies for maintenance of wars and alliances before they are signified in parliament – which the two wars against the States of the United Provinces since your Majesty's happy Restoration, and the League made with them in January 1667[–8] for preservation of the Spanish Netherlands, sufficiently prove, without troubling your Majesty with instances of greater antiquity. From which usage if we should depart, the precedent might be of dangerous consequence in future times, though your Majesty's goodness gives us great security during your Majesty's reign, which we beseech God long to continue.

This consideration prompted us, in our last Address to your Majesty before our late recess, humbly to mention to your Majesty our hopes that before our meeting again your Majesty's alliances might be so fixed as that your Majesty might be graciously pleased to impart them to us in parliament, that so our earnest desires of supplying your Majesty for prosecuting those great ends we had humbly laid before your Majesty might meet with no impediment or obstruction, being highly sensible of the necessity of supporting as well as making the alliances humbly desired in our former Addresses; and which we still conceive so important to the safety of your Majesty and your kingdom that we cannot, without unfaithfulness to your Majesty and those we represent, omit upon all occasions humbly to beseech your Majesty, as we now do, to enter into a league, offensive and defensive, with the States General of the United Provinces against the growth and power of the French king and for the preservation of the Spanish Netherlands, and to make such other alliances with such other of the Confederates as your Majesty shall think fit and useful to that end . . .   *CJ*, IX, 425

(b) Commons debate on the Address, 25 May

Sir Joseph Williamson [Secretary of State]. He agrees as far in the end of the Address as any gentleman does, but he fears that the success will show, that this way will not do it. He cannot but think this is a new thing, and that it will be far from acknowledging the king's condescension, and that we encroach upon his prerogative . . . Why must alliances, offensive and defensive, be the matter of the Address? The people cannot consider it; that is proper only for the royal breast. Defensive consideration is more proper for the people; he never knew an *offensive* league declared here before. You are told that the parliament advised the Palatinate War. There is nothing too great for this House, but he never knew anything done of this nature, but the House was first called up to it. They were called to consult the Palatinate War, and of the late Dutch War. If there be no precedent of it, and if but one, he begs of gentlemen to consider what reception this Address will have, though from the best and kindest of princes from such a House of Commons. You desire freedom of speech and privilege of parliament. The king has but few prerogatives, as coining money, and making peace and war, and they are as landmarks, and are known; they are but few, and a curse is upon him that removes them. You are told of the alliances that saved Holland, &c. He will not compare those with the fears upon you at present, but in Queen Elizabeth's time, before she could be brought to a league offensive and defensive with them, we had two cautionary towns, and a fort, put into our hands. You by this hasty Address are cut off from all hopes of any such caution from them. He has acquitted himself as his allegiance and duty to this House obliges him, and he knows not what to advise you. But would have reasons as strong in the thing as may be, before you go to the king with this Address . . .   Grey, *Debates*, IV, 379

(c) The King's Reply, 28 May

Gentlemen,

Could I have been silent, I would rather have chosen to be so than to call to mind things so unfit for you to meddle with as are contained in some part of your Address, wherein you have entrenched upon so undoubted a right of the Crown that I am confident it will appear in no age (when the sword was not drawn) that the prerogative of making peace and war hath been so dangerously invaded. You do not content yourselves with desiring me to enter into such leagues as may be for the safety of the kingdom, but you tell me what sort of leagues they must be, and with whom. And, as your Address is worded, it is more liable to be understood to be by your leave than your request that I should make such other alliances as I please with other of the Confederates. Should I suffer this fundamental power of making peace and war to be so far invaded (though but once) as to have the manner and circumstances of leagues prescribed to me by parliament, it is plain that no prince or state would any longer believe that the sovereignty of England rests in the Crown; nor could I think myself to signify any more to foreign princes than the empty sound of a king. Wherefore you may rest assured, that no condition shall make me depart from, or lessen, so essential a part of the monarchy. And I am willing to believe so well of this House of Commons, that I am confident these ill consequences are not intended by you . . .   *CJ*, IX, 426

III. RELIGION

Religion, and especially the Roman Catholic religion, was the *damnosa hereditas* of the Stuarts. Rumours were rife in the 1650s that Charles II had been converted to Rome in exile, and in his first letter to the Speaker of the House of Commons in 1660 he felt it necessary to affirm his loyalty to Protestantism, and assure him 'that neither the unkindness of those of the same faith towards us, nor the civilities and obligations from those of a contrary profession (of both of which we have had abundant evidence), could in the least degree startle us, or make us swerve from it'.[29] But, as we have seen, the Act for the Preservation of the King in 1661 barred from public office anyone who should 'maliciously and advisedly publish or affirm the king to be a heretic or a papist, or that he endeavours to introduce popery'.[30]

Charles certainly had a strong inclination towards Rome, though he was sensible enough not to indulge it to the full until he was on his deathbed, and his personal debt to the Catholics who had effected his escape from England after his defeat at Worcester was one of the few obligations he consistently recognised. Nor was the climate of opinion in 1660 apparently inimical to some measure of toleration; in contrast to the Long Parliament, the attitude of the Commonwealth government towards Catholics had been indifferent, and that of the Protector almost benevolent.[31] Indeed, under the pressure of an alliance with a Catholic power, France, Cromwell had to give undertakings similar to those made by James I and Charles I in similar circumstances.[32]

---

[29] *CJ*, VIII, 5a.

[30] 13 Car. II, st. 1, c. 1, *SR*, V, 304, printed in Browning, *Documents*, p. 64.

[31] Again (see pp. 167, 244 above), the treatment of Catholic priests is a useful indicator; only two were executed between 1646 and 1660. Cf. Hardacre, *The Royalists during the Puritan Revolution*, p. 89.

[32] Hardacre, *op. cit.*, pp. 117–20; Robert S. Paul, *The Lord Protector* (1955), p. 327; Firth, *Last Years*, I, 77–8. However, it was ominous that once Cromwell allied himself with parliament in 1657 it tried to drive him towards persecution. The Humble Petition and Advice (no. **95**, p. 326 above) excluded from parliament not only recusants but their husbands, fathers and fathers-in-law.

Clandestine negotiations between Catholic spokesmen and the Protector were resumed with Clarendon on his return.[33]

Apart from this, we must assume that Charles was anxious, if only for the sake of public tranquillity, to fulfil his conditional promise made at Breda of a 'liberty for tender consciences', and he was conscious of the economic and social benefits of general toleration, as it was practised in states like Brandenburg, the Netherlands and (at this stage) France. Accordingly on 17 March 1662 he sent down to the Lords two provisos to be added to the Uniformity Bill then before them. One confirmed his 'supreme power and authority in ecclesiastical affairs', which gave him the right, he said, to dispense from the provisions of the act all those who were not ministers of the Church, and was so clearly in favour of the Catholics that the Lords rejected it two days later.[34] The second proviso merely gave him the power to dispense ministers of whose loyalty he was assured from the necessity of wearing the surplice or using the sign of the cross in baptism. This passed the Lords, but it was thrown out by the Commons on 22 April.[35]

As a result Charles seriously considered suspending the Act of Uniformity altogether, and on 10 June the Privy Council consulted the judges and the bishops.[36] But the judges queried the legality of the suspending power, and the proposal was dropped. On 26 December Charles made one final effort. He issued a long declaration defending himself against charges of ill faith, undue tolerance of Catholics, and an ambition to set up military government, and he suggested that parliament in its next session pass an act 'as may enable us to exercise with a more universal satisfaction that power of dispensing which we conceive to be inherent in us' (**112**).[37] It was an ill-judged and incautiously drafted pronouncement, and the tone of approval with which he referred to his Catholic subjects was long remembered against him. In his speech at the opening of the next session, 18 February 1663, he again defended himself against charges of partiality to the Catholics and explained that he had no wish to admit them to office under the Crown. In their reply, on 27 February, the Commons accepted these assurances with gratitude but politely dismissed his proposed 'dispensation act'.[38] After a long delay Charles returned an evasive answer which left the question hanging.

However, the king's right to dispense occasional individuals from compliance with certain statutes was not seriously questioned, and throughout his reign the Catholics who had assisted Charles in his escape after the battle of Worcester enjoyed the benefit of such dispensations. Nor were the penal laws enforced with any vigour, despite the general tendency to attribute the outbreak of the Great Fire of London in 1666 to the Catholics. In 1669 Charles even issued orders that the act of 1581[39] be not enforced,

---

[33] Hardacre, *op. cit.*, pp. 137-9; Miller, *Popery and Politics*, pp. 95, 98.

[34] *LJ*, XI, 411; *House of Lords Manuscripts*, XI, no. 3699.

[35] *CJ*, VIII, 414; *HMC, 7th Report*, pp. 162-3.

[36] George R. Abernethy, 'Clarendon and the Declaration of Indulgence', *Jnl Eccl. History*, XI (1960), 62.

[37] This is sometimes called the 'First Declaration of Indulgence'. This is harmless enough, though inaccurate, provided the edict of 1672 is not described as the 'Second Declaration of Indulgence'. The first was a request to parliament to pass an enabling act; the second was a suspension by proclamation of existing legislation.

[38] They told him that it would 'establish schism by a law'; *PH*, IV, 262.

[39] Making it treason to convert the king's subjects to Rome, etc., Elton *Tudor Constitution*, pp. 431-3. (But he did not tamper with the much more savage act of 1585, *ibid.*, p. 433-7.)

and though parliament made him withdraw this in 1671 his Reply to the Commons made a distinction unknown in law between Catholics born and Catholic converts.[40]

On the other hand, any desire he might have had to mitigate the penal laws against Protestant Dissenters was also frustrated. His power to dispense individuals from compliance with such laws was well recognised, but the accepted convention was that it could not be applied to large numbers, or whole categories, of men, nor could a dispensation from the Uniformity Act restore an ejected minister to his living. Therefore in March 1672, in circumstances which are still mysterious but were probably connected with his aborted promise in the Treaty of Dover to declare himself a Catholic, thus laying himself open to blackmail, Charles issued a Declaration of Indulgence, suspending by virtue of his 'supreme power in ecclesiastical matters' all penal legislation for religion (113). The only limit to complete religious freedom was that Protestant ministers must be licensed by a magistrate and Catholics were not allowed to worship in public. But the judges were hostile, as they had been in 1662, and when parliament met again, in February 1673, the Commons asserted that Elizabeth I's Act of Supremacy (on which Charles was presumably relying) did not stretch that far, and that statutes could only be suspended by subsequent statutes. Charles was forced to cancel his Declaration (114), and what was more, accept the Test Act, which aped the Long Parliament's Sequestration Ordinance of 1643 (p. 244 above) in imposing a doctrinal as distinct from a political oath (115). Office-holders were also obliged to take the oaths of Allegiance and Supremacy in open court and provide documentary proof that they had recently taken communion in the established Church. (This last proviso also barred Protestant Dissenters, perhaps unintentionally.)

The Test Act revealed that Clifford, the Lord Treasurer, and the king's brother and heir presumptive, James, Duke of York, were concealed Catholics. Combined with parliament's rampant suspicion of Louis XIV's France, this induced a state of tension which persisted down the 1670s and eventually erupted in the Popish Plot scare of 1678–9, provoked by the mendacious revelations of Titus Oates and other unscrupulous informers, which brought down the Earl of Danby, threw Charles's counsels into chaos, and obliged him in January 1679 to dissolve the parliament elected in 1661 and summon three others in two years.[41] Understandably, in 1678 parliament resolved that the fact that James was a Catholic had encouraged the perpetrators of this supposed plot, though neither then nor later did it venture to suggest that he was privy to it. The next parliament, in 1679, re-affirmed this, and the second Exclusion Parliament, in 1680, brought in a bill to exclude him from the succession, which was defeated in the Lords in November 1680 amid scenes of high excitement and political hysteria (117). A similar bill was introduced in the Oxford Parliament in March 1681, but was lost when it was dissolved after only seven days.

The bent of this agitation was almost entirely political, and it is arguable that the aristocratic leaders of the Exclusionist faction, which first acquired the label 'Whig'

---

[40] J. A. Williams, 'English Catholicism under Charles II', *Recusant History*, VII (1963), 123; Kenyon, *Popish Plot*, p. 15.

[41] Apart from Jones, *The First Whigs*, and Haley's life of *Shaftesbury*, there are now two monographs wholly or substantially devoted to this episode (Kenyon, *Popish Plot*, and Miller, *Popery and Politics*, esp. ch. 8), and I have therefore not felt it necessary to cover it in detail, nor give specific references.

during this crisis, were as much concerned with a reduction in the authority of the monarchy as the elimination of the 'Catholic menace'. Actual persecution of Catholics – particularly lay Catholics – was not as fierce as it is often assumed, and parliament showed little interest in reinforcing the penal statutes against them.[42] Apart from the Habeas Corpus Amendment Act of 1679 (p. 401 below), the only mark it left on the statute book was the second Test Act of November 1678 (**116**), which enlarged and reinforced the simple declaration laid down in the act of 1673, and barred Catholics from the House of Lords and from Court.

Obviously this crisis raised fundamental questions about the sanctity, legal or otherwise, of hereditary succession, which were to re-emerge at the Revolution,[43] but for the moment it died down remarkably quickly. In fact, the excesses of the Whigs, which seemed likely to provoke a civil war for the second time in this century, in the end produced a full-blown Tory reaction, strongly supported by the Church of England, which had been steadily behind the king throughout.[44] Additionally fortified by an increased income, Charles therefore lived out the rest of his reign in peace. His drive to confiscate borough charters on a large scale by writs of *quo warranto*, including the charters of many parliamentary boroughs, even strengthened his position (pp. 448–9 below). His brother not only succeeded him in 1685 with an ease which would have been incredible even four years before, but he also faced the most loyal and docile parliament in the seventeenth century.

James II's subsequent descent to disaster is well enough known. His practice of Catholicism publicly was acceptable enough, and could be regarded as more honest than his brother's. Nor was it unreasonable that he should suspend the operation of the penal laws against his co-religionists.[45] But encroachment on the Test Acts was quite another thing. Raising new regiments to deal with Monmouth's Rebellion in the summer of 1685, James extended to England a practice already adopted in Ireland, of dispensing Catholic army officers from the test by letters patent. In November Parliament angrily refused to sanction this procedure, and was prorogued, never to meet again (though it was not dissolved until July 1687). He then turned to the courts of law, and secured an endorsement for his policy in the collusive action *Godden* v. *Hales* in 1686 (pp. 447–9 below).

This enabled him to place a few token Catholics on the Privy Council, but it was not to be expected that a class which had been excluded from higher education and the

---

[42] In fact, they were more interested in relaxing the persecution of Protestant Dissenters. See Henry Horwitz, 'Protestant Reconciliation in the Exclusion Crisis', *Jnl Eccl. Hist.*, xv (1964), 201–17; also C. E. Fryer, 'The Royal Veto under Charles II', *EHR*, xxxii (1917), 103–11.

[43] Betty Behrens, 'The Whig Theory of the Constitution in the reign of Charles II', *Camb. Hist. Jnl*, vii (1941), 42–71, and Carolyn Andervont Edie, 'Succession and Monarchy: the Controversy of 1679–81', *Amer. Hist. Review*, lxx (1965), 350–70.

[44] References to 1641 and 1642 were common during the crisis, and were always taken to be significant. The Whig Sir Henry Capel protested in 1680, 'Parliament brought in the king without blood, but of late still we are told that the Church is in danger, and the actions of 1641 thrown amongst us' (Grey, *Debates*, vii, 362). See also R. A. Beddard, in Jones, *Restored Monarchy*, pp. 172–5.

[45] On 27 February 1685 he issued instructions that no proceedings were to be taken against Catholics who had been sufferers in the Great Rebellion, or were descended from such sufferers, or who had testified to their loyalty to the Crown since then – an extremely broad and inclusive specification. In March 1687 even this thin pretence was abandoned (*CSPD 1685*, no. 243, *Calendars of Treasury Books*, viii, 176, 1262).

professions for the past century would provide more than a trickle of recruits to government, and James's cynical expectation that the lifting of the tests would produce a flood of new converts was never realised. (Paradoxically, his government and household remained overwhelmingly Protestant to the very end.) In fact, over the year 1686 he was driven back increasingly on the Protestant Dissenters. The enforcement of the penal legislation against them, which had been more stringent and vigorous since 1681 than at any other previous time, was quietly relaxed, and in October 1686 he began a purge designed to remove the more obdurate Anglican–Tory magistrates on a nationwide scale.[46] In 1687, though with considerable hesitation, he moved over to a policy of complete religious toleration, which culminated in the issue of his Declaration of Indulgence, or 'Edict of Toleration' as it is sometimes known, in April 1687 (**118**).

The judges were suspected of being as wary of the suspending power as they had been in 1672, which is probably why James's Declaration was much less bold than his brother's. It suspended the penal laws, against both Catholics and Protestants, outright, but with regard to the Test Act of 1673 it merely ordered that the oaths and declaration therein required of all office-holders should not be tendered; the offer of individual dispensations in addition suggests a certain lack of self-confidence, and the whole was made dependent on the subsequent approval of parliament, though it was blithely assumed that this was not in doubt.[47]

However, despite James's efforts to mould the constituencies to his will, he had to put off the election of a new parliament until September 1688, when it was too late.[48] In the meanwhile he gratuitously dragged the whole question out into the open by re-issuing his Declaration in April 1688 and ordering it to be read from the pulpits of the established Church. The Archbishop of Canterbury and six of his bishops petitioned against this order, on the grounds that the suspending power had been declared illegal by parliament in 1673, and were indicted for seditious libel (pp. 396–7 below). Their acquittal underlined the doubts always held by many judges, and it set James firmly on the downward path leading to his fall. The Bill of Rights in 1689 effectively made future monarchs subject to the provisions of the Test Act, and abolished the suspending power outright, though it only condemned the dispensing power 'as it hath been assumed and exercised of late'.[49]

Strangely enough, the English Catholics did not share in the ruin of their great patron, perhaps because his efforts on their behalf had only served to expose their weakness. In the winter of 1689–90 many priests fled abroad in panic, a few who remained were imprisoned, but none were proceeded against at law. A new act passed in May 1689 forbad recusants to come within ten miles of London, but there is no sign that it was any more effective than the proclamations to this effect issued in 1678 and 1679.[50] From 1692 lay Catholics were obliged to pay double land tax, but this seems to

---

[46] Glassey, *Appointment of Justices*, pp. 70–1.

[47] Many Protestant office-holders, Godolphin and Sir Edward Herbert prominent amongst them, rather provocatively insisted on continuing to comply with the Test Act, appearing in Chancery or King's Bench to take the oaths and tender their certificates.

[48] Kenyon, *Sunderland*, ch. 6; J. R. Jones, *The Revolution of 1688* (1972), ch. 6.

[49] Williams, *Eighteenth-Century Constitution*, p. 28.

[50] 1 Wm & M., c. 9, printed Costin and Watson, I, 61–3.

have cancelled out their liabilities under the act of 1581.[51] The very last penal law, in 1700, was a reaction to the alarming number of priests who had returned to the English mission after the Peace of Ryswick.[52] It effectively commuted the death sentence on priests to life imprisonment, and the clauses forbidding Catholics to purchase or inherit land were easily evaded with the aid of a competent conveyancer. The Catholic problem was no longer a political issue, and if the Catholic community declined over the next hundred years, as it manifestly did, it was not because of persecution.

112. His Majesty's declaration to all his loving subjects, 26 December 1662

. . . Our principal aim [in this declaration] is to apply proper antidotes to all those venomous insinuations by which (as we are certainly informed) some of our subjects of inveterate and unalterable ill principles do daily endeavour to poison the affections of our good people by misleading their understandings, and that principally by four sorts of most false and malicious scandals . . .

The first, by suggesting unto them, that having attained our ends in re-establishing our regal authority, and gaining the power into our own hands by a specious condescension to a general Act of Indemnity, we intend nothing less than the observation of it; but on the contrary by degrees to subject the persons and estates of all such who stand in need of that law to future revenge, and to give them up to the spoil of those who had lost their fortunes in our service.

Secondly, that upon pretence of plots and practices against us, we intend to introduce a military way of government in this kingdom.

Thirdly, that having made use of such solemn promises from Breda, and in several declarations since, of ease and liberty to tender consciences, instead of performing any part of them, we have added straiter fetters than ever, and new rocks of scandal to the scrupulous, by the Act of Uniformity.

Fourthly and lastly, . . . that at the same time [as] we deny a fitting liberty to those other sects of our subjects, whose consciences will not allow them to conform to the religion established by law, we are highly indulgent to papists, not only exempting them from the penalties of the law, but even to such a degree of countenance and encouragement as may even endanger the Protestant Religion.

★   ★   ★

As for the third, concerning the non-performance of our promises, we remember well the very words of those from Breda, viz:

We do declare a liberty to tender consciences, and that no man shall be disquieted or

---

[51] W. R. Ward, *The English Land Tax in the Eighteenth Century* (Oxford 1953), pp. 32–3; J. Anthony Williams, 'The Problem of the Double Land Tax', *Dublin Review*, Spring 1959, p. 32. In 1723 Walpole tried to levy an additional aid of £100,000 on recusants, but ten years later only £63,000 had been collected, and the experiment was abandoned.

[52] 11 Wm III, c. 4, printed Williams, *Eighteenth-Century Constitution*, pp. 331–3.

called in question for differences of opinion in matters of religion which do not disturb the peace of the kingdom; and that we shall be ready to consent to such an Act of Parliament as upon mature deliberation shall be offered to us for the full granting that indulgence.

We remember well the confirmations we have made of them since upon several occasions in parliament, and as all these things are still fresh in our memory, so are we still firm in the resolution of performing them to the full. But it must not be wondered at, since that parliament to which those promises were made in relation to an Act never thought fit to offer us any to that purpose, and being so zealous as we are (and by the Grace of God shall ever be) for the maintenance of the true Protestant religion, finding it so shaken (not to say overthrown) as we did, we should give its establishment the precedency before matters of indulgence to dissenters from it. But that once done (as we hope it is sufficiently by the Bill of Uniformity), we are glad to lay hold on this occasion to renew unto all our subjects concerned in those promises of indulgence by a true tenderness of conscience this assurance:

That as in the first place we have been zealous to settle the uniformity of the Church of England, in discipline, ceremony and government, and shall ever constantly maintain it; so as for what concerns the penalties upon those who (living peaceable) do not conform thereunto through scruple and tenderness of misguided conscience, but modestly and without scandal perform their devotions in their own way, we shall make it our special care so far forth as in us lies, without invading the freedom of parliament, to incline their wisdom at this next approaching sessions to concur with us in the making some such act for that purpose as may enable us to exercise with a more universal satisfaction that power of dispensing which we conceive to be inherent in us. Nor can we doubt of their cheerful co-operating with us in a thing wherein we do conceive ourselves so far engaged, both in honour and in what we owe to the peace of our dominions, which we profess we can never think secure whilst there shall be a colour left to the malicious and disaffected to inflame the minds of so many multitudes upon the score of conscience, with despair of ever obtaining any effect of our promise for their case.

In the last place, as to that most pernicious and injurious scandal, so artificially spread and fomented, of our favour to papists; as it is but a repetition of the same detestable arts by which all the late calamities have been brought upon this kingdom in the time of our royal father of blessed memory (who, though the most pious and zealous Protestant that ever reigned in this nation, could never wash off the stains cast upon him by that malice, but by his martyrdom), we conceive all our subjects should be sufficiently prepared against that poison by memory of those disasters, especially since nothing is more evident than that the wicked authors of this scandal are such as seek to involve all good Protestants under the odious name of papists, or popishly affected. Yet we cannot but say upon this occasion that our education and course of life in the true Protestant religion has been such, and our constancy in the profession of it so eminent in our most desperate conditions abroad among Roman Catholic princes, when the appearance of receding from it had been the likeliest way in all human forecast to have procured us the most powerful assistances of our re-establishment, that should any of our subjects give but the least admission of that scandal unto their beliefs we should look upon it as the most unpardonable offence that they can be guilty of towards us.

'Tis true, that as we shall always according to justice retain, so we think it may become us to avow to the world a due sense we have of the greatest part of our Roman Catholic subjects of this kingdom having deserved well from our royal father of blessed memory, and from us, and even from the Protestant religion itself, in adhering to us with their lives and fortunes for the maintenance of our Crown in the religion established against those who under the name of zealous Protestants employed both fire and sword to overthrow them both. We shall with as much freedom profess unto the world, that it is not our intention to exclude our Roman Catholic subjects, who have so demeaned themselves, from all share in the benefit of such an act as in pursuance of our promises the wisdom of our parliament shall think fit to offer unto us for the ease of tender consciences. It might appear no less than injustice, that those who deserved well and continued to do so should be denied some part of that mercy which we have obliged ourselves to afford to ten times the number of such who have not done so. Besides, such are the capital laws in force against them, although[53] justified in their rigour by the times wherein they were made, we profess it would be grievous unto us to consent to the execution of them, by putting any of our subjects to death for their opinions in matter of religion only. But at the same time that we declare our little liking of those sanguinary ones, and our gracious intentions already expressed to such of our Roman Catholic subjects as shall live peaceably, modestly and without scandal, we would have them all know, that if for doing what their duties and loyalties obliged them to, or from our acknowledgment of their well-deserving, they shall have the presumption to hope for a toleration of their profession, or a taking away either those marks of distinction, or of our displeasure, which in a well-governed kingdom ought always to be set upon dissenters from the religion of the state, or to obtain the least remission in the strictness of those laws which either are or shall be made to hinder the spreading of their doctrine, to the prejudice of the true Protestant religion; or that upon our expressing (according to Christian charity) our dislike for bloodshed for religion only, priests shall take the boldness to appear and avow

[53] Original reads *as though*.

themselves, to the offence and scandal of good Protestants, and of the laws in force against them, they shall quickly find we know as well to be severe, when wisdom requires, as indulgent when charity and sense of merit challenge it from us . . .   Cardwell, *Annals*, II, 312–13, 316–19

113. The Declaration of Indulgence, 1672

His Majesty's Declaration to all his loving subjects [15 March 1672]

Our care and endeavours for the preservation of the rights and interests of the Church have been sufficiently manifested to the world by the whole course of our government since our happy restoration, and by the many and frequent ways of coercion that we have used for reducing all erring or dissenting persons, and for composing the unhappy differences in matters of religion which we found among our subjects upon our return. But it being evident by the sad experience of twelve years that there is very little fruit of all those forcible courses, we think ourself obliged to make use of that supreme power in ecclesiastical matters which is not only inherent in us but hath been declared and recognised to be so by several statutes and acts of parliament; and therefore we do now accordingly issue this our Declaration, as well for the quieting the minds of our good subjects in these points, for inviting strangers in this conjuncture to come and live under us, and for the better encouragement of all to a cheerful following of their trade and callings, from whence we hope by the blessing of God to have many good and happy advantages to our government; as also for preventing for the future the danger that might otherwise arise from private meetings and seditious conventicles.

And in the first place we declare our express resolution, meaning and intention to be, that the Church of England be preserved and remain entire in its doctrine, discipline and government, as now it stands established by law; and that this be taken to be, as it is, the basis, rule and standard of the general and public worship of God, and that the orthodox, conformable clergy do receive and enjoy the revenues belonging thereunto; and that no person, though of a different opinion and persuasion, shall be exempt from paying his tithes or other dues whatsoever. And further, we declare that no person shall be capable of holding any benefice or preferment of any kind in this our kingdom of England who is not exactly conformable.

We do in the next place declare our will and pleasure to be, that the execution of all and all manner of penal laws in matters ecclesiastical, against whatsoever sort of nonconformists or recusants, be immediately suspended; and all judges, judges of assize and gaol-delivery, sheriffs, justices of the peace, mayors, bailiffs and other officers whatsoever, whether ecclesiastical or civil, are to take notice of it, and pay due obedience thereunto.

And that there may be no pretence for any of our subjects to continue their illegal meetings and conventicles, we do declare that we shall from time to time allow a sufficient number of places, as they shall be desired, in all parts of this our kingdom, for the use of such as do not conform to the Church of England, to meet and assemble in in order to their public worship and devotion, which places shall be open and free to all persons.

But to prevent such disorders and inconveniences as may happen by this our indulgence, if not duly regulated, and that they may be the better protected by the civil magistrate, our express will and pleasure is that none of our subjects do presume to meet in any place until such place be allowed, and the teacher of that congregation be approved by us.

And lest any should apprehend that this restriction should make our said allowance and approbation difficult to be obtained, we do further declare that this our indulgence, as to the allowance of the public places of worship and approbation of the teachers, shall extend to all sorts of nonconformists and recusants, except the recusants of the Roman Catholic religion, to whom we shall in no way allow public places of worship, but only indulge them their share in the common exemption from the execution of the penal laws, and the exercise of their worship in their private houses only.

And if after this our clemency and indulgence any of our subjects shall presume to abuse this liberty and shall preach seditiously, or to the derogation of the doctrine, discipline or government of the Established Church, or shall meet in places not allowed by us, we do hereby give them warning, and declare, that we will proceed against them with all imaginable severity; and we will let them see we can be as severe to punish such offenders, when so justly provoked, as we are indulgent to truly tender consciences.

Cardwell, *Annals*, II, 333–7

114. The king's surrender, 1673

(a) The King's Reply,[54] *24 February 1673*

His Majesty hath received an Address from you, and he hath seriously considered of it, and returneth you this answer.

That he is very much troubled that that Declaration, which he put out for ends so necessary to the quiet of his kingdom, and especially in that conjuncture, should have proved the cause of disquiet in his House of Commons, and give occasion to the questioning of his power in ecclesiastics, which he finds not done in the reigns of any of his ancestors. He is sure he never had thoughts of using it otherwise than as it hath been entrusted in him, to the peace and establishment of the Church of England, and the ease of all his

[54] To the Commons' Address of the 14th requesting him to withdraw the Declaration of Indulgence.

subjects in general; neither did he pretend to the right of suspending any laws wherein the properties, rights or liberties of any of his subjects are concerned; nor to alter anything in the established doctrine or discipline of the Church of England; but his only design in this was, to take off the penalties the statutes inflict upon Dissenters, and which he believes, when well considered of, you yourselves would not wish executed according to the rigour and letter of the law. Neither hath he done this with any thought of avoiding or precluding the advice of his parliament, and if any bill shall be offered him, which shall appear more proper to attain the aforesaid ends, and secure the peace of the Church and Kingdom, when tendered in due manner to him, he will show how readily he will concur in all ways that shall appear good for the kingdom.

CJ, IX, 256

(b) The Commons Answer, 26 February 1673

Most Gracious Sovereign,

We, your Majesty's most humble and loyal subjects, the knights, citizens and burgesses in this present parliament assembled, do render to your sacred Majesty our most dutiful thanks, for that, to our unspeakable comfort, your Majesty hath been pleased so often to reiterate unto us those gacious promises and assurances of maintaining the religion now established, and the liberties and properties of your people, and we do not in the least measure doubt but that your Majesty had the same gracious intentions, in giving satisfaction to your subjects, by your answer to our last petition and address. Yet upon a serious consideration thereof we find that the said answer is not sufficient to clear the apprehensions that may justly remain in the minds of your people, by your Majesty's having claimed a power to suspend penal statutes in matters ecclesiastical, and which your Majesty does still seem to assert in the said Answer to be entrusted in the Crown, and never questioned in the reigns of any of your ancestors. Wherein we humbly conceive your Majesty hath been very much misinformed, since no such power was ever claimed or exercised by any of your Majesty's predecessors; and if it should be admitted might tend to the interrupting of the free course of the laws, and altering the legislative power, which hath always been acknowledged to reside in your Majesty, and your two Houses of Parliament.

We do therefore, with unanimous consent, become again most humble suitors unto your sacred Majesty, that you would be pleased to give us a full and satisfactory answer to our said petition and address; and that your Majesty would take such effectual order that the proceedings in this matter may not for the future be drawn into consequence or example.   *Ibid.*, 257

[On 7 March Charles cancelled the Declaration.]

115. 25 Car. II, c. 2: An Act for preventing dangers which may happen from Popish recusants, 1673

For preventing dangers which may happen from popish recusants, and quieting the minds of his Majesty's good subjects, be it enacted . . . that all and every person or persons, as well peers as commoners, that shall bear any office or offices, civil or military, or shall receive any pay, salary, fee or wages by reason of any patent of trust from or under his Majesty, or any of his Majesty's predecessors, or by his or their authority derived from him or them within the realm . . ., or shall be of the household or in the service or employment of his Majesty or of his royal Highness the Duke of York, who shall inhabit, reside or be within the city of London or Westminster or within thirty miles distant from the same on the first day of the Easter Term . . . 1673 . . ., all and every the said persons shall personally appear before the end of the said term, or of Trinity Term next following, in his Majesty's High Court of Chancery or in his Majesty's Court of King's Bench, and there in public and open court between the hours of nine of the clock and twelve . . . take the several oaths of supremacy and allegiance, which oath of allegiance is contained in a statute made in the third year of King James;[55] . . . and that all and every of the said respective persons and officers, not having taken the said oaths in the said respective courts as aforesaid, shall on or before the first day of August, 1673, at the Quarter Sessions for that county or place where he or they shall be, inhabit or reside on the twentieth day of May, take the said oaths in open court . . .; and the said respective officers aforesaid shall also receive the sacrament of the Lord's Supper according to the usage of the Church of England at or before the first day of August, 1673, in some parish church upon the Lord's Day, commonly called Sunday, immediately after the Divine Service and sermon . . . And every of the said persons in the respective court where he takes the said oaths shall first deliver a certificate of such his receiving the said sacrament as aforesaid under the hands of the respective minister and churchwarden, and shall then make proof of the truth thereof by two credible witnesses at the least upon oath, all which shall be inquired of and put upon record in the respective courts.

III. And be it further enacted . . . that all and every the person and persons aforesaid that do or shall neglect or refuse to take the said oaths and sacrament . . . shall be *ipso facto* adjudged incapable and disabled in law to all intents and purposes whatsoever to have, occupy or enjoy the said office or offices, employment or employments . . .

---

[55] No. **55**, p. 168 above.

IV. And be it further enacted that all and every such person and persons that . . . after such neglect or refusal shall execute any of the said offices of employments . . ., being lawfully convicted . . ., shall be disabled from thenceforth to sue or use any action . . . in course of law, or to prosecute any suit in any court of equity, or to be guardian of any child, or executor or administrator of any person, or capable of any legacy, or deed of gifts, or to bear any office within this realm . . ., and shall forfeit the sum of five hundred pounds . . .

★   ★   ★

VIII. And be it further enacted . . . that at the same time when the persons concerned in this act shall take the aforesaid oaths of supremacy and allegiance, they shall likewise make and subscribe this Declaration under the same penalties and forfeitures as by this act is appointed:

I, A. B., do declare that I do believe that there is not any transubstantiation in the sacrament of the Lord's Supper, or in the elements of bread and wine, at or after the consecration thereof by any person whatsoever.

Of which subscription there shall be the like register kept as of the taking the oaths aforesaid.

★   ★   ★

SR, v, 782–5

116. 30 Car. II, st. 2, c. 1: An Act for the more effectual preserving the King's person and government by disabling Papists from sitting in either House of Parliament, 1678

Forasmuch as divers good laws have been made for preventing the increase and danger of popery in this kingdom, which have not had the desired effects by reason of the free access which popish recusants have had to his Majesty's Court, and by reason of the liberty which of late some of the recusants have had or taken to sit and vote in Parliament; wherefore, and for the safety of his Majesty's royal person and government, be it enacted by the king's most excellent Majesty . . . that from and after . . . 1 December 1678 no person that now is or hereafter shall be a Peer of this realm or member of the House of Peers shall vote or make his proxy in the House of Peers, or sit there during any debate . . ., nor any person that now is or hereafter shall be a Member of the House of Commons shall vote in the House of Commons or sit there during any debate in the said House of Commons after their Speaker is chosen until such Peer or Member shall from time to time respectively and in manner following first take the several oaths of allegiance and supremacy, and make, subscribe and audibly repeat this declaration following:

I, A. B., do solemnly and sincerely, in the presence of God, profess, testify and declare that I do believe that in the sacrament of the Lord's Supper there is not any transubstantiation of the elements of bread and wine into the body and blood of Christ at or after the consecration thereof by any person whatsoever; and that the invocation or adoration of the Virgin Mary or any other saint, and the sacrifice of the mass as they are now used in the Church of Rome, are superstitious and idolatrous. And I do solemnly, in the presence of God, profess, testify and declare that I do make this declaration and every part thereof in the plain and ordinary sense of the words read unto me, as they are commonly understood by English Protestants, without any evasion, equivocation or mental reservation whatsoever, and without any dispensation already granted me for this purpose by the Pope or any other authority or person whatsoever, and without any hope of any such dispensation from any person or authority whatsoever, or without thinking that I am or can be acquitted before God or Man or absolved of this declaration or any part thereof, although the Pope, or any other person or persons or power whatsoever should dispense with or annul the same, or declare that it was null and void from the beginning.

Which said oaths and declaration shall be in this and every succeeding parliament solemnly and publicly made and subscribed . . .

II. And be it further enacted that after the said first day of December every Peer of this realm . . ., and every Peer of the kingdom of Scotland or of the kingdom of Ireland, being of the age of one and twenty years and upwards, not having taken the said oaths and made and subscribed the said declaration, and every Member of the House of Commons . . . as aforesaid . . ., and every person now or hereafter convicted of Popish recusancy, who hereafter shall at any time . . . come advisedly into and remain in the presence of the king's Majesty or queen's Majesty, or shall come into the Court, or house where they or any of them reside, . . . shall incur and suffer all the pains, penalties, forfeitures and disabilities in this act mentioned or contained . . .

★ ★ ★

XI. Provided always that nothing in this act contained shall extend to his royal Highness the Duke of York. *SR*, v, 894-6

117. The Exclusion Bill, November 1680

Whereas James, Duke of York, is notoriously known to have been perverted from the Protestant to the popish religion, whereby not only great encouragement hath been given to the popish party to enter into and carry on most devilish and horrid plots and conspiracies for the destruction of his Majesty's sacred person and government, and for the extirpation of the true

Protestant religion, but also if the said duke should succeed to the imperial crown of this realm, nothing is more manifest than that a total change of religion within these kingdoms would ensue.

For the prevention whereof, be it therefore enacted by and with the advice and consent of the Lords spiritual and temporal and the Commons in this present parliament assembled, and by the authority of the same, that the said James, Duke of York, shall be and is by authority of the present parliament excluded and made for ever incapable to inherit, possess or enjoy the imperial crown of this realm and of the kingdom of Ireland and the dominions and territories to them or either of them belonging, or to have, exercise or enjoy any dominion, power, jurisdiction or authority within the same . . .

[2.] And be it further enacted by the authority aforesaid that if the said James, Duke of York, shall at any time hereafter challenge, claim, or attempt to possess or enjoy, or shall take upon him to use or exercise any dominion, power, authority or jurisdiction within the said kingdoms . . . as king or chief magistrate of the same, that then he, the said James, Duke of York, for every such offence shall be deemed and adjudged guilty of high treason, and shall suffer the pains, penalties and forfeitures as in cases of high treason; and further, that if any person or persons whatsoever shall assist, aid, maintain, abet, or willingly adhere unto the said James, Duke of York, in such his challenge, claim or attempt, or shall of themselves attempt or endeavour to put or bring the said James, Duke of York, into the possession or exercise of any regal power, jurisdiction or authority within the kingdoms or dominions aforesaid, or shall by writing or preaching advisedly publish, maintain or declare that he hath any right, title or authority to exercise the office of king or chief magistrate . . ., that then every such person shall be deemed and adjudged guilty of high treason . . .

[3.] And be it further enacted . . . that if the said James, Duke of York, shall at any time from and after the fifth day of November in the year of our Lord God 1680 return or come into or within any of the kingdoms or dominions aforesaid, that then he . . . shall be deemed and adjudged guilty of high treason . . . And further, that if any person or persons whatsoever shall be aiding or assisting unto such return of the said James, Duke of York, that then every such person shall be deemed and adjudged guilty of high treason . . .

*   *   *

[5.] And be it further enacted and declared . . . that it shall and may be lawful to and for all magistrates, officers and other subjects whatsoever . . . to apprehend and secure the said James, Duke of York, and every other person offending in the premises, and with him or them in case of resistance to fight and him or them by force to subdue, for all which actings and for so doing they are and shall be by virtue of this act saved harmless and indemnified.

[6.] Provided . . . that nothing in this act contained shall be construed, deemed or adjudged to disable any person from inheriting or enjoying the imperial crown of the realms and dominions aforesaid . . ., but that in case the said James, Duke of York, shall survive his now Majesty and the heirs of his Majesty's body, the said imperial crown shall descend to and be enjoyed by such person and persons successively during the lifetime of the said James, Duke of York, as should have inherited and enjoyed the same in case the said James, Duke of York, were naturally dead, anything in this act contained to the contrary notwithstanding.   *House of Lords MSS, 1678–1688*, pp. 195–7

118. Declaration of Indulgence, 1687

King James the Second his gracious declaration to all his loving subjects for liberty of conscience [4 April 1687]

It having pleased Almighty God not only to bring us to the imperial crown of these kingdoms through the greatest difficulties, but to preserve us by a more than ordinary providence upon the throne of our royal ancestors, there is nothing now that we so earnestly desire as to establish our government on such a foundation as may make our subjects happy, and unite them to us by inclination as well as duty. Which we think can be done by no means so effectually as by granting to them the free exercise of their religion for the time to come, and add that to the perfect enjoyment of their property, which has never been in any case invaded by us since our coming to the crown. Which being the two things men value most, shall ever be preserved in these kingdoms during our reign over them, as the truest methods of their peace and our glory.

We cannot but heartily wish, as it will easily be believed, that all the people of our dominions were members of the Catholic Church, yet we humbly thank Almighty God it is and hath of long time been our constant sense and opinion (which upon divers occasions we have declared), that conscience ought not to be constrained, nor people forced in matters of mere religion. It has ever been directly contrary to our inclination, as we think it is to the interest of government, which it destroys by spoiling trade, depopulating countries and discouraging strangers; and finally, that it never obtained the end for which it was employed. And in this we are the more confirmed by the reflections we have made upon the conduct of the four last reigns. For after all the frequent and pressing endeavours that were used in each of them to reduce this kingdom to an exact conformity in religion, it is visible the success has not answered the design, and that the difficulty is invincible. We therefore, out of our princely care and affection unto all our loving subjects, that they may live at ease and quiet, and for the increase of trade and encouragement of strangers, have thought fit by virtue of our royal prerogative to issue forth this our Declaration of Indulgence, making no doubt of the concurrence of our two houses of parliament when we shall think it convenient for them to meet.

In the first place we do declare, that we will protect and maintain our archbishops, bishops and clergy, and all other our subjects of the Church of England in the free exercise of their religion as by law established, and in the quiet and full enjoyment of all their possessions, without any molestation or disturbance whatsoever.

We do likewise declare, that it is our royal will and pleasure that from henceforth the execution of all and all manner of penal laws in matters ecclesiastical, for not coming to church, or not receiving the sacrament, or for any other nonconformity to the religion established, or for or by reason of the exercise of religion in any manner whatsoever, be immediately suspended; and the further execution of the said penal laws and every of them is hereby suspended.

And to the end that by the liberty hereby granted the peace and security of the government in the practice thereof may not be endangered, we have thought fit, and do hereby straitly charge and command all our loving subjects, that as we do freely give them leave to meet and serve God after their own way and manner, be it in private houses or places purposely hired or built for that use, so that they take especial care, that nothing be preached or taught amongst them which may any ways tend to alienate the hearts of our people from us or our government, and that their meetings and assemblies be peaceably, openly and publicly held, and all persons freely admitted to them, and that they do signify and make known to some one or more of the next justices of the peace, what place or places they set apart for their uses.

And that all our subjects may enjoy such their religious assemblies with greater assurance and protection, we have thought it requisite, and do hereby command, that no disturbance of any kind be made or given unto them, under pain of our displeasure, and to be further proceeded against with the utmost severity.

And forasmuch as we are desirous to have the benefit of the service of all our loving subjects, which by the law of nature is inseparably annexed to and inherent in our royal person; and that none of our subjects may for the future be under any discouragement or disability (who are otherwise well inclined and fit to serve us) by reason of some oaths or tests that have been usually administered on such occasions, we do hereby further declare, that it is our royal will and pleasure that the oaths commonly called 'the oaths of supremacy and allegiance', and also the several tests and declarations mentioned in the acts of parliament made in the 25th and 30th years of the reign of our late royal brother, King Charles II, shall not at any time hereafter be required to be taken, declared or subscribed by any person or persons whatsoever who is or shall be employed in any office or place of trust either civil or military under us, or in our government. And we do further declare it to be our pleasure and intention from time to time hereafter to grant our royal dispensations under our Great Seal to all our loving subjects so to be employed, who shall not take the said oaths, or subscribe or declare the said tests or declarations in the above-mentioned acts and every of them.

And to the end that all our loving subjects may receive and enjoy the full benefit and advantage of our gracious indulgence hereby intended, and may be acquitted and discharged from all pains, penalties, forfeitures and disabilities by them or any of them incurred or forfeited, or which they shall or may at any time hereafter be liable to, for or by reason of their nonconformity, or the exercise of their religion, and from all suits, troubles or disturbances for the same, we do hereby give our free and ample pardon unto all nonconformists, recusants and other our loving subjects for all crimes and things by them committed or done contrary to the penal laws formerly made relating to religion and the profession or exercise thereof; hereby declaring that this our royal pardon and indemnity shall be as good and effectual to all intents and purposes as if every individual person had been therein particularly named, or had particular pardons under our Great Seal, which we do likewise declare shall from time to time be granted unto any person or persons desiring the same, willing and requiring our judges, justices and other officers to take notice of and obey our royal will and pleasure herein before declared.

And although the freedom and assurance we have hereby given in relation to religion and property might be sufficient to remove from the minds of our loving subjects all fears and jealousies in relation to either, yet we have thought fit further to declare, that we will maintain them in all their properties and possessions, as well of church and abbey lands as in any other their lands and properties whatsoever. 　　　Cardwell, *Annals*, II, 359–63

IV. THE JUDICIARY

The law, naturally, was the key to seventeenth-century history; both the king and his critics or opponents continually appealed to it in justification. But the tradition of impartiality expressed by Coke had been largely abandoned in the 1620s and 1630s, or so it seemed, and the prestige of the high courts suffered accordingly (pp. 90–1 above). Subsequently the profession as a whole had been assailed by strong agitation for law reform during the Interregnum, and though its successful resistance to this movement confirmed its innate strength, it was left in no doubt of the unpopularity of many of its functions and activities.[56] At the Restoration Charles II continued the practice forced on his father in 1641, of giving high court judges patents *quamdiu se bene*

[56] Pp. 303–4 above, and Veall, *Popular Movement for Law Reform*, esp. ch. 11.

gesserint, but after Clarendon's fall in 1667 he reverted to patents *durante bene placito*, and subsequently dismissed or suspended judges at will, for political reasons or sometimes for no apparent reason at all.[57] As for the judges themselves, their reputation is coloured by the prominence of men like Scroggs, Jenner and Jeffreys, who were atrocious bullies in Westminster Hall and apparently complaisant toadies at Whitehall, and were credited with an inadequate knowledge of the law they claimed to administer.

There were exceptions, of course. Sir Matthew Hale, whose career as a high court judge, and eventually Chief Justice of King's Bench, spanned the years 1654 to 1676, maintained and developed the juristic tradition of Sir Edward Coke, though his greatest work, *The History of the Common Law of England*, was not published until 1713.[58] It is also worth remembering that Heneage Finch, first Earl of Nottingham, Lord Keeper 1673–4, Lord Chancellor 1674–82, is still regarded as 'the father of modern equity', and that it was in this reign that the strict settlement, that potent innovation in the land law, achieved its perfected form.[59] Nor is it necessary to suppose that the legal learning of the more uncouth judges, like Scroggs and Jeffreys, was as deficient as their political enemies said it was.[60] As for their court room manners, especially in criminal cases and state trials, these arose in part from the need to obtain certain verdicts, despite the unreliability of a great deal of the Crown's evidence and the untrustworthiness of many juries. To us the verdicts given against the Catholics accused of treason in 1678 and 1679, and against Lord Russell and Algernon Sidney in 1683, to mention only the most prominent, are shocking, and the manner in which they were obtained still more so; but it was an accepted tradition going back more than a hundred years that given the inadequate machinery at the state's disposal for the detection of treason, and the heinousness of the crime, those accused of it must be found guilty at all costs.[61]

Moreover, much of the bullying practised by the judges, particularly at assizes, was provoked by the need to handle ignorant or partisan juries, who refused to accept their allotted role as neutral arbiters and could no longer be disciplined by Star Chamber. In 1667 Lord Chief Justice Keeling was summoned to the Bar of the House of Commons for bullying and harrying juries, and even disparaging Magna Carta (**119**). Though he disdained to make an apology the House took no action against him, but it passed a resolution that the fining and imprisoning of juries for giving a verdict against the

[57] A. F. Havighurst, 'The Judiciary and Politics in the Reign of Charles II', *Law Quarterly Review*, LXVI (1950), 62–78, 229–52, and 'James II and the Twelve Men in Scarlet', *ibid.*, LXIX (1953), 522–46, are indispensable; see also Holdsworth, *History of English Law*, VI, 500ff. The latest and in many ways the best discussion of the whole question is by Howard Nenner, *By Colour of Law: Legal Culture and Constitutional Politics 1660–1689* (Chicago 1977).

[58] See Charles M. Gray's introduction to the Chicago University Press reprint of 1971, and Pocock, *Ancient Constitution*, pp. 170–81.

[59] B. English and J. Saville, *Strict Settlement: a Guide for Historians* (Hull 1983), ch. 2; Lloyd Bonfield, *Marriage Settlements 1601–1740* (Cambridge 1983), ch. 4. For Nottingham see D. E. C. Yale's introduction to his edition of *Lord Nottingham's Chancery Cases*, vol. I (Selden Society LXXIII, 1957).

[60] J. P. Kenyon, 'The Acquittal of Sir George Wakeman', *HJ*, XIV (1971), 694–5; G. W. Keeton, *Lord Chancellor Jeffreys and the Stuart Cause* (1965), *passim*.

[61] For Tudor practice, see Elton, *Tudor Constitution*, pp. 80–2. As he remarks, 'It is a mistake to judge these matters solely by the famous cases', and acquittals were possible even at the height of the Popish Plot; see Kenyon, *art. cit.*

judge's summing-up was illegal. In 1670 this was upheld by King's Bench. Edward Bushel, a juryman at the London Court of Sessions, was imprisoned for refusing to bring in a verdict against the Quakers Penn and Mead. On a writ of habeas corpus into King's Bench Lord Chief Justice Vaughan found in favour of the prisoner, and declared that judges could not punish jurymen for their verdict unless there was evidence of corruption. But it should be noticed that Vaughan was very far from asserting the modern doctrine of the jury's absolute impartiality; on the contrary, he argued from the commonsense medieval notion that the jury, drawn from the neighbourhood, knew more about the facts of the case and the parties concerned than the judge; and his idea of what constituted 'discreet and lawful assistance of the jury' is very far from our own (**120**). We notice that in 1687 Mr Justice Holloway of King's Bench could admit quite naturally, in an aside, that he had 'solicited and menaced' an assize jury at Reading in an attempt to secure a conviction (**124**).

Otherwise the main handicap under which a defendant laboured, certainly in trials for treasons and felony, was that he was not allowed the services of counsel except on points of law, he could not subpoena witnesses or put them on oath, and he was not allowed a copy of the indictment beforehand. Even Jeffreys thought that this last was hard, and said so in 1684 (**122**); his reference to the need to change procedure by act of parliament looks forward to the Trials for Treason Act of 1696.[62] On the other hand, presiding as Lord Steward at Lord Delamere's trial in 1686, he argued that the admittance of barristers would merely clog and retard the proceedings.[63] (It should be remembered that the judge, like the prosecuting officer at modern courts-martial, was expected to act as 'prisoner's friend', particularly in the cross-examination of witnesses.)

In fact, until 1681 there is no sign that the Crown was using its wide powers, and the authority of the judges, against its opponents in any systematic way. Even that doughty Whig lawyer Henry Hallam, writing in 1827, committed himself to the surprising statement that 'the fundamental privileges of the subject were less invaded, the prerogative swerved into fewer excesses, during the reign of Charles II than perhaps in any former period of equal length'.[64] What did occasion alarm was the king's power of arbitrary arrest and detention, which the Petition of Right had failed to remove. The Act of 1641 abolishing Star Chamber (p. 204 above) decreed that any man imprisoned by order of king or Council could sue out a writ of habeas corpus in King's Bench or Common Pleas, and that upon return of that writ the gaoler must certify the true cause of imprisonment. But this did not cover commitment by the orders of a secretary of state, which was increasingly common. Moreover, there was doubt as to whether a judge could issue a writ in vacation, and which courts should issue it in term; gaolers were often ordered to delay returning the writ; judges could delay issuing it, then postpone the hearing on its return; the king's prisoners were often carried from gaol to gaol, calling for the issue of a new writ each time, and sometimes

---

[62] Williams, *Eighteenth-Century Constitution*, pp. 53–6.
[63] Nenner, *op. cit.*, p. 31.
[64] *Constitutional History of England* (Everyman edn), III, 1. See also Howard Nenner's defence of the Stuart kings' use of the judiciary, *op. cit.*, pp. 61–74. He concludes that Charles II 'worked within the rules' (p. 64), and his opponents did not.

they were taken to Scilly or the Channel Islands, where the writ did not run. One of the articles in Clarendon's impeachment in 1667 accused him of imprisoning the king's subjects in 'remote garrisons, islands and other places', and indeed many doubtful characters left over from the Interregnum, like John Lambert, were taken out of circulation in this way. (Not that this was anything new; Charles I had sent Prynne to Jersey, and Cromwell, Lilburne.)

As a result various bills were introduced, in 1668, 1670 and 1674, to reform various aspects of habeas corpus procedure, but they were all abortive.[65] Meanwhile Secretary of State Coventry was criticised in 1674 for having a man arrested on his verbal order, and in 1677 it was found that his colleague Williamson was issuing general warrants 'on suspicion of seditious practices'.[66] With political tension mounting, it is not surprising that further bills were introduced in 1675 and 1677, but they too were lost. It was not until the first Exclusion Parliament of 1679, with the government besieged, that it was found possible to combine all these previous bills in the Habeas Corpus Amendment Act (121), which laid down a watertight procedure for the issue of the writ, set a time limit for its hearing, frustrated equivocation on the part of judges or gaolers, and forbad the transportation of remand prisoners overseas. It passed the Lords, in mysterious circumstances, on the last day of the session.[67] It at once became much more difficult for the government to take men up on suspicion, and many of those implicated in the Rye House Plot or Monmouth's Rebellion probably owed their lives to it. James II's dislike of it testified to its effectiveness, as does the decision to suspend it temporarily in 1689, and again in 1715.

To us the main problem was the independence of the judiciary, but it is not clear that contemporaries felt the same. Even a staunch parliamentarian like William Petyt feared 'the spectre of uncontrolled judicial discretion',[68] and this was confirmed in 1674, when a bill was introduced in the Commons to regulate judges' salaries and confirm their tenure. It was strongly opposed, and eventually defeated, by a number of back-benchers who were normally no friends of the monarchy, but who feared that if the judges were given absolute security they would evolve into a separate species of political man, accountable to nobody.[69] Nor is it a fact that insecurity of tenure weakened the resolve of the judges. They contested the legality of Cromwell's ordinances in 1655 (p. 304 above), they were averse to Charles II's proposal to dispense ministers from the provisions of the Uniformity Act in 1662, and reluctant to acknowledge his suspension of the penal laws ten years later. This last provoked the first clear dismissals for political reasons in this reign, but in the absence of a subsequent test case the result is ambiguous. The next time undue pressure was brought to bear on the judges it was from parliament, for it was this that almost certainly led to the dismissal of four judges without cause shown in April 1679; and it is a sign of Charles's growing self-confidence that he felt able in turn to dismiss Sir Robert Atkyns and Sir

---

[65] Holdsworth, IX, 115–17.   [66] Grey, *Debates*, II, 424–5, IV, 261ff.

[67] Godfrey Davies and E. L. Klotz, 'The Habeas Corpus Act of 1679 in the House of Lords', *HLQ*, III (1940), 469; Helen A. Nutting, 'The Most Wholesome Law', *Amer. Hist. Review*, LXV (1960), 527.

[68] Nenner, *op. cit.*, p. 109. Nenner also reminds us that the idea that the judiciary 'belonged' to parliament, or had an affinity with it, is a Whig myth (*ibid.*, pp. 61–2).

[69] Grey, *Debates*, II, 415–20 (13 February 1674).

Francis Pemberton, puisne judges of Common Pleas and King's Bench respectively, in February 1680. He subsequently resisted the strongest pressure, inside parliament and without, to dismiss Lord Chief Justice Scroggs, and only pensioned him off in April 1681, when this pressure had died away. It is rather surprising that Scroggs was replaced by Pemberton, who was then transferred to Common Pleas in December 1682 to make way for Sir Edmund Saunders. It is difficult to detect the reasoning behind these changes, but we should beware of leaping to a sinister explanation. Similarly it was perfectly natural that Jeffreys, a seasoned professional and former Recorder of London, should succeed Saunders on his death a year later.

Finally, the much more business-like and consistent pressure applied by James II was ultimately counter-productive. Too many historians have stood aghast at the sweeping changes he made, without realising that they only gave him a short-term, tactical advantage. In Westminster Hall he won every battle, then lost the war.

He canvassed the judges in the first few weeks of his reign, as to whether he could continue to collect the taxation voted to Charles II for his life in advance of parliamentary confirmation. All went well. They agreed with little demur – though the Convention Parliament in 1689 took a different view. However, when he consulted them again on the validity of his dispensing power at the end of the year he had to dismiss Sir William Gregory and Sir Cresswell Levinz, and a test case was laid on in March 1686. One Godden, coachman to the Catholic Sir Edward Hales, accused him of holding the king's commission without having complied with the Test Act, and was given the verdict at Rochester Assizes. Pleading a dispensation under the Great Seal, Hales then appealed to King's Bench, but before the case came on, in June, James dismissed the Chief Justice of Common Pleas, Sir Thomas Jones, and the Chief Baron of Exchequer, Sir William Montague, together with two puisne judges, Charlton and Nevill. Lord Chief Justice Herbert was a convinced supporter of the dispensing power, but by a strained device the judges from the other high courts were also dragged in (**123**). All but one agreed with Herbert, and there is no real reason to doubt their honesty; though very few judges had ever acknowledged the king's suspending power most of them had always acknowledged the dispensing power.

However, Sir Robert Sawyer, Attorney-General, and Heneage Finch, Solicitor-General, who had office respectively since 1681 and 1679, and had led for the Crown in all the most notorious treason trials of the last five years, declined the invidious task of prosecuting Hales. Finch was dismissed in favour of Sir Thomas Powys, but Sawyer remained, despite his well-publicised refusal to draw up patents of dispensation for Roman Catholics – even the king's natural son, Berwick. His survival for nearly two years is typical of the confusion in the judiciary and the legal profession at this time, and the only conceivable reason for it is that his obvious successor was Jeffreys' *bête noire*, William Williams.[70] But in December 1687, when Sawyer at last gave way to Powys, Williams had to be offered the vacant solicitor-generalship.

As for Jeffreys, the arch-villain of Whig historiography, though his conduct of the Bloody Assizes in 1685 clinched his appointment as Lord Chancellor that autumn, he

---

[70] Jeffreys was not the only one who detested Williams; see LCJ Wright's spiteful and apparently unprovoked remark during the trial of the seven bishops, p. 409 below.

soon fell foul of the king. A loyal Protestant, he objected to the decision to send an envoy to Rome in 1686, and he was very nearly destroyed in an abortive palace coup that December.[71] There were constant rumours of his dismissal, or even his transfer to Dublin as Lord Lieutenant, and many legal appointments in 1687 and 1688 were made against his advice. His successor as Chief Justice of King's Bench, Sir Edward Herbert, was his constant enemy.

Moreover, despite the purge of 1686, James continued to have difficulty with his judges, notably on the key question of desertion from the army. 7 Hen. VII, c. 1. had made this a felony in certain circumstances, and this had been expanded and confirmed by 3 Hen. VIII, c. 5; but some held that the latter act had been repealed under Mary Tudor, and though in 1601, in the 'Case of Soldiers', the judges had denied this, and confirmed that desertion was punishable at Common Law, the question was still wide open.[72] It became increasingly important with the steady growth of James II's army. Sir John Holt, Recorder of London, declined to convict a deserter brought before him early in 1687, but in April King's Bench was asked to grant execution against another deserter, convicted at Reading assizes, so that he could be shot before his regiment at Plymouth. Lord Chief Justice Herbert, supported by Sir Francis Wythens, ruled against the Crown (**124**). Wythens was at once dismissed, with Holt, but as the chief supporter of the dispensing power Herbert was too important to be sacrificed. Instead he was ordered to change places with Sir Robert Wright, Chief Justice of Common Pleas, who at once granted the Crown's application.

This should have had a chastening effect on Herbert, but he went ahead and voted, as a member of the Commission for Ecclesiastical Causes, against the condemnation of the Fellows of Magdalen College, Oxford, in December.[73] But many of his fellow judges were no more reliable, and the prosecution of the Seven Bishops in 1688 went sadly awry. On 27 April James re-issued his Declaration of Indulgence (p. 378 above), and on 4 May he ordered it to be read on two successive Sundays in all the churches of the Anglican communion. On 18 May the Archbishop of Canterbury and six of his bishops presented a petition to the king asking him to withdraw the order on the grounds that the suspending power had been specifically rejected by parliament in 1673 (**125**). When the petition was published next day they were charged with seditious libel.[74]

The trial had strong elements of the grotesque. Defence counsel included a former lord chief justice (Pemberton), another ex-judge (Levinz), and the former attorney- and solicitor-generals (Sawyer and Finch). This, and the eminence of the accused, made the proceedings more decorous than usual, and the judges had to vent their spleen on Solicitor-General Williams, who in effect conducted the case for the Crown. (Attorney-General Powys was so incompetent that he had omitted to furnish proof that the bishops had ever submitted a petition at all, so that his case almost collapsed at

---

[71] Kenyon, *Sunderland*, p. 176; Keeton, *op. cit.*, pp. 357–8, 367, 369–70.

[72] Holdsworth, VI, 228ff.

[73] Havighurst, *Law Quarterly Review*, LXIX, 536–7. Sir Thomas Jenner, a judge almost as notorious as Jeffreys, voted with him, which shows yet again that such men were not necessarily time-servers.

[74] Roger Thomas, 'The Seven Bishops and their Petition', *Jnl Eccl. History*, XII (1961), 56–70.

the outset.) In the end Lord Chief Justice Wright allowed the pleading to degenerate into a discussion of the suspending power, though in his summing-up he insisted that it had nothing to do with the case. The puisne judges, Sir Richard Holloway and Sir John Powell, then intervened to argue cogently against the suspending power, and in favour of acquittal, and the attempt of Sir Richard Alibone, a Catholic appointed to the bench the year before, to refute them was distinguished more by energy than good sense (**126**). The jury returned a verdict of not guilty and the following day Holloway and Powell were dismissed. The doubts of three generations of judges concerning the suspending power were sustained, and it was demonstrated again that no judge could be permanently bought or bullied.

119. Lord Chief Justice Keeling

[Commons, 16 October 1667]

The Lord Chief Justice Keeling was complained of by some of the House for his severe and illegal fining and imprisoning juries . . . A committee was nominated and appointed to inquire into the matter and complaint and to make a report thereof to the House, to the intent that a course may be taken that judges may not at their wills and pleasures impose fines and imprison or affront either grand juries or petty juries for giving and adhering to their verdicts. Milward, *Diary*, pp. 88–9

[11 December 1667]

Sir Thomas Gower reports from the committee the following articles of accusation against the Lord Chief Justice Keeling:

1. That he imposed upon the consciences of the grand jury of Somersetshire, to find a verdict contrary to their judgments, and bound them to their good behaviour. Sir Hugh Wyndham . . . he reproached for being the head of a faction, for no other cause than finding a bill according to his conscience. He drew the verdict and made the jury find it. Sir Hugh said he was the king's servant and a Member of Parliament . . .; he told the grand jury they were his servants, and he would make the best in England stoop.

2. In an indictment for murder [at Devon assizes], which the jury found manslaughter because they found no malice prepense, he told them they must be ruled by him in matter of law, and forced them to find the bill murder. The man was executed accordingly, without reprieve, notwithstanding the address of the gentlemen of the bench to him . . .

3. One before him speaking of Magna Carta, he said, 'Magna Farta? what ado with this have we?'

[The committee recommended that he be impeached, but the House after some debate decided to hear him at the bar.] Grey, *Debates*, I, 62–3

[12 December 1667]

The Lord Chief Justice Keeling came to the bar. A chair was set for him, . . . but he stood . . .

As to the slight speaking of the Magna Carta, he affirmed that it being long since he did not remember, . . . but it might be possible, Magna Carta being often and ignorantly pressed upon him, that he did utter that indecent expression; but as he doth not remember neither can it reasonably be imagined that he should speak these words in any dishonour to that great charter, for it is evidently known to all men his great loyalty to his sovereign and laws . . .

The case in Devonshire was this. A weaver, having divers servants and apprentices, gave order to a servant and authority to oversee them and in his absence correct the younger prentices . . . A prentice boy . . . neglecting his work, this servant beat him about the head with a broomstick, . . . of which the boy died within two or three hours. The jury would find this manslaughter; he caused them to go out again and bring it in murder . . . 'And though I was petitioned', said the chief justice, 'by Sir Thomas Clifford[75] for his reprieve, yet I confess I did not grant it, because I do acknowledge I am very strict and severe against highway robbers and in case of blood.'

The case in Somersetshire was this. The grand jury was of persons of great [wealth] and ability, [such] as Sir Hugh Wyndham and others; they brought in a bill of a man that was killed, *per infortuniam*.[76] The chief justice told them they ought to bring in the bill either *billa vera* or else *ignoramus*. 'I also told them', said he, 'they had . . . to examine anything that shall be brought before them by proofs; and if they find the proofs to be slight or not material, then to find it *ignoramus*, and if it be sufficiently proved, then to bring it in *billa vera*, and then to leave it to the trial of the court . . .

'Notwithstanding, the grand jury would not alter . . . I desired them better to consider of it that night, but at the next day they were of the same judgment, and told me they were resolved not to alter from it, whereupon I fined some of them £20 a man, bound them to their good behaviour, and to appear at the King's Bench bar the next term. Notwithstanding, I offered them to withdraw their fine and recognisance for the good behaviour if they would submit, which they refused, and the matter came to a hearing, and the judges with one consent said that I was in the right, and had done no more but what was just and lawful . . .'

I . . . am very confident that he made a very good and sufficient defence to everything charged upon him as to the point of integrity and justice[77] but without doubt he had failed in point of passion and discretion.

---

[75] Of Ugbrooke, a confidant of Charles II and his brother, and one of the coming men in the government.
[76] By misadventure. They were usurping the functions of an inquest jury.
[77] Four other similar cases were taken into consideration.

After he was withdrawn it came to a debate of four hours at least. Many did aggravate, others did extenuate his failings. In the close the House passed two votes:

1. First, that the late proceedings and precedents in fining and imprisoning juries for giving in their verdict was illegal, and that a bill be brought in to prevent the like for the future.

2. Secondly, that there shall be no further prosecution or proceedings against the chief justice upon this charge.   Milward, *Diary*, pp. 166–70

120. Bushel's Case, King's Bench, 1670

[Edward Bushel, a member of the jury at the London sessions, had refused to convict two Quakers of holding an unlawful conventicle. He was imprisoned by the presiding magistrate for giving a verdict against a judge's direction in a matter of law, but he sued out a writ of *habeas corpus* in King's Bench.]

LCJ Vaughan . . . If the meaning of these words, 'Finding against the direction of the court in matter of law', be that if the judge, having heard the evidence given in court (for he knows no other), shall tell the jury, 'Upon this evidence, the law is for the plaintiff, or for the defendant, and you are under the pain of fine and imprisonment to find accordingly', then the jury ought of duty to do so, every man sees that the jury is but a troublesome delay, great charge, and of no use in determining right and wrong, and therefore the trials by them may be better abolished than continued – which were a strange, new-found conclusion, after a trial so celebrated for many hundreds of years.

For if the judge, from the evidence, shall by his own judgment first resolve upon any trial what the fact is, and so knowing the fact shall then resolve what the law is, and order the jury penally to find accordingly, what either necessary or convenient use can be fancied of juries, or to continue trials by them at all?

But if the jury be not obliged in all trials to follow such directions, if given, but only in some sort of trials (as, for instance, in trials for criminal matters upon indictments or appeals), why then the consequence will be, though not in all yet in criminal trials, the jury (as of no material use) ought to be either omitted or abolished, which were the greater mischief to the people than to abolish them in civil trials. And how the jury should in any other manner . . . find against the direction of the court in matter of law is really not conceivable.

True it is, if it fall out upon some special trial that the jury being ready to give their verdict, and before it is given the judge shall ask whether they find such a particular thing propounded by him, or whether they find the matter of fact to be such as a witness or witnesses have deposed; and the jury answer, they find the matter of fact to be so. If then the judge shall declare, the matter of fact being by you so found to be, the law is for the plaintiff, and you are to find accordingly for him; if notwithstanding they find for the defendant, this may be thought a finding in matter of law against the direction of the court, for in that case the jury first declare the fact, as it is found by themselves, to which fact the judge declares how the law is consequent.

And this is ordinary: when the jury find unexpectedly for the plaintiff or defendant the judge will ask, how do you find such a fact in particular? And upon their answer he will say, then it is for the defendant, though they found for the plaintiff, or *e contrario*, and thereupon they rectify their verdict. And in these cases the jury, and not the judge, resolve and find what the fact is. Wherefore always in discreet and lawful assistance of the jury the judge his direction is hypothetical and upon supposition, and not positive, and upon coercion . . .

It is true, if the jury were to have no other evidence for the fact but what is deposed in court the judge might know their evidence, and the fact from it, equally as they, and so direct what the law were in the case, though even then the judge and jury might honestly differ in the result from the evidence as well as two judges may, which often happens. But the evidence which the jury have of the fact is much other than that, for:

1. Being returned of the vicinage whence the cause of the action ariseth, the law supposeth them thence to have sufficient knowledge to try the matter in issue (and so they must) though no evidence were given on either side in court; but to this evidence the judge is a stranger.

2. They may have evidence from their own personal knowledge, by which they may be assured, and sometimes are, that what is deposed in court is absolutely false; but to this the judge is a stranger . . .

* * *

7. To what end is the jury to be returned out of the vicinage whence the cause of the action ariseth? To what end must hundredors be of the jury, whom the law supposeth to have nearer knowledge of the fact that those of the vicinage in general? . . . To what end must they have such a certain freehold, and be *probi et legales homines*, and not of affinity with the parties concerned? . . . To what end must they undergo the heavy punishment of a villainous judgment, if after all this they implicitly must give a verdict by the dictates and authority of another man, under pains of fines and imprisonment, when sworn to do it according to the best of their own knowledge? . . .

* * *

The chief justice delivered the opinion of the court, and accordingly the prisoners were discharged.   *ST*, VI, 1006–12

121. The Habeas Corpus Amendment Act, 1679

31 Car. II, c. 2. *An Act for the better securing the liberty of the subject and for prevention of imprisonments beyond the seas.*

Whereas great delays have been used by sheriffs, gaolers and other officers to whose custody any of the king's subjects have been committed for criminal or supposed criminal matters in making returns of writs of habeas corpus to them directed, . . . contrary to their duty and the known law of the land, whereby many of the king's subjects have been and hereafter may be long detained in prison in such cases where by law they are bailable, to their great charge and vexation. For the prevention whereof . . . be it enacted . . . that whensoever any person or persons shall bring any habeas corpus directed unto any sheriff or sheriff's gaoler, minister or other persons whatsoever for any person in his or their custody . . . the said officer or officers . . . shall within three days after the service thereof as aforesaid (unless the commitment aforesaid was for treason or felony plainly and specially expressed in the warrant of commitment) . . . bring or cause to be brought the body of the party so committed . . . before the lord chancellor, or lord keeper of the Great Seal of England for the time being, or the judges or barons of the said court from whence the said writ shall issue or . . . is made returnable, . . . and shall likewise then certify the true causes of his detainer or imprisonment . . .

[If the court was more than 20 miles from the prison the gaoler was allowed ten days, and if more than 100, twenty days.]

II. And to the intent that no sheriff, gaoler or other officer may pretend ignorance of the import of any such writ, be it enacted . . . that all such writs shall be marked in this manner, *per statutum tricesimo primo Caroli Secundi regis*, and shall be signed by the person that awards the same.

And if any person or persons shall be or stand committed or detained as aforesaid for any crime, unless for treason or felony, . . . in the vacation time and out of term, it shall and may be lawful to and for the person or persons so committed . . . to appeal or complain to the lord chancellor or lord keeper or any of his Majesty's justices . . .; and the said lord chancellor . . . [etc.] are hereby authorised and required . . . to award and grant a habeas corpus . . . returnable immediate[ly] before . . . [him]. And upon service thereof . . . the officer . . . in whose custody the party is so committed or detained shall within the times respectively before limited bring such prisoner . . . before the said lord chancellor . . . [etc.] . . . And thereupon within two days after the party shall be brought before them the said lord chancellor . . . [etc.] shall discharge the said prisoner from his imprisonment, taking his or their recognisance . . . for his or their appearance in the court of King's Bench the term following, or at the next assizes, sessions or general gaol-delivery of and for such county, city or place where the commitment was . . . as the case shall require; . . . unless it shall appear . . . that the party so committed is detained . . . for such matters or offences for the which by the law the prisoner is not bailable.

*   *   *

VI. Provided always . . . that if any person or persons shall be committed for high treason or felony . . ., [and] upon his prayer or petition in open court the first week of the term or the first day of the sessions of oyer and terminer or general gaol-delivery to be brought to his trial, shall not be indicted some time in the next term [or] sessions . . . after such commitments, it shall and may be lawful to and for the judges . . . to set at liberty the prisoner upon bail, unless it appear to . . . [them] upon oath that the witnesses for the king could not be produced the same term . . . And if any person or persons committed as aforesaid . . . shall not be indicted and tried the second term . . . after his commitment . . . he shall be discharged from his imprisonment.

VII. Provided always that nothing in this act shall extend to discharge out of prison any person charged in debt, or other action or with process in any civil cause . . .

VIII. Provided always . . . that if any person or persons, subjects of this realm, shall be committed to any prison or in custody of any officer or officers whatsoever for any criminal or supposed criminal matter, that the said person shall not be removed from the said prison and custody into the custody of any other officer or officers unless it be by habeas corpus or some other legal writ . . .

*   *   *

X. And be it enacted . . . that a habeas corpus . . . may be directed and run into any county palatine, the Cinque Ports or other privileged places within the kingdom of England, dominion of Wales or town of Berwick-upon-Tweed, and the islands of Jersey or Guernsey, any law or usage to the contrary notwithstanding.

XI. And for preventing illegal imprisonments in prisons beyond the seas, be it further enacted . . . that no subject of this realm . . . shall or may be sent prisoner into Scotland, Ireland, Jersey, Guernsey, Tangier, or into any parts, garrisons, islands or places beyond the seas which are or at any time hereafter shall be within or without the dominions of his Majesty, his heirs or successors, and that every such imprisonment is hereby enacted and adjudged to be illegal . . .

*   *   *

122. *Rex* v. *Rosewall*, King's Bench, 26 November 1684, for high treason

Mr Pollexfen. My lord, I have one word to move for myself, and the others that are appointed to be of counsel for Mr Rosewall. We think it our duty to apply ourselves to your lordship for this favour; that, to enable us the better to do our duty for the person for whom we are assigned, your lordship and the court would please to order that we may have a copy of the indictment. We do acknowledge that it is not a usual thing to have copies granted (though there be no express law that we know against it) in capital matters . . .

LCJ Jeffreys. Look you, if you speak to me privately, as to my own particular opinion, it is hard for me to say that there is any express resolution of the law in the matter; but the practice has always been to deny a copy of the indictment. And therefore if you ask me as a judge to have a copy of the indictment delivered to you in a case of high treason I must answer you, show me any precedents where it was done. For there are abundance of cases in the law which seem hard in themselves, but the law is so because the practice has been so, and we cannot alter the practice of the law without an act of parliament. I think it is a hard case that a man should have counsel to defend himself for a two penny trespass, and his witness examined upon oath; but if he steal, commit murder or felony, nay, high treason, where life, estate, honour and all are concerned, he shall neither have counsel, nor his witnesses examined upon oath. But yet you know as well as I that the practice of the law is so; and the practice is the law.

Pollexfen. My lord, we heard the other day the indictment read . . ., but we desire such a copy as may enable us to argue as we ought to do, and as the court will expect from us, being assigned by the court.

LCJ . . . It is hard, I confess, and so are many other things in the law; but I am wonderfully tender of making precedents, and therefore if it has not been practised I do not see how we can do it.   *ST*, x, 266–8

123. *Godden* v. *Hales*, King's Bench, 16 June 1686

[Arthur Godden, Sir Edward Hales's coachman, brought a collusive action against him for holding a colonel's commission without complying with the Test Act. On 29 March Hales was convicted at Rochester assizes, but he pleaded a dispensation under the Great Seal and appealed to King's Bench, Lord Chief Justice Herbert presiding.]

LCJ This is a case of great consequence, but of as little difficulty as ever any case was that raised so great an expectation, for if the king cannot dispense with this statute he cannot dispense with any penal law whatsoever . . .

There is no law whatsoever but may be dispensed with by the supreme law-giver; as the laws of God may be dispensed with by God himself; as it appears by God's command to Abraham to offer up his son Isaac. So likewise the law of Man may be dispensed with by the legislator, for a law may either be too wide or too narrow, and there may be many cases which may be out of the conveniences which did induce the law to be made; for it is impossible for the wisest law-maker to foresee all the cases that may be or are to be remedied, and therefore there must be a power somewhere, able to dispense with these laws. But as to the case of simony that is objected by the other side, that is against the laws of God, and a special offence, and therefore *malum in se*, which I do agree the king cannot dispense with . . .

The case of the sheriff is a much stronger case than this, and comes up to it in every particular, for that statute[78] doth disable the party to take and the king to grant; and there is also a clause in that statute which says that the patent shall be void notwithstanding any *non obstante* to the contrary, . . . and yet by the opinion of all the judges of England the king has a power of dispensing with that statute . . .

[However, on the strained plea that this doubt about the statute of sheriffs affected the whole administration of justice, Herbert adjourned the case to take the opinion of the judges of common pleas and the barons of the Exchequer. Of the other 11 judges all but one fully concurred with him, and on 21 June, when the hearing was resumed, he so reported.]

. . . We think we may very well declare the opinion of the court to be that the king may dispense in this case; and the judges go upon these grounds:

1. That the kings of England are sovereign princes.
2. That the laws of England are the king's laws.
3. That therefore 'tis an inseparable prerogative in the kings of England to dispense with penal laws in particular cases, and upon particular necessary reasons.
4. That of those reasons and those necessities the king himself is sole judge . . .
5. That this is not a trust invested in or granted to the king by the people, but the ancient remains of the sovereign power and prerogative of the kings of England, which never yet was taken from them, nor can be. And therefore, such a dispensation appearing upon record to come time enough to save him from the forfeiture, judgment ought to be given for the defendant.

ST, XI, 1196–9

[78] 27 Hen. VIII, c. 24 (§ 2).

124. The deserter's case, 1687[79]

Upon Tuesday the 19th [April] a soldier that was for running away from his colours condemned at Reading [assizes] by Mr Justice Holloway was brought to the King's Bench bar. The counsel, Mr Attorney-General, Sir Robert Sawyer, said that the soldier was condemned in Berkshire, that he should be executed at Plymouth, where the regiment or company that he was of did now quarter. And he did therefore move that the conviction of the soldier and the judgment against him to die that were brought up with him might be filed in that court.

The court (i.e. my Lord Chief Justice Herbert) said, 'You would not have us file them before we hear them read?' So they were both read. The lord chief justice said: 'They shall be filed, or rather, taken into the care and custody of the court.' The counsel, Mr Attorney General, moved that the court would award execution against the prisoner. The court . . . said, 'What have you more to urge?' 'Nothing at all.' 'Have you any precedents to strengthen your motion with?' He answered, 'No'. The chief justice said that he did think there had no question at all risen upon that act[80] till of late days, [and] that the majority of his brethren had delivered their opinion that a soldier ought to be condemned to die upon that act.[81] He had spent as much time as his leisure would admit him, and many serious thoughts upon it, for it was a great case, and concerned life, which if it were taken away by mistake there remains no remedy; but he could not reach or comprehend those reasons that induced his brethren to be of that opinion. His judgment was well known in that case, for he had declared it very publicly, and the more he thought of it the more he was confirmed therein, and he could never concur to award execution for a man to die upon an offence which the law did not condemn him for, as he did in his judgment and conscience verily believe it did not that man. But he was but one, and it belongs most properly to you brother Holloway, to award execution who condemned him . . .

He said further, if this act had reached the case he would have said it had been a very useful and very necessary act. Now the peace cannot be preserved without an army, but the act does not reach the case, and I can never concur to award execution against that man the law condemns not . . .

Mr Justice Wythens said he had and would serve the king in all things that he could possibly, and so would all that court he was sure, and desired the king's counsel . . . to acquaint his Majesty so with great earnestness, but hoped he

---

[79] The defendant was so much a cipher that his name is uncertain; it is variously given as Beale or Dale.

[80] Either 7 Hen. VII, c. 1 or 3 Hen. VIII, c. 5. See p. 396 above.

[81] Presumably a reference to the Case of Soldiers, 1601, in which the judges decided that by virtue of the above acts desertion was a felony.

should be excused in case of blood, for he could not concur to award execution against a person tried by another court.

The chief justice told him, 'Do not insist upon that reason, Brother, for it has nothing in it. If the law condemned him I would proceed, though I had not heard the trial.'

Mr Justice Holloway he gave the narrative of the trial, and said he would have had a Frenchman that was charged with the same crimes convicted that he thought a very cunning knave, and have had this man [ac]quitt[ed]; but the jury [ac]quitted the Frenchman and found this, though indeed he had solicited and menaced the jury very much to find him guilty, for otherwise they had not. Although he went to his Majesty when he came to town out of his circuit, and gave him an account of the whole matter, and interceded with the king for his pardon,[82] but the king answered, he had done like a just judge in condemning him, and he would do like a just general in executing him. But he was so dejected and confounded in the court that he was like to sink down.

Then Mr Justice Powell he spoke [so] low that nobody could hear him, though the chief justice desired him twice to speak up, saying it was a very great case, and in a public court, and he desired that all that was said that day might be heard by all the court that there were so well able to judge. But he did not speak up, thereupon the chief justice said, 'I will repeat so much of my brother's discourse as I plainly heard. He saith he thinks this court cannot award execution against the prisoner to die in any county but where he was condemned, and desired time to consult precedents.'

In the close the conviction and condemnation were not filed but taken into the custody of the court, and the prisoner to be safely kept until the court sent for him again . . .

The chief justice called his man Hyde, and sent him to Whitehall, it was supposed to inquire whether his Majesty was at leisure. His man came again, and the chief justice presently rose out of the court and went to Whitehall.

Dr Williams's Library, *Morrice Entring Book*, 2, ff. 98–100

125. The Petition of the Seven Bishops, 18 May 1688

To the King's Most Excellent Majesty:

The humble petition of William, Archbishop of Canterbury, and of divers of the suffragan bishops of that province, now present with him, in behalf of themselves, and others of their absent brethren, and of the clergy of their respective dioceses,
Humbly sheweth,

---

[82] Presumably on the grounds that he was only 17, and had originally been pressed for short-term service against Monmouth in 1685.

That the great averseness they find in themselves in the distributing and publishing in all their churches your Majesty's late Declaration for liberty of conscience proceeds neither from any want of duty and obedience to your Majesty (our holy mother the Church of England being both in her principles and constant practice unquestionably loyal, and having to her great honour been more than once publicly acknowledged to be so by your gracious Majesty), nor yet from any want of due tenderness to Dissenters, in relation to whom they are willing to come to such a temper as shall be thought fit, when that matter shall be considered and settled in parliament and Convocation; but among many other considerations from this especially, because that Declaration if founded upon such a dispensing power as hath been often declared illegal in parliament, and particularly in the years 1662[–3], 1672[–3], and in the beginning of your Majesty's reign, and is a matter of so great moment and consequence to the whole nation, both in Church and state, that your petitioners cannot in prudence, honour or conscience so far make themselves parties to it as the distribution of it all over the nation, and the solemn publication of it once and again even in God's house, and in the time of his divine service, must amount to in common and reasonable construction. Your petitioners therefore most humbly and earnestly beseech your Majesty, that you will be graciously pleased not to insist upon their distributing and reading your Majesty's said Declaration.

And your petitioners shall ever pray, etc.

[*Signed.*]   William Cantuar   William St Asaph
             Thomas Bath & Wells   Francis Ely
             John Chichester   Thomas Peterborough
             Jonathan Bristol.

Cardwell, Annals, ii, 367–70

126. The trial of the Seven Bishops, King's Bench, 29 June 1688

★   ★   ★

Mr Justice Holloway. Mr Solicitor, there is one thing I would fain be satisfied in: you say the bishops have no power to petition the king?

Solicitor General. Not out of parliament, Sir.

Holloway. Pray give me leave, sir. Then, the king having made such a declaration of a general toleration and liberty of conscience, and afterwards he comes and requires the bishops to disperse this declaration, this, they say, they cannot do, because they apprehend it is contrary to law, and contrary to their function. What can they do, if they may not petition?

SG I'll tell you what they should have done, sir. If they were commanded to do anything against their conscience they should have acquiesced till the meeting of the parliament. (*At which some people in the court hissed.*)

Attorney General. This is very fine indeed! I hope the court and the jury will take notice of this carriage.

SG My lord, it is one thing for a man to submit to his prince if the king lay a command upon him that he cannot obey, and another thing to affront him. If the king will impose upon a man what he cannot do, he must acquiesce; but shall he come and fly in the face of his prince? Shall he say it is illegal, and the prince acts against prudence, honour or conscience, and throw dirt in the king's face? Sure that is not permitted; that is libelling with a witness.

LCJ Truly, Mr Solicitor, I am of opinion that the bishops might petition the king, but this is not the right of way bringing it in. I am not of that mind that they cannot petition the king out of parliament, but if they may petition, yet they ought to have done it after another manner. For if they may in this reflective way petition the king, I am sure it will make the government very precarious.

Mr Justice Powell. Mr Solicitor, it would have been too late to stay for a parliament, for it was to have been distributed by such a time.

SG They might have lain under it and submitted.

Powell. No, they would have run into contempt of the king's commands, without petitioning the king not to insist upon it; and if they had petitioned, and not have shown the reason why they could not obey, it would have been looked upon as a piece of sullenness, and that they would have been blamed for as much on the other side.

⋆　⋆　⋆

LCJ [After a review of the prosecution's evidence, and proof of the delivery and publication of the petition.] Gentlemen, after this was proved, then the defendants came to their part; and these gentlemen that were of counsel for my lords let themselves into their defence by notable learned speeches, by telling you that my lords and bishops are guardians to the Church. They have read you a clause of a statute made in Queen Elizabeth's time,[83] by which they say my lords the bishops were under a curse if they did not take care of that law. Then they show you some records; one in Richard II's time which they could make little of, by reason their witness could not read it; but it was, in short, a liberty given to the king to dispense with the statute of provisors. Then they show you some journals of parliament, first in the year 1662[-3], where the king, had granted an indulgence, and the House of Commons declared it was not fit to be done, unless it were by act of parliament, . . . and so likewise

[83] Act of Uniformity, 1559, § 4 printed *PCD*, pp. 17–18.

. . . in 1672[–3], which is all nothing but addresses and votes, or orders of the House, or discourses, . . . but these are not declarations in parliament . . . A declaration in parliament is a law, and that must be by the king, Lords and Commons . . . In all these things (as far as I can observe) nothing can be gathered out of them one way or the other; it is nothing but discourses. Sometimes this dispensing power[84] has been allowed, as in Richard II's time, and sometimes it has been denied; and the king did once waive it. Mr Solicitor tells you the reason, there was a lump of money in the case; but I wonder indeed to hear it come from him.

SG My lord, I never gave my vote for money, I assure you.

LCJ . . . The truth of it is, the dispensing power is out of the case, it is only a word used in the petition. But truly, I will not take upon me to give my opinion in the question, to determine that now, for it is not before me. The only question before me is – and so it is before you, gentlemen, it being a question of fact – whether here be a certain proof of a publication? And then the next question is a question of law indeed, whether if there be a publication proved it be a libel . . .?

Now, gentlemen, anything that shall disturb the government, or make mischief and a stir among the people, is certainly within the case of *libellis famosis*, and I must in short give you my opinion, I do take it to be a libel. Now, this being a point of law, if my brothers have anything to say to it, I suppose they will deliver their opinions.

Holloway. Look you, gentlemen, it is not usual for any person to say anything after the chief justice has summed up the evidence; it is not according to the course of the court. But this is a case of an extraordinary nature, and there being a point of law in it it is very fit everybody should deliver their own opinion. The question is, whether this petition of my lords the bishops is a libel or no. Gentlemen, the end and intention of every action is to be considered, and likewise in this case we are to consider the nature of the offence that these noble persons are charged with; it is for delivering a petition which, according as they have made their defence, was with all the humility and decency that could be; so that if there was no ill intent, and they were not (as it is not, nor can be pretended they were) men of evil lives, or the like, to deliver a petition cannot be a fault, it being the right of every subject to petition. If you are satisfied there was an ill intention, of sedition or the like, you ought to find them guilty; but if there be nothing in the case that you find, but only that they did deliver a petition to save themselves harmless, and to free themselves from blame, by showing the reason of their disobedience to the king's command, which they apprehended to be a grievance to them, and which they could not

---

[84] Here and throughout, the term 'dispensing power' was used to cover the power to suspend a statute as well as the power to dispense individuals from the provisions of a statute.

in conscience give obedience to, I cannot think it is a libel. It is left to you, gentlemen, but that is my opinion.

LCJ Look you, by the way, brother, I did not ask you to sum up the evidence (for that is not usual), but only to deliver your opinion whether it be a libel or no

Powell. Truly I cannot see, for my part, anything of sedition, or any other crime, fixed upon these reverend fathers, my lords the bishops. For, gentlemen, to make it a libel it must be false, it must be malicious, and it must tend to sedition. As to the falsehood, I see nothing that is offered by the king's counsel, nor anything as to malice; it was presented with all the humility and decency that became the king's subjects to approach their prince with . . .

Gentlemen, we must consider what they say is illegal in it. They say, they apprehend the declaration is illegal because it is founded upon a dispensing power which the king claims, to dispense with the laws concerning ecclesiastical affairs. Gentlemen, I do not remember in any case in all our law . . . that there is any such power in the king, and the case must turn upon that. In short, if there be no such dispensing power in the king, then that can be no libel which they presented to the king, which says that the declaration, being founded upon such a pretended power, is illegal . . . I can see no difference, nor know of one in law, between the king's power to dispense with laws ecclesiastical and his power to dispense with any other laws whatsoever. If this be once allowed of, there will need no parliament; all the legislature will be in the king, which is a thing worth considering, and I leave the issue to God and your consciences.

Mr Justice Alibone[85] . . . I think in the first place, that no man can take upon him to write against the actual exercise of the government, unless he have leave from the government, but he makes a libel, be what he writes true or false. For if once we come to impeach the government by way of argument it is the argument that makes it the government or not the government . . .

Then I lay down this for my next position, that no private man can take upon him to write concerning the government at all, for what has any private man to do with the government if his interest be not stirred or shaken? It is the business of the government to manage matters relating to the government; it is the business of subjects to mind only their own properties and interests . . .

I do agree that every man may petition the government or the king in a matter that relates to his own private interest, but to meddle with a matter that relates to the government, I do not think my lords the bishops had any power to do more than any others. When the House of Lords and Commons are in being, it is a proper way of applying to the king; there is all the openness in the world for those that are Members of Parliament to make what addresses they

---

[85] Sir Richard Alibone, a Roman Catholic appointed in April 1687.

please to the government, for the rectifying, altering, regulating and making of what law they please, but if every man shall come and interpose his advice, I think there can never be an end of advising the government. I think there was an instance of this in King James's time, when by a solemn resolution it was declared to be a high misdemeanour, and next to treason, [to petition] the king to put the penal laws in execution.

Powell. Brother, I think you do mistake a little.

Alibone. Brother, I dare rely upon that I am right. It was so declared by all the judges.

SG The Puritans presented a petition to that purpose, and in it they said if it would not be granted they would come with a great number.[86]

Powell. Aye, there it is.

Alibone. I tell you, Mr Solicitor, the resolution of the judges is, that such a petition is next door to treason . . .

Mr Pollexfen. They threatened, unless their request was granted, several thousands of the king's subjects would be discontented.

Powell. That is the reason of that judgment, I affirm it.

Alibone. But then I'll tell you, brother, again . . . for any man to raise a report that the king will or will not permit a toleration, if either of these be disagreeable to the people, whether he may or not, it is against law. For we are not to measure things from any truth they have in themselves, but from that aspect they have upon the government, for there may be every tittle of a libel true, and yet it may be a libel still . . . This is my opinion as to law in general. I will not debate the prerogatives of the king nor the privileges of the subject, but as this fact is, I think these venerable bishops did meddle with that which did not belong to them; they took upon them, in a petition, to contradict the actual exercise of the government, which I think no particular persons, or singular body, may do.

[This concluded the case. The jury stayed out all night and next morning about ten brought in a verdict of 'not guilty'.]   *ST*, XII, 416–17, 424–9

[86] Though everyone is rather confused, the reference is clearly to the Northamptonshire Petition of 1605, see pp. 113–14 above.

CHAPTER 11

LORDS AND COMMONS

Regrettably, the study of the House of Lords in the reigns of Charles II and James II is not so much in its infancy as in the womb.[1] Yet it is in this period that we must look for the origins of that ascendancy which the peerage, and to some extent the House of Lords, were to enjoy in the next century. This is not a development which could reasonably have been foreseen in 1660.

The decimation of the peerage in the fifteenth and early sixteenth centuries had reduced their numbers to 57 on Elizabeth's accession. She was cautious of making good these losses, so that in 1603 the figure stood at 55. Her House of Lords was small, intimate and select, and should probably be seen as an extension of the Council. However, the enormous additions made by James I and Charles I, many of them through the agency of Buckingham, and some of them by outright sale, brought the numbers in 1628 up to 126.[2]

As Lawrence Stone points out in his epic study of the aristocracy, this quite sudden 'inflation of honours' lowered the overall status of the peerage at the same time as their general prestige and their self-confidence was in decline. Their economic strength was faltering, because of injudicious investment and incompetent land management, and because of the hysterical wave of over-spending and over-consumption which for one reason or another overcame the Jacobean Court. This, and the prolonged residence of many noblemen in London, eroded that seigneurial allegiance which had been the basis of their power in the localities. In the absence of foreign war, and the disappearance of the Border, one of their main functions, which they shared with the Continental aristocracies, of leadership in war, was in abeyance. All these factors were accentuated by the ennoblement of men who were felt to be socially or financially inadequate, and led to faction squabbles within the nobility. It also produced a nobility which was for the most part new and inexperienced, without a class tradition to draw upon; in 1628 44 per cent of the House of Lords were first generation peers, 57 per cent first or second generation.[3]

In these circumstances what is surprising is the Lords' resistance to any attempt to make them a mere extension of the Court.[4] The revival of impeachment in 1621 and 1624, even if it was partly a reflection of Court faction, added to their prestige and assisted their wider claims to function as a court of law (above, pp. 88–9). A strong opposition to the Duke of Buckingham built up round the wealthy and influential

---

[1] A. S. Turberville, 'The House of Lords in the Reign of Charles II', *EHR*, XLIV (1929), 400–7, XLV (1930), 58–77, is in the main a superficial narrative, with notable gaps and some inaccuracies. Maxwell P. Schoenfield, *The Restored House of Lords* (The Hague 1967), is moderately useful for the period it covers (1660–2).

[2] Stone, *Aristocracy*, pp. 121, 758, and ch. 3 *passim*.

[3] Stone, *op. cit.*, p. 121.

[4] Russell, *Parliaments and Politics*, p. 16.

Herbert brothers, Earls of Pembroke and Montgomery, who eventually had to be bought out. With regard to the Earl of Arundel and the Earl of Bristol in 1626 Charles I reluctantly agreed that he could not withhold a peer's writ of summons (*GCD*, pp. 44–5); in other words, they were not under his direct control as head of the peerage, but an independent constituent of parliament. Subsequently the Lords took an important if largely passive role in the framing of the Petition of Right.[5]

By this time the economic position of the peerage, and of large landowners in general, was improving under the stimulus of increasing rents; many of them had benefited permanently from the unwise largesse of the Crown, others found their profit in urban development, especially in London, and Court service.[6] Also, though contemporaries were worried by what they saw as a decline in class deference, in general old habits died hard, and the lords were still seen as a class above and apart. Here the stabilisation in number in the 1630s no doubt helped; if there were 126 peers in 1628 there were only 121 at the end of 1641, and even the wholesale creations made by Charles I in the war years, largely for money, plus the Restoration honours list, only brought their numbers up to 170 in 1661. Charles I's decision to summon the peers to a Great Council at York in September 1640 was an obvious attempt to use them as a buffer between himself and the Commons, an attempt which found theoretical expression in his Answer to the Nineteen Propositions in June 1642 (no. **9**, p. 18 above).

In between there is much work still to be done. Gardiner's formative narrative of the first two sessions of the Long Parliament treated the Lords as a kind of punchbag for a militant House of Commons, and Anthony Fletcher's revision of Gardiner in 1981 set much the same tone. Other historians have swung much too far in the other direction, arguing that opposition was centred on and directed from the Lords, to the extent that the Great Rebellion takes on the dimensions of an aristocratic coup.[7] However, there has always been a persistent tradition, beginning with Clarendon, that the premature death of Francis, 4th Earl of Bedford, in May 1641 removed a vital link between the king and some kind of aristocratic clique which might have guided him to safety.[8] In fact, it now looks as though Charles's liaison with a party in the Lords did not cease with Bedford's death, and in the Lords' aversion to ecclesiastical anarchy and their stubborn resistance to the Commons' attempts to tamper with their own membership (by excluding the bishops and the Catholic peers) he had powerful weapons at his disposal.[9] Even after the trauma of the Irish Rebellion he was trying with some success to build up a party in the Lords led by the Earl of Bristol and his son, Lord Digby; in December 1641 Digby very nearly persuaded the House to adjourn to a place outside

[5] Russell, *op. cit.*, pp. 369–74. The best study of an opposition nobleman of the period is Kevin Sharpe's 'The Earl of Arundel, his Circle, and the Opposition', in *Faction*, pp. 209–44.

[6] For rentals see Stone, *op. cit.*, p. 198, and the tables on pp. 760–1.

[7] Paul Christianson, 'The Causes of the English Revolution: a Reappraisal', *JBS*, xv (1976), 40–75, and 'The Peers, the People and Parliamentary Management in the First Six Months of the Long Parliament', *JMH*, xlix (1977), 575–99; Clayton Roberts, 'The Earl of Bedford and the Coming of the English Revolution', *ibid.*, 600–16, and James Farnell, 'The Social and Intellectual Basis of London's Role in the English Civil Wars', *ibid.*, 641–60. But see the comments of J. H. Hexter and Derek Hirst, *ibid.*, l (1978), 1–71.

[8] Clarendon, *History*, iii, 191–2.

[9] Sheila Lambert is working towards a new interpretation in 'The Opening of the Long Parliament', *HJ*, xxvii (1984), 265–87, esp. pp. 279ff.

London on the grounds that the impartiality of its proceedings was being undermined by threats of mob violence. Had he succeeded the Great Rebellion might have been stifled at the outset – or it might have erupted nine months early, of course.[10]

In the end, of course, the peers, like the nation as a whole, were hopelessly split by the events of 1642, particularly the Attempt on the Five Members and the wrangle over the Militia Ordinance. A steady trickle of individual peers to York to join the king enabled the Commons to push through the bill excluding the bishops from the Lords at last in February 1642. By the end of 1642 the Lords had been reduced to a nucleus of about 30, out of 121; Firth calculates that roughly half the peerage actively supported the king, a quarter the Parliament, while the rest stood neutral or were incapacitated in some way.[11] In other words, the proportion of neutrals amongst the peers was probably much lower than amongst the gentry, but given their social prominence this need not surprise us.

If holders of Scots and Irish peerages are included, the regimental and corps leadership of the parliamentary armies in 1642 was almost as aristocratic as the king's, until the Self-Denying Ordinance cleared out the Members of both Houses in 1645. Numbers had now dwindled to about 25, but the House continued to take a full part in proceedings, and in 1646 and 1647 it vigorously asserted its powers of original jurisdiction against John Lilburne; Lilburne appealed to the Commons without result, and after the army's occupation of London in August 1647 it was said that Ireton and Cromwell had promised the Earl of Manchester that the Lords would be safeguarded. Certainly the Heads of the Proposals assumed their survival, though it would have forbidden them to exercise jurisdiction against commoners 'without the concurring judgment of the House of Commons'.[12]

Cromwell and Ireton continued to defend the House of Lords in their confrontation with the Levellers over the winter of 1647–8, which is a pointer to the Protector's thinking ten years later; various schemes were put forward, including a merger of the two Houses on the Scots model, but without result.[13] In its negotiations with the king parliament continued to assume the future existence of the House of Lords, presumably with a veto, though in the Four Bills of December 1647, and again in the Newport Treaty in November 1648, it made the admission of new peers to the House subject to the Commons' approval.[14] But the Newport Treaty was rejected by the army, and though its Remonstrance in November 1648 did not refer directly to the Lords, its supersession was implied by the demand that sovereign power be vested in the elected representative of the people, 'without further appeal to any created standing power' (p. 290 above). The Lords' refusal to sanction the king's trial then

---

[10] See p. 181 above. In the circumstances it was always open to the King to pack the Lords by large-scale new creations. If this did occur to him or his advisers, and there is no proof it did, it was no doubt rejected for fear of an adverse reaction from the existing lords; on their side the Commons would not wish to appear to be tampering any further, even in a negative way, with the composition of the Upper House. However, the point emerged in the last article of the Nineteen Propositions (p. 225 above), which would have allowed the king to continue creating peers, but would have barred their entry to parliament unless with the approval of both Houses. This proviso was repeated in the Propositions of Uxbridge (1644) and Newcastle and in the Heads of the Proposals.

[11] C. H. Firth, *The House of Lords during the Civil War* (1910), p. 115.

[12] P. 270 above; Firth, *op. cit.*, ch. 5, esp. pp. 159, 171–2, 173.

[13] *Ibid.*, pp. 179–88. [14] *GCD*, pp. 340–1; Firth, *op. cit.*, p. 201.

ensured their doom. Cromwell was prominent amongst those who argued for its retention, but as early as 6 February 1649 (before a decision had been reached on the kingship) the Commons voted to abolish the House of Lords as 'useless and dangerous to the people of England'.[15]

But the House of Lords continued to be, in John Pocock's words, 'the great unchronicled actor in English political history'. He goes on to say that Charles I's Answer to the Nineteen Propositions 'was in large measure a bid for its support, and the Humble Petition and Advice in large measure an attempt to find an equivalent for it'.[16] If this is true, and it obviously is, then the refusal of that veteran rebel Lord Saye and Sele to join Cromwell's Other House in 1657, and his successful bid to prevent that other rebel, Lord Wharton, joining it, neatly unites these two episodes. For the arguments Saye and Sele used on his friend were taken bodily from the Answer to the Nineteen Propositions (**127**), and they illustrate the perdurability of aristocratic pretensions in a revolutionary age.[17] He and Wharton were amongst the ten peers who took their seats on 25 April 1660, when the Convention assembled.

The reconstitution of the House of Lords in 1660 has been described many times.[18] The 'Presbyterian' peers, those dogged survivors of the Interregnum who turned up in April 1660, hoped to enforce the provisions of the Newport Treaty, but they were successively overborne by the entry of the 'young lords', who had succeeded to their titles during the Interregnum, and, much more controversially, the 'new lords', created since 1642. After that the return of the remaining royalist peers, from exile or rural retirement, was a foregone conclusion, but the pre-war House was not fully reconstituted until the bishops resumed their seats for the second session of 1661.

Clarendon's speech dismissing the Convention Parliament in December 1660 (**128**) re-affirmed the new government's faith in the Lords not only as a constitutional buffer at Westminster but also as individual spokesmen for the established order in the provinces. In 1661, after the coronation, there were 170 lay peers; in 1685 there were 181. This reflects Charles II's care in his choice of peers, a pattern probably set by Clarendon, who took a high and awful view of the dignity of a peer, as he did of most things. (So far as we know, no peerages were sold after 1660 either.) Our impression is – though in the absence of detailed research it must remain an impression – that between 1660 and 1688 the grant of peerages was geared to services rendered or to be expected, in central government or in the localities. Apart from the royal bastards and sometimes their mothers, the grant of 'ornamental' or 'grace-and-favour' peerages was abandoned. In other words, the later Stuarts were working towards the concept of a 'service' or 'business' nobility.

In these two reigns it is also clear that a fairly consistent effort was being made to mould local government and public opinion through the lord lieutenant, who was emerging as a key political figure. There is evidence that Danby was keenly aware of this, and one of his first requests to Charles II in 1675, when he began the task of rallying support to the monarchy, was that 'he would be pleased to consider and

[15] Though the necessary ordinance was not passed until 19 March; GCD, pp. 387–8.

[16] The Political Works of James Harrington (Cambridge 1977), Intro., p. 128.

[17] He had affirmed his faith in mixed government in 1640; Weston, English Constitutional Theory, p. 21, n. 25.

[18] Firth, op. cit., ch. 9; Schoenfield, op. cit., ch. 4; Turberville, art. cit. (pt 1), pp. 400–1.

review his commission of lieutenancy, deputy lieutenancy and justices of the peace, to the end that none ill affected may be continued, . . . and that preference in all counties may be given to those . . . who have actually been in arms or sufferers for your Majesty or royal father, and to the sons of such'.[19] James II's wholesale revision of the lieutenancy in 1687–8 was only the culmination of a process which had begun in the winter of 1679–80 with the wholesale removal of the Exclusionist peers,[20] and though its wisdom may be doubted it demonstrated the importance the government attached to the office. The activities of the Duke of Norfolk in 1685 and 1688 demonstrate the seigneurial power of a great nobleman (no. **146**, p. 463 below).

This seigneurial power was enhanced by a rise in the prosperity of the large landowners, amongst whom the nobility were predominant. The large estate offered more scope for skilled management and improvement, it steadily increased in size through intermarriage, and it was held together by the legal mechanism of the strict settlement; furthermore, a system of non-graduated direct taxation tended to favour the wealthy, a point of considerable importance as the land tax came to be used with increasing frequency in the 1660s and 1670s.[21] Habakkuk's original thesis placed the starting date for this process in about 1680, but Stone reminds us that the nobility had already profited indirectly from the heavy direct taxation of the Civil Wars and interregnum, which reached a climax in 1660–1 as parliament strained to pay off the New Model Army, and they received preferential treatment in the Restoration Land Settlement, particularly because of the facility with which they could float private acts of parliament to resume their estates.[22]

At the Restoration the Lords also made a strenuous attempt to resume the pre-war practice by which they taxed themselves separately, through a committee of senior peers headed by the Lord Chancellor and Lord Treasurer and appointed by the king.[23] In the Poll Tax Act of 1660 they succeeded; they were allowed to nominate their own collector, and a committee of appeal was set up consisting of eight peers, headed by the Duke of Albemarle. (Clearly no peer was in danger of being over-assessed.) Two supplementary acts first extended this protection to peers' families and households, then stiffened the appeals committee by the addition of ten further members, including the lord chancellor, and made it responsible for supervising the collection as well.[24] The same procedure was adopted for the Poll Tax of 1666, this time with an

---

[19] Browning, *Danby*, II, 66. Browning gives us a tantalising glimpse of Danby's concern for this area of patronage in 'Parties and Party Organisation', 4 *TRHS*, xxx (1948), 32–3, but he does not follow this up in his biography. However, R. W. Ketton-Cremer describes Charles and Danby's efforts to build up a new Court party in Norfolk through the lord lieutenancy in 'The End of the Pastons', *Norfolk Portraits* (1944), pp. 22–57. See also J. H. Plumb's general remarks in *Sir Robert Walpole*, 1 (1956), pp. 42–4.

[20] Jones, *The First Whigs*, p. 120.

[21] H. J. Habakkuk, 'English Landownership 1680–1740', *Econ. Hist. Review*, x (1940), 2–17. His thesis has been contested to some extent, mainly because of its narrow evidential base, but it fits too well into the general picture of the rise of the nobility over this period to be discarded. Habakkuk returns to this theme, though tangentially, in 'The Rise and Fall of English Landed Families 1600–1800' (2 pts), 5 *TRHS*, xxix (1979), 187–207, xxx (1980), 199–221.

[22] Schoenfield, *op. cit.*, ch. 6; Stone, *Aristocracy*, p. 198.

[23] See 1 Car. I, c. 6 (1625), § xvi, and 3 Car. I, c. 8 (1628), § xix, *SR*, v, 15, 47. In 1641 a committee of 25 was named in the act; 16 Car. I, c. 2, § x, *ibid.*, 72–3.

[24] 12 Car. II, c. 9, §§ xv, xviii, c. 11, § vii, c. 28, § xii, *ibid.*, 225, 226, 278. Cf. Schoenfield, *op. cit.*, pp. 143–4. Their contributions to the militia under the act of 1662 were also assessed and collected separately; *ibid.*, 363.

appeal committee of 32; in the Subsidy Act of 1671 and the Poll Tax Act of 1678, they again secured their own collector, but not an appeals committee.[25] Unfortunately they were not so successful with the monthly assessment. In the first Assessment Act in 1660 the best they could do was to add the clause, 'Provided that nothing herein contained shall be drawn into example to the prejudice of the ancient rights belonging to the peers of this realm', and this was repeated in the second Assessment Act of that year.[26] A similar proviso was inserted in the great Assessment Act of 1661, for £1,260,000, though this time they were associated with the lords spiritual and, rather demeaningly, with universities, colleges, schools, almshouses and hospitals.[27] This seems to have been merely a precautionary form of words; it is not found in the Hearth Tax Act of 1662, nor in the three Assessment Acts passed during the Second Dutch War. It subsequently appears in the Assessment Act of 1673 (with the addition of the Cinque Ports), and again in that of 1678,[28] but not in the similar acts of 1677 and 1679.

Directly related to this was the question of the Lords' right to initiate or amend money bills. In 1661, clearly to test the issue, they introduced a minor bill to raise money for road repairs at Westminster; but the Commons incontinently rejected it, and a similar measure sent down to them in 1665. The Lords tried again for the last time in 1677, with a bill 'for the better payment of church rates', but the Commons simply ignored it.[29] Here the Lords' case was weak, but they were much more pertinacious, and initially more successful, in defending their right to amend money bills. Thus they amended the Poll Tax Act of 1660, and even deleted from the Post Office Act a clause allowing MPs to frank their own letters; in 1663 they successfully amended three further secondary money bills, though in 1662 their amendments to another bill were rejected on principle – perhaps because it was essentially the Westminster highways bill they had tried to initiate the year before.[30]

But it was a different matter in 1671, when the Lords tried to amend a major finance bill, imposing new import duties. The Commons reacted with indignation, and resolutions flew to and fro; the Lords had to give way, but the dispute rumbled on until the prorogation (**130**).[31] In 1677 the Lords' attempt to amend the Assessment Act was again rebuffed, and in 1678 the Commons strongly objected to their amending the date for disbanding the army in a further Assessment Act, necessary though this was. After a series of irritable exchanges the Commons passed a resolution unequivocally affirming their sole right to amend as well as initiate such bills (**130**). The Lords made their last such attempt, without avail, in 1679. They never accepted the principle and it was categorically denied in 1740, and again in 1763, by no less an authority than Lord Hardwicke, but the issue was never tested.[32]

The constitutional implications for the future were less serious than they might have

[25] 18, 19 Car. II, c. 1, §§ XXIII, XXXII, *ibid.*, 594, 595; 22, 23 Car. II, c. 3, § XXXV, 29, 30 Car. II, c. 1, § XXIV, *ibid.*, 699, 857.
[26] 12 Car. II, c. 27, § IX, c. 29, § IV, *ibid.*, 269, 283.
[27] 13 Car. II, st. 2, c. 3, § XXVII, *ibid.*, 348.
[28] 25 Car. II, c. 1, § XXX, 30 Car. II, c. 1, § LXV, *ibid.*, 752, 880.
[29] Schoenfield, *op. cit.*, p. 171; Turberville, *art. cit.* (pt 2), pp. 64–5.
[30] Schoenfield, *op. cit.*, p. 172; Turberville, *art. cit.*, p. 65.
[31] Turberville, *loc. cit.*
[32] P. C. Yorke, *Philip Yorke Earl of Hardwicke* (1913), I, 195, III, 383.

seemed. It gave the Commons the power to render any bill immune from amendment in the Upper House by incorporating it in a money bill, but like the Crown's right to swamp the Lords by new creations, it was highly controversial and on the rare occasions on which it was invoked it was usually counter-productive – as with the Irish Land Grants bill in 1700 and the Occasional Conformity bill of 1704. It could also work the other way; the Junto peers effectively defeated the Occasional Conformity bill of 1702 by amending the financial penalties it imposed. But in practical terms, and in the circumstances of the 1670s, it was clearly inequitable; if the Lords had no control over money bills, then they should have the right to tax themselves. As Lord Holles said in 1678:

> In [former] times the Lords and Commons did join in the gift, and the one could not give without the other, except they had otherwise agreed on it amongst themselves; and that they would give separately, as they have sometimes done, but rarely.[33]

In fact, the Lords could not easily translate their economic and social ascendency into constitutional terms, and this is seen also in their unavailing attempt to preserve a right of original jurisdiction. They had freely exercised this right in the Middle Ages, when they were in any case not easily distinguishable from the King's Great Council; it had lapsed with the rise of new conciliar courts under the Tudors, but it had been revived in the special case of impeachment in the 1620s, and thereafter they occasionally, and uncontroversially, accepted original pleas not initiated by the Commons. They had unquestioned power to subpoena witnesses and put them on oath, and in the 1640s, with the loss of Star Chamber, they came into their own, effectively as the judicial wing of the Long Parliament. The Commons viewed with complacency their campaign against the Levellers and other 'anti-social' elements, and their abolition in 1649 left a gap. When the Commons tried to proceed against the Quaker leader James Nayler in 1656 Cromwell had to remind them that they had no power of jurisdiction. After the Restoration the Lords continued to exercise their right of original jurisdiction fairly freely; in fact, one lawyer remarked in 1663, 'The jurisdiction of the Star Chamber is now transformed into the House of Lords, but somewhat in a nobler way.'[34]

The Commons did not agree, and they found a test case in Skinner v. The East India Company (129). In 1666 Thomas Skinner, an 'interloper' – that is, a merchant infringing the monopoly of the Indies trade granted to the East India Company by its charter – petitioned the king, protesting at the Company's seizure of his goods in Sumatra in 1659. The Privy Council tried to mediate and failed, and in January 1667 Charles referred the matter to the House of Lords, since it was doubtful whether the courts of Common Law had jurisdiction outside the realm except in the case of crimes committed on the high seas. The judges had no such doubts, but nevertheless in October 1667 the Lords proceeded to the assessment of damages against the Company, and its directors petitioned the House of Commons, querying the Lords' right to act at all, and pointing out that part of the damages would fall on MPs who were also

---

[33] qu. Schoenfield, op. cit., p. 172 (slightly amended).   [34] Holdsworth, History of English Law, I, 367.

members of the Company. Despite a two months' adjournment beyond Christmas, the dispute dragged on into the following May, 1668, when the Commons voted that the Lords had exceeded their jurisdiction, and were also guilty of a grave breach of privilege. The Lords, predictably, passed a bullish counter-resolution (**129b**). Parliament was then prorogued until October 1669, but as soon as it met the case proceeded, and the Commons took notice of the fact that during the recess the Lords had imprisoned one of their own members, Sir Samuel Barnardiston, deputy governor of the East India Company. This produced another fierce Commons' resolution (**129c**), and Charles ordered another prorogation, until February 1670, when he prevailed on both Houses to abandon the case and expunge all references to it from their journals.[35] Thus the issue was left drawn, but in fact the Lords made no further attempt to act as a court of first instance, except in cases of impeachment.

However, their right to act as a court of appeal was another matter. In 1675 Thomas Shirley appealed to the Lords against a Chancery decree in favour of Sir John Fagg, MP, and the Commons took this up as a breach of privilege.[36] They denied the Lords' right to hear appeals from Chancery, and arrested four barristers due to appear in a similar case pending (**131**). Both Houses were now in a fine frenzy. The Commons imprisoned Fagg for putting in an answer to Shirley's plea before the Lords, and they dismissed their own sergeant-at-arms when he released the four barristers at the request of Black Rod. On 4 June the Lords resolved to proceed with no further business until they received satisfaction. *Shirley* v. *Fagg* easily survived a short prorogation, from June to October, but during the long prorogation that followed, from November 1675 to February 1677, it and all its attendant disputes were quietly dropped. The appellate jurisdiction of the House of Lords was not called in question again.

It was a narrow decision, but in this case as in other aspects of Stuart government constitutional appearances did not reflect political reality. The Lords was a small, intimate, effective body, with a day-to-day working personnel of less than a hundred.[37] They embodied an enormous concentration of wealth, and even the poorest of them enjoyed an assured and elevated status. They were the king's personal counsellors by right, with immediate access to his person, and they were shielded from the hazards of re-election. And they were very ready to fulfil the role envisaged for them by Charles I, though not always in the way he had intended. Thus they defeated the Exclusion Bill in 1680, but in 1685 they took a decisive stand against James II's employment of Catholic army officers, when the Commons, after a brief flicker of independence, were supinely preparing to vote him more money for that army. And the more we examine the Glorious Revolution which followed, the more it appears as an aristocratic coup, both in its planning and execution, with the gentry – as was only proper – accepting the leadership of their seigneurial lords.[38]

[35] *CJ*, IX, 126. Cf. *ST*, VI, 721–2.   [36] Turberville, *art. cit.*, (pt. II), p. 71–4.

[37] Notice that in November 1680 the Exclusion Bill was defeated in the Lords 63:30. Yet this was one of the most contentious divisions of the whole reign, for which whips had been imposed by both sides.

[38] See, for instance, Browning, *Danby*, I, ch. 17; David H. Hosford, *Nottingham, Nobles and the North* (Springfield, Ohio 1976); J. P. Kenyon, *The Nobility in the Revolution of 1688* (Hull 1963).

127. Cromwell's Other House

Viscount Saye and Sele to Lord Wharton, 29 December 1657[39]
My lord,

. . . [As] for this which I take to be the cause of your writing at this time, I shall clearly and sincerely declare unto you my judgment therein, and what my practice will be according thereunto. For the government of this kingdom according to the right constitution thereof and execution agreeable thereunto, I think it to be the best in the world, being a mixture of three lawful governments in that manner that it hath the quintessence of them all, and thereby also the one is a boundary unto the other, whereby they are kept from falling into the extremes which either apart are apt to slip into, monarchy into tyranny, and aristocracy into oligarchy, democracy into anarchy. Now the chiefest remedy and prop to uphold this frame and building and keep it standing and steady is, and experience hath shown it to be, the peers of England, and their power and privileges in the House of Lords. They have been as the beam keeping both scales, king and people, in an even posture, without encroachments one upon another to the hurt and damage of both. Long experience hath made it manifest that they have preserved the just rights and liberties of the people against the tyrannical usurpation of kings, and have also as steps and stairs upheld the crown from falling and being cast down upon the floor, by the insolency of the multitude, from the throne of government. This being so, will it not be as most unjust so most dishonourable for any ancient peer of England to make himself a *felo de se* both to the nobility of England and to [the] just and rightly constituted government of the kingdom by being made a party and indeed a stalking horse and vizard to carry on the design of overthrowing the House of Peers, and in place thereof to bring in and set up a house chosen at the pleasure of him that hath taken power into his hands to do what he will, and by this House that must be carried on, as picked out for that purpose, and altered and new chosen as time and occasion shall require, [and] some five or six lords called to sit with them, who may give some countenance to the design, which for my part I am resolved never to do, nor be guilty of seeming to allow thereof, but rather to profess and bare witness against it. A barebones parliament, as they call it, without choice of the people at all, is not worse than this, which is laying aside the peers of England who by birth are to sit, and picking out a company to make another House of in their places at the pleasure of him that will rule, and withal call a few Lords, thereby causing them to disown their own rights and the rights of all the nobility of England, daubing over the business in this manner, to their perpetual shame who shall yield thereunto.

[39] Clearly Wharton had sought Saye and Sele's advice, though his letter is not extant. Of the 63 persons summoned, seven were peers of England, of whom only two accepted. See Firth, *Last Years*, I, 11–15.

For my part this is my resolution: if a writ be sent me I will lay it by me and sit still; if I be sent for by force I cannot withstand it, but when I come up I will speak that I hope by God's assistance which shall be just in his sight and just to this government being now about unjustly to be subverted.

My lord, for your lawyers I look upon them as weathercocks, which will turn about with the wind for their own advantage, which I wish they did not love more than truly. With them therefore where there is might there is right, it is dominion if it succeed, but rebellion if it miscarry; a good argument for pirates upon the sea and for thieves upon the highway, fitter for hobbs [*sic*] and atheists than good men and christians . . .

EHR, x (1895), 106–7 (ed. C. H. Firth)

128. Clarendon addresses the Lords

Speech to both Houses on the dissolution of the Convention Parliament, 29 December 1660

. . . Your Lordships will easily recover that estimation and reverence that is due to your high condition, by the exercise and practice of that virtue from whence your honours first sprang; the example of your justice and piety will inflame the hearts of the people towards you, and from your practice they will make a judgment of the king himself. They know very well that you are not only admitted to his presence but to his conversation, and even in a degree to his friendship, for you are his Great Council. By your example they will form their own manners, and by yours they will make a guess at the king's. Therefore under that obligation you will cause your piety, your justice, your affability and your charity to shine as bright as possible before them. They are too much in love with England, too partial to it, who believe it the best country in the world; there is better earth and a better air, and a better, that is a warmer, sun in other countries; but we are no more than just, when we say that England is an enclosure of the best people in the world when they are well informed and instructed; a people in sobriety of conscience the most devoted to God Almighty; in the integrity of their affections the most dutiful to the king; in their good manners and inclinations most regardful and loving to the nobility; no nobility in Europe so entirely loved by the people; there may be more awe and fear and terror of them, but no such love towards them as in England.

I beseech your lordships, do not undervalue this love. They have looked upon your lordships, and they will look upon your lordships again, as the greatest examples and patterns of duty to the king, as the greatest security and protection from injury and injustice, and for their enjoying whatever is due to them by the law, and as the most proper mediators and interposers to the king, if by any failure of justice they should be exposed to any oppression and violence. And this by the exercise of your justice and kindness towards them will make them the more abhor and abominate that party upon which a commonwealth [*sc*. republic] must be founded, because it would extirpate, or suppress, or deprive them of their beloved nobility, which are such a support and security to their full happiness . . .   *LJ*, XI, 238[40]

129. *Skinner* v. *The East India Company*, 1668–70

(a) Commons, 2 May 1668

Resolved:

1. That the Lords' taking cognisance of the matter set forth and contained in the petition of Thomas Skinner, merchant, against the governor and company of merchants trading to the East Indies, concerning the taking away the petitioner's ship and goods, and assaulting his person, and their Lordships' overruling the plea of the said governor and company, the said cause coming before their House originally, only upon the complaint of the said Skinner, being a common plea, is not agreeable to the law of the land, and tending to deprive the subject of his right, ease and benefit due to him by the said laws.

2. That the Lords' taking cognisance of the right and title of the island in the petition mentioned, and giving damages thereupon against the said governor and company, is not warranted by the laws of this kingdom.

3. That the said Thomas Skinner, in commencing and prosecuting a suit by petition in the House of Lords against the Company of Merchants trading to the East Indies (wherein several Members of this House are parties concerned with the said company, in particular interests and estates), and in procuring judgment therein, with directions to be served upon the governor, being a Member of this House, . . . is [guilty of] a breach of the privilege of this House.   *PH*, IV, 422–3

(b) Lords, 7 May 1668

It was resolved, That the House of Commons entertaining the scandalous petition of the East India Company against the Lords' House of Parliament, and their proceedings, examinations and votes thereupon had and made, are a breach of the privileges of the House of Peers, and contrary to the fair correspondency which ought to be between the two Houses, and unexampled in former times, [and]

That the House of Lords taking cognisance of the cause of Thomas Skinner, merchant, a person highly oppressed and injured in East India by the governor and company of merchants of London trading thither, and overruling the plea of the said company, and adjudging five thousand pounds damages thereupon against the said governor and company, is agreeable to the laws of the land and well warranted by the law and custom of parliament, and justified by many

---

[40] For a further extract from the same speech, see no. **100**, p. 347 above.

parliamentary precedents, ancient and modern. *HMC, 8th Report*, pp. 172–3

(c) [Immediately upon the adjournment the Lords sent for Sir Samuel Barnardiston, MP, deputy governor of the East India Company, who had presented the company's petitions, denying the jurisdiction of the Lords in this case. He was fined £300, but refused to pay, and was imprisoned until 10 August. As a result, next session the Commons passed the following resolutions.]

1. That it is an inherent right of every commoner of England to prepare and present petitions to the House of Commons in case of grievance, and the House of Commons to receive the same; in evidence whereof, it is one of the first works that is done by the Commons, to appoint a grand committee to receive petitions and informations of grievances.

2. That it is the undoubted right and privilege of the Commons to judge and determine concerning the nature and matter of such petitions, how far they are fit or unfit to be received; and that in no age they found any person presenting a grievance by way of petition to the House of Commons, and received by them, that was ever censured by the Lords, without complaint by the Commons.

3. That no court whatsoever hath power to judge or censure any petition presented to the House of Commons, and received by them, unless transmitted from thence, or the matter complained of by them; and that no suitors for justice in any inferior court in law or equity are therefore punishable criminally, though untrue, or suable by way of action in any other court; but are only subject to a moderate fine or amercement by that court, unless in some cases specially provided by act of parliament, as appeals, or the like. In case men should be punishable in other courts for presenting petitions to the House of Commons, it may deter his Majesty's subjects from seeking redress of their grievances, and frustrate the principal end for which parliaments were ordained.

4. Whereas a petition from the East India Company was presented to the House by Sir Samuel Barnardiston and others, complaining of grievances therein, which the Lords have censured under the notion of a scandalous paper or libel, the said censure, and proceeding of the Lords against the said Sir Samuel, are contrary to and a subversion of the rights and privileges of the House of Commons, and liberties of the commons of England; and further, no petition, or any matter depending in the House of Commons, can be taken notice of by the Lords without breach of privilege, unless permitted by the House of Commons.

5. That the continuance upon record of the judgment given by the Lords, and complained of by the Commons in the last session of parliament, in the case of Thomas Skinner and the East India Company, is prejudicial to the rights of the commons of England. *PH*, IV, 423–3

130. Finance bills

[Commons, 13 April 1671]

The House then proceeded to the reading the amendments and clauses sent from the Lords, to the bill for an imposition on foreign commodities, which were once read.

And the first amendments sent from the Lords being for changing the proportion of the impositions on white sugars from one penny per pound to halfpenny half-farthing, was read the second time, and debated.

Resolved, &c., *nemine contradicente*, that in all aids given to the king by the Commons the rate or tax ought not to be altered by the Lords.

[Conference, 20 April 1671]

. . . Their Lordships had neither reason nor precedent offered by the Commons to back that resolution, but were told that this was a right so fundamentally settled in the Commons that they could not give reasons for it, for that would be a weakening of the Commons' right and privilege.

Yet the Lords in parliament, upon full consideration thereof . . . are come to this resolution, *nemine contradicente*:

That the power exercised by the House of Peers in making the amendments and abatements in the bill . . . [in question], both as to the matter, measure and time concerning the rates and impositions on merchandise, is a fundamental, inherent and undoubted right of the House of Peers, from which they cannot depart.

Reasons
★   ★   ★

4ly, If this right should be denied, the Lords have not a negative voice allowed them in bills of this nature, for if the Lords, who have the power of treating, advising, giving counsel and applying remedies, cannot amend, abate or refuse a bill in part, by what consequence of reason can they enjoy a liberty to reject the whole? When the Commons shall think fit to question it, they may pretend the same grounds for it.

5ly, In any case of judicature, which is undoubtedly and indisputably the peculiar right and privilege of the House of Lords, if their Lordships send down a bill to the Commons for giving judgment in a legislative way they allow and acknowledge the same right in the Commons to amend, change and alter such bills as the Lords have exercised in this bill of impositions sent up by the Commons.

6ly, By this new maxim of the House of Commons a hard and ignoble choice is left to the Lords, either to refuse the Crown supplies when they are most necessary, or to consent to ways and proportions of aid which neither their own judgment or interest, nor the good of the government and people, can admit.

7ly, If positive assertion can introduce a right, what security have the Lords that the House of Commons shall not in other bills (pretended to be for the general good of the commons, whereof they will conceive themselves the fittest judges) claim the same peculiar privilege, in exclusion of any deliberation or alteration of the Lords, when they shall judge it necessary or expedient.

★　★　★

[Two days later parliament was prorogued, and did not meet again until 4 February 1673, by which time the matter was apparently forgotten.]

CJ, IX, 235, 239

(b) [On 21 June 1678 the Lords took into consideration the Supply Bill for the disbandment of the army, and amended the clause which stated that the troops in England must be disbanded by 30 June. The Commons, without a leg to stand on, argued the point, but had to give way, especially since by that time 30 June was passed.[41] The act was amended to read '30 July', three days more grace than the Lords had suggested, but to save their face the Commons passed this Resolution.]

[Commons, 3 July 1678]

Resolved, etc., That all aids and supplies, and aids to his Majesty in Parliament, are the sole gift of the Commons; and all bills for the granting of any such aids and supplies ought to begin with the Commons; and that it is the undoubted and sole right of the Commons to direct, limit and appoint in such bills the ends, purposes, considerations, conditions, limitations and qualifications of such grants, which ought not to be changed or altered by the House of Lords.

CJ, IX, 509

131. *Shirley* v. *Fagg*, 1675

[Lords, 17 May 1675]

Then the lord keeper . . . gave the House a report of the effect of the late conference; which was to communicate to their lordships, by Sir Richard Temple (who said he was appointed by the House of Commons to communicate to you), a resolve of that House, *videlicet*:

Resolved, &c., that the appeal brought by Doctor Shirley in the House of Lords against Sir John Fagg, a Member of the House of Commons, and the

[41] *LJ*, XIII, 257, 262, 265.

proceeding thereupon, is a breach of the undoubted rights and privileges of the House of Commons, and therefore the Commons desire that there be no further proceedings in that case before their lordships.

The House took the matter of this conference into consideration, and after a serious debate made this declaration following:

The Lords do order and declare, that it is the undoubted right of the Lords, in judicature, to receive and determine in time of parliament appeals from inferior courts, though a member of either House be concerned therein, that there may be no failure of justice in the land; and from this right, and the exercise thereof, the Lords will not depart.   *LJ*, XII, 694

BOOK IV

GOVERNMENT

For forms of government let fools contest.
Whate'er is best administer'd is best.

POPE

CHAPTER 12

THE PRIVY COUNCIL

Ostensibly the organisation and method of the Privy Council changed little in this period. It was still the prime executive authority of government, and was unusual amongst the nations of the West in that it could initiate executive or judicial action of its own accord. But the steady rise in its numbers, defying all efforts to restrain it, threatened its status as a policy-making body, and led to the evolution of a committee structure which resulted by the reign of James II in the emergence of a 'Cabinet Council'.[1]

Thomas Cromwell in the 1530s had reduced the size of the King's Council from more than 40 members to less than 20, forming a new Privy Council composed entirely of major office-holders. Elizabeth adhered strictly to this practice; in fact by the end of her reign she had reduced it to 13 – the Archbishop of Canterbury, the Lord Treasurer, the Lord Keeper, the Lord Chief Justice, the Lord Admiral, the Lord Chamberlain, the Master of the Horse, the Comptroller and Vice-Chamberlain of the Household, the Secretaries of State, the Chancellor of Exchequer, and the Earl of Shrewsbury (the only non-office-holder).

On his accession James I at once doubled the size of the Council, to 26; it was then held at that figure for some years (20 in 1610, 28 in 1617). It was generally felt that this inflation lowered the prestige of the individual councillor and made it more difficult to impose secrecy; no doubt there was some truth in this, but Elton argues that in fact Elizabeth's later Councils were too small, they placed too much of a burden on individuals, and they offered too little encouragement to ambitious men outside government.[2] By 1623 it had crept up to 25, with the accession of Charles I it rose to 40, and in 1630 it stood at 42.

However, much of its business was now routine, often of a trifling nature. It had to sift all petitions to the Crown, and settle many disputes of a legal or quasi-legal nature, particularly those involving merchants on the high seas. The orders governing the sitting of the Privy Council on Charles I's accession, and renewed in 1628, were largely concerned with the conduct of this kind of routine business.[3] Also many councillors, probably appointed as a mark of favour, rarely attended, and the registers for 1629–30 show that business was commonly transacted by 12 or 13, sometimes as few as five; on one occasion three. In the 12 months ending 31 May 1630 the Council met 99 times. The Lord Privy Seal attended 83 meetings, making him easily first, followed by the

---

[1] See in general E. R. Turner, *The Privy Council of England 1603–1784* (2 vols., Baltimore 1927–8), a useful but ill-digested compilation of facts. For the Council under the Tudors, see Elton, *Tudor Constitution*, pp. 88–94, and 'Tudor Government: the Points of Contact, II. The Council', 5 *TRHS*, xxv (1975), 195–211.

[2] Elton, *art. cit.*, pp. 209–11. Cf. Willson, *Privy Councillors*, pp. 22–3.

[3] *APC 1627–8*, pp. 331–2.

Lord Keeper (73), and the two Secretaries of State (75, 73). The Lord President (69) was not particularly diligent, nor was the Lord Chamberlain or the Lord Steward (39, 25). (It is a sign of the times that the Archbishop of York attended 32 meetings and Richard Neale, bishop of Winchester, 47.) On the other hand we must conclude that the Earls of Exeter (23), Bridgewater (18), Carlisle (19) and Holland (11), and Viscounts Wilmot and Wimbledon (10, 6), were very much courtesy members.[4] The king himself only sat nine times, and it is not always apparent what brought him. On two occasions, 29 July, 15 November 1629, the privilege of the peerage was involved, but the rest were very much routine; for instance, on 4 December 1629 he heard an acrimonious dispute between the University of Cambridge and the City, over the price of victuals, and on 12 May following he received a long petition from the inhabitants of the East Riding of Yorkshire complaining about flooding.[5]

In fact, there are signs that the Privy Council had now lost most of its functions as a policy-making or even an advisory body. Top secret matters like the Spanish Marriage negotiations 1621–4 were discussed at meetings between the king and nine chosen councillors, and in 1621 and 1624 James experimented with a Council of War which included several men who were not councillors at all.[6] In the printed *Acts of the Privy Council* for 1626 the Duke of Buckingham features extensively as Lord High Admiral, also Lord Lieutenant of Buckinghamshire and Middlesex, but no one would gather that he was the king's chief confidant, still less that he had been impeached by the House of Commons. The Petition of Right, similarly, leaves not a ripple on the Council registers. On 3 March 1629 the Council did issue warrants for the arrest of Sir John Eliot and eight other MPs and their imprisonment in the Tower, but on the 6th it returned to its more usual concerns: the transport of corn into the Low Countries, and barley into Ireland; the long-running dispute between one Captain Turner and one Lawrence Burrows; a dispute between the customs officers at Bridgewater and Lewis Lashbrooke and John Baker, and so on.[7] The king's public policy, and the public declarations to which it gave rise, like the proclamation of 10 March 1629 (no. **26**, p. 71 above), were presumably discussed and drafted elsewhere, no doubt in small, *ad hoc* committees which have left no written record, and we are fortunate that the treachery of Sir Henry Vane has left us an account of a famous meeting of the 'Scottish Committee' on 5 May 1640, consisting of the king, Strafford, Laud, Juxon, the Duke of Hamilton, Lord Cottington, the two Secretaries of State, Vane and Windebank, and the Lord General, the Earl of Northumberland (**132**). The parliamentary opposition always viewed such secret councils with suspicion, and in the Nineteen Propositions in 1642 they demanded that the Privy Council be reduced to a maximum of 25 and made responsible for all policy decisions, a demand still being voiced, in fact, in the Act of Settlement in 1701.

From the Restoration onwards there was a tendency for the Privy Council to grow steadily larger, and inevitably policy making tended to devolve onto a smaller group,

---

[4] *APC 1629–30*, pp. v–viii. It is strange that Sir Humphrey May, Vice-Chamberlain of the Household, attended 56 meetings, his colleague the Treasurer (Sir Thomas Edmondes) only 14.

[5] *Ibid.*, pp. 101–2, 177, 198, 378–9.

[6] E. H. Carlyle, 'Committees of Council under the earlier Stuarts', *EHR*, xxi (1906), 673–85; *TCD*, p. 380.

[7] *APC 1628–9*, pp. 351ff.

the 'cabinet council', a committee of the Council proper. Its formal powers – of summons and interrogation notably – depended on its members' status as privy councillors.[8] However, such developments were regarded with some disfavour, even by some of those directly concerned in them, and in 1668 an attempt was made to revitalise the Privy Council by reforming its committee structure. Standing committees were instituted on foreign affairs, trade, the navy and grievances, and it was laid down that henceforward no matter was to be decided until it had been before the appropriate committee, but conversely no matter was to be dealt with by a committee unless it had been referred to it by the Council proper (**133**).

From the first the Committee for Foreign Affairs was recognised as the senior committee, and it was the only one which was excepted from the general rule forbidding committees to discuss matters not referred to them by the Council. Nor was it necessarily confined to foreign affairs; it was instructed to supervise the correspondence between the king's ministers and the justices of the peace 'concerning the temper of the kingdom', and it dealt with other matters of high policy as well. In November 1672, for instance, it advised the king on the nomination of a new Speaker, and in December it discussed the dismissal of two judges.[9] Sir Joseph Williamson's notes in September 1678 show that it was capable of breaking off its discussion of the Peace of Nijmegen and all its attendant complexities in order to consider the affairs of the borough of Chichester (**136**).

However, it was the committee's association in the public mind with the king's dubious foreign policy which made it an object of suspicion, and early in the Exclusion Crisis Charles II decided to kill two birds with one stone; he made a bid for popularity by dissolving the hated 'Secret Committee', and at the same time he tried to reduce the Privy Council to manageable proportions.[10] On 21 April 1679 he dismissed his existing Privy Council *en bloc* and swore in another of 30; 15 office-holders and 15 others (ten peers and five commoners); and agreed to take no major decisions without its advice – a reform remarkably like that demanded of Charles I in the Nineteen Propositions (**137**).

Nevertheless, only two days later the Committee on Foreign Affairs was revived in the transparent disguise of a 'Committee of Intelligence', consisting of the Lord President, the Lord Chamberlain, the Captain-General of the army, the two Secretaries of State, the First Lord of the Treasury, Viscount Halifax and Sir William Temple.[11] The only innovation was the inclusion of two men without office, Halifax and Temple (though Temple was still technically envoy to the Netherlands). The duties of this Committee were not limited to foreign affairs, of course; it drafted some at least of the King's Messages to Parliament in the session October 1680 to January 1681, it probably discussed the summons or dissolution of parliament, and it certainly discussed delicate matters like the execution of the penal laws against Catholics. Meanwhile Charles's promise to consult the Privy Council at all times was quietly forgotten, especially since the Exclusion Crisis left it with several members, and even

---

[8] William Anson, 'The Cabinet in the Seventeenth and Eighteenth Centuries', *EHR*, XXIX (1914), 58.
[9] *Law Quarterly Review*, LXVI (1950), 72–3 (Havighurst).
[10] E. R. Turner, 'The Privy Council of 1679', *EHR*, XXX (1915), 251–70.
[11] *Ibid.*, p. 265; Godfrey Davies, 'Council and Cabinet 1679–1688', *EHR*, XXXVII (1922), 55.

officers of state, whom the king did not entirely trust. In 1681 we find one such, the Lord Privy Seal, the Earl of Anglesey, complaining that the Committee of Intelligence was not referring important foreign policy matters to the Council, a practice staunchly defended by Sir Leoline Jenkins, now the senior Secretary of State (**138**). (Anglesey was dismissed a year later.)

These tendencies were accentuated under James II, perhaps because of the religious divisions his policy provoked, and he tended to transact his business in smaller and smaller committees and with increasing informality. A French visitor, the young Marquis de Torcy, records that towards the end of 1687 he was taking important decisions in a camarilla consisting of himself, the Earl of Sunderland and the Jesuit Edward Petre (**139**), and foreign ambassadors often referred to a 'Catholic Council' which had no constitutional status at all and whose composition can only be guessed at. The Privy Council still met to transact routine business, but the King regarded it with such contempt that on several occasions in 1688 he simply sat by himself with the clerks to issue council orders.[12]

However, James II was nothing if not natural; he behaved precisely as the mood took him, and his impatience with formalities and his tendency to take advice from a few intimates were unusual only in that he tried to give his practice some familiar constitutional form. Throughout the century, behind the formal apparatus of councils, cabinets and committees lay the simple, usually quite easy, relationship between the king and one or two trusted ministers or advisers. The really important decisions were taken in complete privacy, leaving no surviving records, and we are lucky to possess the Earl of Danby's notes for what he obviously anticipated would be a difficult audience with Charles II in 1677 (**134**).[13]

Danby was usually given the informal title of 'chief minister', but in this century it was never clear whether it was attached to any particular office or not. By the early eighteenth century the Treasury had established a primacy over the other departments of state, but whether the head of the Treasury enjoyed automatic seniority over the other ministers was another matter, and it was certainly not true of the period prior to 1667. No one would have called Lord Buckhurst (1603–8), the Earl of Portland (1628–35) or the Earl of Southampton (1660–7) chief ministers, though they were all Lord Treasurers. The title was most often accorded after the Restoration to the minister responsible for parliament and especially for a cantankerous House of Commons.

But there was still a prejudice against the ascendancy of any one minister, a prejudice felt equally by the king and by parliament, and one which persisted into the 1730s. In fact, James II, who would brook no rival, established division of authority as a principle. When he dismissed his Lord Treasurer, the Earl of Rochester, in January 1687, he announced that thenceforward he would appoint no man to the great executive offices of state, lord treasurer, lord high admiral or captain-general, unless he

[12] This hapened on 26 February, 4, 10, 18, 25 March, 8, 19, 22 April, 19, 20 May, 10 July, 26 August and 1 October 1688 (*PRO*, Privy Council Registers). Most of these 'meetings' were to issue orders for the regulation of individual corporations, but on 10 March he swore in a new lord lieutenant for Sussex, on 26 August he dealt with East India Company business, and on 1 October he issued Dartmouth's sailing orders.

[13] The most revealing account of confidential discussions between minister and monarch is Halifax's notes of his conversations with William III in 1689 and 1690; see Williams, *Eighteenth-Century Constitution*, pp. 60–4.

was of the blood royal. This was a natural development, confirmed by William III, though not by Anne. It is common to say that in these circumstances the king was 'acting as his own prime minister', with a somewhat derogatory implication, but in fact he was merely behaving as a seventeenth-century monarch should. The time was not ripe for the emergence of a prime minister, just as it was not ripe for the emergence of a cabinet in any real sense; and the 'cabinet council' remained an executive instrument of the king's, who summoned it and usually presided over it. It is even arguable that the presence of a chief minister with unquestioned authority, like Buckingham in the 1620s or Clarendon in the 1660s, suggests a serious weakness in the monarch concerned at that time. In other cases – that of Danby, for instance, or Laud – this primacy was more imagined than real.

Finally, in any review of seventeenth-century government we are struck by the substantial immunity enjoyed by the king's ministers. As we have seen (p. 361 above) impeachment was a cumbersome and largely ineffective weapon, which obliged the Commons to resort to 'overkill', to accuse the minister concerned of capital crimes when really their only purpose was to drive him permanently out of office. This was effected in 1667, with Clarendon, and in 1679, with Danby, but only with the substantial co-operation of the king himself, assisted by the Lords. Impeachment failed against Strafford and Laud, though in Laud's case, in the middle of a civil war, conditions were as propitious as they were ever likely to be. In both cases the Commons had to resort to attainder, but after 1660 this was reserved for men actually in rebellion – notably Argyll and Monmouth in 1685. Attempts to remove ministers by the less conclusive means of an Address – Lauderdale in 1677, Halifax and Scroggs in 1680 – were simply ignored. The truth is, whether the Commons wanted to remove a minister by attainder, impeachment or simply an address, the Lords' co-operation was essential, and the Lords, who still provided most of the king's ministers, were chary of condemning a man for 'crimes' which any one of them might find himself committing in future years. Lord Carnarvon's speech in 1678, against the committal of Danby on charges of impeachment, was an amusing squib, but it went right to the heart of the House's attitude in such cases (**135**).

132. The Committee on Scots Affairs, 5 May 1640

LLIr[reland, Strafford].[14] No danger in undertaking this war. Whether the Scots are to be reduced or no?

To reduce them by force, as the state of this kingdom stands.

If his Majesty had not declared himself so soon, he would have declared himself for no war with Scotland, they would have given him plentifully.

The City to be called [upon] immediately and quickened to lend one hundred thousand pounds.

[14] This abbreviated heading is crossed out in the MS, and some have attributed the speech to the Lord General, the Earl of Northumberland. But Northumberland, in his dual role as Lord Admiral, is credited with the next speech. At Strafford's trial none of those present that day were clear as to precisely what had been said and by whom. See Timmis, *Thine is the Kingdom*, pp. 110–18.

The shipping money may be put vigorously upon collection. These two ways will furnish his Majesty plentifully, to go on with arms and war for Scotland.

The manner of the war.

Stopping of the trade of Scotland no prejudice, so they had the trade free with England for their cattle.

A defensive war, altogether against it.

Offensive war into the kingdom; his opinion [a] few months will make an end of the war.

Do you invade them.

L[ord] Ad[miral, Northumberland]. If no more money than what proposed, how then to make an offensive war? A difficulty whether to do nothing or to let them alone, or go on with a vigorous war.

LLIr[eland]. Go vigorously on or let them alone, no defensive war, loss of honour and reputation. The quiet of England will [not?] hold out long.

You will languish as between Saul and David.

Go on with a vigorous war, as you first designed, loosed and absolved from all rules of government, being reduced to extreme necessity, everything is to be done that power might admit, and that you are to do.

They refusing, you are acquitted towards God and man, you have an army in Ireland, you may employ here to reduce this kingdom.

Confident as anything under heaven Scotland shall not hold out five months.

One summer well employed will do it.

Venture all I had, I would carry it or lose it.

Whether a defensive war as impossible as an offensive, or whether to let them alone.

L. Arch[bishop, Laud]. Tried all ways, and refused all ways; by the law of God you should have subsistance, and ought to have it, and lawful to take it.

L. Cott[ington]. Leagues abroad they may make and will, and therefore the defence of this kingdom.

The Lower House are weary both of king and Church. All ways shall be just to raise monies by this unavoidable necessity, therefore, to be used being lawful.

LLIr. Commission of array to be put in execution, they are to bring them to the Borders.

In reason of state you have power, when they are there, to use them at the king's pay, if any of the lords can show you a better way let them do it.

(Ob[jection]. Town full of nobility, who will talk of it.)

He will make them smart for it.

House of Lords MSS, HMC 3rd Report, p. 3

133. The Council Reforms of 1668

[Privy Council minutes, 12 February 1668]

Order for regulation and establishment of the Commitees of the Privy Council. His Majesty upon the 31st of January last caused an Order to be read and passed[15] for establishing a future regulation of the committees of his Privy Council; and some additions being since held necessary to be made thereunto, the same were this day read and allowed of, as follows.

His Majesty having among other the important parts of his affairs taken into his princely consideration the way and method of managing matters at the Council Board, and reflecting that his councils would have more reputation if they were put into a more settled and established course, has thought fit to appoint certain Standing Committees for several businesses, together with regular days and places for their assembling, in such sort as follows.

1. *Foreign Affairs.* The Committee of Foreign Affairs to consist of these persons following (besides his royal Highness,[16] who is understood to be of all committees where he pleases to be), viz., Prince Rupert, Lord Keeper [Bridgeman], Lord Privy Seal [Robartes], Duke of Buckingham, Duke of Albemarle, Duke of Ormond, Lord Arlington and Mr Secretary Morrice; to which committee his Majesty doth also hereby refer the corresponding with justices of the peace, and other his Majesty's officers and ministers in the several counties of the kingdom, concerning the temper of the kingdom, etc. The constant day for this committee to meet to be every Monday, besides such other days wherein any extraordinary occasion shall oblige them to assemble; and the place of their meeting to be at the Lord Arlington's lodgings in Whitehall.

2. *Navy.* Such matters as concern the admiralty and navy, as also all military matters, fortifications, etc., so far as they are fit to be brought to the Council Board without intermeddling with what concerns the proper officers (unless it shall by them be so desired), his Majesty is pleased that they be under the consideration of the following committee, viz., Prince Rupert, Duke of Albemarle, Lord Chamberlain, Earl of Anglesey, Earl of Carlisle, Earl of Craven, Lord Arlington, Lord Berkeley, Lord Ashley, Mr Comptroller, Mr Vice Chamberlain, Mr Secretary Morrice, Sir William Coventry and Sir John Duncombe; the usual day of meeting to be Wednesday, and oftener as he that presides shall direct; and the place to be the Council Chamber, and hereof three or more of them to be a quorum.

3. *Trade.* A committee for the business of trade, under whose consideration

---

[15] Merely a formal order setting up the four Standing Committees. See Turner, *Privy Council*, II, 266–7.
[16] James, Duke of York.

is to come whatsoever concerns his Majesty's foreign plantations, as also what relates to his kingdoms of Scotland and Ireland, in such matters only relating to either of those kingdoms as properly belong to the cognisance of the Council Board, [and] the Isles of Jersey and Guernsey; which is to consist of the Lord Privy Seal, Duke of Buckingham, Duke of Ormond, Earl of Ossory, Earl of Bridgewater, Earl of Anglesey, Earl of Lauderdale, Lord Arlington, Lord Holles, Lord Ashley, Mr Comptroller, Mr Vice Chamberlain, Mr Secretary Morrice, Sir William Coventry; the usual day of meeting to be every Thursday in the Council Chamber, and oftener as he that presides shall direct, and hereof three or more of them to be a quorum . . .

4. *Complaints and Grievances.* A committee to whom all petitions of complaint and grievance are to be referred, in which his Majesty hath thought fit hereby particularly to prescribe not to meddle with property, or what relates to *meum* and *tuum*. And to this committee his Majesty is pleased that all matters which concern acts of state, or of the Council, be referred; the persons to be the Archbishop of Canterbury, Lord Keeper, Lord Privy Seal, Lord Great Chamberlain, Lord Chamberlain, Earl of Bridgewater, Earl of Anglesey, Earl of Bath, Earl of Carberry, Viscount Fitzhardinge, Lord Arlington, Lord Holles, Lord Ashley, Mr Secretary Morrice, Mr Chancellor of the duchy [of Lancaster] and Sir John Duncombe; the constant days to be Fridays in the Council Chamber.

And his Majesty's further meaning is that to these two last committees any of the Council may have liberty to come and vote, and that his two principal secretaries of state be ever understood to be of all committees . . .

And for the better carrying on of business at these several committees his Majesty thinks fit, and accordingly is pleased to appoint, that each of these committees be assigned to the particular care of some one person, who is constantly to attend it. In that of the navy and military matters his royal Highness may preside if he so please, or else the lord general [Albemarle]; in foreign matters, the Lord Arlington; in matters of state and grievances, the Lord Keeper.

All things relating to the Treasury in England or Ireland [are] to be immediately referred to the Lords Commissioners of the Treasury, from whence it may come again to the Council Board, in case the matter be of such a nature as they cannot or would not willingly give their determination therein.

Besides which aforesaid committees, if there shall happen anything extraordinary, that requires advice of any mixed nature, other than what is before determined, his Majesty's meaning and intention is that particular committees be in such cases appointed for them, as hath been hitherto accustomed, . . . and that as on the one side nothing is hereafter to be resolved in Council till the matter has been first examined and [shall] have received the opinion of some committee or other, so on the other hand that nothing be referred to any committee until it hath been first read at the board, except in foreign affairs . . .   *PRO, PC* 2/10, 176–7

134. Earl of Danby, 'Memorandums'[17] in June 1677 for the king

The necessity of having officers to assist me, having neither time to labour as I ought to do in his Majesty's other concerns, nor to think of improving his revenue; nor dare I trust that anything I would do for his service shall not be exposed to public knowledge.

That nothing is more necessary than to let the world see he will reward and punish, and that no longer time must be lost therein, for that people begin already to think he will do neither. That nothing can spoil his affairs at home but unsteadiness of resolution in those steps he has begun, and want of vigour to discountenance all such as pretend to others.

Note here the variety of opposition this must meet:

As the persuasive arguments of the dissenters,

Their conjunction with others,

The no possibility of convincing some, and the discouragement that gives.

Memorandum: Bishop Duresme [Durham], Colonel Norton, the Test. F. Munson, Coleman, Talbot.

Till he can fall into the humour of the people he can never be great nor rich, and while differences continue prerogative must suffer, unless he can live without parliament.

That the condition of this revenue will not permit that.

As to foreign affairs, I cannot as a councillor but consider them in the first place as they stand with the interest of England, and then I am for concerning the peace with the prince of Orange to his satisfaction, and making the alliance strict with him, by which many advantages may accrue to us, as the flag from Spain, great advantages in trade from them, etc. Whereas I know none from France . . . I shall only boldly affirm that were the king of France in the place of the king of England his actions have shown he would not forgo so many of his greatest concerns both at home and abroad for ten times as many good words as we have received, especially when a peace made in favour of him shall maintain our ill humour here; and I could never see what useful help we can receive from him when the peace shall be made.

But against this also there will be strong opposition from mistaken opinions, and whilst the king will remain almost single in his opinion against all others in his kingdom it will also be necessary to show upon what foundations he will build or maintain himself . . .   Browning, *Danby*, II, 69–71

---

[17] In the sense of notes, for a subsequent audience.

135. Impeachment as a double-edged weapon, 1678

The Earl of Carnarvon's speech to the House of Lords, 23 December 1678
[The Commons had brought up articles of impeachment against the Earl of Danby, and requested his immediate committal for trial. This occasioned a debate which 'was carried on with much heat on both sides'.][18]

The Earl of Carnarvon.[19] My Lords, I understand but little of Latin, but a good deal of English, and not a little of the English history, from which I have learnt the mischiefs of such kind of prosecutions as these, and the ill fate of the prosecutors. I could bring many instances, and those very ancient; but, my lords, I shall go no farther back than the latter end of Queen Elizabeth's reign, at which time the Earl of Essex was run down by Sir Walter Rawleigh. My Lord Bacon, he ran down Sir Walter Rawleigh, and your lordships know what became of my Lord Bacon. The Duke of Buckingham, he ran down my Lord Bacon, and your lordships know what happened to the Duke of Buckingham. Sir Thomas Wentworth, afterwards Earl of Strafford, ran down the Duke of Buckingham, and you all know what became of him. Sir Harry Vane, he ran down the Earl of Strafford, and your lordships know what became of Sir Harry Vane. Chancellor Hyde [Clarendon], he ran down Sir Harry Vane, and your lordships know what became of the Chancellor. Sir Thomas Osborne, now Earl of Danby, ran down Chancellor Hyde; but what will become of the Earl of Danby, your lordships best can tell. But let me see that man that dare run the Earl of Danby down, and we shall soon see what will become of him.

This being pronounced with a remarkable humour and tone, the Duke of Buckingham, both surprised and disappointed, after his way, cried out, 'The man is inspired! and claret has done the business.'

[The debate was adjourned to the 26th, and on the 27th the Lords refused the Commons' request.]

PH, IV, 1073

136. The Committee of Intelligence: Sir Joseph Williamson's Notes, 8 September 1678[20]

Mediation. Sir L[eoline] Jenkins, 29 Aug., 2 Sept. [Lawrence] Hyde, 30 Aug., 3 Sept.[21] The two or three points in difference between France and

[18] For a detailed account of the circumstances, see Browning, *Danby,* I, 307–10.

[19] Charles Dormer, 2nd Earl, hereditary Chief Avernor and Keeper of the King's Hawks, had never spoken before in the House, though he had been sitting since 1660. I am grateful to Dr Sheila Lambert for drawing my attention to this speech.

[20] The king was absent at the Newmarket Autumn Meeting. Unfortunately Williamson does not give us the personnel of the committee, nor tell us who took the chair. Its principal role here seems to be to discuss the latest despatches from English envoys abroad and from foreign powers and suggest suitable replies or courses of action for the king's later approval. For the background see K. H. D. Haley, 'English Policy at the Peace Congress of Nijmegen', in *The Peace of Nijmegen 1676–1678/9,* ed. J. A. H. Bots (Amsterdam 1980), pp. 145–55.

[21] Jenkins was England's representative at Nijmegen, Hyde at The Hague.

Spain, that had been proposed to be referred to the king and the states, are by a resolution of the states, as is said, 'evocated', taken singly to themselves, leaving out the king, and not a word of excuse for it towards the king, &c., so as, all the other points having been agreed, the peace is looked on as made, &c.

Denmark and Brandenburg have memorials depending since this day sennight to offer to join with the king, if he will go on with the war, &c.

Now that the peace is as good as signed, nay signed, &c., the ships ordered to be discharged, &c., that were hired to carry over men, &c.; they in Holland are jealous [suspicious] of our troops continuing to be sent over, and even Spain, as if we would keep some of their towns. Stop now put to the men going over, seeing the peace is as good as signed.

Danes' Memorial – In the case put or any other case that shall be found to be the case of his Majesty's treaties with Denmark, the king, as he has always done, will make good whatever he is obliged to by his treaties, &c.

Brandenburg – An answer by letter to be made him. Thank him. He knows how ready the king was to have taken any further measures that should have been useful for the common cause. It did not stick at the king, but elsewhere. That now things have taken another ply abroad. Glad of the Elector's good inclinations to continue united to the king. Shall ever find the king so, &c.

Nimeguen – Sir L. Jenkins to see with the several ministers of the Confederates what instructions they have as to the point of the guarantee of the treaty now to be made. That the king is ready; to know what sort of guarantee, &c. That the king writ so to the Hague, too, Sir W[illiam] Temple having had that point principally in his instructions.

Elector Palatine – Memorial 6 Sept. Send it and commend it by Sir L. Jenkins, and the king will do it to Count Waldstein and Bouillon, &c.

Chichester – The king resolves to hear the matter in Council on his return, of which they shall have notice. In the meantime commands the mayor to take care to preserve the peace, &c., and that it will become the persons excepted against not to act till the matter be heard, &c.[22]

Hague – Sir W. Temple to be minded of the point of the guarantee, whether he hath spoke with the prince, what he says to it, &c. To proceed on it immediately for fear of being prevented by France, &c. Now that the peace between France and Spain is signed or certainly will be so before this comes to hand, Mr Hyde may return; nay must, because of the parliament.

Parliament – Look over the list, and all in Ireland to be early recalled, and so from beyond seas, &c.   *CSPD 1678*, pp. 397–8

[22] The king in fact wrote to the mayor on 14 September (*CSPD 1678*, p. 404). The dispute concerned the improper election of certain additional members to the town's council.

137. The king's speech in Council, 21 April 1679[23]

His Majesty gives you all thanks for your service to him here, and for all the good advices you have given him, which might have been more frequent if the great number of this Council had not made it unfit for the secrecy and dispatch that are necessary in many great affairs. This forced him to use a small number of you in a foreign committee, and sometimes the advice of some few of them (upon such occasions) for many years past. He is sorry for the ill success he has found in this course, and sensible of the ill posture of affairs from that, and some unhappy accidents which have raised great jealousies and dissatisfaction among his good subjects, and thereby left the Crown and government in a condition too weak for those dangers we have reason to fear both at home and abroad.

These his Majesty hopes may yet be prevented by a course of wise and steady counsels for the future . . . To this end he has resolved to lay aside the use he may have hitherto made of any single ministry or private advices, or foreign committees for the general direction of his affairs, and to constitute such a Privy Council as may not only by its number be fit for the consultation and digestion of all business, both domestic and foreign, but also by the choice of them out of the several parts this state is composed of may be best informed in the true constitutions of it, and thereby the most able to counsel him in all the affairs and interests of this Crown and nation. And by the constant advice of such a Council his Majesty is resolved hereafter to govern his kingdoms, together with the frequent use of his Great Council of parliament, which he takes to be the true ancient constitution of this state and government.

Now for the greater dignity of this Council his Majesty resolves their constant number shall be limited to that of thirty, and for their greater authority there shall be fifteen of his chief officers, who shall be privy councillors by their places; and for the other fifteen he will choose ten out of the several ranks of the nobility, and five commoners of the realm whose known abilities, interest and esteem in the nation shall render them without any supposition of either betraying or mistaking the true interests of the kingdom and consequently of advising him ill.

In the first place therefore, and to take care of the Church, his Majesty will have the Archbishop of Canterbury and [the] Bishop of London for the time being; and to inform him well in what concerns the laws, the Lord Chancellor and one of the lord chief justices; for the navy and stores . . . the [Lord High] Admiral and [the] Master of the Ordnance; for the Treasury, the [Lord] Treasurer and [the] Chancellor of the Exchequer (or, whenever any of these charges are in commission, then the first commissioner to serve in their room).

[23] Delivered by the Lord Chancellor.

The rest of the fifteen shall be the lord privy seal, the master of the horse, [the] lord steward and lord chamberlain of his Household, the groom of the stole and the two secretaries of state. And these shall be all the offices of his kingdom to which the dignity of a privy councillor shall be annexed. The other (15) his Majesty has resolved, and hopes he has not chosen ill. His Majesty intends besides to have such princes of his blood as he shall at any time call to this board, being here in court, a president of the Council whenever he shall find it necessary, and the secretary for Scotland . . . But these, being uncertain, he reckons not of the constant number of thirty, which shall never be exceeded.

. . . His Majesty was also pleased to declare that he would have all his affairs here debated freely, of what kind soever they were, and therefore absolutely [in] secrecy. His Majesty was also pleased to declare that he would communicate this alteration of the Council unto both Houses of Parliament in a few words. *EHR*, xxvii (1912), 684–5[24]

138. The Council and the Committee of Intelligence, 1681

Sir Leoline Jenkins, Secretary of State, to his junior colleague the Earl of Conway, 5 October 1681[25]

My Lord Privy Seal . . . [at Council today] was pleased to fall upon the Secretaries of State, for that they did not communicate to the Council those matters of importance that the peace of the kingdoms and the repose of Christendom did depend upon, or to that effect, saying that they came thither to hear news and causes.

Thereupon I took the liberty to assert, that it was the duty of the Secretaries so to manage those correspondencies that his Majesty should direct, and that he should have a constant and punctual account of it; but that they were not at liberty to carry any part of their intelligences to the Council, unless his Majesty directed it specifically so to be done, [and] that I for my part had always governed myself by that rule, because I thought it a duty that lay indispensably upon me.

My Lord was pleased to reply, that Mr Secretary's answer was such an answer as was never offered by a Secretary to a Privy Council before; however that he could not find fault with the answer, for it was constant to the practice of later years. My Lord Falconberg[26] likewise was pleased to allow of what I

---

[24] From 'Inner and Outer Cabinet and Privy Council from William III to George II', by H. W. V. Temperley.

[25] Conway was in attendance on the king, who was again at Newmarket. On this occasion Prince Rupert took the chair.

[26] Apart from Prince Rupert, Lord Privy Seal Anglesey and Jenkins, the councillors present were Falconberg, the Earls of Bath and Craven, and the Archbishop of Canterbury and the Bishop of London, none of them senior ministers; which demonstrates the nature of the problem.

answered, but found fault with the present constitution of the Council, and confessed that it was not a debate proper for this Council. There was nothing resolved on, but that those who found themselves aggrieved with the constitution of the Council as now it is might complain to his Majesty when he returned . . .   *EHR*, xxviii (1913), 131[27]

139. The Privy Council in 1687

[Memoir by the Marquis de Torcy, October 1687]

It is usually held once a week, and the king of England is present. When he has come to a decision in his privy chamber with the ministers he has summoned to him, he imparts it to the Council for form's sake, and they usually have it several days before it is published . . . Besides the Privy Council there is usually another held every Sunday in the king's presence. It is called the Cabinet Council. Despatches are read there, and they deliberate on the answers that are to be sent. Those present at this Council are Prince George [of Denmark], the Lord Chancellor [Jeffreys], the Earl of Sunderland [Lord President], Lord Arundel [Lord Privy Seal], the Earl of Middleton [Secretary of State], Lord Godolphin,[28] the Duke of Ormonde [Lord Steward] and Lord Dartmouth.[29] Mr Bridgeman, the Earl of Sunderland's first secretary, acts as secretary to this Council. The most important business is transacted in the privy chamber of the king of England, and he takes the most important decisions there with Lord Sunderland, Father Petre, or others whom he calls to him.

PRO, 31/3/174, 134

[27] H. W. V. Temperley, 'Documents Illustrating the Powers of the Privy Council in the Seventeenth Century'.

[28] Commissioner of the Treasury and Chamberlain to the Queen. The absence of the First Lord of the Treasury, the Catholic Lord Bellasys, is perhaps meaningful, perhaps not.

[29] Master-General of the Ordnance and Admiral of the Fleet. But he may have sat as one of James's oldest personal friends.

CHAPTER 13

LOCAL GOVERNMENT

The workhorse of local government continued to be the justice of the peace. His duties were multifarious: as well as administering the criminal law in minor cases he executed an increasing number of economic, social and ecclesiastical statutes. He sought out and detained Roman priests, and later Dissenting ministers, he destroyed 'massing stuff' and objects of superstition, he fixed wages, had vagabonds flogged, decided the paternity of bastards, held down the price of corn and other basic foodstuffs, supervised the repair of roads and bridges, protected the manufacture of favoured products like saltpetre, and much, much more. Moreover, he was the king's officer in each locality – often the only one – charged with the exposition and the defence of royal policy, and expected to provide the central government with an unceasing stream of information, especially in the field of 'security'. Before 1640 he had to have a keen eye for papists and separatists, from 1640 to 1660 for 'malignants' and 'delinquents', and after 1660 for republicans and 'Oliverians'. It is not surprising that an active royalist like Sir Peter Leicester delivered charges which read like political tracts (**144**).

However, even if he was chosen by and for the central government, the JP was selected from among a limited number of men, and he was a native of the county and usually of the division of the county for which he acted. The centrifugal tendency of the Commission of the Peace, the danger that its members would come to regard themselves as representatives of the localities against the government, was always present, and James I and Charles I made recurrent efforts to limit their jurisdiction and place them under stricter supervision.

The most convenient agents of supervision were the assize judges, who visited each county at least once a year and met most of the JPs. In 1616 James I, as one manifestation of his abiding interest in the law, chose to harangue the judges in Star Chamber before they departed on circuit (no. **30**, pp. 84–6) above), a practice intermittently maintained through the 1620s, though often by the agency of the Lord Chancellor. The judges were expected to retail the relevant parts of this discourse to the justices of the peace and the grand jury at the subsequent assizes, and since it was not uncommon for more than a hundred freeholders to be impannelled for jury service at any one assize they comprised a sizeable audience of influential men.[1] The articles issued by the judges to the justices in 1618 or thereabouts give a view of some of their activities (**140**); conversely, James I insisted that his judges report in full to the Council on their return, not just use the formulaic 'omnia bene'.

In 1616 and 1617 James went on to review the Commission of the Peace nationwide, removing 142 justices and appointing 209 new ones, though these figures are not all

---

[1] J. S. Morrill, *The Cheshire Grand Jury 1625–1659* (Leicester 1976), pp. 9–12.

that impressive when we remember that there were at least 1,600 men on the Commission.[2] His aim seems to have been increased efficiency, though additions to the bench were not necessarily the right approach; it was a recurrent contemporary complaint that there were too many JPs and not enough of them were active.[3] Prior to 1660 there seems to have been surprisingly little attempt to bring political pressure to bear on JPs, though the reasons are probably to be found in the technical difficulty of carrying out a wholesale purge.[4] In 1626 and 1627 Charles I bore down hard on individual JPs who refused the forced loan, but in the general uproar this particular aspect of the crisis occasioned no adverse comment (see p. 52 above). In 1637 sheriffs were ordered to report to the government all JPs who had refused to pay ship-money or assist in its collection, but apparently the sheriffs ignored it and the matter was forgotten.[5]

However, the period of Charles I's 'personal government' did witness a concerted effort by the central authorities to regularise and re-invigorate the activities of JPs in what we would call the field of social welfare. In times of dearth or plague it had been customary for the government to issue 'books of orders', reminding justices of the need to implement the Poor Laws or impose strict quarantine regulations. The economic crisis of 1629–30, when the stop in trade imposed by the London merchants aggravated the effect of some poor harvests and was accompanied by an epidemic of plague, prompted the Privy Council to do more. In 1630 it issued two books of orders, on dearth and plague, followed in January 1631 by the great Book of Orders, more ambitious and extensive than its predecessors (**141**). Eight basic orders required the justices to meet singly in each hundred once a month and receive the reports of the constables on the administration of the poor laws and take a rough census of the vagabonds and rogues in the district. A series of supplementary directions pointed to methods, statutory or otherwise, for enforcing the law in such cases. Justices were then to report to the sheriff, who would in return report to the assize judges, and they to a special commission of the Privy Council set up for each county. This machinery was strengthened in 1632 by a proclamation ordering all the landed nobility and gentry to repair to their country seats and stay there, busying themselves with local government and the welfare of their social inferiors (**142**). James I had issued similar proclamations, and so had Charles I in 1626, but these had been short-term measures. The proclamation of 1632 was of indefinite duration and strictly enforced.[6]

The policy behind the Book of Orders used to be regarded as an important manifestation of the fussy paternalism of Charles I and Archbishop Laud, or even the mythical policy of 'Thorough' associated with the names of Laud and Strafford. In fact it was initiated and pushed through by the Lord Privy Seal, the Earl of Manchester, and his brother, Lord Montagu, with some assistance from another concerned nobleman, Viscount Wimbledon, and the famous London physician Sir Theodore Mayerne; and

[2] B. W. Quintrell, 'The Making of Charles I's Book of Orders', *EHR*, xcv (1980), 559.

[3] J. H. Gleason, *The Justices of the Peace 1558–1640*, pp. 63–4; G. C. F. Forster, 'The English Local Community and Local Government 1603–25', in Smith, *James VI and I*, pp. 208–9, Cf. Fletcher, *Sussex*, p. 128.

[4] See Glassey, *Politics and the Appointment of Justices*, ch. 1.

[5] Gleason, *op. cit.*, p. 81.

[6] Stone, *Aristocracy*, pp. 397–8.

when every allowance is made for their fear that famine, disease and poor living conditions might lead to acute social disorder it was an impressive attempt to achieve a higher standard of social justice.[7] Its practical effect is difficult to assess, and no doubt varied from county to county according to the zeal and efficiency of the justices and the nature and the seriousness of the problems they faced.[8] As for any political reaction, we must beware of falling into the Whig trap of believing that everything and anything undertaken by the government in the 1630s was received as an attempt to extend central authority and resented accordingly.[9] The enforcement of the apprenticeship regulations was generally unpopular, and no doubt the increased burden of work imposed on magistrates was not exactly welcome, but there was a strong community of interest between Court and Country in keeping the lower classes contented, or at least not discontented. Government pressure was maintained to an extraordinary degree, up to 1635 by the Council and after that by the assize judges, but there is no sign of general dissatisfaction; it certainly did not feature as a grievance in the Long Parliament, and there is some suggestion that the impetus of the Book of Orders continued into the war years.[10] And though this fell away in the Interregnum, the innovation of the petty sessions, in which one justice conducted routine business, was lasting and generally beneficial.

In the Civil Wars and Interregnum the justices of the peace, as a body representing the county's social elite, and its main contact with the government, were overshadowed by the County Committee, though this organ was abandoned or dissolved in most counties after 1649. Royalists who were not removed from the bench tended to hold aloof, and even in 'parliamentary' counties new recruits were usually drawn from a slightly lower social class, lacking the influence of the old guard magistrates.[11] Yet there was certainly no decline in efficiency on the part of the new benches, in some cases the opposite.[12] However, the frequent fluctuations in the nature and structure of central government undoubtedly weakened its control over the localities. The appointment of the major-generals in 1655 must be seen in part as an attempt to overcome that weakness, and it was, of course, a resounding failure (p. 303

[7] Quintrell, art. cit., and Paul Slack, 'Books of Orders: the Making of English Social Policy 1577–1631', 5 TRHS, xxx (1980), 1–22.

[8] Barnes gives a glowing report for Somerset; Somerset 1625–1640, pp. 196–201. So, more generally, does E. M. Leonard, The Early History of English Poor Relief (Cambridge 1900), pp. 194–5, 248–66; in fact, she states that 'the survival of the English system of poor relief is owing to . . . the Book of Orders' (p. 268). W. K. Jordan, Philanthropy in England 1480–1660 (1959), pp. 134–5, is more sceptical, and according to Morrill it was a complete failure in Cheshire, (Cheshire, pp. 247–8).

[9] There are signs of this in Slack, art. cit., pp. 18–21.

[10] Leonard, op. cit., p. 268. Barnes, op. cit., pp. 178–201, gives Somerset a clean bill of health, with the exception of some resentment over apprentices (pp. 184–6). For Lincolnshire Clive Holmes is even more bland; Seventeenth-Century Lincolnshire (Lincoln 1980), pp. 110–12. John Morrill thinks magistrates resented the imposition of uniformity but adduces little evidence; The Revolt of the Provinces (1976), p. 22. For a summary, on the whole favourable, see L. M. Hill, 'County Government in Caroline England', in Russell, Origins, pp. 80–3.

[11] This is the conclusion to be drawn from Fletcher, Sussex, pp. 132–4, 288, 295–6; Morrill, Cheshire, ch. 6 passim; Underdown, Pride's Purge, ch. 10; idem, 'Settlement in the Counties 1653–8', in Aylmer, Interregnum, pp. 165–82. But the question of class is notoriously difficult, see Underdown, 'Community and Class; Theories of Local Politics in the English Revolution', in Barbara C. Malament, ed., After the Reformation (Manchester 1980), pp. 147–65.

[12] Aylmer, State's Servants, pp. 305–17. Morrill is emphatically of the opinion that the Cheshire bench was more active and successful than its pre-war counterpart (Cheshire, pp. 233–53), and there is some suggestion of this in Sussex (Fletcher, Sussex, p. 115).

above). With the re-establishment of the old guard magistracy, which is one of the least noticed results of the Restoration,[13] this independence of central government was confirmed, and it was accentuated by the loss of Star Chamber and the decline in the prestige and thus the authority of the Privy Council. There was a kind of informal truce between the capital and the provinces which some have seen as an unholy alliance. One of its manifestations was the Poor Law of 1662, the notorious Act of Settlement, which divided the nation into the landed sheep and the landless goats. The latter could now be removed from the parish in which they were settled back to the parish of their birth if they were in danger of being a charge on the rates, even if they were able and willing to work, and according to one critic the act 'made the most effectual and extensive invasion of the rights of Englishmen which had ever been attempted since the Conquest'.[14]

A similar distinction between landowners and the rest was made by the Game Act of 1671 (**143**), the most stringent and comprehensive of the famous game laws. It gave gamekeepers the power to enter the houses to search for guns, nets and sporting dogs, which those below the rank of esquire were forbidden to own; it gave a single justice – often the landowner concerned – power to award summary punishment, and the decision of Quarter Sessions, staffed by the neighbouring landowners, was final. Such blatant class legislation confirmed the social ascendancy of the squirearchy, but in the end their administration of the game laws, 'grossly partial, selfishly biased, and swayed by consideration of their own class interest even to the verge of corruption', wrecked the reputation of the rural justices and in the long term made an important contribution to their ultimate downfall.[15]

Charles II and James II would probably have cared little for all this if the country interest had not shown a tendency to coalesce into an obstructive force at Westminster as a Country Party. As it was, several Country Party JPs were removed in Kent and Norfolk in 1677 and 1678, as the preliminary to a more thoroughgoing purge carried out over the winter of 1679–80, and renewed in the summer after the receipt of reports from the assize judges. It was carried out in a businesslike manner by a committee consisting of the Lord Chancellor, the Lord President and the secretaries of state, presumably acting on the advice of the lord lieutenants as well as the judges, and a further purge was carried out in 1681. Here as in most aspects of local government the authorities were hampered by bureaucratic inertia at Whitehall and by sheer ignorance; it was difficult to tell which men were actually on the Commission of the Peace for any given county, or which had died, let alone what their party complexion was; and this led to a sprinkling of paradoxical errors, with some Whigs being dismissed, others retained, others even inserted. But after a further comb-out in 1682–3 there is no doubt that Charles II had attained a loyal and compliant magistracy.[16]

[13] In fact, this old guard began to filter back in some counties with the establishment of a more monarchical Protectorate in 1657; in Sussex the process even began in 1656. See Fletcher, *Sussex*, pp. 311, 316, and Underdown, *Somerset*, pp. 185–6.

[14] Qu. Sidney and Beatrice Webb, *English Local Government*, VII (*English Poor Law History*, pt I), 321. Extracts from the act are printed in Browning, *Documents*, p. 464.

[15] Webb, *op. cit.*, I (*Parish and County*), 597–9. See P. B. Munsche, *Gentlemen and Poachers: the English Game Laws 1671–1831* (Cambridge 1981).

[16] Glassey, *op. cit.*, pp. 10–12, 45–57 *passim*.

This improved control was largely exercised through the lord lieutenant. His authority had been enhanced by Charles I's search for an 'Exact Militia', from 1625 to 1638. He had never attained it, and it had proved a source of friction between himself and the landed classes which was quite as important as ship-money and perhaps more so.[17] But it did cause him to choose his county lieutenants with care, and his decision in 1625 to give them the right to appoint their own deputy lieutenants was an important accretion of patronage and enhanced their status in the eyes of the county.

After 1660 the military effectiveness of the militia if anything declined; cetainly it failed James II in Monmouth's Rebellion in 1685, and he decided to abandon it.[18] Though we should not forget that in one important respect its authority was crucial; after Venner's Rising in 1661 Charles II took good care of the Lieutenancy of London, and it enabled him to keep control of the capital throughout the Exclusion Crisis.[19] And if his military status declined, the civilian powers of the lord lieutenant steadily increased. He became the prime channel through which government patronage at local level – magistracies, mining rights, leases of Crown lands, governorships of forts and castles – was distributed. Great care was taken in his appointment, and he was almost invariably a substantial landowner in his county, and usually the head of an old-established noble family (see p. 415 above). His vice-regal status implied permanence, and by convention he was only removable for lunacy or gross disloyalty; in some counties the office was virtually hereditary in one family.[20] But in 1673 and 1674 Charles II was prompt to remove the Duke of Buckingham and the Earl of Shaftesbury from their lieutenancies when they went into opposition, and the remaining Whig lord lieutenants were removed during the Exclusion Crisis or immediately afterwards.

Thus the lord lieutenant, with his hand-picked deputies, and the senior county justices in whose appointment he had usually participated, constituted a remarkably powerful and stable political machine. A man with the wealth and prestige of a Duke of Norfolk was almost supreme in his dukedom, able, with a suitable show of consultation, to choose parliamentary candidates almost at will, and able, too, to give the leadership badly needed by the gentry at times of national crisis (146). This system reached its apogee in the parliamentary elections of 1685, when the government's success owed almost everything to a concerted drive by the nobility and the senior county gentry, led by their lord lieutenants.[21]

From the beginning the Restoration government displayed an unprecedented interest in elections, and especially borough elections. In view of later events it is

---

[17] Lindsay Boynton, *The Elizabethan Militia 1558–1638* (1967), ch. 8 *passim*, esp. pp. 244–57, 275, 287–91. For the acute friction arising from the Crown's demand that the counties pay the muster masters, see A. Hassell Smith, 'Militia Rates and Militia Statutes 1558–1663', in *The English Commonwealth 1547–1640*, ed. Peter Clark *et al.* (Leicester 1979), pp. 93–110, and Esther S. Cope, 'Politics without Parliament: the Dispute about Muster Masters' Fees in Shropshire in the 1630s', *HLQ*, XLV (1982), 271–84. Notice that the Commons were arguing with James I about muster masters as early as 1606, p. 59 above.

[18] John Miller, 'The Militia and the Army in the Reign of James II', *HJ*, XVI (1973), 659–79.

[19] David Allen, 'The Role of the London Trained Bands in the Exclusion Crisis 1678–81', *EHR*, LXXXVII (1972), 287–303.

[20] J. R. Western, *Monarchy and Revolution* (1972), p. 49.

[21] R. H. George, 'Parliamentary Elections and Electioneering in 1685', 4 *TRHS*, XIX (1936), 167–95.

significant that James, Duke of York, was closely associated with the efforts which were made in the 1660s to bring the parliamentary boroughs under closer control from Whitehall.[22] Parliament frustrated the government's attempt to perpetuate the powers of the commissioners appointed under the Corporation Act for three years to regulate the corporations (p. 337 above), and without them the act proved difficult to enforce, but they never gave up entirely. In 1668 orders were issued for the strict enforcement of the act, and a decision made in 1663 to issue writs of *quo warranto* against boroughs which had not renewed their charters since the Restoration seems to have been carried out, at least in part.[23] In 1681 a really determined effort was made to enforce the Act, and the clause was invoked which allowed the county justices to act if the borough failed to put its own house in order (p. 352 above). In 1682 began the famous campaign by writs of *quo warranto*, which led to the forfeiture of 62 charters by the end of the reign. The new charters gave the king the right to remove members of corporations, though not usually to nominate replacements.

The prolonged and bitter resistance put up by the City of London,[24] and the pious horror with which these proceedings were regarded after the Revolution of 1688, have tended to leave us with an impression of aggressive and bullying violence. However, though Bristol at first refused, it gave way in 1684, and outside London no other city put up more than a token resistance. True, it was touch and go for a time at Norwich, and the Earl of Yarmouth, the Lord Lieutenant, had to bring all his influence to bear; but in most cases local magnates easily persuaded 'their' boroughs to comply (then flaunted their success at Whitehall), and most members of corporations hoped by a ready compliance to secure extra privileges for their towns and thereby confirm their own ascendancy.[25] The negotiations between the Earl of Huntingdon and the corporation of Leicester are typical enough (**145**).

Emboldened by his brother's success, James II made an even more vigorous attempt to mould the localities to his will. Parting company with the Church of England in 1686, in the following winter he embarked on a thorough revision of the Commission of the Peace with the aim of including as many Catholic gentry and office holders as possible, though the former were often disabled from acting because of the government's neglect to add a clause dispensing them from the provisions of the Test Act.[26] In the autumn of 1687 the lord lieutenants were ordered to put to the deputy lieutenants and JPs in their county the notorious Three Questions: would they live in amity with their neighbours, of whatever religious persuasion; if elected to parliament, would they support the repeal of the Test Acts; or would they support the election of candidates so minded? The returns, mainly adverse, provoked a further remodelling of the magistracy, and the wholesale dismissal of deputy lieutenants and

---

[22] Western, *op. cit.*, pp. 70ff.; J. H. Sacret, 'The Restoration Government and the Municipal Corporations', *EHR*, XLV (1930), 232–59. However, John Miller now argues that Charles II's purpose (as distinct from James II's) was not to influence parliamentary elections but simply to regain control of local government; 'The Crown and the Boroughs in the Reign of Charles II', *EHR*, C (1985), 53–84.

[23] G. C. F. Forster, 'Government in Provincial England under the Later Stuarts', 5 *TRHS*, XXXIII (1983), 44–6.

[24] Jennifer Levin, *The Charter Controversy in the City of London 1660–1668* (1969).

[25] John T. Evans, *Seventeenth-Century Norwich* (Oxford 1979), pp. 280–92; Western, *op. cit.*, p. 74; Levin, *op. cit.*, ch. 6.

[26] Glassey, *op. cit.*, pp. 70–7; Miller, *Popery and Politics*, pp. 269–72.

lord lieutenants. By the end of the year 14 lord lieutenants had been replaced, usually by Catholics.[27] At the same time James began regulating the charters of corporations where he had the power, and issuing further writs of *quo warranto* where he did not.

The effectiveness of this campaign in securing a compliant parliament must always be doubtful, because the elections for his next parliament were never held. In fact, James only proceeded against half the parliamentary corporations, and remodelling of their membership did not necessarily affect the franchise and therefore the outcome of a parliamentary election.[28] He was probably relying too much on the example of the election of 1685, though at the same time he was destroying the loyalist alliance in the provinces which had made that victory possible.[29] On a practical level the decision to replace the 9th Earl of Derby as Lord Lieutenant of Lancashire by an obscure Irish Catholic nobleman, Caryll, Viscount Molyneux, made no sense, and the decision to make the Duke of Newcastle Lord Lieutenant of Yorkshire as well as Nottingham-shire left the former county wide open in 1688.

But it is apparent that James's government was still hampered at every turn by lack of information on the localities. This was one of the primary difficulties of government throughout the century, and though it is true that James's own purges, of the judiciary as well as the magistracy, had cut off many reliable sources of information, to a great extent it was a problem he had inherited. It is apparent, for instance, that no seventeenth–century government even possessed a record of the various parliamentary boroughs and their franchises; nor did the House of Commons. As a result in 1688, for the first time in the modern era, the government made a determined effort to secure this and similar information. In April 1688 agents were despatched from London to recruit support for the government in the localities and establish correspondents in each town and county who would disseminate govern-ment propaganda, verbal or printed. They were asked to report on the parliamentary franchise, to identify the local leaders who got out the vote, to assess the effectiveness of the 'regulation' of boroughs and to test the loyalty of local customs and excise officers. In August, with an election in the offing, they were sent out again (**147**). Their reports arrived too late to benefit James, and it seems that they were not even received into the government archives;[30] so after the Revolution governments were in the same state of ignorance as their predecessors. On the other hand, though James's electoral activities and his interference in local government were sharply criticised in William's Declaration of 30 September 1688, the Bill of Rights contained no direct reference to them, and no legislation was passed to prevent a recurrence.[31] It was clearly felt that James's activities had been so unconventional and contrary to custom that they could be safely ignored.

[27] Glassey, *op. cit.*, pp. 77ff. The returns of answers to the Three Questions are analysed by John Carswell, *The Descent on England* (1969), App. A.

[28] Western, *op. cit*, p. 72. Levin, *op. cit.*, p. 113, prints a useful list of parliamentary boroughs whose charters were *not* remodelled 1681–8.

[29] In any case there was a limit to compliance even in 1685, and the government could not place its candidates at will. See *CSPD 1685*, nos. 92, 381, 393, 410, 489, 520.

[30] Some disappeared, others remained in the possession of William Bridgeman, under-secretary to the Southern department. These are now in the Bodleian Library, and were printed by Sir George Duckett in 1882.

[31] Williams, *Eighteenth-Century Constitution*, nos. **2**, **10**.

140. The assize judges' Instruction to Justices of the Peace, 1618

Directions for the Justices, whereof we expect an account at the next Assize, because we are to give an account to the King of our proceedings in this and other things

1. To levy the 12*d*. [fine] upon absentees from Church according [to] the statutes of 1 Elizabeth c. 2 and 3 James [c. 4].

2. Inquire of such as attribute any jurisdiction or pre-eminence to the Pope or See of Rome within the king's dominions.

3. They are to be careful that the constables and churchwardens of every parish once every year present to them at their Quarter Sessions the names of all recusants within their several parishes, with the names of all their children above nine years old and the names of all their servants, retainers or sojourners in their houses and for how many months they have kept such servants, sojourners and retainers that are recusants.

4. To urge the oath of allegiance to all recusants in their several divisions, to summon them by warrant to appear before them at a fit time and place, to return the names of such as make default to appear before you at the next coming of the judges of assize.

5. It is required that they be careful and diligent to execute the statutes of raising money to the relief of the poor which cannot work, for buying hemp, flax, wool and other necessaries to set them to work which are able, and to bind children apprentices whose parents are not able to breed them well, and to take yearly account of churchwardens and overseers.

6. For suppressing of all wanderers and rogues a strict account to be taken by them of the several constables and officers how rogues be punished, and that watches be straitly set for that purpose.

7. The house of correction to be established with all things fitting, and once a year a strict account to be taken of the maintaining the stock.

8. That the Statute for Labourers be duly observed for servants and day labourers. Dissolute or idle servants to be sent to the house of correction.

9. That no alehouse be suffered without licence.[32]

10. The licenced to be bound according to law.

11. That alehousekeepers and their sureties be sufficient.

12. All recognisances to be returned to the Clerk of the Peace.

13. Prosecution to be made upon presentments against alehousekeepers.

14. Not to license retainers, officers, recusants or bailiffs of hundreds to keep alehouse[s]; or any dwelling in any unfitting places, but in the heart of the town, not in corners.

15. In towns that are not thoroughfares few or no alehouses [to be allowed].

---

[32] For the establishment's obsession with alehouses, which dictated clauses 9–17, see Peter Clark, *The English Alehouse 1200–1830* (1983), ch. 8.

16. That inns, taverns and alehouses keep the assize for selling drink according to the statute.

17. No alehousekeepers to suffer the people of that town to tipple in their houses, nor to bear with alehouse-haunters, but to execute the law upon them both.

18. To be careful for repair of bridges and highways according to the laws.

19. Allow whom you think fit to brew and bake for poor artificers and housekeepers.

20. Alehousekeepers to be allowed by justices of the same hundred where they dwell and to be certified to the Clerk of the Peace; and no other justices to meddle therewith unless it be in open Sessions.

B. W. Quintrell, ed., *Proceedings of the Lancashire Justices of the Peace at the Sheriff's Table during Assize Week 1578–1694*, Proceedings Lancashire and Cheshire Record Society, CXXXX (1981), pp. 176–7

141. The Book of Orders, 5 January 1631

Orders and Directions, together with a Commission for the better administration of justice and more perfect information of his Majesty, how and by whom the laws and statutes tending to the relief of the poor, the well-ordering and training up of youth in trades, and the reformation of disorders and disordered persons are executed throughout the kingdom . . .

[The Commission]

Charles, by the Grace of God . . . [etc.], to . . . [all the members of the Privy Council], Greeting.

Whereas divers good laws and statutes, most necessary for these times, have during the happy reign of Queen Elizabeth and of our late Father of blessed memory, and since our coming to the crown of England, been with great wisdom, piety and policy made and enacted in parliament, as well for the charitable relief of aged and impotent poor people, not able by their labours to get their livings, and for the training up of youth in honest and profitable trades and mysteries, by putting them forth to be apprentices, as also for the setting to work of idle persons, who being of ability to work in some kind or other do nevertheless refuse to labour, and either wander up and down the city and country begging, or which is worse, maintain themselves by filching and stealing; and for the punishment of sundry rogues and vagabonds, and setting of them to work; and for the suppressing of that odious and loathsome sin of drunkenness, and the repressing of idleness, the root of so many evils, the due execution of which, and the like laws and statutes, would prevent and cut off many offences and crimes of high nature.

And whereas we are informed that the defect of the execution of the said good and politic laws and constitutions in that behalf made proceedeth especially from the neglect of duty in some of our justices of the peace and other officers . . . to whom the care and trust of seeing the said laws be put in execution is . . . principally committed, which remissness and neglect of duty doth grow and arise from this: that by the most of the said laws there are little or no penalties or forfeiture at all inflicted upon the said justices . . . for not performing their duties in that behalf; or if any be, yet partly by reason of the smallness thereof, and partly by reason of their power and authority in their several places, whereby they hold others under them in awe, there are few or no complaints or informations made of the neglects and want of due execution of the offices of the said justices . . . And although the care and diligence of our judges and justices of assize be never so great, yet by reason of the shortness of the assizes and sessions in every county, and multiplicity of business, they neither have due information of the said neglects, nor in those times can take such exact courses as were requisite for redress of such general abuses and inconveniences so highly importing the public good of this our realm, . . . by reason whereof the said justices of peace . . . are now of late in most parts of this our kingdom grown secure in their said negligence, and the said politic and necessary laws and statutes laid aside or little regarded, as laws of small use or consequence . . .

Know ye therefore that we . . . have constituted, authorised and appointed you to be our commissioners, and by these presents do . . . strictly require you, . . . either by examination upon oath, or by all and every such good and lawful means as to you . . . shall seem convenient and requisite from time to time henceforth, to make inquiries, and thereby to inform yourselves how all and every the laws and statutes now in force which any way concern the relief of impotent or poor people, . . . the punishment or setting to work of rogues and vagabonds, . . . the repressing of drunkenness and idleness, the reforming of abuses committed in inns and alehouses, . . . the keeping of watches and wards duly, and how other public services for God, the king and the Common-wealth, are put into practice and executed . . .

★   ★   ★

And we do further by these presents give full power and authority unto you, or any six or more of you, to call unto you for your assistance in the premises . . . all or any of our justices of assize, . . . and to give such directions and instructions . . . as well to our said justices of assize, oyer and terminer and gaol delivery for their several circuits, as also to our justices, mayors, bailiffs and other head officers within cities and boroughs, clerks of the assize and sessions, and other officers . . . as to you . . . shall seem meet and requisite and shall be agreeable to the laws and statutes of this our realm, for the better execution of the laws and statutes in the time to come . . .

And we do hereby further will and require you, that you . . . give unto us a particular and true information of the care and industry of our justices of the peace . . . as upon the said inquiry you shall find diligent in putting the said laws, statutes, orders and directions in execution; . . . and if contrariwise you shall find any of our said justices of peace . . . negligent and remiss in their . . . performance and execution of the said laws and statutes committed to their charge, or the orders and directions given by you, . . . then our pleasure is that you do likewise certify the names of such as you shall find so remiss and negligent, that accordingly order may be taken for their removing and displacing out of the Commission of the Peace, as men unworthy of their said trust and places, as also deserving such further punishment in our court of Star Chamber or otherwise as may by law be inflicted upon them.

★ ★ ★

[The commissioners were authorised to appoint deputies in every county and borough.]

Orders
I

That the justices of peace of every shire within the realm do divide themselves, and allot amongst themselves what justices of the peace, and what hundreds, shall attend monthly at some certain places of the shire. And at this day and place the high constables, petty constables and churchwardens and overseers for the poor of those hundreds shall attend the said justices. And there inquiry shall be made and information taken by the justices how every of these officers in their several places have done their duties in execution of the laws mentioned in the commission annexed, and what persons have offended against any of the said laws.

II

Where neglect or defect is found in any of the said officers in making their presentments condign punishment [is] to be inflicted upon them by the justices according to law.

★ ★ ★

V

For encouragement to men that do inform and prosecute others for offending against these laws or any of them, liberty [is] to be left to the justices of peace . . . to reward the informer or prosecutor out of part of the money levied upon his or their presentments or information.

Though the statute[s] do not prescribe this, yet this is not against the law that gives the penalty to the poor, which penalty nor no part thereof would else come unto the poor but by this means.

VI

That the several justices of peace of every shire do once every three months certify and account in writing to the high sheriff of the county of their proceedings in this way . . .

VII

That the high sheriff, within fourteen days after this account delivered, do send the same over to the justices of assize for that county, or to one of them, and the justice or justices that receive the same [are] to certify it in the beginning of every term next after to the lords commissioners . . .

Directions

★　★　★

II

That stewards to lords and gentlemen, in keeping their leets twice a year, do specially inquire upon those articles that tend to the reformation and punishment of common offences and abuses: as of bakers and brewers, for breaking of assizes; of forestallers and regraters; against tradesmen of all sorts for selling with underweights or at excessive prices, or things unwholesome, or things made in deceit; of people, breakers of houses, common thieves and their receivers; haunters of taverns or alehouses; those that go in good clothes and fare well, and none knows whereof they live; those that be night walkers; builders of cottages and takers in of inmates; offences of victuallers, artificers, workmen and labourers.

★　★　★

V

That the weekly taxations for relief of the poor . . . be in these times of scarcity raised to higher rates in every parish than in times tofore were used; and contributions had from other parishes to help the weaker parishes, especially from those places where depopulations have been . . .

★　★　★

IX

If in any parish there be found any persons that live out of service, or that live idly and will not work for reasonable wages, or live to spend all they have at the alehouse, those persons to be brought by the high constables and petty constables to the justices at their meeting, there to be ordered and punished as shall be found fit.

X

That the correction houses in all counties may be made adjoining to the common prisons, and the gaoler to be made governor of them, that so he may employ to work prisoners committed for final causes, and so they may learn honestly by labour, and not live idly and miserably long in prison, whereby they are made worse when they come out than they were when they went in . . .

XI

That no man harbour rogues in their [sic] barns or out-housings; and the wandering persons with women and children [are] to give account to the constable or justice of peace where they were married, and where their children were christened; for these people live like savages, neither marry, nor bury nor christen, which licentious liberty makes so many delight to be rogues and wanderers.

* * *

142. A proclamation commanding the gentry to keep their residence at their mansions in the country, and forbidding them to make their habitatations in London and places adjoining, 20 June 1632

The king's most excellent Majesty hath observed that of late years a great number of the nobility and gentry, and abler sort of his people, with their families, have resorted to the cities of London and Westminster, and places adjoining, and there made their residence more than in former times, contrary to the ancient usage of the English nation, which hath occasioned divers inconveniences. For where[as] by their residence and abiding in the several counties where their means ariseth, they served the king in several places according to their degree and ranks, in aid of the government, whereby, and by their housekeeping in those parts, the realm was defended and the meaner sort of people were guided, directed and relieved; but by their residence in the said cities . . . they have not employment, but live without doing any service to his Majesty or his people, a great part of their money and substance is drawn from the several counties whence it ariseth, and is spent in the city in excess of apparel provided from foreign parts, to the enriching of other nations and unnecessary consumption of a great part of the treasure of this realm, and in other delights and expenses, even to the wasting of their estates, which is not issued into the parts whence it ariseth, nor are the people of them relieved therewith or by their hospitality, nor yet set on work, as they might and would be were it not for the absence of the principal men out of their counties, and the excessive use of foreign commodities. By this occasion also . . . the prices of all kind of victuals, both in the said cities and divers other places from whence those cities are served are exceedingly increased, and the several counties undefended, the poorer sort are unrelieved, and not guided or governed as they might be in case those persons of quality and respect resided among them.

⋆   ⋆   ⋆

Therefore his Majesty doth straitly charge and command his lords, both spiritual and temporal, the lieutenants and deputy-lieutenants of counties, justices assigned for conservation of the peace, baronets, knights, esquires and gentlemen, and clerks having benefices with cure, or prebends or dignities in cathedral or collegiate churches, and all other his Majesty's subjects of the several parts of the realm that have mansion houses and places of residence in other parts, and are not of his Majesty's Council, or bound to daily attendance on his Highness, his dearest consort the queen, or their children, that before the end of forty days next after the publishing of this proclamation . . . they with their families depart from the cities of London and Westminster, suburbs and liberties thereof, and places adjoining, and resort to the several counties where they usually resided, and there keep their habitations and hospitality, attend their services, and be ready for the defence and guidance of those parts, as their callings, degrees and abilities shall extend, upon such pains as are to be inflicted upon those that shall neglect the public service and defence of the realm, in contempt of his Majesty's royal command; and that as well those hereby commanded to return to their several counties as those which are already there do upon the same pains continue the residence of themselves and their families there . . .

And . . . his Majesty doth charge and command the lord mayor of the city of London, and the aldermen . . . and the justices . . . that of every of them make special observation of all those that shall be disobedient to this our command, and from time to time present their names to some of our counsel learned, whom we do command to take due examination or notice of the qualities of their offences, and to cause prosecution to be had against them in our court of Star Chamber, or any other our courts of justice, as the case shall require . . .

Finally, his Majesty doth hereby declare, that it is his firm resolution to withstand this great and growing evil by all just ways, and by a constant severity towards the offenders in that behalf; for which cause his Majesty doth give this timely warning that none do hereafter presume to offend, nor put themselves to unnecessary charge in providing themselves to return in winter to the said cities and places adjacent, but that they conform themselves to this his royal commandment as they tender their duties to his Majesty, or the good and welfare of their counties and themselves. *SRP*, II, no. 159

143. The Game Act, 1671

22 & 23 Car. II, c. 25: *An Act for the better preservation of the game and for securing warrens not enclosed and the several fishings of this realm*

Whereas divers disorderly persons, laying aside their lawful trades and employments, do betake themselves to the stealing, taking and killing of conies,[33] hares, pheasants, partridges and other game intended to be preserved by former laws, with guns, dogs, tramells,[34] lowbells,[35] hays,[36] and other nets, snares, hare-pipes and other engines, to the great damage of this realm, and prejudice of noblemen, gentlemen and lords of manors and other owners of warrens; for remedy whereof be it enacted . . . that all lords of manors or other royalties not under the degree of esquire may from henceforth by writings under their hands and seals authorise one or more gamekeeper or gamekeepers within their respective manors or royalties, who . . . may take and seize all such guns, bows, greyhounds, setting dogs, lurchers or other dogs to kill hares or conies, ferrets, trammels, lowbells, hays or other nets, hare-pipes, snares or other engines for the taking and killing of conies, hares, pheasants, partridges or other game as within the precincts of such respective manors shall be used by any person or persons who by this act are prohibited to keep or use the same. And moreover that the said gamekeeper or gamekeepers . . . may in the daytime search the houses, outhouses or other places of any such person or persons by this act prohibited to keep or use the same, as upon good ground shall be suspected to have or keep in his or their custody any guns, bows . . . [dogs, nets, etc., as above], and the same . . . to seize, detain and keep, to and for the use of the lord of the manor . . ., or otherwise to cut in pieces or destroy, as things by this act prohibited to be kept by persons of their degree.

II. And it is hereby enacted and declared that all and every person and persons not having lands and tenements, or some other estate of inheritance in his own or his wife's right, of the clear yearly value of one hundred pounds *per annum* or for term of life, or having lease or leases of ninety-nine years or for

---

[33] Rabbits. [34] A semi-permanent net, with side walls and a roof; for birds.
[35] A bell used to lure birds at night. [36] A specialised kind of rabbit net.

any longer term of the clear yearly value of one hundred and fifty pounds, other than the son and heir apparent of an esquire, or other person of higher degree, and the owners and keepers of forests, parks, chases or warrens, being stocked with deer or conies for their necessary use . . ., are hereby declared to be persons by the laws of this realm not allowed to have or keep for themselves or any other person or persons any guns, bows . . . [dogs, nets, etc., as above], but shall be and are hereby prohibited to have, keep or use the same.

[§§ III–IV made it an offence to take rabbits in or near warrens; for offences committed in the warren itself the punishment was treble damages and three months' imprisonment. §§ VI–VII made it an offence to fish protected rivers, weirs, fishponds, etc., and gave justices power to destroy the offenders' equipment.]

VIII. Provided always . . . that if any person or persons shall find him or themselves aggrieved by any judgment that shall happen to be given by any justice of the peace by virtue of this act, it shall and may be lawful for such person or persons so aggrieved to appeal unto the justices of peace in their general Quarter Sessions . . . And such judgment, order or determination as by the said justices shall be made upon the said appeal shall be final to all intents and purposes whatsoever, if no title to land, royalty or fishery be therein concerned.

IX. Provided always . . . that neither this act nor anything therein contained shall extend or be construed to extend to the taking away or abridging of any royalty or prerogative royal of his Majesty, nor to abridge, change or alter any part of the Forest Laws of this realm . . . SR, v, 745–6

144. Sir Peter Leicester's charge to the grand jury at Nether Knotsford, Cheshire, 2 October 1677

The power, office and jurisdiction of justices of peace (saith the Lord Coke . . .) is such a form of subordinate government for the tranquillity and quiet of this realm as no part of the Christian world hath the like, if duly executed; here the streams of justice flow to every man's door. Indeed, the due administration of justice is the main pillar which supports a kingdom, for by justice is the throne established; and not only so, but it renders it also glorious and flourishing in the eyes of others, for justice exalts a nation.

Now administration of justice supposeth a law, whereby justice may be administered; punishment to the transgressors and protection to the innocent; for which there is no law there can be no transgression. And the law always supposeth a power to compel obedience thereunto . . ., the law hath in itself, or carries along with it, a forcing power; for otherwise it cannot be put in execution, and then it is all one, as if it were no law.

It is therefore the sovereign power which supporteth the laws, and that is our Sovereign Lord the king . . . The laws have not their maintenance from the parliament, as some of the late seditious pamphlets do falsely suggest to the people, but from the king; for it is he that makes judges and justices of peace and other officers, for the better execution of the laws; and the power of all the forces in this kingdom are [sic] in the king, as one of his most just and undoubted prerogatives, which we may read in the preamble of the statute of 12 Car. II, c. 6.[37] And therefore, having *jus gladii* only in himself, he is both the prime author and preserver of our laws – nay, it is no longer a law than the supreme power is pleased to allow it so, because he uncontrollable in his actions, and hath no lawful superior on each to control him.

And this power is given him from God, and therefore due to him *jure divino*; wherefore the king is called by the Apostle[38] Θεοῦ διάκονὸς, God's officer or minister, not the people's officer; neither doth he bear the sword in vain. And St Peter strictly chargeth us[39] to submit ourselves to all mankind in authority in regard of the Lord (for so the words in the original do properly signify and import) . . .

We see then the supreme power lodged in his Majesty *jure divino*, by the law of God. Let us now see how it is lodged in him *jure humano*, by the laws of our nation . . .

[And he embarks on a long review of English history, with special emphasis on the illegal encroachments of the bishop of Rome and the conspiracies fomented by his emissaries, culminating in Gunpowder Plot.]

And ever since have these engineers been continually hatching new devices for stirring up rebellions in our nation, and to disturb the peace of Israel. In the reign of King Charles I there was a sort of sectaries called Puritans, these were tickled in the ears by the Jesuits, that the ceremonies of our Church were popish, and that our bishops intended to bring in popery, which animated that party so far that they raised a rebellion against the king, having some principal men to head the faction, and countenanced by some members of the parliament, A.D. 1640, which at last ended with an execrable murder of the said king under the specious show of a court of justice, and then [they] banished his children and set up Oliver Cromwell, called the Protector, 1655. All this we have seen acted with our own eyes.

And now at this present how many Jesuitical pamphlets are daily scattered among the people to ensnare weaker judgments, and to draw them on to raise a new rebellion? And how many kinds of sectaries have we now amongst us, and numerous parties of each sort? To wit, Presbyterians, Anabaptists, Independents, Quakers, and I know not what; all fed by the Jesuitical party now

---

[37] The Militia Act of 1661, no. **102**, p. 349 above.   [38] Paul, Rom. xiii. 4.   [39] 1 Pet. ii. 13.

lurking in every corner of our kingdom, and following the humours and inclinations of the persons everywhere, as they find them to stand affected according to the several sects, purposely to make divisions amongst us, yet all agreeing in this, that they separate from the Church of England and betake themselves into private conventicles, each sect apart by themselves; and hence it was that the statute against seditious conventicles was enacted, 22 Car. II, 1670.[40] But now these sectaries grow so numerous that they build themselves meeting-houses for their own party almost everywhere, to the confronting of authority and the scandal of the true Protestant religion . . .

And therefore, gentlemen, that I may draw to an end (for I hasten), what remains but the counterplotting of these engineers, who are continually undermining the peace both of our Church and state? I mean our old implacable enemies the papists, with all their new enchanted crew of sectaries of all sorts, which will best be done by the putting of all the laws made against them into speedy execution, whereunto we ourselves, every justice of peace in his station, must make it his business strictly to find them out; for the country people are generally so rotten that they will not complain of them, though they see and know of these seditious meetings before their eyes daily.

★   ★   ★

Chetham Society, 3rd ser., v (1953), 87–91

145. Leicester surrenders its Charter, 1684

[Leicester had been a parliamentary stronghold during the Civil Wars, electing radical, even republican MPs, and it was obviously mistrusted by the Restoration government, which in 1661 allowed the franchise to be broadened to include all the freemen. The corporation was also extensively remodelled in 1662 by the commissioners appointed under the Corporation Act, and it received a new charter in 1665. By the 1670s Theophilus, 7th Earl of Huntingdon, had the predominant outside influence on the borough, but at a by-election in 1677 the corporation declined to accept his candidate, the Tory Heneage Finch, and he threatened them then with a *quo warranto*. To the Exclusion Parliaments the corporation steadily returned two local candidates who usually voted against the government, though they cannot be classified as extreme, and the issue was complicated by the sudden adhesion of Huntingdon himself to the Whig cause. However, he soon repented, and by 1683 he was assiduously working is way back into royal favour. He took the precaution of securing a writ of *quo warranto*, to be held in reserve, but he and his local agent, Dr John Geary, Archdeacon of Stow, easily persuaded the corporation to surrender voluntarily, in the hope of regaining their sole right of election.][41]

[40] No. 106, p. 356 above.
[41] R. W. Greaves, 'The Earl of Huntingdon and the Leicester Charter of 1684', *HLQ*, xv (1952), 371–91; *The House of Commons 1660–1690*, ed. Basil Duke Henning (1983), I, 296–7; *Victoria County History: Leicestershire*, IV, 114–18.

Earl of Huntingdon to Dr John Geary, 6 September 1684

. . . I give you many thanks for your great care about the business at Leicester. Whatever you lay out in wine, letters or other charges put to my account. All corporations of England have surrendered and even the most factious, and all are generally subject to the *quo warrantos*, and it is probable such writs will issue against the refusers with greater disadvantage, and if Leicester do surrender, if they desire any enlargement of privileges I believe they may be obtained. For myself, who have the nomination of Steward and Bailiff . . ., I shall readily submit that to the king, from whom I doubt not of confirmation; and I would advise them to consider that it would be a thing of very dangerous consequence and ill report if upon a debate the thing should be rejected, and you may let them know it will be much to their advantage than otherwise if they can be made better . . .

Geary to Huntingdon, 10 September 1684

The last from your Lordship of the 6th of this instant came by a special messenger to my hand upon the 8th, which was the day appointed by the Mayor for the determination of their concern in hand. For I perceived nothing would be done till the merry day was over, which was Friday last [5th]. The Companies and their wives being at the Angel, nothing that day appeared but loyalty to the king and good wishes to your Honour, and I taking the boldness upon my own account to send Mrs Mayoress a gallon of sack to drink your Lordship's health, some others did the like, which made the good women spend sweetly that day. Since, a Hall being called, and the surrendering of the charter put to the vote, it went for it, but only four votes against it. They were Bentley, Brooksby, Harris and Bent. I fear others were well wishers but durst not appear. At Michaelmas, at the coming back of his Majesty [from Newmarket], I conclude they will wait upon your Honour, all attesting their great zeal to your Lordship's noble family. I found there was nothing like sweeting such persons, and my staying two or three days amongst them proselyted them all . . .   Greaves, *art. cit.*, pp. 376–8

Huntingdon to the Mayor, 2 October 1684

I have acquainted his Majesty with the substance of your letter,[42] and he is very pleased that the resolution of the corporation for the surrendering of your charter was a voluntary act, and not the effect of the *quo warranto*. His Majesty expects you should attend him with it some time before the term, upon which there will be a stop of all proceedings upon that writ. And his Majesty hath further commanded me to let you know he shall be ready to grant you another which I hope may be to all your satisfactions, and for myself I have many

---

[42] Of 13 September, formally announcing the corporation's willingness to surrender its charter; printed Greaves, *art. cit.*, pp. 378–9.

reasons to wish you much happiness, but none greater than the opinion I have that you will approve yourselves loyal and obedient subjects.

'*The Meeting of Mr Mayor and several Members of both Companies*',[43] *6 October 1684*

We conceive it may be advantageous to the town if his Majesty will please to grant the corporation the Saturday before Twelfth Day to be added to the other fourthly fair [?quarterly fairs].

Also that his Majesty will please to settle elections of burgesses for parliament for the corporation in both companies, as formerly.

Also to beseech his Majesty to grant the corporation the reversion of the perquisites of the Court Leet and other immunities thereunto belonging.

10 October 1684

It is ordered and agreed at this meeting that Mr Mayor, Mr Recorder [Sir Nathan Wright], Mr Noble, Mr Southwell, Mr Freeman and Mr Goodall are appointed to go to London to surrender the charter and liberties to his Majesty . . .[44]

29 October 1684

It is agreed at this meeting that the common seal shall be affixed to the surrender now to be sent to his Majesty. It is ordered at this meeting that Mr Chamberlain Abney shall carry the surrender to his Majesty to London, and wait upon the Earl of Huntingdon with it, or Mr Recorder or both.

Nathan Wright to the Mayor, 4 November 1684

. . . As to the alterations in the Corporation I can give you very little account of them, yet in a few days I shall I believe be able to satisfy you fully how all matters will be and who displaced. My Lord of H[untingdon] is now upon the inquiry after men and principles, but who he makes up in this affair I know not . . . I have not heard my Lord speak anything lately of making the gentlemen of the county to be justices for the borough, nor do I believe any such thing is intended . . .

Nathan Wright to the Mayor, 2 December 1684

. . . We have now settled all things in the new charter . . . None of your ancient privileges are in the least impaired by it, except as to the common council, which from 48 is now reduced to 36, and the Chamberlains taken away and the two Bailiffs to supply their place and execute their office, and all the members and officers of the corporation are made subject to the pleasure of

[43] These were 'The Twenty-Four' and 'The Forty-Eight', corresponding to a court of aldermen and a common council.

[44] This was put to the vote and rejected, probably as being too expensive. The corporation had already had to borrow money to defray legal expenses.

his Majesty and his successors to be removed, when he shall think fit to have it so; in all other matters you are as formerly.[45]

Records of the Borough of Leicester, ed. Helen Stocks, IV (Cambridge 1923), 559–61

146. A duke in his dukedom

[Henry Howard, 3rd Duke of Norfolk in the second creation, had conformed to the Church of England in 1679, the rest of his great family remaining Catholic. He was already Lord-Lieutenant of Surrey and Berkshire in 1683, when he was also appointed to Norfolk in an attempt to reunite that county after the disastrous feuds of the 1670's.[46] His secretary, Francis Negus, wrote from London to Edward l'Estrange, clerk to the lieutenancy of Norfolk, a few days after the death of Charles II.]

[10 February 1685]

Now that his Majesty hath declared he will call a parliament (and 'tis believed the beginning of May) my lord duke thinks it fit there should be early thoughts had thereof, and commands me to write to you that you do as soon as may be desire the deputy-lieutenants that they will speedily meet in their several divisions and consult the rest of the justices of the peace and militia officers and gentry, in order to the fixing on fit representatives, and more particularly for knights of the county, which being communicated at a general meeting they may so resolve on two persons as may carry it without opposition . . . When the gentry have met, they will please to let my lord duke hear from them . . .

His grace being well assured of Lord Townshend's interest, desires his lordship may be consulted, and his grace desires those near Sir John Holland will take him in at their meetings. *Norfolk Records Society*, xxx (1961), 63

[Two days later Negus sent on a report of events in Surrey, obviously as a model for the Norfolk gentry.]

[12 February 1685]

His grace desired them [the Surrey gentry] to agree amongst themselves to nominate persons that they thought fit to stand for knights, and when they had named three his grace desired they would let their names be written in so many pieces of papers as there were gentlemen who had voices, and that every one would mark two of this [sic] and then fold up the papers and put them in a hat, which being mingled together were opened and counted, and by that means

---

[45] However, the government continued to favour the broad franchise, now vested in those paying scot and lot. Huntingdon was nominated joint recorder with Wright.

[46] See J. R. Jones, 'The First Whig Party in Norfolk', *Durham University Journal*, XLVI (1953), 13, and R. W. Ketton-Cremer, 'The End of the Pastons', in *Norfolk Portraits* (London 1944).

the two that had most voices were resolved on, and everyone declared he would make his interest unanimous for those two, . . . which in all probability may be a means to prevent any contest, nor can anything be more fair, because my lord would by no means nominate who should stand, and his grace is to meet those of Berkshire tomorrow . . .   *HMC, 11th Report*, VII, 106

[L'Estrange's minutes, 26 February 1685]

The deputy-lieutenants . . . being met at the Grand Jury Chamber in the Castle at Norwich with above 100 of the chief gentlemen from all parts of this county, his grace's letter was read, as follows:

London, 21 February 1685

Gentlemen,

I am very sorry my occasions will not permit me to be in Norfolk by the time you have appointed for a general meeting, . . . which I would by no means have deferred; for though I hope the king will find our county of Norfolk so unanimous that we shall nave no opposition made to those that will be named, yet it is good in these cases to be as early as we can; and as I am very sure that you will think of none but such as have approved themselves fit for such a trust, you may be sure that I shall readily concur to whatever you among yourselves shall approve of . . .

After the reading of the aforesaid letter Sir Thomas Hare and Sir Jacob Astley were unanimously agreed upon . . . to be recommended to the county, . . . and accordingly a paper was subscribed by them all to serve Sir Thomas Hare and Sir Jacob Astley with their entire interests at the next election, an account whereof was given to his Grace by his deputy-lieutenants.

Norfolk Records Society, XXX, 65–6

[Rather than accept James II's revision of the magistracy and the lieutenancy in 1688, the duke went to France; but he was not dismissed from his post, and he returned in time to take part in the Revolution.]

[Minutes, 3 December 1688]

Pursuant to orders received from his grace, the deputy-lieutenants, militia officers and other gentlemen[47] were summoned to attend his grace at Lin Regis [King's Lynn] the 7th . . . December by 9 of the clock in the forenoon; who appeared accordingly and accompanied his grace into the market place, where the mayor of Lin, being attended by the aldermen and a great number of people, made this following speech to his grace:

My Lord,

The daily alarms we receive as well from foreign as domestic enemies give us just apprehensions of approaching dangers, which press us to apply

---

[47] Who had all paraded at Norwich on the 1st.

with all earnestness to your grace as our great patron, in a humble confidence to succeed in our expectations that we may be put into such a posture by your grace's direction and conduct as may make us appear as zealous as any in the defence of the Protestant religion, the laws and ancient government of the kingdom, being the desire of many hundreds amongst us who most humbly challenge a right for your grace's protection.

[The duke replied]

I am very much obliged to you and the rest of the body and those here present for your good opinion of me and the confidence you have that I will do what in me lies to support and defend your laws and liberties and the Protestant religion, which I will never deceive you in. And since the coming of the Prince of Orange has given us an opportunity to declare for the defence of them, I can only assure you that no man will venture his life more freely for the defence of the laws, liberty and Protestant religion than I will do . . .

The same day the duke issued orders for the militia horse and foot to move to Lynn. *Ibid.*, pp. 94–5

[13 December 1688]

His grace the duke of Norfolk having an account that the king was withdrawn from Whitehall, went away for London, and ordered summons[es] to be sent to his deputy-lieutenants and other gentlemen to attend at Norwich upon Saturday the 15th instant to be ready to receive such orders as should then be sent.

[15 December]

His grace hearing that the Irish were coming towards Norfolk came back to Thetford, and ordered that his troop of militia horse which was then upon duty at Norwich should forthwith march to Thetford

The same day towards night the following letter was received from his grace and communicated to the gentlemen at Norwich:

Gentlemen,

I suppose it is no news to you that the king is come back to London and that there is a very fair prospect of all things being settled by a parliament . . . I am resolved to go for London, but being informed from thence that all people flock in great numbers thither upon this great occasion, I have deferred my journey till Monday morning [17th] to expect the company of such gentlemen whose own curiosity or the desire that the county of Norfolk may appear as numerous and in as handsome a posture as other counties will strive to do, will incline to keep me company, which though I might be thought to have some private interest in, and that I may take a great deal of pride to appear accompanied by so many worthy and honest gentlemen, who have never left me and whom I will never forsake, I assure you I would not move this if your own and your county's honour were not in my opinion concerned in it as much as . . . [mine].   *Ibid.*, pp. 96–7

147. James II's election agents, April 1688

Memorandum for those that go into the Country to dispose the Corporations to a good Election for Members of Parliament. To be read by them often

It's necessary you weigh well the difficulty of your work, and consider that you will meet with all manner of deceit and combination to frustrate your endeavours; the clergy will engage the gentry, and both endeavour to render you unacceptable, and your work fruitless, if not top upon you false men under the semblance of real friends.

2. Consider the evil effects that will attend a miscarriage in this matter. 'Tis not only a frustration of the good expected, but ruinous to your own interest, and exposing you to contempt. You must expect that no weakness or inadvertency of yours in this work will pass unobserved, and the best of your actions [may be] misrepresented, and every failing magnified, and that hap'ly to the k[ing], or some of his Ministers, which therefore calls for the highest care and circumspection.

4. [*sic*] You have as full an account of the persons and things for each corporation and place, as hath hitherto been collected, which consider from time to time in the respective places as you come to them, and for your guidance in these places, find one or two of the best, prudentest and acceptablest person or persons, and engage them to your assistance, and know from them the temper and humour of the respective persons with whom you are to converse, and accordingly endeavour to suit your discourse to their temper and humour.

2. [*sic*] Take from place to place letters recommendatory, for the strengthening your interest and acceptance, get fit and acceptable persons to accompany you to such gentlemen as you will have occasion to discourse [with], for you must expect to meet with discerning men, and men of great parts, and for that purpose be wary in your expressions and conversation, and be not too ready and open in discourse, till such persons become by their own declarations engaged.

5. 'Tis of very great importance to this service, that very good correspondents be settled in each town, to whom letters and papers to be dispersed may be sent, and who shall receive every post such prints and advices, as shall be fit and proper for them; and this you must consider, that the persons so to be engaged must be right men, not only by inclination, but also men of prudence and interest (if possible).

6. Where the corporations do fix upon their Members, inform yourself fully what probability there is of their election, and what methods will be taken in order thereunto; and when you have fully satisfied yourself that such persons are right, and likely to answer the k[ing]'s expectation, (in which by your instructions you are not restrained to the persons named in your list, in case there be any exceptions to any of them, or fitter persons to be provided), if possibly you can, get the electors to write letters of invitation to such their intended Members, that by subscription under their hands their election may be ascertained [*sc.* made certain], and where they shall be content to elect such as his Majesty shall nominate or recommend, that they do in like manner express their desire that such nomination and appointment be made in order to their election, in which all prudent care is to be had, and the leading persons of such corporations to be consulted.

7. You are from time to time to give an account of all occurences that are material, and of all suggestions, books and libels that are dispersed in prejudice of his Majesty's service.

8. You must be very careful to give a full and distinct account of all the proceedings every post, and therein an impartial account of the sentiments of the persons with whom you converse, their inclinations and resolutions, and what expedients are necessary to render the election certain; which account you are to give, from time to time, to Robert Brent, Esq., at his chamber in the Temple. The respective correspondents are in like manner to send their letters to him, and to follow such directions as from time to time they shall receive from him, or Mr Edward Roberts, to whom they may write, directing their letters to Mr Brent's chamber; but not to give an account of your proceedings to any other person whatever.

9. You are likewise to consider the correspondents in each corporation, whether they are fit and proper, and if not, that others more fit and proper be named, as also to enquire whether the correspondents do disperse the books and papers according to the directions sent them; and particularly whether they are exposed in coffee houses and houses of public entertainment for the information of the country, [so] that in case they be defective therein it may be rectified.

10. You are to send for the persons in the respective counties underwritten, and to desire their help and assistance in managing the trust committed to you, and to engage them and their correspondents, that are in the respective corporations, to manage such matters and things as upon debate you shall find requisite to promote this service, for inclining and disposing men to elect persons you shall agree upon, and engage them in your absence to keep a constant correspondence with Mr Brent or Mr Roberts, that such advice may be sent from time to time as may be proper.

11. You are also to consider what employments such correspondents are capable of, that are in the k[ing]'s disposal, to the end that they may be recommended to such employments as may compensate for the service they have done, or shall do.

12. You are likewise to inspect the present state of each corporation with respect to the magistrates in being, whether there be any in that are not fit and proper, or whether any are omitted to be put into the government, which if placed therein, may be useful and serviceable for promoting and securing good elections, as also any other method and expedients that have a tendency thereunto.

13. You are likewise to consider what mayors and sheriffs in being are active in his Majesty's service, and to be depended upon, and which of them are fit to be removed before the election, either in order to their being chosen to serve in parliament, or to promote the election of others, and to engage the sheriffs to attend in person at the election, not only in the counties but in each respective corporation, and to take care of the returns; and also to give an account of the inclination and behaviour of the respective town clerks, clerks of the peace and sub-sheriffs, whose places render them capable of his Majesty's service, in case they be right, but otherwise dangerous and prejudicial thereunto.

14. Inform yourselves what Members each corporation intend to choose, and if they are contrary to his Majesty's interest, and you find the corporation resolved upon them out of prejudice, consider then how to give a diversion to their intentions by seeming to promote such persons' election, which they observing may create an aversion to them, and dispose them to elect others which they are inclined to, as suspecting those they before designed to have privately warped to the k[ing]'s interest; and thereby room will be made for the electing such as are right.

Persons proposed as assistants to those that go into the country, for:

	Sir Tho. Stanley	
Chester	Will Fermer	all of
	Mr Mainwaring	Chester

	Tim Seymour	
Salop	Rich. Newton	
	Christopher Morrall	of Much Wenlock.

Sir George Duckett, *Penal Laws and Test Act* (1882), pp. 194–7.

BOOKS CITED

This is by no means a comprehensive bibliography. It merely provides a fuller description of those books previously cited by name of author or short title. See also the list of abbreviations on p. xviii.

I. SOURCES AND COLLECTIONS

Abbott, Wilbur C. (ed.) *The Writings and Speeches of Oliver Cromwell*, 4 vols. Cambridge (Mass.) 1937–47.

Browning, Andrew (ed.) *English Historical Documents 1660–1714*. London 1953.

Burton, Thomas. *The Diary of Thomas Burton, Esq., Member in the Parliaments of Oliver and Richard Cromwell*, 4 vols. London 1828.

Cardwell, Edward (ed.) *Documentary Annals of the Reformed Church of England*, 2 vols. Oxford 1844.

(ed.) *Synodalia: a collection of Articles of Religion, Canons and Proceedings of Convocation in the Province of Canterbury*, 2 vols. Oxford 1842.

Clarendon, Edward Hyde, Earl of. *History of the Rebellion and Civil Wars in England*, ed. W. D. Macray. 6 vols. Oxford 1888.

Coke, Sir Edward. *The Reports of Sir Edward Coke*, ed. J. H. Thomas and J. F. Frazer, 13 pts in 6 vols. London 1826.

Commons, House of. *Commons Debates, 1621*, ed. W. Notestein, F. H. Relf and H. Simpson, 7 vols. New Haven 1935.

Debates in the House of Commons in 1625, ed. S. R. Gardiner. Camden Society 1873.

Cope, Esther S., *Proceedings of the Short Parliament of 1640*, Camden Fourth Series, vol. 19 (1977).

Costin, W. C. and Watson, J. S. (eds.) *The Law and Working of the Constitution: Documents 1660–1914*, 2 vols. London 1952.

D'Ewes, Sir Simonds. *The Journal of Sir Simonds d'Ewes from the beginning of the Long Parliament to the opening of the trial of the Earl of Strafford*, ed. W. Notestein. New Haven 1923.

The Journal of Sir Simonds d'Ewes from the first recess of the Long Parliament to the withdrawal of King Charles from London, ed. Wilson H. Coates. New Haven 1942.

Elton, G. R. (ed.) *The Tudor Constitution: Documents and Commentary*, 2nd edn. Cambridge 1982.

Firth, C. H. and Rait, R. S. (eds.) *Acts and Ordinances of the Interregnum, 1642–1660*, 3 vols. London 1911.

Foedera, conventiones, literae et cuiuscunque generis acta publica, ed. T. Rymer and R. Sanderson, 20 vols. London 1704–32.

Foster, Elizabeth R. *Proceedings in Parliament 1610*, 2 vols. New Haven 1966.

Fuller, Thomas, *The Church History of Britain*, ed. J. Nichols, 3 vols. London 1868.

Gardiner, S. R. (ed.) *Notes of the Debates in the House of Lords*. Camden Society 1879.

    (ed.) *Parliamentary Debates in 1610*. Camden Society 1862.

    (ed.) *Reports of Cases in the Courts of Star Chamber and High Commission*. Camden Society 1886.

Godbolt, J. *Reports of Certain Cases arising in the Several Courts of Record at Westminster*. London 1652.

Grey, Anchitel (ed.) *Debates of the House of Commons from the year 1667 to the year 1694*, 10 vols. London 1769.

Haller, W. and Davies, G. (eds.) *The Leveller Tracts 1647–1653*. New York 1944.

James I, King. *Works*. London 1616.

Knafla, Louis A. (ed.) *Law and Politics in Jacobean England: the Tracts of Lord Chancellor Ellesmere*. Cambridge 1977.

Laud, William. *Works*, ed. W. Scott and J. Bliss, 7 vols. Oxford 1847–60.

Lords, House of. *See* Gardiner *and* Relf.

Milward: The Diary of John. ed. Caroline Robbins. Cambridge 1938.

Muddiman, J. G. (ed.) *The Trial of King Charles the First*. Edinburgh 1928.

Pennington, D. H. and Roots, Ivan (eds.) *The Committee at Stafford 1643–1645: the Order Book of the Staffordshire County Committee*. Manchester 1957.

Petyt, William. *Jus Parliamentarium: or the Ancient Power, Jurisdiction, Rights and Liberties of the most high Court of Parliament*. London 1739.

Relf, F. H. (ed.) *Notes of the Debates in the House of Lords . . . 1621, 1625, 1628*. Camden Society 1929.

Rushworth, J. (ed.) *Historical Collections of Private Passages of State*, 8 vols. London 1659–1701.

Speeches and Passages of this Great and Happy Parliament. London 1641.

State Tracts . . . a collection of several treatises relating to the government . . . now published in a body to show the necessity and clear the legality of the late Revolution, 2 vols. London 1693.

Tanner, J. R. (ed.) *Tudor Constitutional Documents*, 2nd edn. Cambridge 1930.

Williams, E. N. (ed.) *The Eighteenth-Century Constitution 1688–1815: Documents and Commentary*. Cambridge 1960.

Woodhouse, A. S. P. (ed.) *Puritanism and Liberty: being the Army Debates . . . [1647–9]*, 2nd edn. London 1950.

II. SECONDARY WORKS

Ashton, Robert. *The English Civil War: Conservatism and Revolution 1603–1649*. London 1978.

Aveling, J. C. H. *The Handle and the Axe: the Catholic Recusants in England from Reformation to Emancipation*. London 1976.

Aylmer, G. E. *The King's Servants: the Civil Service of Charles I, 1625–1642*. London 1961.

The State's Servants: the Civil Service of the English Republic 1649–1660. London 1973.
(ed.) *The Interregnum: the quest for a settlement 1646–1660.* London 1972.

Babbage, Stuart B. *Puritanism and Richard Bancroft.* London 1962.

Barnes, Thomas G. *Somerset 1625–1640: a County's Government during the 'Personal Rule'.* Oxford 1961.

Browning, Andrew, *Thomas Osborne Earl of Danby,* 3 vols. Glasgow 1944–51.

Chandaman, C. D. *The English Public Revenue 1660–1688.* Oxford 1975.

Cockburn, J. S. *A History of English Assizes 1558–1714.* Cambridge 1972.

Dietz, F. C. *English Public Finance 1558–1641.* New York 1932.

Elton, G. R. *Studies in Tudor and Stuart Politics and Government,* 3 vols. Cambridge 1974–83.

Firth, C. H. *The Last Years of the Protectorate,* 2 vols. London 1909.

Fletcher, Anthony. *A County Community in Peace and War: Sussex 1600–1660.* London 1975.
The Outbreak of the English Civil War. London 1981.

Gardiner, S. R. *History of England from the accession of James I to the Outbreak of Civil War, 1603–1642,* 10 vols. London 1883–4.
History of the Great Civil War, 4 vols. London 1893.
History of the Commonwealth and Protectorate, 3 vols. London 1894–1901.

Glassey, Lionel J. K. *Politics and the Appointment of Justices of the Peace 1675–1720.* Oxford 1979.

Gleason, J. H. *The Justices of the Peace in England 1558–1640.* Oxford 1969.

Haley, K. H. D. *The First Earl of Shaftesbury.* Oxford 1968.

Hardacre, P. H. *The Royalists during the Puritan Revolution.* The Hague 1956.

Havran, Martin J. *The Catholics in Caroline England.* Stanford 1962.

Hibbard, Caroline. *Charles I and the Popish Plot.* Chapel Hill 1983.

Hill, Christopher. *Economic Problems of the Church from Archbishop Whitgift to the Long Parliament.* Oxford 1956.

Holdsworth, Sir William. *A History of English Law,* 14 vols. London 1922–64.

Holmes, Clive. *The Eastern Association in the English Civil War.* Cambridge 1974.

Jones, J. R. *The First Whigs: the Politics of the Exclusion Crisis 1678–83.* Oxford 1961.
(ed.) *The Restored Monarchy 1660–1688.* London 1979.

Jones, W. J. *Politics and the Bench: the Judges and the Origins of the English Civil War.* London 1971.

Judson, Margaret A. *The Crisis of the Constitution: an Essay in Constitutional and Political Thought in England 1603–1645.* Rutgers 1949.

Keeler, Mary F. *The Long Parliament 1640–1641.* Philadelphia 1954.

Kenyon, J. P. *The Popish Plot.* London 1972.
Robert Spencer Earl of Sunderland. London 1958.

Kishlansky, Mark A. *The Rise of the New Model Army.* Cambridge 1979.

Malcolm, Joyce L. *Caesar's Due: Loyalty and King Charles 1642–1646.* London 1983.

Manning, Brian. *The English People and the English Revolution.* London 1976.

Miller, John. *Popery and Politics in England 1660–1688.* Cambridge 1973.

Mitchell, Williams B. *The Rise of the Revolutionary Party in the English House of Commons 1603–1629*. New York 1957.

Moir, Thomas L. *The Addled Parliament of 1614*. Oxford 1958.

Morrill, J. S. *Cheshire 1630–1660: County Government and Society during the English Revolution*. Oxford 1974.

    The Revolt of the Provinces: Conservatives and Radicals in the English Civil War 1630–1650. London 1976.

    (ed.) *Reactions to the English Civil War 1642–1649*. London 1982.

Notestein, Wallace. *The House of Commons 1604–1610*. New Haven 1971.

Nuttall, G. F. and Chadwick, O. (eds.) *From Uniformity to Unity 1662–1962*. London 1962.

Pennington, D. H. and Thomas, Keith (eds.) *Puritans and Revolutionaries: Essays in Seventeenth-Century History presented to Christopher Hill*. Oxford 1978.

Pocock, J. G. A. *The Ancient Constitution and the Feudal Law*. Cambridge 1957.

Prall, Stuart A. *The Agitation for Law Reform during the Puritan Revolution 1640–1660*. The Hague 1966.

Prestwich, Menna. *Cranfield: Politics and Profit under the Early Stuarts*. Oxford 1966.

Relf, F. H. *The Petition of Right*. Minneapolis 1917.

Ruigh, Robert. *The Parliament of 1624*. Cambridge (Mass.) 1971.

Russell, Conrad. *The Crisis of Parliaments 1509–1660*. Oxford 1971.

    Parliaments and English Politics 1621–1629. Oxford 1979.

    (ed.) *The Origins of the English Civil War*. London 1973.

Sharpe, Kevin (ed.) *Faction and Parliament: Essays in Early Stuart History*. Oxford 1978.

Shaw, W. A. *A History of the English Church during the Civil Wars and under the Commonwealth*, 2 vols. London 1900.

Smith, Alan G. R. (ed.) *The Reign of James VI and I*. London 1973.

Stone, Lawrence. *The Causes of the English Revolution 1529–1642*. London 1972.

    The Crisis of the Aristocracy 1558–1641. Oxford 1965.

Timmis, John H. *Thine is the Kingdom: the Trial for Treason of Thomas Wentworth Earl of Strafford*. Alabama 1974.

Tite, Colin C. G. *Impeachment and Parliamentary Judicature in Early Stuart England*. London 1974.

Tomlinson, Howard (ed.) *Before the Englsh Civil War: Essays on Early Stuart Politics and Government*. London 1983.

Trevor-Roper, H. R. *Archbishop Laud 1573–1645*, 2nd edn. London 1965.

Underdown, David. *Pride's Purge: Politics in the Puritan Revolution*. Oxford 1971.

    Somerset in the Civil War and Interregnum. Newton Abbott 1973.

Usher, Roland G. *The Reconstruction of the English Church*, 2 vols. New York 1910.

    The Rise and Fall of High Commission, 2nd edn. Oxford 1968.

Veall, Donald. *The Popular Movement for Law Reform 1640–1660*. Oxford 1970.

Watts, Michael R. *The Dissenters: from the Reformation to the French Revolution*. Oxford 1978.

Weston, Corinne C. *English Constitutional Theory and the House of Lords 1556–1832*. London 1965.

White, Stephen D. *Sir Edward Coke and 'The Grievances of the Commonwealth' 1621–1628*. Chapel Hill 1979.

Willcox, W. B. *Gloucestershire: a Study in Local Government 1590–1640*. New Haven 1940.

Willson, David H. *The Privy Councillors in the House of Commons 1604–1629*. Minneapolis 1940.

Zaller, Robert. *The Parliament of 1621*. Berkeley 1971.

INDEX

Figures in bold type are document numbers